STUDENT SOLUTIONS MANUAL

Nancy S. Boudreau

STATISTICS
for BUSINESS
and ECONOMICS
Seventh Edition

McClave • Benson • Sincich

PRENTICE HALL, UPPER SADDLE RIVER, NJ 07458

Acquisitions Editor: *Ann Heath*
Production Editor: *Mindy De Palma*
Cover Designer: *Paul Gourhan*
Special Projects Manager: *Barbara A. Murray*
Supplement Cover Mnaager: *Paul Gourhan*
Editorial Assistant: *Mindy Ince McClard*
Production Coordinator: *Alan Fischer*

 Copyright © 1998 by Prentice-Hall, Inc.
Simon & Schuster / A Viacom Company
Upper Saddle River, NJ 07458

All rights reserved. No part of this book may be
reproduced in any form or by any means,
without permission in writing from the publisher.

Printed in the United States of America

10 9 8 7 6 5 4 3 2

ISBN 0-13-625260-5

Prentice-Hall International (UK) Limited, *London*
Prentice-Hall of Australia Pty. Limited, *Sydney*
Prentice-Hall Canada Inc., *Toronto*
Prentice Hall Hispanoamericana, S.A., *Mexico*
Prentice-Hall of India Private Limited, *New Delhi*
Prentice-Hall of Japan, Inc., *Tokyo*
Simon & Schuster Asia Pte. Ltd., *Singapore*
Editoria Prentice-Hall do Brasil, *Ltda., Rio de Janero*

Contents

Preface		v
Chapter 1	Statistics, Data, and Statistical Thinking	1
Chapter 2	Methods for Describing Sets of Data	5
Chapter 3	Probability	32
Chapter 4	Discrete Random Variables	51
Chapter 5	Continuous Random Variables	69
Chapter 6	Sampling Distributions	93
Chapter 7	Inferences Based on a Single Sample: Estimation with Confidence Intervals	106
Chapter 8	Inferences Based on a Single Sample: Tests of Hypothesis	125
Chapter 9	Inferences Based on Two Samples: Confidence Intervals and Tests of Hypotheses	145
Chapter 10	Simple Linear Regression	174
Chapter 11	Multiple Regression	203
Chapter 12	Introduction to Model Building	228
Chapter 13	Methods for Quality Improvement	256
Chapter 14	Time Series: Descriptive Analyses, Models, and Forecasting	283
Chapter 15	Design of Experiments and Analysis of Variance	319
Chapter 16	Nonparametric Statistics	346
Chapter 17	The Chi-Square Test and the Analysis of Contingency Tables	371
Chapter 18	Decision Analysis	390

Preface

This solutions manual is designed to accompany the text, *Statistics for Business and Economics*, Seventh Edition, by James T. McClave, P. George Benson, and Terry Sincich. It provides answers to most odd-numbered exercises for each chapter in the text. Other methods of solution may also be appropriate; however, the author has presented one that she believes to be most instructive to the beginning Statistics student. The student should first attempt to solve the assigned exercises without help from this manual. Then, if unsuccessful, the solution in the manual will clarify points necessary to the solution. The student who successfully solves an exercise should still refer to the manual's solution. Many points are clarified and expanded upon to provide maximum insight into and benefit from each exercise.

Instructors will also benefit from the use of this manual. It will save time in preparing presentations of the solutions and possibly provide another point of view regarding their meaning.

Some of the exercises are subjective in nature and thus omitted from the Answer Key at the end of *Statistics for Business and Economics*, Seventh Edition. The subjective decisions regarding these exercises have been made and are explained by the author. Solutions based on these decisions are presented; the solution to this type of exercise is often most instructive. When an alternative interpretation of an exercise may occur, the author has often addressed it and given justification for the approach taken.

I would like to thank Kelly Evans for creating the art work and Brenda Dobson for her assistance and for typing this work.

                                                Nancy S. Boudreau
                                                Bowling Green State University
                                                Bowling Green, Ohio

Statistics, Data, and Statistical Thinking   Chapter 1

1.1   Statistics is a science that deals with the collection, classification, analysis, and interpretation of information or data. It is a meaningful, useful science with a broad, almost limitless scope of applications to business, government, and the physical and social sciences.

1.3   The four elements of a descriptive statistics problem are:

1. The population or sample of interest. This is the collection of all the units upon which the variable is measured.
2. One or more variables that are to be investigated. These are the types of data that are to be collected.
3. Tables, graphs, or numerical summary tools. These are tools used to display the characteristic of the sample or population.
4. Conclusions about the data based on the patterns revealed. These are summaries of what the summary tools revealed about the population or sample.

1.5   The first major method of collecting data is from a published source. These data have already been collected by someone else and is available in a published source. The second method of collecting data is from a designed experiment. These data are collected by a researcher who exerts strict control over the experimental units in a study. These data are measured directly from the experimental units. The third method of collecting data is from a survey. These data are collected by a researcher asking a group of people one or more questions. Again, these data are collected directly from the experimental units or people. The final method of collecting data is observationally. These data are collected directly from experimental units by simply observing the experimental units in their natural environment and recording the values of the desired characteristics.

1.7   A population is a set of existing units such as people, objects, transactions, or events. A variable is a characteristic or property of an individual population unit such as height of a person, time of a reflex, amount of a transaction, etc.

1.9   A representative sample is a sample that exhibits characteristics similar to those possessed by the target population. A representative sample is essential if inferential statistics is to be applied. If a sample does not possess the same characteristics as the target population, then any inferences made using the sample will be unreliable.

1.11   A population is a set of existing units such as people, objects, transactions, or events. A process is a series of actions or operations that transform inputs to outputs. A process produces or generates output over time. Examples of processes are assembly lines, oil refineries, and stock prices.

1.13   The data consisting of the classifications A, B, C, and D are qualitative. These data are nominal and thus are qualitative. After the data are input as 1, 2, 3, and 4, they are still nominal and thus qualitative. The only differences between the two data sets are the names of the categories. The numbers associated with the four groups are meaningless.

1.15   a.   The population of interest is all citizens of the United States.

b. The variable of interest is the view of each citizen as to whether the president is doing a good or bad job. It is qualitative.

c. The sample is the 2000 individuals selected for the poll.

d. The inference of interest is to estimate the proportion of all citizens who believe the president is doing a good job.

e. The method of data collection is a survey.

f. It is not very likely that the sample will be representative of the population of all citizens of the United States. By selecting phone numbers at random, the sample will be limited to only those people who have telephones. Also, many people share the same phone number, so each person would not have an equal chance of being contacted. Another possible problem is the time of day the calls are made. If the calls are made in the evening, those people who work in the evening would not be represented.

1.17 a. The depth of tread is a number such as .25 inch, .15 inch, etc. Therefore, it is quantitative.

b. Occupations take on values such as doctor, lawyer, carpenter, etc., which are not numeric. Therefore, it is qualitative.

c. Employment status can take on values such as employed or unemployed, which are not numeric. Therefore, it is qualitative.

d. The time in months can take on values such as 1, 2, 3, etc. Therefore, it is quantitative.

1.19 a. Length of maximum span can take on values such as 15 feet, 50 feet, 75 feet, etc. Therefore, it is quantitative.

b. The number of vehicle lanes can take on values such as 2, 4, etc. Therefore, it is quantitative.

c. The answer to this item is "yes" or "no," which are not numeric. Therefore, it is qualitative.

d. Average daily traffic could take on values such as 150 vehicles, 3,579 vehicles, 53,295 vehicles, etc. Therefore, it is quantitative.

e. Condition can take on values "good," "fair," or "poor," which are not numeric. Therefore, it is qualitative.

f. The length of the bypass or detour could take on values such as 1 mile, 4 miles, etc. Therefore, it is quantitative.

g. Route type can take on values "interstate," U.S.," "state," "county," or "city," which are not numeric. Therefore, it is qualitative.

1.21 a. The population from which the sample was selected is the set of all department store executives.

b. There are two variables measured by the authors. They are job-satisfaction and Machiavellian rating for each of the executives.

c. The sample is the set of 218 department store executives who completed the questionnaire.

d. The method of data collection is a survey.

e. The inference made by the authors is that those executives with higher job-satisfaction scores are likely to have a lower 'mach' rating.

1.23 a. Some possible questions are:

1. In your opinion, why has the banking industry consolidated in the past few years? Check all that apply.

   a. Too many small banks with not enough capital.
   b. A result of the Savings and Loan scandals.
   c. To eliminate duplicated resources in the upper management positions.
   d. To provide more efficient service to the customers.
   e. To provide a more complete list of financial opportunities for the customers.
   f. Other. Please list.

2. Using a scale from 1 to 5, where 1 means strongly disagree and 5 means strongly agree, indicate your agreement to the following statement: "The trend of consolidation in the banking industry will continue in the next five years."

   1 strongly disagree   2 disagree   3 no opinion   4 agree   5 strongly agree

b. The population of interest is the set of all bank presidents in the United States.

c. It would be extremely difficult and costly to obtain information from all 10,000 bank presidents. Thus, it would be more efficient to sample just 200 bank presidents. However, by sending the questionnaires to only 200 bank presidents, one risks getting the results from a sample which is not representative of the population. The sample must be chosen in such a way that the results will be representative of the entire population of bank presidents in order to be of any use.

1.25 a. The population of interest is the collection of all major U.S. firms.

b. The variable of interest is whether the firm offers job-sharing to its employees or not.

c. The sample is the set of 1,035 firms selected.

d. The government might want to estimate the proportion of all firms that offer job-sharing to their employees.

1.27 I. Qualitative; the possible responses are "yes" or "no," which are nonnumerical.

II. Quantitative; age is measured on a numerical scale, such as 15, 32, etc.

III. Quantitative; the rating is measured on a numerical scale from 1 to 10, where the higher the rating the more helpful the *Tutorial* instructions.

IV. Qualitative; the possible responses are "laser printer" or "another type of printer," which are nonnumerical.

V. Qualitative; the speeds can be classified as "slower," "unchanged," or "faster," which are nonnumerical.

VI. Quantitative; the number of people in a household who have used Windows 3.0 at least once is measured on a numerical scale, such as 0, 1, 2, etc.

1.29 a. The process being studied is the distribution of pipes, valves, and fittings to the refining, chemical, and petrochemical industries by Wallace Company of Houston.

b. The variables of interest are the speed of the deliveries, the accuracy of the invoices, and the quality of the packaging of the products.

c. The sampling plan was to monitor a subset of current customers by sending out a questionnaire twice a year and asking the customers to rate the speed of the deliveries, the accuracy of the invoices, and the quality of the packaging minutes. The sample is the total numbers of questionnaires received.

d. The Wallace Company's immediate interest is learning about the delivery process of its distribution of pipes, valves, and fittings. To do this, it is measuring the speed of deliveries, the accuracy of the invoices, and the quality of its packaging from the sample of its customers to make an inference about the delivery process to all customers. In particular, it might use the mean speed of its deliveries to the sampled customers to estimate the mean speed of its deliveries to all its customers. It might use the mean accuracy of its invoices to the sampled customers to estimate the mean accuracy of its deliveries to all its customers. It might use the mean rating of the quality of its packaging to the sampled customers to estimate the mean rating of the quality of its packaging to all its customers.

e. Several factors might affect the reliability of the inferences. One factor is the set of customers selected to receive the survey. If this set is not representative of all the customers, the wrong inferences could be made. Also, the set of customers returning the surveys may not be representative of all its customers. Again, this could influence the reliability of the inferences made.

Methods for Describing Sets of Data

Chapter 2

2.1 First, we find the frequency of the grade A. The sum of the frequencies for all five grades must be 200. Therefore, subtract the sum of the frequencies of the other four grades from 200. The frequency for grade A is:

$$200 - (36 + 90 + 30 + 28) = 200 - 184 = 16$$

To find the relative frequency for each grade, divide the frequency by the total sample size, 200. The relative frequency for the grade B is $36/200 = .18$. The rest of the relative frequencies are found in a similar manner and appear in the table:

Grade on Statistics Exam	Frequency	Relative Frequency
A: 90–100	16	.08
B: 80– 89	36	.18
C: 65– 79	90	.45
D: 50– 64	30	.15
F: Below 50	28	.14
Total	200	1.00

2.3 a. We must first compute the relative frequency for each response. To find the relative frequency, we divide the frequency by the total sample size, 240. For the first category, the relative frequency is $154/240 = .642$. The rest of the relative frequencies are found in a similar manner and are shown in the table.

Response	Number of Investors	Relative Frequency
Seek formal explanation	154	.642
Seek CEO performance review	49	.204
Dismiss CEO	20	.083
Seek no action	17	.071
TOTAL	240	1.000

b. The relative frequency graph is:

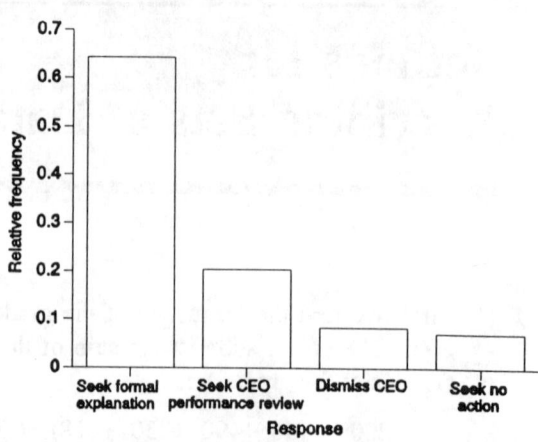

c. If the chief executive officer and the board of directors differed on company strategy, almost 2/3 of the large investors would seek formal explanation (.642). Approximately 20% (.204) would seek CEO performance review. Very few would dismiss the CEO (.083) or would seek no action (.071).

2.5 a. The variable measured by Performark is the length of time it took for each advertiser to respond back.

b. The pie chart is:

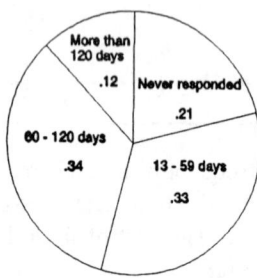

c. Twenty-one percent of .21 × 17,000 = 3,570 of the advertisers never respond to the sales lead.

d. The information from the pie chart does not indicate how effective the "bingo cards" are. It just indicates how long it takes advertisers to respond, if at all.

2.7 a. The variable measured in the survey was the length of time small businesses used the Internet per week.

6 Chapter 2

b. A bar graph of the data is:

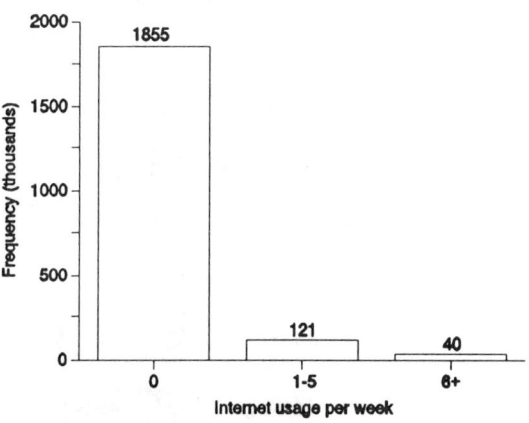

c. The proportion of the 2,016 small businesses that use the Internet on a weekly basis is $(121 + 40)/2{,}016 = 161/2{,}016 = .08$.

2.9 a. From the bar chart, there are approximately 195 transgenic plant trials approved for herbicide tolerance over this period.

b. From the bar chart, there are approximately 90 transgenic plant trials approved for developing virus resistant crops over this period.

c. To modify the bar graph to show relative frequencies, we must first find the total number of transgenic plant trials over the period. From the bar graph, the following are the approximate frequencies:

Trait	Frequency	Relative Frequency
Unspecified	9	9/550 = .016
Multiple Traits	13	13/550 = .024
Herbicide Tolerance	195	195/550 = .355
Crop Production	180	180/550 = .327
Product Quality	103	103/550 = .187
Marker Genes	50	50/550 = .091
Totals	550	1.000

To find the relative frequencies, divide the frequency by the total sample size, 550. The relative frequencies appear in the table above.

Methods for Describing Sets of Data

The bar chart showing the relative frequencies is:

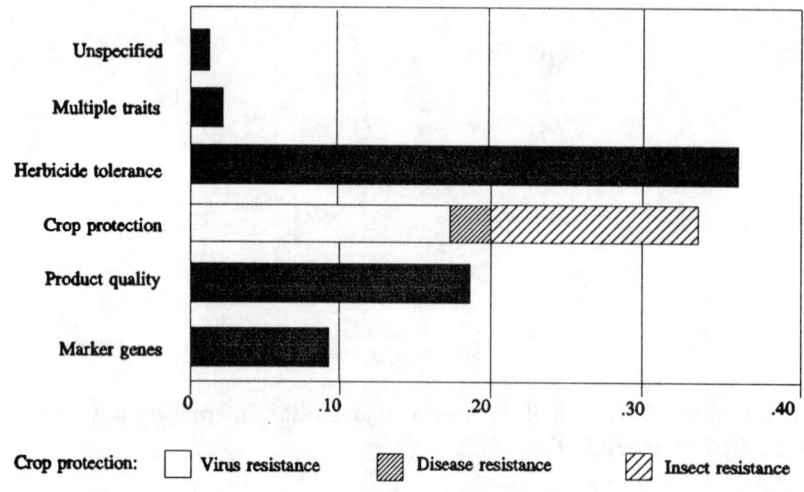

2.11 a. The Pareto diagram is:

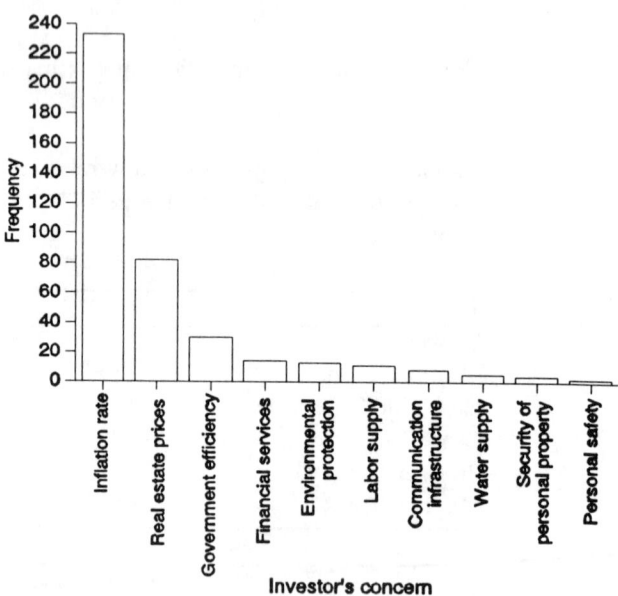

b. The environmental factor of most concern is "Inflation rate" with 233/402 = .58 or 58% of the investors indicating this as their most serious concern. The second most serious concern was "Real Estate prices." Over 20% ((82/402) × 100% = 20.4%) of the investors chose this concern. Each of the other categories were chosen by less than 10% of the investors.

c. Two factors out of 10 represent 20% of the factors. The two factors are "Inflation rate" and "Real estate prices." These two factors represent ((233 + 82)/402 = .78) 78% of the investors. This is very close to 80%.

2.13 To find the number of measurements for each measurement class, multiply the relative frequency by the total number of observations, $n = 500$. The frequency table is:

Measurement Class	Relative Frequency	Frequency
.5 – 2.5	.10	500(.10) = 50
2.5 – 4.5	.15	500(.15) = 75
4.5 – 6.5	.25	500(.25) = 125
6.5 – 8.5	.20	500(.20) = 100
8.5 – 10.5	.05	500(.05) = 25
10.5 – 12.5	.10	500(.10) = 50
12.5 – 14.5	.10	500(.10) = 50
14.5 – 16.5	.05	500(.05) = 25
		500

The frequency histogram is:

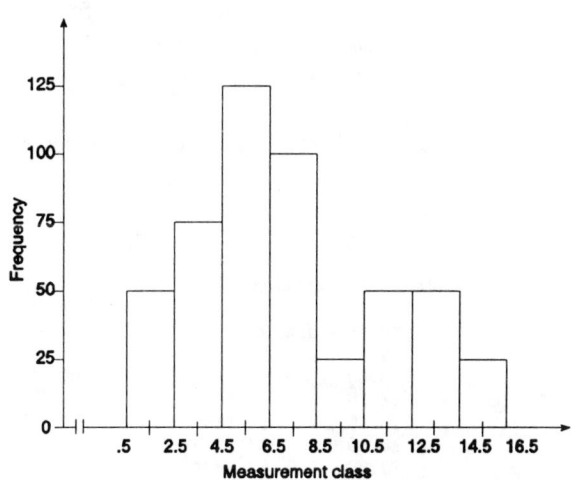

2.15 a. This is a frequency histogram because the number of observations is graphed for each interval rather than the relative frequency.

b. There are 14 measurement classes.

c. There are 49 measurements in the data set.

2.17 a. Almost half (14) of the bid prices were between $99.50 and $102.50. Seventy percent (21) of the bid prices were between $96.50 and $105.50. Only one bid price was greater than $105.50.

b. The total number of bonds with bid prices greater than $96.50 is $3 + 14 + 4 + 1 = 22$. The proportion of the total is $22/33 = .733$.

Methods for Describing Sets of Data

2.19   a.   Using MINITAB, the stem-and-leaf display is:

```
Stem-and-Leaf of PENALTY        N = 38
Leaf Unit = 10000

 (28)    0   ⓪0①①111②②222222③③33334444899
  10     1   ⓪0239
   5     2
   5     3   0
   4     4   0
   3     5
   3     6
   3     7
   3     8   5
   2     9   3
   1    10   0
```

   b.   See the circled leaves in part a.

   c.   Most of the penalties imposed for Clean Air Act violations are relatively small compared to the penalties imposed for other violations. All but one of the penalties for Clean Air Act violations are below the median penalty imposed.

2.21   a.   Using MINITAB, the three frequency histograms are as follows (the same starting point and class interval were used for each):

```
Histogram of C1        N = 25

Tenth Performance

Midpoint    Count
   4.00       0
   8.00       0
  12.00       1   *
  16.00       5   *****
  20.00      10   **********
  24.00       6   ******
  28.00       0
  32.00       2   **
  36.00       0
  40.00       1   *

Histogram of C2        N = 25

Thirtieth Performance

Midpoint    Count
   4.00       1   *
   8.00       9   *********
  12.00      12   ************
  16.00       2   **
  20.00       1   *

Histogram of C3        N = 25

Fiftieth Performance

Midpoint    Count
   4.00       3   ***
   8.00      15   ***************
  12.00       4   ****
  16.00       2   **
  20.00       1   *
```

   b.   The histogram for the tenth performance shows a much greater spread of the observations than the other two histograms. The thirtieth performance histogram shows a shift to the left—implying shorter completion times than for the tenth performance. In addition, the fiftieth performance histogram shows an additional shift to the left compared to that for the thirtieth performance. However, the last shift is not as great as the first shift. This agrees with statements made in the problem.

2.23 a. Most of the observations are below 3000, while two observations are in the high 3000 area and five are 4000 or more. Since SPSS is using a stem which is the 1000's place rounded down to an even number, it is not always possible to determine the actual value of the five largest rates. For example, "8 . 1" could represent a number near 8100 or 9100. The leaves are rounded to the nearest 100. The largest value in the data set is 11,968.23, which is rounded to a representation of "12 . 0".

b. In the second display, the stem is the 1000's place and the leaf is the 100's place. The data seem to be clustering in the 0 to 3000 range with some extreme values.

2.25 a. Using MINITAB, histograms of the two data sets are:

```
Histogram of C1     N = 20           Histogram of C2     N = 20

Manufacturing Companies              Holding Firms

Midpoint   Count                     Midpoint   Count
   0.0      0                           0.0      3    ***
  10.0      6    ******                10.0     11    ***********
  20.0      6    ******                20.0      5    *****
  30.0      2    **                    30.0      0
  40.0      4    ****                  40.0      0
  50.0      0                          50.0      1    *
  60.0      0                          60.0      0
  70.0      2    **                    70.0      0
```

b. The P/E ratios of firms in the manufacturing business tend to be higher than the P/E ratios of firms in the holding business. From the histograms, eight of the 20 manufacturing firms had P/E ratios greater than 30, while only one of the 20 holding firms had a P/E ratio greater than 30.

2.27 a. $\sum x = 3 + 8 + 4 + 5 + 3 + 4 + 6 = 33$

b. $\sum x^2 = 3^2 + 8^2 + 4^2 + 5^2 + 3^2 + 4^2 + 6^2 = 175$

c. $\sum (x - 5)^2 = (3 - 5)^2 + (8 - 5)^2 + (4 - 5)^2 + (5 - 5)^2 + (3 - 5)^2 + (4 - 5)^2 + (6 - 5)^2 = 20$

d. $\sum (x - 2)^2 = (3 - 2)^2 + (8 - 2)^2 + (4 - 2)^2 + (5 - 2)^2 + (3 - 2)^2 + (4 - 2)^2 + (6 - 2)^2 = 71$

e. $(\sum x)^2 = (3 + 8 + 4 + 5 + 3 + 4 + 6)^2 = 33^2 = 1089$

2.29 a. $\sum x = 6 + 0 + (-2) + (-1) + 3 = 6$

b. $\sum x^2 = 6^2 + 0^2 + (-2)^2 + (-1)^2 + 3^2 = 50$

c. $\sum x^2 - \frac{(\sum x)^2}{5} = 50 - \frac{6^2}{5} = 50 - 7.2 = 42.8$

Methods for Describing Sets of Data

2.31 Assume the data are a sample. The sample mean is:

$$\bar{x} = \frac{\sum x}{n} = \frac{3.2 + 2.5 + 2.1 + 3.7 + 2.8 + 2.0}{6} = \frac{16.3}{6} = 2.717$$

The median is the average of the middle two numbers when the data are arranged in order (since $n = 6$ is even). The data arranged in order are: 2.0, 2.1, 2.5, 2.8, 3.2, 3.7. The middle two numbers are 2.5 and 2.8. The median is:

$$\frac{2.5 + 2.8}{2} = \frac{5.3}{2} = 2.65$$

2.33 The mean and median of a symmetric data set are equal to each other. The mean is larger than the median when the data set is skewed to the right. The mean is less than the median when the data set is skewed to the left. Thus, by comparing the mean and median, one can determine whether the data set is symmetric, skewed right, or skewed left.

2.35 a. $\bar{x} = \frac{\sum x}{n} = \frac{7 + \cdots + 4}{6} + \frac{15}{6} = 2.5$

Median $= \frac{3 + 3}{2} = 3$ (mean of 3rd and 4th numbers, after ordering)

Mode $= 3$

b. $\bar{x} = \frac{\sum x}{n} = \frac{2 + \cdots + 4}{13} = \frac{40}{13} = 3.08$

Median $= 3$ (7th number, after ordering)

Mode $= 3$

c. $\bar{x} = \frac{\sum x}{n} = \frac{51 + \cdots + 37}{10} = \frac{496}{10} = 49.6$

Median $= \frac{48 + 50}{2} = 49$ (mean of 5th and 6th numbers, after ordering)

Mode $= 50$

2.37 a. Assume that the data represent a sample.

For the Health Care firms:

$$\bar{x} = \frac{\sum x}{n} = \frac{81,613 + 61,564 + \cdots + 20,441}{10} = \frac{389,569}{10} = 38,956.9$$

The data are arranged in order. Since n is even, the median is the average of the middle two numbers:

$$\text{Median} = \frac{33,437 + 33,072}{2} = \frac{66,509}{2} = 33,254.5$$

For the Banks:

$$\bar{x} = \frac{\sum x}{n} = \frac{33,329 + 26,181 + \cdots + 12,877}{10} = \frac{184,811}{10} = 18,481.1$$

The data are arranged in order. Since *n* is even, the median is the average of the middle two numbers:

$$\text{Median} = \frac{16{,}810 + 15{,}320}{2} = \frac{32{,}130}{2} = 16{,}065$$

b. For the Health Care firms, the mean is larger than the median indicating that the data are skewed to the right. For the Banks, the mean is again larger than the median indicating that the data are skewed to the right.

c. No. If the data set contains an odd number of observations, the median is equal to a value in the data set, namely the middle observation.

d. The market values of the 10 largest health care firms is greater, in general, than the market value of the 10 largest banks. The mean and median market values of the health care firms are larger than the mean and median values of the banks.

2.39 a. In 1980, the median age of the U.S. population was 30. This means that half of the people in the U.S. in 1980 were less than or equal to 30 years old and half were 30 or older. In 2000, the median age is expected to be 36. This means that in 2000, half of the people in the U.S. will be less than or equal to 36 years old and half will be 36 or older. This means the population as a whole is tending to get older.

b. The shift in the median age to 36 in 2000 will mean that there will be proportionally fewer people in the 18 to 30 year age group in 2000 than there was in 1980.

2.43 a. For the "Joint exchange offer with prepack" firms, the mean time is 2.6545 months, and the median is 1.5 months. Thus, the average time spent in bankruptcy for "Joint" firms is 2.6545 months, while half of the firms spend 1.5 months or less in bankruptcy.

For the "No prefiling vote held" firms, the mean time is 4.2364 months, and the median is 3.2 months. Thus, the average time spent in bankruptcy for "No prefiling vote held" firms is 4.2364 months, while half of the firms spend 3.2 months or less in bankruptcy.

For the "Prepack solicitation only" firms, the mean time is 1.8185 months, and the median is 1.4 months. Thus, the average time spent in bankruptcy for "Prepack solicitation only" firms is 1.8185 months, while half of the firms spend 1.4 months or less in bankruptcy.

b. Since the means and medians for the three groups of firms differ quite a bit, it would be unreasonable to use a single number to locate the center of the time in bankruptcy. Three different "centers" should be used.

2.45 a. Assume that the data represent a sample. The mean is:

$$\bar{x} = \frac{\sum x}{n} = \frac{88.3 + 104.3 + \cdots + 87.9}{20} = \frac{1839.8}{20} = 91.99$$

Arranging the data in order, we get:

| 78.5 | 79.2 | 79.9 | 83.2 | 85.1 | 87.9 | 88.1 | 88.3 | 89.8 | 90.0 |
| 91.0 | 91.7 | 93.2 | 94.3 | 94.4 | 95.4 | 102.9 | 103.6 | 104.3 | 119.0 |

Methods for Describing Sets of Data

Since *n* is even, the median is the average of the middle two numbers:

$$\text{Median} = \frac{90.0 + 91.0}{2} = \frac{181.0}{2} = 90.5$$

The mode is the number occurring the most frequently. No number occurs more than once, so all of the numbers are modes.

b. Eliminating the highest number from the data set gives the following:

$$\bar{x} = \frac{\sum x}{n} = \frac{88.3 + 104.3 + \cdots + 87.9}{19} = \frac{1720.8}{19} = 90.57$$

Arranging the data in order, we get:

78.5	79.2	79.9	83.2	85.1	87.9	88.1	88.3	89.8	90.0
91.0	91.7	93.2	94.3	94.4	95.4	102.9	103.6	104.3	

Since *n* is odd, the median is the middle number: Median = 90.0

The mode is the number occurring the most frequently. No number occurs more than once, so all of the numbers are modes.

Dropping the largest number caused the mean to drop from 91.99 to 90.57. The median dropped from 90.5 to 90.0. There was no effect on the mode.

c. Eliminating the two lowest and the two largest values, we get:

79.9	83.2	85.1	87.9	88.1	88.3	89.8	90.0
91.0	91.7	93.2	94.3	94.4	95.4	102.9	103.6

The 80% trimmed mean is:

$$\bar{x} = \frac{\sum x}{n} = \frac{79.9 + 83.2 + \cdots + 102.9}{16} = \frac{1458.8}{16} = 91.175$$

2.47 a. The primary disadvantage of using the range to compare variability of data sets is that the two data sets can have the same range and be vastly different with respect to data variation. Also, the range is greatly affected by extreme measures.

b. The sample variance is the sum of the squared deviations from the sample mean divided by the sample size minus 1. The population variance is the sum of the squared deviations from the population mean divided by the population size.

c. The variance of a data set can never be negative. The variance of a sample is the sum of the *squared* deviations from the mean divided by $n - 1$. The square of any number, positive or negative, is always positive. Thus, the variance will be positive.

The variance is usually greater than the standard deviation. However, it is possible for the variance to be smaller than the standard deviation. If the data are between 0 and 1, the variance will be smaller than the standard deviation. For example, suppose the data set is .8, .7, .9, .5, and .3. The sample mean is:

$$\bar{x} = \frac{\sum x}{n} = \frac{.8 + .7 + .9 + .5 + .3}{.5} = \frac{3.2}{5} = .64$$

The sample variance is:

$$s^2 = \frac{\sum x^2 - \frac{(\sum x)^2}{n}}{n-1} = \frac{2.28 - \frac{3.2^2}{5}}{5-1} = \frac{2.28 - 2.048}{4} = \frac{.325}{4} = .058$$

The standard deviation is $s = \sqrt{.058} = .241$

2.49 a. Range = 4 − 0 = 4

$$s^2 = \frac{\sum x^2 - \frac{(\sum x)^2}{n}}{n-1} = \frac{22 - \frac{8^2}{5}}{4-1} = 2.3 \qquad s = \sqrt{2.3} = 1.52$$

b. Range = 6 − 0 = 6

$$s^2 = \frac{\sum x^2 - \frac{(\sum x)^2}{n}}{n-1} = \frac{63 - \frac{17^2}{7}}{7-1} = 3.619 \qquad s = \sqrt{3.619} = 1.90$$

c. Range = 8 − (−2) = 10

$$s^2 = \frac{\sum x^2 - \frac{(\sum x)^2}{n}}{n-1} = \frac{154 - \frac{30^2}{10}}{10-1} = 7.111 \qquad s = \sqrt{7.111} = 2.67$$

d. Range = 2 − (−3) = 5

$$s^2 = \frac{\sum x^2 - \frac{(\sum x)^2}{n}}{n-1} = \frac{29 - \frac{(-5)^2}{18}}{18-1} = 1.624 \qquad s = \sqrt{1.624} = 1.274$$

2.51 a. $\sum x = 3 + 1 + 10 + 10 + 4 = 28$
$\sum x^2 = 3^2 + 1^2 + 10^2 + 10^2 + 4^2 = 226$

$$\bar{x} = \frac{\sum x}{n} = \frac{28}{5} = 5.6$$

$$s^2 = \frac{\sum x^2 - \frac{(\sum x)^2}{n}}{n-1} = \frac{226 - \frac{28^2}{5}}{5-1} = \frac{69.2}{4} = 17.3 \qquad s = \sqrt{17.3} = 4.1593$$

b. $\sum x = 8 + 10 + 32 + 5 = 55$
$\sum x^2 = 8^2 + 10^2 + 32^2 + 5^2 = 1213$

$$\bar{x} = \frac{\sum x}{n} = \frac{55}{4} = 13.75 \text{ feet}$$

$$s^2 = \frac{\sum x^2 - \frac{(\sum x)^2}{n}}{n-1} = \frac{1213 - \frac{55^2}{4}}{4-1} = \frac{456.75}{3} = 152.25 \text{ square feet}$$

$s = \sqrt{152.25} = 12.339$ feet

c. $\sum x = -1 + (-4) + (-3) + 1 + (-4) + (-4) = -15$
$\sum x^2 = (-1)^2 + (-4)^2 + (-3)^2 + 1^2 + (-4)^2 + (-4)^2 = 59$

Methods for Describing Sets of Data

$$\bar{x} = \frac{\sum x}{n} = \frac{-15}{6} = -2.5$$

$$s^2 = \frac{\sum x^2 - \frac{(\sum x)^2}{n}}{n-1} = \frac{59 - \frac{(-15)^2}{6}}{6-1} = \frac{21.5}{5} = 4.3 \qquad s = \sqrt{4.3} = 2.0736$$

d. $\sum x = \frac{1}{5} + \frac{1}{5} + \frac{1}{5} + \frac{2}{5} + \frac{1}{5} + \frac{4}{5} = \frac{10}{5} = 2$

$\sum x^2 = \left(\frac{1}{5}\right)^2 + \left(\frac{1}{5}\right)^2 + \left(\frac{1}{5}\right)^2 + \left(\frac{2}{5}\right)^2 + \left(\frac{1}{5}\right)^2 + \left(\frac{4}{5}\right)^2 = \frac{24}{25} = .96$

$\bar{x} = \frac{\sum x}{n} = \frac{2}{6} = \frac{1}{3} = .33$ ounce

$s^2 = \frac{\sum x^2 - \frac{(\sum x)^2}{n}}{n-1} = \frac{\frac{24}{25} - \frac{2^2}{6}}{6-1} = \frac{.2933}{5} = .0587$ square ounce

$s = \sqrt{.0587} = .2422$ ounce

2.53 This is one possibility for the two data sets.

Data Set 1: 0, 1, 2, 3, 4, 5, 6, 7, 8, 9
Data Set 2: 0, 0, 1, 1, 2, 2, 3, 3, 9, 9

The two sets of data above have the same range = largest measurement − smallest measurement = 9 − 0 = 9.

The means for the two data sets are:

$\bar{x}_1 = \frac{\sum x}{n} = \frac{0+1+2+3+4+5+6+7+8+9}{10} = \frac{45}{10} = 4.5$

$\bar{x}_2 = \frac{\sum x}{n} = \frac{0+0+1+1+2+2+3+3+9+9}{10} = \frac{30}{10} = 3$

The dot diagrams for the two data sets are shown below.

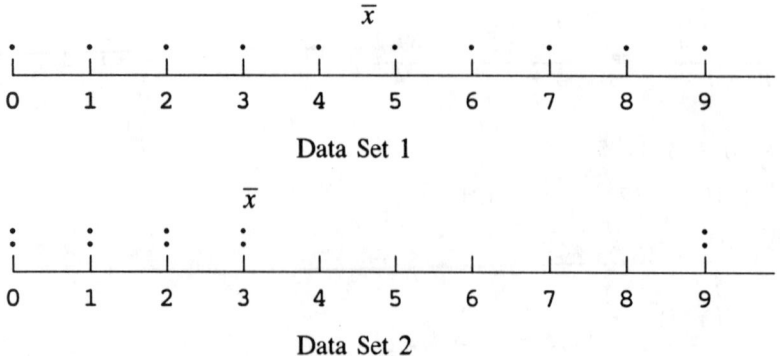

2.55 a. The mean value for the U.S. City Average Index for the data in the table is:

$\bar{x} = \frac{\sum_{i=1}^{n} x_i}{n} = \frac{3607.3}{24} = 150.3042$

The mean value for the Chicago Index for the data in the table is:

$$\bar{x} = \frac{\sum_{i=1}^{n} x_i}{n} = \frac{3622.9}{24} = 150.9542$$

b. For the U.S. City Average Index, the range = largest measurement − smallest measurement
= 153.7 − 146.2 = 7.5

For the Chicago Index, the range = largest measurement − smallest measurement
= 154.3 − 146.5 = 7.8

c. The standard deviation for the U.S. City Average Index is:

$$s = \sqrt{\frac{\sum_{i=1}^{n} x_i^2 - \frac{\left[\sum_{i=1}^{n} x_i\right]^2}{n}}{n-1}} = \sqrt{\frac{542{,}325.89 - \frac{3607.3^2}{24}}{24-1}} = \sqrt{5.8117} = 2.4108$$

The standard deviation for the Chicago Index for the data in the table is:

$$s = \sqrt{\frac{\sum_{i=1}^{n} x_i^2 - \frac{\left[\sum_{i=1}^{n} x_i\right]^2}{n}}{n-1}} = \sqrt{\frac{547{,}054.25 - \frac{3622.9^2}{24}}{24-1}} = \sqrt{7.0609} = 2.6572$$

d. The Chicago Index displays the greater variation about its mean for this time period. This is evident by the larger standard deviation and range for the Chicago Index.

2.57 a. The range is the largest measurement − the smallest measurement = 510.0 − 54.8 = 455.2

$$\sum_{i=1}^{n} x_i = 182.6 + 226.0 + 342.1 + 510.0 + 119.3 + 378.0 + 54.8 = 1812.8$$

$$\sum_{i=1}^{n} x_i^2 = 182.6^2 + 226.0^2 + 342.1^2 + 510.0^2 + 119.3^2 + 378.0^2 + 54.8^2 = 621{,}670.7$$

$$s^2 = \frac{\sum_{i=1}^{n} x_i^2 - \frac{\left[\sum_{i=1}^{n} x_i\right]^2}{n}}{n-1} = \frac{621{,}670.7 - \frac{1812.8^2}{7}}{7-1} = \frac{152{,}207.2943}{6} = 25{,}367.88238$$

$s = \sqrt{25{,}367.88235} = 159.2730$

b. The range is $455.2 million.

The variance is 25,367.88238 million dollars squared.

The standard deviation is $159.2730 million.

c. If America West had a loss of $50 million, the range would increase since the smallest measurement decreased. The data are more spread out now.

Methods for Describing Sets of Data

If America West had a loss of $50 million, the standard deviation would increase since the data set is more spread out. ($s = \sqrt{34{,}069.27667} = 184.5786 > 159.2730$)

2.59   Chebyshev's Rule can be applied to any data set. The Empirical Rule applies only to data sets that are mound-shaped—that are approximately symmetric, with a clustering of measurements about the midpoint of the distribution and that tail off as one moves away from the center of the distribution.

2.61   Since no information is given about the data set, we can only use Chebyshev's Rule.

    a.   Nothing can be said about the percentage of measurements which will fall between $\bar{x} - s$ and $\bar{x} + s$.

    b.   At least 3/4 or 75% of the measurements will fall between $\bar{x} - 2s$ and $\bar{x} + 2s$.

    c.   At least 8/9 or 89% of the measurements will fall between $\bar{x} - 3s$ and $\bar{x} + 3s$.

2.63   a. $\bar{x} = \dfrac{\sum x}{n} = \dfrac{206}{25} = 8.24$

$s^2 = \dfrac{\sum x^2 - \dfrac{(\sum x)^2}{n}}{n-1} = \dfrac{1778 - \dfrac{206^2}{25}}{25-1} = 3.357 \qquad s = \sqrt{s^2} = 1.83$

b.

Interval	Number of Measurements in Interval	Percentage
$\bar{x} \pm s$, or (6.41, 10.07)	18	18/25 = .72 or 72%
$\bar{x} \pm 2s$, or (4.58, 11.90)	24	24/25 = .96 or 96%
$\bar{x} \pm 3s$, or (2.75, 13.73)	25	25/25 = 1 or 100%

    c.   The percentages in part b are in agreement with Chebyshev's Rule and agree fairly well with the percentages given by the Empirical Rule.

    d.   Range = 12 − 5 = 7

$s \approx$ range/4 = 7/4 = 1.75

The range approximation provides a satisfactory estimate of $s = 1.83$ from part a.

2.65   a.   More than half of the spillage amounts are less than or equal to 48 metric tons and almost all (44 out of 50) are below 104 metric tons. There appear to be three outliers, values which are much different than the others. These three values are larger than 216 metric tons.

    b.   From the graph in part a, the data are not mound shaped. Thus, we must use Chebyshev's Rule. This says that at least 8/9 of the measurements will fall within 3 standard deviations of the mean. Since most of the observations will be within 3 standard deviations of the mean, we could use this interval to predict the spillage amount of the next major oil spill. From the printout, the mean is 59.820 and the standard deviation is 53.362. The interval would be:

$\bar{x} \pm 3s \Rightarrow 59.82 \pm 3(53.362) \Rightarrow 59.82 \pm 160.086 \Rightarrow (-100.266, 219.906)$

Since an oil spillage amount cannot be negative, we would predict that the spillage amount of the next major oil spill will be between 0 and 219.906 metric tons.

2.67 a. Since the data are not mound-shaped, the Empirical Rule would not be appropriate for describing bankruptcy times.

b. Chebyshev's Rule says that at least 75% of the data will fall within 2 standard deviations of the mean. From the printout, the mean is 2.549 and the standard deviation is 1.828. The interval $\bar{x} \pm 2s$ is $2.549 \pm 2(1.828)$ or $(-1.107, 6.205)$. Thus, at least 75% of the bankruptcy times should fall within -1.107 and 6.205 months.

c. From the data in Exercise 2.22, 47 of the 49 observations fall in this interval or $47/49 = .959$ or 95.9%. This is at least 75%. It is also very close to the 95% used with the Empirical Rule.

d. Because the data set is skewed to the right, the median is a better estimate of the center of the distribution than the mean. Thus, we would estimate that a firm would be in bankruptcy approximately 1.7 months. From the interval in part b, we would be very confident that the firm would be in bankruptcy no more than 6.2 months.

2.69 a. Since no information is given about the distribution of the velocities of the Winchester bullets, we can only use Chebyshev's Rule to describe the data. We know that at least 3/4 of the velocities will fall within the interval:

$$\bar{x} \pm 2s \Rightarrow 936 \pm 2(10) \Rightarrow 936 \pm 20 \Rightarrow (916, 956)$$

Also, at least 8/9 of the velocities will fall within the interval:

$$\bar{x} \pm 3s \Rightarrow 936 \pm 3(10) \Rightarrow 936 \pm 30 \Rightarrow (906, 966)$$

b. Since a velocity of 1,000 is much larger than the largest value in the second interval in part a, it is very unlikely that the bullet was manufactured by Winchester.

2.71 Since we do not know if the distribution of the heights of the trees is mound-shaped, we need to apply Chebyshev's Rule. We know $\mu = 30$ and $\sigma = 3$. Therefore,

$$\mu \pm 3\sigma \Rightarrow 30 \pm 3(3) \Rightarrow 30 \pm 9 \Rightarrow (21, 39)$$

According to Chebyshev's Rule, at least 8/9 or .89 of the tree heights on this piece of land fall within this interval and at most $\frac{1}{9}$ or .11 of the tree heights will fall above the interval. However, the buyer will only purchase the land if at least $\frac{1000}{5000}$ or .20 of the tree heights are at least 40 feet tall. Therefore, the buyer should not buy the piece of land.

2.73 a. Assume that the data represent a sample. The mean is:

$$\bar{x} = \frac{\sum x}{n} = \frac{-1.0 + 3.9 + (-2.9) + \cdots + (-4.0)}{11} = \frac{-20.1}{11} = -1.83$$

$$s^2 = \frac{\sum x^2 - \frac{(\sum x)^2}{n}}{n-1} = \frac{149.67 - \frac{(-20.1)^2}{11}}{11 - 1} = 11.2942$$

$$s = \sqrt{11.2942} = 3.361$$

b. If we assume that the percent changes in daily circulation is approximately mound-shaped, then we can use the Empirical Rule.

Methods for Describing Sets of Data

The interval $\bar{x} \pm s$ is -1.83 ± 3.361 or $(-5.191, 1.531)$. The Empirical Rule says that approximately 68% of the observations should fall in this interval.

The interval $\bar{x} \pm 2s$ is $-1.83 \pm 2(3.361)$ or $(-8.552, 4.892)$. The Empirical Rule says that approximately 95% of the observations should fall in this interval.

The interval $\bar{x} \pm 3s$ is $-1.83 \pm 3(3.361)$ or $(-11.913, 8.253)$. The Empirical Rule says that approximately all of the observations should fall in this interval.

The relative frequency histogram should look something like the following:

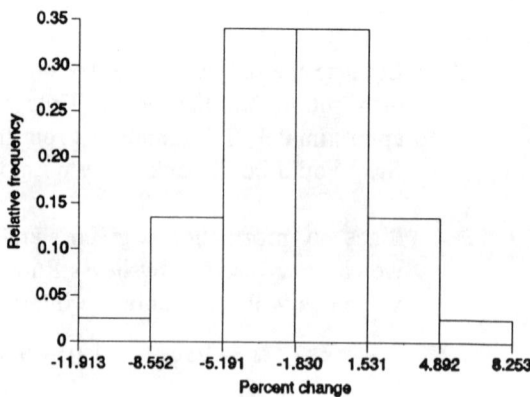

c. No. Almost all of the observations should be within 3 standard deviations of the mean. From the last interval in part b, the largest value should be around 8.3. The 32.4% is much greater than 8.3%. In fact, the 32.4% is more than 10 standard deviations from the mean.

2.75 a. $z = \dfrac{x - \bar{x}}{s} = \dfrac{40 - 30}{5} = 2$ (sample)   2 standard deviations above the mean.

b. $z = \dfrac{x - \mu}{\sigma} = \dfrac{90 - 89}{2} = .5$ (population)   .5 standard deviations above the mean.

c. $z = \dfrac{x - \mu}{\sigma} = \dfrac{50 - 50}{5} = 0$ (population)   0 standard deviations above the mean.

d. $z = \dfrac{x - \bar{x}}{s} = \dfrac{20 - 30}{4} = -2.5$ (sample)   2.5 standard deviations below the mean.

2.77 The 50th percentile of a data set is the observation that has half of the observations less than it. Another name for the 50th percentile is the median.

2.79 a. From the problem, $\mu = 2.7$ and $\sigma = .5$

$$z = \frac{x - \mu}{\sigma} \Rightarrow z\sigma = x - \mu \Rightarrow x = \mu + z\sigma$$

For $z = 2.0$, $x = 2.7 + 2.0(.5) = 3.7$

For $z = -1.0$, $x = 2.7 - 1.0(.5) = 2.2$

For $z = .5$, $x = 2.7 + .5(.5) = 2.95$

For $z = -2.5$, $x = 2.7 - 2.5(.5) = 1.45$

b. For $z = -1.6$, $x = 2.7 - 1.6(.5) = 1.9$

c. If we assume the distribution of GPAs is approximately mound-shaped, we can use the Empirical Rule.

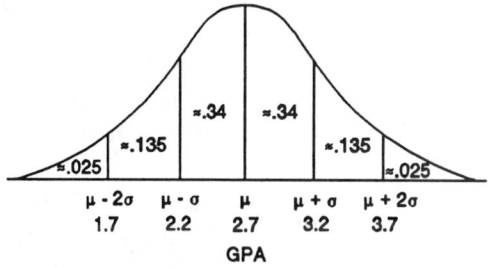

From the Empirical Rule, we know that $\approx .025$ or $\approx 2.5\%$ of the students will have GPAs above 3.7 (with $z = 2$). Thus, the GPA corresponding to summa cum laude (top 2.5%) will be greater than 3.7 ($z > 2$).

We know that $\approx .16$ or 16% of the students will have GPAs above 3.2 ($z = 1$). Thus, the limit on GPAs for cum laude (top 16%) will be greater than 3.2 ($z > 1$).

We must assume the distribution is mound-shaped.

2.81 Since the 90th percentile of the study sample in the subdivision was .00372 mg/L, which is less than the USEPA level of .015 mg/L, the water customers in the subdivision are not at risk of drinking water with unhealthy lead levels.

2.83 a. To calculate the U.S. merchandise trade balance for each of the ten countries, take the exports minus imports.

Country	U.S. Merchandise Trade Balance (in billions)
Brazil	−590
China	−29,494
Egypt	2,296
France	−3,153
Italy	−7,518
Japan	−65,668
Mexico	1,347
Panama	953
Sweden	−2,524
Singapore	−2,339

Methods for Describing Sets of Data

b. To find the z-scores, we must first calculate the sample mean and standard deviation.

$$\bar{x} = \frac{\sum_{i=1}^{n} x_i}{n} = \frac{-106,690}{10} = -10,669$$

$$s^2 = \frac{\sum_{i=1}^{n} x_i^2 - \frac{\left[\sum_{i=1}^{n} x_i\right]^2}{n}}{n-1} = \frac{5,268,827,824 - \frac{(-10,669)^2}{10}}{10-1} = \frac{4,130,552,214}{9} = 458,950,246$$

$$s = \sqrt{458,950,246} = 21,423.1241$$

Japan: $z = \dfrac{x - \bar{x}}{s} = \dfrac{-65,668 - (-10,669)}{21,423.1241} = -2.57$

The relative position of the U.S. trade balance with Japan is 2.57 standard deviations below the mean. This indicates that this measurement is small compared to the other U.S. trade balances.

Egypt: $z = \dfrac{x - \bar{x}}{s} = \dfrac{2,296 - (-10,669)}{21,423.1241} = .61$

The relative position of the U.S. trade balance with Egypt is .61 standard deviation above the mean. This indicates that this measurement is larger than the average of the U.S. trade balances.

2.85   a.   From the printout, the 10th percentile is 0. Ten percent of the observations are less than or equal to 0.

b. From the printout, the 95% percentile is 21. Ninety-five percent of the observations are less than or equal to 21.

c. The z-score for the county with 48 Superfund sites is:

$$z = \frac{x - \bar{x}}{s} = \frac{48 - 5.24}{7.224} = 5.90$$

d. Yes. A score of 48 is almost 6 standard deviations from the mean. We know that for any data set almost all (at least 8/9 using Chebyshev's Rule) of the observations are within 3 standard deviations of the mean. To be almost 6 standard deviations from the mean is very unusual.

2.87   The 25th percentile, or lower quartile, is the measurement that has 25% of the measurements below it and 75% of the measurements above it. The 50th percentile, or median, is the measurement that has 50% of the measurements below it and 50% of the measurements above it. The 75th percentile, or upper quartile, is the measurement that has 75% of the measurements below it and 25% of the measurements above it.

2.89   a.   Median is approximately 39.

b. Q_L is approximately 31.5 (Lower Quartile)

Q_U is approximately 45 (Upper Quartile)

c. $IQR = Q_U - Q_L \approx 45 - 31.5 \approx 13.5$

d. The data set is skewed to the left since the left whisker is longer.

e. 50% of the measurements are to the right of the median and 75% are to the left of the upper quartile.

2.91 a. Using MINITAB, the box plot for sample A is given below.

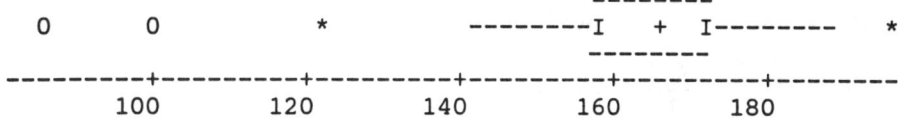

Using MINITAB, the box plot for sample B is given below.

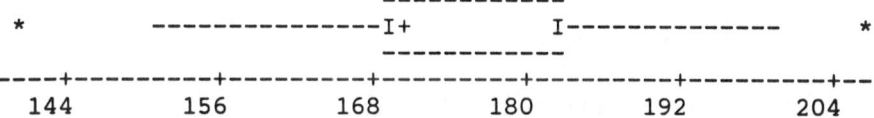

b. The range for sample A is larger than the range for sample B. The descriptive measures for sample A (Q_L, median, and Q_U) are all smaller than those of sample B. Both samples look somewhat symmetric (excluding outliers) since the whiskers on each box plot are the same length on both sides.

In sample A, the measurements 84 and 100 are outliers. These measurements fall outside the outer fences.

$$\begin{aligned} \text{Lower outer fence} &= \text{Lower hinge} - 3(IQR) \\ &\approx 158 - 3(172 - 158) \\ &= 158 - 3(14) \\ &= 116 \end{aligned}$$

In addition, 122 and 196 may be outliers. They lie outside the inner fences. In sample B, 140.4 and 206.4 may be outliers. They lie outside the inner fences.

2.93 a. The median bankruptcy times for "Prepack" and "Joint" firms are almost the same. They are both less than the median bankruptcy time of the "None" firms.

b. The range of the "Prepack" firms is less than the other two, while the range of the "None" firms is the largest. The interquartile range of the "Prepack" firms is less than the other two, while the interquartile range of the "Joint" firms is larger than the other two.

c. No. The interquartile range for the "Prepack" firms is the smallest which corresponds to the smallest standard deviation. However, the second smallest interquartile range corresponds to the "none" firms. The second smallest standard deviation corresponds to the "Joint" firms.

d. Yes. There is evidence of two outliers in the "Prepack" firms. These are indicated by the two *'s. There is also evidence of two outliers in the "None" firms. These are indicated by the two *'s.

Methods for Describing Sets of Data

2.95 a. Using MINITAB, the box plot is:

```
              ---------------
    ---------I    +     I------------    * **            *
              ---------------
    +---------+---------+---------+---------+---------+------
    0        12        24        36        48        60
```

The median is about 18. The data appear to be skewed to the right since there are 4 suspect outliers to the right and none to the left. The variability of the data is fairly small because the IQR is fairly small, approximately $26 - 10 = 16$.

b. The customers associated with the suspected outliers are customers 238, 268, 269, and 264.

c. In order to find the z-scores, we must first find the mean and standard deviation.

$$\bar{x} = \frac{\sum x}{n} = \frac{815}{40} = 20.375$$

$$s^2 = \frac{\sum x^2 - \frac{(\sum x)^2}{n}}{n-1} = \frac{24129 - \frac{815^2}{40}}{40-1} = 192.90705$$

$$s = \sqrt{192.90705} = 13.89$$

The z-scores associated with the suspected outliers are:

Customer 238 $z = \frac{x - \bar{x}}{s} = \frac{47 - 20.375}{13.89} = 1.92$

Customer 268 $z = \frac{49 - 20.375}{13.89} = 2.06$

Customer 269 $z = \frac{50 - 20.375}{13.89} = 2.13$

Customer 264 $z = \frac{64 - 20.375}{13.89} = 3.14$

All but one of the z-scores is greater than 2. These are very unusual values.

2.97 The relative frequency histogram is:

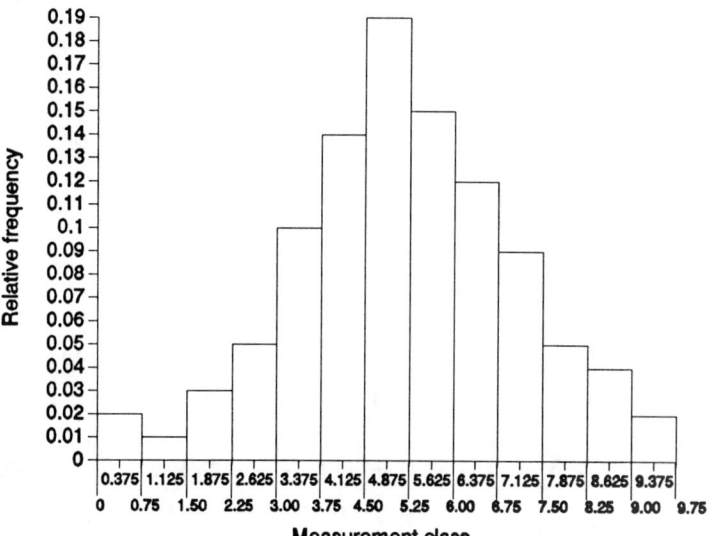

2.99 a. $z = \dfrac{x - \mu}{\sigma} = \dfrac{50 - 60}{10} = -1$

$z = \dfrac{70 - 60}{10} = 1$

$z = \dfrac{80 - 60}{10} = 2$

b. $z = \dfrac{x - \mu}{\sigma} = \dfrac{50 - 60}{5} = -2$

$z = \dfrac{70 - 60}{5} = 2$

$z = \dfrac{80 - 60}{5} = 4$

c. $z = \dfrac{x - \mu}{\sigma} = \dfrac{50 - 40}{10} = 1$

$z = \dfrac{70 - 40}{10} = 3$

$z = \dfrac{80 - 40}{10} = 4$

d. $z = \dfrac{x - \mu}{\sigma} = \dfrac{50 - 40}{100} = .1$

$z = \dfrac{70 - 40}{100} = .3$

$z = \dfrac{80 - 40}{100} = .4$

2.101 a. $\sum x = 13 + 1 + 10 + 3 + 3 = 30$

$\sum x^2 = 13^2 + 1^2 + 10^2 + 3^2 + 3^2 = 288$

$\bar{x} = \sum x = \dfrac{30}{5} = 6$

Methods for Describing Sets of Data   25

$$s^2 = \frac{\sum x^2 - \frac{(\sum x)^2}{n}}{n-1} = \frac{288 - \frac{30^2}{5}}{5-1} = \frac{108}{4} = 27 \qquad s = \sqrt{27} = 5.20$$

b. $\sum x = 13 + 6 + 6 + 0 = 25$
$\sum x^2 = 13^2 + 6^2 + 6^2 + 0^2 = 241$
$\bar{x} = \frac{\sum x}{n} = \frac{25}{4} = 6.25$

$$s^2 = \frac{\sum x^2 - \frac{(\sum x)^2}{n}}{n-1} = \frac{241 - \frac{25^2}{4}}{4-1} = \frac{84.75}{3} = 28.25 \qquad s = \sqrt{28.25} = 5.32$$

c. $\sum x = 1 + 0 + 1 + 10 + 11 + 11 + 15 = 49$
$\sum x^2 = 1^2 + 0^2 + 1^2 + 10^2 + 11^2 + 11^2 + 15^2 = 569$
$\bar{x} = \frac{\sum x}{n} = \frac{49}{7} = 7$

$$s^2 = \frac{\sum x^2 - \frac{(\sum x)^2}{n}}{n-1} = \frac{569 - \frac{49^2}{7}}{7-1} = \frac{226}{6} = 37.67 \qquad s = \sqrt{37.67} = 6.14$$

d. $\sum x = 3 + 3 + 3 + 3 = 12$
$\sum x^2 = 3^2 + 3^2 + 3^2 + 3^2 = 36$
$\bar{x} = \frac{\sum x}{n} = \frac{12}{4} = 3$

$$s^2 = \frac{\sum x^2 - \frac{(\sum x)^2}{n}}{n-1} = \frac{36 - \frac{12^2}{4}}{4-1} = \frac{0}{3} = 0 \qquad s = \sqrt{0} = 0$$

2.103 The range is found by taking the largest measurement in the data set and subtracting the smallest measurement. Therefore, it only uses two measurements from the whole data set. The standard deviation uses every measurement in the data set. Therefore, it takes every measurement into account—not just two. The range is affected by extreme values more than the standard deviation.

2.105 a. In the United Kingdom, conglomerates have increased in each period, from 5% to 9% to 11% to 17%. Companies that have diversified either horizontally or vertically increased from 1950 to 1970 (from 20% to 28% to 49%), and then dropped slightly in 1980 (48%). Companies with a dominant business activity that accounts for more than 70% of revenues stayed relatively the same from 1950 to 1960 (40% to 43%), dropped in 1970, and held relatively constant in 1980 (29% and 27%). Companies with a single business activity held the highest percentage in 1950 (35%) and then dropped steadily until 1980 (20% to 11% to 8%).

In the United States, conglomerates have increased in each period, from 3% to 5% to 13% to 24%. Companies that have diversified either horizontally or vertically increased from 1950 to 1960 (from 27% to 39%), held relatively constant from 1960 to 1970 (39% to 36%), and then increased again from 1970 to 1980 (36% to 54%). Companies with a dominant business activity that accounts for more than 70% of revenues stayed relatively the same from 1950 to 1970 (44% to 40% to 41%), and then dropped in 1980 to 22%. Companies with a single business activity held the highest percentage in 1950 (28%) and then dropped steadily until 1980 (16% to 10% to 0%).

b. One possible set of pie charts for 1990 could be as follows:

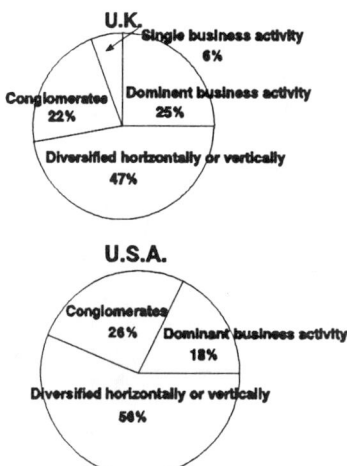

2.107 a. First, we must compute the total processing times by adding the processing times of the three departments. The total processing times are as follows:

Request	Total Processing Time	Request	Total Processing Time	Request	Total Processing Time
1	13.3	17	19.4*	33	23.4*
2	5.7	18	4.7	34	14.2
3	7.6	19	9.4	35	14.3
4	20.0*	20	30.2	36	24.0*
5	6.1	21	14.9	37	6.1
6	1.8	22	10.7	38	7.4
7	13.5	23	36.2*	39	17.7*
8	13.0	24	6.5	40	15.4
9	15.6	25	10.4	41	16.4
10	10.9	26	3.3	42	9.5
11	8.7	27	8.0	43	8.1
12	14.9	28	6.9	44	18.2*
13	3.4	29	17.2*	45	15.3
14	13.6	30	10.2	46	13.9
15	14.6	31	16.0	47	19.9*
16	14.4	32	11.5	48	15.4
				49	14.3*
				50	19.0

Methods for Describing Sets of Data

The stem-and-leaf displays with the appropriate leaves circled are as follows:

```
     Stem-and-leaf of Mkt              Stem-and-leaf of Engr
       Leaf Unit = 0.10                  Leaf Unit = 0.10

    6    0   112446              7    0   4466699
    7    1   3                  14    1   333378⑧
   14    2   ⓪024699            19    2   ①22④6
   16    3   2⑤                 23    3   1568
   22    4   ⓪⓪①577            (5)   4   24688
  (10)   5   0344556889         22    5   233
   18    6   000②2247⑨⑨        19    6   ⓪12③9
    8    7   003⑧               14    7   ②②379
    4    8   ⓪7                  9    8
    2    9                       9    9   66
    2   10   0                   7   10   0
    1   11   0                   6   11   3
                                  5   12   02③
                                  2   13   ⓪
                                  1   14   ④
```

```
    Stem-and-leaf of Accnt           Stem-and-leaf of Total
      Leaf Unit = 0.10                 Leaf Unit = 1.00

   19    0   11111111111②2333444    1    0   1
   (8)   0   55556⑧88               3    0   33
   23    1   00                     5    0   45
   21    1   7⑨                    11    0   666677
   19    2   00②3                  17    0   888999
   15    2                         21    1   0000
   15    3   23                    (5)   1   33333
   13    3   78                    24    1   4④44445555
   11    4                         14    1   66⑦⑦
   11    4                         10    1   ⑧9⑨⑨
   11    5                          6    2   ⓪
   11    5   8                      5    2   ③
   10    6   2                      4    2   ④4
    9    6                        HI   30, ㊱
    9    7   ⓪
    8    7
    8    8   4
   HI  ㊷, ⑩⑤, ⑬⑤, 144,
       ⑱②, 220, ㉚⓪
```

Of the 50 requests, 10 were lost. For each of the three departments, the processing times for the lost requests are scattered throughout the distributions. The processing times for the departments do not appear to be related to whether the request was lost or not. However, the total processing times for the lost requests appear to be clustered towards the high side of the distribution. It appears that if the total processing time could be kept under 17 days, 76% of the data could be maintained, while reducing the number of lost requests to 1.

b. For the Marketing department, if the maximum processing time was set at 6.5 days, 78% of the requests would be processed, while reducing the number of lost requests by 4. For the Engineering department, if the maximum processing time was set at 7.0 days, 72% of the requests would be processed, while reducing the number of lost requests by 5. For the Accounting department, if the maximum processing time was set at 8.5 days, 86% of the requests would be processed, while reducing the number of lost requests by 5.

2.109 a. One reason the plot may be interpreted differently is that no scale is given on the vertical axis. Also, since the plot almost reaches the horizontal axis at 3 years, it is obvious that the bottom of the plot has been cut off. Another important factor omitted is who responded to the survey.

b. A scale should be added to the vertical axis. Also, that scale should start at 0.

2.111 a. Since the mean is greater than the median, the distribution of the radiation levels is skewed to the right.

b. $\bar{x} \pm s \Rightarrow 10 \pm 3 \Rightarrow (7, 13)$; $\bar{x} \pm 2s \Rightarrow 10 \pm 2(3) \Rightarrow (4, 16)$; $\bar{x} \pm 3s \Rightarrow 10 \pm 3(3) \Rightarrow (1, 19)$

Interval	Chebyshev's	Empirical
(7, 13)	At least 0	≈ 68%
(4, 16)	At least 75%	≈ 95%
(1, 19)	At least 88.9%	≈ 100%

Since the data are skewed to the right, Chebyshev's Rule is probably more appropriate in this case.

c. The background level is 4. Using Chebyshev's Rule, at least 75% or .75(50) ≈ 38 homes are above the background level. Using the Empirical Rule, ≈ 97.5% or .975(50) ≈ 49 homes are above the background level.

d. $z = \dfrac{x - \bar{x}}{s} = \dfrac{20 - 10}{3} = 3.333$

It is unlikely that this new measurement came from the same distribution as the other 50. Using either Chebyshev's Rule or the Empirical Rule, it is very unlikely to see any observations more than 3 standard deviations from the mean.

Methods for Describing Sets of Data

2.113 We will use pie charts to demonstrate the increase in part-time and temporary workers in Japan from 1982 to 1992.

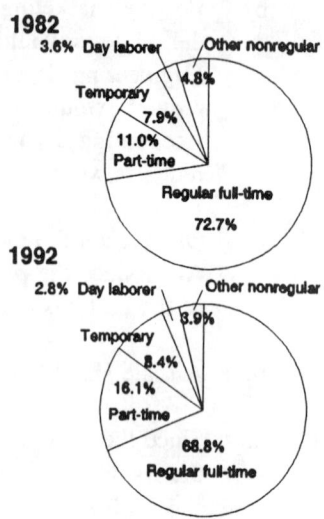

2.115 a. Frequency bar chart.

b. It presents the number of napkins (out of 1000) that fall into each of four categories.

c. Of the 1000 napkins printed, 700 were successful. Another way of saying this is 700/1000 × 100% = 70% of the imprints were successful.

2.119 a. For the High GNP group, we compute the following:

$$\bar{x} = \frac{\sum x}{n} = \frac{3.5 + 6.3 + \cdots + 4.6}{8} = \frac{35.3}{8} = 4.4125$$

$$s^2 = \frac{\sum x^2 - \frac{(\sum x)^2}{n}}{n - 1} = \frac{182.79 - \frac{(35.3)^2}{8}}{8 - 1} = 3.86125$$

$$s = \sqrt{3.86125} = 1.965$$

For the Low GNP group, we compute the following:

$$\text{Median} = \frac{16.9 + 29.4}{2} = 23.15$$

$$s^2 = \frac{\sum x^2 - \frac{(\sum x)^2}{n}}{n - 1} = \frac{162{,}928.01 - \frac{(626.5)^2}{8}}{8 - 1} = 16{,}266.46126$$

$$s = \sqrt{16{,}266.46126} = 127.54$$

b. For the High GNP group, the data appear to be approximately mound-shaped. Thus, we could use either the mean or median as a measure of the middle of the distribution. For this example, the mean and median (4.05) are almost equal to each other.

For the Low GNP group, the data do not appear to be mound-shaped. There are a couple of numbers which are quite large compared to the others. Thus, the median would be a better measure of the middle of the distribution. For this example, the mean (78.3125) is much larger than the median.

2.121   The time series plot for the data is:

Of the 25 observations, only 7 are less than the claimed number of 12 minutes. Thus, the claim that "your hood will be open less than 12 minutes when we service your car" is probably not true.

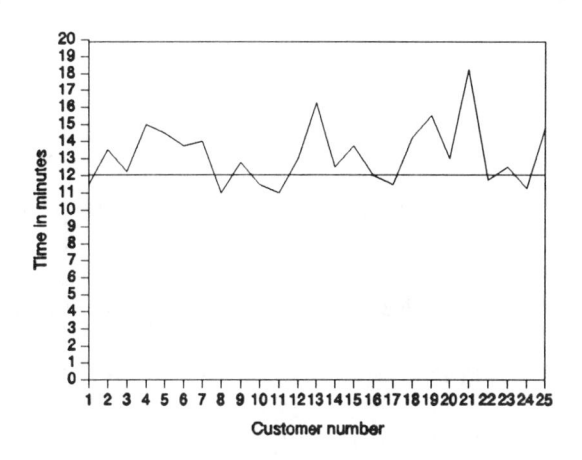

2.123   a.   A relative frequency histogram is:

From the histogram, about a third of the sample scored in the "Very relaxed/confident" category. About an equal amount scored in categories "Very anxious," "Some mild anxiety," and "Generally relaxed/comfortable." Very few scored in the "Anxious/tense" category.

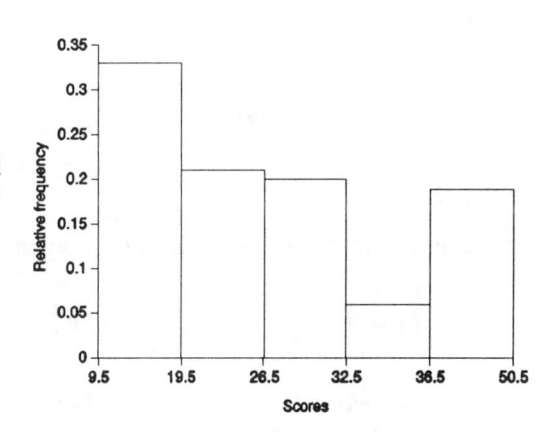

b.   From the tables, the means and standard deviations for the male and female teachers are very similar. The mean for the females is slightly lower than the mean for the males, but the standard deviation is slightly larger. Thus, the average female has a little less anxiety towards computers, but the distribution of female scores is slightly wider than that of the males. But again, these differences are so small that there probably is no difference between male and female teachers concerning their anxiety toward computers.

Methods for Describing Sets of Data

c.   It is not unusual for there to be variation within the samples. The inflation rates in different countries are affected by different characteristics of those countries. It is also not unusual for there to be variation between the samples. The top 10 countries are very similar to each other; thus, the standard deviation is fairly low. The bottom 10 countries are quite a bit different. Thus, it is not unusual for the standard deviation to be quite large.

Probability   Chapter 3

3.1 a. Since the probabilities must sum to 1,

$$P(E_3) = 1 - P(E_1) - P(E_2) - P(E_4) - P(E_5) = 1 - .1 - .2 - .1 - .1 = .5$$

   b. $P(E_3) = 1 - P(E_3) - P(E_2) - P(E_4) - P(E_5)$
       $\Rightarrow 2P(E_3) = 1 - .1 - .2 - .1 \Rightarrow 2P(E_3) = .6 \Rightarrow P(E_3) = .3$

   c. $P(E_3) = 1 - P(E_1) - P(E_2) - P(E_4) - P(E_5) = 1 - .1 - .1 - .1 - .1 = .6$

3.3 $P(A) = P(1) + P(2) + P(3) = .05 + .20 + .30 = .55$
     $P(B) = P(1) + P(3) + P(5) = .05 + .30 + .15 = .50$
     $P(C) = P(1) + P(2) + P(3) + P(5) = .05 + .20 + .30 + .15 = .70$

3.5 If we denote the marbles as B_1, B_2, R_1, R_2, R_3, then the ten equally likely sample points in the sample space would be:

$$S: \begin{bmatrix} (B_1, B_2), (B_1, R_1), (B_1, R_2), (B_1, R_3), (B_2, R_1) \\ (B_2, R_2), (B_2, R_3), (R_1, R_2), (R_1, R_3), (R_2, R_3) \end{bmatrix}$$

Notice that order is ignored, as the only concern is whether or not a marble is selected. Each of these 10 would be equally likely, implying that each occurs with a probability 1/10.

$$P(A) = \frac{1}{10} \qquad P(B) = 6\left[\frac{1}{10}\right] = \frac{6}{10} = \frac{3}{5} \qquad P(C) = 3\left[\frac{1}{10}\right] = \frac{3}{10}$$

3.7 a. The experiment consists of selecting 159 employees and asking each to indicate how strongly he/she agreed or disagreed with the statement "I believe that management is committed to CQI." There are five sample points: "Strongly agree," "Agree," "Neither agree nor disagree," "Disagree," and "Strongly disagree."

   b. Since we have frequencies for each of the sample points, good estimates of the probabilities are the relative frequencies. To find the relative frequencies, divide all of the frequencies by the sample size of 159. The estimates of the probabilities are:

Strongly Agree	Agree	Neither Agree Nor Disagree	Disagree	Strongly Disagree
.189	.403	.258	.113	.038

   c. The probability that an employee agrees or strongly agrees with the statement is .189 + .403 = .592.

   d. The probability that an employee does not strongly agree with the statement is equal to the sum of all the probabilities except that for "strongly agree" = .403 + .258 + .113 + .038 = .812.

3.9 There are $\binom{6}{3} = \frac{6!}{3!3!} = \frac{6 \cdot 5 \cdot 4 \cdot 3 \cdot 2 \cdot 1}{3 \cdot 2 \cdot 1 \cdot 3 \cdot 2 \cdot 1} = 20$ possible ways to select 3 cars from 6. Only one of these combinations includes all three lemons, so the probability that dealer A receives all three lemons is 1/20.

3.11 a. There are 15 sample points and they are the 15 credit card companies.

b. The probability of each sample point corresponds to its relative frequency. The relative frequency for each sample point is the frequency divided by the total sample size of 177.5 million. The probabilities of the sample points are:

	Probabilities
Citibank	24.3/177.5 = .137
Discover/Novus*	33.6/177.5 = .189
MBNA*	12.1/177.5 = .068
First USA*	7.8/177.5 = .044
First Chicago	13.2/177.5 = .074
AT&T Universal*	16.2/177.5 = .091
Household International*	12.2/177.5 = .069
Chase Manhattan	9.8/177.5 = .055
Chemical Bank	6.7/177.5 = .038
Capital One*	5.8/177.5 = .033
Bank of America	9.3/177.5 = .052
Bank One	9.7/177.5 = .055
Advanta*	4.9/177.5 = .028
Bank of New York	5.9/177.5 = .033
Optima (American Express)*	6.0/177.5 = .034
Total	1.000

c. The probability that the account chosen belongs to a nontraditional bank = .189 + .068 + .044 + .091 + .069 + .033 + .028 + .034 = .556. The probability that the account chosen belongs to a traditional bank = .137 + .074 + .055 + .038 + .052 + .055 + .033 = .444.

3.13 a. The odds in favor of an Oxford Shoes win are $\frac{1}{3}$ to $1 - \frac{1}{3} = \frac{2}{3}$ or 1 to 2.

b. If the odds in favor of Oxford Shoes are 1 to 1, then the probability that Oxford Shoes wins is $\frac{1}{1+1} = \frac{1}{2}$.

c. If the odds against Oxford Shoes are 3 to 2, then the odds in favor of Oxford Shoes are 2 to 3. Therefore, the probability that Oxford Shoes wins is $\frac{2}{2+3} = \frac{2}{5}$.

3.15 a. The four classifications are:

  (1) Raise a broad mix of crops
  (2) Raise livestock
  (3) Use chemicals sparingly
  (4) Use techniques for regenerating the soil

Probability

Let us define the following events:

A_1: Raise a broad mix of crops
A_2: Do not raise a broad mix of crops
B_1: Raise livestock
B_2: Do not raise livestock
C_1: Use chemical sparingly
C_2: Do not use chemical sparingly
D_1: Use techniques for regenerating the soil
D_2: Do not use techniques for regenerating the soil

Each farmer is classified as using or not using each of the four techniques. Thus, the sample points are:

$A_1B_1C_1D_1, A_1B_1C_1D_2, A_1B_1C_2D_1, A_1B_2C_1D_1, A_2B_1C_1D_1, A_1B_1C_2D_2,$
$A_1B_2C_1D_2, A_2B_1C_1D_2, A_1B_2C_2D_1, A_2B_1C_2D_1, A_2B_2C_1D_1, A_1B_2C_2D_2,$
$A_2B_1C_2D_2, A_2B_2C_1D_2, A_2B_2C_2D_1, A_2B_2C_2D_2$

b. Since there are 16 classification sets or 16 sample points, the probability of any one sample point is 1/16. The probability that a farmer will be classified as unlikely on all four criteria is:

$P(A_2B_2C_2D_2) = 1/16$

c. The probability that a farmer will be classified as likely on at least three of the criteria is:

$P(A_1B_1C_1D_1) + P(A_1B_1C_1D_2) + P(A_1B_1C_2D_1) + P(A_1B_2C_1D_1) + P(A_2B_1C_1D_1)$
$= 1/16 + 1/16 + 1/16 + 1/16 + 1/16 = 5/16$

3.17 Two events are mutually exclusive if they have no sample points in common. A possible Venn diagram of two mutually exclusive events is:

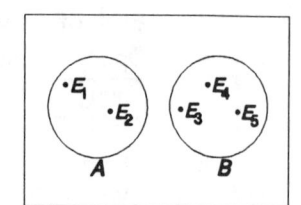

3.19 a. $P(A) = P(E_1) + P(E_2) + P(E_3) + P(E_5) + P(E_6) = \frac{1}{5} + \frac{1}{5} + \frac{1}{5} + \frac{1}{20} + \frac{1}{10} = \frac{15}{20} = \frac{3}{4}$

b. $P(B) = P(E_2) + P(E_3) + P(E_4) + P(E_7) = \frac{1}{5} + \frac{1}{5} + \frac{1}{20} + \frac{1}{5} = \frac{13}{20}$

c. $P(A \cup B) = P(E_1) + P(E_2) + P(E_3) + P(E_4) + P(E_5) + P(E_6) + P(E_7)$
$= \frac{1}{5} + \frac{1}{5} + \frac{1}{5} + \frac{1}{20} + \frac{1}{20} + \frac{1}{10} + \frac{1}{5} = 1$

d. $P(A \cap B) = P(E_2) + P(E_3) = \frac{1}{5} + \frac{1}{5} = \frac{2}{5}$

e. $P(A^c) = 1 - P(A) = 1 - \frac{3}{4} = \frac{1}{4}$

f. $P(B^c) = 1 - P(B) = 1 - \frac{13}{20} = \frac{7}{20}$

g. $P(A \cup A^c) = P(E_1) + P(E_2) + P(E_3) + P(E_4) + P(E_5) + P(E_6) + P(E_7)$
$= \frac{1}{5} + \frac{1}{5} + \frac{1}{5} + \frac{1}{20} + \frac{1}{20} + \frac{1}{10} + \frac{1}{5} = 1$

h. $P(A^c \cap B) = P(E_4) + P(E_7) = \frac{1}{20} + \frac{1}{5} = \frac{5}{20} = \frac{1}{4}$

3.21 The relative frequencies found by dividing the frequencies by $n = 8000$, are given in table form.

		Income		
		(D) Under $20,000	(E) $20,000–$50,000	(F) Over $50,000
Age	(A) Under 25	$\frac{950}{8000}$	$\frac{1000}{8000}$	$\frac{50}{8000}$
	(B) 25–45	$\frac{450}{8000}$	$\frac{2050}{8000}$	$\frac{1500}{8000}$
	(C) Over 45	$\frac{50}{8000}$	$\frac{950}{8000}$	$\frac{1000}{8000}$

a. $P(B) = \frac{450}{8000} + \frac{2050}{8000} + \frac{1500}{8000} = \frac{4000}{8000} = .5$

b. $P(F) = \frac{50}{8000} + \frac{1500}{8000} + \frac{1000}{8000} = \frac{2550}{8000} = .31875$

c. $P(C \cap F) = \frac{1000}{8000} = .125$

d. $P(B \cup C) = \frac{450}{8000} + \frac{2050}{8000} + \frac{1500}{8000} + \frac{50}{8000} + \frac{950}{8000} + \frac{1000}{8000} = \frac{6000}{8000} = .75$

e. $P(A^c) = 1 - P(A) = 1 - \left[\frac{950}{8000} + \frac{1000}{8000} + \frac{50}{8000}\right] = 1 - \frac{2000}{8000} = \frac{6000}{8000} = .75$

f. $P(A^c \cap F) = \frac{1500}{8000} + \frac{1000}{8000} = \frac{2500}{8000} = .3125$

Probability

g. $P(A \cap B) = 0$.   Thus, A and B are mutually exclusive.
    $P(A \cap C) = 0$.   Thus, A and C are mutually exclusive.
    $P(A \cap D) = 950/8000$.   Thus, A and D are not mutually exclusive.
    $P(A \cap E) = 1000/8000$.   Thus, A and E are not mutually exclusive.
    $P(A \cap F) = 50/8000$.   Thus, A and F are not mutually exclusive.
    $P(B \cap C) = 0$.   Thus, B and C are mutually exclusive.
    $P(B \cap D) = 450/8000$.   Thus, B and D are not mutually exclusive.
    $P(B \cap E) = 2050/8000$.   Thus, B and E are not mutually exclusive.
    $P(B \cap F) = 1500/8000$.   Thus, B and F are not mutually exclusive.
    $P(C \cap D) = 50/8000$.   Thus, C and D are not mutually exclusive.
    $P(C \cap E) = 950/8000$.   Thus, C and E are not mutually exclusive.
    $P(C \cap F) = 1000/8000$.   Thus, C and F are not mutually exclusive.
    $P(D \cap E) = 0$.   Thus, D and E are mutually exclusive.
    $P(D \cap F) = 0$.   Thus, D and F are mutually exclusive.
    $P(E \cap F) = 0$.   Thus, E and F are mutually exclusive.

3.23 a. $B \cap C$

   b. A^c

   c. $C \cup B$

   d. $A \cap C^c$

3.25 a. $A \cap B = \{G_1P_1, G_2P_1\}$

   b. $A \cup B = \{G_1G_2, G_1P_1, G_1P_2, G_2P_1, G_2P_2, P_1P_2\}$

   c. $A^c = \{P_1P_2\}$

   d. $P(A) = \dfrac{5}{6}$ $P(B) = \dfrac{3}{6} = \dfrac{1}{2}$ $P(A \cap B) = \dfrac{2}{6} = \dfrac{1}{3}$

   $P(A \cup B) = 1$ $P(A^c) = \dfrac{1}{6}$

   e. $P(A \cup B) = P(A) + P(B) - P(A \cap B) = \dfrac{5}{6} + \dfrac{1}{2} - \dfrac{1}{3} = \dfrac{5 + 3 - 2}{6} = \dfrac{6}{6} = 1$

   No, events A and B are not mutually exclusive because $P(A \cap B) \neq 0$.

3.27 a. A sample point is an event that cannot be decomposed into two or more other events. In this example, there are nine sample points. Let 1 be Warehouse 1, 2 be Warehouse 2, 3 be Warehouse 3, and let R be Regular, S be Stiff, and E be Extra stiff. The sample points are:

   (1, R) (1, S) (1, E)
   (2, R) (2, S) (2, E)
   (3, R) (3, S) (3, E)

   b. The *sample space* of an experiment is the collection of all its sample points.

c. $P(C) = P(3, R) + P(3, S) + P(3, E)$
    $= .11 + .07 + .06$
    $= .24$

d. $P(F) = P(1, E) + P(2, E) + P(3, E)$
    $= 0 + .04 + .06$
    $= .10$

e. $P(A) = P(1, R) + P(1, S) + P(1, E)$
    $= .41 + .06 + 0$
    $= .47$

f. $P(D) = P(1, R) + P(2, R) + P(3, R)$
    $= .41 + .10 + .11$
    $= .62$

g. $P(E) = P(1, S) + P(2, S) + P(3, S)$
    $= .06 + .15 + .07$
    $= .28$

3.29 The following events are defined:

A: {male worker}
B: {female worker}
C: {service worker}
D: {managerial/professional worker}
E: {operator/fabricator/laborers worker}
F: {technical/sales/administrative worker}

a. $P(A \cap C) = .06$

b. $P(D) = P(A \cap D) + P(B \cap D)$
    $= .14 + .13$
    $= .27$

c. $P[(B \cap D) \cup (B \cap E)] = .13 + .04$
    $= .17$

d. $P(F^c) = 1 - P(F) = 1 - [P(A \cap F) + P(B \cap F)]$
    $= 1 - (.11 + .19)$
    $= 1 - .30$
    $= .70$

3.31 a. Yes, the probabilities in the table sum to 1.

$.05 + .16 + .05 + .19 + .32 + .05 + .11 + .05 + .02 = 1$

b. $P(A) = .05 + .16 + .05 = .26$
    $P(B) = .05 + .19 + .11 = .35$
    $P(C) = .05 + .16 + .19 + .32 = .72$
    $P(D) = .05 + .05 + .11 + .05 + .02 = .28$
    $P(E) = .05$

Probability

c. $P(A \cup B) = .05 + .16 + .05 + .19 + .11 = .56$
$P(A \cap B) = .05$
$P(A \cup C) = .05 + .16 + .05 + .19 + .32 = .77$

d. $P(A^c) = 1 - P(A) = 1 - .26 = .74$

The probability that a managerial prospect is not highly motivated is .74. Only about 1/4 of the prospects are highly motivated.

e. The pairs of events that are mutually exclusive have no sample points in common.

$A \cap B$ contains the event "Prospect places in the high motivation category and in the high talent category." Therefore, A and B are not mutually exclusive.

$A \cap C$ contains the event "Prospect places in the high motivation category and in the medium or high talent category." Therefore, A and C are not mutually exclusive.

$A \cap D$ contains the event "Prospect places in the high motivation category and in the low talent category." Therefore, A and D are not mutually exclusive.

$A \cap E$ contains the event "Prospect places in the high motivation category and in the high talent category." Therefore, A and E are not mutually exclusive.

$B \cap C$ contains the event "Prospect places in the high talent category and in the medium or high motivation category." Therefore, B and C are not mutually exclusive.

$B \cap D$ contains the event "Prospect places in the high talent category and in the low motivation category." Therefore, B and D are not mutually exclusive.

$B \cap E$ contains the event "Prospect places in the high talent category and in the high motivation category." Therefore, B and E are not mutually exclusive.

$C \cap D$ contains no events. Therefore, C and D are mutually exclusive.

$C \cap E$ contains the event "Prospect places in the high talent category and in the high motivation category." Therefore, C and E are not mutually exclusive.

$D \cap E$ contains no events. Therefore, D and E are mutually exclusive.

3.33 a. $P(A) = P(E_1) + P(E_2) + P(E_3)$
   $= .2 + .3 + .3$
   $= .8$

$P(B) = P(E_2) + P(E_3) + P(E_5)$
   $= .3 + .3 + .1$
   $= .7$

$P(A \cap B) = P(E_2) + P(E_3)$
   $= .3 + .3$
   $= .6$

b. $P(E_1 \mid A) = \dfrac{P(E_1 \cap A)}{P(A)} = \dfrac{P(E_1)}{P(A)} = \dfrac{.2}{.8} = .25$

$P(E_2 \mid A) = \dfrac{P(E_2 \cap A)}{P(A)} = \dfrac{P(E_2)}{P(A)} = \dfrac{.3}{.8} = .375$

$P(E_3 \mid A) = \dfrac{P(E_3 \cap A)}{P(A)} = \dfrac{P(E_3)}{P(A)} = \dfrac{.3}{.8} = .375$

The original sample point probabilities are in the proportion .2 to .3 to .3 or 2 to 3 to 3.

The conditional probabilities for these sample points are in the proportion .25 to .375 to .375 or 2 to 3 to 3.

c. (1) $P(B \mid A) = P(E_2 \mid A) + P(E_3 \mid A)$
$= .375 + .375$ (from part b)
$= .75$

(2) $P(B \mid A) = \dfrac{P(A \cap B)}{P(A)} = \dfrac{.6}{.8} = .75$ (from part a)

The two methods do yield the same result.

d. If A and B are independent events, $P(B \mid A) = P(B)$.

From part c, $P(B \mid A) = .75$. From part a, $P(B) = .7$.

Since $.75 \neq .7$, A and B are not independent events.

3.35 a. $P(A) = P(E_1) + P(E_3) = .22 + .15 = .37$

b. $P(B) = P(E_2) + P(E_3) + P(E_4) = .31 + .15 + .22 = .68$

c. $P(A \cap B) = P(E_3) = .15$

d. $P(A \mid B) = \dfrac{P(A \cap B)}{P(B)} = \dfrac{.15}{.68} = .2206$

e. $P(B \cap C) = 0$

f. $P(C \mid B) = \dfrac{P(C \cap B)}{P(B)} = \dfrac{0}{.68} = 0$

g. For pair A and B: A and B are not independent because $P(A \mid B) \neq P(A)$ or $.2206 \neq .37$.

For pair A and C:

$P(A \cap C) = P(E_1) = .22$
$P(C) = P(E_1) + P(E_5) = .22 + .1 = .32$
$P(A \mid C) = \dfrac{P(A \cap C)}{P(C)} = \dfrac{.22}{.32} = .6875$

A and C are not independent because $P(A \mid C) \neq P(A)$ or $.6875 \neq .37$.

For pair B and C: B and C are not independent because $P(C \mid B) \neq P(C)$ or $0 \neq .32$.

3.37 a. $P(A \cap C) = 0 \Rightarrow A$ and C are mutually exclusive.
$P(B \cap C) = 0 \Rightarrow B$ and C are mutually exclusive.

b. $P(A) = P(1) + P(2) + P(3) = .20 + .05 + .30 = .55$
$P(B) = P(3) + P(4) = .30 + .10 = .40$
$P(C) = P(5) + P(6) = .10 + .25 = .35$

$P(A \cap B) = P(3) = .30$

$P(A \mid B) = \dfrac{P(A \cap B)}{P(B)} = \dfrac{.30}{.40} = .75$

A and B are independent if $P(A \mid B) = P(A)$. Since $P(A \mid B) = .75$ and $P(A) = .55$, A and B are not independent.

Since A and C are mutually exclusive, they are not independent. Similarly, since B and C are mutually exclusive, they are not independent.

    c.   Using the probabilities of sample points,
$$P(A \cup B) = P(1) + P(2) + P(3) + P(4) = .20 + .05 + .30 + .10 = .65$$

Using the additive rule,
$$P(A \cup B) = P(A) + P(B) - P(A \cap B) = .55 + .40 - .30 = .65$$

Using the probabilities of sample points,
$$P(A \cup C) = P(1) + P(2) + P(3) + P(5) + P(6)$$
$$= .20 + .05 + .30 + .10 + .25 = .90$$

Using the additive rule,
$$P(A \cup C) = P(A) + P(C) - P(A \cap C) = .55 + .35 - 0 = .90$$

3.39   a. $P(A \cap B) = P(A) \cdot P(B) = (.4)(.2) = .08$
              $P(A \mid B) = P(A) = .4$
              $P(A \cup B) = P(A) + P(B) - P(A \cap B) = .4 + .2 - .08 = .52$

    b. $P(A \cap B) = P(A \mid B) \cdot P(B) = (.6)(.2) = .12$

$P(B \mid A) = \dfrac{P(A \cap B)}{P(A)} = \dfrac{.12}{.40} = .30$

3.41   Define the following events:

        A: {Take tough action early}
        B: {Take tough action late}
        C: {Never take tough action}
        D: {Wisconsin}
        E: {Illinois}
        F: {Arkansas}
        G: {Louisiana}

    a. $P(D \cup G) = P(D) + P(G)$ (since D and G are mutually exclusive)

$$= \dfrac{0}{151} + \dfrac{37}{151} + \dfrac{9}{151} + \dfrac{1}{151} + \dfrac{21}{151} + \dfrac{15}{151} = \dfrac{83}{151} = .550$$

    b. $P((D \cup G)^c) = 1 - P(D \cup G)$

$$= 1 - \dfrac{83}{151} = \dfrac{68}{151} = .450$$

    c. $P(C) = \dfrac{9}{151} + \dfrac{11}{151} + \dfrac{6}{151} + \dfrac{15}{151} = \dfrac{41}{151} = .272$

    d. $P(F \cap C) = \dfrac{6}{151} = .040$

e. $P(C \mid F) = \dfrac{P(F \cap C)}{P(F)} = \dfrac{\frac{6}{151}}{\frac{33}{151}} = \dfrac{6}{33} = .182$

f. $P((F \cup G) \mid A) = \dfrac{P((F \cup G) \cap A)}{P(A)} = \dfrac{\frac{5}{151} + \frac{1}{151}}{\frac{7}{151}} = \dfrac{6}{7} = .857$

g. $P(C \mid F) = \dfrac{P(F \cap C)}{P(F)} = \dfrac{\frac{6}{151}}{\frac{33}{151}} = \dfrac{6}{33} = .182$

3.43 a. We will define the events the same as in Exercise 3.10.

There are a total of $9 \times 2 = 18$ sample points for this experiment. There are 9 sources of CO poisoning, and each source of poisoning has 2 possible outcomes, fatal or nonfatal. Suppose we introduce some notation to make it easier to write down the sample points. Let FI = Fire, AU = Auto exhaust, FU = Furnace, K = Kerosene or spaceheater, AP = Appliance, OG = Other gas-powered motors, FP = Fireplace, O = Other, and U = Unknown. Also, let F = Fatal and N = Nonfatal. The 18 sample points are:

| FI, F | AU, F | FU, F | K, F | AP, F | OG, F | FP, F | O, F | U, F |
| FI, N | AU, N | FU, N | K, N | AP, N | OG, N | FP, N | O, N | U, N |

$P(F \mid FI) = 63/116 = .543$

b. $P(AU \mid N) = 178/807 = .221$

c. $P(U \mid F) = 9/174 = .052$

d. The event "not fire or fireplace" would include $AU, FU, K, AP, OG, O,$ and U.

$P(AU \cup FU \cup K \cup AP \cup OG \cup O \cup U \mid N)$
$= (178 + 345 + 18 + 63 + 73 + 19 + 42)/807 = 738/807 = .914$

3.45 Define the following events.

A: {A defective case gets by inspector 1}
B: {A defective case gets by inspector 2}

We want to know

$A \cap B$: {A defective case gets by inspector 1 and inspector 2}.

We know that the two inspectors check the cases independently. Therefore,

$P(A \cap B) = P(A)P(B) = (.05)(.10) = .005$

Probability 41

3.47 Let us define the following events:

  S: {School is a subscriber}
  N: {School never uses the CCN broadcast}
  F: {School uses the CCN broadcast more than five times per week}

From the problem, $P(S) = .40$, $P(N \mid S) = .05$, and $P(F \mid S) = .20$.

a. $P(S \cap N) = P(N \mid S) P(S) = .05(.40) = .02$

b. $P(S \cap F) = P(F \mid S) P(S) = .20(.40) = .08$

3.49 Define the following events:

  A: {Seed carries single spikelets}
  B: {Seed carries paired spikelets}
  C: {Seed produces ears with single spikelets}
  D: {Seed produces ears with paired spikelets}

From the problem, $P(A) = .4$, $P(B) = .6$, $P(C \mid A) = .29$, $P(D \mid A) = .71$, $P(C \mid B) = .26$, and $P(D \mid B) = .74$.

a. $P(A \cap C) = P(C \mid A)P(A) = .29(.4) = .116$

b. $P(D) = P(A \cap D) + P(B \cap D) = P(D \mid A)P(A) + P(D \mid B)P(B) = .71(.4) + .74(.6)$
   $= .284 + .444 = .728$

3.51 Define the following events:

  A: {Selected firm implemented TQM}
  B: {Selected firm's sales increased}

From the information given, $P(A) = 30/100 = .3$, $P(B) = 60/100 = .6$, and $P(A \mid B) = 20/60 = 1/3$.

a. $P(A) = 30/100 = .3$
   $P(B) = 60/100 = .6$

b. If A and B are independent, $P(A \mid B) = P(A)$. However, $P(A \mid B) = 1/3 \neq P(A) = .3$. Thus, A and B are not independent.

c. Now, $P(A \mid B) = 18/60 = .3$. Since $P(A \mid B) = .3 = P(A) = .3$, A and B are independent.

3.53 a. The number of samples of size $n = 3$ elements that can be selected from a population of $N = 600$ is:

$$\binom{N}{n} = \binom{600}{3} = \frac{600!}{3!597!} = \frac{600(599)(598)}{3(2)(1)} = 35{,}820{,}200$$

b. If random sampling is employed, then each sample is equally likely. The probability that any sample is selected is 1/35,820,200.

c. To draw a random sample of three elements from 600, we will number the elements from 1 to 600. Then, starting in an arbitrary position in Table I, Appendix B, we will select three numbers by going either down a column or across a row. Suppose that we start in the first three positions of column 8 and row 17. We will proceed down the column until we select three different numbers, skipping 000 and any numbers between 601 and 999. The first sample drawn will be 448, 298, and 136 (skip 987). The second sample drawn will be 47, 263, and 287. The 20 samples selected are:

Sample Number	Items Selected	Sample Number	Items Selected
1	448, 298, 136	11	345, 420, 152
2	47, 263, 287	12	144, 68, 485
3	153, 147, 222	13	490, 54, 178
4	360, 86, 357	14	428, 297, 549
5	205, 587, 254	15	186, 256, 261
6	563, 408, 258	16	90, 383, 232
7	428, 356, 543	17	438, 430, 352
8	248, 410, 197	18	129, 493, 496
9	542, 355, 208	19	440, 253, 81
10	399, 313, 563	20	521, 300, 15

None of the samples contain the same three elements. Because the probability in part b was so small, it would be very unlikely to have any two samples with the same elements.

3.55   a.   If we randomly select one account from the 5,382 accounts, the probability of selecting account 3,241 is 1/5,382 = .000186.

       b.   To draw a random sample of 10 accounts from 5,382, we will number the accounts from 1 to 5,382. Then, starting in an arbitrary position in Table I, Appendix B, we will select 10 numbers by going either down a column or across a row. Suppose that we start in the first four positions of column 10 and row 5. We will proceed down the column until we select 10 different numbers, skipping 0000 and any numbers between 5,382 and 9,999. The sample drawn will be:

           1505, 4884, 1256, 1798, 3159, 2084, 0827, 2635, 4610, 2217

       c.   No. If the samples are randomly selected, any sample of size 10 is equally likely. The total number of ways to select 10 accounts from 5,382 is:

$$\binom{N}{n} = \binom{5{,}382}{10} = \frac{5{,}382!}{10!\,5{,}372!} = \frac{5{,}382(5381)(5380)\ldots(5373)}{10(9)(8)\ldots(1)} = 5.572377607 \times 10^{30}$$

The probability that any one sample is selected is $1/5.572377607 \times 10^{30}$. Each of the two samples shown have the same probability of occurring.

3.57   a.   Give each stock in the NYSE-Composite Transactions table of the Wall Street Journal a number (1 to m). Using Table I of Appendix B, pick a starting point and read down using the same number of digits as in m until you have n different numbers between 1 and m, inclusive.

3.59   (1)   The probabilities of all sample points must lie between 0 and 1, inclusive.
         (2)   The probabilities of all the sample points in the sample space must sum to 1.

3.61 $P(A \cap B) = .4$, $P(A \mid B) = .8$

Since the $P(A \mid B) = \dfrac{P(A \cap B)}{P(B)}$, substitute the given probabilities into the formula and solve for $P(B)$.

$$.8 = \dfrac{.4}{P(B)} \Rightarrow P(B) = \dfrac{.4}{.8} = .5$$

3.63 a. $P(A \cap B) = 0$

$P(B \cap C) = P(2) = .2$

$P(A \cup C) = P(1) + P(2) + P(3) + P(5) + P(6) = .3 + .2 + .1 + .1 + .2 = .9$

$P(A \cup B \cup C) = P(1) + P(2) + P(3) + P(4) + P(5) + P(6)$
$ = .3 + .2 + .1 + .1 + .1 + .2 = 1$

$P(B^c) = P(1) + P(3) + P(5) + P(6) = .3 + .1 + .1 + .2 = .7$

$P(A^c \cap B) = P(2) + P(4) = .2 + .1 = .3$

$P(B \mid C) = \dfrac{P(B \cap C)}{P(C)} = \dfrac{P(2)}{P(2) + P(5) + P(6)} = \dfrac{.2}{.2 + .1 + .2} = \dfrac{.2}{.5} = .4$

$P(B \mid A) = \dfrac{P(B \cap A)}{P(A)} = \dfrac{0}{P(A)} = 0$

b.   Since $P(A \cap B) = 0$, and $P(A) \cdot P(B) > 0$, these two would not be equal, implying A and B are not independent. However, A and B are mutually exclusive, since $P(A \cap B) = 0$.

c. $P(B) = P(2) + P(4) = .2 + .1 = .3$. But $P(B \mid C)$, calculated above, is .4. Since these are not equal, B and C are not independent. Since $P(B \cap C) = .2$, B and C are not mutually exclusive.

3.65 a. $6! = 6 \cdot 5 \cdot 4 \cdot 3 \cdot 2 \cdot 1 = 720$

b. $\begin{pmatrix} 10 \\ 9 \end{pmatrix} = \dfrac{10!}{9!(10-9)!} = \dfrac{10 \cdot 9 \cdot 8 \cdot \cdots \cdot 1}{9 \cdot 8 \cdot 7 \cdot \cdots \cdot 1 \cdot 1} = 10$

c. $\begin{pmatrix} 10 \\ 1 \end{pmatrix} = \dfrac{10!}{1!(10-1)!} = \dfrac{10 \cdot 9 \cdot 8 \cdot \cdots \cdot 1}{1 \cdot 9 \cdot 8 \cdot \cdots \cdot 1} = 10$

d. $\begin{pmatrix} 6 \\ 3 \end{pmatrix} = \dfrac{6!}{3!(6-3)!} = \dfrac{6 \cdot 5 \cdot 4 \cdot 3 \cdot 2 \cdot 1}{3 \cdot 2 \cdot 1 \cdot 3 \cdot 2 \cdot 1} = 20$

e. $0! = 1$

3.67   Define the following events:

T: {Technical staff}
N: {Nontechnical staff}
U: {Under 20 years with company}
O: {Over 20 years with company}
R_1: {Retire at age 65}
R_2: {Retire at age 68}

The probabilities for each sample point are given in table form.

	U		O	
	T	N	T	N
R_1	$\frac{31}{200}$	$\frac{5}{200}$	$\frac{45}{200}$	$\frac{12}{200}$
R_2	$\frac{59}{200}$	$\frac{25}{200}$	$\frac{15}{200}$	$\frac{8}{200}$

Each sample point consists of three characteristics: type of staff (T or N), years with the company, (U or O), and age plan to retire (R_1 or R_2).

a. $P(T) = P(T \cap U \cap R_1) + P(T \cap U \cap R_2) + P(T \cap O \cap R_1) + P(T \cap O \cap R_2)$

$= \frac{31}{200} + \frac{59}{200} + \frac{45}{200} + \frac{15}{200} = \frac{150}{200} = .75$

b. $P(O) = P(O \cap T \cap R_1) + P(O \cap T \cap R_2) + P(O \cap N \cap R_1) + P(O \cap N \cap R_2)$

$= \frac{45}{200} + \frac{15}{200} + \frac{12}{200} + \frac{8}{200} = \frac{80}{200} = .4$

$P(R_2 \cap O) = P(R_2 \cap O \cap T) + P(R_2 \cap O \cap N) = \frac{15}{200} + \frac{8}{200} = \frac{23}{200} = .115$

Thus, $P(R_2 \mid O) = \frac{P(R_2 \cap O)}{P(O)} = \frac{.115}{.4} = .2875$

c. $P(T) = .75$ from a.

$P(U \cap T) = P(U \cap T \cap R_1) + P(U \cap T \cap R_2) = \frac{31}{200} + \frac{59}{200} = \frac{90}{200} = .45$

Thus, $P(U \mid T) = \frac{P(U \cap T)}{P(T)} = \frac{.45}{.75} = .6$

d. $P(O \cap N \cap R_1) = \frac{12}{200} = .06$

e. If A and B are independent, then $P(A \mid B) = P(A)$ or $P(R_2 \mid T) = P(R_2)$.

$P(A \mid B) = \frac{P(A \cap B)}{P(B)} = \frac{\frac{59}{200} + \frac{15}{200}}{\frac{31}{200} + \frac{59}{200} + \frac{45}{200} + \frac{15}{200}} = \frac{\frac{74}{200}}{\frac{150}{200}} = \frac{74}{150} = .4933$

$P(A) = \frac{59}{200} + \frac{25}{200} + \frac{15}{200} + \frac{8}{200} = \frac{107}{200} = .535$

.4933 ≠ .535; therefore, A and B are not independent events.

f. The employee does not plan to retire at age 68 or the employee is not on the technical staff.

g. Yes, B and E are mutually exclusive events. An employee cannot be on the technical staff and on the nontechnical staff at the same time.

Probability

3.69 Suppose we define the following events:

    A: {Southwest Airline is selected}
    B: {Continental Airline is selected}
    C: {Flight arrived on time}
    D: {Flight was late}

a. Since one airline is to be selected at random, each airline is equally likely. Thus, the probability of selecting any one airline is 1/10.

$$P(A) = 1/10$$
$$P(B) = 1/10$$

b. $P(C \mid B) = 64.1/100 = .641$
    $P(D \mid B) = (100 - 64.1)/100 = 35.9/100 = .359$

c. Since these figures are reported by the airline, these are probably upper bounds. The airlines would want to have a high "on-time" percentage. Thus, they would probably report a percentage that is higher than the actual percentage.

3.71 Define the following events:

    A: {The watch is accurate}
    N: {The watch is not accurate}

Assuming the manufacturer's claim is correct,

$$P(N) = .05 \text{ and } P(A) = 1 - P(N) = 1 - .05 = .95$$

The sample space for the purchase of four of the manufacturer's watches is listed below.

(A, A, A, A) (N, A, A, A) (A, N, N, A) (N, A, N, N)
(A, A, A, N) (A, A, N, N) (N, A, N, A) (N, N, A, N)
(A, A, N, A) (A, N, A, N) (N, N, A, A) (N, N, N, A)
(A, N, A, A) (N, A, A, N) (A, N, N, N) (N, N, N, N)

a. All four watches not being accurate as claimed is the sample point *(N, N, N, N)*.

Assuming the watches purchased operate independently and the manufacturer's claim is correct,

$$P(N, N, N, N) = P(N)P(N)P(N)P(N) = .05^4 = .00000625$$

b. The sample points in the sample space that consist of exactly two watches failing to meet the claim are listed below.

(A, A, N, N) (N, A, A, N)
(A, N, A, N) (N, A, N, A)
(A, N, N, A) (N, N, A, A)

The probability that exactly two of the four watches fail to meet the claim is the sum of the probabilities of these six sample points.

Assuming the watches purchased operate independently and the manufacturer's claim is correct,

$$P(A, A, N, N) = P(A)P(A)P(N)P(N) = (.95)(.95)(.05)(.05) = .00225625$$

All six of the sample points will have the same probability. Therefore, the probability that exactly two of the four watches fail to meet the claim when the manufacturer's claim is correct is

6(0.00225625) = .0135

c. The sample points in the sample space that consist of three of the four watches failing to meet the claim are listed below.

(A, N, N, N)   (N, N, A, N)
(N, A, N, N)   (N, N, N, A)

The probability that three of the four watches fail to meet the claim is the sum of the probabilities of the four sample points.

Assuming the watches purchased operate independently and the manufacturer's claim is correct,

$P(A, N, N, N) = P(A)P(N)P(N)P(N) = (.95)(.05)(.05)(.05) = .00011875$

All four of the sample points will have the same probability. Therefore, the probability that three of the four watches fail to meet the claim when the manufacturer's claim is correct is

4(.00011875) = .000475

If this event occurred, we would tend to doubt the validity of the manufacturer's claim since its probability of occurring is so small.

d. All four watches tested failing to meet the claim is the sample point (N, N, N, N).

Assuming the watches purchased operate independently and the manufacturer's claim is correct,

$P(N, N, N, N) = P(N)P(N)P(N)P(N) = (.05)^4 = .00000625$

Since the probability of observing this event is so small if the claim is true, we have strong evidence against the validity of the claim. However, we do not have conclusive proof that the claim is false. There is still a chance the event can occur (with probability .00000625) although it is extremely small.

3.73   Define the following events:

   A: {Acupoll predicts the success of a particular product}
   B: {Product is successful}

From the problem, we know

   $P(A \mid B) = .89$ and $P(B) = .90$

Thus, $P(A \cap B) = P(A \mid B)P(B) = .89(.90) = .801$

3.75   Define the following events:

   G: {regularly use the golf course}
   T: {regularly use the tennis courts}

Probability

Given: $P(G) = .7$ and $P(T) = .5$

The event "uses neither facility" can be written as $G^c \cap T^c$ or $(G \cup T)^c$. We are given $P(G^c \cap T^c) = P[(G \cup T)^c] = .05$. The complement of the event "uses neither facility" is the event "uses at least one of the two facilities" which can be written as $G \cup T$.

$$P(G \cup T) = 1 - P[(G \cup T)^c] = 1 - .05 = .95$$

From the additive rule, $P(G \cup T) = P(G) + P(T) - P(G \cap T)$
$$\Rightarrow .95 = .7 + .5 - P(G \cap T)$$
$$\Rightarrow P(G \cap T) = .25$$

a. The Venn Diagram is:

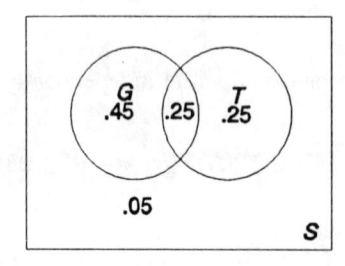

b. $P(G \cup T) = .95$ from above.

c. $P(G \cap T) = .25$ from above.

d. $P(G \mid T) = \dfrac{P(G \cap T)}{P(T)} = \dfrac{.25}{.5} = .5$

3.77 Define the following events:

A: {Family with young children has income above the poverty line, but less than $25,000}
B: {Family with young children has unemployed parents or no parents}
C: {Family with young children has income below the poverty line}

a. $P(A) = (2\% + 22\%)/100\% = 24\%/100\% = .24$

b. $P(B) = (1\% + 7\% + 2\%)/100\% = 10\%/100\% = .1$

c. $P(C) = (7\% + 7\%)/100\% = 14\%/100\% = .14$

3.79 Define the following events:

S_1: {Salesman makes sale on the first visit}
S_2: {Salesman makes a sale on the second visit}

$P(S_1) = .4 \quad P(S_2 \mid S_1^c) = .65$

The sample points of the experiment are:

$S_1 \cap S_2^c$
$S_1^c \cap S_2$
$S_1^c \cap S_2^c$

The probability the salesman will make a sale is:

$$P(S_1 \cap S_2^c) + P(S_1^c \cap S_2) = P(S_1) + P(S_2 \mid S_1^c)P(S_1^c) = .4 + .65(1 - .4) = .4 + .39 = .79$$

3.81 Define the following events:

O_1: {Component #1 operates properly}
O_2: {Component #2 operates properly}
O_3: {Component #3 operates properly}

$P(O_1) = 1 - P(O_1^c) = 1 - .12 = .88$
$P(O_2) = 1 - P(O_2^c) = 1 - .09 = .91$
$P(O_3) = 1 - P(O_3^c) = 1 - .11 = .89$

a. $P(\text{System operates properly}) = P(O_1 \cap O_2 \cap O_3)$
$= P(O_1)P(O_2)P(O_3)$
(since the three components operate independently)
$= (.88)(.91)(.89) = .7127$

b. $P(\text{System fails}) = 1 - P(\text{system operates properly})$
$= 1 - .7127$ (see part a)
$= .2873$

3.83 a. The possible pairs of accounts that could be obtained are:

(0001, 0002) (0001, 0003) (0001, 0004) (0001, 0005)
(0002, 0003) (0002, 0004) (0002, 0005)
(0003, 0004) (0003, 0005)
(0004, 0005)

b. There are 10 possible pairs of accounts that could be obtained. In a random sample, all 10 pairs of accounts have an equal chance of being selected. The probability of selecting any one of the 10 pairs is 1/10. Therefore, the probability of selecting accounts 0001 and 0004 is 1/10.

c. Since only two accounts have a balance of $1,000 (0001 and 0004), the probability of selecting two accounts that each have a balance of $1,000 is 1/10.

Since there are only three accounts that do not have a balance of $1,000 (0002, 0003, and 0005), there are three possible pairs of accounts in which each has a balance other than $1,000 (0002, 0003), (0002, 0005), and (0003, 0005)). Therefore, the probability of selecting a pair of accounts in which each has a balance other than $1,000 is 3/10.

3.85 a. From the problem, we have three students and three hospitals. Suppose we consider the three hospitals as three positions. Using the permutations rule, there are

$$P_3^3 = \frac{3!}{(3-3)!} = \frac{3 \cdot 2 \cdot 1}{1} = 6 \text{ different assignments possible.}$$

These assignments are:

$[S_1H_A \ S_2H_B \ S_3H_C] \ [S_1H_A \ S_3H_B \ S_2H_C]$
$[S_2H_A \ S_1H_B \ S_3H_C] \ [S_2H_A \ S_3H_B \ S_1H_C]$
$[S_3H_A \ S_1H_B \ S_2H_C] \ [S_3H_A \ S_2H_B \ S_1H_C]$

b. Assuming that all of the above assignments are equally likely, the probability of any one of them is 1/6. The probability that student #1 is assigned to hospital B is 2/6 = 1/3.

Probability

3.87   a.   The number of ways $n = 5$ candidates may be selected from the $N = 30$ finalists is:

$$\binom{30}{5} = \frac{30!}{5!25!} = 142{,}506$$

Thus, there are 142,506 sample points for this experiment. Furthermore, since the candidates are to be selected at random, each sample point is equally likely, with probability 1/142,506.

   b.   We must determine the number of sample points which satisfy the event that none of the minority candidates is hired. The event of interest will occur if 0 of the 7 minority candidates is selected and 5 of the 23 nonminority candidates are selected. The number of ways this can occur is:

$$\binom{7}{0}\binom{23}{5} = \frac{7!}{0!7!} \cdot \frac{23!}{5!18!} = 33{,}649$$

Of the 142,506 sample points, 33,649 constitute the event of interest and thus the probability that none of the minority candidates is selected is:

$$\frac{33{,}649}{142{,}506} = .2361$$

   c.   The event that no more than one minority candidate is hired will occur if no minority candidate is hired or if one minority candidate is hired. Thus,

P(No more than one minority candidate is hired)
  $= P$(No minority candidate is hired) $+ P$(One minority candidate is hired)

In part b, we computed

$$P(\text{No minority candidate is hired}) = \frac{33{,}649}{142{,}506}$$

and it remains to compute the probability that exactly one minority candidate is hired.

The experiment contains 142,506 sample points, as shown in part a. The number of these sample points for which 1 of the 7 minority candidates and 4 of the 23 nonminority candidates will be selected is:

$$\binom{7}{1}\binom{23}{4} = \frac{7!}{1!6!} \cdot \frac{23!}{4!19!} = 61{,}985$$

and the probability that exactly one minority candidate will be hired is:

$$\frac{61{,}985}{142{,}506} = .4350$$

Finally, the probability that no more than one minority candidate is hired is:

$$\frac{33{,}649}{142{,}506} + \frac{61{,}985}{142{,}506} = .2361 + .4350 = .6711$$

Discrete Random Variables   Chapter 4

4.1   A random variable is a rule that assigns one and only one value to each sample point of an experiment.

4.3   a.   The closing price of a particular stock on the New York Stock Exchange is discrete. It can take on only a countable number of values.

       b.   The number of shares of a particular stock that are traded on a particular day is discrete. It can take on only a countable number of values.

       c.   The quarterly earnings of a particular firm is discrete. It can take on only a countable number of values.

       d.   The percentage change in yearly earnings between 1996 and 1997 for a particular firm is continuous. It can take on any value in an interval.

       e.   The number of new products introduced per year by a firm is discrete. It can take on only a countable number of values.

       f.   The time until a pharmaceutical company gains approval from the U.S. Food and Drug Administration to market a new drug is continuous. It can take on any value in an interval of time.

4.5   The number of occupied units in an apartment complex at any time is a discrete random variable, as is the number of shares of stock traded on the New York Stock Exchange on a particular day. Two examples of continuous random variables are the length of time to complete a building project and the weight of a truckload of oranges.

4.7   An economist might be interested in the percentage of the work force that is unemployed, or the current inflation rate, both of which are continuous random variables.

4.9   The manager of a clothing store might be concerned with the number of employees on duty at a specific time of day, or the number of articles of a particular type of clothing that are on hand.

4.11   a.   We know $\sum p(x) = 1$. Thus, $p(2) + p(3) + p(5) + p(8) + p(10) = 1$
            $\Rightarrow p(5) = 1 - p(2) - p(3) - p(8) - p(10) = 1 - .15 - .10 - .25 - .25 = .25$

       b. $P(x = 2 \text{ or } x = 10) = P(x = 2) + P(x = 10) = .15 + .25 = .40$

       c. $P(x \leq 8) = P(x = 2) + P(x = 3) + P(x = 5) + P(x = 8) = .15 + .10 + .25 + .25 = .75$

4.13   a.   The sample points are (where H = head, T = tail):

	HHH	HHT	HTH	THH	HTT	THT	TTH	TTT
x = # heads	3	2	2	2	1	1	1	0

b. If each event is equally likely, then $P(\text{sample point}) = \dfrac{1}{n} = \dfrac{1}{8}$

$p(3) = \dfrac{1}{8}$, $p(2) = \dfrac{1}{8} + \dfrac{1}{8} + \dfrac{1}{8} = \dfrac{3}{8}$, $p(1) = \dfrac{1}{8} + \dfrac{1}{8} + \dfrac{1}{8} = \dfrac{3}{8}$, and $p(0) = \dfrac{1}{8}$

c.

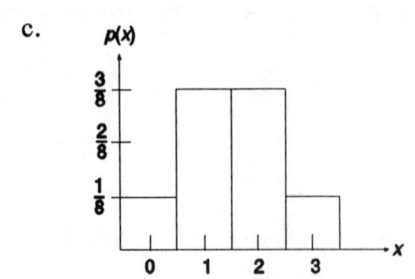

d. $P(x = 2 \text{ or } x = 3) = p(2) + p(3) = \dfrac{3}{8} + \dfrac{1}{8} = \dfrac{4}{8} = \dfrac{1}{2}$

4.15 a. When a die is tossed, the number of spots observed on the upturned face can be 1, 2, 3, 4, 5, or 6. Since the six sample points are equally likely, each one has a probability of 1/6.

The probability distribution of x may be summarized in tabular form:

x	1	2	3	4	5	6
$p(x)$	$\dfrac{1}{6}$	$\dfrac{1}{6}$	$\dfrac{1}{6}$	$\dfrac{1}{6}$	$\dfrac{1}{6}$	$\dfrac{1}{6}$

b. The probability distribution of x may also be presented in graphical form:

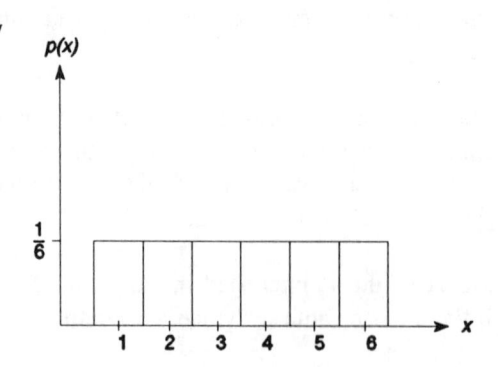

4.17 a. Since the number of observations is very large, the relative frequencies or proportions should reflect the probabilities very well.

b. Let x = household income. Then $P(x > \$200{,}000) = 1.1/100 = .011$
$P(x > \$100{,}000) = 4.1/100 + 1.1/100 = 5.2/100 = .052$
$P(x < \$100{,}000) = 18.5/100 + 19.0/100 + 15.9/100 + 12.8/100 + 9.1/100 + 13.8/100$
$\qquad\qquad\qquad + 5.7/100 = 94.8/100 = .948$
$P(\$30{,}000 < x < \$49{,}999) = 12.8/100 + 9.1/100 = 21.9/100 = .219$

c.

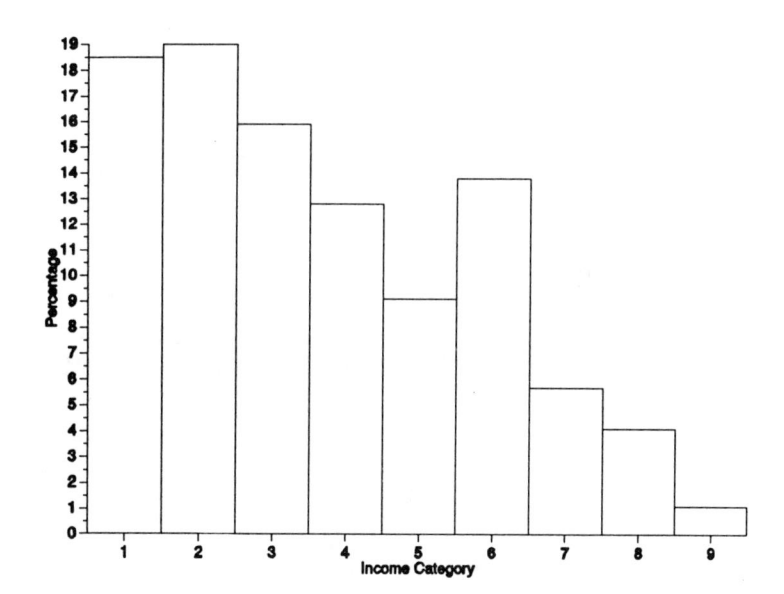

[Bar chart showing Percentage vs Income Category, with bars at categories 1-9 having approximate heights: 18.5, 19, 16, 13, 9, 13.8, 5.5, 4, 1.1]

d. $P(\text{category } 6) = P(\$50{,}000 < x < \$74{,}999) = 13.8/100 = .138$
$P(\text{category 1 or 9}) = P(x < \$10{,}000) + P(x \geq \$200{,}000)$
$= 18.5/100 + 1.1/100 = 19.6/100 = .196$

4.19 a. The properties of valid probability distributions are:

$\sum p(x) = 1$ and $0 \leq p(x) \leq 1$ for all x.

For ARC a_1: $0 \leq p(x) \leq 1$ for all x and $\sum p(x) = .6 + .25 + .1 + .05 = 1.00$
Thus, this is a valid probability distribution.

For ARC a_2: $0 \leq p(x) \leq 1$ for all x and $\sum p(x) = .6 + .3 + .1 = 1.00$
Thus, this is a valid probability distribution.

For ARC a_3: $0 \leq p(x) \leq 1$ for all x and $\sum p(x) = .9 + .1 = 1.00$
Thus, this is a valid probability distribution.

For ARC a_4: $0 \leq p(x) \leq 1$ for all x and $\sum p(x) = .9 + .1 = 1.00$
Thus, this is a valid probability distribution.

For ARC a_5: $0 \leq p(x) \leq 1$ for all x and $\sum p(x) = .9 + .1 = 1.00$
Thus, this is a valid probability distribution.

For ARC a_6: $0 \leq p(x) \leq 1$ for all x and $\sum p(x) = .7 + .25 + .05 = 1.00$
Thus, this is a valid probability distribution.

b. For Arc a_1, $P(x > 1) = P(x = 2) + P(x = 3) = .25 + .6 = .85$

c. For Arc a_2, $P(x > 1) = P(x = 2) = .6$
For Arc a_3, $P(x > 1) = 0$
For Arc a_4, $P(x > 1) = 0$
For Arc a_5, $P(x > 1) = 0$
For Arc a_6, $P(x > 1) = P(x = 2) = .7$

d. Let x_1 = capacity for Arc a_1 and x_2 = capacity for Arc a_2
$P(x_1 > 1 \text{ and } x_2 > 1) = P(x_1 > 1)P(x_2 > 1) = .85(.6) = .51$

Discrete Random Variables

4.21 The population mean, μ, is equal to the expected value of x, $E(x)$. The sample mean, $\bar{x}$, is calculated from a sample.

4.23 a. $\mu = E(x) = \sum xp(x)$
$= 10(.05) + 20(.20) + 30(.30) + 40(.25) + 50(.10) + 60(.10)$
$= .5 + 4 + 9 + 10 + 5 + 6 = 34.5$

$\sigma^2 = E(x - \mu)^2 = \sum (x - \mu)^2 p(x)$
$= (10 - 34.5)^2(.05) + (20 - 34.5)^2(.20) + (30 - 34.5)^2(.30)$
$+ (40 - 34.5)^2(.25) + (50 - 34.5)^2(.10) + (60 - 34.5)^2(.10)$
$= 30.0125 + 42.05 + 6.075 + 7.5625 + 24.025 + 65.025 = 174.75$

$\sigma = \sqrt{174.75} = 13.219$

b.

[Histogram showing p(x) vs x with bars at x=10 (0.05), 20 (0.20), 30 (0.30), 40 (0.25), 50 (0.10), 60 (0.10). Markers indicate $\mu - 2\sigma$, μ, and $\mu + 2\sigma$.]

c. $\mu \pm 2\sigma \Rightarrow 34.5 \pm 2(13.219) \Rightarrow 34.5 \pm 26.438 \Rightarrow (8.062, 60.938)$

$P(8.062 < x < 60.938) = p(10) + p(20) + p(30) + p(40) + p(50) + p(60)$
$= .05 + .20 + .30 + .25 + .10 + .10 = 1.00$

4.25 a. It would seem that the mean of both would be 1 since they both are symmetric distributions centered at 1.

b. $P(x)$ seems more variable since there appears to be greater probability for the two extreme values of 0 and 2 than there is in the distribution of y.

c. For x: $\mu = E(x) = \sum xp(x) = 0(.3) + 1(.4) + 2(.3) = 0 + .4 + .6 = 1$
$\sigma^2 = E[(x - \mu)^2] = \sum (x - \mu)^2 p(x)$
$= (0 - 1)^2(.3) + (1 - 1)^2(.4) + (2 - 1)^2(.3) = .3 + 0 + .3 = .6$

For y: $\mu = E(y) = \sum yp(y) = 0(.1) + 1(.8) + 2(.1) = 0 + .8 + .2 = 1$
$\sigma^2 = E[(y - \mu)^2] = \sum (y - \mu)^2 p(y)$
$= (0 - 1)^2(.1) + (1 - 1)^2(.8) + (2 - 1)^2(.1) = .1 + 0 + .1 = .2$

The variance for x is larger than that for y.

4.27 Let x = bookie's earnings per dollar wagered. Then x can take on values $1 (you lose) and $-5 (you win). The only way you win is if you pick 3 winners in 3 games. If the probability of picking 1 winner in 1 game is .5, then $P(www) = p(w)p(w)p(w) = .5(.5)(.5) = .125$ (assuming games are independent).

Thus, the probability distribution for x is:

x	$p(x)$
$1	.875
$-5	.125

$E(x) = \sum xp(x) = 1(.875) - 5(.125) = .875 - .625 = \$.25$

4.29 a. Let x = number of training units necessary to master the complex computer software program.

$\mu = E(x) = \sum xp(x) = 1(.1) + 2(.25) + 3(.4) + 4(.15) + 5(.1)$
$= .1 + .5 + 1.2 + .6 + .5 = 2.9$

This is the average number of units necessary to master the complex software program.

Median = 3 (first observation where the cumulative probability is $\geq .5$)

At least half of the observations are less than or equal to 3 and at least half of the observations are greater than or equal to 3.

b. $P(x \leq k) \geq .75 \Rightarrow k = 3$
$P(x \leq k) \geq .90 \Rightarrow k = 4$

c. $\mu = E(x) = \sum xp(x) = 1(.25) + 2(.35) + 3(.40) = .25 + .70 + 1.2 = 2.15$

This is smaller than the answer in part a. Again, this is the average number of units necessary to master the complex software program.

Median = 2 (first observation where the cumulative probability is $\geq .5$)

$P(x \leq k) \geq .75 \Rightarrow k = 3$
$P(x \leq k) \geq .90 \Rightarrow k = 3$

4.31 For ARC a_1: $\mu = E(x) = \sum xp(x) = 0(.05) + 1(.10) + 2(.25) + 3(.60) = 2.4$
The mean capacity for ARC a_1 is 2.4

For ARC a_2: $\mu = E(x) = \sum xp(x) = 0(.10) + 1(.30) + 2(.60) = 1.5$
The mean capacity for ARC a_2 is 1.5

For ARC a_3: $\mu = E(x) = \sum xp(x) = 0(.10) + 1(.90) = .90$
The mean capacity for ARC a_3 is .90

For ARC a_4: $\mu = E(x) = \sum xp(x) = 0(.10) + 1(.90) = .90$
The mean capacity for ARC a_4 is .90

For ARC a_5: $\mu = E(x) = \sum xp(x) = 0(.10) + 1(.90) = .90$
The mean capacity for ARC a_5 is .90

For ARC a_6: $\mu = E(x) = \sum xp(x) = 0(.05) + 1(.25) + 2(.70) = 1.65$
The mean capacity for ARC a_6 is 1.65

4.33   a.   The probability the first candidate is qualified is 1/4 = .25. The cost of interviewing one candidate is $1,000.

The probability the second candidate is qualified is 3/4(1/3) = 1/4 = .25. The cost of interviewing two candidates is $2,000.

The cost of interviewing three candidates is $3,000. Since the company will interview no more than three candidates, the probability of $3,000 is 1 − .25 − .25 = .50.

The probability distribution would be:

Cost	p
$1,000	.25
$2,000	.25
$3,000	.50

   b.   The probability that none of the candidates are hired = probability that the fourth candidate is qualified = 3/4(2/3)(1/2)(1/1) = 1/4 = .25.

   c. $\mu = E(x) = \sum xp(x) = \$1,000(.25) + \$2,000(.25) + \$3,000(.5) = \$2,250$

   d.   The expected total cost of the interviewing strategy is $2,250.

4.35   a. $\dfrac{6!}{2!(6-2)!} = \dfrac{6!}{2!4!} = \dfrac{6 \cdot 5 \cdot 4 \cdot 3 \cdot 2 \cdot 1}{(2 \cdot 1)(4 \cdot 3 \cdot 2 \cdot 1)} = 15$

   b. $\binom{5}{2} = \dfrac{5!}{2!(5-2)!} = \dfrac{5!}{2!3!} = \dfrac{5 \cdot 4 \cdot 3 \cdot 2 \cdot 1}{(2 \cdot 1)(3 \cdot 2 \cdot 1)} = 10$

   c. $\binom{7}{0} = \dfrac{7!}{0!(7-0)!} = \dfrac{7!}{0!7!} = \dfrac{7 \cdot 6 \cdot 5 \cdot 4 \cdot 3 \cdot 2 \cdot 1}{(1)(7 \cdot 6 \cdot 5 \cdot 4 \cdot 3 \cdot 2 \cdot 1)} = 1$
       (Note: 0! = 1)

   d. $\binom{6}{6} = \dfrac{6!}{6!(6-6)!} = \dfrac{6!}{6!0!} = \dfrac{6 \cdot 5 \cdot 4 \cdot 3 \cdot 2 \cdot 1}{(6 \cdot 5 \cdot 4 \cdot 3 \cdot 2 \cdot 1)(1)} = 1$

   e. $\binom{4}{3} = \dfrac{4!}{3!(4-3)!} = \dfrac{4!}{3!1!} = \dfrac{4 \cdot 3 \cdot 2 \cdot 1}{(3 \cdot 2 \cdot 1)(1)} = 4$

4.37   a. $P(x = 1) = \dfrac{5!}{1!4!}(.2)^1(.8)^4 = \dfrac{5 \cdot 4 \cdot 3 \cdot 2 \cdot 1}{(1)(4 \cdot 3 \cdot 2 \cdot 1)}(.2)^1(.8)^4 = 5(.2)^1(.8)^4 = .4096$

   b. $P(x = 2) = \dfrac{4!}{2!2!}(.6)^2(.4)^2 = \dfrac{4 \cdot 3 \cdot 2 \cdot 1}{(2 \cdot 1)(2 \cdot 1)}(.6)^2(.4)^2 = 6(.6)^2(.4)^2 = .3456$

   c. $P(x = 0) = \dfrac{3!}{0!3!}(.7)^0(.3)^3 = \dfrac{3 \cdot 2 \cdot 1}{(1)(3 \cdot 2 \cdot 1)}(.7)^0(.3)^3 = 1(.7)^0(.3)^3 = .027$

   d. $P(x = 3) = \dfrac{5!}{3!2!}(.1)^3(.9)^2 = \dfrac{5 \cdot 4 \cdot 3 \cdot 2 \cdot 1}{(3 \cdot 2 \cdot 1)(2 \cdot 1)}(.1)^3(.9)^2 = 10(.1)^3(.9)^2 = .0081$

e. $P(x = 2) = \dfrac{4!}{2!2!}(.4)^2(.6)^2 = \dfrac{4 \cdot 3 \cdot 2 \cdot 1}{(2 \cdot 1)(2 \cdot 1)}(.4)^2(.6)^2 = 6(.4)^2(.6)^2 = .3456$

f. $P(x = 1) = \dfrac{3!}{1!2!}(.9)^1(.1)^2 = \dfrac{3 \cdot 2 \cdot 1}{(1)(2 \cdot 1)}(.9)^1(.1)^2 = 3(.9)^1(.1)^2 = .027$

4.39 a. $\mu = np = 25(.5) = 12.5$

$\sigma^2 = np(1 - p) = 25(.5)(.5) = 6.25$

$\sigma = \sqrt{\sigma^2} = \sqrt{6.25} = 2.5$

b. $\mu = np = 80(.2) = 16$

$\sigma^2 = np(1 - p) = 80(.2)(.8) = 12.8$

$\sigma = \sqrt{\sigma^2} = \sqrt{12.8} = 3.578$

c. $\mu = np = 100(.6) = 60$

$\sigma^2 = np(1 - p) = 100(.6)(.4) = 24$

$\sigma = \sqrt{\sigma^2} = \sqrt{24} = 4.899$

d. $\mu = np = 70(.9) = 63$

$\sigma^2 = np(1 - p) = 70(.9)(.1) = 6.3$

$\sigma = \sqrt{\sigma^2} = \sqrt{6.3} = 2.510$

e. $\mu = np = 60(.8) = 48$

$\sigma^2 = np(1 - p) = 60(.8)(.2) = 9.6$

$\sigma = \sqrt{\sigma^2} = \sqrt{9.6} = 3.098$

f. $\mu = np = 1{,}000(.04) = 40$

$\sigma^2 = np(1 - p) = 1{,}000(.04)(.96) = 38.4$

$\sigma = \sqrt{\sigma^2} = \sqrt{38.4} = 6.197$

4.41 x is a binomial random variable with $n = 4$.

a. If the probability distribution of x is symmetric, $p(0) = p(4)$ and $p(1) = p(3)$.

Since $p(x) = \begin{bmatrix} n \\ x \end{bmatrix} p^x q^{n-x} \quad x = 0, 1, \ldots, n,$

When $n = 4$,

$\begin{bmatrix} 4 \\ 0 \end{bmatrix} p^0 q^4 = \begin{bmatrix} 4 \\ 4 \end{bmatrix} p^4 q^0 \Rightarrow \dfrac{4!}{0!4!} p^0 q^4 = \dfrac{4!}{4!0!} p^4 q^0 \Rightarrow q^4 = p^4 \Rightarrow p = q$

Since $p + q = 1, p = .5$

Therefore, the probability distribution of x is symmetric when $p = .5$.

Discrete Random Variables

b. If the probability distribution of x is skewed to the right, then the mean is greater than the median. Therefore, there are more small values in the distribution (0, 1) than large values (3, 4). Therefore, p must be smaller than .5. Let $p = .2$ and the probability distribution of x will be skewed to the right.

c. If the probability distribution of x is skewed to the left, then the mean is smaller than the median. Therefore, there are more large values in the distribution (3, 4) than small values (0, 1). Therefore, p must be larger than .5. Let $p = .8$ and the probability distribution of x will be skewed to the left.

d. In part a, x is a binomial random variable with $n = 4$ and $p = .5$.

$$p(x) = \binom{4}{x} .5^x .5^{4-x} \quad x = 0, 1, 2, 3, 4$$

$$p(0) = \binom{4}{0} .5^0 .5^4 = \frac{4!}{0!4!} .5^4 = 1(.5)^4 = .0625$$

$$p(1) = \binom{4}{1} .5^1 .5^3 = \frac{4!}{1!3!} .5^4 = 4(.5)^4 = .25$$

$$p(2) = \binom{4}{2} .5^2 .5^2 = \frac{4!}{2!2!} .5^4 = 6(.5)^4 = .375$$

$p(3) = p(1) = .25$ (since the distribution is symmetric)

$p(4) = p(0) = .0625$

The probability distribution of x in tabular form is:

x	0	1	2	3	4
$p(x)$	.0625	.25	.375	.25	.0625

$\mu = np = 4(.5) = 2$

The graph of the probability distribution of x when $n = 4$ and $p = .5$ is as follows.

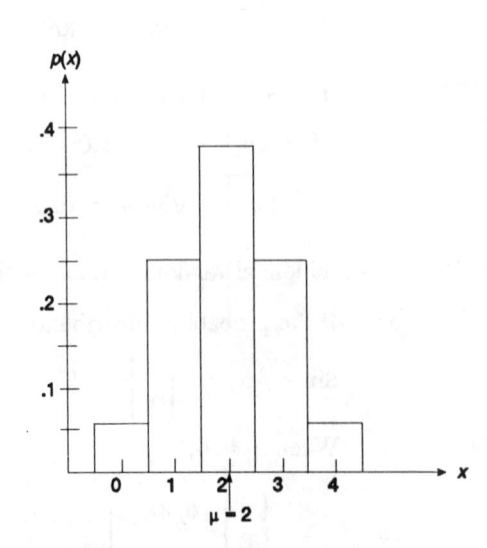

In part b, x is a binomial random variable with $n = 4$ and $p = .2$.

$$p(x) = \binom{4}{x} .2^x .8^{4-x} \qquad x = 0, 1, 2, 3, 4$$

$$p(0) = \binom{4}{0} .2^0 .8^4 = 1(1).8^4 = .4096$$

$$p(1) = \binom{4}{1} .2^1 .8^3 = 4(.2)(.8)^3 = .4096$$

$$p(2) = \binom{4}{2} .2^2 .8^2 = 6(.2)^2(.8)^2 = .1536$$

$$p(3) = \binom{4}{3} .2^3 .8^1 = 4(.2)^3(.8) = .0256$$

$$p(4) = \binom{4}{4} .2^4 .8^0 = 1(.2)^4(1) = .0016$$

The probability distribution of x in tabular form is:

x	0	1	2	3	4
$p(x)$	.4096	.4096	.1536	.0256	.0016

$\mu = np = 4(.2) = .8$

The graph of the probability distribution of x when $n = 4$ and $p = .2$ is as follows:

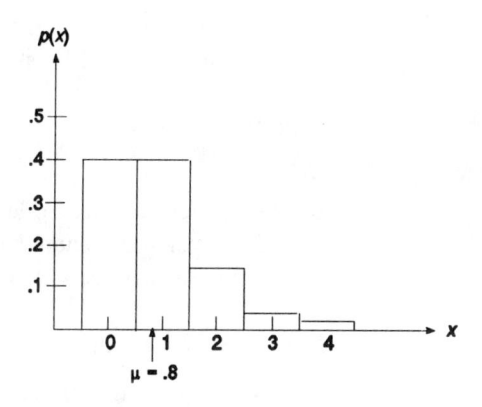

In part c, x is a binomial random variable with $n = 4$ and $p = .8$.

$$p(x) = \binom{4}{x} .8^x .2^{4-x} \qquad x = 0, 1, 2, 3, 4$$

$$p(0) = \binom{4}{0} .8^0 .2^4 = 1(1).2^4 = .0016$$

$$p(1) = \binom{4}{1} .8^1 .2^3 = 4(.8)(.2)^3 = .0256$$

$$p(2) = \binom{4}{2} .8^2 .2^2 = 6(.8)^2(.2)^2 = .1536$$

$$p(3) = \binom{4}{3} .8^3 .2^1 = 4(.8)^3(.2) = .4096$$

$$p(4) = \binom{4}{4} .8^4 .2^0 = 1(.8)^4(1) = .4096$$

Discrete Random Variables

The probability distribution of x in tabular form is:

x	0	1	2	3	4
$p(x)$	.0016	.0256	.1536	.4096	.4096

Note: The distribution of x when $n = 4$ and $p = .2$ is the reverse of the distribution of x when $n = 4$ and $p = .8$.

$\mu = np = 4(.8) = 3.2$

The graph of the probability distribution of x when $n = 4$ and $p = .8$ is as follows:

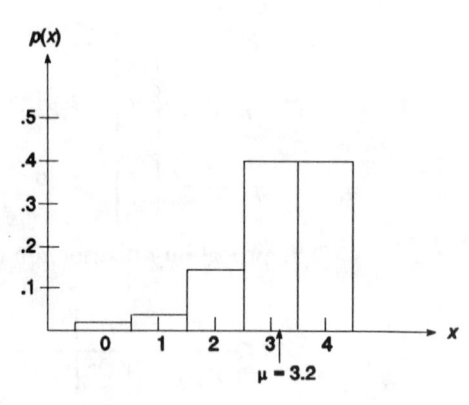

e. In general, when $p = .5$, a binomial distribution will be symmetric regardless of the value of n. When p is less than .5, the binomial distribution will be skewed to the right; and when p is greater than .5, it will be skewed to the left. (Refer to parts a, b, and c.)

4.43 Define the following events:

A: {Taxpayer is audited}
B: {Taxpayer has income less than $50,000}
C: {Taxpayer has income between $50,000 and $99,999}
D: {Taxpayer has income of $100,000 or more}

a. From the information given in the problem,

$P(A \mid B) = 6/1000 = .006$
$P(A \mid C) = 10/1000 = .01$
$P(A \mid D) = 49/1000 = .049$

b. Let x = number of taxpayers with incomes under $50,000 who are audited. Then x is a binomial random variable with $n = 5$ and $p = .006$.

$$P(x = 1) = \binom{5}{1} \frac{5!}{1!(5-1)!} .006^1 .994^{(5-1)} = \frac{5 \cdot 4 \cdot 3 \cdot 2 \cdot 1}{1 \cdot 4 \cdot 3 \cdot 2 \cdot 1} .006^1 .994^4$$

$$= 5(.006)(.976215137) = .0293$$

$$P(x > 1) = 1 - [P(x = 0) + P(x = 1)]$$

$$= 1 - \left[\binom{5}{0} \frac{5!}{0!(5-0)!} .006^0 .994^{(5-0)} + .0293 \right]$$

$$= 1 - \left[\frac{5 \cdot 4 \cdot 3 \cdot 2 \cdot 1}{1 \cdot 5 \cdot 4 \cdot 3 \cdot 2 \cdot 1} .006^0 .994^5 + .0293 \right]$$

$$= 1 - [1(1)(.9704) + .0293] = 1 - .9997 = .0003$$

c. Let x = number of taxpayers with incomes between $50,000 and $99,999 who are audited. Then x is a binomial random variable with $n = 5$ and $p = .01$.

$$P(x = 1) = \binom{5}{1}\frac{5!}{1!(5-1)!}.01^1.99^{(5-1)} = \frac{5 \cdot 4 \cdot 3 \cdot 2 \cdot 1}{1 \cdot 4 \cdot 3 \cdot 2 \cdot 1}.01^1.99^4$$
$$= 5(.01)(.96059601) = .0480$$

$$P(x > 1) = 1 - [P(x = 0) + P(x = 1)]$$
$$= 1 - \left[\binom{5}{0}\frac{5!}{0!(5-0)!}.01^0.99^{(5-0)} + .0480\right]$$
$$= 1 - \left[\frac{5 \cdot 4 \cdot 3 \cdot 2 \cdot 1}{1 \cdot 5 \cdot 4 \cdot 3 \cdot 2 \cdot 1}.01^0.99^5 + .0480\right]$$
$$= 1 - [1(1)(.95099) + .0480] = 1 - .9990 = .0010$$

d. Let x = number of taxpayers with incomes under $50,000 who are audited. Then x is a binomial random variable with $n = 2$ and $p = .006$.

Let y = number of taxpayers with incomes $100,000 or more who are audited. Then y is a binomial random variable with $n = 2$ and $p = .049$.

$$P(x = 0) = \binom{2}{0}\frac{2!}{0!(2-0)!}.006^0.994^{(2-0)} = \frac{2 \cdot 1}{1 \cdot 2 \cdot 1}.006^0.994^2$$
$$= 1(1)(.988036) = .988036$$

$$P(y = 0) = \binom{2}{0}\frac{2!}{0!(2-0)!}.049^0.951^{(2-0)} = \frac{2 \cdot 1}{1 \cdot 2 \cdot 1}.049^0.951^2$$
$$= 1(1)(.904401) = .904401$$

$$P(x = 0)P(y = 0) = .988036(.904401) = .8936$$

e. We must assume that the variables defined as x and y are binomial random variables. We must assume that the trials are identical, the probability of success is the same from trial to trial, and that the trials are independent.

4.45 a. We must assume that the probability that a specific type of ball meets the requirements is always the same from trial to trial and the trials are independent. To use the binomial probability distribution, we need to know the probability that a specific type of golf ball meets the requirements.

b. For a binomial distribution,

$$\mu = np$$
$$\sigma = \sqrt{npq}$$

In this example, n = two dozen = $2 \cdot 12 = 24$.

$p = .10$ (Success here means the golf ball *does not* meet standards.)
$q = .90$
$\mu = np = 24(.10) = 2.4$
$\sigma = \sqrt{npq} = \sqrt{24(.10)(.90)} = 1.47$

Discrete Random Variables

c. In this situation,

p = Probability of success
  = Probability golf ball *does* meet standards
  = .90
$q = 1 - .90 = .10$
$n = 24$
$E(x) = \mu = np = 24(.90) = 21.60$
$\sigma = \sqrt{npq} = \sqrt{24(.10)(.90)} = 1.47$ (Note that this is the same as in part **b**.)

4.47 Assuming the supplier's claim is true,

$$\mu = np = 500(.001) = .5$$
$$\sigma = \sqrt{npq} = \sqrt{500(.001)(.999)} = \sqrt{.4995} = .707$$

If the supplier's claim is true, we would only expect to find .5 defective switches in a sample of size 500. Therefore, it is not likely we would find 4.

Based on the sample, the guarantee is probably inaccurate.

Note: $z = \dfrac{x - \mu}{\sigma} = \dfrac{4 - .5}{.707} = 4.95$

This is an unusually large z-score.

4.49 a. $\mu = E(x) = np = 800(.65) = 520$
  $\sigma = \sqrt{npq} = \sqrt{800(.65)(.35)} = 13.491$

b. Half of the 800 food items is 400. A value of $x = 400$ would have a z-score of:

$$z = \dfrac{x - \mu}{\sigma} = \dfrac{400 - 520}{13.491} = -8.895$$

Since the z-score associated with 400 items is so small (-8.895), it would be virtually impossible to observe less than half without any traces of pesticides if the 65% value was correct.

4.51 The random variable x = number of defective fuses is a binomial random variable with $n = 25$. We will accept a lot if $x < 3$ or $x \leq 2$.

Using Table II, Appendix B:

a. $P(\text{accepting a lot}) = P(x \leq 2) = 1$ when $p = 0$

b. $P(\text{accepting a lot}) = P(x \leq 2) = .998$ when $p = .01$

c. $P(\text{accepting a lot}) = P(x \leq 2) = .537$ when $p = .10$

d. $P(\text{accepting a lot}) = P(x \leq 2) = .009$ when $p = .30$

e. $P(\text{accepting a lot}) = P(x \leq 2) \approx 0$ when $p = .50$

f. $P(\text{accepting a lot}) = P(x \leq 2) \approx 0$ when $p = .80$

g. $P(\text{accepting a lot}) = P(x \leq 2) \approx 0$ when $p = .95$

h. $P(\text{accepting a lot}) = P(x \leq 2) \approx 0$ when $p = 1$

i. A graph of the operating characteristic curve for this sampling plan is shown at right.

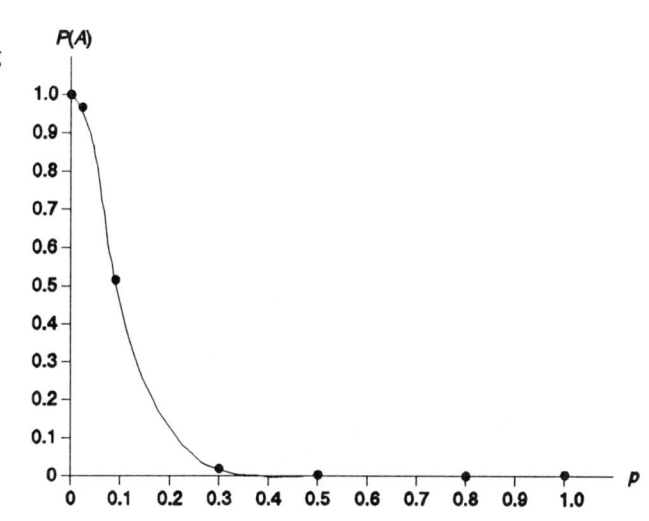

4.53 a. The random variable x is discrete since it can assume a countable number of values (0, 1, 2, ...).

b. This is a Poisson probability distribution with $\lambda = 3$.

c. In order to graph the probability distribution, we need to know the probabilities for the possible values of x. Using Table III of Appendix B with $\lambda = 3$:

$p(0) = .050$
$p(1) = P(x \leq 1) - P(x = 0) = .199 - .050 = .149$
$p(2) = P(x \leq 2) - P(x \leq 1) = .423 - .199 = .224$
$p(3) = P(x \leq 3) - P(x \leq 2) = .647 - .423 = .224$
$p(4) = P(x \leq 4) - P(x \leq 3) = .815 - .647 = .168$
$p(5) = P(x \leq 5) - P(x \leq 4) = .916 - .815 = .101$
$p(6) = P(x \leq 6) - P(x \leq 5) = .966 - .916 = .050$
$p(7) = P(x \leq 7) - P(x \leq 6) = .988 - .966 = .022$
$p(8) = P(x \leq 8) - P(x \leq 7) = .996 - .988 = .008$
$p(9) = P(x \leq 9) - P(x \leq 8) = .999 - .996 = .003$
$p(10) \approx .001$

The probability distribution of x in graphical form is:

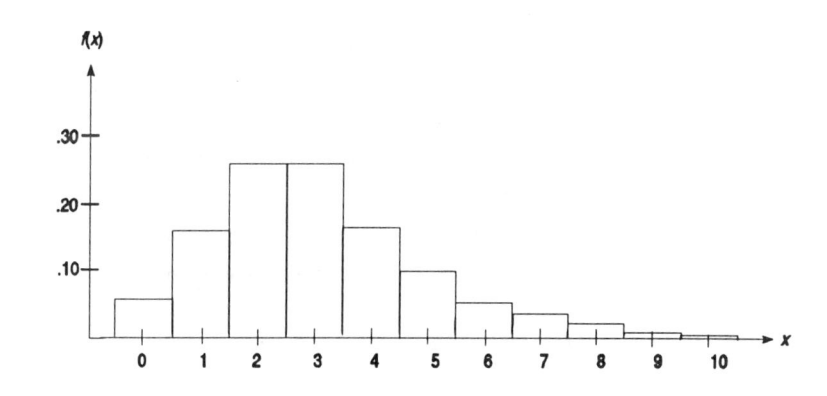

d. $\mu = \lambda = 3$
$\sigma^2 = \lambda = 3$
$\sigma = \sqrt{3} = 1.7321$

Discrete Random Variables

e. The mean of x is the same as the mean of the probability distribution, $\mu = \lambda = 3$.

The standard deviation of x is the same as the standard deviation of the probability distribution, $\sigma = 1.7321$.

4.55 $\mu = \lambda = 1.5$

Using Table III of Appendix B:

a. $P(x \leq 3) = .934$

b. $P(x \geq 3) = 1 - P(x \leq 2) = 1 - .809 = .191$

c. $P(x = 3) = P(x \leq 3) - P(x \leq 2) = .934 - .809 = .125$

d. $P(x = 0) = .223$

e. $P(x > 0) = 1 - P(x = 0) = 1 - .223 = .777$

f. $P(x > 6) = 1 - P(x \leq 6) = 1 - .999 = .001$

4.57 a. $E(x) = \mu = \lambda = 128.6$

$\sigma = \sqrt{\lambda} = \sqrt{128.6} = 11.340$

b. $z = \dfrac{x - \mu}{\sigma} = \dfrac{41 - 128.6}{11.340} = -7.72$

c. Using the formula with $\lambda = 128.6$,

$$P(x \leq 122) = P(x = 0) + P(x = 1) + \cdots + P(x = 122)$$
$$= \dfrac{128.6^0 e^{-128.6}}{0!} + \dfrac{128.6^1 e^{-128.6}}{1!} + \cdots + \dfrac{128.6^{122} e^{-128.6}}{122!}$$

d. The experiment consists of counting the number of bank failures per year. We assume the probability a bank fails in a year is the same for each year. We must also assume that the number of bank failures in one year is independent of the number in any other year.

4.59 a. $\sigma = \sqrt{\sigma^2} = \sqrt{\lambda} = \sqrt{4} = 2$

b. $P(x > 10) = 1 - P(x \leq 10)$
$= 1 - .977$ (Table III, Appendix B)
$= .003$

No. The probability that a sample of air from the plant exceeds the EPA limit is only .003. Since this value is very small, it is not very likely that this will occur.

c. The experiment consists of counting the number of parts per million of vinyl chloride in air samples. We must assume the probability of a part of vinyl chloride appearing in a million parts of air is the same for each million parts of air. We must also assume the number of parts of vinyl chloride in one million parts of air is independent of the number in any other one million parts of air.

4.61 There will not be enough beds if x = the number of newly admitted patients exceeds 4. For $\lambda = 2.5$,

$$P(x > 4) = 1 - P(x \leq 4)$$
$$= 1 - \{P(x = 0) + P(x = 1) + P(x = 2) + P(x = 3) + P(x = 4)\}$$
$$= 1 - \left[\frac{2.5^0 \cdot e^{-2.5}}{0!} + \frac{2.5^1 \cdot e^{-2.5}}{1!} + \frac{2.5^2 \cdot e^{-2.5}}{2!} + \frac{2.5^3 \cdot e^{-2.5}}{3!} + \frac{2.5^4 \cdot e^{-2.5}}{4!}\right]$$
$$= 1 - (.0821 + .2052 + .2565 + .2138 + .1336)$$
$$= 1 - .8912 = .1088$$

4.63 $\mu = \lambda = 3.4$, using Table III, Appendix B:

a. $P(x = 2) = P(x \leq 2) - P(x \leq 1) = .340 - .147 = .193$

b. $P(x \geq 3) = 1 - P(x \leq 2) = 1 - .340 = .660$

c. We need to assume that the probability that an accident occurs in a particular month is the same for all months. The number of accidents that occur in a particular month must all be independent of the number occurring in other months.

4.65 $\mu = \lambda = 3$, using Table III, Appendix B:

$P(x = 3) = P(x \leq 3) - P(x \leq 2) = .647 - .423 = .224$
$P(x = 0) = .050$

The probability that no bulbs fail in one hour is .050. If we let y = number of one hour intervals out of 8 that have no bulbs fail, then y is a binomial random variable with $n = 8$ and $p = .05$. Then, the probability that no bulbs fail in an 8 hour shift is

$$P(y = 8) = \binom{8}{8}.05^8.95^{(8-8)} = \frac{8!}{8!(8-8)!}.05^8.95^0$$
$$= \frac{8 \cdot 7 \cdot 6 \cdot 5 \cdot 4 \cdot 3 \cdot 2 \cdot 1}{8 \cdot 7 \cdot 6 \cdot 5 \cdot 4 \cdot 3 \cdot 2 \cdot 1 \cdot 1}.05^8.95^0 = .05^8$$

We must assume that the 8 one-hour intervals are independent and identical, and that the probability that no bulbs fail is the same for each one-hour interval.

4.67 $p(x) = \binom{n}{x}p^x q^{n-x}$ $x = 0, 1, 2, \ldots, n$

a. $P(x = 3) = p(3) = \binom{7}{3}.5^3.5^4 = \frac{7!}{3!4!}.5^3.5^4 = 35(.125)(.0625) = .2734$

b. $P(x = 3) = p(3) = \binom{4}{3}.8^3.2^1 = \frac{4!}{3!1!}.8^3.2^1 = 4(.512)(.2) = .4096$

c. $P(x = 1) = p(1) = \binom{15}{1}.1^1.9^{14} = \frac{15!}{1!14!}.1^1.9^{14} = 15(.1)(.228768) = .3432$

4.69 From Table II, Appendix B:

a. $P(x = 14) = P(x \leq 14) - P(x \leq 13) = .584 - .392 = .192$

Discrete Random Variables

b. $P(x \leq 12) = .228$

c. $P(x > 12) = 1 - P(x \leq 12) = 1 - .228 = .772$

d. $P(9 \leq x \leq 18) = P(x \leq 18) - P(x \leq 8) = .992 - .005 = .987$

e. $P(8 < x < 18) = P(x \leq 17) - P(x \leq 8) = .965 - .005 = .960$

f. $\mu = np = 20(.7) = 14$

$\sigma^2 = npq = 20(.7)(.3) = 4.2, \sigma = \sqrt{4.2} = 2.049$

g. $\mu \pm 2\sigma \Rightarrow 14 \pm 2(2.049) \Rightarrow 14 \pm 4.098 \Rightarrow (9.902, 18.098)$

$$P(9.902 < x < 18.098) = P(10 \leq x \leq 18) = P(x \leq 18) - P(x \leq 9)$$
$$= .992 - .017 = .975$$

4.71 a. Discrete — The number of damaged inventory items is countable.

b. Continuous — The average monthly sales can take on any value within an acceptable limit.

c. Continuous — The number of square feet can take on any positive value.

d. Continuous — The length of time we must wait can take on any positive value.

4.73 a. $E(x) = \sum xp(x)$
$= 37,500(.14) + 112,500(.3) + 225,000(.2) + 400,000(.17) + 750,000(.1)$
$+ 3,000,000(.09)$
$= 5250 + 33,750 + 45,000 + 68,000 + 75,000 + 270,000$
$= 497,000$

b. $E[(x - \mu)^2] = \sum (x - \mu)^2 p(x)$
$= (37,500 - 497,000)^2(.14) + (112,500 - 497,000)^2(.3)$
$+ (225,000 - 497,000)^2(.2) + (400,000 - 497,000)^2(.17)$
$+ (750,000 - 497,000)^2(.1) + (3,000,000 - 497,000)^2(.09)$
$= 29,559,635,000 + 44,352,075,000 + 14,796,800,000 + 1,599,530,000$
$+ 6,400,900,000 + 563,850,810,000$
$= 660,559,750,000$
$= 6.6055975 \times 10^{11}$

c. The average sales volume for the fabricare firms is $497,000. This is what we expect the sales volume of a randomly selected fabricare firm to be.

The variance in the sales volume of the fabricare firms is 6.6056×10^{11}. This is a measure of the spread of the sales volumes of the firms.

4.75 Define x as the number of invoices in the sample that contain arithmetic errors. The random variable x is a binomial random variable since it fits the characteristics (the invoices are independently chosen with only two possible outcomes). If the accountant's theory is valid, $n = 25$ and $p = .10$.

$$P(x \geq 7) = 1 - P(x \leq 6) = 1 - \sum_{x=0}^{6} p(x) = 1 - .991 \quad \text{(Table II)}$$
$$= .009$$

4.77 a. The number of cars that have mileages within 2 miles per gallon of their EPA projections in a sample of 20 chosen from a finite population is not a binomial random variable since the sample is chosen without replacement from a finite population. However, since the sample is small compared to the population, we could treat it like a binomial random variable for convenience. Therefore, the statement is true.

b. Let x be the number of cars that have mileages within 2 miles per gallon of their EPA projections. For convenience, assume the random variable x is binomial with $n = 20$ and $p = .70$. Using Table II, Appendix B, with $n = 20$ and $p = .70$,

$$P(x < 10) = P(x \leq 9) = .017$$

Therefore, the probability is approximately .017.

4.79 a. In order for the number of deaths to follow a Poisson distribution, we must assume that the probability of a death is the same for any week. We must also assume that the number of deaths in any week is independent of any other week.

The first assumption may not be valid. The probability of a death may not be the same for every week. The number of passengers varies from week to week, so the probability of a death may change.

b. $E(x) = \lambda = 14$.
$\sigma = \sqrt{\lambda} = \sqrt{14} = 3.742$

c. Using Chebyshev's Rule, we know that at most 25% of the measurements are more than 2 standard deviations from the mean. Also, at most 11.1% of the measurements are more than 3 standard deviations from the mean.

$\mu \pm 2\sigma \Rightarrow 14 \pm 2(3.742) \Rightarrow 14 \pm 7.484 \Rightarrow (6.516, 21.484)$
$\mu \pm 3\sigma \Rightarrow 14 \pm 3(3.742) \Rightarrow 14 \pm 11.226 \Rightarrow (2.774, 25.226)$

From this information, at most 25% of the weeks will four or fewer deaths occur. This is not that uncommon.

d. $P(x \leq 4) = .002$ (Using Table III, Appendix B)

This probability is less than the "at most 25%" in part c, which agrees. However, it is much less. With this probability, it would be extremely unlikely to see four or fewer deaths in a week.

4.81 a. $\mu = n \cdot p = 25(.05) = 1.25$
$\sigma = \sqrt{npq} = \sqrt{25(.05)(.95)} = 1.09$

Since μ is not an integer, x could not equal its mean.

Discrete Random Variables

b. The event is $(x \geq 5)$. From Table II with $n = 25$ and $p = .05$:

$$P(x \geq 5) = 1 - P(x \leq 4) = 1 - .993 = .007$$

c. Since the probability obtained in part b is so small, it is unlikely that 5% applies to this agency. The percentage is probably greater than 5%.

4.83 Using Table II with $n = 25$ and $p = .8$:

a. $P(x < 15) = P(x \leq 14) = .006$

b. Since the probability of such an event is so small when $p = .8$, if less than 15 insects die we would conclude that the insecticide is not as effective as claimed.

4.85 Let x = the number of delivery truck breakdowns today and y = the number of delivery truck breakdowns tomorrow. The random variables x and y are Poisson with $\mu = \lambda = 1.5$. Using Table III, Appendix B:

a. $P(x = 2 \cap y = 3) = P(x = 2)P(y = 3)$ (by independence)
$= [P(x \leq 2) - P(x \leq 1)][P(y \leq 3) - P(y \leq 2)]$
$= (.809 - .558)(.934 - .809) = .251(.125) = .0314$

b. $P(x < 2 \cap y > 2) = P(x < 2)P(y > 2)$ (by independence)
$= P(x \leq 1)[1 - P(y \leq 2)]$
$= .558(1 - .809) = .558(.191) = .1066$

Continuous Random Variables — Chapter 5

5.1   a. $f(x) = \dfrac{1}{d-c} \quad (c \leq x \leq d)$

$\dfrac{1}{d-c} = \dfrac{1}{45-20} = \dfrac{1}{25} = .04$

So, $f(x) = \begin{cases} .04 & (20 \leq x \leq 45) \\ 0 & \text{otherwise} \end{cases}$

b. $\mu = \dfrac{c+d}{2} = \dfrac{20+45}{2} = \dfrac{65}{2} = 32.5$

$\sigma = \dfrac{d-c}{\sqrt{12}} = \dfrac{45-20}{\sqrt{12}} = 7.2169$

$\sigma^2 = (7.2169)^2 = 52.0833$

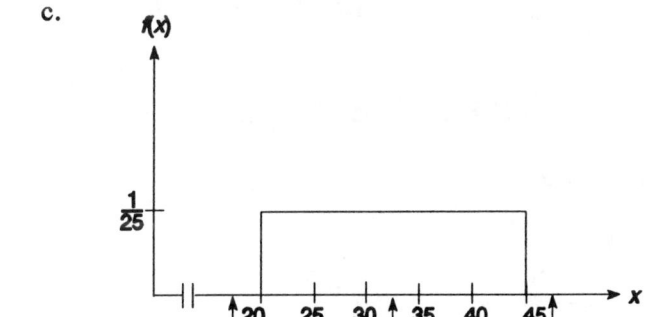

c.

$\mu \pm 2\sigma \Rightarrow 32.5 \pm 2(7.2169) \Rightarrow (18.0662, 46.9338)$

$P(18.0662 < x < 46.9338) = P(20 < x < 45) = (45-20).04 = 1$

5.3   a. $f(x) = \dfrac{1}{d-c} \quad (c \leq x \leq d)$

$\dfrac{1}{d-c} = \dfrac{1}{7-3} = \dfrac{1}{4}$

$f(x) = \begin{cases} \dfrac{1}{4} & (3 \leq x \leq 7) \\ 0 & \text{otherwise} \end{cases}$

b. $\mu = \dfrac{c+d}{2} = \dfrac{3+7}{2} = \dfrac{10}{2} = 5$

$\sigma = \dfrac{d-c}{\sqrt{12}} = \dfrac{7-3}{\sqrt{12}} = \dfrac{4}{\sqrt{12}} = 1.155$

c. $\mu \pm \sigma \Rightarrow 5 \pm 1.155 \Rightarrow (3.845, 6.155)$

$P(\mu - \sigma \leq x \leq \mu + \sigma) = P(3.845 \leq x \leq 6.155) = \dfrac{b-a}{d-c} = \dfrac{6.155 - 3.845}{7 - 3} = \dfrac{2.31}{4} = .5775$

5.5 $f(x) = \dfrac{1}{d-c} = \dfrac{1}{200-100} = \dfrac{1}{100} = .01$

$f(x) = \begin{cases} .01 & (100 \leq x \leq 200) \\ 0 & \text{otherwise} \end{cases}$

$\mu = \dfrac{c+d}{2} = \dfrac{100+200}{2} = \dfrac{300}{2} = 150$

$\sigma = \dfrac{d-c}{\sqrt{12}} = \dfrac{200-100}{\sqrt{12}} = \dfrac{100}{\sqrt{12}} = 28.8675$

a. $\mu \pm 2\sigma \Rightarrow 150 \pm 2(28.8675) \Rightarrow 150 \pm 57.735 \Rightarrow (92.265, 207.735)$

$P(x < 92.265) + P(x > 207.735) = P(x < 100) + P(x > 200)$
$\phantom{P(x < 92.265) + P(x > 207.735)} = 0 + 0$
$\phantom{P(x < 92.265) + P(x > 207.735)} = 0$

b. $\mu \pm 3\sigma \Rightarrow 150 \pm 3(28.8675) \Rightarrow 150 \pm 86.6025 \Rightarrow (63.3975, 236.6025)$

$P(63.3975 < x < 236.6025) = P(100 < x < 200) = (200 - 100)(.01) = 1$

c. From a, $\mu \pm 2\sigma \Rightarrow (92.265, 207.735)$.

$P(92.265 < x < 207.735) = P(100 < x < 200) = (200 - 100)(.01) = 1$

5.7   a. The amount dispensed by the beverage machine is a continuous random variable since it can take on any value between 6.5 and 7.5 ounces.

b. Since the amount dispensed is random between 6.5 and 7.5 ounces, x is a uniform random variable.

$f(x) = \dfrac{1}{d-c} \quad (c \leq x \leq d)$

$\dfrac{1}{d-c} = \dfrac{1}{7.5 - 6.5} = \dfrac{1}{1} = 1$

Therefore, $f(x) = \begin{cases} 1 & (6.5 \leq x \leq 7.5) \\ 0 & \text{otherwise} \end{cases}$

The graph is as follows:

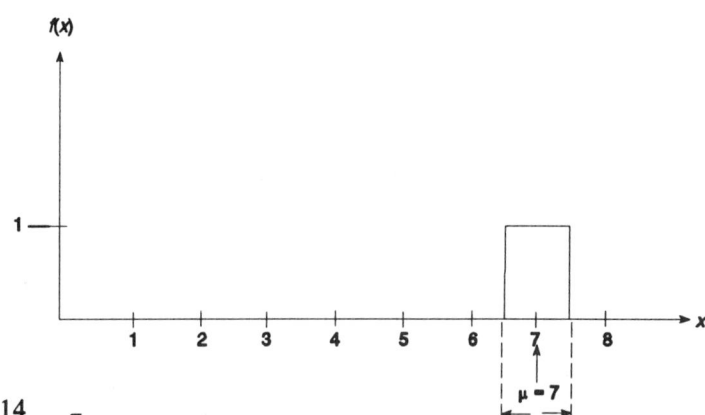

[Graph showing f(x) with a rectangle of height 1 between x=6.5 and x=7.5, with μ=7 and μ±2σ indicated]

c. $\mu = \dfrac{c + d}{2} = \dfrac{6.5 + 7.5}{2} = \dfrac{14}{2} = 7$

$\sigma = \dfrac{d - c}{\sqrt{12}} = \dfrac{7.5 - 6.5}{\sqrt{12}} = .2887$

$\mu \pm 2\sigma \Rightarrow 7 \pm 2(.2887) \Rightarrow 7 \pm .5774 \Rightarrow (6.422, 7.577)$

d. $P(x \geq 7) = (7.5 - 7)(1) = .5$

e. $P(x < 6) = 0$

f. $P(6.5 \leq x \leq 7.25) = (7.25 - 6.5)(1) = .75$

g. The probability that the next bottle filled will contain more than 7.25 ounces is:

$P(x > 7.25) = (7.5 - 7.25)(1) = .25$

The probability that the next 6 bottles filled will contain more than 7.25 ounces is:

$P[(x > 7.25) \cap (x > 7.25) \cap (x > 7.25) \cap (x > 7.25) \cap (x > 7.25) \cap (x > 7.25)]$
$= [P(x > 7.25)]^6 = .25^6 = .0002$

5.9 To construct a relative frequency histogram for the data, we can use 7 measurement classes.

Interval width = $\dfrac{\text{Largest number} - \text{smallest number}}{\text{Number of classes}} = \dfrac{98.0716 - .7434}{7} = 13.9$

We will use an interval width of 14 and a starting value of .74335.

The measurement classes, frequencies, and relative frequencies are given in the table below.

Class	Measurement Class	Class Frequency	Class Relative Frequency
1	.74335 − 14.74335	6	6/40 = .15
2	14.74335 − 28.74335	4	.10
3	28.74335 − 42.74335	6	.15
4	42.74335 − 56.74335	6	.15
5	56.74335 − 70.74335	5	.125
6	70.74335 − 84.74335	4	.10
7	84.74335 − 98.74335	9	.225
		40	1.000

Continuous Random Variables

The histogram looks like the data could be from a uniform distribution. The last class (84.74335 − 98.74335) has a few more observations in it than we would expect. However, we cannot expect a perfect graph from a sample of only 40 observations.

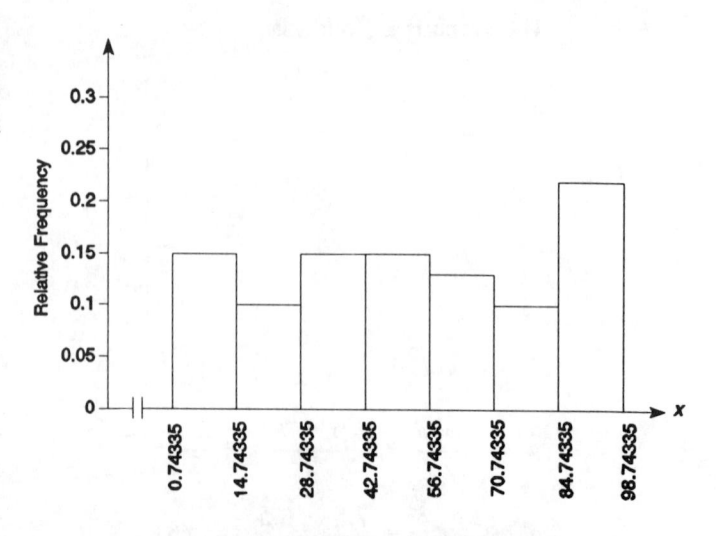

5.11 Let x = number of inches a gouge is from one end of the spindle. Then x has a uniform distribution with $f(x)$ as follows:

$$f(x) = \begin{cases} \dfrac{1}{d-c} = \dfrac{1}{18-0} = \dfrac{1}{18} & 0 \le x \le 18 \\ 0 & \text{otherwise} \end{cases}$$

In order to get at least 14 consecutive inches without a gouge, the gouge must be within 4 inches of either end. Thus, we must find:

$$P(x < 4) + P(x > 14) = (4-0)(1/18) + (18-14)(1/18)$$
$$= 4/18 + 4/18 = 8/18 = .4444$$

5.13 Table IV in the text gives the area between $z = 0$ and $z = z_0$. In this exercise, the answers may thus be read directly from the table by looking up the appropriate z.

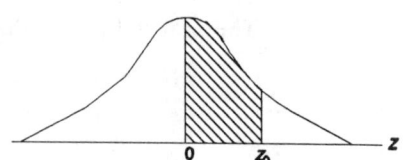

   a. $P(0 < z < 2.0) = .4772$

   b. $P(0 < z < 3.0) = .4987$

   c. $P(0 < z < 1.5) = .4332$

   d. $P(0 < z < .80) = .2881$

5.15 Using Table IV, Appendix B:

   a. $P(z > 1.46) = .5 - P(0 < z \le 1.46)$
       $= .5 - .4279 = .0721$

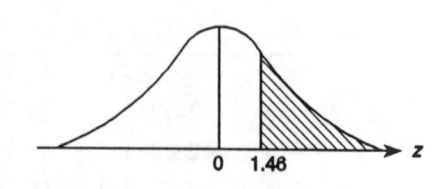

72 Chapter 5

b. $P(x < -1.56) = .5 - P(-1.56 \leq z < 0)$
$= .5 - .4406 = .0594$

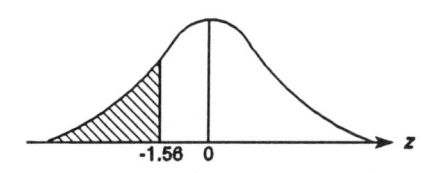

c. $P(.67 \leq z \leq 2.41)$
$= P(0 < z \leq 2.41) - P(0 < z < .67)$
$= .4920 - .2486 = .2434$

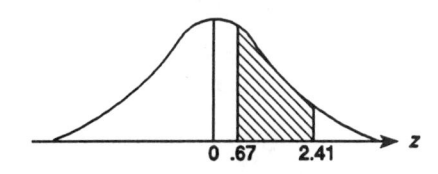

d. $P(-1.96 \leq z < -.33)$
$= P(-1.96 \leq z < 0) - P(-.33 \leq z < 0)$
$= .4750 - .1293 = .3457$

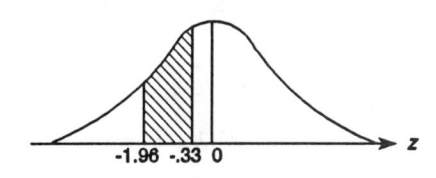

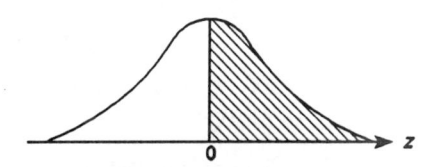

e. $P(z \geq 0) = .5$

f. $P(-2.33 < z < 1.50)$
$= P(-2.33 < z < 0) + P(0 < z < 1.50)$
$= .4901 + .4332 = .9233$

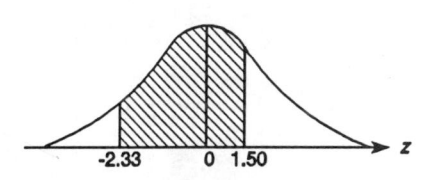

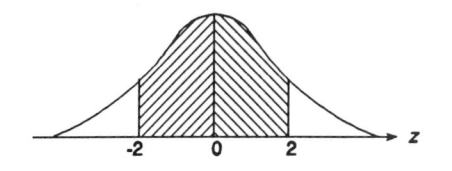

5.17   Using Table IV, Appendix B:

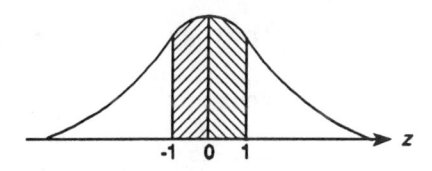

a. $P(-1 \leq z \leq 1)$
$= P(-1 \leq z \leq 0) + P(0 < z \leq 1)$
$= .3413 + .3413 = .6826$

b. $P(-1.96 \leq z \leq 1.96)$
$= P(-1.96 \leq z < 0) + P(0 \leq z \leq 1.96)$
$= .4750 + .4750 = .9500$

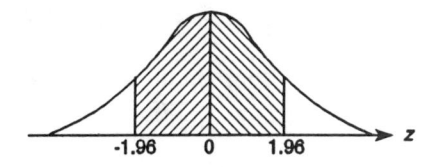

c. $P(-1.645 \leq z \leq 1.645)$
$= P(-1.645 \leq z < 0) + P(0 \leq z \leq 1.645)$
$= .4500 + .4500 = .90$
(using interpolation)

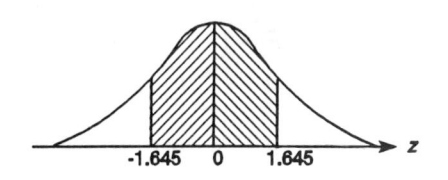

d. $P(-2 \leq z \leq 2)$
$= P(-2 \leq z < 0) + P(0 \leq z \leq 2)$
$= .4772 + .4772 = .9544$

Continuous Random Variables

5.19 Using Table IV of Appendix B:

a. $P(z \leq z_0) = .2090$

$A = .5000 - .2090 = .2910$

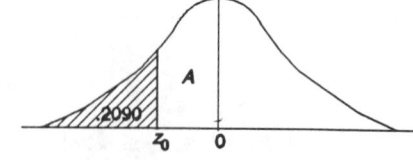

Look up the area .2910 in the body of Table IV; $z_0 = -.81$.

(z_0 is negative since the graph shows z_0 is on the left side of 0.)

b. $P(z \leq z_0) = .7090$

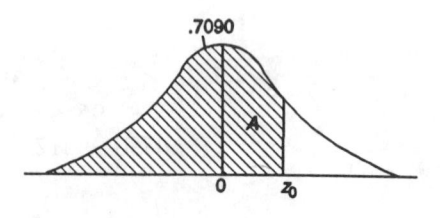

$P(z \leq z_0) = P(z \leq 0) + P(0 \leq z \leq z_0)$
$= .5 + P(0 \leq z \leq z) = .7090$

Therefore, $P(0 \leq z \leq z_0) = .7090 - .5 = .2090$

Look up the area .2090 in the body of Table IV; $z_0 \approx .55$.

c. $P(-z_0 \leq z < z_0) = .8472$

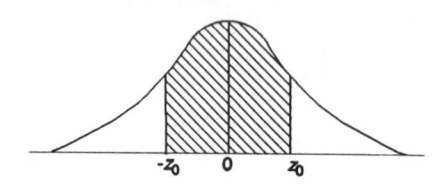

$P(-z_0 \leq z < z_0) = 2P(0 \leq z \leq z_0)$
$2P(0 \leq z \leq z_0) = .8472$

Therefore, $P(0 \leq z \leq z_0) = .4236$.

Look up the area .4236 in the body of Table IV; $z_0 = 1.43$.

d. $P(-z_0 \leq z < z_0) = .1664$

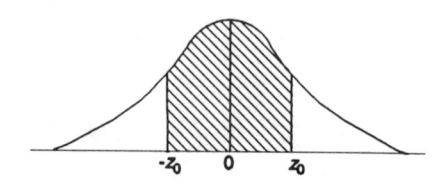

$P(-z_0 \leq z \leq z_0) = 2P(0 \leq z \leq z_0)$
$2P(0 \leq z \leq z_0) = .1664$

Therefore, $P(0 \leq z \leq z_0) = .0832$.

Look up the area .0832 in the body of Table IV; $z_0 = .21$.

e. $P(z_0 \leq z \leq 0) = .4798$

$P(z_0 \leq z \leq 0) = P(0 \leq z \leq -z_0)$

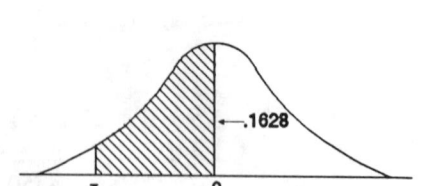

Look up the area .4798 in the body of Table IV; $z_0 = -2.05$.

f. $P(-1 < z < z_0) = .5328$

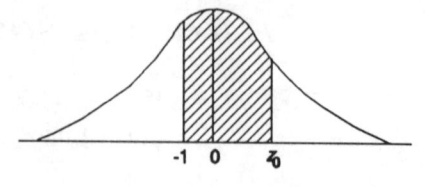

$P(-1 < z < z_0)$
$= P(-1 < z < 0) + P(0 < z < z_0)$
$= .5328$

$P(0 < z < 1) + P(0 < z < z_0) = .5328$

Thus, $P(0 < z < z_0) = .5328 - .3413 = .1915$

Look up the area .1915 in the body of Table IV; $z_0 = .50$.

5.21 a. If $x = 20$, $z = \dfrac{x - \mu}{\sigma} = \dfrac{20 - 30}{4} = -2.5$

b. If $x = 30$, $z = \dfrac{x - \mu}{\sigma} = \dfrac{30 - 30}{4} = 0$

c. If $x = 27.5$, $z = \dfrac{x - \mu}{\sigma} = \dfrac{27.5 - 30}{4} = -.625$

d. If $x = 15$, $z = \dfrac{x - \mu}{\sigma} = \dfrac{15 - 30}{4} = -3.75$

e. If $x = 35$, $z = \dfrac{x - \mu}{\sigma} = \dfrac{35 - 30}{4} = 1.25$

f. If $x = 25$, $z = \dfrac{x - \mu}{\sigma} = \dfrac{25 - 30}{4} = -1.25$

5.23 a. $P(10 \leq x \leq 12) = P\left[\dfrac{10 - 11}{2} \leq z \leq \dfrac{12 - 11}{2}\right]$
$= P(-0.50 \leq z \leq 0.50)$
$= A_1 + A_2$
$= .1915 + .1915 = .3830$

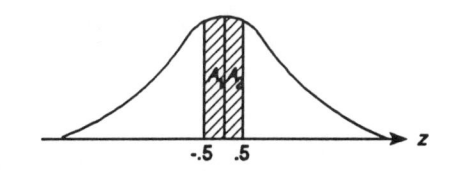

b. $P(6 \leq x \leq 10) = P\left[\dfrac{6 - 11}{2} \leq z \leq \dfrac{10 - 11}{2}\right]$
$= P(-2.50 \leq z \leq -0.50)$
$= P(-2.50 \leq z \leq 0)$
$\quad - P(-0.50 \leq z \leq 0)$
$= .4938 - .1915 = .3023$

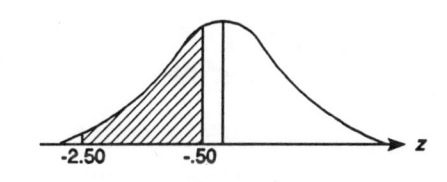

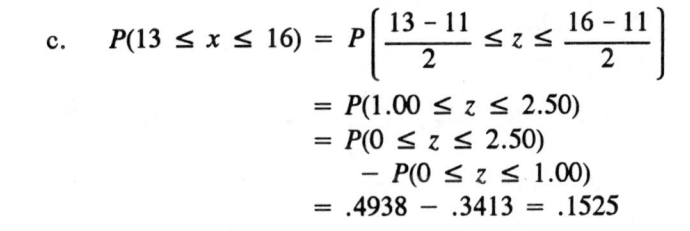

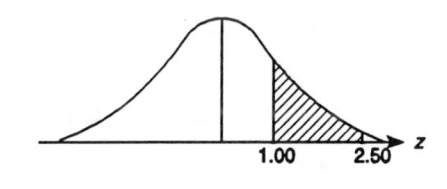

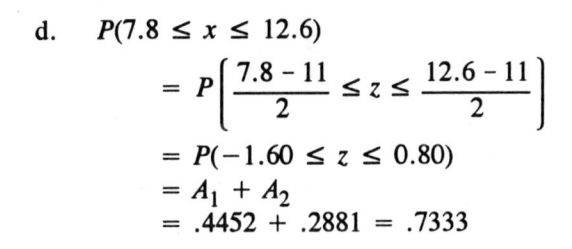

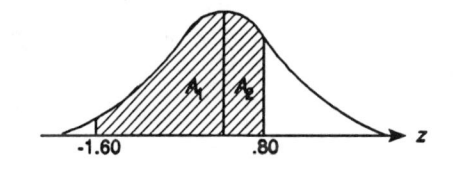

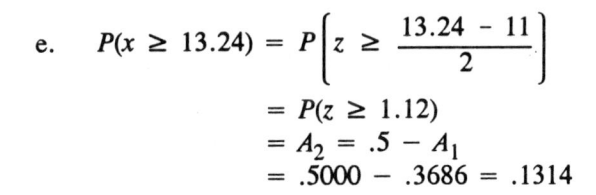

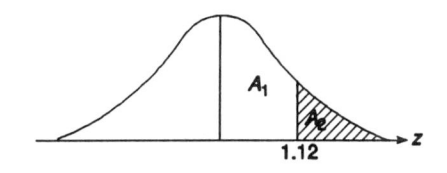

c. $P(13 \leq x \leq 16) = P\left[\dfrac{13 - 11}{2} \leq z \leq \dfrac{16 - 11}{2}\right]$
$= P(1.00 \leq z \leq 2.50)$
$= P(0 \leq z \leq 2.50)$
$\quad - P(0 \leq z \leq 1.00)$
$= .4938 - .3413 = .1525$

d. $P(7.8 \leq x \leq 12.6)$
$= P\left[\dfrac{7.8 - 11}{2} \leq z \leq \dfrac{12.6 - 11}{2}\right]$
$= P(-1.60 \leq z \leq 0.80)$
$= A_1 + A_2$
$= .4452 + .2881 = .7333$

e. $P(x \geq 13.24) = P\left[z \geq \dfrac{13.24 - 11}{2}\right]$
$= P(z \geq 1.12)$
$= A_2 = .5 - A_1$
$= .5000 - .3686 = .1314$

Continuous Random Variables

f. $P(x \geq 7.62) = P\left[z \geq \dfrac{7.62 - 11}{2}\right]$
$= P(z \geq -1.69)$
$= A_1 + A_2$
$= .4545 + .5000 = .9545$

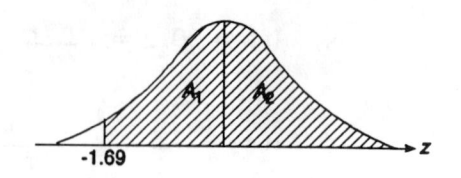

5.25

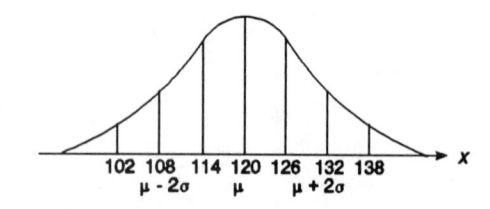

Using Table IV, Appendix B:

a. $P(\mu - 2\sigma \leq x \leq \mu + 2\sigma) = P(-2 \leq z \leq 2)$
$= P(-2 \leq z \leq 0) + P(0 \leq z \leq 2)$
$= .4772 + .4772 = .9544$

b. $P(x \geq 128) = P\left[z \geq \dfrac{128 - 120}{6}\right] = P(z \geq 1.33) = .5 - .4082 = .0918$

c. $P(x \leq 108) = P\left[z \leq \dfrac{108 - 120}{6}\right] = P(z \leq -2) = .5 - .4772 = .0228$

d. $P(112 \leq x \leq 130) = P\left[\dfrac{112 - 120}{6} \leq z \leq \dfrac{130 - 120}{6}\right] = P(-1.33 \leq z \leq 1.67)$
$= P(-1.33 \leq z \leq 0) + P(0 \leq z \leq 1.67)$
$= .4082 + .4525 = .8607$

e. $P(114 \leq x \leq 116) = P\left[\dfrac{114 - 120}{6} \leq z \leq \dfrac{116 - 120}{6}\right] = P(-1 \leq z \leq -.67)$
$= P(-1 \leq z \leq 0) - P(-.67 \leq z \leq 0)$
$= .3413 - .2486 = .0927$

f. $P(115 \leq x \leq 128) = P\left[\dfrac{115 - 120}{6} \leq z \leq \dfrac{128 - 120}{6}\right] = P(-.83 \leq z \leq 1.33)$
$= P(-.83 \leq z \leq 0) + P(0 \leq z \leq 1.33)$
$= .2967 + .4082 = .7049$

5.27 a. Let $x =$ passenger demand. The random variable x has a normal distribution with $\mu = 125$ and $\sigma = 45$.

For the Boeing 727, the probability that the passenger demand will exceed the capacity is:

$P(x > 148) = P\left[z > \dfrac{148 - 125}{45}\right] = P(z > .51) = .5 - .1950 = .3050$

(using Table IV)

For the Boeing 757, the probability that the passenger demand will exceed the capacity is:

$$P(x > 182) = P\left(z > \frac{182 - 125}{45}\right) = P(z > 1.27) = .5 - .3890 = .1020$$

b. For the Boeing 727, the probability that the flight will depart with one or more empty seats is:

$$P(x \leq 147) = P\left(z \leq \frac{147 - 125}{45}\right) = P(z \leq .49) = .5 + .1879 = .6879$$

For the Boeing 757, the probability that the flight will depart with one or more empty seats is:

$$P(x \leq 181) = P\left(z \leq \frac{181 - 125}{45}\right) = P(z \leq 1.24) = .5 + .3925 = .8925$$

c. For the Boeing 727, the probability that the spill is more than 100 passengers is:

$$P(x > 248) = P\left(z > \frac{248 - 125}{45}\right) = P(z > 2.73) = .5 - .4968 = .0032$$

5.29 a. Using Table IV, Appendix B, with $\mu = 20.2$ and $\sigma = .65$,

$$P(20 < x < 21) = P\left(\frac{20 - 20.2}{.65} < z < \frac{21 - 20.2}{.65}\right) = P(-.31 < z < 1.23)$$
$$= P(-.31 < z < 0) + P(0 \leq z < 1.23) = .1217 + .3907 = .5124$$

b. $P(x \leq 19.84) = P\left(z \leq \frac{19.84 - 20.2}{.65}\right) = P(z \leq -.55) = .5 - .2088 = .2912$

Since the probability of observing a sardine with a length of 19.84 cm or smaller is not small ($p = .2912$), this is not an unusual event if the sardine was, in fact, two years old. Thus, it is likely that the sardine is two years old.

c. $P(x \geq 22.01) = P\left(z \geq \frac{22.01 - 20.2}{.65}\right) = P(z \geq 2.78) = .5 - .4973 = .0027$

Since the probability of observing a sardine with a length of 22.01 cm or larger is so small ($p = .0027$), this would be a very unusual event if the sardine was, in fact, two years old. Thus, it is unlikely that the sardine is two years old.

5.31 a. Using Table IV, Appendix B, with $\mu = 8.72$ and $\sigma = 1.10$,

$$P(x < 6) = P\left(z < \frac{6 - 8.72}{1.10}\right) = P(z < -2.47) = .5 - .4932 = .0068$$

Thus, approximately .68% of the games would result in fewer than 6 hits.

b. The probability of observing fewer than 6 hits in a game is $p = .0068$. The probability of observing 0 hits would be even smaller. Thus, it would be extremely unusual to observe a no hitter.

Continuous Random Variables

5.33 Let x = the amount of dye discharged. The random variable x is normally distributed with $\sigma = 4$.

We want P(shade is unacceptable) $\leq .01$

$\Rightarrow P(x > 6) \leq .01$

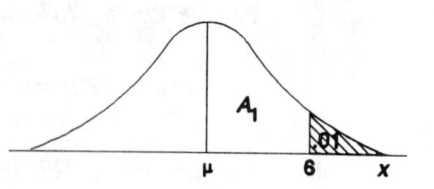

Then $A_1 = .50 - .01 = .49$. Look up the area .49 in the body of Table IV, Appendix B; (take the closest value) $z_0 = 2.33$.

To find μ, substitute into the z-score formula:

$$z = \frac{x - \mu}{\sigma}$$

$$2.33 = \frac{6 - \mu}{.4}$$

$$\mu = 6 - .4(2.33) = 5.068$$

5.35 Let x = monthly rate of return to stock ABC and y = monthly rate of return to stock XYZ. The random variable x is normally distributed with $\mu = .05$ and $\sigma = .03$ and y is normally distributed with $\mu = .07$ and $\sigma = .05$. You have $100 invested in each stock.

a. The average monthly rate of return for ABC stock is $\mu = .05$.
The average monthly rate of return for XYZ stock is $\mu = .07$.
Therefore, stock XYZ has the higher average monthly rate of return.

b. $E(x) = .05$ for each $1.

Since we have $100 invested in stock ABC, the monthly rate of return would be $100(.05) = \$5$.

Therefore, the expected value of the investment in stock ABC at the end of 1 month is $100 + 5 = \$105$.

$E(y) = .07$ for each $1.

Since we have $100 invested in stock XYZ, the monthly rate of return would be $100(.07) = \$7$.

Therefore, the expected value of the investment in stock XYZ at the end of 1 month is $100 + 7 = \$107$.

c. We need to find the probability of incurring a loss for each stock and compare them.

P(incurring a loss on stock ABC)
= P(monthly rate of return is negative on stock ABC)
= $P(x < 0)$

P(incurring a loss on stock XYZ)
= P(monthly rate of return is negative on stock XYZ)
= $P(y < 0)$

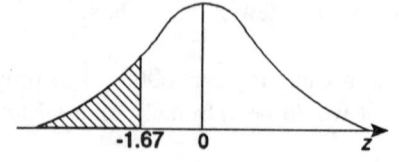

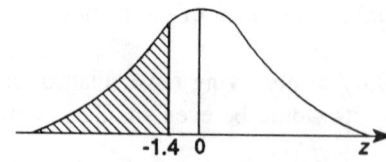

$$P(x < 0) = P\left(z < \frac{0 - .05}{.03}\right) \qquad P(y < 0) = P\left(z < \frac{0 - .07}{.05}\right)$$
$$= P(z < -1.67) \qquad\qquad\qquad = P(z < -1.4)$$
$$= .5000 - .4525 \qquad\qquad\qquad = .5000 - .4192$$
$$= .0475 \text{ (Table IV, Appendix B)} \qquad = .0818 \text{ (Table IV, Appendix B)}$$

Since the probability of incurring a loss is smaller for stock ABC, stock ABC would have a greater protection against occurring a loss next month.

5.37 a. If z is a standard normal random variable,

$Q_L = z_L$ is the value of the standard normal distribution which has 25% of the data to the left and 75% to the right.

Find z_L such that $P(z < z_L) = .25$

$A_1 = .50 - .25 = .25$.

Look up the area $A_1 = .25$ in the body of Table IV of Appendix B; $z_L = -.67$ (taking the closest value). If interpolation is used, $-.675$ would be obtained.

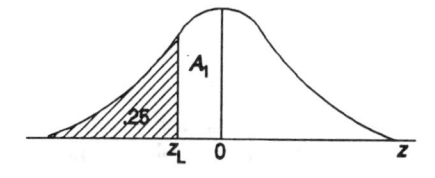

$Q_U = z_U$ is the value of the standard normal distribution which has 75% of the data to the left and 25% to the right.

Find z_U such that $P(z < z_U) = .75$

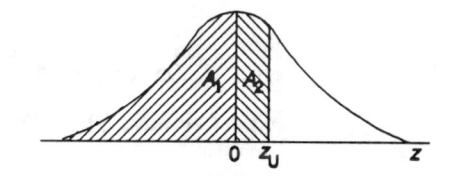

$$A_1 + A_2 = P(z \leq 0) + P(0 \leq z \leq z_U)$$
$$= .5 + P(0 \leq z \leq z_U)$$
$$= .75$$

Therefore, $P(0 \leq z \leq z_U) = .25$.

Look up the area .25 in the body of Table IV of Appendix B; $z_U = .67$ (taking the closest value).

b. Recall that the inner fences of a box plot are located $1.5(Q_U - Q_L)$ outside the hinges (Q_L and Q_U).

To find the lower inner fence,

$$Q_L - 1.5(Q_U - Q_L) = -.67 - 1.5(.67 - (-.67))$$
$$= -.67 - 1.5(1.34)$$
$$= -2.68 \; (-2.70 \text{ if } z_L = -.675 \text{ and } z_U = +.675)$$

The upper inner fence is:

$$Q_U + 1.5(Q_U - Q_L) = .67 + 1.5(.67 - (-.67))$$
$$= .67 + 1.5(1.34)$$
$$= 2.68 \; (+2.70 \text{ if } z_L = -.675 \text{ and } z_U = +.675)$$

c. Recall that the outer fences of a box plot are located $3(Q_U - Q_L)$ outside the hinges (Q_L and Q_U).

Continuous Random Variables

To find the lower outer fence,

$$Q_L - 3(Q_U - Q_L) = -.67 - 3(.67 - (-.67))$$
$$= -.67 - 3(1.34)$$
$$= -4.69 \ (-4.725 \text{ if } z_L = -.675 \text{ and } z_U = +.675)$$

The upper outer fence is:

$$Q_U + 3(Q_U - Q_L) = .67 + 3(.67 - (-.67))$$
$$= .67 + 3(1.34)$$
$$= 4.69 \ (4.725 \text{ if } z_L = -.675 \text{ and } z_U = +.675)$$

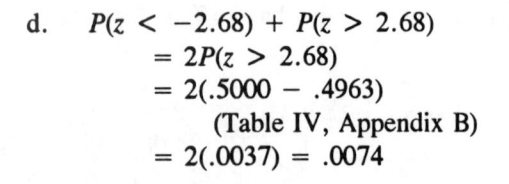

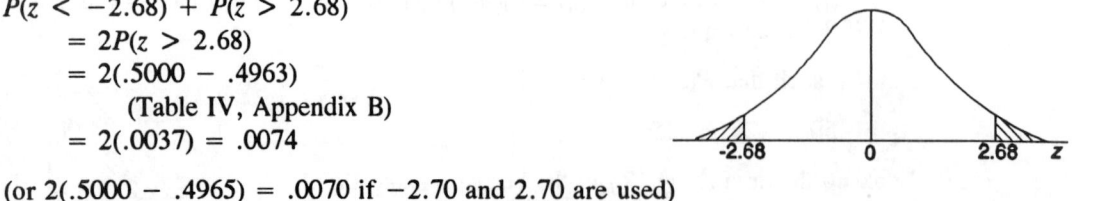

d. $P(z < -2.68) + P(z > 2.68)$
$= 2P(z > 2.68)$
$= 2(.5000 - .4963)$
  (Table IV, Appendix B)
$= 2(.0037) = .0074$

(or $2(.5000 - .4965) = .0070$ if -2.70 and 2.70 are used)

$P(z < -4.69) + P(z > 4.69)$
$= 2P(z > 4.69)$
$\approx 2(.5000 - .5000) \approx 0$

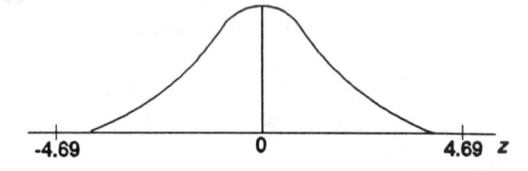

e. In a normal probability distribution, the probability of an observation being beyond the inner fences is only .0074 and the probability of an observation being beyond the outer fences is approximately zero. Since the probability is so small, there should not be any observations beyond the inner and outer fences. Therefore, they are probably outliers.

5.39 It is appropriate to approximate a binomial distribution with a normal distribution when n is large. As a rule of thumb: the interval $\mu \pm 3\sigma$ should lie in the range 0 to n in order for the normal approximation to be adequate.

5.41 a. In order to approximate the binomial distribution with the normal distribution, the interval

$\mu \pm 3\sigma \Rightarrow np \pm 3\sqrt{npq}$ should lie in the range 0 to n.

When $n = 25$ and $p = .7$,

$np \pm 3\sqrt{npq} \Rightarrow 25(.7) \pm 3\sqrt{25(.7)(1 - .7)}$
$\Rightarrow 17.5 \pm 3\sqrt{5.25}$
$\Rightarrow 17.5 \pm 6.87$
$\Rightarrow (10.63, 24.37)$

Since the interval calculated does lie in the range 0 to 25, we can use the normal approximation.

b. $\mu = np = 25(.7) = 17.5$
$\sigma^2 = npq = 25(.7)(.3) = 5.25$

c. $P(x \geq 15) = 1 - P(x \leq 14)$
$= 1 - .098$
$= .902$ (Table II, Appendix B)

d. $P(x \geq 15) \approx P\left[z \geq \dfrac{(15 - .5) - 17.5}{\sqrt{5.25}}\right]$
$\approx P(z \geq -1.31)$
$= .5000 + .4049$
$= .9049$

(Using Table IV in Appendix B.)

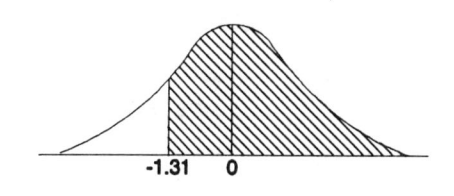

5.43 x is a binomial random variable with $n = 1000$ and $p = .50$.

$\mu \pm 3\sigma \Rightarrow np \pm 3\sqrt{npq} \Rightarrow 1000(.50) \pm 3\sqrt{1000(.5)(.5)}$
$\Rightarrow 500 \pm 3(15.8114)$
$\Rightarrow (452.5658, 547.4342)$

Since the interval lies in the range 0 to 1000, we can use the normal approximation to approximate the probabilities.

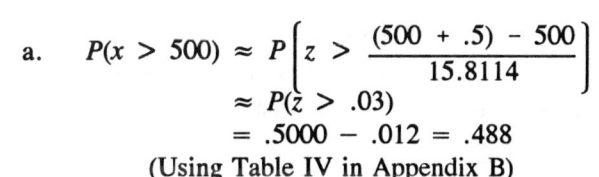

a. $P(x > 500) \approx P\left[z > \dfrac{(500 + .5) - 500}{15.8114}\right]$
$\approx P(z > .03)$
$= .5000 - .012 = .488$

(Using Table IV in Appendix B)

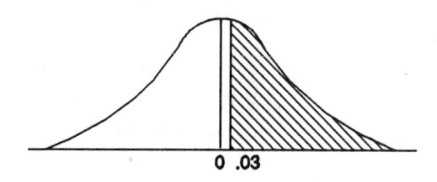

b. $P(490 \leq x < 500)$
$\approx P\left[\dfrac{(490 - .5) - 500}{15.8114} \leq z < \dfrac{(500 - .5) - 500}{15.8114}\right]$
$\approx P(-.66 \leq z < -.03)$
$= P(-.66 \leq z \leq 0) - P(-.03 \leq z \leq 0)$
$= P(0 \leq z \leq .66) - P(0 \leq z \leq .03)$
$= .2454 - .012 = .2334$

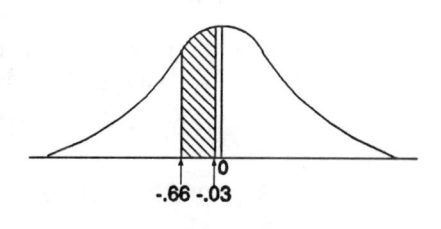

(Using Table IV in Appendix B)

c. $P(x > 1000) = 0$

Since $n = 1000$, the random variable x can only take on the values 0, 1, 2, ... , 1000.

5.45 Let x = number of white-collar employees in good shape who will develop stress related illnesses in a sample of 400. Then x is a binomial random variable with $n = 400$ and $p = .10$. To see if the normal approximation is appropriate for this problem:

$np \pm 3\sqrt{npq} \Rightarrow 400(.1) \pm 3\sqrt{400(.1)(.9)} \Rightarrow 40 \pm 18 \Rightarrow (22, 58)$

Since this interval is contained in the interval 0, $n = 400$, the normal approximation is appropriate.

$P(x > 60) \approx P\left[z > \dfrac{(60 + .5) - 40}{6}\right]$
$= P(z > 3.42) \approx .5000 - .5000 = 0$

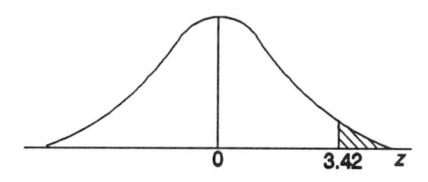

Continuous Random Variables 81

5.47 Let x equal the number of catastrophes due to booster failure.

a. In order to approximate the binomial distribution with the normal distribution, the interval $\mu \pm 3\sigma$ should lie in the range 0 to n.

$$\mu \pm 3\sigma \Rightarrow np \pm 3\sqrt{npq} \Rightarrow 25\left(\frac{1}{35}\right) \pm 3\sqrt{25\left(\frac{1}{35}\right)\left(1 - \frac{1}{35}\right)}$$
$$\Rightarrow .714 \pm 3(.833) \Rightarrow (-1.785, 3.213)$$

Since the interval calculated does not lie in the range 0 to 25, we should not use the normal approximation.

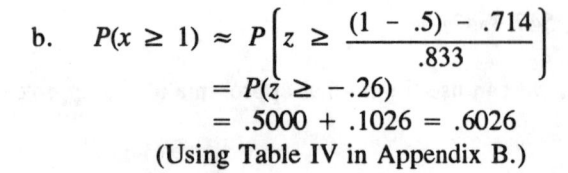

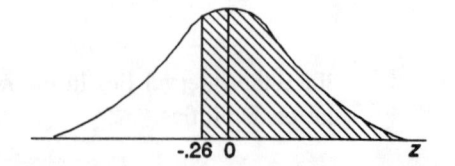

b. $P(x \geq 1) \approx P\left(z \geq \dfrac{(1 - .5) - .714}{.833}\right)$
$= P(z \geq -.26)$
$= .5000 + .1026 = .6026$
(Using Table IV in Appendix B.)

The exact probability is .5155 and the approximate probability is .6026. The approximation is quite a bit off, but this is not surprising since in part a we decided that we should not use the normal approximation.

c. Referring to part a, recalculate the interval $\mu \pm 3\sigma$ using $n = 100$ instead of $n = 25$.

$$\mu \pm 3\sigma \Rightarrow np \pm 3\sqrt{npq} \Rightarrow 100\left(\frac{1}{35}\right) \pm 3\sqrt{100\left(\frac{1}{35}\right)\left(1 - \frac{1}{35}\right)}$$
$$\Rightarrow 2.857 \pm 3(1.666) \Rightarrow (-2.141, 7.855)$$

Since the interval calculated does not lie in the range 0 to 100 we should not use the normal approximation when $n = 100$.

Recalculate the interval $\mu \pm 3\sigma$ using $n = 500$.

$$\mu \pm 3\sigma \Rightarrow np \pm 3\sqrt{npq} \Rightarrow 500\left(\frac{1}{35}\right) \pm 3\sqrt{500\left(\frac{1}{35}\right)\left(1 - \frac{1}{35}\right)}$$
$$\Rightarrow 14.286 \pm 3(3.725) \Rightarrow (3.111, 25.461)$$

Since the interval calculated does lie in the range 0 to 500, we can use the normal approximation when $n = 500$.

Since we can use the normal approximation when $n = 500$, we can use it when $n = 1,000$.

$$\mu \pm 3\sigma \Rightarrow np \pm 3\sqrt{npq} \Rightarrow 1000\left(\frac{1}{35}\right) \pm 3\sqrt{1000\left(\frac{1}{35}\right)\left(1 - \frac{1}{35}\right)}$$
$$\Rightarrow 28.571 \pm 3(5.268) \Rightarrow (12.767, 44.375)$$

Since the interval calculated does lie in the range 0 to 1,000, we can use the normal approximation when $n = 1,000$.

d. x is a binomial random variable with $n = 1000$ and $p = \frac{1}{35}$.

$$P(x > 25) \approx P\left(z > \frac{(25 + .5) - 28.571}{5.268}\right)$$
$$= P(z > -.58)$$
$$= .5000 + .2190 = .7190$$
(Using Table IV in Appendix B.)

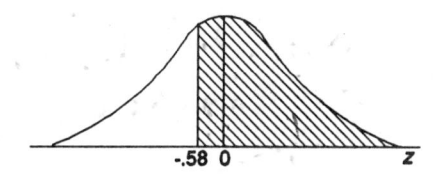

5.49 a. Let x = the number of workers on the job on a particular day out of 50 workers. The random variable x is a binomial random variable with $n = 50$ and $p = .80$ (if 20% are absent, 80% are on the job).

90% of 50 workers $= .9(50) = 45$

$\mu = np = 50(.8) = 40$
$\sigma^2 = npq = 50(.8)(.2) = 8$
$\sigma = \sqrt{\sigma^2} = \sqrt{8} = 2.8284$

$$P(x \geq 45) \approx P\left(z \geq \frac{(45 - .5) - 40}{2.8284}\right)$$
$$\approx P(z \geq 1.59)$$
$$= .5000 - .4441 = .0559$$

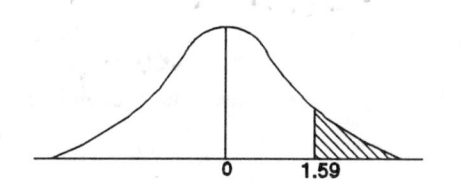

b. $\mu \pm 3\sigma \Rightarrow np \pm 3\sqrt{npq} \Rightarrow 40 \pm 3(2.8284)$ (part a) $\Rightarrow 40 \pm 8.485 \Rightarrow (31.515, 48.485)$

Since the interval lies in the range 0 to 50, we can use the normal approximation to approximate the probability in part a.

c. If the absentee rate is 2%, then 98% of the workers are on the job. Hence, x is a binomial random variable with $n = 50$ and $p = .98$.

$\mu \pm 3\sigma \Rightarrow np \pm 3\sqrt{npq} \Rightarrow 50(.98) \pm 3\sqrt{50(.98)(1 - .98)}$
$\Rightarrow 49 \pm 2.9698$
$\Rightarrow (46.0302, 51.9698)$

Since the interval does not lie in the range 0 to 50, we should not use the normal approximation to approximate the probability in part a.

5.51 a. We must assume that whether one smoke detector is defective is independent of whether any other smoke detector is defective. Also the probability of a smoke detector being defective must remain constant for all smoke detectors. These assumptions seem to be satisfied since a random sample was taken.

b. The random variable x is a binomial random variable with $n = 2000$ and $p = .40$.

$\mu \pm 3\sigma \Rightarrow np \pm 3\sqrt{npq} \Rightarrow 2000(.40) \pm 3\sqrt{2000(.40)(1 - .40)}$
$\Rightarrow 800 \pm 3(21.9089) \Rightarrow 800 \pm 65.7267$
$\Rightarrow (734.2733, 865.7267)$

Continuous Random Variables

Since the interval does lie in the range 0 to 2000, we can use the normal approximation to approximate the probability.

$$P(x \leq 4) \approx P\left[z \leq \frac{(4 + .5) - 800}{21.9089}\right]$$
$$\approx P(z \leq -36.31)$$
$$\approx .5 - .5 = 0$$

c. No, it is not likely that 40% of their detectors are defective. If 40% really were defective, then the probability of four or fewer defectives is approximately zero. But there were only four defectives. Therefore, it is very unlikely that 40% are defective.

d. Yes, it is possible that 40% of the detectors are defective. The probability of four or fewer defectives is approximately zero. It is possible but very, very unlikely.

5.53   a.   If $\lambda = 1$, $a = 1$, then $e^{-\lambda a} = e^{-1} = .367879$

       b.   If $\lambda = 1$, $a = 2.5$, then $e^{-\lambda a} = e^{-2.5} = .082085$

       c.   If $\lambda = 2.5$, $a = 3$, then $e^{-\lambda a} = e^{-7.5} = .000553$

       d.   If $\lambda = 5$, $a = .3$, then $e^{-\lambda a} = e^{-1.5} = .223130$

5.55   Using Table V in Appendix B:

       a. $P(x \leq 3) = 1 - P(x > 3) = 1 - e^{-2.5(3)} = 1 - e^{-7.5} = 1 - .000553 = .999447$

       b. $P(x \leq 4) = 1 - P(x > 4) = 1 - e^{-2.5(4)} = 1 - e^{-10} = 1 - .000045 = .999955$

       c. $P(x \leq 1.6) = 1 - P(x > 1.6) = 1 - e^{-2.5(1.6)} = 1 - e^{-4} = 1 - .018316 = .981684$

       d. $P(x \leq .4) = 1 - P(x > .4) = 1 - e^{-2.5(.4)} = 1 - e^{-1} = 1 - .367879 = .632121$

5.57 $f(x) = \lambda e^{-\lambda x} = e^{-x}$ $(x > 0)$

$\mu = \dfrac{1}{\lambda} = \dfrac{1}{1} = 1$, $\sigma = \dfrac{1}{\lambda} = \dfrac{1}{1} = 1$

       a. $\mu \pm 3\sigma \Rightarrow 1 \pm 3(1) \Rightarrow (-2, 4)$

Since $\mu - 3\sigma$ lies below 0, find the probability that x is more than $\mu + 3\sigma = 4$.

$P(x > 4) = e^{-1(4)} = e^{-4} = .018316$ (using Table V in Appendix B)

       b. $\mu \pm 2\sigma \Rightarrow 1 \pm 2(1) \Rightarrow (-1, 3)$

Since $\mu - 2\sigma$ lies below 0, find the probability that x is between 0 and 3.

$P(x < 3) = 1 - P(x \geq 3) = 1 - e^{-1(3)} = 1 - e^{-3} = 1 - .049787 = .950213$
(using Table V in Appendix B)

c. $\mu \pm .5\sigma \Rightarrow 1 \pm .5(1) \Rightarrow (.5, 1.5)$

$$P(.5 < x < 1.5) = P(x > .5) - P(x > 1.5)$$
$$= e^{-.5} - e^{-1.5}$$
$$= .606531 - .223130$$
$$= .383401 \quad \text{(using Table V in Appendix B)}$$

5.59 a. Let x = length of time elapsed before the winning goal is scored. Then x has an exponential distribution with $\mu = 9.15$ and $\lambda = 1/9.15$.

$$P(x \leq 3) = 1 - P(x > 3) = 1 - e^{-3/9.15} = 1 - e^{-.327869}$$
$$= 1 - .720457 = .279543$$

b. $P(x > 20) = e^{-20/9.15} = e^{-2.185792} = .1123887$

5.61 a. $R(x) = e^{-\lambda x} = e^{-.5x}$

b. $P(x \geq 4) = e^{-.5(4)} = e^{-2} = .135335$ (Table V, Appendix B)

c. $\mu = \dfrac{1}{\lambda} = \dfrac{1}{.5} = 2$

$P(x > \mu) = P(x > 2) = e^{-.5(2)} = e^{-1} = .367879$ (Table V, Appendix B)

d. For all exponential distributions, $\mu = \dfrac{1}{\lambda}$

$P(x > \mu) = P\left[x > \dfrac{1}{\lambda}\right] = e^{-\lambda(1/\lambda)} = e^{-1} = .367879.$ Thus, regardless of the value of λ, the probability that x is larger than the mean is always .367879.

e. $P(x > 5) = e^{-.5(5)} = e^{-2.5} = .082085$ (Table V, Appendix B)

If 10,000 units are sold, approximately 10,000(.082085) = 820.85 will perform satisfactorily for more than 5 years.

$P(x \leq 1) = 1 - P(x > 1) = 1 - e^{-.5(1)} = 1 - e^{-.5} = 1 - .606531 = .39469$

If 10,000 units are sold, approximately 10,000(.393469) = 3934.69 will fail within 1 year.

f. $P(x < a) \leq .05$
$\Rightarrow 1 - P(x \geq a) \leq .05$
$\Rightarrow P(x \geq a) \geq .95$
$\Rightarrow e^{-.5a} \geq .95$

Using Table V, Appendix B, $e^{-.05}$ is closest to .95 (yet larger).

Thus, $.05 = .5a \Rightarrow a = .1$

The warranty should be for approximately .1 year or .1(365) = 36.5 or 37 days.

Continuous Random Variables

5.63   a.   Let x = interarrival time of jobs. Then x has an exponential distribution with a mean of $\mu = 1.25$ minutes and $\lambda = 1/1.25$.

$$P(x \leq 1) = 1 - P(x > 1) = 1 - e^{-1/1.25} = 1 - e^{-.8} = 1 - .449329 = .550671$$

b.   Let y = amount of time the machine operates before breaking down. Then y has an exponential distribution with a mean of $\mu = 540$ minutes and $\lambda = 1/540$.

$$P(y > 720) = e^{-720/540} = e^{-1.333333} = .263597$$

5.65   a. $\mu = 1/\lambda = 1/.004 = 250$

b.   Let x = lifelength of the new halogen bulb. Then x has an exponential distribution with $\lambda = .004$.

$$P(x > 500) = e^{-.004(500)} = e^{-2} = .135335 \text{ (from Table V, Appendix B)}$$

c.   First, we must find the probability of each individual event. Let x = lifelength of the first bulb, and y = lifelength of the second bulb.

$$P(x > 300) = e^{-.004(300)} = e^{-1.2} = .301194 \text{ (from Table V, Appendix B)}$$

$$P(y > 200) = e^{-.004(200)} = e^{-.8} = .449329 \text{ (from Table V, Appendix B)}$$

Since the two events are independent, $P(x > 300 \text{ and } y > 200) = P(x > 300)P(y > 200) = .301194(.449329) = .135335$

d.   For $a = 300$ and $b = 200$, $P(x > a + b) = P(x > 300 + 200) = P(x > 500) = .135335$

From part c, $P(x > 300)P(x > 200) = .135335$.

Thus, $P(x > 500) = P(x > 300)P(x > 200)$.

e.   Let $a = 100$ and $b = 400$. $P(x > a + b) = P(x > 100 + 400) = P(x > 500) = .135335$

$$P(x > 100) = e^{-.004(100)} = e^{-.4} = .670320 \text{ (from Table V, Appendix B)}$$

$$P(x > 400) = e^{-.004(400)} = e^{-1.6} = .201897 \text{ (from Table V, Appendix B)}$$

Since the two events are independent, $P(x > 100 \text{ and } x > 400) = P(x > 100)P(x > 400) = .670320(.201897) = .135336$

f.   In general, $P(x > a + b) = e^{-\lambda(a+b)}$

$P(x > a) = e^{-\lambda a}$ and $P(x > b) = e^{-\lambda b}$.

If the two events are independent,
$$P(x > a \text{ and } x > b) = P(x > a)P(x > b) = e^{-\lambda a}e^{-\lambda b} = e^{-\lambda(a+b)} = P(x > a + b).$$

5.67   a. $f(x) = \begin{cases} \dfrac{1}{d-c} = \dfrac{1}{90-10} = \dfrac{1}{80}, & 10 \leq x \leq 90 \\ 0 & \text{otherwise} \end{cases}$

b. $\mu = \dfrac{c+d}{2} = \dfrac{10+90}{2} = 50$

$\sigma = \dfrac{d-c}{\sqrt{12}} = \dfrac{90-10}{\sqrt{12}} = 23.094011$

c. The interval $\mu \pm 2\sigma \Rightarrow 50 \pm 2(23.094) \Rightarrow 50 \pm 46.188 \Rightarrow (3.812, 96.188)$ is indicated on the graph.

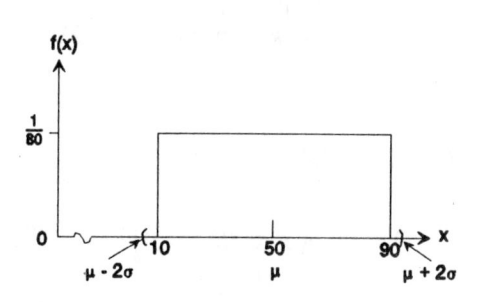

d. $P(x \leq 60) = \text{Base(height)} = (60-10)\dfrac{1}{80} = \dfrac{5}{8} = .625$

e. $P(x \geq 90) = 0$

f. $P(x \leq 80) = \text{Base(height)} = (80-10)\dfrac{1}{80} = \dfrac{7}{8} = .875$

g. $P(\mu - \sigma \leq x \leq \mu + \sigma) = P(50 - 23.094 \leq x \leq 50 + 23.094)$
$= P(26.906 \leq x \leq 73.094)$
$= \text{Base(height)}$
$= (73.094 - 26.906)\left[\dfrac{1}{80}\right] = \dfrac{46.188}{80} = .577$

h. $P(x > 75) = \text{Base(height)} = (90-75)\dfrac{1}{80} = \dfrac{15}{80} = .1875$

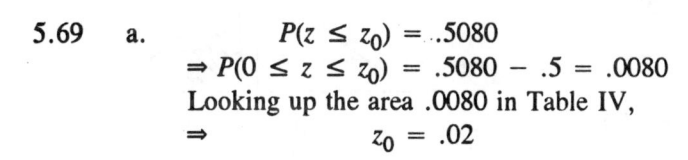

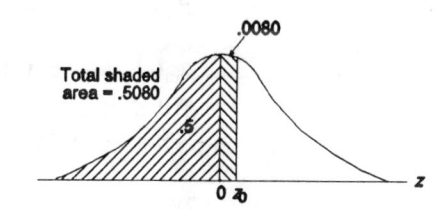

5.69 a. $P(z \leq z_0) = .5080$
$\Rightarrow P(0 \leq z \leq z_0) = .5080 - .5 = .0080$
Looking up the area .0080 in Table IV,
$\Rightarrow \qquad z_0 = .02$

b. $P(z \geq z_0) = .5517$
$\Rightarrow P(z_0 \leq z \leq 0) = .5517 - .5 = .0517$

Looking up the area .0517 in Table IV, $z_0 = -.13$.

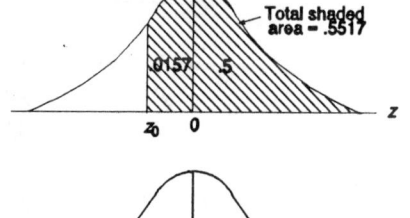

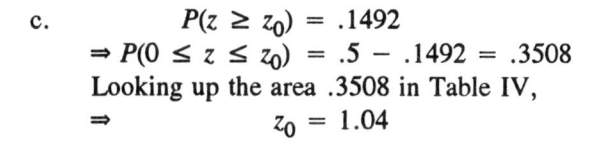

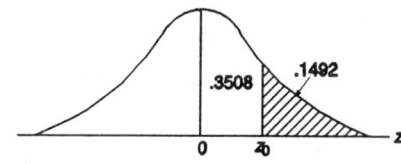

c. $P(z \geq z_0) = .1492$
$\Rightarrow P(0 \leq z \leq z_0) = .5 - .1492 = .3508$
Looking up the area .3508 in Table IV,
$\Rightarrow \qquad z_0 = 1.04$

Continuous Random Variables

d. $P(z_0 \leq z \leq .59) = .4773$
$\Rightarrow P(z_0 \leq z \leq 0) + P(0 \leq z \leq .59) = .4773$

$P(0 \leq z \leq .59) = .2224$

Thus, $P(z_0 \leq z \leq 0) = .4773 - .2224 = .2549$
Looking up the area .2549 in Table IV, $z_0 = -.69$

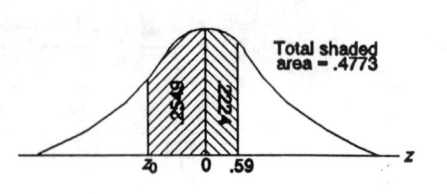

5.71 $\mu = np = 100(.5) = 50$, $\sigma = \sqrt{npq} = \sqrt{100(.5)(.5)} = 5$

a. $P(x \leq 48) = P\left(z \leq \dfrac{(48 + .5) - 50}{5}\right)$

$= P(z \leq -.30)$
$= .5 - .1179 = .3821$

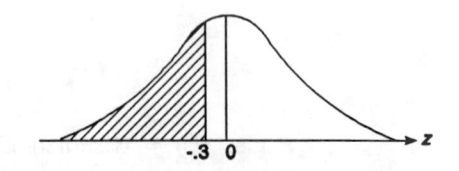

b. $P(50 \leq x \leq 65)$

$= P\left(\dfrac{(50 - .5) - 50}{5} \leq z \leq \dfrac{(65 + .5) - 50}{5}\right)$

$= P(-.10 \leq z \leq 3.10)$
$= .0398 + .5000 = .5398$

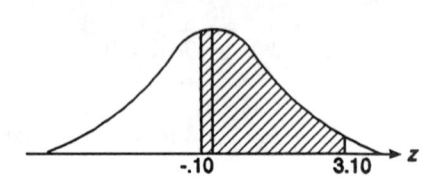

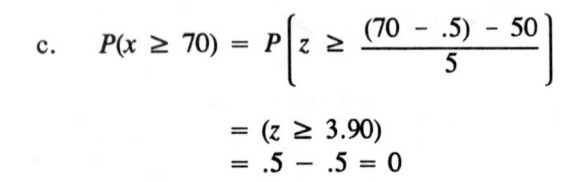

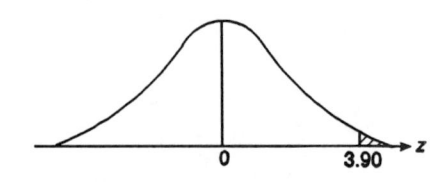

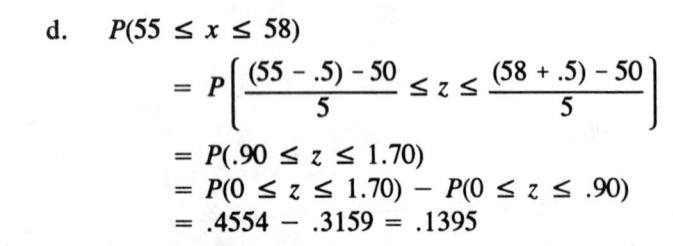

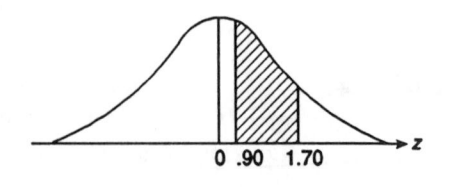

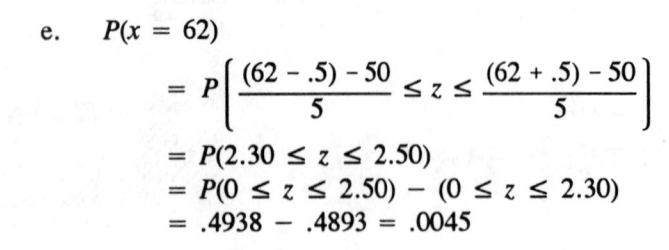

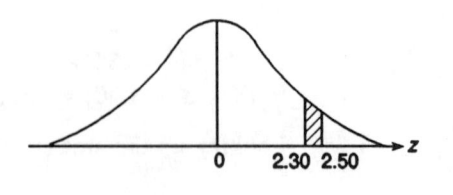

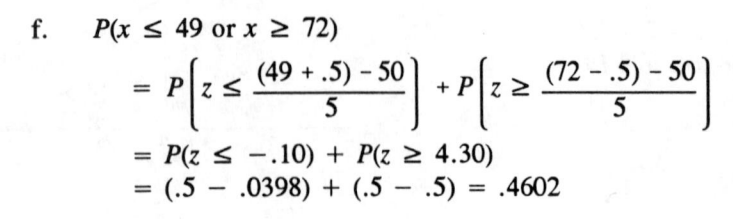

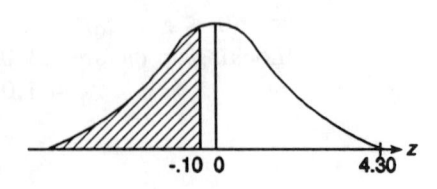

c. $P(x \geq 70) = P\left(z \geq \dfrac{(70 - .5) - 50}{5}\right)$

$= (z \geq 3.90)$
$= .5 - .5 = 0$

d. $P(55 \leq x \leq 58)$

$= P\left(\dfrac{(55 - .5) - 50}{5} \leq z \leq \dfrac{(58 + .5) - 50}{5}\right)$

$= P(.90 \leq z \leq 1.70)$
$= P(0 \leq z \leq 1.70) - P(0 \leq z \leq .90)$
$= .4554 - .3159 = .1395$

e. $P(x = 62)$

$= P\left(\dfrac{(62 - .5) - 50}{5} \leq z \leq \dfrac{(62 + .5) - 50}{5}\right)$

$= P(2.30 \leq z \leq 2.50)$
$= P(0 \leq z \leq 2.50) - (0 \leq z \leq 2.30)$
$= .4938 - .4893 = .0045$

f. $P(x \leq 49 \text{ or } x \geq 72)$

$= P\left(z \leq \dfrac{(49 + .5) - 50}{5}\right) + P\left(z \geq \dfrac{(72 - .5) - 50}{5}\right)$

$= P(z \leq -.10) + P(z \geq 4.30)$
$= (.5 - .0398) + (.5 - .5) = .4602$

5.73   Let y be the profit on a metal part that is produced. Then y is $10, $−2, or $−1, depending where it falls with respect to the tolerance limits.

Let x be the tensile strength of a particular metal part. The random variable x is normally distributed with $\mu = 25$ and $\sigma = 2$.

$$z = \frac{x - \mu}{\sigma} = \frac{21 - 25}{2} = -2$$

$$z = \frac{x - \mu}{\sigma} = \frac{30 - 25}{2} = 2.5$$

$P(y = 10) = P(x$ falls within the tolerance limits$)$
$= P(21 < x < 30) = P(-2 < z < 2.5)$
$= P(-2 < z < 0) + P(0 < z < 2.5)$
$= P(0 < z < 2) + P(0 < z < 2.5)$
$= .4772 + .4938$
$= .9710$

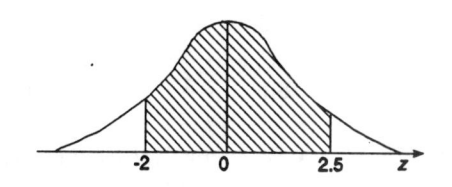

$P(y = -2) = P(x$ falls below the lower tolerance limit$)$
$= P(x < 21) = P(z < -2)$
$= .5000 - P(-2 < z < 0)$
$= .5000 - P(0 < z < 2)$
$= .5000 - .4772$
$= .0228$

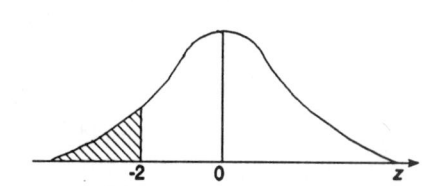

$P(y = -1) = P(x$ falls above the upper tolerance limit$)$
$= P(x > 30) = P(z > 2.5)$
$= .5000 - P(0 < z < 2.5)$
$= .5000 - .4938$
$= .0062$

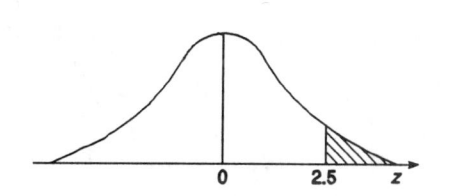

The probability distribution of y is given below:

y	10	−2	−1
p(y)	.9710	.0228	.0062

$E(y) = \sum yp(y) = 10(.9710) + -2(.0228) + -1(.0062)$
$= 9.71 - .0456 - .0062$
$= \$9.6582$

5.75   Let x be the noise level per jet takeoff in a neighborhood near the airport. The random variable x is approximately normally distributed with $\mu = 100$ and $\sigma = 6$.

a. $P(x > 108) = P\left[z > \frac{108 - 100}{6}\right]$
$= P(z > 1.33)$
$= .5000 - P(0 \leq z \leq 1.33)$
$= .5000 - .4082$
$= .0918$

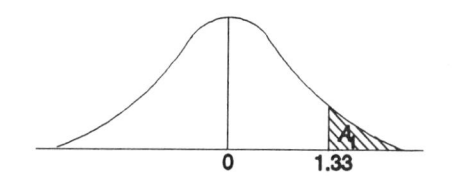

b. $P(x = 100) = 0$

Continuous Random Variables

c. Given $P(x < 105) = .95$ and $\sigma = 6$,

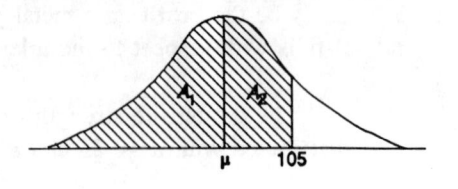

$$P(x < 105) = P(x < \mu) + P(\mu < x < 105)$$
$$= .5 + .45 = A_1 + A_2$$

Looking up the area $A_2 = .45$ in Table IV, $z_0 = 1.645$.

Since $z = 1.645$, $x = 105$ and $\sigma = 6$,

$$z_0 = \frac{x_0 - \mu}{\sigma} \Rightarrow 1.645 = \frac{105 - \mu}{6} \Rightarrow 9.87 = 105 - \mu$$

Hence, $\mu = 95.13$

Since $\mu = 100$, the mean level of noise must be lowered $100 - 95.13 = 4.87$ decibels.

5.77 Let x = interarrival time between patients. Then x is an exponential random variable with a mean of 4 minutes and $\lambda = 1/4$.

a. $P(x < 1) = 1 - P(x \geq 1)$
    $= 1 - e^{-1/4}$
    $= 1 - e^{-.25}$
    $= 1 - .778801$
    $= .221199$

b. Assuming that the interarrival times are independent,
    P(next 4 interarrival times are all less than 1 minute)
    $= \{P(x < 1)\}^4$
    $= .221199^4$
    $= .002394$

c. $P(x > 10) = e^{-10(1/4)}$
    $= e^{-2.5}$
    $= .082085$

5.79 Let x equal the difference between the actual weight and recorded weight (the error of measurement). The random variable x is normally distributed with $\mu = 592$ and $\sigma = 628$.

a. We want to find the probability that the weigh-in-motion equipment understates the actual weight of the truck. This would be true if the error of measurement is positive.

$$P(x > 0) = P\left(z > \frac{0 - 592}{628}\right)$$
$$= P(z > -.94)$$
$$= .5000 + .3264$$
$$= .8264$$

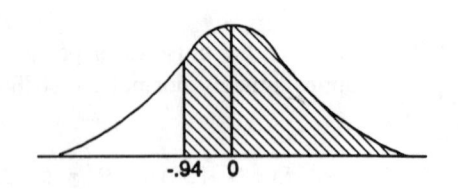

b. P(overstate the weight) $= 1 - P$(understate the weight)
    $= 1 - .8264$
    $= .1736$ (Refer to part a.)

For 100 measurements, approximately $100(.1736) = 17.36$ or 17 times the weight would be overstated.

c. $P(x > 400) = P\left(z > \dfrac{400 - 592}{628}\right)$
$= P(z > -.31)$
$= .5000 + .1217$
$= .6217$

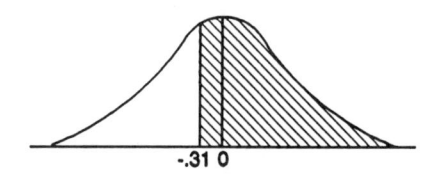

d. We want P(understate the weight) $= .5$

To understate the weight, $x > 0$. Thus, we want to find μ so that $P(x > 0) = .5$

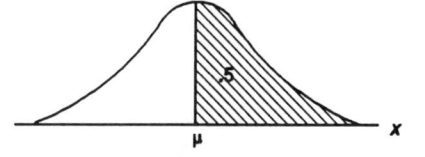

$P(x > 0) = P\left(z > \dfrac{0 - \mu}{628}\right) = .5$

From Table IV, Appendix B, $z_0 = 0$. To find μ, substitute into the z-score formula:

$z_0 = \dfrac{x_0 - \mu}{\sigma} \Rightarrow 0 = \dfrac{0 - \mu}{628} \Rightarrow \mu = 0$

Thus, the mean error should be set at 0.

We want P(understate the weight) $= .4$

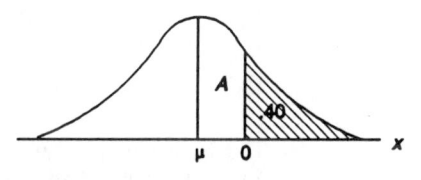

To understate the weight, $x > 0$. Thus, we want to find μ so that $P(x > 0) = .4$

$A = .5 - .40 = .1$. Look up the area .1000 in the body of Table IV, Appendix B, $z_0 = .25$.

To find μ, substitute into the z-score formula:

$z_0 = \dfrac{x_0 - \mu}{\sigma} \Rightarrow .25 = \dfrac{0 - \mu}{628} \Rightarrow \mu = 0 - (.25)628 = -157$

Thus, the mean error should be set at -157.

5.81 Let x = sales per salesperson. Using Table IV, Appendix B:

a. $p_1 = P(x < 100{,}000) = P\left(z < \dfrac{100{,}000 - 180{,}000}{50{,}000}\right) = P(z < -1.6)$
$= .5 - .4452 = .0548$

b. $p_2 = P(100{,}000 \le x \le 200{,}000)$
$= P\left(\dfrac{100{,}000 - 180{,}000}{50{,}000} < z < \dfrac{200{,}000 - 180{,}000}{50{,}000}\right)$
$= P(-1.60 < z < .40) = .4452 + .1554 = .6006$

c. $p_3 = P(x > 200{,}000) = P\left(z > \dfrac{200{,}000 - 180{,}000}{50{,}000}\right) = P(x > .40)$
$= .5 - .1554 = .3446$

Continuous Random Variables

d. Let y = bonus payout. The probability distribution for y is:

y	p(y)
$ 1,000	.0548
$ 5,000	.6006
$10,000	.3446

$$\mu = E(y) = \sum yp(y) = 1000(.0548) + 5000(.6006) + 10,000(.3446)$$
$$= 54.8 + 3003 + 3446$$
$$= \$6503.80$$

5.83 a. (i) $P(0 < z < 1.2) \approx 1.2(4.4 - 1.2)/10 = .384$
(ii) $P(0 < z < 2.5) = .49$
(iii) $P(z > .8) = .5 - P(0 < z < .8) = .5 - .8(4.4 - .8)/10 = .5 - .288 = .212$
(iv) $P(z < 1.0) = .5 + P(0 < z < 1) = .5 + 1(4.4 - 1)/10 = .5 + .34 = .84$

b. Using Table IV, Appendix B:
(i) $P(0 < z < 1.2) = .3849$
(ii) $P(0 < z < 2.5) = .4938$
(iii) $P(z > .8) = .5 - P(0 < z < .8) = .5 - .2881 = .2119$
(iv) $P(z < 1.0) = .5 + P(0 < z < 1) = .5 + .3413 = .8413$

c. For each part, we will take the approximate probability minus the exact probability:
(i) $|.384 - .3849| = .0009$
(ii) $|.49 - .4938| = .0038$
(iii) $|.212 - .2119| = .0001$
(iv)) $|.84 - .8413| = .0013$

All of the absolute differences are less than .0052.

5.85 For $n = 1600$ and $p = .2$, $\mu = np = 1600(.2) = 320$ and $\sigma = \sqrt{npq} = \sqrt{1600(.2)(.8)} = 16$

Using the normal approximation to the binomial and Table IV,

$$P(x \geq 400) \approx P\left(z \geq \frac{(400 - .5) - 320}{16}\right) = P(z \geq 4.97) = .5 - .5 = 0$$

If $p = .2$, the probability of observing 400 or more consumers who favor the product is essentially 0. This implies that p is probably not .2 but larger than .2.

5.87 a. Define x = the number of serious accidents per month. Then x has a Poisson distribution with $\lambda = 2$. If we define y = the time between adjacent serious accidents, then y has an exponential distribution with $\mu = 1/\lambda = 1/2$. If an accident occurs today, the probability that the next serious accident will **not** occur during the next month is:

$$P(y > 1) = e^{-1(2)} = e^{-2} = .135335$$

Alternatively, we could solve the problem in terms of the random variable x by noting that the probability that the next serious accident will **not** occur during the next month is the same as the probability that the number of serious accident next month is zero, i.e.,

$$P(y > 1) = P(x = 0) = \frac{e^{-2}2^0}{0!} = e^{-2} = .135335$$

b. $P(x > 1) = 1 - P(x \leq 1) = 1 - .406 = .594$ (Using Table III in Appendix B with $\lambda = 2$)

Sampling Distributions — Chapter 6

6.1   a–b.   The different samples of $n = 2$ with replacement and their means are:

Possible Samples	$\bar{x}$	Possible Samples	$\bar{x}$
0, 0	0	4, 0	2
0, 2	1	4, 2	3
0, 4	2	4, 4	4
0, 6	3	4, 6	5
2, 0	1	6, 0	3
2, 2	2	6, 2	4
2, 4	3	6, 4	5
2, 6	4	6, 6	6

c.   Since each sample is equally likely, the probability of any 1 being selected is $\frac{1}{4}\left(\frac{1}{4}\right) = \frac{1}{16}$

d. $P(\bar{x} = 0) = \dfrac{1}{16}$

$P(\bar{x} = 1) = \dfrac{1}{16} + \dfrac{1}{16} = \dfrac{2}{16}$

$P(\bar{x} = 2) = \dfrac{1}{16} + \dfrac{1}{16} + \dfrac{1}{16} = \dfrac{3}{16}$

$P(\bar{x} = 3) = \dfrac{1}{16} + \dfrac{1}{16} + \dfrac{1}{16} + \dfrac{1}{16} = \dfrac{4}{16}$

$P(\bar{x} = 4) = \dfrac{1}{16} + \dfrac{1}{16} + \dfrac{1}{16} = \dfrac{3}{16}$

$P(\bar{x} = 5) = \dfrac{1}{16} + \dfrac{1}{16} = \dfrac{2}{16}$

$P(\bar{x} = 6) = \dfrac{1}{16}$

$\bar{x}$	$p(\bar{x})$
0	1/16
1	2/16
2	3/16
3	4/16
4	3/16
5	2/16
6	1/16

e.

6.3   If the observations are independent of each other, then

$P(1, 1) = p(1)p(1) = .2(.2) = .04$
$P(1, 2) = p(1)p(2) = .2(.3) = .06$
$P(1, 3) = p(1)p(3) = .2(.2) = .04$
   etc.

a.

Possible Samples	$\bar{x}$	$p(\bar{x})$	Possible Samples	$\bar{x}$	$p(\bar{x})$
1, 1	1	.04	3, 4	3.5	.04
1, 2	1.5	.06	3, 5	4	.02
1, 3	2	.04	4, 1	2.5	.04
1, 4	2.5	.04	4, 2	3	.06
1, 5	3	.02	4, 3	3.5	.04
2, 1	1.5	.06	4, 4	4	.04
2, 2	2	.09	4, 5	4.5	.02
2, 3	2.5	.06	5, 1	3	.02
2, 4	3	.06	5, 2	3.5	.03
2, 5	3.5	.03	5, 3	4	.02
3, 1	2	.04	5, 4	4.5	.02
3, 2	2.5	.06	5, 5	5	.01
3, 3	3	.04			

Summing the probabilities, the probability distribution of $\bar{x}$ is:

$\bar{x}$	$p(\bar{x})$
1	.04
1.5	.12
2	.17
2.5	.20
3	.20
3.5	.14
4	.08
4.5	.04
5	.01

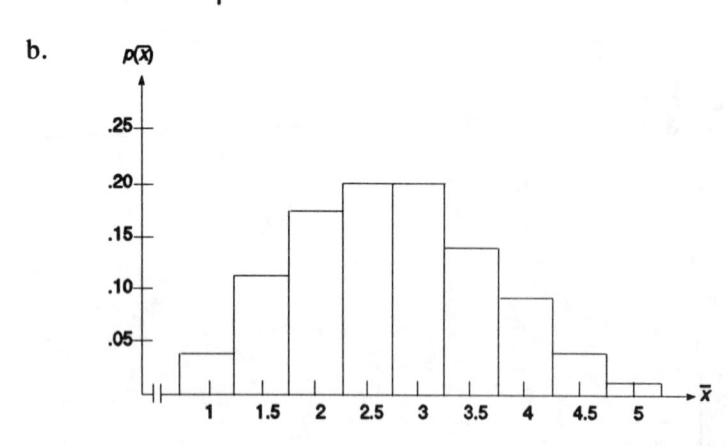

b. [histogram of $p(\bar{x})$ vs $\bar{x}$]

c. $P(\bar{x} \geq 4.5) = .04 + .01 = .05$

d.   No. The probability of observing $\bar{x} = 4.5$ or larger is small (.05).

6.5 a. For a sample of size $n = 2$, the sample mean and sample median are exactly the same. Thus, the sampling distribution of the sample median is the same as that for the sample mean (see Exercise 6.3a).

b. The probability histogram for the sample median is identical to that for the sample mean (see Exercise 6.3b).

6.9 a. $\mu = \sum xp(x) = 2\left(\frac{1}{3}\right) + 4\left(\frac{1}{3}\right) + 9\left(\frac{1}{3}\right) = \frac{15}{3} = 5$

b. The possible samples of size $n = 3$, the sample means, and the probabilities are:

Possible Samples	$\bar{x}$	$p(\bar{x})$	m	Possible Samples	$\bar{x}$	$p(\bar{x})$	m
2, 2, 2	2	1/27	2	4, 4, 4	4	1/27	4
2, 2, 4	8/3	1/27	2	4, 4, 9	17/3	1/27	4
2, 2, 9	13/3	1/27	2	4, 9, 2	5	1/27	4
2, 4, 2	8/3	1/27	2	4, 9, 4	17/3	1/27	4
2, 4, 4	10/3	1/27	4	4, 9, 9	22/3	1/27	9
2, 4, 9	5	1/27	4	9, 2, 2	13/3	1/27	2
2, 9, 2	13/3	1/27	2	9, 2, 4	5	1/27	4
2, 9, 4	5	1/27	4	9, 2, 9	20/3	1/27	9
2, 9, 9	20/3	1/27	9	9, 4, 2	5	1/27	4
4, 2, 2	8/3	1/27	2	9, 4, 4	17/3	1/27	4
4, 2, 4	10/3	1/27	4	9, 4, 9	22/3	1/27	9
4, 2, 9	5	1/27	4	9, 9, 2	20/3	1/27	9
4, 4, 2	10/3	1/27	4	9, 9, 4	22/3	1/27	9
				9, 9, 9	9	1/27	9

The sampling distribution of $\bar{x}$ is:

$\bar{x}$	$p(\bar{x})$
2	1/27
8/3	3/27
10/3	3/27
4	1/27
13/3	3/27
5	6/27
17/3	3/27
20/3	3/27
22/3	3/27
9	1/27
	27/27

$$E(\bar{x}) = \sum \bar{x}p(\bar{x}) = 2\left[\frac{1}{27}\right] + \frac{8}{3}\left[\frac{3}{27}\right] + \frac{10}{3}\left[\frac{3}{27}\right] + 4\left[\frac{1}{27}\right] + \frac{13}{3}\left[\frac{3}{27}\right]$$
$$+ 5\left[\frac{6}{27}\right] + \frac{17}{3}\left[\frac{3}{27}\right] + \frac{20}{3}\left[\frac{3}{27}\right] + \frac{22}{3}\left[\frac{3}{27}\right] + 9\left[\frac{1}{27}\right]$$
$$= \frac{2}{27} + \frac{8}{27} + \frac{10}{27} + \frac{4}{27} + \frac{13}{27} + \frac{30}{27} + \frac{17}{27} + \frac{20}{27} + \frac{22}{27} + \frac{9}{27}$$
$$= \frac{135}{27} = 5$$

Since $\mu = 5$ in part **a**, and $E(\bar{x}) = \mu = 5$, $\bar{x}$ is an unbiased estimator of μ.

c. The median was calculated for each sample and is shown in the table in part **b**. The sampling distribution of m is:

m	$p(m)$
2	7/27
4	13/27
9	7/27
	27/27

$$E(m) = \sum mp(m) = 2\left[\frac{7}{27}\right] + 4\left[\frac{13}{27}\right] + 9\left[\frac{7}{27}\right] = \frac{14}{27} + \frac{52}{27} + \frac{63}{27} = \frac{129}{27} = 4.778$$

$E(m) = 4.778 \neq \mu = 5$. Thus, m is a biased estimator of μ.

d. Use the sample mean, $\bar{x}$. It is an unbiased estimator.

6.13 a. Refer to the solution to Exercise 6.3. The values of s^2 and the corresponding probabilities are listed below:

$$s^2 = \frac{\sum (x^2) - \frac{(\sum x)^2}{n}}{n - 1}$$

For sample 1, 1, $s^2 = \dfrac{2 - \frac{2^2}{2}}{1} = 0$

For sample 1, 2, $s^2 = \dfrac{5 - \frac{3^2}{2}}{1} = .5$

The rest of the values are calculated and shown:

s^2	$p(s^2)$	s^2	$p(s^2)$
0.0	.04	0.5	.04
0.5	.06	2.0	.02
2.0	.04	4.5	.04
4.5	.04	2.0	.06
8.0	.02	0.5	.04
0.5	.06	0.0	.04
0.0	.09	0.5	.02
0.5	.06	8.0	.02
2.0	.06	4.5	.03
4.5	.03	2.0	.02
2.0	.04	0.5	.02
0.5	.06	0.0	.01
0.0	.04		

The sampling distribution of s^2 is:

s^2	$p(s^2)$
0.0	.22
0.5	.36
2.0	.24
4.5	.14
8.0	.04

b. $\sigma^2 = \sum (x - \mu)^2 p(x) = (1 - 2.7)^2(.2) + (2 - 2.7)^2(.3) + (3 - 2.7)^2(.2)$
$\qquad\qquad\qquad\qquad\qquad + (4 - 2.7)^2(.2) + (5 - 2.7)^2(.1)$
$\qquad\qquad\qquad = 1.61$

c. $E(s^2) = \sum s^2 p(s^2) = 0(.22) + .5(.36) + 2(.24) + 4.5(.14) + 8(.04) = 1.61$

d. The sampling distribution of s is listed below, where $s = \sqrt{s^2}$:

s	$p(s)$
0.000	.22
0.707	.36
1.414	.24
2.121	.14
2.828	.04

e. $E(s) = \sum sp(s) = 0(.22) + .707(.36) + 1.414(.24) + 2.121(.14) + 2.828(.04)$
$\qquad\qquad = 1.00394$

Since $E(s) = 1.00394$ is not equal to $\sigma = \sqrt{\sigma^2} = \sqrt{1.61} = 1.269$, s is a biased estimator of σ.

6.15 a. $\mu_{\bar{x}} = \mu = 100$, $\sigma_{\bar{x}} = \dfrac{\sigma}{\sqrt{n}} = \dfrac{\sqrt{100}}{\sqrt{4}} = 5$

Sampling Distributions

b. $\mu_{\bar{x}} = \mu = 100$, $\sigma_{\bar{x}} = \dfrac{\sigma}{\sqrt{n}} = \dfrac{\sqrt{100}}{\sqrt{25}} = 2$

c. $\mu_{\bar{x}} = \mu = 100$, $\sigma_{\bar{x}} = \dfrac{\sigma}{\sqrt{n}} = \dfrac{\sqrt{100}}{\sqrt{100}} = 1$

d. $\mu_{\bar{x}} = \mu = 100$, $\sigma_{\bar{x}} = \dfrac{\sigma}{\sqrt{n}} = \dfrac{\sqrt{100}}{\sqrt{50}} = 1.414$

e. $\mu_{\bar{x}} = \mu = 100$, $\sigma_{\bar{x}} = \dfrac{\sigma}{\sqrt{n}} = \dfrac{\sqrt{100}}{\sqrt{500}} = .447$

f. $\mu_{\bar{x}} = \mu = 100$, $\sigma_{\bar{x}} = \dfrac{\sigma}{\sqrt{n}} = \dfrac{\sqrt{100}}{\sqrt{1000}} = .316$

6.17 a. $\mu = \sum xp(x) = 1(.1) + 2(.4) + 3(.4) + 8(.1) = 2.9$

$\sigma^2 = \sum (x - \mu)^2 p(x) = (1 - 2.9)^2(.1) + (2 - 2.9)^2(.4) + (3 - 2.9)^2(.4) + (8 - 2.9)^2(.1)$
$= .361 + .324 + .004 + 2.601 = 3.29$

$\sigma = \sqrt{3.29} = 1.814$

b. The possible samples, values of $\bar{x}$, and associated probabilities are listed:

Possible Samples	$\bar{x}$	$p(\bar{x})$	Possible Samples	$\bar{x}$	$p(\bar{x})$
1, 1	1	.01	3, 1	2	.04
1, 2	1.5	.04	3, 2	2.5	.16
1, 3	2	.04	3, 3	3	.16
1, 8	4.5	.01	3, 8	5.5	.04
2, 1	1.5	.04	8, 1	4.5	.01
2, 2	2	.16	8, 2	5	.04
2, 3	2.5	.16	8, 3	5.5	.04
2, 8	5	.04	8, 8	8	.01

$P(1, 1) = p(1)p(1) = .1(.1) = .01$
$P(1, 2) = p(1)p(2) = .1(.4) = .04$
$P(1, 3) = p(1)p(3) = .1(.4) = .04$
   etc.

The sampling distribution of $\bar{x}$ is:

$\bar{x}$	$p(\bar{x})$
1	.01
1.5	.08
2	.24
2.5	.32
3	.16
4.5	.02
5	.08
5.5	.08
8	.01
	1.00

c. $\mu_{\bar{x}} = E(\bar{x}) = \sum \bar{x} p(\bar{x}) = 1(.01) + 1.5(.08) + 2(.24) + 2.5(.32) + 3(.16) + 4.5(.02)$
$\qquad + 5(.08) + 5.5(.08) + 8(.01)$
$\qquad = 2.9 = \mu$

$\sigma_{\bar{x}}^2 = \sum (\bar{x} - \mu_{\bar{x}})^2 p(\bar{x}) = (1 - 2.9)^2(.01) + (1.5 - 2.9)^2(.08) + (2 - 2.9)^2(.24)$
$\qquad + (2.5 - 2.9)^2(.32) + (3 - 2.9)^2(.16) + (4.5 - 2.9)^2(.02)$
$\qquad + (5 - 2.9)^2(.08) + (5.5 - 2.9)^2(.08) + (8 - 2.9)^2(.01)$
$\qquad = .0361 + .1568 + .1944 + .0512 + .0016 + .0512 + .3528$
$\qquad + .5408 + .2601$
$\qquad = 1.645$

$\sigma_{\bar{x}} = \sqrt{1.645} = 1.283$

$\sigma_{\bar{x}} = \sigma/\sqrt{n} = 1.814/\sqrt{2} = 1.283$

6.19 a. $\mu_{\bar{x}} = \mu = 20$, $\sigma_{\bar{x}} = \sigma/\sqrt{n} = 16/\sqrt{64} = 2$

b. By the Central Limit Theorem, the distribution of $\bar{x}$ is approximately normal. In order for the Central Limit Theorem to apply, n must be sufficiently large. For this problem, $n = 64$ is sufficiently large.

c. $z = \dfrac{\bar{x} - \mu_{\bar{x}}}{\sigma_{\bar{x}}} = \dfrac{15.5 - 20}{2} = -2.25$

d. $z = \dfrac{\bar{x} - \mu_{\bar{x}}}{\sigma_{\bar{x}}} = \dfrac{23 - 20}{2} = 1.50$

6.21 By the Central Limit Theorem, the sampling distribution of $\bar{x}$ is approximately normal with $\mu_{\bar{x}} = \mu = 30$ and $\sigma_{\bar{x}} = \sigma/\sqrt{n} = 16/\sqrt{100} = 1.6$. Using Table IV, Appendix B:

a. $P(\bar{x} \geq 28) = P\left(z \geq \dfrac{28 - 30}{1.6}\right) = P(z \geq -1.25) = .5 + .3944 = .8944$

b. $P(22.1 \leq \bar{x} \leq 26.8) = P\left(\dfrac{22.1 - 30}{1.6} \leq z \leq \dfrac{26.8 - 30}{1.6}\right) = P(-4.94 \leq z \leq -2)$
$\qquad = .5 - .4772 = .0228$

Sampling Distributions

c. $P(\bar{x} \leq 28.2) = P\left(z \leq \dfrac{28.2 - 30}{1.6}\right) = P(z \leq -1.13) = .5 - .3708 = .1292$

d. $P(\bar{x} \geq 27.0) = P\left(z \geq \dfrac{27.0 - 30}{1.6}\right) = P(z \geq -1.88) = .5 + .4699 = .9699$

6.25 a. For $n = 36$, $\mu_{\bar{x}} = \mu = 406$ and $\sigma_{\bar{x}} = \sigma/\sqrt{n} = 10.1/\sqrt{36} = 1.6833$. By the Central Limit Theorem, the sampling distribution is approximately normal (n is large).

b. $P(\bar{x} \leq 400.8) = P\left(z \leq \dfrac{400.8 - 406}{1.6833}\right) = P(z \leq -3.09) = .5 - .4990 = .0010$
(using Table IV, Appendix B)

c. The first. If the true value of μ is 406, it would be extremely unlikely to observe an $\bar{x}$ as small as 400.8 or smaller (probability .0010). Thus, we would infer that the true value of μ is less than 406.

6.27 a. $\mu_{\bar{x}} = \mu = 89.34$; $\sigma_{\bar{x}} = \dfrac{\sigma}{\sqrt{n}} = \dfrac{7.74}{\sqrt{35}} = 1.3083$

b.

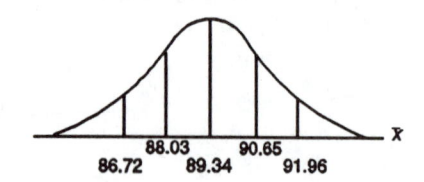

Normal curve with values 86.72, 88.03, 89.34, 90.65, 91.96 on the $\bar{x}$ axis.

c. $P(\bar{x} > 88) = P\left(z > \dfrac{88 - 89.34}{1.3083}\right) = P(z > -1.02) = .5 + .3461 = .8461$
(using Table IV, Appendix B)

d. $P(\bar{x} < 87) = P\left(z < \dfrac{87 - 89.34}{1.3083}\right) = P(z < -1.79) = .5 - .4633 = .0367$
(using Table IV, Appendix B)

6.29 a. By the Central Limit Theorem, the distribution of $\bar{x}$ is approximately normal, with
$\mu_{\bar{x}} = \mu = 157$ and $\sigma_{\bar{x}} = \sigma/\sqrt{n} = 3/\sqrt{40} = .474$.

The sample mean is 1.3 psi below 157 or $\bar{x} = 157 - 1.3 = 155.7$

$P(\bar{x} \leq 155.7) = P\left(z \leq \dfrac{155.7 - 157}{.474}\right) = P(z \leq -2.74) = .5 - .4969 = .0031$
(using Table IV, Appendix B)

If the claim is true, it is very unlikely (probability = .0031) to observe a sample mean 1.3 psi below 157 psi. Thus, the actual population mean is probably not 157 but something lower.

b. $P(\bar{x} \leq 155.7) = P\left(z \leq \dfrac{155.7 - 156}{.474}\right) = P(z \leq -.63) = .5 - .2357 = .2643$
(using Table IV, Appendix B)

The observed sample is more likely if $\mu = 156$ rather than 157.

$$P(\bar{x} \leq 155.7) = P\left(z \leq \frac{155.7 - 158}{.474}\right) = P(z \leq -4.85) = .5 - .5 = 0$$

The observed sample is less likely if $\mu = 158$ rather than 157.

c. $\sigma_{\bar{x}} = \sigma/\sqrt{n} = 2/\sqrt{40} = .316 \qquad \mu_{\bar{x}} = 157$

$$P(\bar{x} \leq 155.7) = P\left(z \leq \frac{155.7 - 157}{.316}\right) = P(z \leq -4.11) = .5 - .5 = 0$$
(using Table IV, Appendix B)

The observed sample is less likely if $\sigma = 2$ rather than 3.

$\sigma_{\bar{x}} = \sigma/\sqrt{n} = 6/\sqrt{40} = .949 \qquad \mu_{\bar{x}} = 157$

$$P(\bar{x} \leq 155.7) = P\left(z \leq \frac{155.7 - 157}{.949}\right) = P(z \leq -1.37) = .5 - .4147 = .0853$$
(using Table IV, Appendix B)

The observed sample is more likely if $\sigma = 6$ rather than 3.

6.31 a. "The sampling distribution of the sample statistic A" is the probability distribution of the variable A.

b. "A" is an unbiased estimator of α if the mean of the sampling distribution of A is α.

c. If both A and B are unbiased estimators of α, then the statistic whose standard deviation is smaller is a better estimator of α.

d. No. The Central Limit Theorem applies only to the sample mean. If A is the sample mean, $\bar{x}$, and n is sufficiently large, then the Central Limit Theorem will apply. However, both A and B cannot be sample means. Thus, we cannot apply the Central Limit Theorem to both A and B.

6.33 By the Central Limit Theorem, the sampling distribution of $\bar{x}$ is approximately normal.

$$\mu_{\bar{x}} = \mu = 19.6, \quad \sigma_{\bar{x}} = \frac{3.2}{\sqrt{68}} = .388$$

a. $P(\bar{x} \leq 19.6) = P\left(z \leq \dfrac{19.6 - 19.6}{.388}\right) = P(z \leq 0) = .5$ (using Table IV, Appendix B)

b. $P(\bar{x} \leq 19) = P\left(z \leq \dfrac{19 - 19.6}{.388}\right) = P(z \leq -1.55) = .5 - .4394 = .0606$
(using Table IV, Appendix B)

c. $P(\bar{x} \geq 20.1) = P\left(z \geq \dfrac{20.1 - 19.6}{.388}\right) = P(z \geq 1.29) = .5 - .4015 = .0985$
(using Table IV, Appendix B)

d. $P(19.2 \leq \bar{x} \leq 20.6) = P\left(\dfrac{19.2 - 19.6}{.388} \leq z \leq \dfrac{20.6 - 19.6}{.388}\right)$

$= P(-1.03 \leq z \leq 2.58) = .3485 + .4951 = .8436$
(using Table IV, Appendix B)

Sampling Distributions

6.37 Given: $\mu = 100$ and $\sigma = 10$

n	1	5	10	20	30	40	50
$\frac{\sigma}{\sqrt{n}}$	10	4.472	3.162	2.236	1.826	1.581	1.414

The graph of $\sigma/\sqrt{n}$ against n is given here:

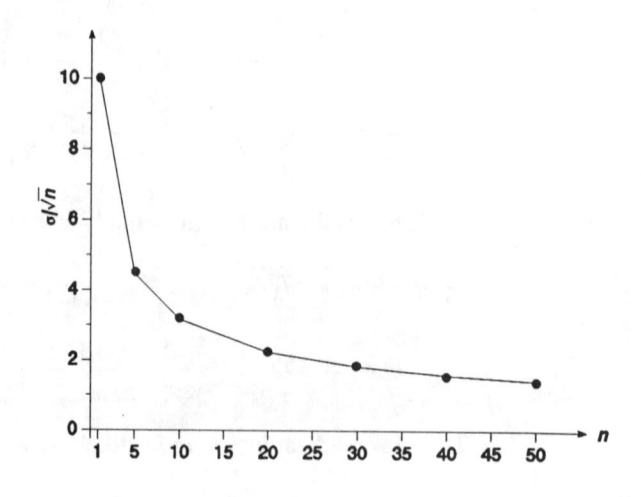

6.39 a. The distribution of x has a mean of $\mu = 26$ and a standard deviation of σ. There is no information given to indicate the shape of the distribution.

b. The distribution of $\bar{x}$ has a mean of $\mu_{\bar{x}} = \mu = 26$ and a standard deviation of $\sigma_{\bar{x}} = \sigma/\sqrt{n}$. Since $n = 200$ is sufficiently large, the Central Limit Theorem says that the sampling distribution of $\bar{x}$ is approximately normal.

c. If $\sigma = 20$, then $\sigma_{\bar{x}} = \sigma/\sqrt{n} = 20/\sqrt{200} = 1.4142$.

$$P(\bar{x} > 26.8) = P\left(z > \frac{26.8 - 26}{1.4142}\right) = P(z > .57) = .5 - .2157 = .2843$$

d. If $\sigma = 10$, then $\sigma_{\bar{x}} = \sigma/\sqrt{n} = 10/\sqrt{200} = .7071$

$$P(\bar{x} > 26.8) = P\left(z > \frac{26.8 - 26}{.7071}\right) = P(z > 1.13) = .5 - .3708 = .1292$$

6.41 a. By the Central Limit Theorem, the sampling distribution of $\bar{x}$ is approximately normal (since $n \geq 30$) with

$$\mu_{\bar{x}} = \mu = 10 \text{ and } \sigma_{\bar{x}} = \frac{\sigma}{\sqrt{n}} = \frac{16}{\sqrt{61}} = 2.0486$$

b. Find the probability of getting a sample mean of 13.49 or larger.

$$P(\bar{x} \geq 13.49) = P\left(z \geq \frac{13.49 - 10}{2.0486}\right)$$
$$= P(z \geq 1.70) = .5 - P(0 \leq z \leq 1.70)$$
$$= .5 - .4554 = .0446$$

This is not a very likely result since the probability is not very large.

c. The random variable x is the difference between the actual number of units sold and the forecast (forecast error). If $\bar{x} = 0$ and $s^2 = 1$, then the forecasts were very accurate since the mean error is 0 and the variance is only 1.

6.43 The mean, μ, of the length of the steel rods is 3 meters with a standard deviation, σ, of .03. By the Central Limit Theorem, the sampling distribution of $\bar{x}$ is approximately normal since $n \geq 30$, and

$$\mu_{\bar{x}} = \mu = 3 \text{ and } \sigma_{\bar{x}} = \frac{\sigma}{\sqrt{n}} = \frac{.03}{\sqrt{100}} = .003$$

a. Since the lots are accepted if the sample mean is 3.005 meters or more and returned if the sample mean is less than 3.005,

$$P(\bar{x} < 3.005) = P\left[z < \frac{3.005 - 3}{.003}\right]$$
$$= P(z < 1.67) = .5 + P(0 < z < 1.67)$$
$$= .5 + .4525 = .9525$$

Thus, $.9525 \times 100 = 95.25\%$ of the lots will be returned to the vendor.

b. We will only accept the lot if the sample mean is 3.005 meters or more. If all the rods are between 2.999 and 3.004 meters in length, then the sample mean must also be between 2.999 and 3.004 meters. Therefore, all of the lots (100%) will be returned to the vendor since the sample mean will never be 3.005 meters or more.

6.45 a. The mean, μ, diameter of the bearings is unknown with a standard deviation, σ, of .001 inch. By the Central Limit Theorem, the sampling distribution of $\bar{x}$ is approximately normal since $n \geq 30$, with

$$\mu_{\bar{x}} = \mu \qquad \sigma_{\bar{x}} = \frac{\sigma}{\sqrt{n}} = \frac{.001}{\sqrt{36}} = .000167$$

Having the sample mean fall within .0001 inch of μ implies $|\bar{x} - \mu| \leq .0001$ or $-.0001 \leq \bar{x} - \mu \leq .0001$.

$$P(-.0001 \leq \bar{x} - \mu \leq .0001)$$
$$= P\left[\frac{-.0001}{.000167} \leq z \leq \frac{.0001}{.000167}\right] = P(-.60 \leq z \leq .60)$$
$$= 2P(0 \leq z \leq .60) = 2(.2257) = .4514$$

b. It will not be affected. Since $n \geq 30$, the sampling distribution of $\bar{x}$ is approximately normal by the Central Limit Theorems regardless of the shape of the distribution of x.

6.47 The mean, μ, of the percentage of alkali in a test specimen of soap is 2% with a standard deviation, σ, of 1%. The sampling distribution of $\bar{x}$ is approximately normal since x is approximately normal and if $n = 4$,

$$\mu_{\bar{x}} = \mu = 2 \qquad \sigma_{\bar{x}} = \frac{\sigma}{\sqrt{n}} = \frac{1}{\sqrt{4}} = .5$$

a. The control limits are located $3\sigma_{\bar{x}}$ above and below μ.

$$3\sigma_{\bar{x}} = 3(.5) = 1.5$$

Therefore, the upper and lower control limits are located 1.5% above and below μ.

b. $\bar{x}$ will fall outside the control limits if it is smaller than $\mu - 3\sigma_{\bar{x}}$ or larger than $\mu + 3\sigma_{\bar{x}}$. If the process is in control,

$$P(\bar{x} < \mu - 3\sigma_{\bar{x}}) + P(\bar{x} > \mu + 3\sigma_{\bar{x}})$$
$$= P\left[z < \frac{\mu - 3\sigma_{\bar{x}} - \mu}{\sigma_{\bar{x}}}\right] + P\left[z > \frac{\mu + 3\sigma_{\bar{x}} - \mu}{\sigma_{\bar{x}}}\right]$$
$$= P(z < -3) + P(z > 3)$$
$$= 2(z > 3)$$
$$= 2(.5 - P(0 < z < 3))$$
$$= 2(.5 - .4987)$$
$$= 2(.0013)$$
$$= .0026$$

c. The process is deemed to be out of control if $\bar{x}$ is outside the control limits. The control limits are located at $\mu \pm 3\sigma_{\bar{x}} \Rightarrow 2 \pm 1.5 \Rightarrow (.5, 3.5)$. If the mean shifts to $\mu = 3\%$,

$$P(\bar{x} < .5) + P(\bar{x} > 3.5)$$
$$= P\left[z < \frac{.5 - 3}{.5}\right] + P\left[z > \frac{3.5 - 3}{.5}\right]$$
$$= P(z < -5) + P(z > 1)$$
$$= .5 - .5 + .5 - .3413$$
$$= .1587$$

6.49 Referring to Exercises 6.47 and 6.48, the mean, μ, of the percentage of alkali in a test specimen of soap is 2% with a standard deviation, σ, of 1%. The sampling distribution of $\bar{x}$ is approximately normal since x is approximately normal and if $n = 4$,

$$\mu_{\bar{x}} = \mu = 2 \qquad \sigma_{\bar{x}} = \frac{\sigma}{\sqrt{n}} = \frac{1}{\sqrt{4}} = .5$$

a. $\bar{x}$ will fall outside the warning limits if it is smaller than $\mu - 1.96\sigma_{\bar{x}}$ or larger than $\mu + 1.96\sigma_{\bar{x}}$. If the process is in control,

$$P(\bar{x} < \mu - 1.96\sigma_{\bar{x}}) + P(\bar{x} > \mu + 1.96\sigma_{\bar{x}})$$
$$= P\left[z < \frac{\mu - 1.96\sigma_{\bar{x}} - \mu}{\sigma_{\bar{x}}}\right] + P\left[z > \frac{\mu + 1.96\sigma_{\bar{x}} - \mu}{\sigma_{\bar{x}}}\right]$$
$$= P(z < -1.96) + P(z > 1.96)$$
$$= 2P(z > 1.96)$$
$$= 2(.5 - .4750)$$
$$= 2(.025)$$
$$= .05$$

b. $P(\bar{x} > \mu + 1.96\sigma_{\bar{x}}) = P(z > 1.96) = .025$ (Refer to part a.)

Therefore, $40 \times .025 = 1$ of the next 40 values of $\bar{x}$ is expected to fall above the upper warning limit.

c. P(next two values of $\bar{x}$ fall below the lower warning limit)
$$= P(\bar{x} < \mu - 1.96\sigma_{\bar{x}})P(\bar{x} < \mu - 1.96\sigma_{\bar{x}}) \text{ (by independence)}$$
$$= P(z < -1.96)P(z < -1.96)$$
$$= .025(.025) \text{ (Refer to part a)}.$$
$$= .000625$$

6.51 a. If x is an exponential random variable, then $\mu = E(x) = 1/\lambda = 60$. The standard deviation of x is $\sigma = 1/\lambda = 60$.

Then, $E(\bar{x}) = \mu_{\bar{x}} = \mu = 60$;

$$V = \sigma_{\bar{x}}^2 = \frac{\sigma^2}{n} = \frac{60^2}{100} = 36$$

b. Because the sample size is fairly large, the Central Limit Theorem says that the sampling distribution of $\bar{x}$ is approximately normal.

c. $P(\bar{x} \leq 30) = P\left(z \leq \dfrac{30 - 60}{\sqrt{36}}\right) = P(z \leq -5.0) \approx .5 - .5 = 0$

Sampling Distributions

Inferences Based on a Single Sample: Estimation with Confidence Intervals Chapter 7

7.1 a. For $\alpha = .10$, $\alpha/2 = .10/2 = .05$. $z_{\alpha/2} = z_{.05}$ is the z-score with .05 of the area to the right of it. The area between 0 and $z_{.05}$ is $.5 - .05 = .4500$. Using Table IV, Appendix B, $z_{.05} = 1.645$.

b. For $\alpha = .01$, $\alpha/2 = .01/2 = .005$. $z_{\alpha/2} = z_{.005}$ is the z-score with .005 of the area to the right of it. The area between 0 and $z_{.005}$ is $.5 - .005 = .4950$. Using Table IV, Appendix B, $z_{.005} = 2.58$.

c. For $\alpha = .05$, $\alpha/2 = .05/2 = .025$. $z_{\alpha/2} = z_{.025}$ is the z-score with .025 of the area to the right of it. The area between 0 and $z_{.025}$ is $.5 - .025 = .4750$. Using Table IV, Appendix B, $z_{.025} = 1.96$.

d. For $\alpha = .20$, $\alpha/2 = .20/2 = .10$. $z_{\alpha/2} = z_{.10}$ is the z-score with .10 of the area to the right of it. The area between 0 and $z_{.10}$ is $.5 - .10 = .4000$. Using Table IV, Appendix B, $z_{.10} = 1.28$.

7.3 a. For confidence coefficient .95, $\alpha = .05$ and $\alpha/2 = .05/2 = .025$. From Table IV, Appendix B, $z_{.025} = 1.96$. The confidence interval is:

$$\bar{x} \pm z_{.025}\frac{s}{\sqrt{n}} \Rightarrow 28 \pm 1.96\frac{\sqrt{12}}{\sqrt{75}} \Rightarrow 28 \pm .784 \Rightarrow (27.216, 28.784)$$

b. $$\bar{x} \pm z_{.025}\frac{s}{\sqrt{n}} \Rightarrow 102 \pm 1.96\frac{\sqrt{22}}{\sqrt{200}} \Rightarrow 102 \pm .65 \Rightarrow (101.35, 102.65)$$

c. $$\bar{x} \pm z_{.025}\frac{s}{\sqrt{n}} \Rightarrow 15 \pm 1.96\frac{.3}{\sqrt{100}} \Rightarrow 15 \pm .0588 \Rightarrow (14.9412, 15.0588)$$

d. $$\bar{x} \pm z_{.025}\frac{s}{\sqrt{n}} \Rightarrow 4.05 \pm 1.96\frac{.83}{\sqrt{100}} \Rightarrow 4.05 \pm .163 \Rightarrow (3.887, 4.213)$$

e. No. Since the sample size in each part was large (n ranged from 75 to 200), the Central Limit Theorem indicates that the sampling distribution of $\bar{x}$ is approximately normal.

7.5 a. For confidence coefficient .95, $\alpha = .05$ and $\alpha/2 = .05/2 = .025$. From Table IV, Appendix B, $z_{.025} = 1.96$. The confidence interval is:

$$\bar{x} \pm z_{\alpha/2}\frac{s}{\sqrt{n}} \Rightarrow 26.2 \pm 1.96\frac{4.1}{\sqrt{70}} \Rightarrow 26.2 \pm .96 \Rightarrow (25.24, 27.16)$$

b. The confidence coefficient of .95 means that in repeated sampling, 95% of all confidence intervals constructed will include μ.

c. For confidence coefficient .99, $\alpha = .01$ and $\alpha/2 = .01/2 = .005$. From Table IV, Appendix B, $z_{.005} = 2.58$. The confidence interval is:

$$\bar{x} \pm z_{\alpha/2}\frac{s}{\sqrt{n}} \Rightarrow 26.2 \pm 2.58\frac{4.1}{\sqrt{70}} \Rightarrow 26.2 \pm 1.26 \Rightarrow (24.94, 27.46)$$

d. As the confidence coefficient increases, the width of the confidence interval also increases.

e. Yes. Since the sample size is 70, the Central Limit Theorem applies. This ensures the distribution of $\bar{x}$ is normal, regardless of the original distribution.

7.7 A point estimator is a single value used to estimate the parameter, μ. An interval estimator is two values, an upper and lower bound, which define an interval with which we attempt to enclose the parameter, μ. An interval estimate also has a measure of confidence associated with it.

7.9 Yes. As long as the sample size is sufficiently large, the Central Limit Theorem says the distribution of $\bar{x}$ is approximately normal regardless of the original distribution.

7.11 a. For confidence coefficient .90, $\alpha = .10$ and $\alpha/2 = .05$. From Table IV, Appendix B, $z_{.01} = 1.645$. The 90% confidence interval is:

$$\bar{x} \pm z_{.05}\sigma_{\bar{x}} \Rightarrow \bar{x} \pm 1.645\frac{\sigma}{\sqrt{n}} \Rightarrow 33.583 \pm 1.645\frac{19.1495}{\sqrt{30}} \Rightarrow 33.583 \pm 5.751$$
$$\Rightarrow (\$27.832, \$39.334)$$

7.13 a. The population of interest to the auditor is the set of all invoices produced since the new billing system was installed.

b. The auditor measured the difference between the actual amount owed the company and the amount indicated on the invoice for 35 randomly selected invoices from all invoices produced by the company's new billing system.

c. For confidence coefficient .98, $\alpha = .02$ and $\alpha/2 = .01$. From Table IV, Appendix B, $z_{.01} = 2.33$. The 98% confidence interval is:

$$\bar{x} \pm z_{.01}\sigma_{\bar{x}} \Rightarrow \bar{x} \pm 2.33\frac{\sigma}{\sqrt{n}} \Rightarrow 1 \pm 2.33\frac{124}{\sqrt{35}} \Rightarrow 1 \pm 48.84 \Rightarrow (\$-47.84, \$49.84)$$

d. We are 98% confident that the mean difference between the actual amount owed the company and the amount indicated on the invoice is between $-47.84 and $49.84.

e. The interval constructed in part d is fairly wide. It appears the new billing system is not very accurate.

7.15 a. For confidence coefficient .90, $\alpha = 1 - .90 = .10$ and $\alpha/2 = .10/2 = .05$. From Table IV, Appendix B, $z_{.05} = 1.645$. The 90% confidence interval for μ is:

$$\bar{x} \pm z_{.05}\sigma_{\bar{x}} \Rightarrow \bar{x} \pm 1.645\frac{\sigma}{\sqrt{n}} \Rightarrow 23.43 \pm 1.645\frac{10.82}{\sqrt{96}} \Rightarrow 23.43 \pm 1.817$$
$$\Rightarrow (21.613, 25.247)$$

b. We are 90% confident the true mean number of years of service lies between 21.613 years and 25.247 years.

c. That you have chosen a random sample where n is sufficiently large to use the normal distribution.

d. Yes, $\bar{x}$ is an unbiased estimate of μ; therefore, $E(\bar{x}) = \mu = E(x)$.

7.17 a. For confidence coefficient .95, $\alpha = .05$ and $\alpha/2 = .025$. From Table IV, Appendix B, $z_{.025} = 1.96$. The confidence interval is:

$$\bar{x} \pm z_{\alpha/2} \frac{s}{\sqrt{n}}$$

Younger: $4.17 \pm 1.96 \dfrac{.75}{\sqrt{241}} \Rightarrow 4.17 \pm .095 \Rightarrow (4.075, 4.265)$

We are 95% confident that the mean job satisfaction score for all adults in the younger age group is between 4.075 and 4.265.

Middle-Age: $4.04 \pm 1.96 \dfrac{.81}{\sqrt{768}} \Rightarrow 4.04 \pm .057 \Rightarrow (3.983, 4.097)$

We are 95% confident that the mean job satisfaction score for all adults in the middle-age age group is between 3.983 and 4.097.

Older: $4.31 \pm 1.96 \dfrac{.82}{\sqrt{677}} \Rightarrow 4.31 \pm .062 \Rightarrow (4.248, 4.372)$

We are 95% confident that the mean job satisfaction score for all adults in the older age group is between 4.248 and 4.372.

b. Let y = number of 95% confidence intervals that do not contain the population mean in 3 trials. Then y is a binomial random variable with $n = 3$ and $p = .05$.

$$P(y \geq 1) = 1 - P(y = 0) = 1 - \binom{3}{0} .05^0 .95^3 = 1 - .857375 = .142625$$

Thus, it is more likely that at least one of three intervals will not contain the population mean than it is for a single confidence interval to miss the population mean.

The probability that a single confidence interval will not contain the population mean is .05.

c. Since the 95% confidence interval for the "older" group does not overlap the 95% confidence interval for the "middle-age" group, there is evidence that the mean satisfaction for the "older" group is higher than that of the "middle-age" group. However, since the 95% confidence interval for the "younger" group does overlap the 95% confidence interval for the "middle age" group, there is no evidence that the mean satisfaction for the "younger" group is higher than that of the "middle-age" group.

7.19 a. For confidence coefficient .80, $\alpha = 1 - .80 = .20$ and $\alpha/2 = .20/2 = .10$. From Table IV, Appendix B, $z_{.10} = 1.28$. From Table VI, with df $= n - 1 = 5 - 1 = 4$, $t_{.10} = 1.533$.

b. For confidence coefficient .90, $\alpha = 1 - .90 = .05$ and $\alpha/2 = .10/2 = .05$. From Table IV, Appendix B, $z_{.05} = 1.645$. From Table VI, with df $= n - 1 = 5 - 1 = 4$, $t_{.05} = 2.132$.

c. For confidence coefficient .95, $\alpha = 1 - .95 = .05$ and $\alpha/2 = .05/2 = .025$. From Table IV, Appendix B, $z_{.025} = 1.96$. From Table VI, with df $= n - 1 = 5 - 1 = 4$, $t_{.025} = 2.776$.

d. For confidence coefficient .98, $\alpha = 1 - .98 = .02$ and $\alpha/2 = .02/2 = .01$. From Table IV, Appendix B, $z_{.01} = 2.33$. From Table VI, with df $= n - 1 = 5 - 1 = 4$, $t_{.01} = 3.747$.

e. For confidence coefficient .99, $\alpha = 1 - .99 = .02$ and $\alpha/2 = .02/2 = .005$. From Table IV, Appendix B, $z_{.005} = 2.575$. From Table VI, with df $= n - 1 = 5 - 1 = 4$, $t_{.005} = 4.604$.

f. Both the t- and z-distributions are symmetric around 0 and mound-shaped. The t-distribution is more spread out than the z-distribution.

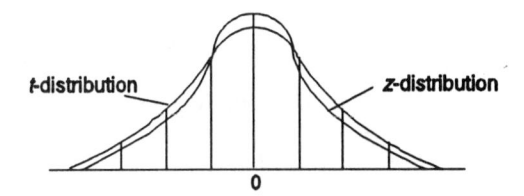

7.21 a. $P(-t_0 < t < t_0) = .95$ where df $= 10$

Because of symmetry, the statement can be written

$P(0 < t < t_0) = .475$ where df $= 10$
$\Rightarrow P(t \geq t_0) = .025$
$t_0 = 2.228$

b. $P(t \leq -t_0 \text{ or } t \geq t_0) = .05$ where df $= 10$

$\Rightarrow 2P(t \geq t_0) = .05$
$\Rightarrow P(t \geq t_0) = .025$ where df $= 10$
$t_0 = 2.228$

c. $P(t \leq t_0) = .05$ where df $= 10$

Because of symmetry, the statement can be written

$\Rightarrow P(t \geq -t_0) = .05$ where df $= 10$
$t_0 = -1.812$

d. $P(t < -t_0 \text{ or } t > t_0) = .10$ where df $= 20$
$\Rightarrow 2P(t > t_0) = .10$
$\Rightarrow P(t > t_0) = .05$ where df $= 20$
$t_0 = 1.725$

e. $P(t \leq -t_0 \text{ or } t \geq t_0) = .01$ where df $= 5$
$\Rightarrow 2P(t \geq t_0) = .01$
$\Rightarrow P(t \geq t_0) = .005$ where df $= 5$
$t_0 = 4.032$

7.23 For this sample,

$$\bar{x} = \frac{\sum x}{n} = \frac{1567}{16} = 97.9375$$

$$s^2 = \frac{\sum x^2 - \frac{(\sum x)^2}{n}}{n - 1} = \frac{155{,}867 - \frac{1567^2}{16}}{16 - 1} = 159.9292$$

$$s = \sqrt{s^2} = 12.6463$$

Inferences Based on a Single Sample: Estimation with Confidence Intervals

a. For confidence coefficient, .80, $\alpha = 1 - .80 = .20$ and $\alpha/2 = .20/2 = .10$. From Table VI, Appendix B, with df $= n - 1 = 16 - 1 = 15$, $t_{.10} = 1.341$. The 80% confidence interval for μ is:

$$\bar{x} \pm t_{.10} \frac{s}{\sqrt{n}} \Rightarrow 97.94 \pm 1.341 \frac{12.6463}{\sqrt{16}} \Rightarrow 97.94 \pm 4.240 \Rightarrow (93.700, 102.180)$$

b. For confidence coefficient, .95, $\alpha = 1 - .95 = .05$ and $\alpha/2 = .05/2 = .025$. From Table VI, Appendix B, with df $= n - 1 = 24 - 1 = 23$, $t_{.025} = 2.131$. The 95% confidence interval for μ is:

$$\bar{x} \pm t_{.025} \frac{s}{\sqrt{n}} \Rightarrow 97.94 \pm 2.131 \frac{12.6463}{\sqrt{16}} \Rightarrow 97.94 \pm 6.737 \Rightarrow (91.203, 104.677)$$

The 95% confidence interval for μ is wider than the 80% confidence interval for μ found in part a.

c. For part a:

We are 80% confident that the true population mean lies in the interval 93.700 to 102.180.

For part b:

We are 95% confident that the true population mean lies in the interval 91.203 to 104.677.

The 95% confidence interval is wider than the 80% confidence interval because the more confident you want to be that μ lies in an interval, the wider the range of possible values.

7.25 a. For confidence coefficient .99, $\alpha = .01$ and $\alpha/2 = .01/2 = .005$. From Table VI, Appendix B, with df $= n - 1 = 3 - 1 = 2$, $t_{.005} = 9.925$. The confidence interval is:

$$\bar{x} \pm t_{.005} \frac{s}{\sqrt{n}} \Rightarrow 49.3 \pm 9.925 \frac{1.5}{\sqrt{3}} \Rightarrow 49.3 \pm 8.60 \Rightarrow (40.70, 57.90)$$

b. We are 99% confident that the mean percentage of B(a)p removed from all soil specimens using the poison is between 40.70% and 57.90%.

c. We must assume that the distribution of the percentages of B(a)p removed from all soil specimens using the poison is normal.

7.27 a. Possible causes for the variation could be different sizes of kitchens, different amounts of remodeling to be done, different costs of living in the different locales, etc.

b. Some preliminary calculations are:

$$\bar{x} = \frac{\sum x}{n} = \frac{258{,}391}{11} = 23{,}490.09$$

$$s^2 = \frac{\sum x^2 - \frac{(\sum x)^2}{n}}{n - 1} = \frac{6{,}154{,}667{,}311 - \frac{23{,}490.09^2}{11}}{11 - 1} = 8{,}503{,}923.1$$

$$s = \sqrt{8{,}503{,}923.1} = 2{,}916.15$$

For confidence coefficient .95, $\alpha = .05$ and $\alpha/2 = .05/2 = .025$. From Table VI, Appendix B, with df $= n - 1 = 11 - 1 = 10$, $t_{.025} = 2.228$. The confidence interval is:

$$\bar{x} \pm t_{\alpha/2}\frac{s}{\sqrt{n}} \Rightarrow 23{,}490.09 \pm 2.228 \frac{2{,}916.15}{\sqrt{11}} \Rightarrow 23{,}490.09 \pm 1{,}958.97$$
$$\Rightarrow (21{,}531.12, 26{,}449.06)$$

We are 95% confident that the true mean kitchen remodeling cost is between $21,531.12 and $26,449.06.

c. Since the data points in this case are means, we are fairly confident that the distribution of data points is normal by the Central Limit Theorem. Thus, the necessary assumption for the small sample estimation of a population mean is met.

7.29 First we make some preliminary calculations:

$$\bar{x} = \frac{\sum x}{n} = \frac{1479.9}{8} = 184.9875$$

$$s^2 = \frac{\sum x^2 - \frac{(\sum x)^2}{n}}{n - 1} = \frac{453{,}375.17 - \frac{1479.9^2}{8}}{8 - 1} = 25{,}658.88124$$

$$s = \sqrt{25{,}658.88124} = 160.1839$$

For confidence coefficient .95, $\alpha = .05$ and $\alpha/2 = .025$. From Table VI, Appendix B, with df $= n - 1 = 8 - 1 = 7$, $t_{.025} = 2.365$. The 95% confidence interval is:

$$\bar{x} \pm t_{.05}\frac{s}{\sqrt{n}} \Rightarrow 184.9875 \pm 2.365 \frac{160.1839}{\sqrt{8}} \Rightarrow 184.9875 \pm 133.9384 \Rightarrow (51.0491, 318.9259)$$

We must assume that the population of private colleges' and universities' endowments are normally distributed.

7.31 a. For confidence coefficient .99, $\alpha = .01$ and $\alpha/2 = .01/2 = .005$. From Table VI, Appendix B, with df $= n - 1 = 22 - 1 = 21$, $t_{.005} = 2.831$. The confidence interval is:

$$\bar{x} \pm t_{\alpha/2}\frac{s}{\sqrt{n}} \Rightarrow 22.455 \pm 2.831 \frac{18.518}{\sqrt{22}} \Rightarrow 22.455 \pm 11.177 \Rightarrow (11.278, 33.632)$$

b. We are 99% confident that the mean number of full-time employees at office furniture dealers in Tampa is between 11.278 and 33.632.

c. In order for the confidence interval to be valid, we must assume that the distribution of the number of full-time employees at all office furniture dealers in Tampa is normal and that the sample was a random sample.

d. If the 22 observations in the sample were the top-ranked furniture dealers in Tampa, then the sample was not a random sample. Thus, the validity of the interval is suspect.

7.33 An unbiased estimator is one in which the mean of the sampling distribution is the parameter of interest, i.e., $E(\hat{p}) = p$.

7.35 The sample size is large enough if $\hat{p} \pm 3\sigma_{\hat{p}}$ lies within the interval (0, 1).

$$\hat{p} \pm 3\sigma_{\hat{p}} \Rightarrow \hat{p} \pm 3\sqrt{\frac{pq}{n}} \Rightarrow \hat{p} \pm 3\sqrt{\frac{\hat{p}\hat{q}}{n}}$$

a. When $n = 400$, $\hat{p} = .10$:

$$.10 \pm 3\sqrt{\frac{.10(1 - .10)}{400}} \Rightarrow .10 \pm .045 \Rightarrow (.055, .145)$$

Since the interval lies completely in the interval (0, 1), the normal approximation will be adequate.

b. When $n = 50$, $\hat{p} = .10$:

$$.10 \pm 3\sqrt{\frac{.10(1 - .10)}{50}} \Rightarrow .10 \pm .127 \Rightarrow (-.027, .227)$$

Since the interval does not lie completely in the interval (0, 1), the normal approximation will not be adequate.

c. When $n = 20$, $\hat{p} = .5$:

$$.5 \pm 3\sqrt{\frac{.5(1 - .5)}{20}} \Rightarrow .5 \pm .335 \Rightarrow (.165, .835)$$

Since the interval lies completely in the interval (0, 1), the normal approximation will be adequate.

d. When $n = 20$, $\hat{p} = .3$:

$$.3 \pm 3\sqrt{\frac{.3(1 - .3)}{20}} \Rightarrow .3 \pm .307 \Rightarrow (-.007, .607)$$

Since the interval does not lie completely in the interval (0, 1), the normal approximation will not be adequate.

7.37 a. The sample size is large enough if the interval $\hat{p} \pm 3\sigma_{\hat{p}}$ does not include 0 or 1.

$$\hat{p} \pm 3\sigma_{\hat{p}} \Rightarrow \hat{p} \pm 3\sqrt{\frac{pq}{n}} \Rightarrow \hat{p} \pm 3\sqrt{\frac{\hat{p}\hat{q}}{n}} \Rightarrow .46 \pm 3\sqrt{\frac{.46(1 - .46)}{225}} \Rightarrow .46 \pm .0997$$
$$\Rightarrow (.3603, .5597)$$

Since the interval lies within the interval (0, 1), the normal approximation will be adequate.

b. For confidence coefficient .95, $\alpha = .05$ and $\alpha/2 = .025$. From Table IV, Appendix B, $z_{.025} = 1.96$. The 95% confidence interval is:

$$\hat{p} \pm z_{.025}\sqrt{\frac{pq}{n}} \Rightarrow \hat{p} \pm 1.96\sqrt{\frac{\hat{p}\hat{q}}{n}} \Rightarrow .46 \pm 1.96\sqrt{\frac{.46(1 - .46)}{225}} \Rightarrow .46 \pm .065$$
$$\Rightarrow (.395, .525)$$

c. We are 95% confident the true value of p will fall between .395 and .525.

d. "95% confidence interval" means that if repeated samples of size 225 were selected from the population and 95% confidence intervals formed, 95% of all confidence intervals will contain the true value of p.

7.39 a. Of the 72 observations, 50 admitted having employees whose performance was affected by drugs or alcohol $\Rightarrow \hat{p} = 50/72 = .694$.

To see if the sample size is sufficiently large:

$$\hat{p} \pm \sigma_{\hat{p}} \Rightarrow \hat{p} \pm 3\sqrt{\frac{pq}{n}} \Rightarrow \hat{p} \pm 3\sqrt{\frac{\hat{p}\hat{q}}{n}} \Rightarrow .694 \pm 3\sqrt{\frac{.694(.306)}{72}} \Rightarrow .694 \pm .163$$
$$\Rightarrow (.531, .857)$$

Since the interval lies within the interval (0, 1), the normal approximation will be adequate.

For confidence coefficient .95, $\alpha = .05$ and $\alpha/2 = .05/2 = .025$. From Table IV, Appendix B, $z_{.025} = 1.96$. The confidence interval is:

$$\hat{p} \pm z_{.05}\sqrt{\frac{pq}{n}} \Rightarrow \hat{p} \pm 1.96\sqrt{\frac{\hat{p}\hat{q}}{n}} \Rightarrow .694 \pm 1.96\sqrt{\frac{.694(.306)}{72}} \Rightarrow .694 \pm .106$$
$$\Rightarrow (.588, .800)$$

b. We must assume that the sample size is sufficiently large and that the sample was randomly selected.

c. We are 95% confident that the proportion of all New Jersey companies with substance abuse problems is between .588 and .800.

d. In repeated sampling, 95% of all intervals constructed will contain the true proportion.

e. One must look at the interval constructed with some skepticism. The problem states that questionnaires were sent to all New Jersey businesses that were members of the Governor's Council. However, the total number mailed out is not given. There were 72 respondents. If there were only 80 questionnaires mailed out, then a return rate of 72 would be quite high. On the other hand, if 500 questionnaires were mailed out a return rate of 72 would not be very good. Also, this sample was self selected, not random. It may not be representative of the entire population. Thus, the interval constructed in part a should be looked at with caution.

7.41 a. First, we must check to see if the sample size is sufficiently large:

Poor: $\hat{p} \pm 3\sigma_{\hat{p}} \approx \hat{p} \pm 3\sqrt{\frac{\hat{p}\hat{q}}{n}} \Rightarrow .155 \pm 3\sqrt{\frac{.155(.845)}{242}} \Rightarrow .155 \pm .070 \Rightarrow (.085, .225)$

Average: $\hat{p} \pm 3\sigma_{\hat{p}} \approx \hat{p} \pm 3\sqrt{\frac{\hat{p}\hat{q}}{n}} \Rightarrow .133 \pm 3\sqrt{\frac{.133(.867)}{212}} \Rightarrow .133 \pm .070 \Rightarrow (.063, .203)$

Good: $\hat{p} \pm 3\sigma_{\hat{p}} \approx \hat{p} \pm 3\sqrt{\frac{\hat{p}\hat{q}}{n}} \Rightarrow .108 \pm 3\sqrt{\frac{.108(.892)}{95}} \Rightarrow .108 \pm .096 \Rightarrow (.012, .204)$

Since all of the intervals are wholly contained in the interval (0, 1), we may conclude that the normal approximation is reasonable for all data sets.

Inferences Based on a Single Sample: Estimation with Confidence Intervals

b. For confidence coefficient .95, $\alpha = .05$ and $\alpha/2 = .025$. From Table IV, Appendix B, $z_{.025} = 1.96$. The confidence interval is:

$$\hat{p} \pm z_{.025}\sqrt{\frac{\hat{p}\hat{q}}{n}}$$

Poor: $.155 \pm 1.96\sqrt{\frac{.155(.845)}{242}} \Rightarrow .155 \pm .046 \Rightarrow (.109, .201)$

Average: $.133 \pm 1.96\sqrt{\frac{.133(.867)}{212}} \Rightarrow .133 \pm .046 \Rightarrow (.087, .179)$

Good: $.108 \pm 1.96\sqrt{\frac{.108(.892)}{95}} \Rightarrow .108 \pm .062 \Rightarrow (.046, .170)$

c. Poor: We are 95% confident that for those who are classified as poor in fitness, the true proportion of all employees of companies that participate in the Health Examination Program who show signs of stress is between .109 and .201.

Average: We are 95% confident that for those who are classified as average in fitness, the true proportion of all employees of companies that participate in the Health Examination Program who show signs of stress is between .087 and .179.

Good: We are 95% confident that for those who are classified as good in fitness, the true proportion of all employees of companies that participate in the Health Examination Program who show signs of stress is between .046 and .170.

7.43 First, we must compute $\hat{p}$: $\hat{p} = \frac{x}{n} = \frac{282,200}{332,000} = .85$

To see if the sample size is sufficiently large:

$$\hat{p} \pm 3\sigma_{\hat{p}} \approx \hat{p} \pm 3\sqrt{\frac{\hat{p}\hat{q}}{n}} \Rightarrow .85 \pm 3\sqrt{\frac{.85(.15)}{332,000}} \Rightarrow .85 \pm .002 \Rightarrow (.848, .852)$$

Since this interval is wholly contained in the interval (0, 1), we may conclude that the normal approximation is reasonable.

For confidence coefficient .99, $\alpha = .01$ and $\alpha/2 = .01/2 = .005$. From Table IV, Appendix B, $z_{.005} = 2.58$. The confidence interval is:

$$\hat{p} \pm z_{.005}\sqrt{\frac{pq}{n}} \approx \hat{p} \pm 2.58\sqrt{\frac{\hat{p}\hat{q}}{n}} \Rightarrow .85 \pm 2.58\sqrt{\frac{.85(.15)}{332,000}} \Rightarrow .85 \pm .002 \Rightarrow (.848, .852)$$

We are 99% confident that the true percentage of items delivered on time by the U.S. Postal Service is between 84.8% and 85.2%.

7.45 a. The point estimate for the proportion of major oil spills that are caused by hull failure is:

$$\hat{p} = \frac{x}{n} = \frac{12}{50} = .24$$

b. To see if the sample size is sufficiently large:

$$\hat{p} \pm 3\sigma_{\hat{p}} \approx \hat{p} \pm 3\sqrt{\frac{\hat{p}\hat{q}}{n}} \Rightarrow .24 \pm 3\sqrt{\frac{.24(.76)}{50}} \Rightarrow .24 \pm .181 \Rightarrow (.059, .421)$$

Since this interval is wholly contained in the interval (0, 1), we may conclude that the normal approximation is reasonable.

For confidence coefficient .95, $\alpha = .05$ and $\alpha/2 = .05/2 = .025$. From Table IV, Appendix B, $z_{.025} = 1.96$. The confidence interval is:

$$\hat{p} \pm z_{.025}\sqrt{\frac{pq}{n}} \approx \hat{p} \pm 1.96\sqrt{\frac{\hat{p}\hat{q}}{n}} \Rightarrow .24 \pm 1.96\sqrt{\frac{.24(.76)}{50}} \Rightarrow .24 \pm .118$$
$$\Rightarrow (.122, .358)$$

We are 95% confident that the true percentage of major oil spills that are caused by hull failure is between .122 and .358.

7.47 To compute the necessary sample size, use

$$n = \frac{(z_{\alpha/2})^2 \sigma^2}{B^2} \text{ where } \alpha = 1 - .95 = .05 \text{ and } \alpha/2 = .05/2 = .025.$$

From Table IV, Appendix B, $z_{.025} = 1.96$. Thus,

$$n = \frac{(1.96)^2(7.2)}{.3^2} = 307.328 \approx 308$$

You would need to take 308 samples.

7.49 a. An estimate of σ is obtained from:

$$\text{range} \approx 4s$$
$$s \approx \frac{\text{range}}{4} = \frac{34 - 30}{4} = 1$$

To compute the necessary sample size, use

$$n = \frac{(z_{\alpha/2})^2 \sigma^2}{B^2} \text{ where } \alpha = 1 - .90 = .10 \text{ and } \alpha/2 = .05.$$

From Table IV, Appendix B, $z_{.05} = 1.645$. Thus,

$$n = \frac{(1.645)^2(1)^2}{.2^2} = 67.65 \approx 68$$

b. A less conservative estimate of σ is obtained from:

$$\text{range} \approx 6s$$
$$s \approx \frac{\text{range}}{6} = \frac{34 - 30}{6} = .6667$$

Thus, $n = \dfrac{(z_{\alpha/2})^2 \sigma^2}{B^2} = \dfrac{(1.645)^2(.6667)^2}{.2^2} = 30.07 \approx 31$

Inferences Based on a Single Sample: Estimation with Confidence Intervals

7.51   For confidence coefficient .90, $\alpha = .10$ and $\alpha/2 = .05$. From Table IV, Appendix B, $z_{.05} = 1.645$.

We know $\hat{p}$ is in the middle of the interval, so $\hat{p} = \dfrac{.54 + .26}{2} = .4$

The confidence interval is $\hat{p} \pm z_{.05}\sqrt{\dfrac{\hat{p}\hat{q}}{n}} \Rightarrow .4 \pm 1.645\sqrt{\dfrac{.4(.6)}{n}}$

We know $.4 - 1.645\sqrt{\dfrac{.4(.6)}{n}} = .26$

$\Rightarrow .4 - \dfrac{.8059}{\sqrt{n}} = .26$

$\Rightarrow .4 - .26 = \dfrac{.8059}{\sqrt{n}} \Rightarrow \sqrt{n} = \dfrac{.8059}{.14} = 5.756$

$\Rightarrow n = 5.756^2 = 33.1 \approx 34$

7.53   a.   The width of a confidence interval is $2B = 2z_{\alpha/2}\dfrac{\sigma}{\sqrt{n}}$

For confidence coefficient .95, $\alpha = 1 - .95 = .05$ and $\alpha/2 = .05/2 = .025$. From Table IV, Appendix B, $z_{.025} = 1.96$.

For $n = 16$,
$$W = 2z_{\alpha/2}\dfrac{\sigma}{\sqrt{n}} = 2(1.96)\dfrac{1}{\sqrt{16}} = 0.98$$

For $n = 25$,
$$W = 2z_{\alpha/2}\dfrac{\sigma}{\sqrt{n}} = 2(1.96)\dfrac{1}{\sqrt{25}} = 0.784$$

For $n = 49$,
$$W = 2z_{\alpha/2}\dfrac{\sigma}{\sqrt{n}} = 2(1.96)\dfrac{1}{\sqrt{49}} = 0.56$$

For $n = 100$,
$$W = 2z_{\alpha/2}\dfrac{\sigma}{\sqrt{n}} = 2(1.96)\dfrac{1}{\sqrt{100}} = 0.392$$

For $n = 400$,
$$W = 2z_{\alpha/2}\dfrac{\sigma}{\sqrt{n}} = 2(1.96)\dfrac{1}{\sqrt{400}} = 0.196$$

b.

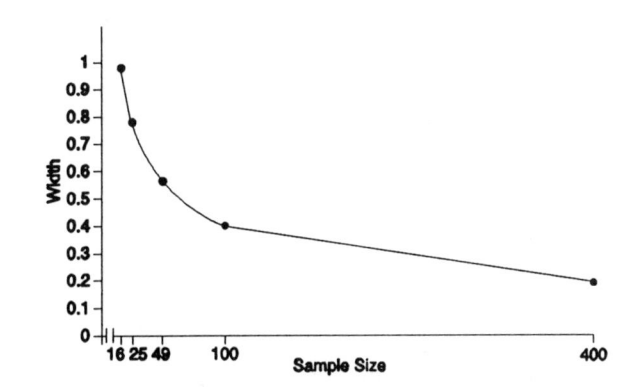

[Graph showing Width vs Sample Size, with Width decreasing from near 1.0 at sample size 16 down to about 0.2 at sample size 400. Points plotted at sample sizes 16, 25, 49, 100, 400.]

7.55 a. Of the 13,000 observations, 2,938 indicated that they were definitely not willing to pay such fees, $\Rightarrow \hat{p} = 2{,}938/13{,}000 = .226$.

To see if the sample size is sufficiently large:

$$\hat{p} \pm 3\sigma_{\hat{p}} \Rightarrow \hat{p} \pm 3\sqrt{\frac{pq}{n}} \Rightarrow \hat{p} \pm 3\sqrt{\frac{\hat{p}\hat{q}}{n}} \Rightarrow .226 \pm 3\sqrt{\frac{.226(.774)}{13{,}000}} \Rightarrow .226 \pm .011$$
$$\Rightarrow (.215, .237)$$

Since the interval lies within the interval (0, 1), the normal approximation will be adequate.

For confidence coefficient .95, $\alpha = .05$ and $\alpha/2 = .05/2 = .025$. From Table IV, Appendix B, $z_{.025} = 1.96$. The confidence interval is:

$$\hat{p} \pm z_{.05}\sqrt{\frac{pq}{n}} \Rightarrow \hat{p} \pm 1.96\sqrt{\frac{\hat{p}\hat{q}}{n}} \Rightarrow .226 \pm 1.96\sqrt{\frac{.226(.774)}{13{,}000}} \Rightarrow .226 \pm .007$$
$$\Rightarrow (.219, .233)$$

We are 95% confident that the proportion definitely unwilling to pay fees is between .219 and .233.

b. The width of the interval is $.233 - .219 = .014$. Since the interval is unnecessarily small, this indicates that the sample size was extremely large.

c. The bound is $B = .02$. For confidence coefficient .95, $\alpha = .05$ and $\alpha/2 = .05/2 = .025$. From Table IV, Appendix B, $z_{.025} = 1.96$. Thus,

$$n = \frac{(z_{\alpha/2})^2 pq}{B^2} = \frac{1.96^2 \cdot .226(.774)}{.02^2} = 1{,}679.97 \approx 1{,}680.$$

Thus, we would need a sample size of 1,680.

7.57 To compute the needed sample size, use

$$n = \frac{(z_{\alpha/2})^2 \sigma^2}{B^2} \text{ where } \alpha = 1 - .95 = .05 \text{ and } \alpha/2 = .05/2 = .025.$$

From Table IV, Appendix B, $z_{.025} = 1.96$.

Inferences Based on a Single Sample: Estimation with Confidence Intervals

Thus, for $s = 10$, $n = \dfrac{(1.96)^2(10)^2}{3^2} = 42.68 \approx 43$

For $s = 20$, $n = \dfrac{(1.96)^2(20)^2}{3^2} = 170.74 \approx 171$

For $s = 30$, $n = \dfrac{(1.96)^2(30)^2}{3^2} = 384.16 \approx 385$

7.59 For confidence coefficient .95, $\alpha = .05$ and $\alpha/2 = .025$. From Table IV, Appendix B, $z_{.025} = 1.96$.

The sample size is $n = \dfrac{z_{\alpha/2}^2 \sigma^2}{B^2} = \dfrac{1.96^2(.75^2)}{.04^2} = 1350.56 \approx 1351$

7.61 To compute the necessary sample size, use

$$n = \dfrac{(z_{\alpha/2})^2 \sigma^2}{B^2} \text{ where } \alpha = 1 - .90 = .10 \text{ and } \alpha/2 = .05.$$

From Table IV, Appendix B, $z_{.05} = 1.645$. Thus,

$$n = \dfrac{(1.645)^2(10)^2}{1^2} = 270.6 \approx 271$$

7.63 For confidence coefficient .95, $\alpha = .05$ and $\alpha/2 = .025$. From Table IV, Appendix B, $z_{.025} = 1.96$. We will assume that the true proportion is approximately .108 from Exercise 7.41.

The sample size is $n = \dfrac{(z_{\alpha/2})^2 pq}{B^2} = \dfrac{(1.96)^2(.108)(.892)}{.01^2} = 3700.8 \approx 3701$

You would need to take $n = 3{,}701$ samples.

7.65 $\sigma_{\bar{x}} = \dfrac{\sigma}{\sqrt{n}} \sqrt{\dfrac{N-n}{N}}$

a. $\sigma_{\bar{x}} = \dfrac{200}{\sqrt{1000}} \sqrt{\dfrac{2500 - 1000}{2500}} = 4.90$

b. $\sigma_{\bar{x}} = \dfrac{200}{\sqrt{1000}} \sqrt{\dfrac{5000 - 1000}{5000}} = 5.66$

c. $\sigma_{\bar{x}} = \dfrac{200}{\sqrt{1000}} \sqrt{\dfrac{10{,}000 - 1000}{10{,}000}} = 6.00$

d. $\sigma_{\bar{x}} = \dfrac{200}{\sqrt{1000}} \sqrt{\dfrac{100{,}000 - 1000}{100{,}000}} = 6.293$

7.67 a. $\hat{\sigma}_{\bar{x}} = \dfrac{s}{\sqrt{n}}\sqrt{\dfrac{N-n}{N}} = \dfrac{50}{\sqrt{2000}}\sqrt{\dfrac{10{,}000 - 2000}{10{,}000}} = 1.00$

b. $\hat{\sigma}_{\bar{x}} = \dfrac{50}{\sqrt{4000}}\sqrt{\dfrac{10{,}000 - 4000}{10{,}000}} = .6124$

c. $\hat{\sigma}_{\bar{x}} = \dfrac{50}{\sqrt{10{,}000}}\sqrt{\dfrac{10{,}000 - 10{,}000}{10{,}000}} = 0$

d. As n increases, $\sigma_{\bar{x}}$ decreases.

e. We are computing the standard error of $\bar{x}$. If the entire population is sampled, then $\bar{x} = \mu$. There is no sampling error, so $\sigma_{\bar{x}} = 0$.

7.69 The approximate 95% confidence interval for p is

$$\hat{p} \pm 2\hat{\sigma}_{\hat{p}} \Rightarrow \hat{p} \pm 2\sqrt{\dfrac{\hat{p}(1-\hat{p})}{n}}\sqrt{\dfrac{N-n}{N}}$$

$$\Rightarrow .42 \pm 2\sqrt{\dfrac{.42(.58)}{1600}}\sqrt{\dfrac{6000-1600}{6000}} \Rightarrow .42 \pm .021 \Rightarrow (.399, .441)$$

7.71 a. The point estimate of the mean value of the parts inventory is $\bar{x} = 156.46$.

b. The estimated standard error is:

$$\hat{\sigma}_{\bar{x}} = \dfrac{s}{\sqrt{n}}\sqrt{\dfrac{N-n}{N}} = \dfrac{209.10}{\sqrt{100}}\sqrt{\dfrac{5{,}000 - 100}{5{,}000}} = 20.6998$$

c. The approximate 95% confidence interval is:

$$\bar{x} \pm 2\hat{\sigma}_{\bar{x}} \Rightarrow \bar{x} \pm 2\left(\dfrac{s}{\sqrt{n}}\right)\sqrt{\dfrac{N-n}{N}} \Rightarrow 156.46 \pm 2\left(\dfrac{209.10}{\sqrt{100}}\right)\sqrt{\dfrac{5{,}000-100}{5{,}000}}$$

$$\Rightarrow 156.46 \pm 41.40 \Rightarrow (115.06, 197.86)$$

We are 95% confident that the mean value of the parts inventory is between $115.06 and $197.86.

d. Since the interval in part c does not include $300, the value of $300 is not a reasonable value for the mean value of the parts inventory.

7.73 For $N = 1{,}500$, $n = 35$, $\bar{x} = 1$, and $s = 124$, the 95% confidence interval is:

$$\bar{x} \pm 2\hat{\sigma}_{\bar{x}} \Rightarrow \bar{x} \pm 2\left(\dfrac{s}{\sqrt{n}}\right)\sqrt{\dfrac{N-n}{N}} \Rightarrow 1 \pm 2\left(\dfrac{124}{\sqrt{35}}\right)\sqrt{\dfrac{1{,}500-35}{1{,}500}}$$

$$\Rightarrow 1 \pm 41.43 \Rightarrow (-40.43, 42.43)$$

We are 95% confident that the mean error of the new system is between $-$40.43 and $42.43.

Inferences Based on a Single Sample: Estimation with Confidence Intervals

7.75 For $N = 251$, $n = 72$, $\hat{p} = .694$, the 95% confidence interval is:

$$\hat{p} \pm 2\hat{\sigma}_{\hat{p}} \Rightarrow \hat{p} \pm 2\sqrt{\frac{\hat{p}(1-\hat{p})}{n}}\sqrt{\frac{(N-n)}{N}}$$

$$\Rightarrow .694 \pm 2\sqrt{\frac{.694(.306)}{72}}\sqrt{\frac{(251-72)}{251}} \Rightarrow .694 \pm .092 \Rightarrow (.602, .786)$$

We are 95% confident that the proportion of all New Jersey's Council business members that have employees with substance abuse problems is between .602 and .786.

7.77 a. $P(t \le t_0) = .05$ where df = 20
$t_0 = -1.725$

b. $P(t \ge t_0) = .005$ where df = 9
$t_0 = 3.250$

c. $P(t \le -t_0 \text{ or } t \ge t_0) = .10$ where df = 8 is equivalent to
$P(t \ge t_0) = .10/2 = .05$ where df = 8
$t_0 = 1.860$

d. $P(t \le -t_0 \text{ or } t \ge t_0) = .01$ where df = 17 is equivalent to
$P(t \ge t_0) = .01/2 = .005$ where df = 17
$t_0 = 2.898$

7.79 a. For confidence coefficient .99, $\alpha = .01$ and $\alpha/2 = .005$. From Table IV, Appendix B, $z_{.005} = 2.58$. The confidence interval is:

$$\bar{x} \pm z_{\alpha/2}\frac{s}{\sqrt{n}} \Rightarrow 32.5 \pm 2.58\frac{30}{\sqrt{225}} \Rightarrow 32.5 \pm 5.16 \Rightarrow (27.34, 37.66)$$

b. The sample size is $n = \frac{(z_{\alpha/2})^2\sigma^2}{B^2} = \frac{2.58^2(30)^2}{.5^2} = 23,963.04 \approx 23,964$

c. "99% confidence" means that if repeated samples of size 225 were selected from the population and 99% confidence intervals constructed for the population mean, then 99% of all the intervals constructed will contain the population mean.

7.81 a. The finite population correction factor is:

$$\sqrt{\frac{(N-n)}{N}} = \sqrt{\frac{(2,000-50)}{2,000}} = .9874$$

b. The finite population correction factor is:

$$\sqrt{\frac{(N-n)}{N}} = \sqrt{\frac{(100-20)}{100}} = .8944$$

c. The finite population correction factor is:

$$\sqrt{\frac{(N-n)}{N}} = \sqrt{\frac{(1,500-300)}{1,500}} = .8944$$

7.83 a. The 95% confidence interval is (298.6, 582.3).

b. We are 95% confident that the mean sales price is between $298,600 and $582,300.

c. "95% confidence" means that in repeated sampling, 95% of all confidence intervals constructed will contain the true mean salary and 5% will not.

d. Since the sample size is small ($n = 20$), we must assume that the distribution of sales prices is normal. From the stem-and-leaf display, it does not appear that the data come from a normal distribution. Thus, this confidence interval is probably not valid.

7.85 a. First we must compute $\hat{p}$: $\hat{p} = \dfrac{x}{n} = \dfrac{89{,}582}{102{,}263} = .876$

To see if the sample size is sufficiently large:

$$\hat{p} \pm 3\sigma_{\hat{p}} \approx \hat{p} \pm 3\sqrt{\dfrac{\hat{p}\hat{q}}{n}} \Rightarrow .876 \pm 3\sqrt{\dfrac{.876(.124)}{102{,}263}} \Rightarrow .876 \pm .003 \Rightarrow (.873, .879)$$

Since this interval is wholly contained in the interval (0, 1), we may conclude that the normal approximation is reasonable.

For confidence coefficient .99, $\alpha = .01$ and $\alpha/2 = .01/2 = .005$. From Table IV, Appendix B, $z_{.005} = 2.58$. The confidence interval is:

$$\hat{p} \pm z_{.005}\sqrt{\dfrac{pq}{n}} \approx \hat{p} \pm 2.58\sqrt{\dfrac{\hat{p}\hat{q}}{n}} \Rightarrow .876 \pm 2.58\sqrt{\dfrac{.876(.124)}{102{,}263}} \Rightarrow .876 \pm .003$$
$$\Rightarrow (.873, .879)$$

We are 99% confident that the true proportion of American adults who believe their health to be good to excellent is between .873 and .879.

7.87 a. For confidence coefficient .95, $\alpha = .05$ and $\alpha/2 = .025$. From Table IV, Appendix B, $z_{.025} = 1.96$. The confidence interval is:

$$\bar{x} \pm z_{\alpha/2}\dfrac{s}{\sqrt{n}}$$

Men: $7.4 \pm 1.96\dfrac{6.3}{\sqrt{159}} \Rightarrow 7.4 \pm .979 \Rightarrow (6.421, 8.379)$

We are 95% confident that the average distance to work for men in the central city is between 6.421 and 8.379 miles.

Women: $4.5 \pm 1.96\dfrac{4.2}{\sqrt{119}} \Rightarrow 4.5 \pm .755 \Rightarrow (3.745, 5.255)$

We are 95% confident that the average distance to work for women in the central city is between 3.745 and 5.255 miles.

b. Men: $9.3 \pm 1.96\dfrac{7.1}{\sqrt{138}} \Rightarrow 9.3 \pm 1.185 \Rightarrow (8.115, 10.485)$

We are 95% confident that the average distance to work for men in the suburbs is between 8.115 and 10.485 miles.

Inferences Based on a Single Sample: Estimation with Confidence Intervals

Women: $6.6 \pm 1.96 \dfrac{5.6}{\sqrt{93}} \Rightarrow 6.6 \pm 1.138 \Rightarrow (5.462, 7.738)$

We are 95% confident that the average distance to work for women in the suburbs is between 5.462 and 7.738 miles.

7.89   a. For confidence coefficient .90, $\alpha = .10$ and $\alpha/2 = .05$. From Table IV, Appendix B, $z_{.05} = 1.645$. The 90% confidence interval is:

$$\bar{x} \pm z_{.05}\dfrac{\sigma}{\sqrt{n}} \Rightarrow \bar{x} \pm 1.645\dfrac{s}{\sqrt{n}} \Rightarrow 12.2 \pm 1.645\dfrac{10}{\sqrt{100}} \Rightarrow 12.2 \pm 1.645$$
$$\Rightarrow (10.555, 13.845)$$

b. For confidence coefficient .99, $\alpha = .01$ and $\alpha/2 = .005$. From Table IV, Appendix B, $z_{.005} = 2.58$.

The sample size is $n = \dfrac{(z_{\alpha/2})^2\sigma^2}{B^2} = \dfrac{(2.58)^2(10)^2}{2^2} = 166.4 \approx 167$

You would need to take $n = 167$ samples.

7.91   a. Of the 24 observations, 20 were 2 weeks of vacation $\Rightarrow \hat{p} = 20/24 = .833$.

To see if the sample size is sufficiently large:

$$\hat{p} \pm 3\sigma_{\hat{p}} \Rightarrow \hat{p} \pm 3\sqrt{\dfrac{pq}{n}} \Rightarrow \hat{p} \pm 3\sqrt{\dfrac{\hat{p}\hat{q}}{n}} \Rightarrow .833 \pm 3\sqrt{\dfrac{.833(.167)}{24}} \Rightarrow .833 \pm .228$$
$$\Rightarrow (.605, 1.061)$$

Since the interval does not lie within the interval (0, 1), the normal approximation will not be adequate.

b. The bound is $B = .02$. For confidence coefficient .95, $\alpha = .05$ and $\alpha/2 = .05/2 = .025$. From Table IV, Appendix B, $z_{.025} = 1.96$. Thus,

$$n = \dfrac{(z_{\alpha/2})^2 pq}{B^2} = \dfrac{1.96^2\,.833(.167)}{.02^2} = 1{,}336.02 \approx 1{,}337.$$

Thus, we would need a sample size of 1,337.

7.93   a. First, we must estimate the standard deviation. The only information that we have is the values of the 20th, 50th, and 80th percentiles. Since the 20th percentile $35,100 is closer to the median, $50,000, than the 80th percentile, $73,000, the data are skewed. From Chebyshev's Rule, we know that at least $1 - 1/k^2$ of the observations are within k standard deviations of the mean. Thus, we want to find k such that $1 - 1/k^2 = .8 - .2 = .6$.

$$1 - 1/k^2 = .6 \Rightarrow k^2 = 1/.4 = 2.5 \Rightarrow k \approx 1.6$$

Thus, there are $2(1.6) = 3.2$ standard deviations in the interval from the 20th percentile to the 80th percentile. The standard deviation can be estimated by:

$$s \approx \dfrac{80\text{th} - 20\text{th}}{3.2} = \dfrac{73{,}000 - 35{,}100}{3.2} = 11{,}843.75$$

For confidence coefficient .98, $\alpha = .02$ and $\alpha/2 = .02/2 = .01$. From Table IV, Appendix B, $z_{.01} = 2.33$. Thus,

$$n = \frac{(z_{\alpha/2})^2 \sigma^2}{B^2} = \frac{2.33^2 (11,843.75)^2}{2,000^2} = 190.4 \approx 191$$

Thus, we would need a sample size of 191.

b. See part a.

c. We must assume that the distribution of salaries next year has a similar shape to the distribution of salaries in the sixth annual salary survey.

7.95 a. We would have to assume that the sample was a random sample. Since n is large, the Central Limit Theorem applies.

b. $\bar{x} = \dfrac{\sum x}{n} = \dfrac{586}{180} = 3.256$

$s^2 = \dfrac{\sum x^2 - \dfrac{(\sum x)^2}{n}}{n - 1} = \dfrac{2,640 - \dfrac{586^2}{180}}{180 - 1} = 4.0908;\ s = \sqrt{4.0908} = 2.0226$

For confidence coefficient .98, $\alpha = .02$ and $\alpha/2 = .02/2 = .01$. From Table IV, Appendix B, $z_{.01} = 2.33$. The 98% confidence interval is:

$$\bar{x} \pm 2.33 \hat{\sigma}_{\bar{x}} \Rightarrow \bar{x} \pm 2.33 \left(\frac{s}{\sqrt{n}}\right)\sqrt{\frac{N-n}{N}} \Rightarrow 3.256 \pm 2.33 \left(\frac{2.0226}{\sqrt{180}}\right)\sqrt{\frac{8,521-180}{8,521}}$$

$$\Rightarrow 3.256 \pm .348 \Rightarrow (2.908, 3.604)$$

We are 98% confident that the mean subscription length is between 2.908 and 3.604 years.

c. Since this is a mail-in survey, the sample is self-selected. Thus, it may not be representative of the population.

7.99 a. For confidence coefficient .99, $\alpha = 1 - .99 = .01$ and $\alpha/2 = .01/2 = .005$. From Table VI, Appendix B, with df $= n - 1 = 9 - 1 = 8$. $t_{.005} = 3.355$. The 99% confidence interval is:

$$\bar{x} \pm t_{.005} \frac{s}{\sqrt{n}} \Rightarrow 985.6 \pm 3.355 \frac{22.9}{\sqrt{9}} \Rightarrow 985.6 \pm 25.610 \Rightarrow (959.990, 1011.210)$$

b. Since 1000 is in the 99% confidence interval, it is not an unusual value for the mean. Thus, based on this confidence interval, the process should not be considered out of control.

c. (a) For confidence coefficient .90, $\alpha = 1 - .90 = .10$ and $\alpha/2 = .10/2 = .05$. From Table VI, Appendix B, with df $= n - 1 = 9 - 1 = 8$, $t_{.05} = 1.860$. The 90% confidence interval is:

$$\bar{x} \pm t_{.05} \frac{s}{\sqrt{n}} \Rightarrow 985.6 \pm 1.860 \frac{22.9}{\sqrt{9}} \Rightarrow 985.6 \pm 14.198 \Rightarrow (971.402, 999.798)$$

Inferences Based on a Single Sample: Estimation with Confidence Intervals

(b) Since 1000 is not in the 90% confidence interval, it is an unusual value for the mean. Thus, it appears the process is out of control based on the 90% confidence interval.

d. We would use the 99% confidence interval. We would have a smaller probability of concluding that the process is out of control when it is not.

e. We must assume that the samples are random and that the breaking strengths are normally distributed.

7.101 For confidence coefficient .95, $\alpha = .05$ and $\alpha/2 = .025$. From Table IV, Appendix B, $z_{.025} = 1.96$. From Exercise 7.100, a good approximation for p is .094. Also, $B = .02$.

The sample size is $n = \dfrac{(z_{\alpha/2})^2 pq}{B^2} = \dfrac{(1.96)^2(.094)(.906)}{.02^2} = 817.9 \approx 818$

You would need to take $n = 818$ samples.

Inferences Based on a Single Sample: Tests of Hypothesis

Chapter 8

8.1 The null hypothesis is the "status quo" hypothesis, while the alternative hypothesis is the research hypothesis.

8.3 The "level of significance" of a test is α. This is the probability that the test statistic will fall in the rejection region when the null hypothesis is true.

8.5 The four possible results are:

1. Rejecting the null hypothesis when it is true. This would be a Type I error.
2. Accepting the null hypothesis when it is true. This would be a correct decision.
3. Rejecting the null hypothesis when it is false. This would be a correct decision.
4. Accepting the null hypothesis when it is false. This would be a Type II error.

8.7 When you reject the null hypothesis in favor of the alternative hypothesis, this does not prove the alternative hypothesis is correct. We are $100(1 - \alpha)\%$ confident that there is sufficient evidence to conclude that the alternative hypothesis is correct.

If we were to repeatedly draw samples from the population and perform the test each time, approximately $100(1 - \alpha)\%$ of the tests performed would yield the correct decision.

8.9 a. Since the company must give proof the drug is safe, the null hypothesis would be the drug is unsafe. The alternative hypothesis would be the drug is safe.

b. A Type I error would be concluding the drug is safe when it is not safe. A Type II error would be concluding the drug is not safe when it is. α is the probability of concluding the drug is safe when it is not. β is the probability of concluding the drug is not safe when it is.

c. In this problem, it would be more important for α to be small. We would want the probability of concluding the drug is safe when it is not to be as small as possible.

8.11 a.

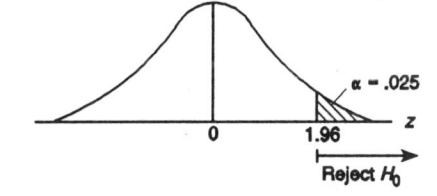

b.

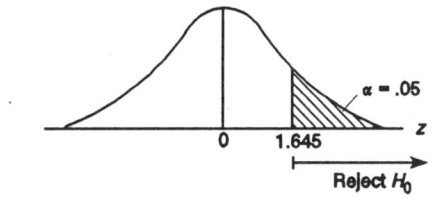

Inferences Based on a Single Sample: Tests of Hypothesis

c.

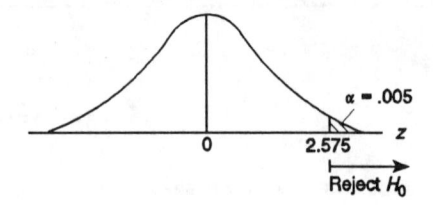

[Graph: normal curve with α = .005, rejection region z > 2.575]

d.

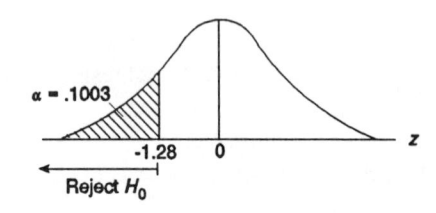

[Graph: normal curve with α = .1003, rejection region z < -1.28]

e.

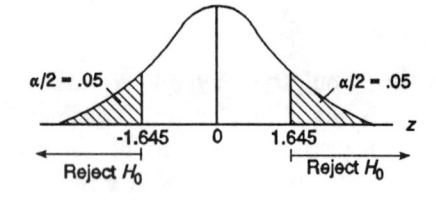

[Graph: normal curve with α/2 = .05 on each side, rejection regions z < -1.645 and z > 1.645]

f.

[Graph: normal curve with α/2 = .005 on each side, rejection regions z < -2.575 and z > 2.575]

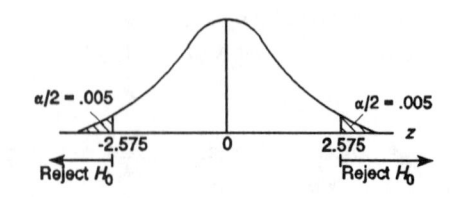

g. $P(z > 1.96) = .025$
$P(z > 1.645) = .05$
$P(z > 2.575) = .005$
$P(z < -1.28) = .1003$
$P(z < -1.645 \text{ or } z > 1.645) = .10$
$P(z < -2.575 \text{ or } z > 2.575) = .01$

8.13 a. $H_0: \mu = 100$
$H_a: \mu > 100$

The test statistic is $z = \dfrac{\bar{x} - \mu_0}{\sigma_{\bar{x}}} = \dfrac{\bar{x} - \mu_0}{\sigma/\sqrt{n}} = \dfrac{110 - 100}{60/\sqrt{100}} = 1.67$

The rejection region requires $\alpha = .05$ in the upper tail of the z-distribution. From Table IV, Appendix B, $z_{.05} = 1.645$. The rejection region is $z > 1.645$.

Since the observed value of the test statistic falls in the rejection region, ($z = 1.67 > 1.645$), H_0 is rejected. There is sufficient evidence to indicate the true population mean is greater than 100 at $\alpha = .05$.

b. $H_0: \mu = 100$
$H_a: \mu \neq 100$

The test statistic is $z = \dfrac{\bar{x} - \mu_0}{\sigma_{\bar{x}}} = \dfrac{110 - 100}{60/\sqrt{100}} = 1.67$

The rejection region requires $\alpha/2 = .05/2 = .025$ in each tail of the z-distribution. From Table IV, Appendix B, $z_{.025} = 1.96$. The rejection region is $z < -1.96$ or $z > 1.96$.

Since the observed value of the test statistic does not fall in the rejection region, ($z = 1.67 \not> 1.96$), H_0 is not rejected. There is insufficient evidence to indicate μ does not equal 100 at $\alpha = .05$.

c. In part **a**, we rejected H_0 and concluded the mean was greater than 100. In part **b**, we did not reject H_0. There was insufficient evidence to conclude the mean was different from 100. Because the alternative hypothesis in part **a** is more specific than the one in **b**, it is easier to reject H_0.

8.15 a. To determine whether the true mean PTSD score of all World War II aviator POWs is less than 16, we test:

H_0: $\mu = 16$
H_a: $\mu < 16$

b. The test statistic is $z = \dfrac{\bar{x} - \mu_0}{\sigma_{\bar{x}}} = \dfrac{9 - 16}{9.32/\sqrt{33}} = -4.31$

The rejection region requires $\alpha = .10$ in the lower tail of the z-distribution. From Table IV, Appendix B, $z_{.10} = 1.28$. The rejection region is $z < -1.28$.

Since the observed value of the test statistic falls in the rejection region ($z = -4.31 < -1.28$), H_0 is rejected. There is sufficient evidence to indicate that the true mean PTSD score of all World War II aviator POWs is less than 16 at $\alpha = .10$.

The practical implications of the test are that the World War II aviator POWs have a lower level PTSD level on the average than the POWs from Vietnam.

c. The sample used in this study was a self-selected sample—only 33 of the 239 located survivors responded. Very often, self-selected respondents are not representative of the population. Here, those former POWs who are more comfortable with their lives may be more willing to respond than those who are less comfortable. Those who are less comfortable may be suffering more from PTSD than those who are more comfortable. Also, it may not be fair to compare the survivors from World War II to the survivors of Vietnam. The World War II survivors are more removed from their imprisonment than those from the Vietnam war. Also, many of the World War II POWs probably are no longer living. Again, those still alive may be the ones who are more comfortable with their lives.

8.17 a. To determine if the process is not operating satisfactorily, we test:

H_0: $\mu = .250$
H_a: $\mu \neq .250$

The test statistic is $z = \dfrac{\bar{x} - \mu_0}{\sigma_{\bar{x}}} = \dfrac{.252475 - .250}{.00223/\sqrt{40}} = 7.02$

The rejection region requires $\alpha/2 = .01/2 = .005$ in each tail of the z-distribution. From Table IV, Appendix B, $z_{.005} = 2.58$. The rejection region is $z < -2.58$ or $z > 2.58$.

Inferences Based on a Single Sample: Tests of Hypothesis

Since the observed value of the test statistic falls in the rejection region ($z = 7.02 > 2.58$), H_0 is rejected. There is sufficient information to indicate the process is performing in an unsatisfactory manner at $\alpha = .01$.

b. α is the probability of a Type I error. A Type I error, in this case, is to say the process is unsatisfactory when, in fact, it is satisfactory. The risk, then, is to the producer since he will be spending time and money to repair a process that is not in error.

β is the probability of a Type II error. A Type II error, in this case, is to say the process is satisfactory when it, in fact, is not. This is the consumer's risk since he could unknowingly purchase a defective product.

8.19 First, we must estimate the standard deviation. We are given that the losses ranged from $208 to $400,000. An estimate of the standard deviation is the range divided by 4 or the range divided by 6. In this case, to be conservative, we will use the range divided by 4.

$$s \approx \frac{400,000 - 208}{4} = 99,948$$

To determine if the true mean loss due to check fraud of mid-sized banks in 1993 exceeds $15,100 per bank, we test:

$H_0: \mu = 15,100$
$H_a: \mu > 15,100$

The test statistic is $z = \dfrac{\bar{x} - \mu_0}{\sigma_{\bar{x}}} = \dfrac{37,443 - 15,100}{99,948/\sqrt{50}} = 1.58$

The rejection region requires $\alpha = .10$ in the upper tail of the z-distribution. From Table IV, Appendix B, $z_{.10} = 1.28$. The rejection region is $z > 1.28$.

Since the observed value of the test statistic falls in the rejection region ($z = 1.58 > 1.28$), H_0 is rejected. There is sufficient evidence to indicate that the true mean loss due to check fraud of mid-sized banks in 1993 exceeds $15,100 per bank at $\alpha = .10$.

8.21 a. To determine if the mean lifetime of the new cartridges exceeds that of the old, we test:

$H_0: \mu = 1,502.5$
$H_a: \mu > 1,502.5$

b. The test statistic is $z = \dfrac{\bar{x} - \mu_0}{\sigma_{\bar{x}}} = \dfrac{1,511.4 - 1,502.5}{35.7/\sqrt{225}} = 3.74$

The rejection region requires $\alpha = .005$ in the upper tail of the z-distribution. From Table IV, Appendix B, $z_{.005} = 2.58$. The rejection region is $z > 2.58$.

Since the observed value of the test statistic falls in the rejection region ($z = 3.74 > 2.58$), H_0 is rejected. There is sufficient evidence to indicate the mean lifetime of the new cartridges exceeds that of the old at $\alpha = .005$.

c. No. The mean lifetime of the old cartridges was 1,511.4 pages and the mean of the new cartridges is 1,502.5 pages. In practical terms, there is not much difference between these two numbers.

d. Yes. There is much less variability among the new cartridges. Thus, they are more similar to each other and the quality is higher.

8.23 To determine if the new drug is effective in reducing the mean time until relief from pain, we test:

$H_0: \mu = 3.5$
$H_a: \mu < 3.5$

The test statistic is $z = \dfrac{\bar{x} - \mu_0}{\dfrac{\sigma}{\sqrt{n}}} = \dfrac{2.8 - 3.5}{\dfrac{1.14}{\sqrt{50}}} = -4.34$

The rejection region requires $\alpha = .10$ in the lower tail of the z-distribution. From Table IV, Appendix B, $z_{.10} = 1.28$. The rejection region is $z < -1.28$.

Since the observed value of the test statistic falls in the rejection region ($z = -4.34 < -1.28$), H_0 is rejected. There is sufficient evidence to indicate the new drug has been effective in reducing the mean time until relief from pain at $\alpha = .10$.

8.25 a. Since the p-value = .10 is greater than $\alpha = .05$, H_0 is not rejected.

b. Since the p-value = .05 is less than $\alpha = .10$, H_0 is rejected.

c. Since the p-value = .001 is less than $\alpha = .01$, H_0 is rejected.

d. Since the p-value = .05 is greater than $\alpha = .025$, H_0 is not rejected.

e. Since the p-value = .45 is greater than $\alpha = .10$, H_0 is not rejected.

8.27 p-value = $P(z \geq 2.17) = .5 - P(0 < z < 2.17) = .5 - .4850 = .0150$
(using Table IV, Appendix B)

8.29 $z = \dfrac{\bar{x} - \mu_0}{\sigma_{\bar{x}}} = \dfrac{49.4 - 50}{4.1/\sqrt{100}} = -1.46$

p-value = $P(z \geq -1.46) = .5 + .4279 = .9279$

There is no evidence to reject H_0 for $\alpha \leq .10$.

8.31 a. The p-value reported by SAS is for a two-tailed test. Thus, $P(z \leq -1.63) + P(z \geq 1.63) = .1032$. For this one-tailed test, the p-value = $P(z \leq -1.63) = .1032/2 = .0516$.

Since the p-value = $.0516 > \alpha = .05$, H_0 is not rejected. There is insufficient evidence to indicate $\mu < 75$ at $\alpha = .05$.

b. For this one-tailed test, the p-value = $P(z \leq 1.63)$. Since $P(z \leq -1.63) = .1032/2 = .0516$, $P(z \leq 1.63) = 1 - .0516 = .9484$.

Since the p-value = $.9484 > \alpha = .10$, H_0 is not rejected. There is insufficient evidence to indicate $\mu < 75$ at $\alpha = .10$.

c. For this one-tailed test, the p-value = $P(z \geq 1.63) = .1032/2 = .0516$.

Since the p-value = $.0516 < \alpha = .10$, H_0 is rejected. There is sufficient evidence to indicate $\mu > 75$ at $\alpha = .10$.

Inferences Based on a Single Sample: Tests of Hypothesis

d. For this two-tailed test, the p-value $= .1032$.

Since the p-value $= .1032 > \alpha = .01$, H_0 is not rejected. There is insufficient evidence to indicate $\mu \neq 75$ at $\alpha = .01$.

8.33 a. To determine whether the true mean one-year rate of return for electric utility stocks exceeded 30%, we test:

H_0: $\mu = 30\%$
H_a: $\mu > 30\%$

b. The test statistic is $z = \dfrac{\bar{x} - \mu_0}{\sigma_{\bar{x}}} = \dfrac{31.929 - 30}{13.4654/\sqrt{63}} = 1.14$

The observed significance level is $p = P(z \geq 1.14) = .5 - .3729 = .1271$ (using Table IV, Appendix B).

c. Since the observed significance level (.1271) is not less than any reasonable value of α, H_0 is not rejected. There is insufficient evidence to indicate the true mean one-year rate of return for electric utility stocks exceeded 30% at $\alpha \leq .10$.

8.35 a. To determine if children in this age group perceive a risk associated with failure to wear helmets, we test:

H_0: $\mu = 2.5$
H_a: $\mu > 2.5$

b. The test statistic is $z = \dfrac{\bar{x} - \mu_0}{\sigma_{\bar{x}}} = \dfrac{3.39 - 2.5}{.80/\sqrt{797}} = 31.41$

p-value $= P(z \geq 31.41) \approx .5 - .5 = 0$

c. There is strong evidence to reject H_0 for any reasonable value of α. There is strong evidence to indicate the mean perceived risk associated with failure to wear helmets is greater than 2.5 for any reasonable value of α.

8.37 a. To determine whether Chinese smokers smoke, on average, more cigarettes a day in 1997 than in 1995, we test:

H_0: $\mu = 16.5$
H_a: $\mu > 16.5$

b. The test statistic is $z = \dfrac{\bar{x} - \mu_0}{\sigma_{\bar{x}}} = \dfrac{17.05 - 16.5}{5.21/\sqrt{200}} = 1.49$

The observed significance level is $p = P(z \geq 1.49) = .5 - .4319 = .0681$ (using Table IV, Appendix B).

Since the observed significance level (.0681) is not less than $\alpha = .05$, H_0 is not rejected. There is insufficient evidence to indicate that Chinese smokers smoke, on average, more cigarettes a day in 1997 than in 1995 at $\alpha = .05$.

If we used $\alpha = .10$, we would reject H_0. There is sufficient evidence to indicate that Chinese smokers smoke, on average, more cigarettes a day in 1997 than in 1995 at $\alpha = .10$.

c. The two-tailed test is inappropriate because we are interested in whether Chinese smokers, on average, smoke more cigarettes now than in 1995. This specifies only one-tail for the test.

8.39 We should use the *t*-distribution in testing a hypothesis about a population mean if the sample size is small, the population being sampled from is normal, and the variance of the population is unknown.

8.41 a. $P(t > 1.440) = .10$
(Using Table VI, Appendix B, with df = 6)

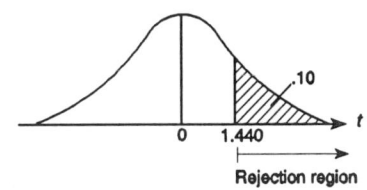

b. $P(t < -1.782) = .05$
(Using Table VI, Appendix B, with df = 12)

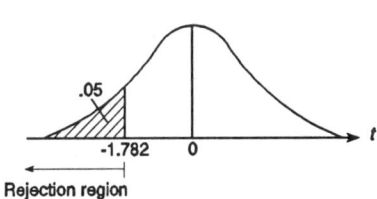

c. $P(t < -2.060) = P(t > 2.060) = .025$
(Using Table VI, Appendix B, with df = 25)

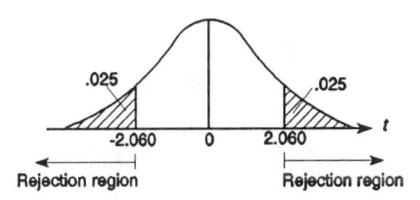

8.43 a. The rejection region requires $\alpha/2 = .05/2 = .025$ in each tail of the *t*-distribution with df = $n - 1 = 14 - 1 = 13$. From Table VI, Appendix B, $t_{.025} = 2.160$. The rejection region is $t < -2.160$ or $t > 2.160$.

b. The rejection region requires $\alpha = .01$ in the upper tail of the *t*-distribution with df = $n - 1$ = 24 - 1 = 23. From Table VI, Appendix B, $t_{.01} = 2.500$. The rejection region is $t > 2.500$.

c. The rejection region requires $\alpha = .10$ in the upper tail of the *t*-distribution with df = $n - 1$ = 9 - 1 = 8. From Table VI, Appendix B, $t_{.10} = 1.397$. The rejection region is $t > 1.397$.

d. The rejection region requires $\alpha = .01$ in the lower tail of the *t*-distribution with df = $n - 1$ = 12 - 1 = 11. From Table VI, Appendix B, $t_{.01} = 2.718$. The rejection region is $t < -2.718$.

e. The rejection region requires $\alpha/2 = .10/2 = .05$ in each tail of the *t*-distribution with df = $n - 1 = 20 - 1 = 19$. From Table VI, Appendix B, $t_{.05} = 1.729$. The rejection region is $t < -1.729$ or $t > 1.729$.

f. The rejection region requires $\alpha = .05$ in the lower tail of the *t*-distribution with df = $n - 1$ = 4 - 1 = 3. From Table VI, Appendix B, $t_{.05} = 2.353$. The rejection region is $t < -2.353$.

Inferences Based on a Single Sample: Tests of Hypothesis

8.45 a. We must assume that a random sample was drawn from a normal population.

b. The hypotheses are:

$$H_0: \mu = 1000$$
$$H_a: \mu > 1000$$

The test statistic is $t = 1.894$.

The p-value is .0382.

There is evidence to reject H_0 for $\alpha > .0382$. There is evidence to indicate the mean is greater than 1000 for $\alpha > .0382$.

c. The hypotheses are:

$$H_0: \mu = 1000$$
$$H_a: \mu \neq 1000$$

The test statistic is $t = 1.894$.

The p-value is $2(.0382) = .0764$.

There is no evidence to reject H_0 for $\alpha = .05$. There is insufficient evidence to indicate the mean is different than 1000 for $\alpha = .05$.

There is evidence to reject H_0 for $\alpha > .0764$. There is evidence to indicate the mean is different than 1000 for $\alpha > .0764$.

8.47 Some preliminary calculations:

$$\bar{x} = \frac{\sum x}{n} = \frac{489}{5} = 97.8 \qquad s^2 = \frac{\sum x^2 - \frac{(\sum x)^2}{n}}{n-1} = \frac{47,867 - \frac{489^2}{5}}{5-1} = 10.7$$

$$s = \sqrt{10.7} = 3.271$$

To determine if the mean recovery percentage of Aldrin exceeds 85% using the new MSPD method, we test:

$$H_0: \mu = 85$$
$$H_a: \mu > 85$$

The test statistic is $t = \dfrac{\bar{x} - \mu_0}{s/\sqrt{n}} = \dfrac{97.8 - 85}{3.271/\sqrt{5}} = 8.75$

The rejection region requires $\alpha = .05$ in the upper tail of the t-distribution with df = $n - 1 = 5 - 1 = 4$. From Table VI, Appendix B, $t_{.05} = 2.132$. The rejection region is $t > 2.132$.

Since the observed value of the test statistic falls in the rejection region ($t = 8.75 > 2.132$), H_0 is rejected. There is sufficient evidence to indicate that the true mean recovery percentage of Aldrin exceeds 85% using the new MSPD method at $\alpha = .05$.

8.49 a. To test whether the mean level is less than 15 ppb, we test:

$$H_0: \mu = 15$$
$$H_a: \mu < 15$$

b. From the printout, the value of the test statistic is $t = -1.732$. The reported p-value is .1112, but this is for a two-tailed test. For this one-tailed test, the p-value = .1112/2 = .0556.

c. There is no evidence to reject H_0 for $\alpha = .05$. There is no evidence to indicate the mean level of phosphorus is less than 15 ppb for $\alpha = .05$.

There is evidence to reject H_0 for $\alpha > .0556$. There is evidence to indicate the mean level of phosphorus is less than 15 ppb for $\alpha > .0556$.

8.51 To determine if the true mean crack intensity of the Mississippi highway exceeds the AASHTO recommended maximum, we test:

H_0: $\mu = .100$
H_a: $\mu > .100$

The test statistic is $t = \dfrac{\bar{x} - \mu_0}{s/\sqrt{n}} = \dfrac{.210 - .100}{\sqrt{.011}/\sqrt{8}} = 2.97$

The rejection region requires $\alpha = .01$ in the upper tail of the t-distribution with df = $n - 1$ = 8 − 1 = 7. From Table VI, Appendix B, $t_{.01} = 2.998$. The rejection region is $t > 2.998$.

Since the observed value of the test statistic does not fall in the rejection region ($t = 2.97 \not> 2.998$), H_0 is not rejected. There is insufficient evidence to indicate that the true mean crack intensity of the Mississippi highway exceeds the AASHTO recommended maximum at $\alpha = .01$.

8.53 The sample size is large enough if the interval $p_0 \pm 3\sigma_{\hat{p}}$ is contained in the interval (0, 1).

a. $p_0 \pm 3\sqrt{\dfrac{p_0 q_0}{n}} \Rightarrow .975 \pm 3\sqrt{\dfrac{(.975)(.025)}{900}} \Rightarrow .975 \pm .016 \Rightarrow (.959, .991)$

Since the interval is contained in the interval (0, 1), the sample size is large enough.

b. $p_0 \pm 3\sqrt{\dfrac{p_0 q_0}{n}} \Rightarrow .01 \pm 3\sqrt{\dfrac{(.01)(.99)}{125}} \Rightarrow .01 \pm .027 \Rightarrow (-.017, .037)$

Since the interval is not contained in the interval (0, 1), the sample size is not large enough.

c. $p_0 \pm 3\sqrt{\dfrac{p_0 q_0}{n}} \Rightarrow .75 \pm 3\sqrt{\dfrac{(.75)(.25)}{40}} \Rightarrow .75 \pm .205 \Rightarrow (.545, .955)$

Since the interval is contained in the interval (0, 1), the sample size is large enough.

d. $p_0 \pm 3\sqrt{\dfrac{p_0 q_0}{n}} \Rightarrow .75 \pm 3\sqrt{\dfrac{(.75)(.25)}{15}} \Rightarrow .75 \pm .335 \Rightarrow (.415, 1.085)$

Since the interval is not contained in the interval (0, 1), the sample size is not large enough.

e. $p_0 \pm 3\sqrt{\dfrac{p_0 q_0}{n}} \Rightarrow .62 \pm 3\sqrt{\dfrac{(.62)(.38)}{12}} \Rightarrow .62 \pm .420 \Rightarrow (.120, 1.040)$

Since the interval is not contained in the interval (0, 1), the sample size is not large enough.

8.55 a. $z = \dfrac{\hat{p} - p_0}{\sqrt{\dfrac{p_0 q_0}{n}}} = \dfrac{.83 - .9}{\sqrt{\dfrac{.9(.1)}{100}}} = -2.33$

b. The denominator in Exercise 8.54 is $\sqrt{\dfrac{.7(.3)}{100}} = .0458$ as compared to $\sqrt{\dfrac{.9(.1)}{100}} = .03$ in part a. Since the denominator in this problem is smaller, the absolute value of z is larger.

c. The rejection region requires $\alpha = .05$ in the lower tail of the z-distribution. From Table IV, Appendix B, $z_{.05} = 1.645$. The rejection region is $z < -1.645$.

Since the observed value of the test statistic falls in the rejection region ($z = -2.33 < -1.645$), H_0 is rejected. There is sufficient evidence to indicate the population proportion is less than .9 at $\alpha = .05$.

d. The p-value $= P(z \le -2.33) = .5 - .4901 = .0099$ (from Table IV, Appendix B). Since the p-value is less than $\alpha = .05$, H_0 is rejected.

8.57 From Exercise 7.36, $n = 50$ and since p is the proportion of consumers who do not like the snack food, $\hat{p}$ will be:

$$\hat{p} = \dfrac{\text{Number of 0's in sample}}{n} = \dfrac{29}{50} = .58$$

First, check to see if the normal approximation will be adequate:

$$p_0 \pm 3\sigma_{\hat{p}} \Rightarrow p_0 \pm 3\sqrt{\dfrac{pq}{n}} \approx p_0 \pm 3\sqrt{\dfrac{p_0 q_0}{n}} \Rightarrow .5 \pm 3\sqrt{\dfrac{.5(1 - .5)}{50}} \Rightarrow .5 \pm .2121$$
$$\Rightarrow (.2879, .7121)$$

Since the interval lies completely in the interval (0, 1), the normal approximation will be adequate.

a. H_0: $p = .5$
H_a: $p > .5$

The test statistic is $z = \dfrac{\hat{p} - p_0}{\sigma_{\hat{p}}} = \dfrac{\hat{p} - p_0}{\sqrt{\dfrac{p_0 q_0}{n}}} = \dfrac{.58 - .5}{\sqrt{\dfrac{.5(1 - .5)}{50}}} = 1.13$

The rejection region requires $\alpha = .10$ in the upper tail of the z-distribution. From Table IV, Appendix B, $z_{.10} = 1.28$. The rejection region is $z > 1.28$.

Since the observed value of the test statistic does not fall in the rejection region ($z = 1.13 \not> 1.28$), H_0 is not rejected. There is insufficient evidence to indicate the proportion of customers who do not like the snack food is greater than .5 at $\alpha = .10$.

b. p-value $= P(z \geq 1.13) = .5 - .3708 = .1292$

8.59 a. To test the hypothesis that less than 40% of the residents of Los Angeles County have earthquake insurance, we test:

$H_0: p = .4$
$H_a: p < .4$

b. $\hat{p} = \dfrac{x}{n} = \dfrac{133}{337} = .395$

The test statistic is $z = \dfrac{\hat{p} - p_0}{\sqrt{\dfrac{p_0 q_0}{n}}} = \dfrac{.395 - .4}{\sqrt{\dfrac{.4(.6)}{337}}} = -.19$

The rejection region requires $\alpha = .10$ in lower tail of the z-distribution. From Table IV, Appendix B, $z_{.10} = 1.28$. The rejection region is $z < -1.28$.

Since the observed value of the test statistic does not fall in the rejection region ($z = -.19 \not< -1.28$), H_0 is not rejected. There is insufficient evidence to indicate that less than 40% of the residents of Los Angeles County have earthquake insurance at $\alpha = .10$.

c. The p-value $= P(z \leq -.19)$. From Table IV, Appendix B, $P(z \leq -.19) = .5 - .0753 = .4247$. Since the p-value is not less than $\alpha = .10$, H_0 is not rejected.

8.61 First, check to see if the normal approximation is adequate:

$p_0 \pm 3\sigma_{\hat{p}} \Rightarrow p_0 \pm 3\sqrt{\dfrac{p_0 q_0}{n}} \Rightarrow .5 \pm 3\sqrt{\dfrac{(.5)(.5)}{7000}} \Rightarrow .5 \pm .018 \Rightarrow (.482, .518)$

Since the interval falls completely in the interval (0, 1), the normal distribution will be adequate.

To determine if there was a placebo effect, we test:

$H_0: p = .5$
$H_a: p > .5$

The test statistic is $z = \dfrac{\hat{p} - p_0}{\sqrt{\dfrac{p_0 q_0}{n}}} = \dfrac{.7 - .5}{\sqrt{\dfrac{(.5)(.5)}{7000}}} = 33.47$

The rejection region requires $\alpha = .05$ in the upper tail of the z-distribution. From Table IV, Appendix B, $z_{.05} = 1.645$. The rejection region is $z > 1.645$.

Since the observed value of the test statistic falls in the rejection region ($z = 33.47 > 1.645$), H_0 is rejected. There is sufficient evidence to indicate that the true proportion of patients who improved (while on the placebo) is greater than .5 at $\alpha = .05$.

8.63 a. First, check to see if the normal approximation is adequate:

$p_0 \pm 3\sigma_{\hat{p}} \Rightarrow p_0 \pm 3\sqrt{\dfrac{p_0 q_0}{n}} \Rightarrow .25 \pm 3\sqrt{\dfrac{(.25)(.75)}{159}} \Rightarrow .25 \pm .103 \Rightarrow (.147, .353)$

Inferences Based on a Single Sample: Tests of Hypothesis

Since the interval falls completely in the interval (0, 1), the normal distribution will be adequate.

$$\hat{p} = \frac{x}{n} = \frac{124}{159} = .786$$

To determine if the percentage of truckers who suffer from sleep apnea differs from 25%, we test:

H_0: $p = .25$
H_a: $p \neq .25$

The test statistic is $z = \dfrac{\hat{p} - p_0}{\sqrt{\dfrac{p_0 q_0}{n}}} = \dfrac{.786 - .25}{\sqrt{\dfrac{(.25)(.75)}{159}}} = 15.61$

The rejection region requires $\alpha/2 = .10/2 = .05$ in each tail of the z-distribution. From Table IV, Appendix B, $z_{.05} = 1.645$. The rejection region is $z < -1.645$ or $z > 1.645$.

Since the observed value of the test statistic falls in the rejection region ($z = 15.61 > 1.645$), H_0 is rejected. There is sufficient evidence to indicate that the percentage of truckers who suffer from sleep apnea differs from 25% at $\alpha = .05$.

b. The observed significance level is the *p*-value and is:

$$p\text{-value} = P(z \geq 15.61) + P(z \leq -15.61) \approx (.5 - .5) + (.5 - .5) = 0$$

Since the *p*-value is so small, we would reject H_0 for any reasonable value of α. There is sufficient evidence to indicate that the percentage of truckers who suffer from sleep apnea differs from 25%.

c. The inference from a confidence interval and a test of hypothesis must agree because the same numbers are used in both if the same level of significance is used.

8.65 The power of a test increases when:

1. The distance between the null and alternative values of μ increases.
2. The value of α increases.
3. The sample size increases.

8.67 a. By the Central Limit Theorem, the sampling distribution of $\bar{x}$ is approximately normal with $\mu_{\bar{x}} = \mu = 500$ and

$$\sigma_{\bar{x}} = \frac{\sigma}{\sqrt{n}} = \frac{100}{\sqrt{25}} = 20.$$

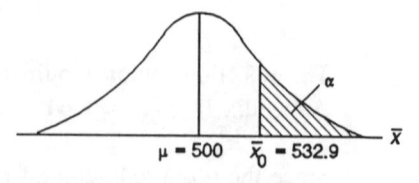

b. $\bar{x}_0 = \mu_0 + z_\alpha \sigma_{\bar{x}} = \mu_0 + z_\alpha \dfrac{\sigma}{\sqrt{n}}$ where $z_\alpha = z_{.05} = 1.645$ from Table IV, Appendix B.

Thus, $\bar{x}_0 = 500 + 1.645 \dfrac{100}{\sqrt{25}} = 532.9$

c. The sampling distribution of $\bar{x}$ is approximately normal by the Central Limit Theorem with $\mu_{\bar{x}} = \mu = 550$ and

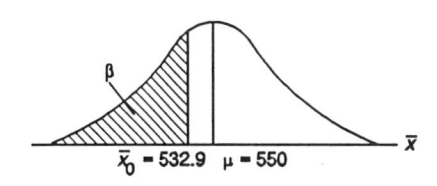

$$\sigma_{\bar{x}} = \frac{\sigma}{\sqrt{n}} = \frac{100}{\sqrt{25}} = 20.$$

d. $\beta = P(\bar{x}_0 < 532.9 \text{ when } \mu = 550) = P\left(z < \frac{532.9 - 550}{100/\sqrt{25}}\right) = P(z < -.86)$

$= .5 - .3051 = .1949$

e. Power $= 1 - \beta = 1 - .1949 = .8051$

8.69 a. The sampling distribution of $\bar{x}$ will be approximately normal (by the Central Limit Theorem) with $\mu_{\bar{x}} = \mu = 75$ and $\sigma_{\bar{x}} = \frac{\sigma}{\sqrt{n}} = \frac{15}{\sqrt{49}} = 2.143$.

b. The sampling distribution of $\bar{x}$ will be approximately normal (by the Central Limit Theorem) with $\mu_{\bar{x}} = \mu = 70$ and $\sigma_{\bar{x}} = \frac{\sigma}{\sqrt{n}} = \frac{15}{\sqrt{49}} = 2.143$.

c. First, find $\bar{x}_0 = \mu_0 - z_\alpha \sigma_{\bar{x}} = \mu_0 - z_\alpha \frac{\sigma}{\sqrt{n}}$ where $z_{.10} = 1.28$ from Table IV, Appendix B.

Thus, $\bar{x}_0 = 75 - 1.28 \frac{15}{\sqrt{49}} = 72.257$

Now, find $\beta = P(\bar{x}_0 > 72.257 \text{ when } \mu = 70) = P\left(z > \frac{72.257 - 70}{15/\sqrt{49}}\right)$

$= P(z > 1.05) = .5 - .3531 = .1469$

d. Power $= 1 - \beta = 1 - .1469 = .8531$

8.71 a. The sampling distribution of $\bar{x}$ will be approximately normal (by the Central Limit Theorem) with $\mu_{\bar{x}} = \mu = 30$ and $\sigma_{\bar{x}} = \frac{\sigma}{\sqrt{n}} = \frac{1.2}{\sqrt{121}} = .109$.

b. The sampling distribution of $\bar{x}$ will be approximately normal (CLT) with $\mu_{\bar{x}} = \mu = 29.8$ and $\sigma_{\bar{x}} = \frac{\sigma}{\sqrt{n}} = \frac{1.2}{\sqrt{121}} = .109$.

c. First, find $\bar{x}_{0,L} = \mu_0 - z_{\alpha/2}\sigma_{\bar{x}} = \mu_0 - z_{\alpha/2}\frac{\sigma}{\sqrt{n}}$

where $z_{.05/2} = z_{.025} = 1.96$ from Table IV, Appendix B.

Thus, $\bar{x}_{0,L} = 30 - 1.96 \frac{1.2}{\sqrt{121}} = 29.79$

$\bar{x}_{0,U} = \mu_0 + z_{\alpha/2}\sigma_{\bar{x}} = \mu_0 + z_{\alpha/2}\frac{\sigma}{\sqrt{n}} = 30 + 1.96 \frac{1.2}{\sqrt{121}} = 30.21$

Inferences Based on a Single Sample: Tests of Hypothesis

Now, find $\beta = P(29.79 < \bar{x} < 30.21$ when $\mu = 29.8)$

$$= P\left[\frac{29.79 - 29.8}{1.2/\sqrt{121}} < z < \frac{30.21 - 29.8}{1.2/\sqrt{121}}\right]$$

$$= P(-.09 < z < 3.76)$$
$$= .0359 + .5 = .5359$$

d. $\beta = P(29.79 < \bar{x} < 30.21$ when $\mu = 30.4) = P\left[\frac{29.79 - 30.4}{1.2/\sqrt{121}} < z < \frac{30.21 - 30.4}{1.2/\sqrt{121}}\right]$

$$= P(-5.59 < z < -1.74)$$
$$= .5 - .4591 = .0409$$

8.73 a. To determine if the true mean salary of IMA members in New York is higher than the national average, we test:

H_0: $\mu = 56,391$
H_a: $\mu > 56,391$

The test statistic is $z = \dfrac{\bar{x} - \mu_0}{\sigma_{\bar{x}}} = \dfrac{62,770 - 56,391}{28,972/\sqrt{122}} = 2.43$

The rejection region requires $\alpha = .05$ in the upper tail of the z-distribution. From Table IV, Appendix B, $z_{.05} = 1.645$. The rejection region is $z > 1.645$.

Since the observed value of the test statistic falls in the rejection region ($z = 2.43 > 1.645$), H_0 is rejected. There is sufficient evidence to indicate that the true mean salary of IMA members in New York is higher than the national average at $\alpha = .05$.

b. First find:

$$\bar{x}_0 = \mu_0 + z_\alpha \sigma_{\bar{x}} = \mu_0 + z_\alpha \frac{\sigma}{\sqrt{n}} \text{ where } z_\alpha = 1.645 \text{ from Table IV, Appendix B.}$$

Thus, $\bar{x}_0 = 56,391 + 1.645 \dfrac{28,972}{\sqrt{122}} = 60,705.84$

The power of the test is:

$$\text{Power} = P(\bar{x} > 60,705.84 \mid \mu = 66,391) = P\left[z > \frac{60,705.84 - 66,391}{28,972/\sqrt{122}}\right]$$
$$= P(z > -2.17) = .5 + .4850 = .9850$$

8.75 First, find $\bar{x}_0$ such that $P(\bar{x} < \bar{x}_0) = .05$.

$$P(\bar{x} < \bar{x}_0) = P\left[z < \frac{\bar{x}_0 - 10}{1.2/\sqrt{48}}\right] = P(z < z_0) = .05.$$

From Table IV, Appendix B, $z_0 = -1.645$.

Thus, $z_0 = \dfrac{\bar{x}_0 - 10}{1.2/\sqrt{48}} \Rightarrow \bar{x}_0 = -1.645(.173) + 10 = 9.715$

The probability of a Type II error is:

$$\beta = P(\bar{x} \geq 9.715 \mid \mu = 9.5) = P\left(z \geq \dfrac{9.715 - 9.5}{1.2/\sqrt{48}}\right) = P(z \geq 1.24) = .5 - .3925 = .1075$$

8.77 The smaller the p-value associated with a test of hypothesis, the stronger the support for the **alternative** hypothesis. The p-value is the probability of observing your test statistic or anything more unusual, given the null hypothesis is true. If this value is small, it would be very unusual to observe this test statistic if the null hypothesis were true. Thus, it would indicate the alternative hypothesis is true.

8.79 There is not a direct relationship between α and β. That is, if α is known, it does not mean β is known because β depends on the value of the parameter in the alternative hypothesis and the sample size. However, as α decreases, β increases for a fixed value of the parameter and a fixed sample size.

8.81 a. $H_0: \mu = 80$
$H_a: \mu < 80$

The test statistic is $t = \dfrac{\bar{x} - \mu_0}{s/\sqrt{n}} = \dfrac{72.6 - 80}{\sqrt{19.4}/\sqrt{20}} = -7.51$

The rejection region requires $\alpha = .05$ in the lower tail of the t-distribution with df $= n - 1 = 20 - 1 = 19$. From Table VI, Appendix B, $t_{.05} = 1.729$. The rejection region is $t < -1.729$.

Since the observed value of the test statistic falls in the rejection region ($-7.51 < -1.729$), H_0 is rejected. There is sufficient evidence to indicate that the mean is less than 80 at $\alpha = .05$.

b. $H_0: \mu = 80$
$H_a: \mu \neq 80$

The test statistic is $t = \dfrac{\bar{x} - \mu_0}{s/\sqrt{n}} = \dfrac{72.6 - 80}{\sqrt{19.4}/\sqrt{20}} = -7.51$

The rejection region requires $\alpha/2 = .01/2 = .005$ in each tail of the t-distribution with df $= n - 1 = 20 - 1 = 19$. From Table VI, Appendix B, $t_{.005} = 2.861$. The rejection region is $t < -2.861$ or $t > 2.861$.

Since the observed value of the test statistic falls in the rejection region ($-7.51 < -2.861$), H_0 is rejected. There is sufficient evidence to indicate that the mean is different from 80 at $\alpha = .01$.

8.83 a. $H_0: \mu = 8.3$
$H_a: \mu \neq 8.3$

The test statistic is $z = \dfrac{\bar{x} - \mu_0}{\sigma_{\bar{x}}} = \dfrac{8.2 - 8.3}{.79/\sqrt{175}} = -1.67$

Inferences Based on a Single Sample: Tests of Hypothesis

The rejection region requires $\alpha/2 = .05/2 = .025$ in each tail of the z-distribution. From Table IV, Appendix B, $z_{.025} = 1.96$. The rejection region is $z < -1.96$ or $z > 1.96$.

Since the observed value of the test statistic does not fall in the rejection region ($-1.67 \not< -1.96$), H_0 is not rejected. There is insufficient evidence to indicate that the mean is different from 8.3 at $\alpha = .05$.

b. $H_0: \mu = 8.4$
$H_a: \mu \neq 8.4$

The test statistic is $z = \dfrac{\bar{x} - \mu_0}{\sigma_{\bar{x}}} = \dfrac{8.2 - 8.4}{.79/\sqrt{175}} = -3.35$

The rejection region is the same as part b, $z < -1.96$ or $z > 1.96$.

Since the observed value of the test statistic falls in the rejection region ($-3.35 < -1.96$), H_0 is rejected. There is sufficient evidence to indicate that the mean is different from 8.4 at $\alpha = .05$.

8.85 a. The hypotheses would be:

H_0: Individual does not have the disease
H_a: Individual does have the disease

b. A Type I error would be: Conclude the individual has the disease when in fact he/she does not. This would be a false positive test.

A Type II error would be: Conclude the individual does not have the disease when in fact he/she does. This would be a false negative test.

c. If the disease is serious, either error would be grave. Arguments could be made for either error being more grave. However, I believe a Type II error would be more grave: Concluding the individual does not have the disease when he/she does. This person would not receive critical treatment, and may suffer very serious consequences. Thus, it is more important to minimize β.

8.87 a. To determine if the claim can be rejected, we test:

$H_0: \mu = .25$
$H_a: \mu < .25$

The test statistic is $z = \dfrac{\hat{p} - p_0}{\sqrt{\dfrac{p_0 q_0}{n}}} = \dfrac{.190 - .25}{\sqrt{\dfrac{.25(.75)}{195}}} = -1.93$

Since no α was given, we will use $\alpha = .05$. The rejection region requires $\alpha = .05$ in the lower tail of the z-distribution. From Table IV, Appendix B, $z_{.05} = 1.645$. The rejection region is $z < -1.645$.

Since the observed value of the test statistic falls in the rejection region ($z = -1.93 < -1.645$), H_0 is rejected. There is sufficient evidence to reject the claim that the "more than 25% of all U.S. businesses will have Web sites by the middle of 1995" at $\alpha = .05$.

b. This sample was self-selected and may not be representative of the population. The sample of readers who received the questionnaires was randomly selected. However, only 195 out of 1,500 returned the questionnaires. Usually those who return questionnaires have strong opinions one way or another, and thus, those responding to the questionnaire may not be representative.

8.89 a. The test statistic is $t = \dfrac{\bar{x} - \mu_0}{s/\sqrt{n}} = \dfrac{1173.6 - 1100}{36.3/\sqrt{3}} = 3.512$

The p-value $= P(t \geq 3.512)$. From Table VI with df $= n - 1 = 3 - 1 = 2$, $.025 < p$-value $< .05$.

b. The p-value $= .0362 = P(t \geq 3.512)$. Since this p-value is fairly small, there is evidence to reject H_0 for $\alpha > .0362$. There is evidence to indicate the mean length of life of a certain mechanical component is longer than 1100 hours.

c. A Type I error would be of most concern for this test. A Type I error would be concluding the mean lifetime is greater than 1100 hours when in fact the mean lifetime is not greater than 1100.

d. It is rather questionable whether a sample of 3 is representative of the population. If the sample is representative, then the conclusion is warranted.

8.91 a. First, check to see if n is large enough:

$$p_0 \pm 3\sigma_{\hat{p}} \Rightarrow p_0 \pm 3\sqrt{\dfrac{p_0 q_0}{n}} \Rightarrow .5 \pm 3\sqrt{\dfrac{.5(.5)}{250}} \Rightarrow .5 \pm .095 \Rightarrow (.405, .595)$$

Since the interval lies within the interval (0, 1), the normal approximation will be adequate.

To determine if there is evidence to reject the claim that no more than half of all manufacturers are dissatisfied with their trade promotion spending, we test:

H_0: $p = .5$
H_a: $p > .5$

The test statistic is $z = \dfrac{\hat{p} - p_0}{\sqrt{\dfrac{p_0 q_0}{n}}} = \dfrac{.91 - .5}{\sqrt{\dfrac{.5(.5)}{250}}} = 12.97$

The rejection region requires $\alpha = .02$ in the upper tail of the z-distribution. From Table IV, Appendix B, $z_{.02} = 2.05$. The rejection region is $z > 2.05$.

Since the observed value of the test statistic falls in the rejection region ($z = 12.97 > 2.05$), H_0 is rejected. There is sufficient evidence to reject the claim that no more than half of all manufacturers are dissatisfied with their trade promotion spending at $\alpha = .02$.

b. The observed significance level is p-value $= P(z \geq 12.97) \approx .5 - .5 = 0$. Since this p-value is so small, H_0 will be rejected for any reasonable value of α.

Inferences Based on a Single Sample: Tests of Hypothesis

c. First, we must define the rejection region in terms of $\hat{p}$.

$$\hat{p} = p_0 + z_\alpha \sigma_{\hat{p}} = .5 + 2.05\sqrt{\frac{.5(.5)}{250}} = .565$$

$$\beta = P(\hat{p} < .565 \mid p = .55) = P\left(z < \frac{.565 - .55}{\sqrt{\frac{.55(.45)}{250}}}\right) = P(z < .48) = .5 + .1844 = .6844$$

8.93 a. To determine if the production process should be halted, we test:

$H_0: \mu = 3$
$H_a: \mu > 3$

where μ = mean amount of PCB in the effluent.

The test statistic is $z = \dfrac{\bar{x} - \mu_0}{\sigma_{\bar{x}}} = \dfrac{3.1 - 3}{.5/\sqrt{50}} = 1.41$

The rejection region requires $\alpha = .01$ in the upper tail of the z-distribution. From Table IV, Appendix B, $z_{.01} = 2.33$. The rejection region is $z > 2.33$.

Since the observed value of the test statistic does not fall in the rejection region, ($z = 1.41 \not> 2.33$), H_0 is not rejected. There is insufficient evidence to indicate the mean amount of PCB in the effluent is more than 3 parts per million at $\alpha = .01$. Do not halt the manufacturing process.

b. As plant manager, I do not want to shut down the plant unnecessarily. Therefore, I want $\alpha = P(\text{shut down plant when } \mu = 3)$ to be small.

c. The p-value is $p = P(z \geq 1.41) = .5 - .4207 = .0793$. Since the p-value is not less than $\alpha = .01$, H_0 is not rejected.

8.95 a. No, it increases the risk of falsely rejecting H_0, i.e., closing the plant unnecessarily.

b. First, find $\bar{x}_0$ such that $P(\bar{x} > \bar{x}_0) = P(z > z_0) = .05$.

From Table IV, Appendix B, $z_0 = 1.645$

$$z = \frac{\bar{x}_0 - \mu}{\sigma/\sqrt{n}} \Rightarrow 1.645 = \frac{\bar{x}_0 - 3}{.5/\sqrt{50}} \Rightarrow \bar{x}_0 = 3.116$$

Then, compute:

$$\beta = P(\bar{x}_0 \leq 3.116 \text{ when } \mu = 3.1) = P\left(z \leq \frac{3.116 - 3.1}{.5/\sqrt{50}}\right) = P(z \leq .23) = .5 + .0910 = .5910$$

Power $= 1 - \beta = 1 - .5910 = .4090$

c. The power of the test increases as α increases.

8.97 a. Type II error is concluding the newsletter does not significantly increase the odds of winning when in fact it does.

b. First, calculate the value of $\hat{p}$ that corresponds to the border between the acceptance region and the rejection region.

$P(\hat{p} > p_0) = P(z > z_0) = .05$. From Table IV, Appendix B, $z_0 = 1.645$.

$$z = \frac{\hat{p} - p_0}{\sqrt{\frac{p_0 q_0}{n}}} \Rightarrow \hat{p}_0 = p_0 + 1.645\sigma_{\hat{p}} = .5 + 1.645\sqrt{\frac{.5(.5)}{50}} = .5 + .116 = .616$$

$\beta = P(\hat{p} \leq .616$ when $p = .55)$

$= P\left(z < \frac{.616 - .55}{\sqrt{\frac{.55(.45)}{50}}}\right) = P(z \leq .94) = .5 + .3264 = .8264$

c. If n increases, the probability of a Type II error would decrease.

First, calculate the value of $\hat{p}$ that corresponds to the border between the acceptance region and the rejection region.

$$\hat{p} = p_0 + 1.645\sigma_{\hat{p}_0} = .5 + 1.645\sqrt{\frac{.5(.5)}{100}} = .5 + .082 = .582$$

$\beta = P(\hat{p} \leq .582$ when $p = .55)$

$= P\left(z \leq \frac{.582 - .55}{\sqrt{\frac{.55(.45)}{100}}}\right) = P(z \leq .64) = .5 + .2389 = .7389$

8.99 a. To determine whether the mean amount of tuition and fees in 1996–1997 was significantly larger than in 1995–1996, we test:

H_0: $\mu = 12,432$
H_a: $\mu > 12,432$

b. The test statistic is $z = \dfrac{\bar{x} - \mu_0}{\sigma_{\bar{x}}} = \dfrac{13,016 - 12,432}{1,721/\sqrt{30}} = 1.86$

The p-value is $p = P(z \geq 1.86) = .5 - .4686 = .0314$

Since the p-value is so small, H_0 would be rejected for $\alpha = .05$. There is sufficient evidence to indicate that the mean amount for tuition and fees in 1996–1997 was significantly larger than in 1995–1996 at $\alpha = .05$.

c. Statistical significance indicates that the mean amount of tuition and fees differs in 1996–1997 from the mean amount in 1995–96 in a statistical sense. Practical significance indicates whether the difference in the mean amount of tuition and fees is meaningful to the average person. Here, the mean difference between 1995–96 and 1996–97 is approximately $584. For most people, this would be a meaningful difference.

8.101 a. The value of the test statistic is $t = 2.408$. The p-value is .0304, which corresponds to a two-tailed test.

Inferences Based on a Single Sample: Tests of Hypothesis

$P(t \geq 2.408) + P(t \leq -2.408) = .0304$. Since the p-value is less than $\alpha = .10$, H_0 is rejected. There is sufficient evidence to indicate the mean beta coefficient of high technology stock is different than 1.

b. The p-value would be $.0304/2 = .0152$.

8.103 From Exercise 8.102, the rejection region is $z < -2.33$.

$$z = \frac{\bar{x}_0 - \mu_0}{\sigma/\sqrt{n}} \Rightarrow \bar{x}_0 = z_\alpha \frac{\sigma}{\sqrt{n}} + \mu_0 = -2.33\left(\frac{21}{\sqrt{50}}\right) + 880 = 873.1$$

For $\mu = 875$, $\beta = P(\bar{x} \geq 873.1) = P\left(z \geq \dfrac{873.1 - 875}{\dfrac{21}{\sqrt{50}}}\right) = P(z \geq -.64) = .5 + .2389 = .7389$

Power $= 1 - \beta = 1 - .7389 = .2611$

Inferences Based on Two Samples: Confidence Intervals and Tests of Hypotheses Chapter 9

9.1 a. $\mu_1 \pm 2\sigma_{\bar{x}_1} \Rightarrow \mu_1 \pm 2\dfrac{\sigma_1}{\sqrt{n_1}} \Rightarrow 150 \pm 2\dfrac{\sqrt{900}}{\sqrt{100}} \Rightarrow 150 \pm 6 \Rightarrow (144, 156)$

b. $\mu_2 \pm 2\sigma_{\bar{x}_2} \Rightarrow \mu_2 \pm 2\dfrac{\sigma_2}{\sqrt{n_2}} \Rightarrow 150 \pm 2\dfrac{\sqrt{1600}}{\sqrt{100}} \Rightarrow 150 \pm 8 \Rightarrow (142, 158)$

c. $\mu_{\bar{x}_1-\bar{x}_2} = \mu_1 - \mu_2 = 150 - 150 = 0$

$\sigma_{\bar{x}_1-\bar{x}_2} = \sqrt{\dfrac{\sigma_1^2}{n_1} + \dfrac{\sigma_2^2}{n_2}} = \sqrt{\dfrac{900}{100} + \dfrac{1600}{100}} = \sqrt{\dfrac{2500}{100}} = 5$

d. $(\mu_1 - \mu_2) \pm 2\sqrt{\dfrac{\sigma_1^2}{n_1} + \dfrac{\sigma_2^2}{n_2}} \Rightarrow (150 - 150) \pm 2\sqrt{\dfrac{900}{100} + \dfrac{1600}{100}} \Rightarrow 0 \pm 10 \Rightarrow (-10, 10)$

e. The variability of the difference between the sample means is greater than the variability of the individual sample means.

9.3 a. For confidence coefficient .95, $\alpha = .05$ and $\alpha/2 = .025$. From Table IV, Appendix B, $z_{.025} = 1.96$. The confidence interval is:

$(\bar{x}_1 - \bar{x}_2) \pm z_{.025}\sqrt{\dfrac{\sigma_1^2}{n_1} + \dfrac{\sigma_2^2}{n_2}} \Rightarrow (5{,}275 - 5{,}240) \pm 1.96\sqrt{\dfrac{150^2}{400} + \dfrac{200^2}{400}}$

$\Rightarrow 35 \pm 24.5 \Rightarrow (10.5, 59.5)$

We are 95% confident that the difference between the population means is between 10.5 and 59.5.

b. The test statistic is $z = \dfrac{(\bar{x}_1 - \bar{x}_2) - (\mu_1 - \mu_2)}{\sqrt{\dfrac{\sigma_1^2}{n_1} + \dfrac{\sigma_2^2}{n_2}}} = \dfrac{(5275 - 5240) - 0}{\sqrt{\dfrac{150^2}{400} + \dfrac{200^2}{400}}} = 2.8$

The p-value of the test is $P(z \leq -2.8) + P(z \geq 2.8) = 2P(z \geq 2.8) = 2(.5 - .4974)$
$= 2(.0026) = .0052$

Inferences Based on Two Samples: Confidence Intervals and Tests of Hypotheses

Since the *p*-value is so small, there is evidence to reject H_0. There is evidence to indicate the two population means are different for $\alpha > .0052$.

    c.   The *p*-value would be half of the *p*-value in part **b**. The *p*-value = $P(z \geq 2.8) = .5 - .4974 = .0026$. Since the *p*-value is so small, there is evidence to reject H_0. There is evidence to indicate the mean for population 1 is larger than the mean for population 2 for $\alpha > .0026$.

    d.   The test statistic is $z = \dfrac{(\bar{x}_1 - \bar{x}_2) - (\mu_1 - \mu_2)}{\sqrt{\dfrac{\sigma_1^2}{n_1} + \dfrac{\sigma_2^2}{n_2}}} = \dfrac{(5275 - 5240) - 25}{\sqrt{\dfrac{150^2}{400} + \dfrac{200^2}{400}}} = .8$

The *p*-value of the test is $P(z \leq -.8) + P(z \geq .8) = 2P(z \geq .8) = 2(.5 - .2881) = 2(.2119) = .4238$

Since the *p*-value is so large, there is no evidence to reject H_0. There is no evidence to indicate that the difference in the 2 population means is different from 25 for $\alpha \leq .10$.

    e.   We must assume that we have two independent random samples.

9.5   a.   No. Both populations must be normal.

    b.   No. Both populations variances must be equal.

    c.   No. Both populations must be normal.

    d.   Yes.

    e.   No. Both populations must be normal.

9.7   a. $s_p^2 = \dfrac{(n_1 - 1)s_1^2 + (n_2 - 1)s_2^2}{n_1 + n_2 - 2} = \dfrac{(25 - 1)120 + (25 - 1)100}{25 + 25 - 2} = \dfrac{5280}{48} = 110$

    b. $s_p^2 = \dfrac{(20 - 1)12 + (10 - 1)20}{20 + 10 - 2} = \dfrac{408}{28} = 14.5714$

    c. $s_p^2 = \dfrac{(6 - 1).15 + (10 - 1).2}{6 + 10 - 2} = \dfrac{2.55}{14} = .1821$

    d. $s_p^2 = \dfrac{(16 - 1)3000 + (17 - 1)2500}{16 + 17 - 2} = \dfrac{85,000}{31} = 2741.9355$

    e. s_p^2 falls near the variance with the larger sample size.

9.9   a. $\sigma_{\bar{x}_1 - \bar{x}_2} = \sqrt{\dfrac{\sigma_1^2}{n_1} + \dfrac{\sigma_2^2}{n_2}} = \sqrt{\dfrac{9}{100} + \dfrac{16}{100}} = \sqrt{.25} = .5$

b. The sampling distribution of $\bar{x}_1 - \bar{x}_2$ is approximately normal by the Central Limit Theorem since $n_1 \geq 30$ and $n_2 \geq 30$.

$\mu_{\bar{x}_1 - \bar{x}_2} = \mu_1 - \mu_2 = 10$

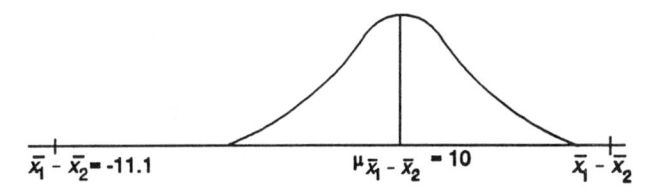

c. $\bar{x}_1 - \bar{x}_2 = 15.5 - 26.6 = -11.1$

Yes, it appears that $\bar{x}_1 - \bar{x}_2 = -11.1$ contradicts the null hypothesis $H_0: \mu_1 - \mu_2 = 10$.

d. The rejection region requires $\alpha/2 = .025 = .05/2$ in each tail of the z-distribution. From Table IV, Appendix B, $z_{.025} = 1.96$. The rejection region is $z < -1.96$ or $z > 1.96$.

e. $H_0: \mu_1 - \mu_2 = 10$
$H_a: \mu_1 - \mu_2 \neq 10$

The test statistic is $z = \dfrac{(\bar{x}_1 - \bar{x}_2) - 10}{\sqrt{\dfrac{\sigma_1^2}{n_1} + \dfrac{\sigma_2^2}{n_2}}} = \dfrac{(15.5 - 26.6) - 10}{.5} = -42.2$

The rejection region is $z < -1.96$ or $z > 1.96$. (Refer to part **d**.)

Since the observed value of the test statistic falls in the rejection region ($z = -42.2 < -1.96$), H_0 is rejected. There is sufficient evidence to indicate the difference in the population means is not equal to 10 at $\alpha = .05$.

9.11 a. The test statistic is $z = -1.576$ and the p-value $= .1150$. Since the p-value is not small, there is no evidence to reject H_0 for $\alpha \leq .10$. There is insufficient evidence to indicate the two population means differ for $\alpha \leq .10$.

b. If the alternative hypothesis had been one-tailed, the p-value would be half of the value for the two-tailed test. Here, p-value $= .1150/2 = .0575$.

There is no evidence to reject H_0 for $\alpha = .05$. There is insufficient evidence to indicate the mean for population 1 is less than the mean for population 2 at $\alpha = .05$.

There is evidence to reject H_0 for $\alpha > .0575$. There is sufficient evidence to indicate the mean for population 1 is less than the mean for population 2 at $\alpha > .0575$.

9.13 a. $s_p^2 = \dfrac{(n_1 - 1)s_1^2 + (n_2 - 1)s_2^2}{n_1 + n_2 - 2} = \dfrac{(17 - 1)3.4^2 + (12 - 1)4.8^2}{17 + 12 - 2} = 16.237$

The test statistic is $t = \dfrac{(\bar{x}_1 - \bar{x}_2) - 0}{\sqrt{s_p^2 \left(\dfrac{1}{n_1} + \dfrac{1}{n_2}\right)}} = \dfrac{(5.4 - 7.9) - 0}{\sqrt{16.237 \left(\dfrac{1}{17} + \dfrac{1}{12}\right)}} = -1.646$

The p-value = $P(t \le -1.646) + P(t \ge 1.646) = 2P(t \ge 1.646)$.

Using Table VI with df = $n_1 + n_2 = 17 + 12 - 2 = 27$, $P(t \ge 1.646)$ is between .05 and .10. Thus, $2(.05) < p$-value $< 2(.10)$ or $.10 < p$-value $< .20$.

These values correspond to those found in the printout.

Since the p-value is not small, there is no evidence to reject H_0. There is no evidence to indicate the means are different for $\alpha \le .10$.

b. For confidence coefficient .95, $\alpha = .05$ and $\alpha/2 = .025$. From Table VI, Appendix B, with df = $n_1 + n_2 - 2 = 17 + 12 - 2 = 27$, $t_{.025} = 2.052$. The confidence interval is:

$$(\bar{x}_1 - \bar{x}_2) \pm t_{.025}\sqrt{s_p^2\left[\frac{1}{n_1} + \frac{1}{n_2}\right]} \quad \text{where } t \text{ has 27 df}$$

$$\Rightarrow (5.4 - 7.9) \pm 2.052\sqrt{16.237\left[\frac{1}{17} + \frac{1}{12}\right]} \Rightarrow -2.50 \pm 3.12 \Rightarrow (-5.62, 0.62)$$

9.15 a. Let μ_1 = mean age of nonpurchasers and μ_2 = mean age of purchasers.

To determine if there is a difference in the mean age of purchasers and nonpurchasers, we test:

H_0: $\mu_1 - \mu_2 = 0$
H_a: $\mu_1 - \mu_2 \ne 0$

The test statistic is $t = 1.9557$ (from printout).

The rejection region requires $\alpha/2 = .10/2 = .05$ in each tail of the t-distribution with df = $n_1 + n_2 - 2 = 20 + 20 - 2 = 38$. From Table VI, Appendix B, $t_{.05} \approx 1.684$. The rejection region is $t < -1.684$ or $t > 1.684$.

Since the observed value of the test statistic falls in the rejection region ($t = 1.9557 > 1.684$), H_0 is rejected. There is sufficient evidence to indicate the mean age of purchasers and nonpurchasers differ at $\alpha = .10$.

b. The necessary assumptions are:

1. Both sampled populations are approximately normal.
2. The population variances are equal.
3. The samples are randomly and independently sampled.

c. The observed significance level is $p = .0579$. Since the p-value is less than α (.0579 < .10), H_0 is rejected. This is the same result as in part a.

d. For confidence coefficient .90, $\alpha = 1 - .90 = .10$ and $\alpha/2 = .10/2 = .05$. From Table VI, Appendix B, with df = 38, $t_{.05} \approx 1.684$. The confidence interval is:

$$(\bar{x}_2 - \bar{x}_1) \pm t_{.05}\sqrt{s_p^2\left[\frac{1}{n_2} + \frac{1}{n_1}\right]} \Rightarrow (39.8 - 47.2) \pm 1.684\sqrt{143.1684\left[\frac{1}{20} + \frac{1}{20}\right]}$$

$$\Rightarrow -7.4 \pm 6.382 \Rightarrow (-13.772, -1.028)$$

We are 90% confident that the difference in mean ages between purchasers and nonpurchasers is between -13.772 and -1.028.

9.17   a.   To determine if the merged firms generally have smaller price earnings ratios, we test:

H_0: $\mu_1 = \mu_2$
H_a: $\mu_1 < \mu_2$

where μ_1 = mean price earnings ratio for merged firms, and
μ_2 = mean price earnings ratio for nonmerged firms.

The test statistic is $z = \dfrac{(\bar{x}_1 - \bar{x}_2) - 0}{\sqrt{\dfrac{\sigma_1^2}{n_1} + \dfrac{\sigma_2^2}{n_2}}} = \dfrac{(7.295 - 14.666) - 0}{\sqrt{\dfrac{7.374^2}{44} + \dfrac{16.089^2}{44}}} = \dfrac{-7.371}{2.6681} = -2.76$

The rejection region requires $\alpha = .05$ in the lower tail of the z-distribution. From Table IV, Appendix B, $z_{.05} = -1.645$. The rejection region is $z < -1.645$.

Since the observed value of the test statistic falls in the rejection region ($z = -2.76 < -1.645$), H_0 is rejected. There is sufficient evidence to indicate the mean price earnings ratio for merged firms is smaller than that for nonmerged firms at $\alpha = .05$.

     b.   The p-value is $P(z \leq -2.76) = .5 - .4971 = .0029$.

     c.   No. If the price-earnings ratios cannot be negative, the populations cannot be normal because the standard deviations for both groups are larger than the means. Thus, there can be no observations more than one standard deviation below the mean.

     d.   Since the sample sizes are large ($n_1 = n_2 = 44$), the Central Limit Theorem says the sampling distributions of $\bar{x}_1$ and $\bar{x}_2$ are normal. Thus, our answer to part c does not impact the validity of the inference.

9.19   a.   If we consider those currently in the Senate as a sample of all those who could be in the Senate, then we cannot answer the question. In order to answer the question, we must know the standard deviations of the ages for both groups of senators. If we assume that those currently in the Senate as populations rather than samples, then we could answer the question. We would assume that the mean ages would be population means rather than sample means.

     b.   Let μ_1 = mean age at which the 13 retiring senators began their service and μ_2 = mean age at which the other retiring senators began their service. To determine if the 13 senators who decided to retire in 1995–1996 began their careers at a younger average age than did the rest of their colleagues, we test:

H_0: $\mu_1 - \mu_2 = 0$
H_a: $\mu_1 - \mu_2 < 0$

9.21   a.   To determine if the mean annual percentage turnover for U.S. plants exceeds that for Japanese plants, we test:

H_0: $\mu_1 - \mu_2 = 0$
H_a: $\mu_1 - \mu_2 > 0$

The test statistic is $t = 4.46$ (from printout).

The rejection region requires $\alpha = .05$ in the upper tail of the t-distribution with df = $n_1 + n_2 - 2 = 5 + 5 - 2 = 8$. From Table VI, Appendix B, $t_{.05} = 1.860$. The rejection region is $t > 1.860$.

Since the observed value of the test statistic falls in the rejection region ($t = 4.46 > 1.860$), H_0 is rejected. There is sufficient evidence to indicate the mean annual percentage turnover for U.S. plants exceeds that for Japanese plants at $\alpha = .05$.

b. The observed significance is $.0031/2 = .00155$.

Since the p-value is so small, there is evidence to reject H_0 for $\alpha > .005$.

c. The necessary assumptions are:

1. Both sampled populations are approximately normal.
2. The population variances are equal.
3. The samples are randomly and independently sampled.

There is no indication that the populations are not normal. Both sample variances are similar, so there is no evidence the population variances are unequal. There is no indication the assumptions are not valid.

9.23 a. Let μ_1 = mean number of cigarettes per week for the treatment group and μ_2 = mean number of cigarettes per week for the control group.

For confidence coefficient .95, $\alpha = .05$ and $\alpha/2 = .025$. From Table VI, Appendix B, with df = $n_1 + n_2 - 2 = 35 + 17 - 2 = 50$, $t_{.025} \approx 2.021$. The confidence interval is:

$$(\bar{x}_1 - \bar{x}_2) \pm t_{.025} \sqrt{s_p^2 \left(\frac{1}{n_1} + \frac{1}{n_2}\right)}$$

For Beginning time period:

$$s_p^2 = \frac{(n_1 - 1)s_1^2 + (n_2 - 1)s_2^2}{n_1 + n_2 - 2} = \frac{(35 - 1)71.20^2 + (17 - 1)67.45^2}{35 + 17 - 2} = 4903.06$$

$$\Rightarrow (165.09 - 159.00) \pm 2.021 \sqrt{4903.06 \left(\frac{1}{35} + \frac{1}{17}\right)}$$

$$\Rightarrow 6.09 \pm 41.835 \Rightarrow (-35.745, 47.925)$$

We are 95% confident that the difference in the mean number of cigarettes smoked per week for the two groups is between -35.745 and 47.925.

For First follow-up period:

$$s_p^2 = \frac{(n_1 - 1)s_1^2 + (n_2 - 1)s_2^2}{n_1 + n_2 - 2} = \frac{(35 - 1)69.08^2 + (17 - 1)66.80^2}{35 + 17 - 2} = 4672.91$$

$$\Rightarrow (105.00 - 157.24) \pm 2.021 \sqrt{4672.91 \left(\frac{1}{35} + \frac{1}{17}\right)}$$

$$\Rightarrow -52.24 \pm 40.842 \Rightarrow (-93.082, -11.398)$$

We are 95% confident that the difference in the mean number of cigarettes smoked per week for the two groups is between -93.082 and -11.398.

For Second follow-up period:

$$s_p^2 = \frac{(n_1 - 1)s_1^2 + (n_2 - 1)s_2^2}{n_1 + n_2 - 2} = \frac{(35 - 1)69.08^2 + (17 - 1)65.73^2}{35 + 17 - 2} = 4627.53$$

$$\Rightarrow (111.11 - 159.52) \pm 2.021 \sqrt{4627.53 \left(\frac{1}{35} + \frac{1}{17}\right)}$$

$$\Rightarrow -48.41 \pm 40.643 \Rightarrow (-89.053, -7.767)$$

We are 95% confident that the difference in the mean number of cigarettes smoked per week for the two groups is between -89.053 and -7.767.

For Third follow-up period:

$$s_p^2 = \frac{(n_1 - 1)s_1^2 + (n_2 - 1)s_2^2}{n_1 + n_2 - 2} = \frac{(35 - 1)67.59^2 + (17 - 1)64.41^2}{35 + 17 - 2} = 4434.08$$

$$\Rightarrow (120.20 - 157.88) \pm 2.021 \sqrt{4434.08 \left(\frac{1}{35} + \frac{1}{17}\right)}$$

$$\Rightarrow -37.68 \pm 39.784 \Rightarrow (-77.464, 2.104)$$

We are 95% confident that the difference in the mean number of cigarettes smoked per week for the two groups is between -77.464 and 2.104.

For Fourth follow-up period:

$$s_p^2 = \frac{(n_1 - 1)s_1^2 + (n_2 - 1)s_2^2}{n_1 + n_2 - 2} = \frac{(35 - 1)74.09^2 + (17 - 1)67.01^2}{35 + 17 - 2} = 5169.65$$

$$\Rightarrow (123.63 - 162.17) \pm 2.021 \sqrt{5169.65 \left(\frac{1}{35} + \frac{1}{17}\right)}$$

$$\Rightarrow -38.54 \pm 42.958 \Rightarrow (-81.498, 4.418)$$

We are 95% confident that the difference in the mean number of cigarettes smoked per week for the two groups is between -81.498 and 4.418.

b. For each time period, we must make the following assumptions:

1. Both populations being sampled from are normal
2. The two population variances are equal.
3. Independent random samples are selected from each population.

9.25 a. Let μ_1 = mean rate for cable companies with no competition and μ_2 = mean rate for cable companies with competition.

To determine if the mean rate for cable companies with no competition is higher than that for companies with competition, we test:

$H_0: \mu_1 - \mu_2 = 0$
$H_a: \mu_1 - \mu_2 > 0$

b. Some preliminary calculations are:

$$\bar{x}_1 = \frac{\sum x_1}{n_1} = \frac{144.83}{6} = 24.138$$

$$s_1^2 = \frac{\sum x_1^2 - \frac{(\sum x_1)^2}{n_1}}{n_1 - 1} = \frac{3552.3193 - \frac{144.83^2}{6}}{5} = 11.2729$$

$$\bar{x}_2 = \frac{\sum x_2}{n_2} = \frac{119.2}{6} = 19.867$$

$$s_2^2 = \frac{\sum x_2^2 - \frac{(\sum x_2)^2}{n_2}}{n_2 - 1} = \frac{2391.7322 - \frac{119.2^2}{6}}{5} = 4.7251$$

$$s_p^2 = \frac{(n_1 - 1)s_1^2 + (n_2 - 1)s_2^2}{n_1 + n_2 - 2} = \frac{5(11.2729) + 5(4.7251)}{6 + 6 - 2} = 7.999$$

The test statistic is $t = \dfrac{(\bar{x}_1 - \bar{x}_2) - D_0}{\sqrt{s_p^2 \left(\dfrac{1}{n_1} + \dfrac{1}{n_2}\right)}} = \dfrac{24.138 - 19.867 - 0}{\sqrt{7.999\left(\dfrac{1}{6} + \dfrac{1}{6}\right)}} = 2.616$

The p-value = $P(t \geq 2.616)$. Using Table VI, Appendix B, with df = $n_1 + n_2 - 2 = 6 + 6 - 2 = 10$, $.01 < p\text{-value} < .025$. Since the p-value is less than $\alpha = .05$, there is evidence to reject H_0. There is sufficient evidence to indicate the mean rate for cable companies with no competition is higher than that for companies with competition for $\alpha = .05$.

c. We must assume:

1. Both populations sampled from are normally distributed.
2. The variances for the two populations are equal.
3. Independent random samples were selected from each population.

9.27 a. The rejection region requires $\alpha = .05$ in the upper tail of the t-distribution with df = $n_D - 1 = 12 - 1 = 11$. From Table VI, Appendix B, $t_{.05} = 1.796$. The rejection region is $t > 1.796$.

b. From Table VI, with df = $n_D - 1 = 24 - 1 = 23$, $t_{.10} = 1.319$. The rejection region is $t > 1.319$.

c. From Table VI, with df = $n_D - 1 = 4 - 1 = 3$, $t_{.025} = 3.182$. The rejection region is $t > 3.182$.

d. From Table VI, with df = $n_D - 1 = 8 - 1 = 7$, $t_{.01} = 2.998$. The rejection region is $t > 2.998$.

9.29 Let μ_1 = mean of population 1 and μ_2 = mean of population 2.

a. H_0: $\mu_D = 0$
H_a: $\mu_D < 0$ where $\mu_D = \mu_1 - \mu_2$

b. The test statistic is $t = -5.29$ and the p-value = .0002.

Since the p-value is so small, there is evidence to reject H_0. There is evidence to indicate the mean for population 2 is larger than the mean for population 1 for $\alpha > .0002$.

c. The confidence interval is $(-5.284, -2.116)$. We are 95% confident the difference in the 2 population means is between -5.284 and -2.116.

d. We must assume that the population of differences is normal, and the sample of differences is randomly selected.

9.31 Some preliminary calculations:

Pair	Difference $x - y$
1	$55 - 44 = 11$
2	$68 - 55 = 13$
3	$40 - 25 = 15$
4	$55 - 56 = -1$
5	$75 - 62 = 13$
6	$52 - 38 = 14$
7	$49 - 31 = 18$

$$\bar{x}_D = \frac{\sum x_D}{n_D} = \frac{83}{7} = 11.86$$

$$s_D^2 = \frac{\sum x_D^2 - \frac{(\sum x_D)^2}{n_D}}{n_D - 1} = \frac{1205 - \frac{83^2}{7}}{7 - 1} = 36.8095$$

$$s_D = \sqrt{s_D^2} = \sqrt{36.8095} = 6.0671$$

a. H_0: $\mu_D = 10$
H_a: $\mu_D \neq 10$ where $\mu_D = (\mu_1 - \mu_2)$

The test statistic is $t = \dfrac{\bar{x}_D - D_0}{s_D/\sqrt{n_D}} = \dfrac{11.86 - 10}{6.0671/\sqrt{7}} = \dfrac{1.86}{2.2931} = .81$

The rejection region requires $\alpha/2 = .05/2 = .025$ in each tail of the t-distribution with df $= n_D - 1 = 7 - 1 = 6$. From Table VI, Appendix B, $t_{.025} = 2.447$. The rejection region is $t < -2.447$ or $t > 2.447$.

Since the observed value of the test statistic does not fall in the rejection region ($t = .81 \not> 2.447$), H_0 is not rejected. There is insufficient evidence to conclude $\mu_D \neq 10$ at $\alpha = .05$.

b. p-value $= P(t \leq -.81) + P(t \geq .81) = 2P(t \geq .81)$

Using Table VI, Appendix B, with df $= 6$, $P(t \geq .81)$ is greater than .10.

Thus, $2P(t \geq .81)$ is greater than .20.

The probability of observing a value of t as large as .81 or as small as $-.81$ if, in fact, $\mu_D = 10$ is greater than .20. We would conclude that there is insufficient evidence to suggest $\mu_D \neq 10$.

9.33 Some preliminary calculations are:

Working Days	Difference (Design 1 − Design 2)
8/16	−53
8/17	−271
8/18	−206
8/19	−266
8/20	−213
8/23	−183
8/24	−118
8/25	−87

$\bar{x}_D = \dfrac{\sum x_D}{n_D} = \dfrac{-1{,}397}{8} = -174.625$

$s_D^2 = \dfrac{\sum x_D^2 - \dfrac{(\sum x_D)^2}{n_D}}{n_D - 1} = \dfrac{289{,}793 - \dfrac{(-1{,}397)^2}{8}}{8 - 1} = 6{,}548.839$

$s_D = \sqrt{s_D^2} = \sqrt{6{,}548.839} = 80.925$

a. For confidence coefficient .95, $\alpha = .05$ and $\alpha/2 = .05/2 = .025$. From Table VI, Appendix B, with df $= n_D - 1 = 8 - 1 = 7$, $t_{.025} = 2.365$. The 95% confidence interval is:

$\bar{x}_D \pm t_{.025} \dfrac{s_D}{\sqrt{n_D}} \Rightarrow -174.625 \pm 2.365 \dfrac{80.925}{\sqrt{8}} \Rightarrow -174.625 \pm 67.666$

$\Rightarrow (-242.291, -106.959)$

We are 95% confident that the difference in mean daily output of the two designs is between -242.291 and -106.959.

b. We must assume that the population of differences is normal and that the sample of differences is randomly selected.

c. Yes. Since 0 is not contained in the confidence interval and the endpoints are both negative, there is evidence to indicate that Design 2 is superior to Design 1.

9.35 Some preliminary calculations are:

$$\bar{x}_1 = \frac{\sum x_1}{n_1} = \frac{64.3}{6} = 10.7167 \qquad \bar{x}_2 = \frac{\sum x_2}{n_2} = \frac{61.8}{6} = 10.3$$

$$s_1^2 = \frac{\sum x_1^2 - \frac{(\sum x_1)^2}{n_1}}{n_1 - 1} = \frac{704.43 - \frac{64.3^2}{6}}{6 - 1} = 3.0697$$

$$s_2^2 = \frac{\sum x_2^2 - \frac{(\sum x_2)^2}{n_2}}{n_2 - 1} = \frac{653.06 - \frac{61.8^2}{6}}{6 - 1} = 3.304$$

$$s_p^2 = \frac{(n_1 - 1)s_1^2 + (n_2 - 1)s_2^2}{n_1 + n_2 - 2} = \frac{(6 - 1)3.0697 + (6 - 1)3.304}{6 + 6 - 2} = 3.18685$$

a. To determine if there is a difference in the mean strength of the two types of shocks, we test:

$H_0: \mu_1 - \mu_2 = 0$
$H_a: \mu_1 - \mu_2 \neq 0$

The test statistic is $t = \dfrac{(\bar{x}_1 - \bar{x}_2) - D_0}{\sqrt{s_p^2 \left(\dfrac{1}{n_1} + \dfrac{1}{n_2}\right)}} = \dfrac{(10.7167 - 10.3) - 0}{\sqrt{3.18685 \left(\dfrac{1}{6} + \dfrac{1}{6}\right)}} = .40$

The rejection region requires $\alpha/2 = .05/2 = .025$ in each tail of the t-distribution with df $= n_1 + n_2 - 2 = 6 + 6 - 2 = 10$. From Table VI, Appendix B, $t_{.025} = 2.228$. The rejection region is $t < -2.228$ or $t > 2.228$.

Since the observed value of the test statistic does not fall in the rejection region ($t = .40 \not> 2.228$), H_0 is not rejected. There is insufficient evidence to indicate a difference between the mean strengths for the two types of shocks at $\alpha = .05$.

b. For confidence coefficient .95, $\alpha = 1 - .95 = .05$ and $\alpha/2 = .05/2 = .025$. From Table VI, Appendix B, with df $= n_1 + n_2 - 2 = 6 + 6 - 2 = 10$, $t_{.025} = 2.228$. The confidence interval is:

$$(\bar{x}_1 - \bar{x}_2) \pm t_{.025}\sqrt{s_p^2 \left(\frac{1}{n_1} + \frac{1}{n_2}\right)} \Rightarrow (10.7167 - 10.3) \pm 2.228\sqrt{3.18685\left(\frac{1}{6} + \frac{1}{6}\right)}$$
$$\Rightarrow .4167 \pm 2.2963 \Rightarrow (-1.8796, 2.7130)$$

We are 95% confident the mean strength of the manufacturer's shock exceeds the mean strength of the competitor's shock by anywhere from -1.8796 to 2.7130.

c. The confidence interval obtained in part b is wider than that found in Exercise 9.34. This interval is wider because the standard deviation is larger for the independent samples than for the matched-pair design.

d. The results of an unpaired analysis are **not** valid when the data are collected from a paired experiment. The assumption of independent samples is not valid.

9.37 a. Let μ_D = mean difference in inflation forecasts between June 1995 and January 1996. To determine if the group of economists was more optimistic about prospects for low inflation in late 1996 than it was for late 1995, we test:

$H_0: \mu_D = 0$
$H_a: \mu_D > 0$

b. Some preliminary calculations are:

Economist	Difference (June 1995 – January 1996)
Maureen Allyn	.7
Wayne Angell	.3
David Blitzer	–.1
Michael Cosgrove	.5
Gail Fosler	–.1
Irwin Kellner	1.0
Donald Ratajczak	.6
Thomas Synott	.3
John Williams	.7

$$\bar{x}_D = \frac{\sum x_D}{n_D} = \frac{3.9}{9} = .4333$$

$$s_D^2 = \frac{\sum x_D^2 - \frac{(\sum x_D)^2}{n_D}}{n_D - 1} = \frac{2.79 - \frac{(3.9)^2}{9}}{9 - 1} = .1375$$

$$s_D = \sqrt{s_D^2} = \sqrt{.1375} = .3708$$

$H_0: \mu_D = 0$
$H_a: \mu_D > 0$

The test statistic is $t = \dfrac{\bar{x}_D}{\frac{s_D}{\sqrt{n_D}}} = \dfrac{.4333}{\frac{.3708}{\sqrt{9}}} = 3.506$

The rejection region requires $\alpha = .05$ in the upper tail of the t-distribution with df = $n_D - 1$ = 9 – 1 = 8. From Table VI, Appendix B, $t_{.05} = 1.860$. The rejection region is $t > 1.860$.

Since the observed value of the test statistic falls in the rejection region ($t = 3.506 > 1.860$), H_0 is rejected. There is sufficient evidence to indicate that the group of economists was more optimistic about prospects for low inflation in late 1996 than it was for late 1995 at $\alpha = .05$.

9.39 Let μ_1 = mean number of swims by male rat pups and μ_2 = mean number of swims by female rat pups. Then $\mu_D = \mu_1 - \mu_2$. To determine if there is a difference in the mean number of swims required by male and female rat pups, we test:

H_0: $\mu_D = 0$
H_a: $\mu_D \neq 0$

The test statistic is $t = 0.46$ (from printout)

The p-value is $p = 0.65$.

Since the p-value is greater than α ($p = .65 > .10$), H_0 is not rejected. There is insufficient evidence to indicate there is a difference in the mean number of swims required by male and female rat pups at $\alpha = .10$.

9.41 Remember that $\hat{p}_1$ and $\hat{p}_2$ can be viewed as means of the number of successes per n trials in the respective samples. Therefore, when n_1 and n_2 are large, $\hat{p}_1 - \hat{p}_2$ is approximately normal by the Central Limit Theorem.

9.43 a. The rejection region requires $\alpha = .01$ in the lower tail of the z-distribution. From Table IV, Appendix B, $z_{.01} = 2.33$. The rejection region is $z < -2.33$.

b. The rejection region requires $\alpha = .025$ in the lower tail of the z-distribution. From Table IV, Appendix B, $z_{.025} = 1.96$. The rejection region is $z < -1.96$.

c. The rejection region requires $\alpha = .05$ in the lower tail of the z-distribution. From Table IV, Appendix B, $z_{.05} = 1.645$. The rejection region is $z < -1.645$.

d. The rejection region requires $\alpha = .10$ in the lower tail of the z-distribution. From Table IV, Appendix B, $z_{.10} = 1.28$. The rejection region is $z < -1.28$.

9.45 For confidence coefficient .95, $\alpha = 1 - .95 = .05$ and $\alpha/2 = .05/2 = .025$. From Table IV, Appendix B, $z_{.025} = 1.96$. The 95% confidence interval for $p_1 - p_2$ is approximately:

a. $(\hat{p}_1 - \hat{p}_2) \pm z_{\alpha/2} \sqrt{\dfrac{\hat{p}_1 \hat{q}_1}{n_1} + \dfrac{\hat{p}_2 \hat{q}_2}{n_2}} \Rightarrow (.65 - .58) \pm 1.96 \sqrt{\dfrac{.65(1 - .65)}{400} + \dfrac{.58(1 - .58)}{400}}$
$\Rightarrow .07 \pm .067 \Rightarrow (.003, .137)$

b. $(\hat{p}_1 - \hat{p}_2) \pm z_{\alpha/2} \sqrt{\dfrac{\hat{p}_1 \hat{q}_1}{n_1} + \dfrac{\hat{p}_2 \hat{q}_2}{n_2}} \Rightarrow (.31 - .25) \pm 1.96 \sqrt{\dfrac{.31(1 - .31)}{180} + \dfrac{.25(1 - .25)}{250}}$
$\Rightarrow .06 \pm .086 \Rightarrow (-.026, .146)$

c. $(\hat{p}_1 - \hat{p}_2) \pm z_{\alpha/2} \sqrt{\dfrac{\hat{p}_1 \hat{q}_1}{n_1} + \dfrac{\hat{p}_2 \hat{q}_2}{n_2}} \Rightarrow (.46 - .61) \pm 1.96 \sqrt{\dfrac{.46(1 - .46)}{100} + \dfrac{.61(1 - .61)}{120}}$
$\Rightarrow -.15 \pm .131 \Rightarrow (-.281, -.019)$

9.47 $\hat{p} = \dfrac{n_1 \hat{p}_1 + n_2 \hat{p}_2}{n_1 + n_2} = \dfrac{55(.7) + 65(.6)}{55 + 65} = \dfrac{78}{120} = .65$ $\hat{q} = 1 - \hat{p} = 1 - .65 = .35$

H_0: $p_1 - p_2 = 0$
H_a: $p_1 - p_2 > 0$

Inferences Based on Two Samples: Confidence Intervals and Tests of Hypotheses

The test statistic is $z = \dfrac{(\hat{p}_1 - \hat{p}_2) - 0}{\sqrt{\hat{p}\hat{q}\left[\dfrac{1}{n_1} + \dfrac{1}{n_2}\right]}} = \dfrac{(.7 - .6) - 0}{\sqrt{.65(.35)\left[\dfrac{1}{55} + \dfrac{1}{65}\right]}} = \dfrac{.1}{.08739} = 1.14$

The rejection region requires $\alpha = .05$ in the upper tail of the z-distribution. From Table IV, Appendix B, $z_{.05} = 1.645$. The rejection region is $z > 1.645$.

Since the observed value of the test statistic does not fall in the rejection region ($z = 1.14 \not> 1.645$), H_0 is not rejected. There is insufficient evidence to indicate the proportion from population 1 is greater than that for population 2 at $\alpha = .05$.

9.49 a. Let p_1 = error rate for supermarkets and p_2 = error rate for department stores. To see if the samples are sufficiently large:

$$\hat{p}_1 \pm 3\sigma_{\hat{p}_1} \Rightarrow \hat{p}_1 \pm 3\sqrt{\dfrac{p_1 q_1}{n_1}} \Rightarrow \hat{p}_1 \pm 3\sqrt{\dfrac{\hat{p}_1 \hat{q}_1}{n_1}} \Rightarrow .0347 \pm 3\sqrt{\dfrac{.0347(.9653)}{800}}$$
$$\Rightarrow .0347 \pm .0194 \Rightarrow (.0153, .0541)$$

$$\hat{p}_2 \pm 3\sigma_{\hat{p}_2} \Rightarrow \hat{p}_2 \pm 3\sqrt{\dfrac{p_2 q_2}{n_2}} \Rightarrow \hat{p}_2 \pm 3\sqrt{\dfrac{\hat{p}_2 \hat{q}_2}{n_2}} \Rightarrow .0915 \pm 3\sqrt{\dfrac{.0915(.9085)}{900}}$$
$$\Rightarrow .0915 \pm .0288 \Rightarrow (.0627, .1203)$$

Since both intervals lie within the interval (0, 1), the normal approximation will be adequate.

b. For confidence coefficient .98, $\alpha = .02$ and $\alpha/2 = .02/2 = .01$. From Table IV, Appendix B, $z_{.01} = 2.33$. The 95% confidence interval is:

$$(\hat{p}_1 - \hat{p}_2) \pm z_{.01}\sqrt{\dfrac{\hat{p}_1 \hat{q}_1}{n_1} + \dfrac{\hat{p}_2 \hat{q}_2}{n_2}}$$
$$\Rightarrow (.0347 - .0915) \pm 2.33\sqrt{\dfrac{.0347(.9653)}{800} + \dfrac{.0915(.9085)}{900}} \Rightarrow -.0568 \pm .0270$$
$$\Rightarrow (-.0838, -.0298)$$

We are 98% confident that the difference in the error rates between supermarkets and department stores is between $-.0838$ and $-.0298$.

c. We must assume that the sample sizes are sufficiently large and that the two samples were independently and randomly selected.

9.51 To determine if there is a difference in the proportions of consumer/commercial and industrial product managers who are at least 40 years old, we could use either a test of hypothesis or a confidence interval. Since we are asked only to determine if there is a difference in the proportions, we will use a test of hypothesis.

Let p_1 = proportion of consumer/commercial product managers at least 40 years old and p_2 = proportion of industrial product managers at least 40 years old.

$\hat{p}_1 = .40$ $\hat{q}_1 = 1 - \hat{p}_1 = 1 - .40 = .60$
$\hat{p}_2 = .54$ $\hat{q}_2 = 1 - \hat{p}_2 = 1 - .54 = .46$

$\hat{p} = \dfrac{n_1\hat{p}_1 + n_2\hat{p}_2}{n_1 + n_2} = \dfrac{93(.40) + 212(.54)}{93 + 212} = .497$ $\hat{q} = 1 - \hat{p} = 1 - .497 = .503$

To see if the samples are sufficiently large:

$\hat{p}_1 \pm 3\sigma_{\hat{p}_1} \Rightarrow \hat{p}_1 \pm 3\sqrt{\dfrac{p_1 q_1}{n_1}} \Rightarrow \hat{p}_1 \pm 3\sqrt{\dfrac{\hat{p}_1 \hat{q}_1}{n_1}} \Rightarrow .40 \pm 3\sqrt{\dfrac{.40(.60)}{93}}$
$\Rightarrow .40 \pm .152 \Rightarrow (.248, .552)$

$\hat{p}_2 \pm 3\sigma_{\hat{p}_2} \Rightarrow \hat{p}_2 \pm 3\sqrt{\dfrac{p_2 q_2}{n_2}} \Rightarrow \hat{p}_2 \pm 3\sqrt{\dfrac{\hat{p}_2 \hat{q}_2}{n_2}} \Rightarrow .54 \pm 3\sqrt{\dfrac{.54(.46)}{212}}$
$\Rightarrow .54 \pm .103 \Rightarrow (.437, .643)$

Since both intervals lie within the interval (0, 1), the normal approximation will be adequate.

To determine if there is a difference in the proportions of consumer/commercial and industrial product managers who are at least 40 years old, we test:

H_0: $p_1 - p_2 = 0$
H_a: $p_1 - p_2 \neq 0$

The test statistic is $z = \dfrac{(\hat{p}_1 - \hat{p}_2) - 0}{\sqrt{\hat{p}\hat{q}\left[\dfrac{1}{n_1} + \dfrac{1}{n_2}\right]}} = \dfrac{(.40 - .54) - 0}{\sqrt{.497(.503)\left[\dfrac{1}{93} + \dfrac{1}{212}\right]}} = -2.25$

We will use $\alpha = .05$. The rejection region requires $\alpha/2 = .05/2 = .025$ in each tail of the z-distribution. From Table IV, Appendix B, $z_{.025} = 1.96$. The rejection region is $z < -1.96$ or $z > 1.96$.

Since the observed value of the test statistic falls in the rejection region ($z = -2.25 < -1.96$), H_0 is rejected. There is sufficient evidence to indicate that there is a difference in the proportions of consumer/commercial and industrial product managers who are at least 40 years old at $\alpha = .05$.

Since the test statistic is negative, there is evidence to indicate that the industrial product managers tend to be older than the consumer/commercial product managers.

9.53 a. Let p_1 = proportion of new fathers using the program and p_2 = proportion of new fathers that wants to participate.

To determine if there is a difference in the proportion of new fathers using the program and the proportion of new fathers who wants to participate, we test:

H_0: $p_1 - p_2 = 0$
H_a: $p_1 - p_2 \neq 0$

b. The sample sizes are large enough if the interval $\hat{p}_i \pm 3\sigma_{\hat{p}_i}$ is contained in the interval (0, 1).

$$\hat{p}_1 = \frac{x_1}{n_1} = \frac{9}{96} = .094 \qquad \hat{p}_2 = \frac{x_2}{n_2} = \frac{35}{100} = .35$$

$$\hat{p}_1 \pm 3\sigma_{\hat{p}_1} \Rightarrow \hat{p}_1 \pm 3\sqrt{\frac{\hat{p}_1 \hat{q}_1}{n_1}} \Rightarrow .094 \pm 3\sqrt{\frac{.094(.906)}{96}} \Rightarrow .094 \pm .089 \Rightarrow (.005, .183)$$

$$\hat{p}_2 \pm 3\sigma_{\hat{p}_2} \Rightarrow \hat{p}_2 \pm 3\sqrt{\frac{\hat{p}_2 \hat{q}_2}{n_2}} \Rightarrow .35 \pm 3\sqrt{\frac{.35(.65)}{100}} \Rightarrow .35 \pm .143 \Rightarrow (.207, .493)$$

Since both intervals are contained in the interval (0, 1), the normal approximation is valid.

c. $\hat{p} = \dfrac{x_1 + x_2}{n_1 + n_2} = \dfrac{9 + 35}{96 + 100} = .224 \qquad \hat{q} = 1 - \hat{p} = 1 - .224 = .776$

The test statistic is $z = \dfrac{(\hat{p}_1 - \hat{p}_2) - 0}{\sqrt{\hat{p}\hat{q}\left(\dfrac{1}{n_1} + \dfrac{1}{n_2}\right)}} = \dfrac{(.094 - .35) - 0}{\sqrt{.224(.776)\left(\dfrac{1}{96} + \dfrac{1}{100}\right)}} = -4.30$

The p-value $= P(z \le -4.30) + P(z \ge 4.30) = 2P(z \ge 4.30) \approx 2(.5 - .5) = 0$.

Since the p-value is less than $\alpha = .05$, there is very strong evidence to reject H_0 for $\alpha = .05$. There is sufficient evidence to indicate that there is a difference in the proportion of new fathers using the program and the proportion of new fathers who wants to participate at $\alpha = .05$.

d. We must assume that the sample sizes are large enough to use the normal approximation and that the two samples are random and independent.

9.55 a. Let p_1 = proportion of employees in the Poor fitness category who show signs of stress and p_2 = proportion of employees in the Average fitness category who show signs of stress. To determine if a greater proportion of employees in the Poor fitness category show signs of stress than those in the Average fitness category, we test:

$H_0: p_1 - p_2 = 0$
$H_a: p_1 - p_2 > 0$

b. $\hat{p} = \dfrac{n_1 \hat{p}_1 + n_2 \hat{p}_2}{n_1 + n_2} = \dfrac{242(.155) + 212(.133)}{242 + 212} = .145$

The test statistic is $z = \dfrac{(\hat{p}_1 - \hat{p}_2) - 0}{\sqrt{\hat{p}\hat{q}\left(\dfrac{1}{n_1} + \dfrac{1}{n_2}\right)}} = \dfrac{(.155 - .133) - 0}{\sqrt{.145(.855)\left(\dfrac{1}{242} + \dfrac{1}{212}\right)}} = .664$

The rejection region requires $\alpha = .10$ in the upper tail of the z-distribution. From Table IV, Appendix B, $z_{.10} = 1.28$. The rejection region is $z > 1.28$.

Since the observed value of the test statistic does not fall in the rejection region ($z = .664 > 1.28$), H_0 is not rejected. There is insufficient evidence to indicate that a greater proportion of employees in the Poor fitness category show signs of stress than those in the Average fitness category for $\alpha = .10$.

c. Let p_3 = proportion of employees in the Good fitness category who show signs of stress. To determine if a greater proportion of employees in the Poor fitness category show signs of stress than those in the Good fitness category, we test:

H_0: $p_1 - p_3 = 0$
H_a: $p_1 - p_3 > 0$

d. The test statistic is $z = 1.11$ and the p-value $= .1335$. Since the p-value is not small, there is no evidence to reject H_0. There is insufficient evidence to indicate that a greater proportion of employees in the Poor fitness category show signs of stress than those in the Good fitness category for $\alpha \leq .10$.

From these data, there is no evidence to indicate fitness level has a bearing on whether an individual shows signs of stress. This does not necessarily imply that fitness level has no bearing on whether an individual shows signs of stress. We just do not have enough evidence to say that it does have a bearing.

9.57 $n_1 = n_2 = \dfrac{(z_{\alpha/2})^2(\sigma_1^2 + \sigma_2^2)}{B^2}$

For confidence coefficient .95, $\alpha = 1 - .95 = .05$ and $\alpha/2 = .05/2 = .025$. From Table IV, Appendix B, $z_{.025} = 1.96$.

$n_1 = n_2 = \dfrac{1.96^2(14 + 14)}{1.8^2} = 33.2 \approx 34$

9.59 a. For confidence coefficient .99, $\alpha = 1 - .99 = .01$ and $\alpha/2 = .01/2 = .005$. From Table IV, Appendix B, $z_{.005} = 2.58$.

$n_1 = n_2 = \dfrac{(z_{\alpha/2})^2(p_1q_1 + p_2q_2)}{B^2} = \dfrac{2.58^2(.4(1 - .4) + .7(1 - .7))}{.01^2} = \dfrac{2.99538}{.0001}$
$= 29{,}953.8 \approx 29{,}954$

b. For confidence coefficient .90, $\alpha = 1 - .90 = .10$ and $\alpha/2 = .10/2 = .05$. From Table IV, Appendix B, $z_{.05} = 1.645$. Since we have no prior information about the proportions, we use $p_1 = p_2 = .5$ to get a conservative estimate. For a width of .05, the bound is .025.

$n_1 = n_2 = \dfrac{(z_{\alpha/2})^2(p_1q_1 + p_2q_2)}{B^2} = \dfrac{(1.645)^2(.5(1 - .5) + .5(1 - .5))}{.025^2} = 2164.82 \approx 2165$

c. From part b, $z_{.05} = 1.645$.

$n_1 = n_2 = \dfrac{(z_{\alpha/2})^2(p_1q_1 + p_2q_2)}{B^2} = \dfrac{(1.645)^2(.2(1 - .2) + .3(1 - .3))}{.03^2} = \dfrac{1.00123}{.0009}$
$= 1112.48 \approx 1113$

Inferences Based on Two Samples: Confidence Intervals and Tests of Hypotheses

9.61 For confidence coefficient .90, $\alpha = 1 - .90 = .10$ and $\alpha/2 = .10/2 = .05$. From Table IV, Appendix B, $z_{.05} = 1.645$. Since no information is given about the values of p_1 and p_2, we will be conservative and use .5 for both. A width of .04 means the bound is $.04/2 = .02$.

$$n_1 = n_2 = \frac{(z_{\alpha/2})^2(p_1q_1 + p_2q_2)}{B^2} = \frac{(1.645)^2(.5(.5) + .5(.5))}{.02^2} = 3{,}382.5 \approx 3{,}383$$

9.63 For confidence coefficient .90, $\alpha = 1 - .90 = .10$ and $\alpha = .10/2 = .05$. From Table IV, Appendix B, $z_{.05} = 1.645$. Since prior information is given about the values of p_1 and p_2, we will use these values as estimators. Thus, $p_1 = p_2 = .5$. A width of .10 means the bound is $.10/2 = .05$.

$$n_1 = n_2 = \frac{(z_{\alpha/2})^2(p_1q_1 + p_2q_2)}{B^2} = \frac{(1.645)^2(.5(.5) + .5(.5))}{.05^2} = 541.2 \approx 542$$

9.65 For probability .95, $\alpha = 1 - .95 = .05$ and $\alpha/2 = .05/2 = .025$. From Table IV, Appendix B, $z_{.025} = 1.96$. Since we have no prior information about the proportions, we use $p_1 = p_2 = .5$ to get a conservative estimate.

$$n_1 = n_2 = \frac{(z_{\alpha/2})^2(p_1q_1 + p_2q_2)}{B^2} = \frac{(1.96)^2(.5(1 - .5) + .5(1 - .5))}{.02^2} = \frac{1.9208}{.0004} = 4{,}802$$

9.67 a. For confidence coefficient .95, $\alpha = .05$ and $\alpha/2 = .025$. From Table IV, Appendix B, $z_{.025} = 1.96$.

$$n_1 = n_2 = \frac{(z_{\alpha/2})^2(p_1q_1 + p_2q_2)}{B^2} = \frac{1.96^2((.155)(.845) + (.108)(.892))}{.04^2} = 545.8 \approx 546$$

b. Let p_1 = proportion of employees in the Poor fitness category who show signs of stress and p_2 = proportion of employees in the Good fitness category who show signs of stress. To determine if a greater proportion of employees in the Poor fitness category show signs of stress than those in the Good fitness category, we test:

$H_0: p_1 - p_2 = 0$
$H_a: p_1 - p_2 > 0$

$$\hat{p} = \frac{n_1\hat{p}_1 + n_2\hat{p}_2}{n_1 + n_2} = \frac{546(.155) + 546(.108)}{546 + 546} = .1315$$

The test statistic is $z = \dfrac{(\hat{p}_1 - \hat{p}_2) - 0}{\sqrt{\hat{p}\hat{q}\left(\dfrac{1}{n_1} + \dfrac{1}{n_2}\right)}} = \dfrac{(.155 - .108) - 0}{\sqrt{.1315(.8685)\left(\dfrac{1}{546} + \dfrac{1}{546}\right)}} = 2.30$

The p-value = $P(z \geq 2.30) = .5 - .4893 = .0107$. Since this p-value is so small, there is evidence to reject H_0. There is sufficient evidence to indicate that a greater proportion of employees in the Poor fitness category show signs of stress than those in the Good fitness category for $\alpha > .0107$.

9.69 a. With $\nu_1 = 9$ and $\nu_2 = 6$, $F_{.05} = 4.10$.

b. With $v_1 = 18$ and $v_2 = 14$, $F_{.01} \approx 3.57$. (Since $v_1 = 18$ is not given, we estimate the value between those for $v_1 = 15$ and $v_1 = 20$.)

c. With $v_1 = 11$ and $v_2 = 4$, $F_{.025} \approx 8.805$. (Since $v_1 = 11$ is not given, we estimate the value by averaging those given for $v_1 = 10$ and $v_1 = 12$.)

d. With $v_1 = 20$ and $v_2 = 5$, $F_{.10} = 3.21$.

9.71 a. Reject H_0 if $F > F_{.10} = 1.74$. (From Table VII, Appendix B, with $v_1 = 30$ and $v_2 = 20$.)

b. Reject H_0 if $F > F_{.05} = 2.04$. (From Table VIII, Appendix B, with $v_1 = 30$ and $v_2 = 20$.)

c. Reject H_0 if $F > F_{.025} = 2.35$. (From Table IX.)

d. Reject H_0 if $F > F_{.01} = 2.78$. (From Table X.)

9.73 a. The rejection region requires $\alpha = .05$ in the upper tail of the F-distribution with $v_1 = n_1 - 1 = 25 - 1 = 24$ and $v_2 = n_2 - 1 = 20 - 1 = 19$. From Table IX, Appendix B, $F_{.05} = 2.11$. The rejection region is $F > 2.11$ (if $s_1^2 > s_2^2$).

b. The rejection region requires $\alpha = .05$ in the upper tail of the F-distribution with $v_1 = n_2 - 1 = 15 - 1 = 14$ and $v_2 = n_1 - 1 = 10 - 1 = 9$. From Table IX, Appendix B, $F_{.05} \approx 3.01$. The rejection region is $F > 3.01$ (if $s_2^2 > s_1^2$).

c. The rejection region requires $\alpha/2 = .10/2 = .05$ in the upper tail of the F-distribution. If $s_1^2 > s_2^2$, $v_1 = n_1 - 1 = 21 - 1 = 20$ and $v_2 = n_2 - 1 = 31 - 1 = 30$. From Table IX, Appendix B, $F_{.05} = 1.93$. The rejection region is $F > 1.93$. If $s_1^2 < s_2^2$, $v_1 = n_2 - 1 = 30$ and $v_2 = n_1 - 1 = 20$. From Table IX, $F_{.05} = 2.04$. The rejection region is $F > 2.04$.

d. The rejection region requires $\alpha = .01$ in the upper tail of the F-distribution with $v_1 = n_2 - 1 = 41 - 1 = 40$ and $v_2 = n_1 - 1 = 31 - 1 = 30$. From Table XI, Appendix B, $F_{.01} = 2.30$. The rejection region is $F > 2.30$ (if $s_2^2 > s_1^2$).

e. The rejection region requires $\alpha/2 = .05/2 = .025$ in the upper tail of the F-distribution. If $s_1^2 > s_2^2$, $v_1 = n_1 - 1 = 7 - 1 = 6$ and $v_2 = n_2 - 1 = 16 - 1 = 15$. From Table X, Appendix B, $F_{.025} = 3.14$. The rejection region is $F > 3.14$. If $s_1^2 < s_2^2$, $v_1 = n_2 - 1 = 15$ and $v_2 = n_1 - 1 = 6$. From Table X, Appendix B, $F_{.025} = 5.27$. The rejection region is $F > 5.27$.

9.75 a. To determine if the variance for population 2 is greater than that for population 1, we test:

H_0: $\sigma_1^2 = \sigma_2^2$
H_a: $\sigma_1^2 < \sigma_2^2$

The test statistic is $F = \dfrac{s_2^2}{s_1^2} = \dfrac{2.9729^2}{1.4359^2} = 4.29$

Inferences Based on Two Samples: Confidence Intervals and Tests of Hypotheses

The rejection region requires $\alpha = .05$ in the upper tail of the F-distribution with $\nu_1 = n_2 - 1 = 5 - 1 = 4$ and $\nu_2 = n_1 - 1 = 6 - 1 = 5$. From Table VIII, Appendix B, $F_{.05} = 5.19$. The rejection region is $F > 5.19$.

Since the observed value of the test statistic does not fall in the rejection region ($F = 4.29 \not> 5.19$), H_0 is not rejected. There is insufficient evidence to indicate the variance for population 2 is greater than that for population 1 at $\alpha = .05$.

b. The p-value is $P(F \geq 4.29)$. From Tables VII and VIII, with $\nu_1 = 4$ and $\nu_2 = 5$,

$$.05 < P(F \geq 4.29) < .10$$

There is no evidence to reject H_0 for $\alpha < .05$ but there is evidence to reject H_0 for $\alpha = .10$.

9.77 a. Let σ_1^2 = variance in inspection errors for novice inspectors and σ_2^2 = variance in inspection errors for experienced inspectors. Since we wish to determine if the data support the belief that the variance is lower for experienced inspectors than for novice inspectors, we test:

$$H_0: \sigma_1^2 = \sigma_2^2$$
$$H_a: \sigma_1^2 > \sigma_2^2$$

The test statistic is $F = \dfrac{\text{Larger sample variance}}{\text{Smaller sample variance}} = \dfrac{s_1^2}{s_2^2} = \dfrac{8.643^2}{5.744^2} = 2.26$

The rejection region requires $\alpha = .05$ in the upper tail of the F-distribution with $\nu_1 = n_1 - 1 = 12 - 1 = 11$ and $\nu_2 = n_2 - 1 = 12 - 1 = 11$. From Table IX, Appendix B, $F_{.05} \approx 2.82$ (using interpolation). The rejection region is $F > 2.82$.

Since the observed value of the test statistic does not fall in the rejection region ($F = 2.26 \not> 2.82$), H_0 is not rejected. The sample data do not support her belief at $\alpha = .05$.

b. The p-value = $P(F \geq 2.26)$ with $\nu_1 = 11$ and $\nu_2 = 11$. Checking Tables VIII, IX, X, and XI in Appendix B, we find $F_{.10} = 2.23$ and $F_{.05} = 2.82$. Since the observed value of F exceeds $F_{.10}$ but is less than $F_{.05}$, the observed significance level for the test is less than .10. So $.05 < p\text{-value} < .10$.

9.79 a. Let σ_1^2 = variance of the order-to-delivery times for the Persian Gulf War and σ_2^2 = variance of the order-to-delivery times for Bosnia.

To determine if the variances of the order-to-delivery times for the Persian Gulf and Bosnia shipments are equal, we test:

$$H_0: \dfrac{\sigma_1^2}{\sigma_2^2} = 1$$

$$H_a: \dfrac{\sigma_1^2}{\sigma_2^2} \neq 1$$

The test statistic is $F = 8.29$ (from printout).

The p-value is $p = 0.007$ (from printout). Since the p-value is less than α ($p = .007 < .05$), H_0 is rejected. There is sufficient evidence to indicate the variances of the order-to-delivery times for the Persian Gulf and Bosnia shipments differ at $\alpha = .05$.

 b. No. One assumption necessary for the small sample confidence interval for $(\mu_1 - \mu_2)$ is that $\sigma_1^2 = \sigma_2^2$. For this problem, there is evidence to indicate that $\sigma_1^2 \neq \sigma_2^2$.

9.81 a. $s_p^2 = \dfrac{(n_1 - 1)s_1^2 + (n_1 - 1)s_2^2}{n_1 + n_2 - 2} = \dfrac{11(74.2) + 13(60.5)}{12 + 14 - 2} = 66.7792$

H_0: $\mu_1 - \mu_2 = 0$
H_a: $\mu_1 - \mu_2 > 0$

The test statistic is $t = \dfrac{(\bar{x}_1 - \bar{x}_2) - 0}{\sqrt{s_p^2 \left[\dfrac{1}{n_1} + \dfrac{1}{n_2}\right]}} = \dfrac{(17.8 - 15.3) - 0}{\sqrt{66.7792 \left[\dfrac{1}{12} + \dfrac{1}{14}\right]}} = .78$

The rejection region requires $\alpha = .05$ in the upper tail of the t-distribution with df $= n_1 + n_2 - 2 = 12 + 14 - 2 = 24$. From Table VI, Appendix B, for df = 24, $t_{.05} = 1.711$. The rejection region is $t > 1.711$.

Since the observed value of the test statistic does not fall in the rejection region ($0.78 \not> 1.711$), H_0 is not rejected. There is insufficient evidence to indicate that $\mu_1 > \mu_2$ at $\alpha = .05$.

 b. For confidence coefficient .99, $\alpha = .01$ and $\alpha/2 = .01/2 = .005$. From Table VI, Appendix B, with df $= n_1 + n_2 - 2 = 12 + 14 - 2 = 24$, $t_{.005} = 2.797$. The confidence interval is:

$(\bar{x}_1 - \bar{x}_2) \pm t_{.005} \sqrt{s_p^2 \left[\dfrac{1}{n_1} + \dfrac{1}{n_2}\right]} \Rightarrow (17.8 - 15.3) \pm 2.797 \sqrt{66.7792 \left[\dfrac{1}{12} + \dfrac{1}{14}\right]}$
$\Rightarrow 2.50 \pm 8.99 \Rightarrow (-6.49, 11.49)$

 c. For confidence coefficient .99, $\alpha = .01$ and $\alpha/2 = .01/2 = .005$. From Table IV, Appendix B, $z_{.005} = 2.58$.

$n_1 = n_2 = \dfrac{(z_{\alpha/2})^2 (\sigma_1^2 + \sigma_2^2)}{B^2} = \dfrac{(2.58)^2 (74.2 + 60.5)}{2^2} = 224.15 \approx 225$

9.83 a. For confidence coefficient .90, $\alpha = .10$ and $\alpha/2 = .05$. From Table IV, Appendix B, $z_{.05} = 1.645$. The confidence interval is:

$(\bar{x}_1 - \bar{x}_2) \pm z_{.05} \sqrt{\dfrac{s_1^2}{n_1} + \dfrac{s_2^2}{n_2}} \Rightarrow (12.2 - 8.3) \pm 1.645 \sqrt{\dfrac{2.1}{135} + \dfrac{3.0}{148}}$
$\Rightarrow 3.90 \pm .31 \Rightarrow (3.59, 4.21)$

b. H_0: $\mu_1 - \mu_2 = 0$
H_a: $\mu_1 - \mu_2 \neq 0$

The test statistic is $z = \dfrac{(\bar{x}_1 - \bar{x}_2) - 0}{\sqrt{\dfrac{s_1^2}{n_1} + \dfrac{s_2^2}{n_2}}} = \dfrac{(12.2 - 8.3) - 0}{\sqrt{\dfrac{2.1}{135} + \dfrac{3.0}{148}}} = 20.60$

The rejection region requires $\alpha/2 = .01/2 = .005$ in each tail of the z-distribution. From Table IV, Appendix B, $z_{.005} = 2.58$. The rejection region is $z < -2.58$ or $z > 2.58$.

Since the observed value of the test statistic falls in the rejection region (20.60 > 2.58), H_0 is rejected. There is sufficient evidence to indicate that $\mu_1 \neq \mu_2$ at $\alpha = .01$.

c. For confidence coefficient .90, $\alpha = .10$ and $\alpha/2 = .05$. From Table IV, Appendix B, $z_{.05} = 1.645$.

$$n_1 = n_2 = \dfrac{(z_{\alpha/2})^2(\sigma_1^2 + \sigma_2^2)}{B^2} = \dfrac{(1.645)^2(2.1 + 3.0)}{.2^2} = 345.02 \approx 346$$

9.85 a. This is a paired difference experiment.

Pair	Difference (Pop. 1 − Pop. 2)
1	6
2	4
3	4
4	3
5	2

$\bar{x}_D = \dfrac{\sum x_D}{n_D} = \dfrac{19}{5} = 3.8$ $s_D^2 = \dfrac{\sum x_D^2 - \dfrac{(\sum x_D)^2}{n_D}}{n_D - 1} = \dfrac{81 - \dfrac{19^2}{5}}{5 - 1} = 2.2$

$s_D = \sqrt{2.2} = 1.4832$

H_0: $\mu_D = 0$
H_a: $\mu_D \neq 0$

The test statistic is $t = \dfrac{\bar{x}_D - 0}{s_D/\sqrt{n_D}} = \dfrac{3.8 - 0}{1.4832/\sqrt{5}} = 5.73$

The rejection region requires $\alpha/2 = .05/2 = .025$ in each tail of the t-distribution with df = $n - 1 = 5 - 1 = 4$. From Table VI, Appendix B, $t_{.025} = 2.776$. The rejection region is $t < -2.776$ or $t > 2.776$.

Since the observed value of the test statistic falls in the rejection region (5.73 > 2.776), H_0 is rejected. There is sufficient evidence to indicate that the population means are different at $\alpha = .05$.

b. For confidence coefficient .95, $\alpha = .05$ and $\alpha/2 = .025$. Therefore, we would use the same t value as above, $t_{.025} = 2.776$. The confidence interval is:

$$\bar{x}_D \pm t_{\alpha/2} \frac{s_D}{\sqrt{n_D}} \Rightarrow 3.8 \pm 3.8 \pm 2.776 \frac{1.4832}{\sqrt{5}} \Rightarrow 3.8 \pm 1.84 \Rightarrow (1.96, 5.64)$$

c. The sample of differences must be randomly selected from a population of differences which has a normal distribution.

9.87 If the p-value is less than α, reject H_0. Otherwise, do not reject H_0.

a. p-value $= .0429 < .05 \Rightarrow$ Reject H_0

b. p-value $= .1984 \not< .05 \Rightarrow$ Do not reject H_0

c. p-value $= .0001 < .05 \Rightarrow$ Reject H_0

d. p-value $= .0344 < .05 \Rightarrow$ Reject H_0

e. p-value $= .0545 \not< .05 \Rightarrow$ Do not reject H_0

f. p-value $= .9633 \not< .05 \Rightarrow$ Do not reject H_0

g. We must assume:

1. Both sampled populations are normal.
2. Both population variances are equal.
3. Samples are random and independent.

9.89 From Exercise 9.88, $\bar{x}_D = 205.243$, $s_D^2 = 38{,}916.9195$, and $s_D = 197.2737$. For confidence coefficient .95, $\alpha = 1 - .95 = .05$ and $\alpha/2 = .05/2 = .025$. From Table VI, Appendix B, with df $= n_D - 1 = 7 - 1 = 6$, $t_{.025} = 2.447$. The confidence interval is:

$$\bar{x}_D \pm t_{.025} \frac{s_D}{\sqrt{n_D}} \Rightarrow 205.243 \pm 2.447 \left[\frac{197.2737}{\sqrt{7}}\right] \Rightarrow 205.243 \pm 182.454$$
$$\Rightarrow (22.789, 387.697)$$

We are 95% confident the difference between 1995 and 1994 R&D expenditures is between 22,789 and 387.697 million dollars.

9.91 For confidence coefficient .90, $\alpha = 1 - .90 = .10$ and $\alpha/2 = .10/2 = .05$. From Table IV, Appendix B, $z_{.05} = 1.645$. We estimate $p_1 = p_2 = .5$.

$$n_1 = n_2 = \frac{(z_{\alpha/2})^2(p_1 q_1 + p_2 q_2)}{B^2} = \frac{(1.645)^2(.5(.5) + .5(.5))}{.05^2} = 541.205 \approx 542$$

9.93 a. Since there are large differences among the canisters, a paired difference experiment was conducted to eliminate the differences from canister to canister.

b. To determine if there is a difference in the mean exhalation rates between PCHD and EERF, we test

$H_0: \mu_1 - \mu_2 = 0$
$H_a: \mu_1 - \mu_2 \neq 0$

The test statistic is $t = \dfrac{\bar{x}_D - 0}{s_D/\sqrt{n_D}} = \dfrac{84.17 - 0}{408.92/\sqrt{15}} = .80$

The rejection region requires $\alpha/2 = .05/2 = .025$ in each tail of the t-distribution with df = $n_D - 1 = 15 - 1 = 14$. From Table VI, Appendix B, $t_{.025} = 2.145$. The rejection region is $t < -2.145$ or $t > 2.145$.

Since the observed value of the test statistic does not fall in the rejection region $(.80 \not> 2.145)$, H_0 is not rejected. There is insufficient evidence to indicate that there is a difference in the mean exhalation rates between PCHD and EERF at $\alpha = .05$.

c. For confidence coefficient .95, $\alpha = .05$ and $\alpha/2 = .025$. From Table VI, Appendix B, with df = $n_D - 1 = 15 - 1 = 14$, $t_{.025} = 2.145$. The confidence interval is:

$\bar{x}_D \pm t_{\alpha/2} s_D/\sqrt{n_D} \Rightarrow 84.17 \pm (2.145)\dfrac{408.92}{\sqrt{15}} \Rightarrow 84.17 \pm 226.47 \Rightarrow (-142.30, 310.64)$

We are 95% confident the difference in mean measurements between PCHD and EERF is between -142.30 and 310.64. Since 0 is in the interval, it implies there is no significant difference between the mean measurements. This supports the test in part **b**.

9.95 Let μ_1 = mean initial performance of stayers and μ_2 = mean initial performance of leavers.

To determine if the mean initial performance differs for stayers and leavers, we test:

$H_0: \mu_1 - \mu_2 = 0$
$H_a: \mu_1 - \mu_2 \neq 0$

The test statistic is $z = \dfrac{(\bar{x}_1 - \bar{x}_2) - 0}{\sqrt{\dfrac{s_1^2}{n_1} + \dfrac{s_2^2}{n_2}}} = \dfrac{(3.51 - 3.24) - 0}{\sqrt{\dfrac{.51^2}{174} + \dfrac{.52^2}{355}}} = 5.68$

Since no α is given, we will use $\alpha = .05$. The rejection region requires $\alpha/2 = .05/2 = .025$ in each tail of the z-distribution. For Table IV, Appendix B, $z_{.025} = 1.96$. The rejection region is $z < -1.96$ or $z > 1.96$.

Since the observed value of the test statistic falls in the rejection region ($z = 5.68 > 1.96$), H_0 is rejected. There is sufficient evidence to indicate the mean initial performance differs for stayers and leavers at $\alpha = .05$.

Let μ_1 = mean rate of career advancement of stayers and μ_2 = mean rate of career advancement of leavers.

To determine if the mean rate of career advancement differs for stayers and leavers, we test:

$H_0: \mu_1 - \mu_2 = 0$
$H_a: \mu_1 - \mu_2 \neq 0$

The test statistic is $z = \dfrac{(\bar{x}_1 - \bar{x}_2) - 0}{\sqrt{\dfrac{s_1^2}{n_1} + \dfrac{s_2^2}{n_2}}} = \dfrac{(0.43 - 0.31) - 0}{\sqrt{\dfrac{.20^2}{174} + \dfrac{.31^2}{355}}} = 5.36$

Since no α is given, we will use $\alpha = .05$. The rejection region is $z < -1.96$ or $z > 1.96$ (from above).

Since the observed value of the test statistic falls in the rejection region ($z = 5.36 > 1.96$), H_0 is rejected. There is sufficient evidence to indicate the mean rate of career advancement differs for stayers and leavers at $\alpha = .05$.

Let μ_1 = mean final performance appraisal of stayers and μ_2 = mean final performance appraisal of leavers.

To determine if the mean final performance appraisal differs for stayers and leavers, we test:

$H_0: \mu_1 - \mu_2 = 0$
$H_a: \mu_1 - \mu_2 \neq 0$

The test statistic is $z = \dfrac{(\bar{x}_1 - \bar{x}_2) - 0}{\sqrt{\dfrac{s_1^2}{n_1} + \dfrac{s_2^2}{n_2}}} = \dfrac{(3.78 - 3.15) - 0}{\sqrt{\dfrac{.62^2}{174} + \dfrac{.68^2}{355}}} = 10.63$

Since no α is given, we will use $\alpha = .05$. The rejection region is $z < -1.96$ or $z > 1.96$ (from above).

Since the observed value of the test statistic falls in the rejection region ($z = 10.63 > 1.96$), H_0 is rejected. There is sufficient evidence to indicate the mean final performance appraisal differs for stayers and leavers at $\alpha = .05$.

9.97   Some preliminary calculations are:

Supervisor	Difference (Pre-test − Post-test)
1	−15
2	1
3	−7
4	−8
5	−4
6	−13
7	−8
8	2
9	−10
10	−7

Inferences Based on Two Samples: Confidence Intervals and Tests of Hypotheses

$$\bar{x}_D = \frac{\sum x_D}{n_D} = \frac{-69}{10} = -6.9$$

$$s_D^2 = \frac{\sum x_D^2 - \frac{(\sum x_D)^2}{n_D}}{n_D - 1} = \frac{741 - \frac{(-69)^2}{10}}{10 - 1} = \frac{264.9}{9} = 29.4333$$

$$s_D = \sqrt{29.4333} = 5.4252$$

a. To determine if the training program is effective in increasing supervisory skills, we test:

H_0: $\mu_D = 0$
H_a: $\mu_D < 0$

The test statistic is $t = \dfrac{\bar{x}_D - 0}{\frac{s_D}{\sqrt{n_D}}} = \dfrac{-6.9 - 0}{\frac{5.4252}{\sqrt{10}}} = -4.02$

The rejection region requires $\alpha = .10$ in the lower tail of the t-distribution with df $= n_D - 1 = 10 - 1 = 9$. From Table VI, Appendix B, $t_{.10} = 1.383$. The rejection region is $t < -1.383$.

Since the observed value of the test statistic falls in the rejection region ($t = -4.02 < -1.383$), H_0 is rejected. There is sufficient evidence to indicate the training program is effective in increasing supervisory skills at $\alpha = .10$.

b. From the printout, the p-value is $p = .0030$. The probability of observing a test statistic of -4.02 or anything lower is $.0030$ when H_0 is true. This is very unusual if H_0 is true. There is evidence to reject H_0 for $\alpha > .003$.

9.99 To determine if there is a difference in job satisfaction for the two groups, we test:

H_0: $\mu_1 - \mu_2 = 0$
H_a: $\mu_1 - \mu_2 \neq 0$

where μ_1 = mean rating for workers who believe in the existence of a class system,
and μ_2 = mean rating for workers who do not believe in the existence of a class system.

The test statistic is $z = \dfrac{(\bar{x}_1 - \bar{x}_2) - 0}{\sqrt{\frac{s_1^2}{n_1} + \frac{s_2^2}{n_2}}} = \dfrac{(5.42 - 5.19) - 0}{\sqrt{\frac{1.24^2}{175} + \frac{1.17^2}{277}}} = 1.963$

The p-value of this test is just under .05. (If the test statistic had been 1.960, the p-value would have been exactly .05). Thus, if a level of significance of .05 or more was desired, it would be possible to reject H_0 and conclude that there is a difference in job satisfaction for the two different sociocultural type of workers. If a level of significance less than .05 was desired, we would fail to reject H_0 and conclude that there was not enough evidence to conclude that such a difference existed.

9.101 a. For each measure, let μ_1 = mean job satisfaction for day-shift nurses and μ_2 = mean job satisfaction for night-shift nurses. To determine whether a difference in job satisfaction exists between day-shift and night-shift nurses, we test:

H_0: $\mu_1 - \mu_2 = 0$
H_a: $\mu_1 - \mu_2 \neq 0$

b. Hours of work: The p-value = .813. Since the p-value is so large, there is no evidence to reject H_0. There is insufficient evidence to indicate a difference in mean job satisfaction exists between day-shift and night-shift nurses on hours of work for $\alpha \leq .10$.

Free time: The p-value = .047. Since the p-value is so small, there is evidence to reject H_0. There is sufficient evidence to indicate a difference in mean job satisfaction exists between day-shift and night-shift nurses on free time for $\alpha > .047$.

Breaks: The p-value = .0073. Since the p-value is so small, there is evidence to reject H_0. There is sufficient evidence to indicate a difference in mean job satisfaction exists between day-shift and night-shift nurses on breaks for $\alpha > .0073$.

c. We must make the following assumptions for each measure:

1. The job satisfaction scores for both day-shift and night-shift nurses are normally distributed.
2. The variances of job satisfaction scores for both day-shift and night-shift nurses are equal.
3. Random and independent samples were selected from both populations of job satisfaction scores.

9.103 Some preliminary calculations are:

$$s_1^2 = \frac{\sum x_1^2 - \frac{(\sum x_1)^2}{n_1}}{n_1 - 1} = \frac{10{,}251 - \frac{225^2}{5}}{5 - 1} = \frac{126}{4} = 31.5$$

$$s_2^2 = \frac{\sum x_2^2 - \frac{(\sum x_2)^2}{n_2}}{n_2 - 1} = \frac{10{,}351 - \frac{227^2}{5}}{5 - 1} = \frac{45.2}{4} = 11.3$$

Let σ_1^2 = variance for instrument A and σ_2^2 = variance for instrument B. Since we wish to determine if there is a difference in the precision of the two machines, we test:

H_0: $\sigma_1^2 = \sigma_2^2$
H_a: $\sigma_1^2 \neq \sigma_2^2$

The test statistic is $F = \dfrac{\text{Larger sample variance}}{\text{Smaller sample variance}} = \dfrac{s_1^2}{s_2^2} = \dfrac{31.5}{11.3} = 2.79$

The rejection region requires $\alpha/2 = .10/2 = .05$ in the upper tail of the F-distribution with $\nu_1 = n_1 - 1 = 5 - 1 = 4$ and $\nu_2 = n_2 - 1 = 5 - 1 = 4$. From Table IX, Appendix B, $F_{.05} = 6.39$. The rejection region is $F > 6.39$.

Inferences Based on Two Samples: Confidence Intervals and Tests of Hypotheses

Since the observed value of the test statistic does not fall in the rejection region ($F = 2.79 \not> 6.39$), H_0 is not rejected. There is insufficient evidence of a difference in the precision of the two instruments at $\alpha = .10$.

9.105 For confidence coefficient .95, $\alpha = .05$ and $\alpha/2 = .025$. From Table IV, Appendix B, $z_{.025} = 1.96$.

$$n_1 = n_2 = \frac{(z_{\alpha/2})^2(p_1q_1 + p_2q_2)}{B^2} = \frac{1.96^2(.395(.605) + .293(.707))}{.03^2} = 1904.26 \approx 1905$$

9.107 a. The sample sizes for each of the 3 areas are large enough to use the methods of this section if the intervals

$$\hat{p}_i \pm 3\sigma_{\hat{p}_i} \Rightarrow \hat{p}_i \pm 3\sqrt{\frac{\hat{p}_i\hat{q}_i}{n_i}} \text{ do not contain 0 or 1.}$$

For Age:

$$\hat{p}_1 = \frac{x_1}{n_1} = \frac{19}{207} = .092 \qquad \hat{p}_2 = \frac{x_2}{n_2} = \frac{96}{153} = .627$$

$$\hat{p}_1 \pm 3\sigma_{\hat{p}_1} \Rightarrow .092 \pm 3\sqrt{\frac{.092(.908)}{207}} \Rightarrow .092 \pm .06 \Rightarrow (.032, .152)$$

$$\hat{p}_2 \pm 3\sigma_{\hat{p}_2} \Rightarrow .627 \pm 3\sqrt{\frac{.627(.373)}{153}} \Rightarrow .627 \pm .117 \Rightarrow (.51, .744)$$

Since neither interval contains 0 or 1, the sample sizes are large enough to use the methods of this section in the area age.

For Education:

$$\hat{p}_1 = \frac{x_1}{n_1} = \frac{195}{207} = .942 \qquad \hat{p}_2 = \frac{x_2}{n_2} = \frac{116}{153} = .758$$

$$\hat{p}_1 \pm 3\sigma_{\hat{p}_1} \Rightarrow .942 \pm 3\sqrt{\frac{.942(.058)}{207}} \Rightarrow .942 \pm .049 \Rightarrow (.893, .991)$$

$$\hat{p}_2 \pm 3\sigma_{\hat{p}_2} \Rightarrow .758 \pm 3\sqrt{\frac{.758(.242)}{153}} \Rightarrow .758 \pm .104 \Rightarrow (.654, .862)$$

Since neither interval contains 0 or 1, the sample sizes are large enough to use the methods of this section in the area education.

For Employment:

$$\hat{p}_1 = \frac{x_1}{n_1} = \frac{19}{207} = .092 \qquad \hat{p}_2 = \frac{x_2}{n_2} = \frac{47}{153} = .307$$

$$\hat{p}_1 \pm 3\sigma_{\hat{p}_1} \Rightarrow .092 \pm 3\sqrt{\frac{.092(.908)}{207}} \Rightarrow .092 \pm .06 \Rightarrow (.032, .152)$$

$$\hat{p}_2 \pm 3\sigma_{\hat{p}_2} \Rightarrow .307 \pm 3\sqrt{\frac{.307(.693)}{153}} \Rightarrow .307 \pm .112 \Rightarrow (.195, .419)$$

Since neither interval contains 0 or 1, the sample sizes are large enough to use the methods of this section in the area employment.

b. To determine if Fortune 500 CEO's and entrepreneurs differ in terms of being fired or dismissed, we test:

H_0: $p_1 - p_2 = 0$
H_a: $p_1 - p_2 \neq 0$

The test statistic is $z = \dfrac{(\hat{p}_1 - \hat{p}_2) - 0}{\sqrt{\hat{p}\hat{q}\left[\dfrac{1}{n_1} + \dfrac{1}{n_2}\right]}}$

where $\hat{p}_1 = .092$, $\hat{p}_2 = .307$, and $\hat{p} = \dfrac{x_1 + x_2}{n_1 + n_2} = \dfrac{19 + 47}{207 + 153} = .183$

Thus, $z = \dfrac{(.092 - .307) - 0}{\sqrt{.183(.817)\left[\dfrac{1}{207} + \dfrac{1}{153}\right]}} = -5.22$

The rejection region requires $\alpha/2 = .05/2 = .025$ in each tail of the z-distribution. From Table IV, Appendix B, $z_{.025} = 1.96$. The rejection region is $z < -1.96$ or $z > 1.96$.

Since the observed value of the test statistic falls in the rejection region ($z = -5.22 < -1.96$), H_0 is rejected. There is sufficient evidence to indicate that Fortune 500 CEO's and entrepreneurs differ in terms of being fired or dismissed at $\alpha = .05$.

c. For confidence level .99, $\alpha = .01$ and $\alpha/2 = .01/2 = .005$. From Table IV, Appendix B, $z_{.005} = 2.58$. The confidence interval is:

$(\hat{p}_1 - \hat{p}_2) \pm z_{.01}\sqrt{\dfrac{\hat{p}_1\hat{q}_1}{n_1} + \dfrac{\hat{p}_2\hat{q}_2}{n_2}} \Rightarrow (.092 - .307) \pm 2.58\sqrt{\dfrac{.092(.908)}{207} + \dfrac{.307(.693)}{153}}$
$\Rightarrow -.215 \pm .109 \Rightarrow (-.324, -.106)$

We are 99% confident that the difference in the fractions of CEOs and entrepreneurs who have been fired or dismissed from a job is between $-.324$ and $-.106$.

d. The confidence interval provides more information. The test of hypothesis just indicates if a difference exists. The confidence interval provides the range of values in which we would expect to find the difference.

Inferences Based on Two Samples: Confidence Intervals and Tests of Hypotheses

Simple Linear Regression — Chapter 10

10.1 a.

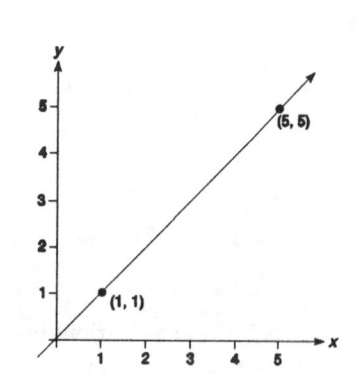

b.

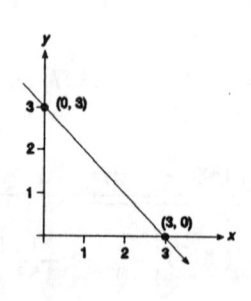

c.

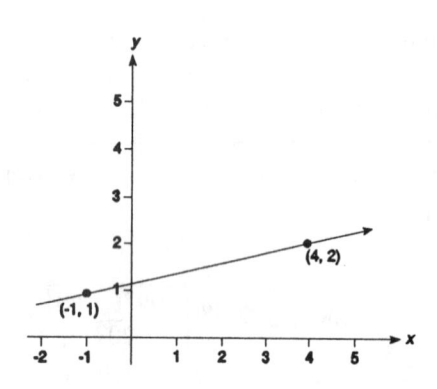

d.

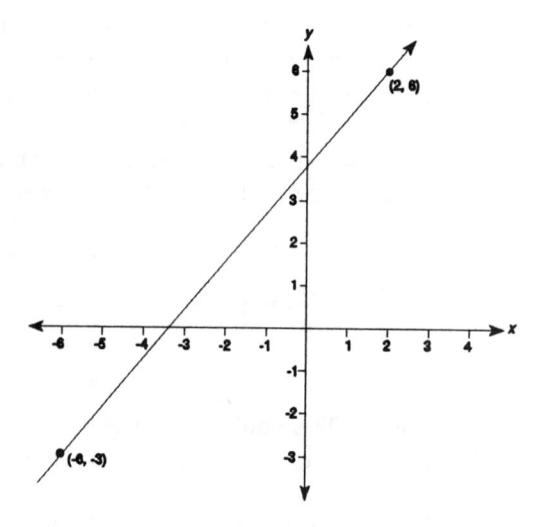

10.3 The two equations are:

$$4 = \beta_0 + \beta_1(-2) \text{ and } 6 = \beta_0 + \beta_1(4)$$

Subtracting the first equation from the second, we get

$$\begin{aligned} 6 &= \beta_0 + 4\beta_1 \\ -(4 &= \beta_0 - 2\beta_1) \\ \hline 2 &= 6\beta_1 \end{aligned} \Rightarrow \beta_1 = \frac{2}{6} = \frac{1}{3}$$

Substituting $\beta_1 = \frac{1}{3}$ into the first equation, we get:

$$4 = \beta_0 + \frac{1}{3}(-2) \Rightarrow \beta_0 = 4 + \frac{2}{3} = \frac{14}{3}$$

The equation for the line is $y = \frac{14}{3} + \frac{1}{3}x$.

10.5 To graph a line, we need two points. Pick two values for x, and find the corresponding y values by substituting the values of x into the equation.

a. Let $x = 0 \Rightarrow y = 4 + (0) = 4$
and $x = 2 \Rightarrow y = 4 + (2) = 6$

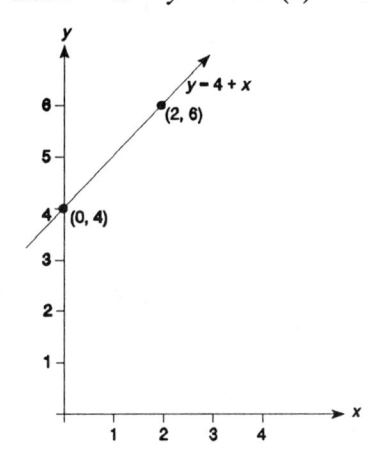

b. Let $x = 0 \Rightarrow y = 5 - 2(0) = 5$
and $x = 2 \Rightarrow y = 5 - 2(2) = 1$

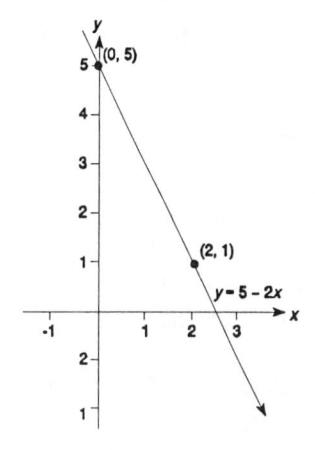

c. Let $x = 0 \Rightarrow y = -4 + 3(0) = -4$
and $x = 2 \Rightarrow y = -4 + 3(2) = 2$

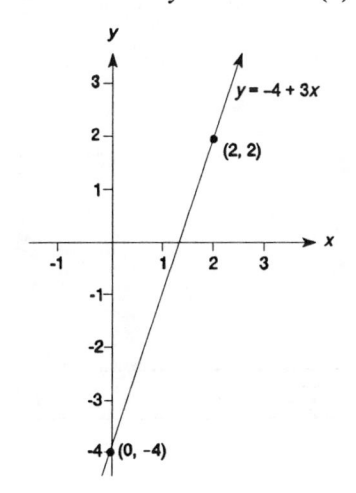

d. Let $x = 0 \Rightarrow y = -2(0) = 0$
and $x = 2 \Rightarrow y = -2(2) = -4$

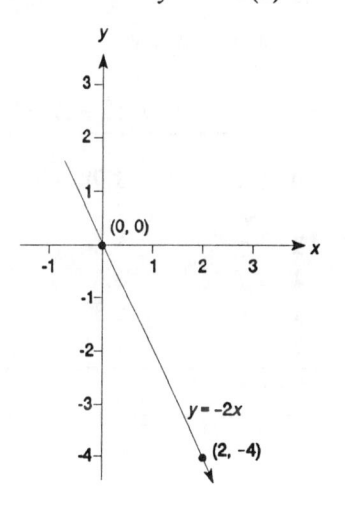

e. Let $x = 0 \Rightarrow y = 0$
and $x = 2 \Rightarrow y = 2$

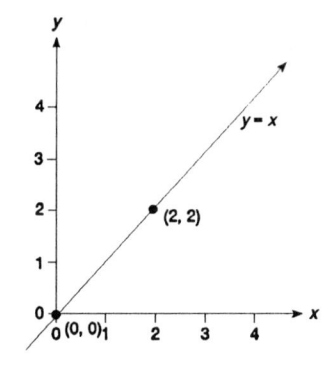

f. Let $x = 0 \Rightarrow y = .5 + 1.5(0) = .5$
and $x = 2 \Rightarrow y = .5 + 1.5(2) = 3.5$

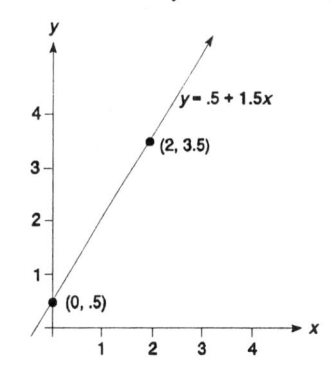

Simple Linear Regression

10.7 A deterministic model does not allow for random error or variation, whereas a probabilistic model does. An example where a deterministic model would be appropriate is:

Let y = cost of a 2 × 4 piece of lumber and
x = length (in feet)

The model would be $y = \beta_1 x$. There should be no variation in price for the same length of wood.

An example where a probabilistic model would be appropriate is:

Let y = sales per month of a commodity and
x = amount of money spent advertising

The model would be $y = \beta_0 + \beta_1 x + \epsilon$. The sales per month will probably vary even if the amount of money spent on advertising remains the same.

10.9 No. The random error component, ϵ, allows the values of the variable to fall above or below the line.

10.11 From Exercise 10.10, $\hat{\beta}_0 = 7.10$ and $\hat{\beta}_1 = -.78$.

The fitted line is $\hat{y} = 7.10 - .78x$. To obtain values for $\hat{y}$, we substitute values of x into the equation and solve for $\hat{y}$.

a.

x	y	$\hat{y} = 7.10 - .78x$	$(y - \hat{y})$	$(y - \hat{y})^2$
7	2	1.64	.36	.1296
4	4	3.98	.02	.0004
6	2	2.42	−.42	.1764
2	5	5.54	−.54	.2916
1	7	6.32	.68	.4624
1	6	6.32	−.32	.1024
3	5	4.76	.24	.0576
			$\sum(y - \hat{y}) = 0.02$	SSE = $\sum(y - \hat{y})^2 = 1.2204$

b.

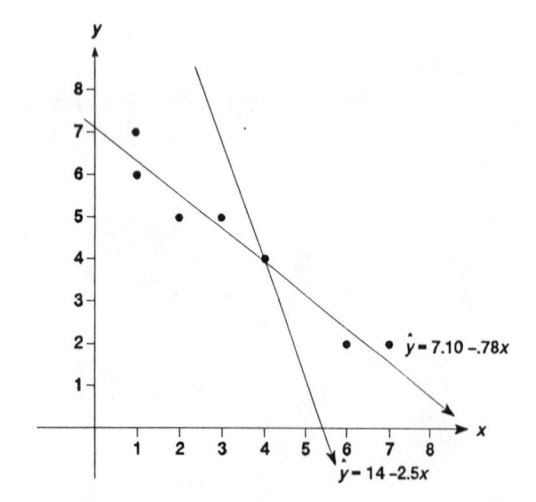

c.

x	y	$\hat{y} = 14 - 2.5x$	$(y - \hat{y})$	$(y - \hat{y})^2$
7	2	−3.5	5.5	30.25
4	4	4	0	0
6	2	−1	3	9
2	5	9	−4	16
1	7	11.5	−4.5	20.25
1	6	11.5	−5.5	30.25
3	5	6.5	−1.5	2.25
			$\sum(y - \hat{y}) = -7$	SSE = 108.00

10.13 a.

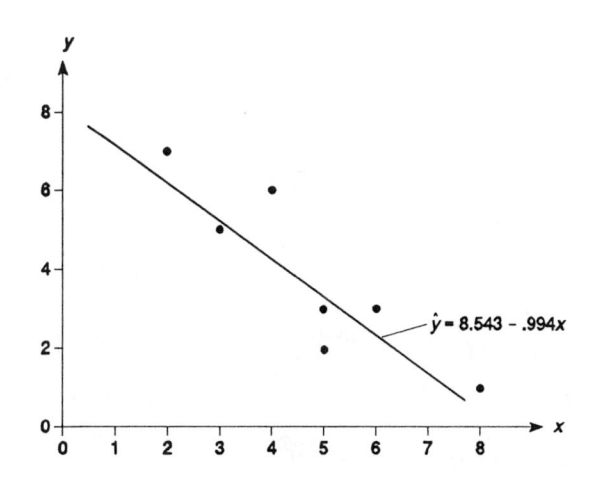

b. Looking at the scattergram, x and y appear to have a negative linear relationship.

c. From the printout, $\hat{\beta}_1 = -.9939$ and $\hat{\beta}_0 = 8.543$

d. The least squares line is $\hat{y} = 8.543 - .994x$. The line is plotted in part a. It appears to fit the data well.

e. $\hat{\beta}_0 = 8.543$ Since $x = 0$ is not in the observed range, $\hat{\beta}_0$ has no meaning other than the y-intercept.

$\hat{\beta}_1 = -.994$ The estimated change in the mean value of y for each unit change in x is −.994. These interpretations are valid only for values of x in the range from 2 to 8.

Simple Linear Regression

10.15 a. It appears as salary increases, the retaliation index decreases.

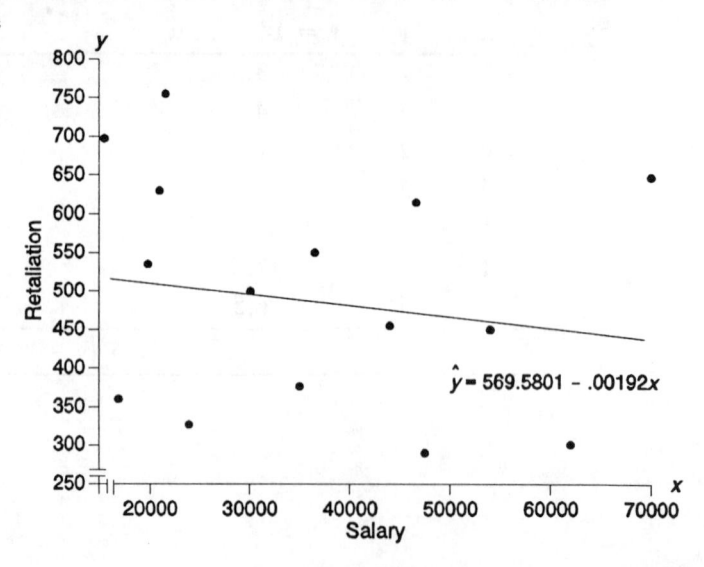

$\hat{y} = 569.5801 - .00192x$

b. $\sum x = 544{,}100 \qquad \sum y = 7{,}497 \qquad \sum xy = 263{,}977{,}000$
$\sum x^2 = 23{,}876{,}290{,}000$

$\bar{x} = \dfrac{\sum x}{n} = \dfrac{544{,}100}{15} = 36{,}273.333 \qquad \bar{y} = \dfrac{\sum y}{n} = \dfrac{7{,}497}{15} = 499.8$

$SS_{xy} = \sum xy - \dfrac{(\sum x)(\sum y)}{n} = 263{,}977{,}000 - \dfrac{(544{,}100)(7{,}497)}{15}$
$= 263{,}977{,}000 - 271{,}941{,}180 = -7{,}964{,}180$

$SS_{xx} = \sum x^2 - \dfrac{(\sum x)^2}{n} = 23{,}876{,}290{,}000 - \dfrac{(544{,}100)^2}{15}$
$= 23{,}876{,}290{,}000 - 19{,}736{,}320{,}670 = 4{,}139{,}969{,}330$

$\hat{\beta}_1 = \dfrac{SS_{xy}}{SS_{xx}} = \dfrac{-7{,}964{,}180}{4{,}139{,}969{,}330} = -.001923729 \approx -.00192$

$\hat{\beta}_0 = \bar{y} - \hat{\beta}_1 \bar{x} = 499.8 - (-.001923729)(36{,}273.333)$
$= 499.8 + 69.78007144 = 569.5800714 \approx 569.5801$

$\hat{y} = 569.5801 - .00192x$

c. The least squares line supports the answer because the line has a negative slope.

d. $\hat{\beta}_0 = 569.5801$ \qquad This has no meaning because $x = 0$ is not in the observed range.

e. $\hat{\beta}_1 = -.00192$ \qquad When the salary increases by \$1, the mean retaliation index is estimated to decrease by .00192. This is meaningful for the range of x from \$16,900 to \$70,000.

10.17 a. You should expect to have a positive relationship since the higher batting average, the more hits and ultimately the more games won.

b. Yes, it seems there is a positive linear relationship. As batting averages increase, the number of games won also increases.

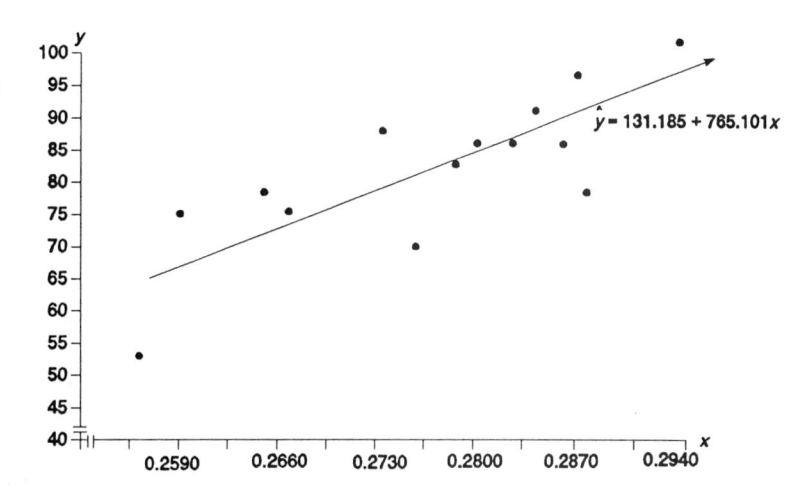

$\hat{y} = 131.185 + 765.101x$

c. From the printout, $\hat{\beta}_0 = -131.18519$ and $\hat{\beta}_1 = 765.101228$.

The least squares line is $\hat{y} = -131.185 + 765.101x$.

d. The line is plotted on the graph in part b. The line presents an adequate fit.

e. The mean number of games won appears to be fairly strongly related to a team's batting average because the points lie close to the line. However, there are more factors to a game than batting, such as pitcher's performance.

f. $\hat{\beta}_0 = -131.18519$ Since $x = 0$ is not in the observed range, $\hat{\beta}_0$ is simply the estimated y-intercept.

$\hat{\beta}_1 = 755.101$ Since x cannot increase by one full unit, we will interpret this value in terms of a .01 increase. For each .01 increase in team batting average, the mean number of games won is estimated to increase by 7.55101.

10.19 a. $\sum x_i = 1,635$ $\sum x_i^2 = 575,825$ $\sum x_i y_i = 111,100$

$\sum y_i = 366$ $\sum y_i^2 = 28,948$

$SS_{xy} = \sum x_i y_i - \dfrac{\sum x_i \sum y_i}{n} = 111,100 - \dfrac{1,635(366)}{5} = -8582$

$SS_{xx} = \sum x_i^2 - \dfrac{(\sum x_i)^2}{n} = 575,825 - \dfrac{1,635^2}{5} = 41,180$

$\hat{\beta}_1 = \dfrac{SS_{xy}}{SS_{xx}} = \dfrac{-8582}{41,180} = -.208402137 \approx -.208$

$\hat{\beta}_0 = \bar{y} - \hat{\beta}_1 \bar{x} = 73.2 - (-.208402137)(327) = 141.3474988 \approx 141.347$

The least squares line is $\hat{y} = 141.347 - .208x$.

Simple Linear Regression

b. The plot of the data is:

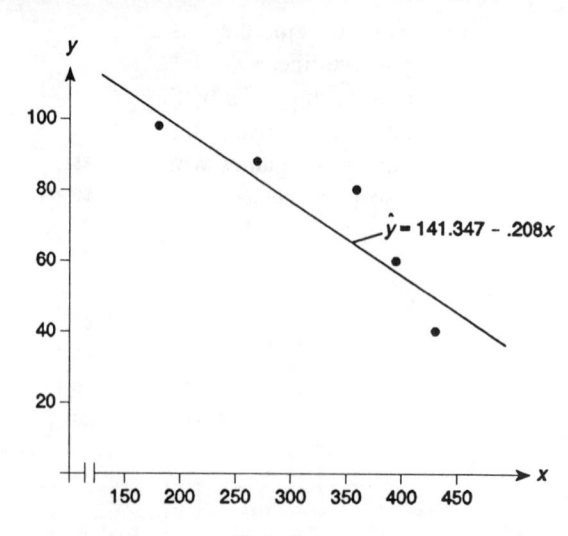

c. $\hat{\beta}_0 = 5.053$ This has no meaning since $x = 0$ is not in the observed range.

$\hat{\beta}_1 = .208$ As the number of suppliers increases by 1, the percent of products that meet final test quality inspection is estimated to decrease by .208.

10.21   a.   The plot of the data is:

It appears that as the age of the firm increases, the number of employees at fast-growing firms increases linearly. However, it does not appear to be a strong linear relationship. The points are not bunched very close to the line.

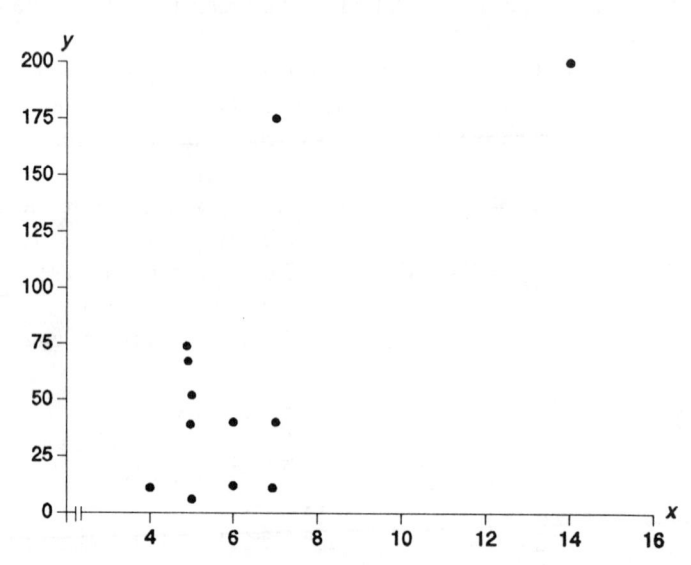

b. From the printout, $\hat{\beta}_0 = -51.361607$ and $\hat{\beta}_1 = 17.754464$.

$\hat{\beta}_0 = -51.361607$. Since $x = 0$ is not in the observed range, $\hat{\beta}_0$ is just an estimate of the y-intercept.

$\hat{\beta}_1 = 17.754464$. For each additional year of age, the mean number of employees is estimated to increase by 17.754464.

10.23   a. $s^2 = \dfrac{\text{SSE}}{n-2} = \dfrac{8.34}{26-2} = .3475$

b. We would expect most of the observations to be within $2s$ of the least squares line. This is:

$2s = 2\sqrt{.3475} \approx 1.179$

10.25 $SSE = SS_{yy} - \hat{\beta}_1 SS_{xy}$

where $SS_{yy} = \sum y_i^2 - \dfrac{(\sum y_i)^2}{n}$

For Exercise 10.10,

$$\sum y_i^2 = 159 \qquad \sum y_i = 31$$

$$SS_{yy} = 159 - \dfrac{31^2}{7} = 159 - 137.2857143 = 21.7142857$$

$$SS_{xy} = -26.2857143 \qquad \hat{\beta}_1 = -.779661017$$

Therefore, $SSE = 21.7142857 - (-.779661017)(-26.2857143) = 1.22033896 \approx 1.2203$

$$s^2 = \dfrac{SSE}{n-2} = \dfrac{1.22033896}{7-2} = .244067792, \quad s = \sqrt{.244067792} = .4960$$

We would expect most of the observations to fall within $2s$ or $2(.4940)$ or $.988$ units of the least squares prediction line.

For Exercise 10.13,

$$\sum x_i = 33 \quad \sum y_i = 27 \quad \sum x_i y_i = 104 \quad \sum x_i^2 = 179 \quad \sum y_i^2 = 133$$

$$SS_{xy} = \sum x_i y_i - \dfrac{(\sum x_i \sum y_i)}{n} = 104 - \dfrac{(23)(27)}{7} = 104 - 127.2857143 = -23.2857143$$

$$SS_{xx} = \sum x_i^2 - \dfrac{(\sum x_i)^2}{n} = 179 - \dfrac{(33)^2}{7} = 179 - 155.5714286 = 23.4285714$$

$$S_{yy} = \sum y_i^2 - \dfrac{(\sum y_i)^2}{n} = 133 - \dfrac{(27)^2}{7} = 133 - 104.1428571 = 28.8571429$$

$$\hat{\beta}_1 = \dfrac{SS_{xy}}{S_{xx}} = \dfrac{-23.2857143}{23.4285714} = -.99390244$$

$$SSE = SS_{yy} - \hat{\beta}_1 SS_{xy} = 28.8571429 - (.99390244)(-23.2857143)$$
$$= 28.8571429 - 23.14372824 = 5.71341466$$

$$s^2 = \dfrac{SSE}{n-2} = \dfrac{5.71341466}{7-2} = 1.142682932 \quad s = \sqrt{1.142682932} = 1.0690$$

We would expect most of the observations to fall within $2s$ or $2(1.0690)$ or 2.1380 units of the least squares prediction line.

10.27 a. From the printout, $SSE = 623.85737$, $s^2 = MSE = 51.98811$, and $s = $ Standard error $= 7.21028$.

b. We would expect that most of the observations will fall within $2s$ or $2(7.21028) = 14.42056$ games of their predicted values.

10.29 a. $\sum x = 55 \qquad \sum x^2 = 899 \qquad \sum xy = 154.89$
$\sum y = 14.49 \qquad \sum y^2 = 42.0817$

$$SS_{xy} = \sum xy - \dfrac{\sum x \sum y}{n} = 154.89 - \dfrac{55(14.49)}{5} = -4.55$$

Simple Linear Regression

$$SS_{xx} = \sum x^2 - \frac{(\sum x)^2}{n} = 899 - \frac{55^2}{5} = 294$$

$$SS_{yy} = \sum y^2 - \frac{(\sum y)^2}{n} = 42.0817 - \frac{14.49^2}{5} = .08968$$

$$\hat{\beta}_1 = \frac{SS_{xy}}{SS_{xx}} = \frac{-4.55}{294} = -.01547619 \approx -.015$$

$$\hat{\beta}_0 = \bar{y} - \hat{\beta}_1 \bar{x} = 2.898 - (-.01547619)(11) = 3.068238095 \approx 3.068$$

The least squares line is $\hat{y} = 3.068 - .015x$.

b. The graph of the data is:

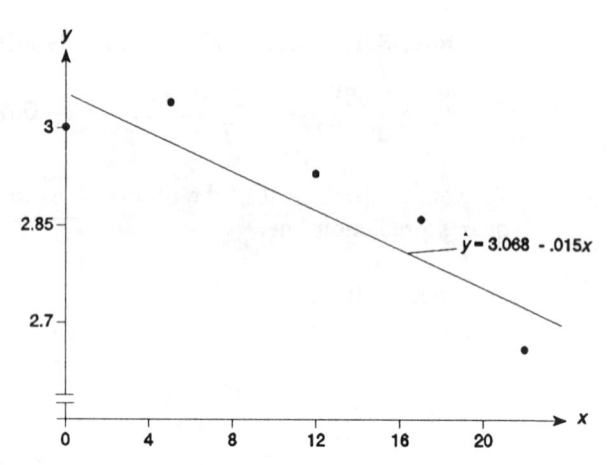

c. For $x = 10$, $\hat{y} = 3.068 - .015(10) = 2.918$
For $x = 16$, $\hat{y} = 3.068 - .015(16) = 2.828$

d. $SSE = SS_{yy} - \hat{\beta}_1 SS_{xy} = .08968 - (-.01547619)(-4.55) = .019263335$

$$s^2 = \frac{SSE}{n-2} = \frac{.019263335}{5-2} = .0064211 \qquad s = \sqrt{.0064211} = .0801$$

e. We would expect almost all of the predicted values to fall within $2s$ or $2(.0801)$ or $.1602$ of their observed values.

10.31 a. For confidence coefficient .95, $\alpha = 1 - .95 = .05$ and $\alpha/2 = .05/2 = .025$. From Table VI, Appendix B, with df $= n - 2 = 12 - 2 = 10$, $t_{.025} = 2.228$.

The 95% confidence interval for β_1 is:

$$\hat{\beta}_1 \pm t_{.025} s_{\hat{\beta}_1} \text{ where } s_{\hat{\beta}_1} = \frac{s}{\sqrt{SS_{xx}}} = \frac{3}{\sqrt{35}} = .5071$$

$$\Rightarrow 31 \pm 2.228(.5071) \Rightarrow 31 \pm 1.13 \Rightarrow (29.87, 32.13)$$

For confidence coefficient .90, $\alpha = 1 - .90 = .10$ and $\alpha/2 = .10/2 = .05$. From Table VI, Appendix B, with df $= 10$, $t_{.05} = 1.812$.

The 90% confidence interval for β_1 is:

$$\hat{\beta}_1 \pm t_{.05} s_{\hat{\beta}_1} \Rightarrow 31 \pm 1.812(.5071) \Rightarrow 31 \pm .92 \Rightarrow (30.08, 31.92)$$

b. $s^2 = \dfrac{SSE}{n-2} = \dfrac{1960}{18-2} = 122.5, s = \sqrt{s^2} = 11.0680$

For confidence coefficient, .95, $\alpha = 1 - .95 = .05$ and $\alpha/2 = .05/2 = .025$. From Table VI, Appendix B, with df $= n - 2 = 18 - 2 = 16$, $t_{.025} = 2.120$. The 95% confidence interval for β_1 is:

$$\hat{\beta}_1 \pm t_{.025} s_{\hat{\beta}_1} \text{ where } s_{\hat{\beta}_1} = \dfrac{s}{\sqrt{SS_{xx}}} = \dfrac{11.0680}{\sqrt{30}} = 2.0207$$

$$\Rightarrow 64 \pm 2.120(2.0207) \Rightarrow 64 \pm 4.28 \Rightarrow (59.72, 68.28)$$

For confidence coefficient .90, $\alpha = 1 - .90 = .10$ and $\alpha/2 = .10/2 = .05$. From Table VI, Appendix B, with df $= 16$, $t_{.05} = 1.746$.

The 90% confidence interval for β_1 is:

$$\hat{\beta}_1 \pm t_{.05} s_{\hat{\beta}_1} \Rightarrow 64 \pm 1.746(2.0207) \Rightarrow 64 \pm 3.53 \Rightarrow (60.47, 67.53)$$

c. $s^2 = \dfrac{SSE}{n-2} = \dfrac{146}{24-2} = 6.6364, s = \sqrt{s^2} = 2.5761$

For confidence coefficient .95, $\alpha = 1 - .95 = .05$ and $\alpha/2 = .05/2 = .025$. From Table VI, Appendix B, with df $= n - 2 = 24 - 2 = 22$, $t_{.025} = 2.074$. The 95% confidence interval for β_1 is:

$$\hat{\beta}_1 \pm t_{.025} s_{\hat{\beta}_1} \text{ where } s_{\hat{\beta}_1} = \dfrac{s}{\sqrt{SS_{xx}}} = \dfrac{2.5761}{\sqrt{64}} = .3220$$

$$\Rightarrow -8.4 \pm 2.074(.322) \Rightarrow -8.4 \pm .67 \Rightarrow (-9.07, -7.73)$$

For confidence coefficient .90, $\alpha = 1 - .90 = .10$ and $\alpha/2 = .10/2 = .05$. From Table VI, Appendix B, with df $= 22$, $t_{.05} = 1.717$.

The 90% confidence interval for β_1 is:

$$\hat{\beta}_1 \pm t_{.05} s_{\hat{\beta}_1} \Rightarrow -8.4 \pm 1.717(.322) \Rightarrow -8.4 \pm .55 \Rightarrow (-8.95, -7.85)$$

10.33 From Exercise 10.32 $\hat{\beta}_1 = .8214, s = 1.1922, SS_{xx} = 28$, and $n = 7$.

For confidence coefficient .80, $\alpha = 1 - .80 = .20$ and $\alpha/2 = .20/2 = .10$. From Table VI, Appendix B, with df $= n - 2 = 7 - 2 = 5$, $t_{.10} = 1.476$. The 80% confidence interval for β_1 is:

$$\hat{\beta}_1 \pm t_{.025} s_{\hat{\beta}_1} \text{ where } s_{\hat{\beta}_1} = \dfrac{s}{\sqrt{SS_{xx}}} = \dfrac{1.1922}{\sqrt{28}} = .2253$$

$$\Rightarrow .8214 \pm 1.476(.2253) \Rightarrow .8214 \pm .3325 \Rightarrow (.4889, 1.1539)$$

For confidence coefficient .98, $\alpha = 1 - .98 = .02$ and $\alpha/2 = .02/2 = .01$. From Table VI, Appendix B, with df $= 5$, $t_{.01} = 3.365$.

The 98% confidence interval for β_1 is:

$$\hat{\beta}_1 \pm t_{.01} s_{\hat{\beta}_1} \Rightarrow .8214 \pm 3.365(.2253) \Rightarrow .8214 \pm .7581 \Rightarrow (.0633, 1.5795)$$

10.35   a.   For $n = 100$, df $= n - 2 = 100 - 2 = 98$. From Table VI with df $= 98$, p-value $= P(t > 6.572) + P(t < -6.572) = 2P(t > 6.572) < 2(.0005) = .0010$. Since this p-value is very small, we would reject H_0. There is sufficient evidence to indicate the slope is not 0. Thus, there is evidence to indicate sales price and square feet of living space are linearly related.

   b.   For each additional square foot of living space, the price of the house is estimated to increase from $49.1 to $90.9. This is valid only for houses with square footage between 1,500 and 4,000. The interval could be made narrower by decreasing the level of confidence.

10.37   a.   To determine if x and y are linearly related, we test:

H_0: $\beta_1 = 0$
H_a: $\beta_1 \neq 0$

The test statistic is $t = 4.98$.

The p-value is .001. Since the p-value is less than $\alpha = .01$, H_0 is rejected at $\alpha = .01$. There is sufficient evidence to indicate that x and y are linearly related.

   b.   Since the model is adequate, it is reasonable to use it to predict values of y.

For $x = 3$, $\hat{y} = .202 + .135x = .202 + .135(3) = .607$. This value is meaningful only if $x = 3$ is within the observed range.

10.39   a.   To determine whether the number of employees is positively linearly related to age of a fast-growing firm, we test:

H_0: $\beta_1 = 0$
H_a: $\beta_1 > 0$

The test statistic is $t = \dfrac{\hat{\beta}_1 - 0}{s_{\hat{\beta}_1}} = 3.384$ (from printout).

The p-value is $.0070/2 = .0035$. Since the p-value is less than $\alpha = .01$, H_0 is rejected. There is sufficient evidence to indicate that the number of employees is positively linearly related to age of a fast-growing firm at $\alpha > .0035$.

   b.   For confidence coefficient .99, $\alpha = 1 - .99 = .01$ and $\alpha/2 = .005$. From Table VI, Appendix B, with df $= n - 2 = 12 - 2 = 10$, $t_{.005} = 3.169$. The confidence interval is:

$\hat{\beta}_1 \pm t_{.005}\, s_{\hat{\beta}_1} \Rightarrow 17.754 \pm 3.169(5.2467) \Rightarrow 17.754 \pm 16.627 \Rightarrow (1.127, 34.381)$

We are 99% confident that for each additional year of age, the mean number of employees will increase by anywhere from 1.127 to 34.381.

10.41   a.   From the printout, the fitted line is $\hat{y} = 12.71 + 1.50x$.

   b.   To determine whether the straight-line model contributes information for the prediction of overhead costs, we test:

H_0: $\beta_1 = 0$
H_a: $\beta_1 \neq 0$

The test statistic is $t = \dfrac{\hat{\beta}_1 - 0}{s_{\hat{\beta}_1}} = 18.258$

The rejection region requires $\alpha/2 = .05/2 = .025$ in each tail of the t-distribution with df $= n - 2 = 12 - 2 = 10$. From Table VI, Appendix B, $t_{.025} = 2.228$. The rejection region is $t > 2.228$ or $t < -2.228$.

Since the observed value of the test statistic falls in the rejection region ($t = 18.258 > 2.228$), H_0 is rejected. There is sufficient evidence to indicate the straight-line model contributes information for the prediction of overhead costs at $\alpha = .05$.

c. The assumption of independence of error terms may be inappropriate since the data are collected sequentially.

10.43 From Exercise 10.15,

$SS_{xx} = 4{,}362{,}209{,}330 \qquad \hat{\beta}_1 = -.002186456$
$SS_{xy} = -9{,}537{,}780$

$\sum y_i = 7497 \qquad \sum y_i^2 = 4{,}061{,}063$

$SS_{yy} = \sum y_i^2 - \dfrac{(\sum y_i)^2}{n} = 4{,}061{,}063 - \dfrac{7497^2}{15} = 314062.4$

$SSE = SS_{yy} - \hat{\beta}_1 SS_{xy} = 314062.4 - (-.002186456)(-9{,}537{,}780) = 293208.4637$

$s^2 = \dfrac{SSE}{n-2} = \dfrac{293208.4637}{15-2} = 22554.49721 \quad s = \sqrt{22554.49721} = 150.1815$

To determine if extent of retaliation is related to whistle blower's power, we test:

$H_0: \beta_1 = 0$
$H_a: \beta_1 \neq 0$

The test statistic is $t = \dfrac{\hat{\beta}_1 - 0}{s_{\hat{\beta}_1}} = \dfrac{-.0022}{\dfrac{150.1815}{\sqrt{4362209330}}} = -.96$

The rejection region requires $\alpha/2 = .05/2 = .025$ in each tail of the t-distribution with df $= n - 2 = 15 - 2 = 13$. From Table VI, Appendix B, $t_{.025} = 2.160$. The rejection region is $t > 2.160$ or $t < -2.160$.

Since the observed value of the test statistic does not fall in the rejection region ($t = -.96 \not< -2.160$), H_0 is not rejected. There is insufficient evidence to indicate the extent of retaliation is related to the whistle blower's power at $\alpha = .05$. This agrees with Near and Miceli.

10.45 a. If $r = .7$, there is a positive relationship between x and y. As x increases, y tends to increase. The slope is positive.

b. If $r = -.7$, there is a negative relationship between x and y. As x increases, y tends to decrease. The slope is negative.

c. If $r = 0$, there is a 0 slope. There is no relationship between x and y.

Simple Linear Regression

d. If $r^2 = .64$, then r is either .8 or $-.8$. The relationship between x and y could be either positive or negative.

10.47 a. From Exercises 10.10 and 10.25,

$$r^2 = 1 - \frac{SSE}{SS_{yy}} = 1 - \frac{1.22033896}{21.7142857} = 1 - .0562 = .9438$$

94.38% of the total sample variability around $\bar{y}$ is explained by the linear relationship between y and x.

b. From Exercises 10.13 and 10.25,

$$r^2 = 1 - \frac{SSE}{SS_{yy}} = 1 - \frac{5.71341466}{28.8571429} = .8020$$

80.20% of the total sample variability around $\bar{y}$ is explained by the linear relationship between y and x.

10.49 a. $r = .14$. Because this value is close to 0, there is a very weak positive linear relationship between math confidence and computer interest for boys.

b. $r = .33$. Because this value is fairly close to 0, there is a weak positive linear relationship between math confidence and computer interest for girls.

10.51 a. Some preliminary calculations:

$$\sum x = 195 \quad \sum x^2 = 8,425 \quad \sum xy = 14,700 \quad \sum y = 355 \quad \sum y^2 = 26,125$$

$$SS_{xy} = \sum xy - \frac{(\sum x)(\sum y)}{n} = 14,700 - \frac{195(355)}{5} = 855$$

$$SS_{xx} = \sum x^2 - \frac{(\sum x)^2}{n} = 8,425 - \frac{195^2}{5} = 820$$

$$SS_{yy} = \sum y^2 - \frac{(\sum y)^2}{n} = 26,125 - \frac{355^2}{5} = 920$$

$$r = \frac{SS_{xy}}{\sqrt{SS_{xx}SS_{yy}}} = \frac{855}{\sqrt{820(920)}} = .9844$$

b. The coefficient of correlation is .9844. There is a very strong positive linear relationship between views of American and Asian managers. Even though the coefficient of correlation is close to one, the values of the Asian managers are approximately 30 points higher in each case than the values of the American managers.

10.53 From the printout, $r^2 = $ R Square $= .57873$

57.9% of the sample variability around the sample mean S&P 500 stock composite average is explained by the linear relationship between the interest rate and the S&P 500 stock composite average.

From the printout, $r = -.7607$

The relationship between interest rate and S&P stock composite average is negative since $r < 0$. The relationship is not particularly strong because $-.7607$ is not that close to -1.

10.55 a.

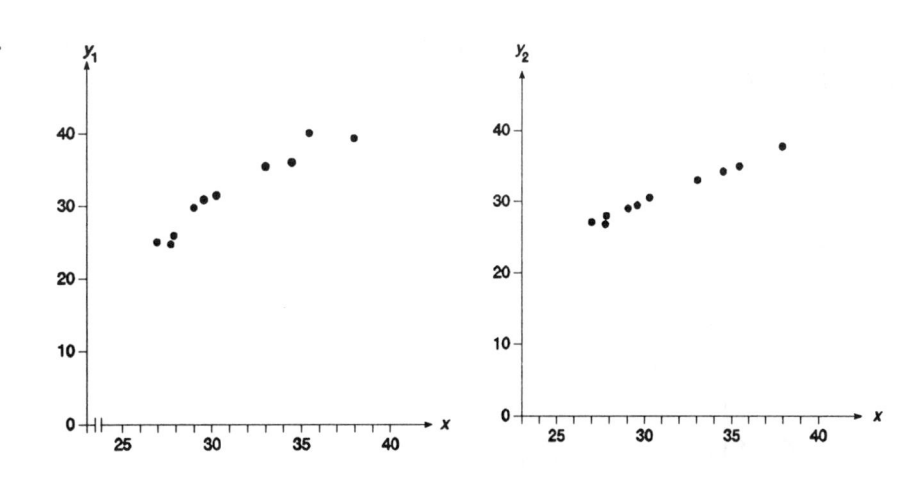

[Two scatterplots: left shows y_1 vs x with points rising from about (27, 25) to (38, 40); right shows y_2 vs x with points rising from about (27, 27) to (38, 38), both spanning x from 25 to 40.]

b. It appears that the weigh-in-motion reading after calibration adjustment is more highly correlated with the static weight of trucks than prior to calibration adjustment. The scattergram is closer to a straight line.

c. Some preliminary calculations are:

$$\sum x = 312.8 \quad \sum x^2 = 9911.42 \quad \sum xy_1 = 10{,}201.41$$

$$\sum y_1 = 320.2 \quad \sum y_1^2 = 10{,}543.68 \quad n = 10$$

$$\sum y_2 = 311.2 \quad \sum y_2^2 = 9809.52 \quad \sum xy_2 = 9859.84$$

$$SS_{xy_1} = \sum xy_1 - \frac{\sum x \sum y_1}{n} = 10{,}201.41 - \frac{312.8(320.2)}{10} = 185.554$$

$$SS_{xx} = \sum x^2 - \frac{(\sum x)^2}{n} = 9911.42 - \frac{312.8^2}{10} = 127.036$$

$$SS_{y_1 y_1} = \sum y_1^2 - \frac{(\sum y_1)^2}{n} = 10{,}543.68 - \frac{320.2^2}{10} = 290.876$$

$$SS_{xy_2} = \sum xy_2 - \frac{\sum x \sum y_2}{n} = 9859.84 - \frac{312.8(311.2)}{10} = 125.504$$

$$SS_{y_2 y_2} = \sum y_2^2 - \frac{(\sum y_2)^2}{n} = 9809.52 - \frac{311.2^2}{10} = 124.976$$

$$r_1 = \frac{SS_{xy_1}}{\sqrt{SS_{xx} SS_{y_1 y_1}}} = \frac{185.554}{\sqrt{127.036(290.876)}} = .9653$$

$$r_2 = \frac{SS_{xy_2}}{\sqrt{SS_{xx} SS_{y_2 y_2}}} = \frac{125.504}{\sqrt{127.036(124.976)}} = .9960$$

$r_1 = .9563$ implies the static weight of trucks and weigh-in-motion prior to calibration adjustment have a strong positive linear relationship.

$r_2 = .996$ implies the static weight of trucks and weigh-in-motion after calibration adjustment have a stronger positive linear relationship.

The closer r is to 1 indicates the more accurate the weigh-in-motion readings are.

Simple Linear Regression

d. Yes. If the weigh-in-motion readings were all exactly the same distance below (or above) the actual readings, r would be 1.

10.57 a.

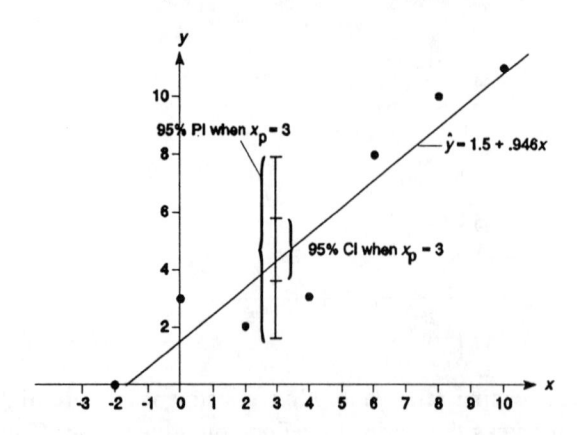

b. Some preliminary calculations are:

$$\sum x_i = 28 \quad \sum x_i^2 = 224 \quad \sum x_i y_i = 254 \quad \sum y_i = 37 \quad \sum y_i^2 = 307$$

$$SS_{xy} = \sum x_i y_i - \frac{\sum x_i \sum y_i}{n} = 254 - \frac{28(37)}{7} = 106$$

$$SS_{xx} = \sum x_i^2 - \frac{(\sum x_i)^2}{n} = 224 - \frac{28^2}{7} = 112$$

$$SS_{yy} = \sum y_i^2 - \frac{(\sum y_i)^2}{n} = 307 - \frac{37^2}{7} = 111.4285714$$

$$\hat{\beta}_1 = \frac{SS_{xy}}{SS_{xx}} = \frac{106}{112} = .946428571$$

$$\hat{\beta}_0 = \bar{y} - \hat{\beta}_1 \bar{x} = \frac{37}{7} - .946428571\left(\frac{28}{7}\right) = 1.5$$

The least squares line is $\hat{y} = 1.5 + .946x$.

c. $SSE = SS_{yy} - \hat{\beta}_1 SS_{xy} = 111.4285714 - (.946428571)(106) = 11.1071429$

$$s^2 = \frac{SSE}{n - 2} = \frac{11.1071429}{7 - 2} = 2.22143$$

d. The form of the confidence interval is:

$$\hat{y} \pm t_{\alpha/2} s \sqrt{\frac{1}{n} + \frac{(x_p - \bar{x})^2}{SS_{xx}}} \text{ where } s = \sqrt{s^2} = \sqrt{2.22143} = 1.4904$$

For $x_p = 3$, $\hat{y} = 1.5 + .946(3) = 4.338$ and $\bar{x} = \frac{28}{7} = 4$

For confidence coefficient .90, $\alpha = 1 - .90 = .10$ and $\alpha/2 = .10/2 = .05$. From Table VI, Appendix B, $t_{.05} = 2.015$ with df $= n - 2 = 7 - 2 = 5$.

The 90% confidence interval is:

$$4.338 \pm 2.015(1.4904)\sqrt{\frac{1}{7} + \frac{(3-4)^2}{112}} \Rightarrow 4.338 \pm 1.170 \Rightarrow (3.168, 5.508)$$

e. The form of the prediction interval is:

$$\hat{y} \pm t_{\alpha/2}s\sqrt{1 + \frac{1}{n} + \frac{(x_p - \bar{x})^2}{SS_{xx}}}$$

The 90% prediction interval is:

$$4.338 \pm 2.015(1.4904)\sqrt{1 + \frac{1}{7} + \frac{(3-4)^2}{112}} \Rightarrow 4.338 \pm 3.223 \Rightarrow (1.115, 7.561)$$

f. The 95% prediction interval for y is wider than the 95% confidence interval for the mean value of y when $x_p = 3$.

The error of predicting a particular value of y will be larger than the error of estimating the mean value of y for a particular x value. This is true since the error in estimating the mean value of y for a given x value is the distance between the least squares line and the true line of means, while the error in predicting some future value of y is the sum of two errors—the error of estimating the mean of y plus the random error that is a component of the value of y to be predicted.

10.59 a. The form of the confidence interval is:

$$\bar{y} \pm t_{\alpha/2}\frac{s}{\sqrt{n}} \text{ where } \bar{y} = \frac{\sum y}{n} = \frac{22}{10} = 2.2$$

$$s^2 = \frac{\sum y^2 - \frac{(\sum y)^2}{n}}{n - 1} = \frac{82 - \frac{(22)^2}{10}}{10 - 1} = 3.7333 \text{ and } s = 1.9322$$

For confidence coefficient .95, $\alpha = 1 - .95 = .05$ and $\alpha/2 = .05/2 = .025$. From Table VI, Appendix B, $t_{.025} = 2.262$ with df $= n - 1 = 10 - 1 = 9$. The 95% confidence interval is:

$$2.2 \pm 2.262\frac{1.9322}{\sqrt{10}} \Rightarrow 2.2 \pm 1.382 \Rightarrow (.818, 3.582)$$

Simple Linear Regression

b.

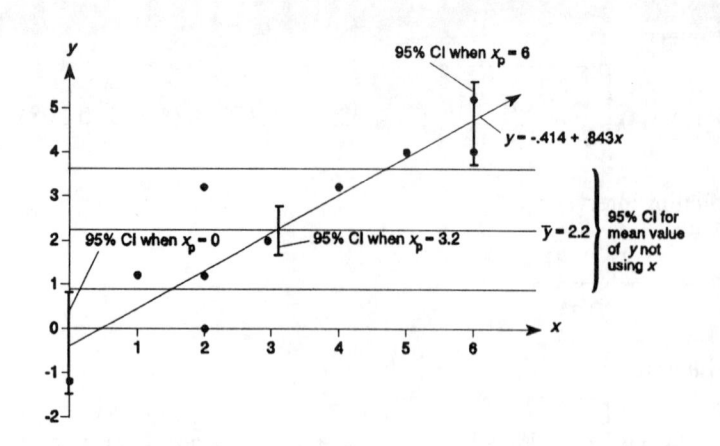

c. The confidence intervals computed in Exercise 10.58 are much narrower than that found in part a. Thus, x appears to contribute information about the mean value of y.

d. From Exercise 10.58, $\hat{\beta}_1 = .843$, $s = .8619$, $SS_{xx} = 38.9$, and $n = 10$.

H_0: $\beta_1 = 0$
H_a: $\beta_1 \neq 0$

The test statistic is $t = \dfrac{\hat{\beta}_1 - 0}{s_{\hat{\beta}_1}} = \dfrac{\hat{\beta}_1 - 0}{\dfrac{s}{\sqrt{SS_{xx}}}} = \dfrac{.843 - 0}{\dfrac{.8619}{\sqrt{38.9}}} = 6.10$

The rejection region requires $\alpha/2 = .05/2 = .025$ in each tail of the t-distribution with df $= n - 2 = 10 - 2 = 8$. From Table VI, Appendix B, $t_{.025} = 2.306$. The rejection region is $t > 2.306$ or $t < -2.306$.

Since the observed value of the test statistic falls in the rejection region ($t = 6.10 > 2.306$), H_0 is rejected. There is sufficient evidence to indicate the straight-line model contributes information for the prediction of y at $\alpha = .05$.

10.61 a. The scatterplot of the data is:

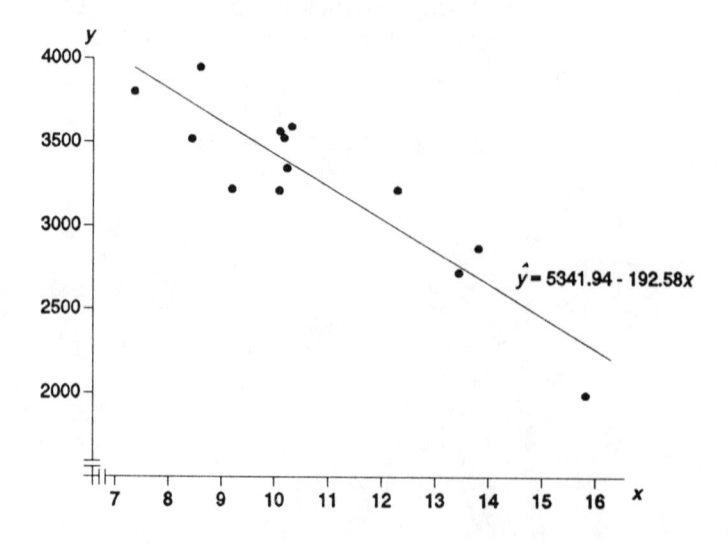

b. From the printout, the least squares line is:

$$\hat{y} = 5341.9 - 192.58x$$

See the plot in part a.

c. To determine if a straight-line model provides useful information about the relationship between annual sales of existing single-family homes and mortgage interest rates, we test:

$H_0: \beta_1 = 0$
$H_a: \beta_1 \neq 0$

The test statistic is $t = \dfrac{\hat{\beta}_1 - 0}{s_{\hat{\beta}_1}} = -7.09$ (from printout).

The rejection region requires $\alpha/2 = .05/2 = .025$ in each tail of the t-distribution with df = $n - 2 = 13 - 2 = 11$. From Table VI, Appendix B, $t_{.025} = 2.201$. The rejection region is $t > 2.201$ or $t < -2.201$.

Since the observed value of the test statistic falls in the rejection region ($t = -7.09 < -2.201$), H_0 is rejected. There is sufficient evidence to indicate that mortgage interest rates contribute information for the prediction of the annual sales of existing single-family homes at $\alpha = .05$.

d. From the printout, $r^2 = .820$.

82.0% of the sample variability of the annual sales of existing single-family homes about their means is explained by the linear relationship between interest rates and annual sales of existing single-family homes.

e. The confidence interval is: (3269.9, 3562.4)

We are 95% confident that the mean number of existing single family homes sold when the average annual mortgage interest rate is 10% is between 3,269.9 and 3,562.4.

f. The prediction interval is: (2893.7, 3938.6)

We are 95% confident that the actual number of existing single family homes sold when the average annual mortgage interest rate is 10% is between 2,893.7 and 3,938.6.

g. The width of the prediction interval for an actual value of y is always larger than the width of the confidence interval for the mean value of y. The prediction interval takes into account two variances: the variance for locating the mean and the variance of y once the mean has been located.

10.63 a. To determine the usefulness of the model, we test:

$H_0: \beta_1 = 0$
$H_a: \beta_1 \neq 0$

The test statistic is $t = \dfrac{\hat{\beta}_1 - 0}{s_{\hat{\beta}_1}} = 15.35$ (from printout).

Simple Linear Regression

The rejection region requires $\alpha/2 = .05/2 = .025$ in each tail of the t-distribution with df = $n - 2 = 20 - 2 = 18$. From Table VI, Appendix B, $t_{.025} = 2.101$. The rejection region is $t > 2.101$ or $t < -2.101$.

Since the observed value of the test statistic falls in the rejection region ($t = 15.35 > 2.101$), H_0 is rejected. There is sufficient evidence to indicate the model is useful at $\alpha = .05$. Therefore, the monthly sales is useful in predicting the number of managers at $\alpha = .05$.

b. For confidence coefficient .90, $\alpha = 1 - .90 = .10$ and $\alpha/2 = .10/2 = .05$. From Table VI, Appendix B, $t_{.05} = 1.734$ with df = 18.

For $x_p = 39$, $\bar{x} = \dfrac{\sum x}{n} = \dfrac{540}{20} = 27$, and $\hat{y} = 5.325 + .5861(39) = 28.1829$.

The form of the prediction interval is:

$$\hat{y} \pm t_{\alpha/2} s \sqrt{1 + \frac{1}{n} + \frac{(x_p - \bar{x})^2}{SS_{xx}}} \Rightarrow 28.183 \pm 1.734(2.5664)\sqrt{1 + \frac{1}{20} + \frac{(39 - 27)^2}{4{,}518}}$$
$$\Rightarrow 28.183 \pm 4.629 \Rightarrow (23.554, 32.812)$$

c. We are 90% confident the actual number of managers needed when 39 units are sold is between 23.55 and 32.81.

10.65 a. The dependent variable should be Indirect Manufacturing Labor Costs. The cost driver or independent variable is the machine hours. Thus, the Indirect Manufacturing Labor cost will be the dependent variable.

b. The scatterplot of the data is:

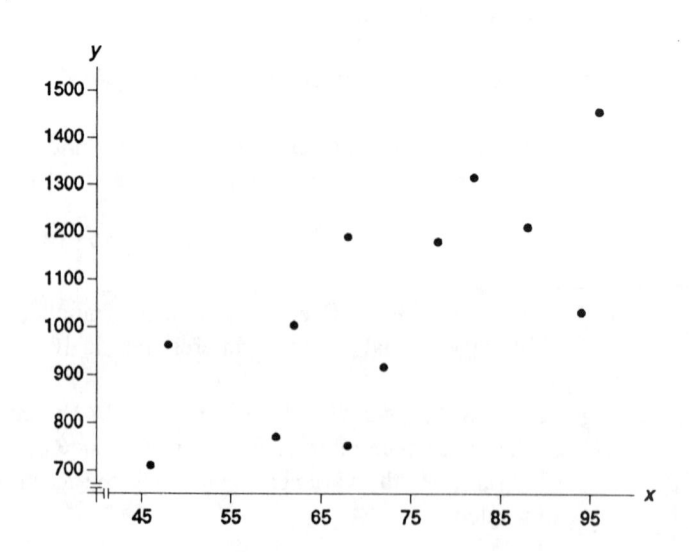

c. Some preliminary calculations:

$$\sum x = 862 \qquad \sum x^2 = 64{,}900 \qquad \sum xy = 928{,}716$$
$$\sum y = 12{,}501 \qquad \sum y^2 = 13{,}630{,}615$$

$$SS_{xy} = \sum xy - \frac{(\sum x)(\sum y)}{n} = 928{,}716 - \frac{862(12{,}501)}{12} = 30{,}727.5$$

$$SS_{xx} = \sum x^2 - \frac{(\sum x)^2}{n} = 64{,}900 - \frac{862^2}{12} = 2{,}979.666667$$

$$SS_{yy} = \sum y^2 - \frac{(\sum y)^2}{n} = 13{,}630{,}615 - \frac{12{,}501^2}{12} = 607{,}698.25$$

$$\hat{\beta}_1 = \frac{SS_{xy}}{SS_{xx}} = \frac{30{,}727.5}{2{,}979.666667} = 10.31239511 \approx 10.312$$

$$\hat{\beta}_0 = \bar{y} - \hat{\beta}_1 \bar{x} = \frac{12{,}501}{12} - \frac{10.31239511(862)}{12} = 300.9762846 \approx 300.976$$

The least squares equation is $\hat{y} = 300.976 + 10.312x$.

d. $SSE = SS_{yy} - \hat{\beta}_1 SS_{xy} = 607{,}698.25 - 10.31239511(30{,}727.5) = 290{,}824.1293$

$$s^2 = \frac{SSE}{n-2} = \frac{290{,}824.1293}{12-2} = 29{,}082.41293 \qquad s = \sqrt{29{,}082.41293} = 170.5356647$$

$$s_{\hat{\beta}_1} = \frac{s}{\sqrt{SS_{xx}}} = \frac{170.5356647}{\sqrt{2{,}979.66667}} = 3.1241$$

To determine if the model was useful, we test:

$H_0: \beta_1 = 0$
$H_a: \beta_1 \neq 0$

The test statistic is $t = \dfrac{\hat{\beta}_1 - 0}{s_{\hat{\beta}_1}} = \dfrac{10.312 - 0}{3.1241} = 3.301$

The rejection region requires $\alpha/2 = .05/2 = .025$ in each tail of the t-distribution with df $= n - 2 = 12 - 2 = 10$. From Table VI, Appendix B, $t_{.025} = 2.228$. The rejection region is $t < -2.228$ or $t > 2.228$.

Since the observed value of the test statistic falls in the rejection region ($t = 3.301 > 2.228$), H_0 is rejected. There is sufficient evidence to indicate that the model is useful at $\alpha = .05$.

e. $r^2 = 1 - \dfrac{SSE}{SS_{yy}} = 1 - \dfrac{290{,}824.1293}{607{,}698.25} = .5214$

52.14% of the variability in the Labor Costs about their means is explained by the linear relationship between Labor Costs and Machine Hours.

f. The form of the prediction interval is:

$$\hat{y} \pm t_{\alpha/2} s \sqrt{1 + \frac{1}{n} + \frac{(x_p - \bar{x})^2}{SS_{xx}}}$$

Suppose $x_p = 50$. $\hat{y} = 300.976 + 10.312(50) = 816.596$

For confidence coefficient .95, $\alpha = 1 - .95 = .05$ and $\alpha/2 = .05/2 = .025$. From Table VI, Appendix B, with df $= n - 2 = 12 - 2 = 10$, $t_{.025} = 2.228$. The prediction interval is:

$$816.596 \pm 2.228(170.5357)\sqrt{1 + \frac{1}{12} + \frac{(50 - 71.8333)^2}{2{,}979.66667}} \Rightarrow 816.596 \pm 423.664$$
$$\Rightarrow (392.932,\ 1{,}240.260)$$

Simple Linear Regression

We are 95% confident that the actual labor costs for 50 machine hours will be between 392.932 and 1,240.260.

10.67 a. $\hat{\beta}_1 = \dfrac{SS_{xy}}{SS_{xx}} = \dfrac{-88}{55} = -1.6$, $\hat{\beta}_0 = \bar{y} - \hat{\beta}_1 \bar{x} = 35 - (-1.6)(1.3) = 37.08$

The least squares line is $\hat{y} = 37.08 - 1.6x$.

b.

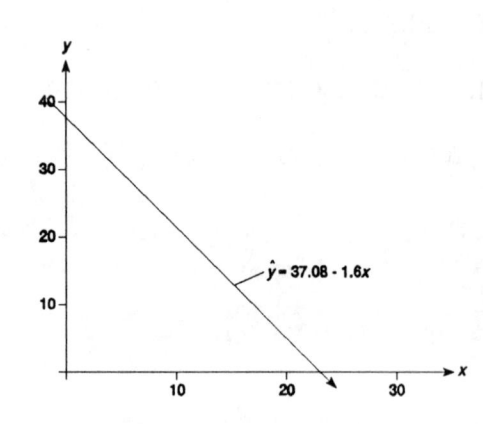

c. $SSE = SS_{yy} - \hat{\beta}_1 SS_{xy} = 198 - (-1.6)(-88) = 57.2$

d. $s^2 = \dfrac{SSE}{n-2} = \dfrac{57.2}{15-2} = 4.4$

e. For confidence coefficient .90, $\alpha = 1 - .90 = .10$ and $\alpha/2 = .10/2 = .05$. From Table VI, Appendix B, with df $= n - 2 = 15 - 2 = 13$, $t_{.05} = 1.771$. The 90% confidence interval for β_1 is:

$$\hat{\beta}_1 \pm t_{\alpha/2} \dfrac{s}{\sqrt{SS_{xx}}} \Rightarrow -1.6 \pm 1.771 \dfrac{\sqrt{4.4}}{\sqrt{55}} \Rightarrow -1.6 \pm .501 \Rightarrow (-2.101, -1.099)$$

We are 90% confident the change in the mean value of y for each unit change in x is between -2.101 and -1.099.

f. For $x_p = 15$, $\hat{y} = 37.08 - 1.6(15) = 13.08$

The 90% confidence interval is:

$$\hat{y} \pm t_{\alpha/2} s \sqrt{\dfrac{1}{n} + \dfrac{(x_p - \bar{x})^2}{SS_{xx}}} \Rightarrow 13.08 \pm 1.771(\sqrt{4.4}) \sqrt{\dfrac{1}{15} + \dfrac{(15-1.3)^2}{55}}$$

$$\Rightarrow 13.08 \pm 6.929 \Rightarrow (6.151, 20.009)$$

g. The 90% prediction interval is:

$$\hat{y} \pm t_{\alpha/2} s \sqrt{1 + \dfrac{1}{n} + \dfrac{(x_p - \bar{x})^2}{SS_{xx}}} \Rightarrow 13.08 \pm 1.771(\sqrt{4.4}) \sqrt{1 + \dfrac{1}{15} + \dfrac{(15-1.3)^2}{55}}$$

$$\Rightarrow 13.08 \pm 7.862 \Rightarrow (5.218, 20.942)$$

10.69   a.

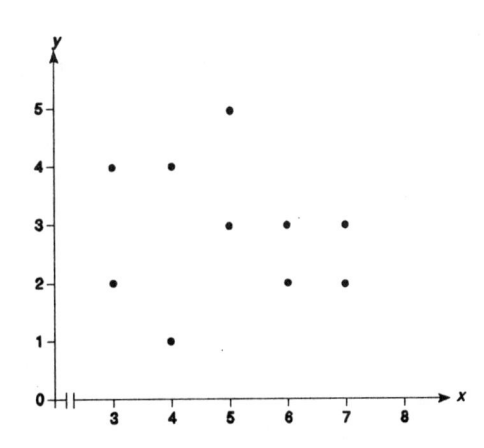

b.   Some preliminary calculations are:

$$\sum x = 50 \qquad \sum x^2 = 270 \qquad \sum xy = 143$$
$$\sum y = 29 \qquad \sum y^2 = 97$$

$$SS_{xy} = \sum xy - \frac{\sum x \sum y}{n} = 143 - \frac{50(29)}{10} = -2$$

$$SS_{xx} = \sum x^2 - \frac{(\sum x)^2}{n} = 270 - \frac{50^2}{10} = 20$$

$$SS_{yy} = \sum y^2 - \frac{(\sum y)^2}{n} = 97 - \frac{29^2}{10} = 12.9$$

$$r = \frac{SS_{xy}}{\sqrt{SS_{xx} SS_{yy}}} = \frac{-2}{\sqrt{20(12.9)}} = -.1245$$

$$r^2 = 2(-.1245)^2 = .0155$$

c.   Some preliminary calculations are:

$$\hat{\beta}_1 = \frac{SS_{xy}}{SS_{xx}} = \frac{-2}{20} = -.1$$

$$SSE = SS_{yy} = \hat{\beta}_1 SS_{xy} = 12.9 - (-.1)(-2) = 12.7$$

$$s^2 = \frac{SSE}{n-2} = \frac{12.7}{10-2} = 1.5875 \qquad s = \sqrt{1.5875} = 1.25996$$

To determine if x and y are linearly correlated, we test:

H_0: $\beta_1 = 0$
H_a: $\beta_1 \neq 0$

The test statistic is $t = \dfrac{\hat{\beta}_1 - 0}{\dfrac{s}{\sqrt{SS_{xx}}}} = \dfrac{-.1 - 0}{\dfrac{1.25996}{\sqrt{20}}} = -.35$

The rejection requires $\alpha/2 = .10/2 = .05$ in the each tail of the t-distribution with df $= n - 2 = 10 - 2 = 8$. From Table VI, Appendix B, $t_{.05} = 1.86$. The rejection region is $t > 1.86$ or $t < -1.86$.

Simple Linear Regression

Since the observed value of the test statistic does not fall in the rejection region ($t = -.35 \not< -1.86$), H_0 is not rejected. There is insufficient evidence to indicate that x and y are linearly correlated at $\alpha = .10$.

10.71 a. The plot of the data is:

It appears that there is a linear relationship between order size and time. As order size increases, the time tends to increase.

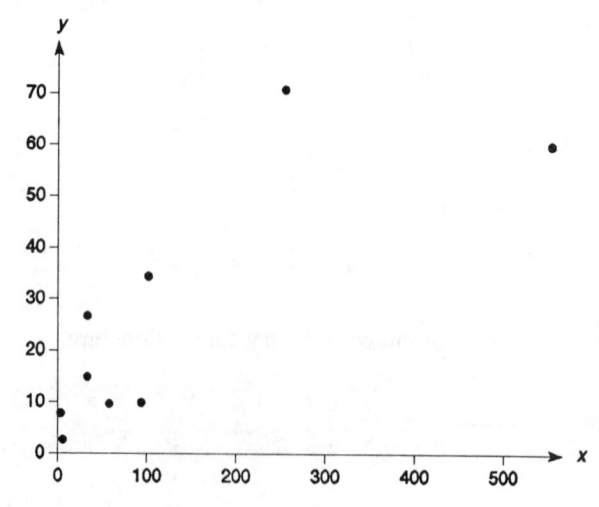

b. Some preliminary calculations are:

$$\sum x_i = 1149 \qquad \sum x_i^2 = 398{,}979 \qquad \sum x_i y_i = 58{,}102$$

$$\sum y_i = 239 \qquad \sum y_i^2 = 11{,}093$$

$$SS_{xy} = \sum x_i y_i - \frac{\sum x_i \sum y_i}{n} = 58{,}102 - \frac{1149(239)}{9} = 27{,}589.66667$$

$$SS_{xx} = \sum x_i^2 - \frac{(\sum x_i)^2}{n} = 398{,}979 - \frac{1149^2}{9} = 252{,}290$$

$$SS_{yy} = \sum y_i^2 - \frac{(\sum y_i)^2}{n} = 11{,}093 - \frac{239^2}{9} = 4746.222222$$

$$\hat{\beta}_1 = \frac{SS_{xy}}{SS_{xx}} = \frac{27{,}589.66667}{252{,}290} = .109356957 \approx .10936$$

$$\hat{\beta}_0 = \bar{y} - \hat{\beta}_1 \bar{x} = \frac{239}{9} - (.109356957)\frac{1149}{9} = 12.59431738 \approx 12.594$$

$$SSE = SS_{yy} - \hat{\beta}_1 SS_{xy} = 4746.222222 - (.109356957)(27{,}589.66667)$$
$$= 1729.10023$$

$$s^2 = \frac{SSE}{n-2} = \frac{1729.10023}{9-2} = 247.0143186 \qquad s = \sqrt{s^2} = 15.7167$$

The least squares line is $\hat{y} = 12.594 + .10936x$.

c. To determine if the mean time to fill an order increases with the size of the order, we test:

$H_0: \beta_1 = 0$
$H_a: \beta_1 > 0$

The test statistic is $t = \dfrac{\hat{\beta}_1 - 0}{s_{\hat{\beta}_1}} = \dfrac{.1094 - 0}{\dfrac{15.7167}{\sqrt{252{,}290}}} = 3.50$

The rejection region requires $\alpha = .05$ in the upper tail of the t-distribution. From Table VI, Appendix B, $t_{.05} = 1.895$, with df $= n - 2 = 9 - 2 = 7$. The rejection region is $t > 1.895$.

Since the observed value of the test statistic falls in the rejection region ($t = 3.50 > 1.895$), H_0 is rejected. There is sufficient evidence to indicate the mean time to fill an order increases with the size of the order for $\alpha = .05$.

d. For confidence coefficient .95, $\alpha = 1 - .95 = .05$ and $\alpha/2 = .05/2 = .025$. From Table VI, Appendix B, $t_{.025} = 2.365$ with df $= n - 2 = 9 - 2 = 7$.

The confidence interval is:

$$\hat{y} \pm t_{\alpha/2} s \sqrt{\dfrac{1}{n} + \dfrac{(x_p - \bar{x})^2}{SS_{xx}}}$$

For $x_p = 150$, $\hat{y} = 12.594 + .10936(150) = 28.998$, and $\bar{x} = \dfrac{1149}{9} = 127.6667$

$$28.988 \pm 2.365(15.7167)\sqrt{\dfrac{1}{9} + \dfrac{(150 - 127.6667)^2}{252{,}290}} \Rightarrow 28.988 \pm 12.500$$
$$\Rightarrow (16.498, 41.498)$$

10.73 Some preliminary calculations:

$\sum x = 15{,}734 \qquad \sum x^2 = 30{,}945{,}562 \qquad \sum xy = 50{,}900{,}475$
$\sum y = 25{,}929 \qquad \sum y^2 = 125{,}301{,}381$

$SS_{xy} = \sum xy - \dfrac{(\sum x)(\sum y)}{n} = 50{,}900{,}475 - \dfrac{15{,}734(25{,}929)}{8} = -95{,}385.75$

$SS_{xx} = \sum x^2 - \dfrac{(\sum x)^2}{n} = 30{,}945{,}562 - \dfrac{15{,}734^2}{8} = 717.5$

$SS_{yy} = \sum y^2 - \dfrac{(\sum y)^2}{n} = 125{,}301{,}381 - \dfrac{25{,}929^2}{8} = 41{,}262{,}250.87$

$\hat{\beta}_1 = \dfrac{SS_{xy}}{SS_{xx}} = \dfrac{-95{,}385.75}{717.5} = -132.9418118 \approx -132.9418$

$\hat{\beta}_0 = \bar{y} - \hat{\beta}_1 \bar{x} = \dfrac{25{,}929}{8} - \dfrac{-132.9418118(15{,}734)}{8} = 264{,}704.4334$

The least squares equation is $\hat{y} = 264{,}704.4334 - 132.9418x$.

$SSE = SS_{yy} - \hat{\beta}_1 SS_{xy} = 41{,}262{,}250.87 - (-132.9418118(-95{,}385.75)) = 28{,}581{,}496.44$

$s^2 = \dfrac{SSE}{n-2} = \dfrac{28{,}581{,}496.44}{8-2} = 3{,}572{,}687.055 \qquad s = \sqrt{3{,}572{,}687.055} = 1{,}890.155299$

$s_{\hat{\beta}_1} = \dfrac{s}{\sqrt{SS_{xx}}} = \dfrac{1{,}890.155299}{\sqrt{717.5}} = 70.5645$

Simple Linear Regression

To determine if the model was useful, we test:

H_0: $\beta_1 = 0$
H_a: $\beta_1 \neq 0$

The test statistic is $t = \dfrac{\hat{\beta}_1 - 0}{s_{\hat{\beta}_1}} = \dfrac{-135.942 - 0}{70.5645} = -1.926$

The rejection region requires $\alpha/2 = .05/2 = .025$ in each tail of the t-distribution with df $= n - 2 = 8 - 2 = 6$. From Table VI, Appendix B, $t_{.025} = 2.447$. The rejection region is $t < -2.447$ or $t > 2.447$.

Since the observed value of the test statistic does not fall in the rejection region ($t = -1.926 \not< -2.447$), H_0 is not rejected. There is insufficient evidence to indicate that the model is useful at $\alpha = .05$.

For this model,

$$r^2 = 1 - \dfrac{SSE}{SS_{yy}} = 1 - \dfrac{28{,}581{,}496.44}{41{,}262{,}250.87} = .3073$$

Thus only 30.73% of the sample variability of the number of outlets can be explained by the linear relationship between number of outlets and year the company began franchising.

10.75 a. A scatterplot of the data is:

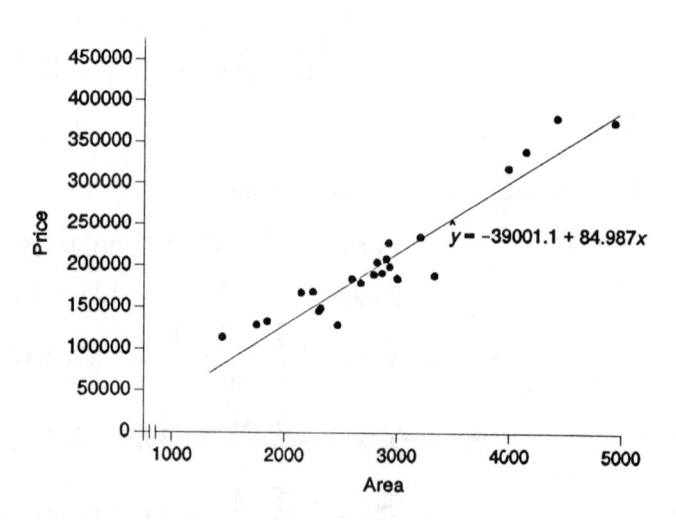

b. From the printout, the least squares line is $\hat{y} = -39{,}001 + 84.987x$.

c. r^2 = R-square = .8983

89.83% of the sample variability in price is explained by the linear relationship between price and area.

d. To determine if living area contributes information for predicting the price of a home, we test:

H_0: $\beta_1 = 0$
H_a: $\beta_1 \neq 0$

The test statistic is $t = 13.942$ (from printout).

The *p*-value is .0001.

Since the *p*-value is less than $\alpha = .05$, H_0 is rejected. There is sufficient evidence to indicate living area contributes information for predicting the price of a home at $\alpha = .05$.

e. For confidence coefficient .95, $\alpha = 1 - .95 = .05$ and $\alpha/2 = .05/2 = .025$. From Table VI, Appendix B, $t_{.025} = 2.074$ with df = n − 2 = 24 − 2 = 22. The confidence interval is:

$$\hat{\beta}_1 \pm t_{\alpha/2} s_{\hat{\beta}_1} \Rightarrow 84.987 \pm 2.074(6.0957) \Rightarrow 84.987 \pm 12.642 \Rightarrow (72.345, 97.629)$$

Since 0 is not in the confidence interval, it is not a likely value for $\beta_1 \Rightarrow$ reject H_0. This corresponds to the conclusion in **d**.

f. The observed significance level is .0001. Since this is less than $\alpha = .05$, H_0 is rejected in part **d**.

g. From the 25th observation on the printout, the point estimate for price when $x_p = 3000$ is $\hat{y} = 215,960$. The 95% confidence interval is (205,524, 226,396). We are 95% confident that the mean selling price will be between 205,524 and 226,396 for houses with 3,000 square feet.

10.77 a. $\hat{\beta}_0$(INTERCEP) = −99045
$\hat{\beta}_1$(AREA) = 102.814048

b. To determine if energy consumption is positively linearly related to the shell area, we test:

H_0: $\beta_1 = 0$
H_a: $\beta_1 > 0$

The test statistic is $t = 6.483$ (from printout).

The rejection region requires $\alpha = .10$ in the upper tail of the *t*-distribution with df = n − 2 = 22 − 2 = 20. From Table VI, Appendix B, $t_{.10} = 1.325$. The rejection region is $t > 1.325$.

Since the observed value of the test statistic falls in the rejection region ($t = 6.483 > 1.325$), H_0 is rejected. There is sufficient evidence to indicate that energy consumption is positively linearly related to the shell area at $\alpha = .10$.

c. Since this is a one-tailed test but the output calculates the *p*-value for a two-tailed test, the observed significance level is:

$$\frac{1}{2}\left(\text{Prob} > |T|\right) \leq \frac{1}{2}(.0001) = .00005$$

This is the probability of observing our value of t (6.483) or anything larger if $\beta_1 = 0$. Since this probability is so small, there is strong evidence to reject H_0.

d. r^2 = R-Square = .6776

67.76% of the total sample variability in energy consumption around its mean is explained by the linear relationship between energy consumption and shell area.

e. From the printout, for $x_p = 8000$, $\hat{y} = 723,467$ (observation 23).

The 95% prediction interval is (−631,806, 2,078,740).

This interval is so large and includes negative BTU's; it is not very useful.

Simple Linear Regression

10.79 a. The scattergram is:

From the plot, it appears that there is a positive linear relationship between job evaluation points and salary.

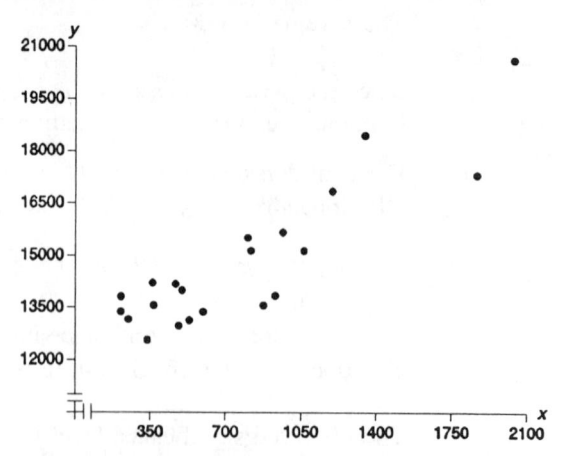

b. From the printout, the least squares line is $\hat{y} = 12{,}024 + 3.581616x$.

$\hat{\beta}_0 = 12{,}024$. This has no meaning since $x = 0$ is not in the observed range.

$\hat{\beta}_1 = 3.581616$. We estimate that the mean salary will increase by \$3.581616 for each additional job evaluation point.

c. $r^2 = $ R-square $= .7972$. 79.72% of the total sample variability of the salary values around their mean is explained by the linear relationship between salary and job evaluation points.

d. To determine if the straight-line model provides useful information about the relationship between salary and job evaluation points, we test:

H_0: $\beta_1 = 0$
H_a: $\beta_1 \neq 0$

The test statistic is $t = 8.641$ (from the printout).

The p-value associated with this test is .0001. Since this p-value is so small, there is strong evidence to reject H_0. There is sufficient evidence to indicate the straight-line model provides useful information about the relationship between salary and job evaluation points for $\alpha > .0001$.

e. A point estimate for a fair salary when the job evaluation score is 800 is:

$\hat{y} = \$14{,}888.9$ (from printout for observation #22)

The 95% prediction interval is (\$12,862.60, \$16,915.30). We are 95% confident that the actual salary for a job receiving an evaluation score of 800 is between \$12,862.60 and \$16,915.30.

10.81 We will duplicate the analyses from problem 10.65. We will then make some comments comparing the two analyses. These analyses should then be incorporated into a written report.

a. The dependent variable should be Indirect Manufacturing Labor Costs. The cost driver or independent variable is the Direct Manufacturing Labor-Hours. Thus, the Indirect Manufacturing Labor Cost will be the dependent variable.

b. The scatterplot of the data is:

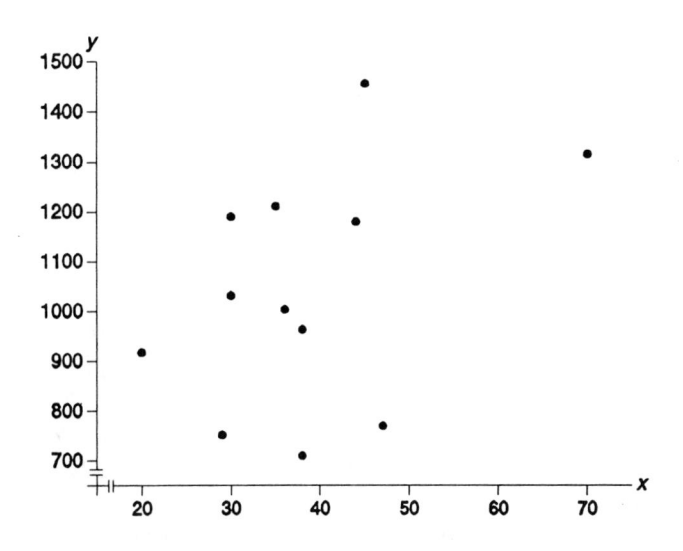

c. Some preliminary calculations:

$$\sum x = 462 \qquad \sum x^2 = 19{,}520 \qquad \sum xy = 494{,}661$$
$$\sum y = 12{,}501 \qquad \sum y^2 = 13{,}630{,}615$$

$$SS_{xy} = \sum xy - \frac{(\sum x)(\sum y)}{n} = 494{,}661 - \frac{462(12{,}501)}{12} = 13{,}372.5$$

$$SS_{xx} = \sum x^2 - \frac{(\sum x)^2}{n} = 19{,}520 - \frac{462^2}{12} = 1{,}733$$

$$SS_{yy} = \sum y^2 - \frac{(\sum y)^2}{n} = 13{,}360{,}615 - \frac{12{,}501^2}{12} = 607{,}698.25$$

$$\hat{\beta}_1 = \frac{SS_{xy}}{SS_{xx}} = \frac{13{,}372.5}{1{,}733} = 7.716387767 \approx 7.716$$

$$\hat{\beta}_0 = \bar{y} - \hat{\beta}_1 \bar{x} = \frac{12{,}501}{12} - \frac{7.716387767(462)}{12} = 744.669071 \approx 744.669$$

The least squares equation is $\hat{y} = 744.669 + 7.716x$.

d. $SSE = SS_{yy} - \hat{\beta}_1 SS_{xy} = 607{,}698.25 - 7.716387767(13{,}372.5) = 504{,}510.8546$

$$s^2 = \frac{SSE}{n-2} = \frac{504{,}510.8546}{12-2} = 50{,}451.08546 \qquad s = \sqrt{50{,}451.08546} = 224.6131908$$

$$s_{\hat{\beta}_1} = \frac{s}{\sqrt{SS_{xx}}} = \frac{224.6131908}{\sqrt{1733}} = 5.39555$$

To determine if the model was useful, we test:

$$H_0: \beta_1 = 0$$
$$H_a: \beta_1 \neq 0$$

The test statistic is $t = \dfrac{\hat{\beta}_1 - 0}{s_{\hat{\beta}_1}} = \dfrac{7.716 - 0}{5.39555} = 1.430$

Simple Linear Regression

The rejection region requires $\alpha/2 = .05/2 = .025$ in each tail of the t-distribution with df = $n - 2 = 12 - 2 = 10$. From Table VI, Appendix B, $t_{.025} = 2.228$. The rejection region is $t < -2.228$ or $t > 2.228$.

Since the observed value of the test statistic does not fall in the rejection region ($t = 1.430 \not> 2.228$), H_0 is not rejected. There is insufficient evidence to indicate that the model is useful at $\alpha = .05$.

e. For this model,
$$r^2 = 1 - \frac{SSE}{SS_{yy}} = 1 - \frac{504,510.8546}{607,698.25} = .1698$$

16.98% of the variability in the Labor Costs about their means is explained by the linear relationship between Labor Costs and Direct Manufacturing Labor Costs.

f. The form of the prediction interval is:

$$\hat{y} \pm t_{\alpha/2} s \sqrt{1 + \frac{1}{n} + \frac{(x_p - \bar{x})^2}{SS_{xx}}}$$

Suppose $x_p = 50$. $\hat{y} = 744.669 + 7.716(950) = 1,130.469$

For confidence coefficient .95, $\alpha = 1 - .95 = .05$ and $\alpha/2 = .05/2 = .025$. From Table VI, Appendix B, with df = $n - 2 = 12 - 2 = 10$, $t_{.025} = 2.228$. The prediction interval is:

$$1,130.469 \pm 2.228(224.6132)\sqrt{1 + \frac{1}{12} + \frac{(50 - 38.5)^2}{1,733}} \Rightarrow 1,130.469 \pm 538.906$$
$$\Rightarrow (591.563, 1,669.375)$$

We are 95% confident that the actual labor costs for 50 Direct Manufacturing Labor-Hours will be between 591.563 and 1,669.375.

Of these two cost functions, the first should be used to predict Indirect Manufacturing Labor Cost. There was a significant linear relationship between Indirect Manufacturing Labor Cost and Machine-Hours. There was not a significant linear relationship between Indirect Manufacturing Labor Cost and Direct Manufacturing Labor-Hours. The r^2 for first function was .521, while the r^2 for the second cost function was .1698. In addition, the standard deviation for the first cost function ($s = 170.536$) was much smaller than for the second cost function ($s = 224.6132$).

Multiple Regression — Chapter 11

11.1   a. $\hat{\beta}_0 = 506.346067, \hat{\beta}_1 = -941.900226, \hat{\beta}_2 = -429.060418$

     b. $\hat{y} = 506.346 - 941.900x_1 - 429.060x_2$

     c.   SSE = 151,015.72376, MSE = 8883.27787, s = Root MSE = 94.25114

         We expect about 95% of the y-values to fall within $\pm 2s$ or $\pm 2(94.25114)$ or ± 188.50228 units of the fitted regression equation.

     d. $H_0: \beta_1 = 0$
             $H_a: \beta_1 \neq 0$

         The test statistic is $t = \dfrac{\hat{\beta}_1 - 0}{s_{\hat{\beta}_1}} = \dfrac{-941.900226}{275.08555975} = -3.424$

         The rejection region requires $\alpha/2 = .05/2 = .025$ in each tail of the t-distribution with df $= n - (k + 1) = 20 - (2 + 1) = 17$. From Table VI, Appendix B, $t_{.025} = 2.110$. The rejection region is $t < -2.110$ or $t > 2.110$.

         Since the observed value of the test statistic falls in the rejection region ($t = -3.424 < -2.110$), H_0 is rejected. There is sufficient evidence to indicate $\beta_1 \neq 0$ at $\alpha = .05$.

     e.   For confidence coefficient .95, $\alpha = .05$ and $\alpha/2 = .025$. From Table VI, Appendix B, with df $= n - (k + 1) = 20 - (2 + 1) = 17$, $t_{.025} = 2.110$. The 95% confidence interval is:

$$\hat{\beta}_2 \pm t_{.025} s_{\hat{\beta}_2} \Rightarrow -429.060 \pm 2.110(379.8527) \Rightarrow -429.060 \pm 801.4322$$
$$\Rightarrow (-1230.4922, 372.3722)$$

11.3   a. $H_0: \beta_2 = 0$
             $H_a: \beta_2 \neq 0$

         The test statistic is $t = \dfrac{\hat{\beta}_2 - 0}{s_{\hat{\beta}_2}} = \dfrac{.47 - 0}{.15} = 3.133$

         The rejection region requires $\alpha/2 = .05/2 = .025$ in each tail of the t-distribution with df $= n - (k + 1) = 25 - (2 + 1) = 22$. From Table VI, Appendix B, $t_{.025} = 2.074$. The rejection region is $t < -2.074$ or $t > 2.074$.

         Since the observed value of the test statistic falls in the rejection region ($t = 3.133 > 2.074$), H_0 is rejected. There is sufficient evidence to indicate the true relationship is given by the quadratic model at $\alpha = .05$.

     b. $H_0: \beta_2 = 0$
             $H_a: \beta_2 > 0$

The test statistic is the same as in part a, $t = 3.133$.

The rejection region requires $\alpha = .05$ in the upper tail of the t-distribution with df = 22. From Table VI, Appendix B, $t_{.05} = 1.717$. The rejection region is $t > 1.717$.

Since the observed value of the test statistic falls in the rejection region ($t = 3.133 > 1.717$), H_0 is rejected. There is sufficient evidence to indicate the quadratic curve opens upward at $\alpha = .05$.

c. $F = t^2 = 3.133^2 = 9.816$

d. No. The F statistic can only be used to test whether the parameter is equal to 0 or not.

11.5 a. The output from using SAS is:

```
DEPENDENT VARIABLE:  Y
   SOURCE              DF      SUM OF SQUARES     MEAN SQUARE       F VALUE
   MODEL                2         15.03047619      7.51523810        686.17
   ERROR                4          0.04380952      0.01095238        PR > F
   CORRECTED TOTAL      6         15.07428571                        0.0001


   R-SQUARE           C.V.           ROOT MSE         Y MEAN
   0.997094          2.6639         0.10465362       3.92857143

                                    T FOR H0:                     STD ERROR OF
   PARAMETER        ESTIMATE      PARAMETER=0      PR > |T|        ESTIMATE
   INTERCEPT        1.09523810       11.99          0.0003         0.09134917
   X                1.63571429       22.94          0.0001         0.07130942
   X*X             -0.15952381      -13.97          0.0002         0.01141865
```

SSE = .04380952, s^2 = MSE = .01095238

b. H_0: $\beta_2 = 0$
H_a: $\beta_2 \neq 0$

The test statistic is $t = \dfrac{\hat{\beta}_2 - 0}{s_{\hat{\beta}_2}} = \dfrac{-.1595 - 0}{.01141865} = -13.97$

The rejection region requires $\alpha/2 = .05/2 = .025$ in each tail of the t-distribution with df = $n - (k + 1) = 7 - (2 + 1) = 4$. From Table VI, Appendix B, $t_{.025} = 2.776$. The rejection region is $t < -2.776$ or $t > 2.776$.

Since the observed value of the test statistic falls in the rejection region ($t = -13.97 < -2.776$), H_0 is rejected. There is sufficient evidence to indicate the second-order term provides information for the prediction of y at $\alpha = .05$.

c. $\hat{y} = 1.095 + 1.636x - .1595x^2$

d. PLOT OF Y*X SYMBOL USED IS *
   PLOT OF YHAT*X SYMBOL USED IS +

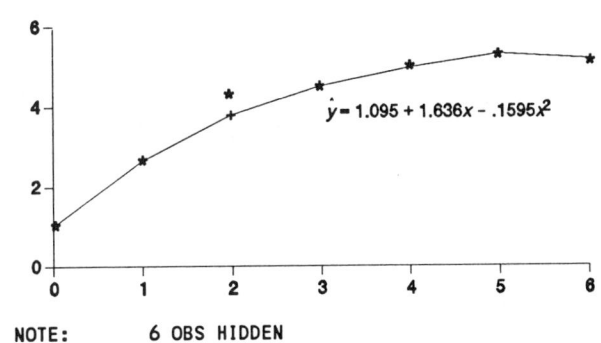

$\hat{y} = 1.095 + 1.636x - .1595x^2$

NOTE: 6 OBS HIDDEN

The prediction equation fits the data very well.

11.7 $\hat{\beta}_0 = 39.05$ The estimated y-intercept is 39.05.

$\hat{\beta}_1 = -5.41$ The mean profitability is estimated to decrease by 5.41 units for each 1 unit increase in state population per inn, holding room rate, square root of median income, and number of college students within 4 miles constant.

$\hat{\beta}_2 = 5.86$ The mean profitability is estimated to increase by 5.86 units for each 1 unit increase in room rate, holding state population per inn, square root of median income, and number of college students within 4 miles constant.

$\hat{\beta}_3 = -3.09$ The mean profitability is estimated to decrease by 3.09 units for each 1 unit increase in square root of median income, holding state population per inn, room rate, and number of college students within 4 miles constant.

$\hat{\beta}_4 = 1.75$ The mean profitability is estimated to increase by 1.75 units for each 1 unit increase in number of college students with 4 miles, holding state population per inn, room rate, and square root of median income constant.

11.9 a. $\hat{y} = 20.0911 - .6705x + .0095x^2$

b. It appears that the relationship between time to assemble and months of experience is fairly linear. It is possible the quadratic term is significant, but not likely.

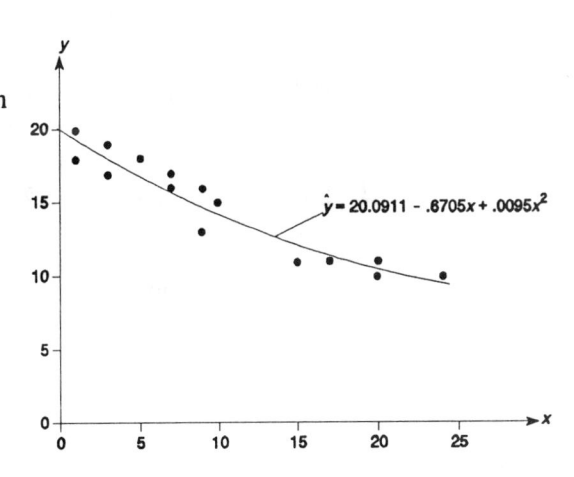

$\hat{y} = 20.0911 - .6705x + .0095x^2$

c. $H_0: \beta_2 = 0$
   $H_a: \beta_2 \neq 0$

The test statistic is $t = \dfrac{\hat{\beta}_2 - 0}{s_{\hat{\beta}_2}} = \dfrac{.0095 - 0}{.00632580} = 1.51$

Multiple Regression

The rejection region requires $\alpha/2 = .01/2 = .005$ in each tail of the t-distribution with df = $n - (k + 1) = 15 - (2 + 1) = 12$. From Table VI, Appendix B, $t_{.005} = 3.055$. The rejection region is $t < -3.055$ or $t > 3.055$.

Since the observed value of the test statistic does not fall in the rejection region ($t = 1.51 \not> 3.055$), H_0 is not rejected. There is insufficient evidence to indicate $\beta_2 \neq 0$ at $\alpha = .01$.

d. Some preliminary calculations are:

$$\sum x = 151 \qquad \sum x^2 = 2295 \qquad \sum xy = 1890$$
$$\sum y = 222 \qquad \sum y^2 = 3456$$

$$SS_{xy} = \sum xy - \frac{\sum x \sum y}{n} = 1890 - \frac{151(222)}{15} = -344.8$$

$$SS_{xx} = \sum x^2 - \frac{(\sum x)^2}{n} = 2295 - \frac{151^2}{15} = 774.9333333$$

$$SS_{yy} = \sum y^2 - \frac{(\sum y)^2}{n} = 3456 - \frac{222^2}{15} = 170.4$$

$$\hat{\beta}_1 = \frac{SS_{xy}}{SS_{xx}} = \frac{-344.8}{774.933333} = -.4449415 \approx -.445$$

$$\hat{\beta}_0 = \bar{y} - \hat{\beta}_1 \bar{x} = \frac{222}{15} - (-.4449415)\left[\frac{151}{15}\right] = 19.27907777 = 19.279$$

The reduced fitted model is $\hat{y} = 19.279 - .445x$.

e. β_1 = change in mean time to complete task for each additional month of experience.

Some preliminary calculations are:

$$SSE = SS_{yy} - \hat{\beta}_1 SS_{xy} = 170.4 - (-.4449415)(-344.8) = 16.9841708$$

$$s^2 = \frac{SSE}{n-2} = \frac{16.9841708}{15-2} = 1.30647, \; s = \sqrt{1.30647} = 1.143$$

For confidence coefficient .90, $\alpha = .10$ and $\alpha/2 = .05$. From Table VI, Appendix B, with df = $n - (k + 1) = 15 - (1 + 1) = 13$, $t_{.05} = 1.771$. The confidence interval is:

$$\hat{\beta}_1 \pm t_{.05} \, s_{\hat{\beta}_1} \Rightarrow -.445 \pm 1.771\left[\frac{1.143}{\sqrt{774.93333}}\right] \Rightarrow -.445 \pm .0727 \Rightarrow (-.5177, -.3723)$$

11.11 a. Using SAS, the printout is:

```
Model: MODEL1
Dependent Variable: Y

                     Analysis of Variance

                        Sum of        Mean
Source        DF       Squares       Square      F Value     Prob>F

Model          3     1683.60264     561.20088      7.653      0.0029
Error         14     1026.59267      73.32805
C Total       17     2710.19531

      Root MSE       8.56318     R-square     0.6212
      Dep Mean      41.52083     Adj R-sq     0.5400
      C.V.          20.62381
```

```
                        Parameter Estimates
                     Parameter      Standard     T for H0:
        Variable DF  Estimate       Error        Parameter=0    Prob > |T|

        INTERCEP 1   -72.557628     44.91381281  -1.615         0.1285
        X1       1    -0.058299      0.19927559  -0.293         0.7742
        X2       1    84.925174     22.27654857   3.812         0.0019
        X3       1    -0.022018      0.03018773  -0.729         0.4778
```

The least squares prediction equation is:

$$\hat{y} = -72.558 - .058x_1 + 84.925x_2 - .022x_3.$$

b. The standard deviation is $s =$ Root MSE $= 8.56318$. Most of the observations will fall within $\pm 2s$ or $\pm 2(8.56318)$ or ± 17.126 units of their predicted values.

c. To determine if the price of Ford stock decreases as the yen rate increases, we test:

H_0: $\beta_1 = 0$
H_a: $\beta_1 < 0$

The test statistic is $t = -0.293$.

The p-value for the test is $.7742/2 = .3871$. Since the p-value is not less than α ($p = .3871$ $\not< \alpha = .05$), H_0 is not rejected. There is insufficient evidence to indicate the price of Ford stock decreases as the yen rate increases holding all the other variables constant at $\alpha = .05$.

d. $\hat{\beta}_2 = 84.925$. The mean price of Ford stock is estimated to increase by 84.925 for each 1 unit increase in Deutsche mark exchange rate, holding Japanese yen exchange rate and S & P 500 Index constant.

11.13 a. The two statistics, SSE and R^2, seem to imply a good fit of the data since SSE is small and $R^2 = .87$, which is fairly close to 1.

b. H_0: $\beta_1 = \beta_2 = \beta_3 = \beta_4 = \beta_5 = 0$
H_a: At least one $\beta_i \neq 0$, for $i = 1, 2, ..., 5$

The test statistic is $F = \dfrac{R^2/k}{(1 - R^2)/[n - (k + 1)]}$

$$F = \frac{.87/5}{(1 - .87)/(30 - (5 + 1))} = \frac{.174}{.00542} = 32.12$$

The rejection region requires $\alpha = .05$ in the upper tail of the F-distribution with $\nu_1 = k = 5$ and $\nu_2 = n - (k + 1) = 30 - (5 + 1) = 24$. From Table VIII, Appendix B, $F_{.05} = 2.62$. The rejection region is $F > 2.62$.

Since the observed value of the test statistic falls in the rejection region ($F = 32.12 > 2.62$), H_0 is rejected. There is sufficient evidence to indicate the model is useful in predicting y at $\alpha = .05$.

11.15 a. Some preliminary calculations are:

$$\text{SSE} = \sum (y_i - \hat{y}_i)^2 = 12.37, \text{df} = n - (k + 1) = 20 - (2 + 1) = 17$$

Multiple Regression

$$SS(\text{Total}) = \sum(y - \bar{y})^2 = 23.75, \text{df} = n - 1 = 20 - 1 = 19$$

$$SS(\text{Model}) = SS(\text{Total}) - SSE = 23.75 - 12.37 = 11.38, \text{df} = k = 2$$

$$MS(\text{Model}) = \frac{SSR}{k} = \frac{11.38}{2} = 5.69$$

$$MS(\text{Error}) = \frac{SSE}{n - (k + 1)} = \frac{12.37}{17} = .72765$$

$$F = \frac{MS(\text{Model})}{MS(\text{Error})} = \frac{5.69}{.72765} = 7.82$$

The analysis of variance table is:

Source	df	SS	MS	F
Model	2	11.38	5.69	7.82
Error	17	12.37	.72765	
Total	19	23.75		

$$R^2 = 1 - \frac{SSE}{SS(\text{Total})} = 1 - \frac{12.37}{23.75} = .4792$$

b. H_0: $\beta_1 = \beta_2 = 0$
    H_a: At least one $\beta_i \neq 0$, $i = 1, 2$

The test statistic is $F = \dfrac{MS(\text{Model})}{MS(\text{Error})} = \dfrac{5.69}{.72765} = 7.82$ or

$$F = \frac{R^2/k}{(1 - R^2)/[n - (k + 1)]} = \frac{.4792/2}{(1 - .4792)/[20 - (2 + 1)]} = 7.82$$

The rejection region requires $\alpha = .05$ in the upper tail of the F-distribution with df = $\nu_1 = k = 2$ and $\nu_2 = n - (k + 1) = 17$. From Table VIII, Appendix B, $F_{.05} = 3.59$. The rejection region is $F > 3.59$.

Since the observed value of the test statistic falls in the rejection region ($F = 7.82 > 3.59$), H_0 is rejected. There is sufficient evidence to indicate the model is useful in predicting y at $\alpha = .05$.

11.17 a. The least squares prediction equation is:

$$\hat{y} = -4.30 - .002x_1 + .336x_2 + .384x_3 + .067x_4 - .143x_5 + .081x_6 + .134x_7$$

b. To determine if the model is adequate, we test:

H_0: $\beta_1 = \beta_2 = \beta_3 = \beta_4 = \beta_5 = \beta_6 = \beta_7 = 0$
H_a: At least one $\beta_i \neq 0$, $i = 1, 2, 3, ..., 7$

The test statistic is $F = 111.1$ (from printout).

The rejection region requires $\alpha = .05$ in the upper tail of the F-distribution with $\nu_1 = k = 7$ and $\nu_2 = n - (k + 1) = 268 - (7 + 1) = 260$. From Table VIII, Appendix B, $F_{.05} \approx 2.01$. The rejection region is $F > 2.01$.

Since the observed value of the test statistic falls in the rejection region ($F = 111.1 > 2.01$), H_0 is rejected. There is sufficient evidence to indicate that the model is adequate for predicting the logarithm of the audit fees at $\alpha = .05$.

c. $\hat{\beta}_3 = .384$. For each additional subsidiary of the auditee, the mean of the logarithm of audit fee is estimated to increase by .384 units.

d. To determine if the $\beta_4 > 0$, we test:

$H_0: \beta_4 = 0$
$H_a: \beta_4 > 0$

The test statistic is $t = 1.76$ (from table).

The p-value for the test is .079. Since the p-value is not less than α ($p = .079 \not< \alpha = .05$), H_0 is not rejected. There is insufficient evidence to indicate that $\beta_4 > 0$, holding all the other variables constant, at $\alpha = .05$.

e. To determine if the $\beta_1 < 0$, we test:

$H_0: \beta_1 = 0$
$H_a: \beta_1 < 0$

The test statistic is $t = -0.049$ (from table).

The p-value for the test is .961. Since the p-value is not less than α ($p = .961 \not< \alpha = .05$), H_0 is not rejected. There is insufficient evidence to indicate that $\beta_1 < 0$, holding all the other variables constant, at $\alpha = .05$. There is insufficient evidence to indicate that the new auditors charge less than incumbent auditors.

11.19 a. $R^2 = .51$. This means that 51% of the sample variation in the operating margins is explained by the model containing population per inn, room rate, median income, and college enrollment.

b. To determine if the model is adequate, we test:

$H_0: \beta_1 = \beta_2 = \beta_3 = \beta_4 = 0$
$H_a:$ At least one $\beta_i \neq 0$, $i = 1, 2, 3, 4$

The test statistic is $F = \dfrac{R^2/k}{(1 - R^2)/[n - (k + 1)]} = \dfrac{.51/4}{(1 - .51)/[57 - (4 + 1)]} = 13.53$

The rejection region requires $\alpha = .05$ in the upper tail of the F-distribution with $\nu_1 = k = 4$ and $\nu_2 = n - (k + 1) = 57 - (4 + 1) = 52$. From Table VIII, Appendix B, $F_{.05} \approx 3.01$. The rejection region is $F > 3.01$.

Since the observed value of the test statistic falls in the rejection region ($F = 13.53 > 3.01$), H_0 is rejected. There is sufficient evidence to indicate that the model is adequate for predicting operating margin at $\alpha = .05$.

11.21 a. A model including the interaction term is:

$E(y) = \beta_0 + \beta_1 x_1 + \beta_2 x_2 + \beta_3 x_1 x_2$

b. To determine if the effect of treatment on spelling score depends on disease intensity, we test:

H_0: $\beta_3 = 0$
H_a: $\beta_3 \neq 0$

The p-value is $p = .02$. Since the p-value is less than α ($p = .02 < .05$), H_0 is rejected. There is sufficient evidence to indicate that the effect of treatment on spelling score depends on disease intensity at $\alpha = .05$.

c. Since the two variables interact, the main effects may be covered up by the interaction effect. Thus, tests on main effects should not be made. Also, the interpretation of the coefficients of the main effects should be interpreted with caution. Since the independent variables interact, the effect of one independent variable on the dependent variable depends on the level of the second independent variable.

11.23 a. $\hat{y} = 295.33 - 480.84x_1 - 829.46x_2 + .0079x_3 + 2.3608x_4$

b. $s = $ Root MSE $= 46.76747$. We would expect about 95% of all observations to fall within $\pm 2s$ or $\pm 2(46.76747)$ or ± 93.53494 units of the fitted regression line.

c. To determine if the model is useful, we test:

H_0: $\beta_1 = \beta_2 = \beta_3 = \beta_4 = 0$
H_a: At least one $\beta_i \neq 0$, $i = 1, 2, 3, 4$

The test statistic is $F = \dfrac{\text{MS(Model)}}{\text{MSE}} = \dfrac{61634.26485}{2187.19604} = 28.18$

The rejection region requires $\alpha = .025$ in the upper tail of the F-distribution with numerator df $= k = 4$ and denominator df $= n - (k + 1) = 20 - (4 + 1) = 15$. From Table IX, Appendix B, $F_{.025} = 3.80$. The rejection region is $F > 3.80$.

Since the observed value of the test statistic falls in the rejection region ($F = 28.18 > 3.80$), H_0 is rejected. There is sufficient evidence to indicate the model is useful at $\alpha = .025$.

The observed significance level is p-value $\leq .0001$.

d. To determine if an increase in the number of for-profit beds would decrease the survival size, we test:

H_0: $\beta_1 = 0$
H_a: $\beta_1 < 0$

The test statistic is $t = \dfrac{\hat{\beta}_1 - 0}{s_{\hat{\beta}_1}} = \dfrac{-480.8376}{150.3905} = -3.197$

The rejection region requires $\alpha = .05$ in the lower tail of the t-distribution with df $= n - (k + 1) = 20 - (4 + 1) = 15$. From Table VI, Appendix B, $t_{.05} = 1.753$. The rejection region is $t < -1.753$.

Since the observed value of the test statistic falls in the rejection region ($t = -3.197 < -1.753$), H_0 is rejected. There is sufficient evidence to indicate that as the number of for-profit beds increases, the survival size decreases at $\alpha = .05$.

11.25 a. The value $R^2 = .87$. 87% of the sample variation in attitude is explained by the regression model containing gender, years of experience, years squared, and the interaction between gender and years of experience.

b. H_0: $\beta_1 = \beta_2 = \beta_3 = \beta_4 = 0$
H_a: At least one $\beta_i \neq 0$, for $i = 1, 2, ..., 4$

The test statistic $F = \dfrac{R^2/k}{\dfrac{1 - R^2}{(n - (k + 1))}}$ where $k = 4$, $n = 40$

$= \dfrac{.87/4}{(1 - .87)/(40 - (4 + 1))} = \dfrac{.2175}{.0037} = 58.56$

The rejection region requires $\alpha = .05$ in the upper tail of the F-distribution with $\nu_1 = k = 4$ and $\nu_1 = n - (k + 1) = 40 - (4 + 1) = 35$. From Table VIII, Appendix B, $F_{.05} \approx 2.69$. The rejection region is $F > 2.69$.

Since the observed value of the test statistic falls in the rejection region ($F = 58.56 > 2.69$), H_0 is rejected. There is sufficient evidence to indicate the model is useful in predicting attitude at $\alpha = .05$. Attitude is related to at least one of the independent variables.

c. To determine if the interaction between sex and years of experience is useful in the prediction model, we test:

H_0: $\beta_4 = 0$
H_a: $\beta_4 \neq 0$

The test statistic is $t = \dfrac{\hat{\beta}_4}{s_{\hat{\beta}_4}} = \dfrac{-1}{.02} = -50$

The rejection region requires $\alpha/2 = .05/2 = .025$ in each tail of the t-distribution with df $= n - (k + 1) = 40 - (4 + 1) = 35$. From Table VI, Appendix B, $t_{.025} \approx 2.042$. The rejection region is $t < -2.042$ or $t > 2.042$.

Since the observed value of the test statistic falls in the rejection region ($t = -50 < -2.042$), H_0 is rejected. There is sufficient evidence to indicate the interaction between sex and years of experience is useful in the prediction model at $\alpha = .05$.

d. For $x_1 = 0$, $\hat{y} = 50 + 5(0) + 6x_2 - .2x_2^2 - 0(x_2)$
$= 50 + 6x_2 - .2x_2^2$
For $x_1 = 1$, $\hat{y} = 50 + 5(1) + 6x_2 - .2x_2^2 - x_2$
$= 55 + 5x_2 - .2x_2^2$

Multiple Regression

$x_1 = 0$		$x_1 = 1$	
x_2	$\hat{y}$	x_2	$\hat{y}$
0	50	0	55
2	61.2	2	64.2
4	70.8	4	71.8
6	78.8	6	77.8
8	85.2	8	82.2
10	90	10	85

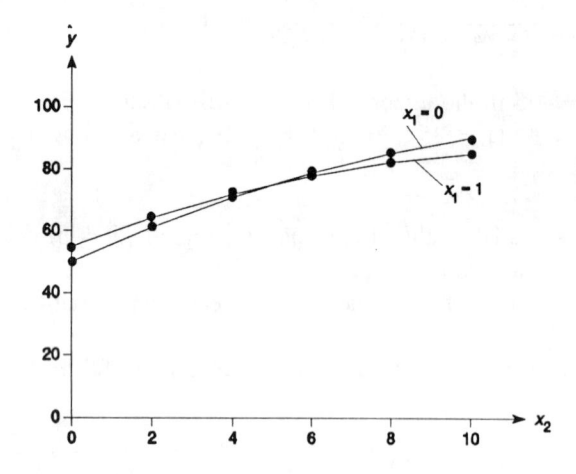

11.27 a. The hypothesized model is:

$$E(y) = \beta_0 + \beta_1 x_1 + \beta_2 x_2 + \beta_3 x_3 + \beta_4 x_4 + \beta_5 x_5$$

β_0 = y-intercept. It has no interpretation in this model.

β_1 = difference in the mean salaries between males and females, all other variables held constant.

β_2 = difference in the mean salaries between whites and nonwhites, all other variables held constant.

β_3 = change in the mean salary for each additional year of education, all other variables held constant.

β_4 = change in the mean salary for each additional year of tenure with firm, all other variables held constant.

β_5 = change in the mean salary for each additional hour worked per week, all other variables held constant.

b. The least squares equation is:

$$\hat{y} = 15.491 + 12.774 x_1 + .713 x_2 + 1.519 x_3 + .32 x_4 + .205 x_5$$

$\hat{\beta}_0$ = estimate of the y-intercept. It has no interpretation in this model.

$\hat{\beta}_1$: We estimate the difference in the mean salaries between males and females to be $12.774, all other variables held constant.

$\hat{\beta}_2$: We estimate the difference in the mean salaries between whites and nonwhites to be $.713, all other variables held constant.

$\hat{\beta}_3$: We estimate the change in the mean salary for each additional year of education to be $1.519, all other variables held constant.

$\hat{\beta}_4$: We estimate the change in the mean salary for each additional year of tenure with firm to be $.320, all other variables held constant.

$\hat{\beta}_5$: We estimate the change in the mean salary for each additional hour worked per week to be $.205, all other variables held constant.

c. $R^2 = .240$. 24% of the total variability of salaries is explained by the model containing gender, race, educational level, tenure with firm, and number of hours worked per week.

To determine if the model is useful for predicting annual salary, we test:

H_0: $\beta_1 = \beta_2 = \beta_3 = \beta_4 = \beta_5 = 0$
H_a: At least one $\beta_i \neq 0$

The test statistic is $F = \dfrac{R^2/k}{(1 - R^2)/[n - (k + 1)]} = \dfrac{.24/5}{(1 - .24)/[191 - (5 + 1)]} = 11.68$

The rejection region requires $\alpha = .05$ in the upper tail of the F-distribution with numerator df $= k = 5$ and denominator df $= n - (k + 1) = 191 - (5 + 1) = 185$. From Table VIII, Appendix B, $F_{.05} \approx 2.21$. The rejection region is $F > 2.21$.

Since the observed value of the test statistic falls in the rejection region ($F = 11.68 > 2.21$), H_0 is rejected. There is sufficient evidence to indicate the model containing gender, race, educational level, tenure with firm, and number of hours worked per week is useful for predicting annual salary for $\alpha = .05$.

d. To determine if male managers are paid more than female managers, we test:

H_0: $\beta_1 = 0$
H_a: $\beta_1 > 0$

The p-value given for the test $< .05/2 = .025$. Since the p-value is less than $\alpha = .05$, there is evidence to reject H_0. There is evidence to indicate male managers are paid more than female managers, holding all other variables constant, for $\alpha > .025$.

e. The salary paid an individual depends on many factors other than gender. Thus, in order to adjust for other factors influencing salary, we include them in the model.

f. Interaction between gender and tenure indicates that the effect of gender on salary depends on the number of years with the firm. If interaction is present, then the difference in mean salary between males and females will depend on the length of tenure with the firm. One example of this would be that males and females are hired in at the same starting salary, but the difference in mean salary grows as the tenure grows.

11.29   In multiple regression, as in simple regression, the confidence interval for the mean value of y is narrower than the prediction interval of a particular value of y. When predicting an actual value, the variability includes the variability in locating the mean plus the variability of the actual observations.

11.31   In the residual plot for the straight-line model, there is a definite mound shape to the plot. This implies there is a need for a quadratic term in the model.

In the residual plot for the quadratic model, there is no longer a mound shape evident. The quadratic term seemed to help. From Exercise 11.14, the standard deviation for the quadratic model is $s = .43$. Two standard deviations from the mean is $\pm 2(.43) \Rightarrow \pm .86$. There are no points more than 2 standard deviations from the mean for the quadratic model.

In Exercise 11.14, part d, there was sufficient evidence to indicate the squared term was needed in the model at $\alpha = .05$. This agrees with our conclusion from analyzing the residual plots.

11.33   a.   Using SAS, the output is:

```
Model: MODEL1
Dependent Variable: Y

                        Analysis of Variance

                       Sum of         Mean
Source          DF    Squares        Square      F Value    Prob>F

Model            2  451880491.97  225940245.98    68.246    0.0001
Error           12   39727837.366   3310653.1138
C Total         14  491608329.33

     Root MSE        1819.52002     R-square      0.9192
     Dep Mean        7796.33333     Adj R-sq      0.9057
     C.V.              23.33815

                        Parameter Estimates

                 Parameter      Standard      T for H0:
Variable   DF    Estimate         Error      Parameter=0    Prob > |T|

INTERCEP    1   -754.710621    895.50272971    -0.843       0.4158
X1          1    217.492953     21.96107356     9.904       0.0001
X2          1      0.713124      0.32771107     2.176       0.0502

         Dep Var   Predict   Std Err   Lower95%   Upper95%
Obs         Y       Value    Predict    Mean       Mean     Residual

  1      10012.0   10936.6   706.111    9398.1    12475.1    -924.6
  2        326.0    -427.3   875.328   -2334.4     1479.9     753.3
  3      13376.0   14284.8   900.768   12322.2    16247.4    -908.8
  4      13767.0   10787.9   667.900    9332.7    12243.2    2979.1
  5        662.0     48.9802 849.391   -1801.7     1899.6     613.0
  6        857.0    221.7    805.108   -1532.5     1975.8     635.3
  7       1259.0   1006.9    799.652    -735.3     2749.2     252.1
  8      18842.0  18310.2   1203.299   15688.4    20932.0     531.8
  9       6763.0   8097.0    962.192    6000.6    10193.5   -1334.0
 10      16681.0  12833.4   1149.628   10328.6    15338.2    3847.6
 11       7094.0   9270.0    675.130    7799.1    10741.0   -2176.0
 12      10021.0  11247.4    680.765    9764.2    12730.7   -1226.4
 13       5142.0   6491.1    483.221    5438.2     7543.9   -1349.1
 14       5104.0   5113.0    570.484    3870.1     6356.0     -9.0317
 15       7039.0   8723.1    476.450    7685.0     9761.2   -1684.1
 16          .     -180.7    831.264   -1991.8     1630.5       .

Sum of Residuals                          0
Sum of Squared Residuals          39727837.366
Predicted Resid SS (Press)        75899078.696

                        Correlation Analysis

                   2 'VAR' Variables:   X1        X2
```

214   *Chapter 11*

```
                        Simple Statistics

Variable        N       Mean    Std Dev       Sum    Minimum    Maximum
X1             15    33.2047   23.7673       498.1     1.4400    82.3000
X2             15     1864.0    1592.7     27960.0    20.0000     5269.0
```

Pearson Correlation Coefficients / Prob > |R| under Ho: Rho=0 / N = 15

```
                        X1              X2
        X1           1.00000         0.36332
                        0.0            0.1832

        X2           0.36332         1.00000
                        0.1832          0.0
```

The fitted regression line is $\hat{y} = -754.711 + 217.493x_1 + .713x_2$.

b. From the printout, the 95% confidence interval is $(-1991.8, 1630.5)$ (from the 16th observation). We are 95% confident that mean sales revenue for companies with 1,000 employees and R&D expenditures of $500 million is between $-1,991.8$ and $1,630.5$ million dollars.

c. There do not appear to be any signs of multicollinearity. We would expect there to be a positive relationship between sales and number of employees and between sales and R&D expense. The estimated coefficients are both positive as expected.

d. There does not appear to be any multicollinearity in this problem. The correlation between the two independent variables is .36332. This is not very large.

11.35 a. For the model fit with 25 observations:

$$\hat{y}_1 = 2.370 + .009x_1 + .354x_2$$

For the model fit with 26 observations:

$$\hat{y}_2 = 2.036 + .016x_1 + .394x_2$$

$\hat{\beta}_0$ decreased for the new model while $\hat{\beta}_1$ and $\hat{\beta}_2$ increased.

For the model fit with 25 observations:

$\hat{\beta}_0 = 2.370$ This is the y-intercept. It has no other meaning.

$\hat{\beta}_1 = .00919$ For each additional one-thousand dollars of income, we estimate the mean food consumption will increase by $9.19, for a fixed household size.

$\hat{\beta}_2 = .354$ For each additional person in the household, we estimate the mean food consumption will increase by $354.00 for a fixed household income.

For the model fit with 26 observations:

$\hat{\beta}_0 = 2.036$ This is the y-intercept. It has no other meaning.

$\hat{\beta}_1 = .01556$ For each additional one-thousand dollars of income, we estimate the mean food consumption will increase by $15.56, for a fixed household size.

$\hat{\beta}_2 = .394$ For each additional person in the household, we estimate the mean food consumption will increase by $394.00, for a fixed household income.

b. For the first model ($n = 25$):

s = Root MSE = .35014

In predicting the 1996 food consumption expenditure, we would expect 95% of the observations to lie within $\pm 2s \Rightarrow \pm 2(.3501) \Rightarrow \pm .7002$ thousand dollars of the mean food consumption expenditure.

For the second model ($n = 26$):

s = Root MSE = .62859

In predicting the 1996 food consumption expenditure, we would expect 95% of the observations to lie within $\pm 2s \Rightarrow \pm 2(.6286) \Rightarrow \pm 1.2572$ thousand dollars of the mean food consumption expenditure.

c. For the first model ($n = 25$):

H_0: $\beta_1 = \beta_2 = 0$
H_a: At least one $\beta_i \neq 0$, $i = 1, 2$

The test statistic is $F_1 = \dfrac{\text{MSR}}{\text{MSE}} = \dfrac{6.39219}{.12260} = 52.138$

The rejection region requires $\alpha = .05$ in the upper tail of the F-distribution with $\nu_1 = k = 2$ and $\nu_2 = n - (k + 1) = 25 - (2 + 1) = 22$. From Table VIII, Appendix B, $F_{.05} = 3.44$. The rejection region is $F_1 > 3.44$.

Since the observed value of the test statistic falls in the rejection region ($F = 52.138 > 3.44$), H_0 is rejected. There is sufficient evidence to indicate the model is useful for predicting the 1996 food consumption expenditure at $\alpha = .05$.

For the second model ($n = 26$):

H_0: $\beta_1 = \beta_2 = 0$
H_a: At least one $\beta_i \neq 0$, $i = 1, 2$

The test statistic is $F_2 = \dfrac{\text{MSR}}{\text{MSE}} = \dfrac{8.89934}{.39512} = 22.523$

The rejection region requires $\alpha = .05$ in the upper tail of the F-distribution with $\nu_1 = k = 2$ and $\nu_2 = n - (k + 1) = 26 - (2 + 1) = 23$. From Table VIII, Appendix B, $F_{.05} = 3.42$. The rejection region is $F_2 > 3.42$.

Since the observed value of the test statistic falls in the rejection region ($F_2 = 22.523 > 3.42$), H_0 is rejected. There is sufficient evidence to indicate the model is useful for predicting the 1996 food consumption expenditure at $\alpha = .05$.

d. For the first model ($n = 25$):

The standard error for $\hat{\beta}_2$ is .03518 (from printout).

For confidence coefficient .95, $\alpha = 1 - .95 = .05$ and $\alpha/2 = .05/2 = .025$. From Table VI, Appendix B, with df = 22, $t_{.025} = 2.074$. The confidence interval is:

$$\hat{\beta}_2 \pm t_{.025} s_{\hat{\beta}_2} \Rightarrow .354 \pm 2.074(.03518) \Rightarrow .354 \pm .0730 \Rightarrow (.218, .427)$$

For the second model ($n = 26$):

The standard error for $\hat{\beta}_2$ is .06239 (from printout).

For confidence coefficient .95, $\alpha = 1 - .95 = .05$ and $\alpha/2 = .05/2 = .025$. From Table VI, Appendix B, with df = 23, $t_{.025} = 2.069$. The confidence interval is:

$$\hat{\beta}_2 \pm t_{.025} s_{\hat{\beta}_2} \Rightarrow .394 \pm 2.069(.06239) \Rightarrow .394 \pm .1291 \Rightarrow (.2649, .4109)$$

e. For the first model ($n = 25$):

We are 95% confident the actual food consumption is between $3,421.90 and $4,904.80 when income is $41,100 and size is 4.

For the second model ($n = 26$):

We are 95% confident the actual food consumption is between $2,923.30 and $5,577.30 when income is $41,100 and size is 4.

f. With the 26th observation, the standard deviation for the model increases to almost double the old amount. This brings the test statistic down and increases the width of the confidence interval for β_2. The observation appears to have a large amount of influence.

11.37 The stem-and-leaf display for the first model's residuals, ($n = 25$), appears to be somewhat normal. However when the 26th observation is included, the stem-and-leaf display becomes skewed to the right. The 26th observation has destroyed the normality of the residuals.

11.39 From the printout, the standard deviation is $s = 24.68$. Two standard deviations is $2(24.68) = 49.36$ and 3 standard deviations is $3(24.68) = 74.04$. There is one observation with a residual that is more than 2 standard deviations from zero (observation 25) but less than 3 standard deviations from zero. This observation is a possible outlier.

11.41 a. Variables that are moderately or highly correlated have correlation coefficients of .5 or higher in absolute value. There are only two pairs of variables which are moderately or highly correlated. They are "year GRE taken" and "years in graduate program" ($r = -.602$), and "race" and "foreign status" ($r = -.515$).

b. When independent variables that are highly correlated with each other are included in a regression model, the results may be confusing. Highly correlated independent variables contribute overlapping information in the prediction of the dependent variable. The overall global test can indicate that the model is useful in predicting the dependent variable, while the individual t-tests on the independent variables can indicate that none of the independent variables are significant. This happens because the individual t-tests tests for the significance of an independent variable after the other independent variables are taken into account. Usually, only one of the independent variables that are highly correlated with each other are included in the regression model.

Multiple Regression

11.43   a.   To determine if at least one of the β parameters is not zero, we test:

H_0: $\beta_1 = \beta_2 = \beta_3 = \beta_4 = 0$
H_a: At least one $\beta_i \neq 0$

The test statistic is $F = \dfrac{R^2/k}{(1 - R^2)/[n - (k + 1)]} = \dfrac{.83/4}{(1 - .83)/[25 - (4 + 1)]} = 24.41$

The rejection region requires $\alpha = .05$ in the upper tail of the F-distribution with numerator df $= k = 4$ and denominator df $= n - (k + 1) = 25 - (4 + 1) = 20$. From Table VII, Appendix B, $F_{.05} = 2.87$. The rejection region is $F > 2.87$.

Since the observed value of the test statistic falls in the rejection region ($F = 24.41 > 2.87$), H_0 is rejected. There is sufficient evidence to indicate at least one of the β parameters is nonzero at $\alpha = .05$.

b. H_0: $\beta_1 = 0$
H_a: $\beta_1 < 0$

The test statistic is $t = \dfrac{\hat{\beta}_1 - 0}{s_{\hat{\beta}_1}} = \dfrac{-2.43 - 0}{1.21} = -2.01$

The rejection region requires $\alpha = .05$ in the lower tail of the t-distribution with df $= n - (k + 1) = 25 - (4 + 1) = 20$. From Table VI, Appendix B, $t_{.05} = 1.725$. The rejection region is $t < -1.725$.

Since the observed value of the test statistic falls in the rejection region ($t = -2.01 < -1.725$), H_0 is rejected. There is sufficient evidence to indicate β_1 is less than 0 at $\alpha = .05$.

c. H_0: $\beta_2 = 0$
H_a: $\beta_2 > 0$

The test statistic is $t = \dfrac{\hat{\beta}_2 - 0}{s_{\hat{\beta}_2}} = \dfrac{.05 - 0}{.16} = .31$

The rejection region requires $\alpha = .05$ in the upper tail of the t-distribution. From part **b** above, the rejection region is $t > 1.725$.

Since the observed value of the test statistic does not fall in the rejection region ($t = .31 \not> 1.725$), H_0 is not rejected. There is insufficient evidence to indicate β_2 is greater than 0 at $\alpha = .05$.

d. H_0: $\beta_3 = 0$
H_a: $\beta_3 \neq 0$

The test statistic is $t = \dfrac{\hat{\beta}_3 - 0}{s_{\hat{\beta}_3}} = \dfrac{.62 - 0}{.26} = 2.38$

The rejection region requires $\alpha/2 = .05/2 = .025$ in each tail of the t-distribution with df $= 20$. From Table VI, Appendix B, $t_{.025} = 2.086$. The rejection region is $t < -2.086$ or $t > 2.086$.

Since the observed value of the test statistic falls in the rejection region ($t = 2.38 > 2.086$), H_0 is rejected. There is sufficient evidence to indicate β_3 is different from 0 at $\alpha = .05$.

11.45 The confidence interval for the mean value of y gives a range within which we would expect the mean to fall. Once this mean value has been located, the actual values of y can still vary around the mean. Therefore, the variance for predicting the actual value of y includes the variation due to locating the mean plus the variation of y around its mean. Thus, the prediction interval must always be larger than the confidence interval for the mean.

11.47 a. Using MINITAB,

```
MTB > regr c1 2 c2 c3

The regression equation is
y = -50.5 + 7.37 x1 + 2.23 x2

Predictor        Coef         Stdev        t-ratio       p-value
Constant       -50.489        6.407         -7.88         0.000
x1               7.3694       0.8155         9.04         0.000
x2               2.2324       0.7604         2.94         0.012

s = 8.070        R-sq = 87.3%      R-sq(adj) = 85.2%

Analysis of Variance

SOURCE           DF           SS           MS            F        p-value
Regression        2         5361.8       2680.9        41.16      0.000
Error            12          781.5         65.1
Total            14         6143.3
```

The fitted regression model is $\hat{y} = -50.489 + 7.3694x_1 + 2.2324x_2$

b. Again using MINITAB,

```
MTB > regr c1 3 c2-c4

The regression equation is
y = -22.5 + 2.04 x1 - 2.81 x2 + 1.03 x1x2

Predictor        Coef         Stdev        t-ratio       p-value
Constant       -22.505        3.678         -6.12         0.000
x1               2.0352       0.6274         3.24         0.008
x2              -2.8072       0.5912         -4.75        0.000
x1x2             1.0296       0.1083         9.51         0.000

s = 2.777        R-sq = 98.6%      R-sq(adj) = 98.2%

Analysis of Variance

SOURCE           DF           SS           MS            F        p-value
Regression        3         6058.5       2019.5       261.92      0.000
Error            11           84.8          7.7
Total            14         6143.3
```

The fitted regression model is $\hat{y} = -22.505 + 2.0352x_1 - 2.8072x_2 + 1.0296x_1x_2$

c. The significances of all three *t* ratios in the interaction model of part **b** imply that all three terms aid in the prediction of *y* (all have *p*-values less than 0.01). Thus, the model in part **b** best describes the relationship between y_1, x_1 and x_2. This is further substantiated by the larger R^2 in this model.

Multiple Regression

d. Comparable results are reached with SAS, shown below.

```
Model: FIRST
Dep Variable: Y
                         Analysis of Variance

                    Sum of          Mean
Source      DF      Squares         Square       F Value     Prob>F

Model        2     5361.81021      2680.90511    41.164      0.0001
Error       12      781.52312        65.12693
C Total     14     6143.33333

      Root MSE       8.07013     R-Square     0.8728
      Dep Mean      -5.66667     Adj R-Sq     0.8516
      C.V.        -142.41398

                       Parameter Estimates
                   Parameter      Standard      T for H0:
Variable    DF      Estimate        Error       Parameter=0    Prob > |T|

INTERCEP     1     -50.489180     6.40691271      -7.880        0.0001
X1           1       7.369395     0.81552896       9.036        0.0001
X2           1       2.232353     0.76035721       2.936        0.0125
```

11.49 a. The first order model for $E(y)$ as a function of the first five independent variables is:

$$E(y) = \beta_0 + \beta_1 x_1 + \beta_2 x_2 + \beta_3 x_3 + \beta_4 x_4 + \beta_5 x_5$$

b. To test the utility of the model, we test:

H_0: $\beta_1 = \beta_2 = \beta_3 = \beta_4 = \beta_5 = 0$
H_a: At least one $\beta_i \neq 0$, $i = 1, 2, 3, 4, 5$

The test statistic is $F = 34.47$.

The p-value is $p < .001$. Since the p-value is so small, there is sufficient evidence to indicate the model is useful for predicting GSI at $\alpha > .001$.

$R^2 = .469$ 46.9% of the variability in the GSI scores is explained by the model including the first five independent variables.

c. The first order model for $E(y)$ as a function of the first seven independent variables is:

$$E(y) = \beta_0 + \beta_1 x_1 + \beta_2 x_2 + \beta_3 x_3 + \beta_4 x_4 + \beta_5 x_5 + \beta_6 x_6 + \beta_7 x_7$$

d. $R^2 = .603$ 60.3% of the variability in the GSI scores is explained by the model including the first seven independent variables.

e. Since the p-values associated with the variables DES and PDEQ-SR are both less than .001, there is evidence that both variables contribute to the prediction of GSI, adjusted for all the other variables already in the model for $\alpha > .001$.

11.51 The correlation coefficient between Importance and Replace is .2682. This correlation coefficient is fairly small and would not indicate a problem with multicollinearity between Importance and Replace. The correlation coefficient between Importance and Support is .6991. This correlation coefficient is fairly large and would indicate a potential problem with multicollinearity between Importance and Support. Probably only one of these variables should be included in the regression model. The correlation coefficient between Replace and Support is $-.0531$. This correlation coefficient is very small and would not indicate a problem with multicollinearity between Replace and Support. Thus, the model could probably include Replace and one of the variables Support or Importance.

11.53 To determine if plant A has a lower mean assembly time than plant B, we test:

H_0: $\beta_2 = 0$
H_a: $\beta_2 < 0$

The test statistic is $t = \dfrac{\hat{\beta}_2 - 0}{s_{\hat{\beta}_2}} = \dfrac{-.53}{.48} = -1.10$

The rejection region requires $\alpha = .01$ in the lower tail of the t-distribution with df $= n - (k + 1)$ $= 42 - (2 + 1) = 39$. From Table VI, Appendix B, $t_{.01} \approx 2.423$. The rejection region is $t < -2.423$.

Since the observed value of the test statistic does not fall in the rejection region ($t = -1.10 \not< -2.423$), H_0 is not rejected. There is insufficient evidence to indicate plant A had a lower mean assembly time than plant B at $\alpha = .01$.

11.55 a. $\hat{\beta}_1 = -.0945$ is the estimated change in the mean wage for each additional unit of business course work in high school, all other variables constant.

$\hat{\beta}_2 = -.032$ is the estimated change in the mean wage for each additional unit of college prep work in high school, all other variables constant.

$\hat{\beta}_3 = .009$ is the estimated change in the mean wage for each additional unit in math aptitude, all other variables constant.

$\hat{\beta}_4 = -.0028$ is the estimated change in the mean wage for each additional unit in the high school grade-point average, all other variables constant.

$\hat{\beta}_5 = .007$ is the estimated change in the mean wage for each additional unit in socioeconomic status, all other variables constant.

$\hat{\beta}_6 = .105$ is the estimated difference in the mean wage between married and single people, all other variables held constant.

$\hat{\beta}_7 = .469$ is the estimated change in the mean wage for each additional unit of on-the-job training, all other variables constant.

b. For all, the hypotheses are:

H_0: $\beta_i = 0$
H_a: $\beta_i \neq 0$

The rejection region for all tests requires $\alpha/2 = .01/2 = .005$ in each tail of the t-distribution with df $= n - (k + 1) = 60 - (7 + 1) = 52$. From Table VI, Appendix B, $t_{.005} \approx 2.704$. The rejection region is $t < -2.704$ or $t > 2.704$.

The null hypothesis will be rejected for tests for β_3, β_5, and β_6. The null hypothesis will not be rejected for β_1, β_2, β_4, and β_7.

Multiple Regression

c. For confidence coefficient .99, $\alpha = .01$ and $\alpha/2 = .01/2 = .005$. From Table VI, Appendix B, with df $= n - (k + 1) = 60 - (7 + 1) = 53$, $t_{.005} \approx 2.68$. The confidence interval is:

$$\hat{\beta}_5 \pm t_{.005} s_{\hat{\beta}_5} \Rightarrow .007 \pm 2.68 (.001225) \Rightarrow .007 \pm .0033 \Rightarrow (.0037, .0103)$$

d. We are 99% confident the true value of β_5 is between .0037 and .0103. We are 99% confident that the mean future wages will increase between .0037 and .0103 for each additional unit change in socioeconomic status, all other variables held constant.

11.57 a. The proposed model would be:

$$E(y) = \beta_0 + \beta_1 x_1 + \beta_2 x_2 + \beta_3 x_3 + \beta_4 x_4 + \beta_5 x_5 + \beta_6 x_6 + \beta_7 x_7$$

b. Using SAS, the printout is:

```
Model: MODEL1
Dependent Variable: Y

                        Analysis of Variance

                         Sum of        Mean
        Source    DF    Squares       Square      F Value     Prob>F

        Model      7    7.95777      1.13682       5.292      0.0074
        Error     11    2.36324      0.21484
        C Total   18   10.32101

            Root MSE      0.46351    R-square     0.7710
            Dep Mean      0.97684    Adj R-sq     0.6253
            C.V.         47.44963

                         Parameter Estimates

                    Parameter     Standard     T for H0:
        Variable  DF  Estimate       Error     Parameter=0   Prob > |T|

        INTERCEP  1   0.998082    0.24754163      4.032       0.0020
        X1        1  -0.022429    0.00503909     -4.451       0.0010
        X2        1   0.155711    0.07429092      2.096       0.0600
        X3        1  -0.017187    0.01185959     -1.449       0.1752
        X4        1  -0.009527    0.00961942     -0.990       0.3433
        X5        1   0.421421    0.10078189      4.182       0.0015
        X6        1   0.417123    0.43770177      0.953       0.3611
        X7        1  -0.155244    0.14858185     -1.045       0.3185
```

The fitted regression line is:

$$\hat{y} = .998 - .022x_1 + .156x_2 - .017x_3 - .010x_4 + .421x_5 + .417x_6 - .155x_7$$

To determine if the model is useful, we test:

H_0: $\beta_1 = \beta_2 = \beta_3 = \beta_4 = \beta_5 = \beta_6 = \beta_7 = 0$
H_a: At least one $\beta_i \neq 0$, for $i = 1, 2, ..., 7$

The test statistic is $F = 5.292$.

The rejection region requires $\alpha = .05$ in the upper tail of the F-distribution with $\nu_1 = k = 7$ and $\nu_2 = n - (k + 1) = 19 - (7 + 1) = 11$. From Table VIII, Appendix B, $F_{.05} = 3.01$. The rejection region is $F > 3.01$.

Since the observed value of the test statistic falls in the rejection region ($F = 5.292 > 3.01$), H_0 is rejected. There is sufficient evidence to indicate the model is useful for predicting voltage at $\alpha = .05$.

$R^2 = .7710$. Thus, 77.10% of the sample variation of voltage is explained by the model containing the seven independent variables.

The estimate of the standard deviation is $s = .464$.

$\hat{\beta}_0 = .998$.   This is simply the estimate of the y-intercept.

$\hat{\beta}_1 = -.022$.   For each unit increase in disperse phase volume, we estimate that the mean voltage will decrease by .022 units, holding all other variables constant.

$\hat{\beta}_2 = .156$.   For each unit increase in salinity, we estimate that the mean voltage will increase by .156 units, holding all other variables constant.

$\hat{\beta}_3 = -.017$.   For each unit increase in temperature, we estimate that the mean voltage will decrease by .017 units, holding all other variables constant.

$\hat{\beta}_4 = -.010$.   For each unit increase in time delay, we estimate that the mean voltage will decrease by .010 units, holding all other variables constant.

$\hat{\beta}_5 = .421$.   For each unit increase in surfactant concentration, we estimate that the mean voltage will increase by .421 units, holding all other variables constant.

$\hat{\beta}_6 = .417$.   For each unit increase in S:T ratio, we estimate that the mean voltage will increase by .417 units, holding all other variables constant.

$\hat{\beta}_7 = -.155$.   For each unit increase in solid particles, we estimate that the mean voltage will decrease by .155 units, holding all other variables constant.

d.   For experiment 14,

$$\hat{y} = .998 - .022(80) + .156(1) - .017(23) - .010(24) + .421(2) + .417(.25) - .155(2) = -.60075$$

e.   By including the interaction terms, it implies that the relationship between voltage and volume fraction of the disperse phase depend on the levels of salinity and surfactant concentration.

A possible sketch of the relationship is:

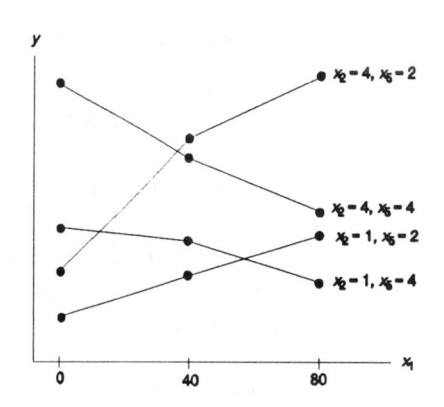

f.   Using SAS, the printout is:

```
Model: MODEL1
Dependent Variable: Y
                         Analysis of Variance
                         Sum of        Mean
     Source      DF      Squares       Square     F Value    Prob>F

     Model        5      7.01028       1.40206     5.505     0.0061
     Error       13      3.31073       0.25467
     C Total     18     10.32101
```

Multiple Regression

```
        Root MSE           0.50465      R-square        0.6792
        Dep Mean           0.97684      Adj R-sq        0.5558
        C.V.              51.66138

                          Parameter Estimates
                      Parameter    Standard    T for H0:
        Variable  DF   Estimate     Error      Parameter=0   Prob > |T|

        INTERCEP  1    0.905732    0.28546326      3.173       0.0073
        X1        1   -0.022753    0.00831751     -2.736       0.0170
        X2        1    0.304719    0.23660006      1.288       0.2202
        X5        1    0.274741    0.22704807      1.210       0.2478
        X1X2      1   -0.002804    0.00378998     -0.740       0.4725
        X1X5      1    0.001579    0.00394692      0.400       0.6956

                          Dep Var   Predict   Std Err  Lower95%  Upper95%
        Obs  X1  X2  X5     Y       Value    Predict   Predict   Predict   Residual

         1   40  1   2   0.6400    0.8640    0.185    -0.2969    2.0248   -0.2240
         2   80  1   4   0.8000    0.7701    0.309    -0.5082    2.0484    0.0299
         3   40  4   4   3.2000    2.1174    0.264     0.8869    3.3480    1.0826
         4   80  4   2   0.4800    0.2092    0.305    -1.0645    1.4828    0.2708
         5   40  1   4   1.7200    1.5398    0.309     0.2617    2.8178    0.1802
         6   80  1   2   0.3200   -0.0320    0.283    -1.2820    1.2181    0.3520
         7   40  4   2   0.6400    1.4416    0.292     0.1824    2.7009   -0.8016
         8   80  4   4   0.6800    1.0113    0.298    -0.2553    2.2779   -0.3313
         9   40  1   2   0.1200    0.8640    0.185    -0.2969    2.0248   -0.7440
        10   80  1   4   0.8800    0.7701    0.309    -0.5082    2.0484    0.1099
        11   40  4   4   2.3200    2.1174    0.264     0.8869    3.3480    0.2026
        12   80  4   2   0.4000    0.2092    0.305    -1.0645    1.4828    0.1908
        13   40  1   4   1.0400    1.5398    0.309     0.2617    2.8178   -0.4998
        14   80  1   2   0.1200   -0.0320    0.283    -1.2820    1.2181    0.1520
        15   40  4   2   1.2800    1.4416    0.292     0.1824    2.7009   -0.1616
        16   80  4   4   0.7200    1.0113    0.298    -0.2553    2.2779   -0.2913
        17    0  0   0   1.0800    0.9057    0.285    -0.3468    2.1583    0.1743
        18    0  0   0   1.0800    0.9057    0.285    -0.3468    2.1583    0.1743
        19    0  0   0   1.0400    0.9057    0.285    -0.3468    2.1583    0.1343

        Sum of Residuals                         0
        Sum of Squared Residuals              3.3107
        Predicted Resid SS (Press)            6.5833
```

The fitted regression line is:

$$\hat{y} = .906 - .023x_1 + .350x_2 + .275x_5 - .003x_1x_2 + .002x_1x_5$$

To determine if the model is useful, we test:

H_0: $\beta_1 = \beta_2 = \beta_3 = \beta_4 = \beta_5 = 0$
H_a: At least one $\beta_i \neq 0$, for $i = 1, 2, ..., 5$

The test statistic is $F = 5.505$.

The rejection region requires $\alpha = .05$ in the upper tail of the F-distribution with $\nu_1 = k = 5$ and $\nu_2 = n - (k + 1) = 19 - (5 + 1) = 13$. From Table VIII, Appendix B, $F_{.05} = 3.03$. The rejection region is $F > 3.03$.

Since the observed value of the test statistic falls in the rejection region ($F = 5.505 > 3.03$), H_0 is rejected. There is sufficient evidence to indicate the model is useful for predicting voltage at $\alpha = .05$.

$R^2 = .6792$. Thus, 67.92% of the sample variation of voltage is explained by the model containing the three independent variables and two interaction terms.

The estimate of the standard deviation is $s = .505$.

Comparing this model to that fit in part a, the model in part a appears to fit the data better. The model in part a has a higher R^2 (.7710 vs .6792) and a smaller estimate of the standard deviation (.464 vs .505).

g. $\hat{\beta}_0 = .906.$ This is simply the estimate of the y-intercept.

$\hat{\beta}_1 = -.023.$ For each unit increase in disperse phase volume, we estimate that the mean voltage will decrease by .023 units, holding salinity and surfactant concentration at 0.

$\hat{\beta}_2 = .305.$ For each unit increase in salinity, we estimate that the mean voltage will increase by .305 units, holding disperse phase volume and surfactant concentration at 0.

$\hat{\beta}_3 = .275.$ For each unit increase in surfactant concentration, we estimate that the mean voltage will increase by .275 units, holding disperse phase volume and salinity at 0.

$\hat{\beta}_4 = -.003.$ This estimates the difference in the slope of the relationship between voltage and disperse phase volume for each unit increase in salinity, holding surfactant concentration constant.

$\hat{\beta}_5 = .002.$ This estimates the difference in the slope of the relationship between voltage and disperse phase volume for each unit increase in surfactant concentration, holding salinity constant.

g. Observation #14 has x_1 at the high level and both x_2 and x_5 at the low level. The 95% prediction interval is $(-1.2820, 1.2181)$. We are 95% confident that the actual voltage will be between -1.282 and 1.2181 when $x_1 = 80$, $x_2 = 1$, and $x_5 = 2$.

11.59 a. For a sunny weekday, $x_1 = 0$ and $x_2 = 1$:

$x_3 = 70 \Rightarrow \hat{y} = 250 - 700(0) + 100(1) + 5(70) + 15(0)(70) = 700$
$x_3 = 80 \Rightarrow \hat{y} = 250 - 700(0) + 100(1) + 5(80) + 15(0)(80) = 750$
$x_3 = 90 \Rightarrow \hat{y} = 800$
$x_3 = 100 \Rightarrow \hat{y} = 850$

For a sunny weekend, $x_1 = 1$ and $x_2 = 1$:

$x_3 = 70 \Rightarrow \hat{y} = 250 - 700(1) + 100(1) + 5(70) + 15(1)(70) = 1050$
$x_3 = 80 \Rightarrow \hat{y} = 250 - 700(1) + 100(1) + 5(80) + 15(1)(80) = 1250$
$x_3 = 90 \Rightarrow \hat{y} = 1450$
$x_3 = 100 \Rightarrow \hat{y} = 1650$

Multiple Regression

[Graph: Predicted day's attendance vs Predicted high temperature (x_3), showing two lines — "Sunny weekend" (steeper) and "Sunny weekday" (shallower), with temperature ranging from 60 to 100 and attendance from 600 to 1800.]

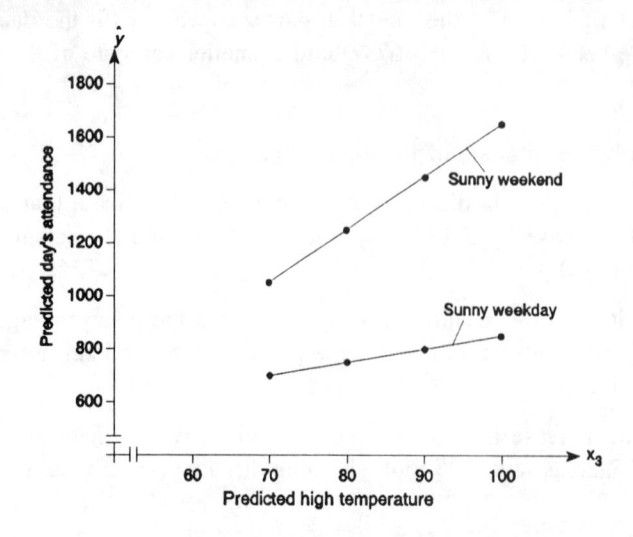

For both sunny weekdays and sunny weekend days, as the predicted high temperature increases, so does the predicted day's attendance. However, the predicted day's attendance on sunny weekend days increases at a faster rate than on sunny weekdays. Also, the predicted day's attendance is higher on sunny weekend days than on sunny weekdays.

b. To determine if the interaction term is a useful addition to the model, we test:

H_0: $\beta_4 = 0$
H_a: $\beta_4 \neq 0$

The test statistic is $t = \dfrac{\hat{\beta}_4}{s_{\hat{\beta}_4}} = \dfrac{15}{3} = 5$

The rejection region requires $\alpha/2 = .05/2 = .025$ in each tail of the t-distribution with df = $n - (k + 1) = 30 - (4 + 1) = 25$. From Table VI, Appendix B, $t_{.025} = 2.06$. The rejection region is $t < -2.06$ or $t > 2.06$.

Since the observed value of the test statistic falls in the rejection region ($t = 5 > 2.06$), H_0 is rejected. There is sufficient evidence to indicate the interaction term is a useful addition to the model at $\alpha = .05$.

c. For $x_1 = 0$, $x_2 = 1$, and $x_3 = 95$,

$\hat{y} = 250 - 700(0) + 100(1) + 5(95) + 15(0)(95) = 825$

d. The width of the interval in Exercise 11.58e is $1245 - 645 = 600$, while the width is $850 - 800 = 50$ for the model containing the interaction term. The smaller the width of the interval, the smaller the variance. This implies that the interaction term is quite useful in predicting daily attendance. It has reduced the unexplained error.

e. Because an interaction term including x_1 is in the model, the coefficient corresponding to x_1 must be interpreted with caution. For all observed values of x_3 (temperature), the interaction term value is greater than 700.

11.61   From the plot of the residuals against x_1, there is a general mound shape to the data. This indicates that adding x_1^2 to the model might provide significant information to the model. From the plot of the residuals against x_2, there is no apparent mound or bowl shape. This indicates that adding x_2^2 to the model would not add significantly to the model.

11.63   The residual plots of the residuals against x_1 and against x_2 for the second-order model indicate there is no mound or bowl shape in either graph. This implies that second-order is the highest order necessary. We have eliminated the mound shape from the plot of the residuals against x_1 for the first-order model. From the plots and the results of the tests in Exercise 11.61, it appears the second order model is preferable for predicting GPA.

Introduction to Model Building — Chapter 12

12.1   a.   The variable "minimum road distance" is measured on a numerical scale, so it is a quantitative variable.

b.   The variable "length of time" is measured on a numerical scale, so it is a quantitative variable.

c.   The variable "percentage of workers" is measured on a numerical scale, so it is a quantitative variable.

d.   The variable "whether or not the province borders France or Switzerland" is not measured on a numerical scale, so it is a qualitative variable.

e.   The variable "rate of unemployment" is measured on a numerical scale, so it is a quantitative variable.

f.   The variable "ratio of union members to population" is measured on a numerical scale, so it is a quantitative variable.

g.   The variable "product sectors" is measured on a numerical scale, so it is a quantitative variable.

12.3   a.   1.   The "Quantitative GMAT score" is measured on a numerical scale, so it is a quantitative variable.
2.   The "Verbal GMAT score" is measured on a numerical scale, so it is a quantitative variable.
3.   The "Undergraduate GPA" is measured on a numerical scale, so it is a quantitative variable.
4.   The "First-year graduate GPA" is measured on a numerical scale, so it is a quantitative variable.
5.   The "Student cohort" is measured on a numerical scale, so it is a quantitative variable.

b.   The variables quantitative GMAT score, verbal GMAT score, undergraduate GPA, and first-year graduate GPA should all be positively correlated to final GPA. The variable student cohort could be negatively correlated to final GPA.

c.   There are no qualitative variables among the list of variables.

12.5   a.   The variable "Flextime of the position applied for" is not measured on a numerical scale, so it is a qualitative variable.

b.   The variable "level of day care support required" is not measured on a numerical scale, so it is a qualitative variable.

c.   The variable "spousal transfer support required" is not measured on a numerical scale, so it is a qualitative variable.

d. The variable "number of days allowed for family sick leave" is measured on a numerical scale, so it is a quantitative variable.

e. The variable "marital status" is not measured on a numerical scale, so it is a qualitative variable.

f. The variable "number of children" is measured on a numerical scale, so it is a quantitative variable.

g. The variable "gender" is not measured on a numerical scale, so it is a qualitative variable.

12.7 a. Since the graph is a straight line, it is first-order.

$\beta_0 = 10$, the y-intercept. β_1 is $\frac{\Delta y}{\Delta x}$.

The line goes through the points (0, 10), (20, 20). Thus,

$$\beta_1 = \frac{10 - 20}{0 - 20} = \frac{-10}{-20} = .5$$

b. Since the graph is a straight line, it is first-order.

$\beta_0 = 80$, the y-intercept. β_1 is $\frac{\Delta y}{\Delta x}$.

The line goes through the points (0, 80), (80, 40). Thus,

$$\beta_1 = \frac{80 - 40}{0 - 80} = \frac{40}{-80} = -.5$$

12.9 a. $E(y) = 2 + 3x$. The order of the polynomial is first-order. To graph the line, we need to pick two values of x and find the corresponding values of $E(y)$.

For $x = 0$, $E(y) = 2 + 3(0) = 2$
$x = 2$, $E(y) = 2 + 3(2) = 8$

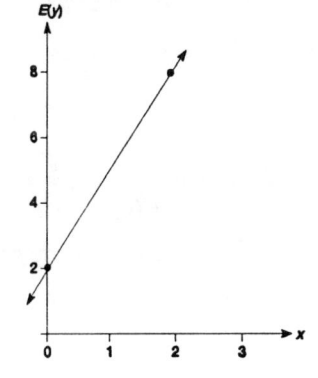

b. $E(y) = 2 + 3x^2$. The order of the polynomial is second-order.

For $x = 0$, $E(y) = 2 + 3(0^2) = 2$
$x = 1$, $E(y) = 2 + 3(1^2) = 5$
$x = 2$, $E(y) = 2 + 3(2^2) = 14$
$x = 3$, $E(y) = 2 + 3(3^2) = 29$

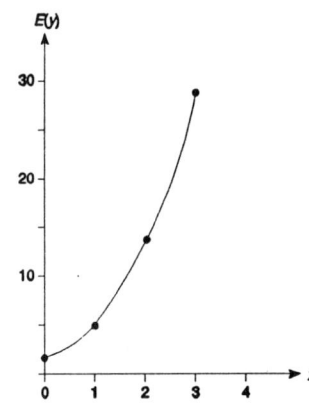

Introduction to Model Building

c. $E(y) = 1 + 2x + 2x^2 + x^3$. The order of the polynomial is third-order.

For $x = 0$, $E(y) = 1 + 2(0) + 2(0^2) + 0^3 = 1$
$x = 1$, $E(y) = 1 + 2(1) + 2(1^2) + 1^3 = 6$
$x = 2$, $E(y) = 1 + 2(2) + 2(2^2) + 2^3 = 21$
$x = 3$, $E(y) = 1 + 2(3) + 2(3^2) + 3^3 = 52$

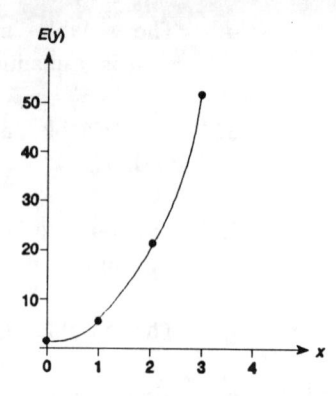

d. $E(y) = 2x + 2x^2 + x^3$. The order of the polynomial is third-order.

For $x = 0$, $E(y) = 2(0) + 2(0^2) + 0^3 = 0$
$x = 1$, $E(y) = 2(1) + 2(1^2) + 1^3 = 5$
$x = 2$, $E(y) = 2(2) + 2(2^2) + 2^3 = 20$
$x = 3$, $E(y) = 2(3) + 2(3^2) + 3^3 = 51$

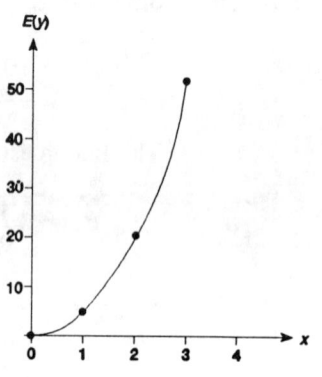

e. $E(y) = 2 - 3x^2$. The order of the polynomial is second-order.

For $x = 0$, $E(y) = 2 - 3(0^2) = 2$
$x = 1$, $E(y) = 2 - 3(1^2) = -1$
$x = 2$, $E(y) = 2 - 3(2^2) = -10$
$x = 3$, $E(y) = 2 - 3(3^2) = -25$

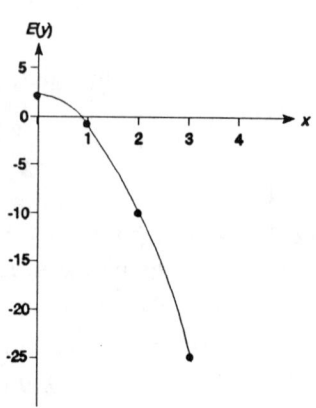

f. $E(y) = -2 + 3x$. The order of the polynomial is first-order.

For $x = 0$, $E(y) = -2 + 3(0) = -2$
$x = 2$, $E(y) = -2 + 3(2) = 4$

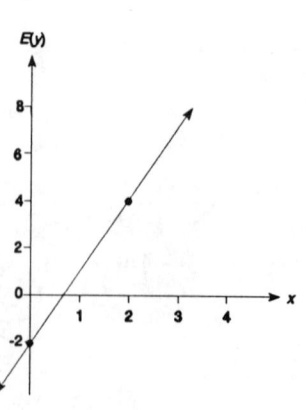

12.11 a. The least squares prediction equation is $\hat{y} = 63.1 + 1.17x - .0374x^2$.

b. To plot this second-order equation, we pick several values of x and find the corresponding values of $\hat{y}$.

For $x = 0$, $\hat{y} = 63.1 + 1.17(0) - .0374(0^2) = 63.1$
$x = 1$, $\hat{y} = 63.1 + 1.17(1) - .0374(1^2) = 64.2326$
$x = 2$, $\hat{y} = 63.1 + 1.17(2) - .0374(2^2) = 65.2904$
$x = 4$, $\hat{y} = 63.1 + 1.17(4) - .0374(4^2) = 67.1816$
$x = 6$, $\hat{y} = 63.1 + 1.17(6) - .0374(6^2) = 68.7736$
$x = 10$, $\hat{y} = 63.1 + 1.17(10) - .0374(10^2) = 71.06$
$x = 15$, $\hat{y} = 63.1 + 1.17(15) - .0374(15^2) = 72.2350$
$x = 20$, $\hat{y} = 63.1 + 1.17(20) - .0374(20^2) = 71.54$

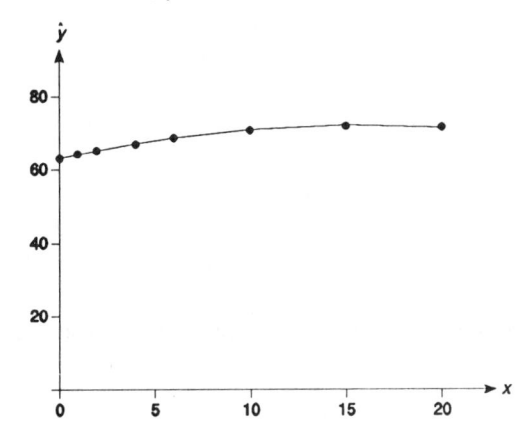

c. The hypotheses are:

H_0: $\beta_2 = 0$
H_a: $\beta_2 < 0$

d. The test statistic is $t = -3.03$ (from printout).

The rejection region requires $\alpha = .05$ in the lower tail of the t-distribution with df $= n - (k + 1) = 17 - (2 + 1) = 14$. From Table VI, Appendix B, $t_{.05} = 1.761$. The rejection region is $t < -1.761$.

Since the observed value of the test statistic falls in the rejection region ($t = -3.03 < -1.761$), H_0 is rejected. There is sufficient evidence to indicate that y decreases at an increasing rate as x increases at $\alpha = .05$.

12.13 a. Because the company suspects that new and old copiers require more service calls than those in the middle, the model would be

$$E(y) = \beta_0 + \beta_1 x + \beta_2 x^2$$

where y = number of service calls
x = age of copier

b. $\beta_0 > 0$ and $\beta_2 > 0$. Since the parabola will open upwards (number of service calls larger for young and old machines), both β_0 and β_2 will be greater than 0.

12.15 The model would be $E(y) = \beta_0 + \beta_1 x + \beta_2 x^2$. Since the value of y is expected to increase and then decrease as x gets larger, β_2 will be negative. A sketch of the model would be:

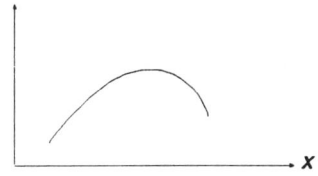

Introduction to Model Building

12.17   a.   A model that would allow the assembly time to decrease and then increase would be

$$E(y) = \beta_0 + \beta_1 x + \beta_2 x^2$$

where y = assembly time
x = time since lunch
β_0 = y-intercept
β_1 = shifts parabola to right or left
β_2 = rate of curvature

b.   The sketch of the model is:

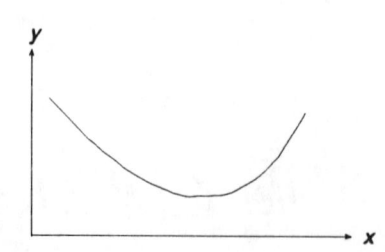

12.19   To determine if the rate of increase in output per unit increase of input decreases as the input increases, we test:

H_0: $\beta_2 = 0$
H_a: $\beta_2 < 0$

The test statistic is $t = \dfrac{\hat{\beta}_2}{s_{\hat{\beta}_2}} = \dfrac{-.03231}{.00489} = -6.60$

The rejection region requires $\alpha = .05$ in the lower tail of the t-distribution with df = $n - (k + 1)$ = 25 - (2 + 1) = 22. From Table VI, Appendix B, $t_{.05} = 1.717$. The rejection region is $t < -1.717$.

Since the observed value of the test statistic falls in the rejection region (t = $-6.60 < -1.717$), H_0 is rejected. There is sufficient evidence to indicate the rate of increase decreases as the input increases at $\alpha = .05$.

12.21   a.   The first-order model is $E(y) = \beta_0 + \beta_1 x_1 + \beta_2 x_2$

b.   The model including the interaction term is $E(y) = \beta_0 + \beta_1 x_1 + \beta_2 x_2 + \beta_3 x_1 x_2$

c.   The complete second-order model is $E(y) = \beta_0 + \beta_1 x_1 + \beta_2 x_2 + \beta_3 x_1 x_2 + \beta_4 x_1^2 + \beta_5 x_2^2$

12.23   a.   The response surface is a twisted plane.

b.   The contour line when $x_1 = 0$ is $E(y) = 4 - 0 + 2x_2 + 0(x_2) = 4 + 2x_2$

The contour line when $x_1 = 1$ is $E(y) = 4 - 1 + 2x_2 + x_2 = 3 + 3x_2$

The contour line when $x_1 = 2$ is $E(y) = 4 - 2 + 2x_2 + 2x_2 = 2 + 4x_2$

The plots are:

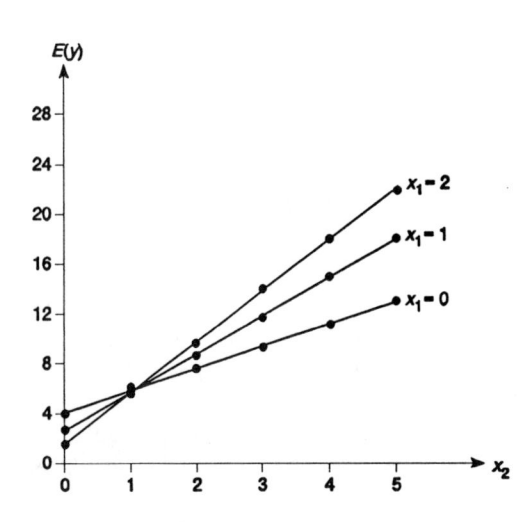

c. The interactive term x_1x_2 allows the contour lines to be non-parallel.

d. When $x_1 = 0$, the contour line is $E(y) = 4 + 2x_2$. For each unit change in x_2, $E(y)$ increases by 2 units.

When $x_1 = 1$, the contour line is $E(y) = 3 + 3x_2$. For each unit change in x_2, $E(y)$ increases by 3 units.

When $x_1 = 2$, the contour line is $E(y) = 2 + 4x_2$. For each unit change in x_2, $E(y)$ increases by 4 units.

e. When $x_1 = 2$ and $x_2 = 4$, $E(y) = 18$. When $x_1 = 0$ and $x_2 = 5$, $E(y) = 14$. Thus, the change in $E(y)$ is from 18 to 14 or -4.

12.25 a. The prediction equation is:
$$\hat{y} = -2.55 + 3.82x_1 + 2.63x_2 - 1.29x_1x_2$$

b. The response surface is a twisted plane, since the equation contains an interaction term.

c. For $x_2 = 1$, $\hat{y} = -2.55 + 3.82x_1 + 2.63(1) - 1.29x_1(1)$
$= .08 + 2.53x_1$

For $x_2 = 3$, $\hat{y} = -2.55 + 3.82x_1 + 2.63(3) - 1.29x_1(3)$
$= 5.34 - .05x_1$

For $x_2 = 5$, $\hat{y} = -2.55 + 3.82x_1 + 2.63(5) - 1.29x_1(5)$
$= 10.6 - 2.63x_1$

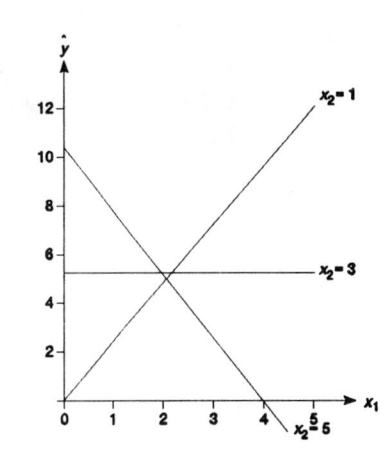

d. If x_1 and x_2 interact, the effect of x_1 on y is different at different levels of x_2. When $x_2 = 1$, as x_1 increases, $\hat{y}$ also increases. When $x_2 = 5$, as x_1 increases, $\hat{y}$ decreases.

Introduction to Model Building

e. The hypotheses are:

$$H_0: \beta_3 = 0$$
$$H_a: \beta_3 \neq 0$$

f. The test statistic is $t = \dfrac{\hat{\beta}_3}{s_{\hat{\beta}_3}} = \dfrac{-1.285}{.1594} = -8.06$

The rejection region requires $\alpha/2 = .01/2 = .005$ in each tail of the t-distribution with df $= n - (k + 1) = 15 - (3 + 1) = 11$. From Table VI, Appendix B, $t_{.005} = 3.106$. The rejection region is $t < -3.106$ or $t > 3.106$.

Since the observed value of the test statistic falls in the rejection region ($t = -8.06 < -3.106$), H_0 is rejected. There is sufficient evidence to indicate that x_1 and x_2 interact at $\alpha = .01$.

12.27 a. The complete second-order model is:

$$E(y) = \beta_0 + \beta_1 x_1 + \beta_2 x_2 + \beta_3 x_1 x_2 + \beta_4 x_1^2 + \beta_5 x_2^2$$

b. The terms in the model that allow for curvilinear relationships are:

$\beta_4 x_1^2$ and $\beta_5 x_2^2$

12.31 a. The prediction equation is:

$$\hat{y} = 149.5 + .472 x_1 - .099 x_2 - .00054 x_1^2 + .000015 x_2^2$$

b. Because the estimates of β_3 and β_4 have different signs, the surface is saddle-shaped.

c. To determine if the model is useful, we test:

$$H_0: \beta_1 = \beta_2 = \beta_3 = \beta_4 = 0$$
$$H_a: \text{At least one } \beta_i \neq 0$$

The test statistic is $F = \dfrac{\text{MSR}}{\text{MSE}} = \dfrac{1500.52}{47.40} = 31.66$

The rejection region requires $\alpha = .01$ in the upper tail of the F-distribution with $\nu_1 = k = 4$ and $\nu_2 = n - (k + 1) = 16 - (4 + 1) = 11$. From Table X, Appendix B, $F_{.01} = 5.67$. The rejection region is $F > 5.67$.

Since the observed value of the test statistic falls in the rejection region ($F = 31.66 > 5.67$), H_0 is rejected. There is sufficient evidence to indicate the model is useful for predicting quarterly sales at $\alpha = .01$.

d. It appears the variation in air conditioner sales could be adequately explained by a less complex model since the estimates of the coefficients β_3 and β_4 are very close to 0 and the t values associated with each are small. We could probably use the model $E(y) = \beta_0 + \beta_1 x_1 + \beta_2 x_2$

12.33 a. H_a: At least one $\beta_i \neq 0$, $i = 3, 4, 5$

b. First, fit the complete second-order model. Find the sum of squares for error and call it SSE_c. Then, fit the reduced model, or the first-order model. Find the sum of squares for error and call it SSE_r.

The test statistic is $F = \dfrac{(SSE_r - SSE_c)/(k - g)}{SSE_c/[n - (k + 1)]}$ where k is the number of terms in the complete model besides β_0, g is the number of terms in the reduced model besides β_0, and n is the sample size.

c. $\nu_1 = k - g = 5 - 2 = 3$ and $\nu_2 = n - (k + 1) = 30 - (5 + 1) = 24$.

12.35 By adding variables to the model, SSE will decrease or stay the same. Thus, $SSE_c \leq SSE_r$. The only circumstance under which we will reject H_0 is if SSE_c is much smaller than SSE_r. If SSE_c is much smaller than SSE_r, F will be large. Thus, the test is only one-tailed.

12.37 a. To determine whether the complete model contributes information for the prediction of y, we test:

H_0: $\beta_1 = \beta_2 = \beta_3 = \beta_4 = \beta_5 = 0$
H_a: At least one of the β's is not 0, $i = 1, 2, 3, 4, 5$

b. The test statistic is $F = \dfrac{MSR}{MSE} = \dfrac{982.31}{53.84} = 18.24$

The rejection region requires $\alpha = .05$ in the upper tail of the F-distribution with $\nu_1 = k = 5$ and $\nu_2 = n - (k + 1) = 40 - (5 + 1) = 34$. From Table VIII, Appendix B, $F_{.05} \approx 2.53$. The rejection region is $F > 2.53$.

Since the observed value of the test statistic falls in the rejection region ($F = 18.24 > 2.53$), H_0 is rejected. There is sufficient evidence to indicate that the complete model contributes information for the prediction of y at $\alpha = .05$.

c. To determine whether a second-order model contributes more information than a first-order model for the prediction of y, we test:

H_0: $\beta_3 = \beta_4 = \beta_5 = 0$
H_a: At least one of the parameters, β_3, β_4, or β_5, is not 0

d. The test statistic is $F = \dfrac{(SSE_r - SSE_c)/(k - g)}{SSE_c/[n - (k + 1)]} = \dfrac{(3197.16 - 1830.44)/(5 - 2)}{1830.44/(40 - (5 + 1))}$

$= \dfrac{455.5733}{53.8365} = 8.46$

The rejection region requires $\alpha = .05$ in the upper tail of the F-distribution with $\nu_1 = k - g = 3$ and $\nu_2 = n - (k + 1) = 40 - (5 + 1) = 34$. From Table VIII, Appendix B, $F_{.05} \approx 2.92$. The rejection region is $F > 2.92$.

Since the observed value of the test statistic falls in the rejection region ($F = 8.46 > 2.92$), H_0 is rejected. There is sufficient evidence to indicate the second-order model contributes more information than a first-order model for the prediction of y at $\alpha = .05$.

e. The second-order model, based on the test result in part d.

12.39 a. Using MINITAB, the output from fitting a complete second-order model is:

```
* NOTE *     X1 is highly correlated with other predictor variables
* NOTE *     X2 is highly correlated with other predictor variables
* NOTE *     X1X2 is highly correlated with other predictor variables
```

Introduction to Model Building

```
The regression equation is
Y = 172788 - 10739 X1 - 499 X2 - 20.2 X1X2 + 198 X1SQ + 14.7 X2SQ

Predictor      Coef       Stdev     t-ratio      p
Constant     172788       97785       1.77    0.084
X1           -10739        2789      -3.85    0.000
X2             -499        1444      -0.35    0.731
X1X2         -20.20       21.36      -0.95    0.350
X1SQ         197.57       22.60       8.74    0.000
X2SQ         14.678       8.819       1.66    0.103

s = 13132      R-sq = 95.9%      R-sq(adj) = 95.5%

Analysis of Variance

SOURCE       DF          SS              MS            F         p
Regression    5   1.70956E+11     34191134720      198.27     0.000
Error        42     7242915328      172450368
Total        47   1.78199E+11

SOURCE       DF      SEQ SS
X1            1   1.56067E+11
X2            1       13214024
X1X2          1     1686339840
X1SQ          1    12711371776
X2SQ          1      477704384

Unusual Observations
Obs.    X1         Y        Fit   Stdev.Fit   Residual   St.Resid
 14    62.9    203288    235455      6002      -32167     -2.75R
 22    45.4     27105     58567      3603      -31462     -2.49R
 34    28.2     28722     15156     11311       13566      2.03RX
 43    64.3    230329    248054      8790      -17725     -1.82 X
 47    63.9    212309    240469      4904      -28160     -2.31R

R denotes an obs. with a large st. resid.
X denotes an obs. whose X value gives it large influence.
```

b. To test the hypothesis H_0: $\beta_4 = \beta_5 = 0$, we must fit the reduced model

$$E(y) = \beta_0 + \beta_1 x_1 + \beta_2 x_2 + \beta_3 x_1 x_2$$

Using MINITAB, the output from fitting the reduced model is:

```
* NOTE *    X1X2 is highly correlated with other  predictor variables

The regression equation is
Y = - 476768 + 11458 X1 + 3404 X2 - 64.4 X1X2

Predictor      Coef       Stdev     t-ratio      p
Constant    -476768      100852      -4.73    0.000
X1            11458        1874       6.11    0.000
X2             3404        1814       1.88    0.067
X1X2         -64.35       33.77      -1.91    0.063

s = 21549      R-sq = 88.5%      R-sq(adj) = 87.8%

Analysis of Variance

SOURCE       DF          SS              MS            F         p
Regression    3   1.57767E+11     52588867584      113.25     0.000
Error        44    20431990784      464363424
Total        47   1.78199E+11

SOURCE       DF      SEQ SS
X1            1   1.56067E+11
X2            1       13214024
X1X2          1     1686339840

Unusual Observations
Obs.    X1         Y        Fit   Stdev.Fit   Residual   St.Resid
 34    28.2     28722    -59713    11922       88435      4.93RX
 38    66.5    290411    250350     9553       40061      2.07R
 43    64.3    230329    202899    11574       27430      1.51 X

R denotes an obs. with a large st. resid.
X denotes an obs. whose X value gives it large influence.
```

The test is:

H_0: $\beta_4 = \beta_5 = 0$
H_a: At least one $\beta_i \neq 0$, for $i = 4, 5$

The test statistic is $F = \dfrac{(\text{SSE}_r - \text{SSE}_c)/(k - g)}{\text{SSE}_c/[n - (k + 1)]}$

$= \dfrac{(20{,}431{,}990{,}784 - 7{,}242{,}915{,}328)/(5 - 3)}{7{,}242{,}915{,}328/[48 - (5 + 1)]} = 38.24$

The rejection region requires $\alpha = .05$ in the upper tail of the F-distribution with $\nu_1 = k - g = 5 - 3 = 2$ and $\nu_2 = n - (k + 1) = 48 - (5 + 1) = 42$. From Table VIII, Appendix B, $F_{.05} \approx 3.23$. The rejection region is $F > 3.23$.

Since the observed value of the test statistic falls in the rejection region ($F = 38.24 > 3.23$), H_0 is rejected. There is sufficient evidence to indicate that at least one of the quadratic terms contributes to the prediction of monthly collision claims at $\alpha = .05$.

c. From part **b**, we know at least one of the quadratic terms is significant. From part **a**, it appears that none of the terms involving x_2 may be significant.

Thus, we will fit the model with just x_1 and x_1^2. The MINITAB output is:

```
The regression equation is
Y = 185160 - 11580 X1 + 196 X1SQ

Predictor       Coef      Stdev    t-ratio        p
Constant      185160      54791       3.38    0.002
X1           -11580        2182      -5.31    0.000
X1SQ         195.54       21.64       9.04    0.000

s = 13219       R-sq = 95.6%    R-sq(adj) = 95.4%

Analysis of Variance

SOURCE        DF           SS             MS           F         p
Regression     2  1.70335E+11    85167357952      487.36     0.000
Error         45     7863868416      174752624
Total         47  1.78199E+11

SOURCE        DF       SEQ SS
X1             1  1.56067E+11
X1SQ           1    14267676672

Unusual Observations
Obs.      X1         Y         Fit   Stdev.Fit   Residual   St.Resid
  10    35.8     28957       21200        5825       7757      0.65 X
  14    62.9    203288      230397        4044     -27109     -2.15R
  22    45.4     27105       62456        2856     -35351     -2.74R
  34    28.2     28722       14099       11344      14623      2.15RX
  38    66.5    290411      279798        6189      10613      0.91 X
  47    63.9    212309      243611        4570     -31302     -2.52R

R denotes an obs. with a large st. resid.
X denotes an obs. whose X value gives it large influence.
```

To see if any of the terms involving x_2 are significant, we test:

H_0: $\beta_2 = \beta_3 = \beta_5 = 0$
H_a: At least one $\beta_i \neq 0$, for $i = 2, 3, 5$

Introduction to Model Building

The test statistic is $F = \dfrac{(SSE_r - SSE_c)/(k - g)}{SSE_c/[n - (k + 1)]}$

$= \dfrac{(7,863,868,416 - 7,242,915,328)/(5 - 2)}{7,242,915,328/[48 - (5 + 1)]} = 1.20$

The rejection region requires $\alpha = .05$ in the upper tail of the F-distribution with $\nu_1 = k - g = 5 - 2 = 3$ and $\nu_2 = n - (k + 1) = 48 - (5 + 1) = 42$. From Table VIII, Appendix B, $F_{.05} \approx 2.84$. The rejection region is $F > 2.84$

Since the observed value of the test statistic does not fall in the rejection region ($F = 1.20 \not> 2.84$), H_0 is not rejected. There is insufficient evidence to indicate that any of the terms involving x_2 contribute to the model at $\alpha = .05$.

Thus, it appears that the best model is $E(y) = \beta_0 + \beta_1 x_1 + \beta_2 x_1^2$. The model does not support the analyst's claim. In the model above, the estimate for β_2 is positive. This would indicate that the higher claims are for both the young and the old. Also, there is no evidence to support the claim that there are more claims when the temperature goes down.

12.41 a. The complete second-order model is:

$$E(y) = \beta_0 + \beta_1 x_1 + \beta_2 x_2 + \beta_3 x_1 x_2 + \beta_4 x_1^2 + \beta_5 x_2^2$$

The SAS output is:

```
DEP VARIABLE: Y
ANALYSIS OF VARIANCE

                    SUM OF          MEAN
SOURCE      DF     SQUARES        SQUARE       F VALUE      PROB>F

MODEL        5   38638.97257    7727.79451     289.894      0.0001
ERROR        6     159.94409      26.65734905
C TOTAL     11   38798.91667

        ROOT MSE    5.163076     R-SQUARE    0.9959
        DEP MEAN  104.0833       ADJ R-SQ    0.9924
        C.V.        4.960521

PARAMETER ESTIMATES

                     PARAMETER       STANDARD     T FOR H0:
VARIABLE    DF       ESTIMATE        ERROR        PARAMETER=0     PROB > |T|

INTERCEP     1      -214.50642      38.67967128     -5.546         0.0015
X1           1        -0.90993997    0.15211450     -5.982         0.0010
X2           1        78.68346134   11.56158360      6.806         0.0005
X1X2         1         0.14279555    0.02035520      7.015         0.0004
X1SQ         1        -0.000136976   0.000138603    -0.988         0.3612
X2SQ         1        -5.98714362    0.86370441     -6.932         0.0004
```

The fitted model is $\hat{y} = -214.5 - .91x_1 + 78.68x_2 + .14x_1x_2 - .0001x_1^2 - 5.99x_2^2$

b. To determine if the complete second-order model is useful for forecasting sales, we test:

H_0: $\beta_1 = \beta_2 = \beta_3 = \beta_4 = \beta_5 = 0$
H_a: At least one $\beta_i \neq 0$, $i = 1, 2, 3, 4, 5$

The test statistic is $F = \dfrac{MSR}{MSE} = \dfrac{7727.79451}{26.65735} = 289.89$

The rejection region requires $\alpha = .05$ in the upper tail of the F-distribution with $\nu_1 = k = 5$ and $\nu_2 = n - (k + 1) = 12 - (5 + 1) = 6$. From Table VIII, Appendix B, $F_{.05} = 4.39$. The rejection region is $F > 4.39$.

Since the observed value of the test statistic falls in the rejection region ($F = 289.89 > 4.39$), H_0 is rejected. There is sufficient evidence to indicate the complete second-order model is useful for forecasting sales at $\alpha = .05$.

c. For $x_1 = 400$ and $x_2 = 12$,

$$\hat{y} = -214.50642 - .90993997(400) + 78.68346134(12) + .1427955(400)(12) - .000136976(400^2) - 5.98714362(12^2) = 167.073$$

Thus, the forecast for next year's sales is $167,073.

12.43 a. The complete second-order model is:

$$E(y) = \beta_0 + \beta_1 x_1 + \beta_2 x_2 + \beta_3 x_3 + \beta_4 x_1 x_2 + \beta_5 x_1 x_3 + \beta_6 x_2 x_3 + \beta_7 x_1^2 + \beta_8 x_2^2 + \beta_9 x_3^2$$

b. The first-order model is $E(y) = \beta_0 + \beta_1 x_1 + \beta_2 x_2 + \beta_3 x_3$

c. The prediction equation for the second-order model is:

$$\hat{y} = 655.8 - 57.33 x_1 - 3.39 x_2 - 28.27 x_3 + .224 x_1 x_2 + 2.20 x_1 x_3 + .089 x_2 x_3 + .453 x_1^2 + .004 x_2^2 + .208 x_3^2$$

The prediction equation for the first-order model is:

$$\hat{y} = 131.9 + 2.73 x_1 + .05 x_2 - 2.59 x_3$$

d. To determine if the second-order terms are useful, we test:

$H_0: \beta_4 = \beta_5 = \cdots = \beta_9 = 0$
$H_a:$ At least one $\beta_i \neq 0$, $i = 4, 5, ..., 9$

The test statistic is $F = \dfrac{(SSE_r - SSE_c)/(k - g)}{SSE_c[n - (k + 1)]}$

$$= \dfrac{(1539.8862 - 654.7947)/(9 - 3)}{654.7947/[20 - (9 + 1)]} = \dfrac{147.51525}{65.47947} = 2.25$$

The rejection region requires $\alpha = .05$ in the upper tail of the F-distribution with $\nu_1 = k - g = 9 - 3 = 6$ and $\nu_2 = n - (k + 1) = 20 - (9 + 1) = 10$. From Table VIII, Appendix B, $F_{.05} = 3.22$. The rejection region is $F > 3.22$.

Since the observed value of the test statistic does not fall in the rejection region ($F = 2.25 \not> 3.22$), H_0 is not rejected. There is insufficient evidence to indicate the second-order terms are useful at $\alpha = .05$.

12.45 The model is $E(y) = \beta_0 + \beta_1 x_1 + \beta_2 x_2$

where $x_1 = \begin{cases} 1 & \text{if the variable is at level 2} \\ 0 & \text{otherwise} \end{cases}$ $x_2 = \begin{cases} 1 & \text{if the variable is at level 3} \\ 0 & \text{otherwise} \end{cases}$

β_0 = mean value of y when qualitative variable is at level 1.
β_1 = difference in mean value of y between level 2 and level 1 of qualitative variable.
β_2 = difference in mean value of y between level 3 and level 1 of qualitative variable.

12.47 a. The least squares prediction equation is:

$$\hat{y} = 80 + 16.8x_1 + 40.4x_2$$

b. $\hat{\beta}_1$ estimates the difference in the mean value of the dependent variable between level 2 and level 1 of the independent variable.

$\hat{\beta}_2$ estimates the difference in the mean value of the dependent variable between level 3 and level 1 of the independent variable.

c. The hypothesis H_0: $\beta_1 = \beta_2 = 0$ is the same as H_0: $\mu_1 = \mu_2 = \mu_3$.

The hypothesis H_a: At least one of the parameters β_1 and β_2 differs from 0 is the same as H_a: At least one mean (μ_1, μ_2, or μ_3) is different.

d. The test statistic is $F = \dfrac{\text{MSR}}{\text{MSE}} = \dfrac{2059.5}{83.3} = 24.72$

The rejection region requires $\alpha = .05$ in the upper tail of the test statistic with $\nu_1 = k = 2$ and $\nu_2 = n - (k + 1) = 15 - (2 + 1) = 12$. From Table VIII, Appendix B, $F_{.05} = 3.89$. The rejection region is $F > 3.89$.

Since the observed value of the test statistic falls in the rejection region ($F = 24.72 > 3.89$), H_0 is rejected. There is sufficient evidence to indicate at least one of the means is different at $\alpha = .05$.

12.49 a. Let $x_1 = \begin{cases} 1 & \text{if Referral} \\ 0 & \text{otherwise} \end{cases}$ and $x_2 = \begin{cases} 1 & \text{if On premise} \\ 0 & \text{otherwise} \end{cases}$

The model would be: $E(y) = \beta_0 + \beta_1 x_1 + \beta_2 x_2$

b. β_0 = mean job preference score for no day care support.

β_1 = difference in mean job preference score between referral day care support and no day care support.

β_2 = difference in mean job preference score between on premise day care support and no day care support.

c. To determine if the mean job preference scores differ among the three levels of day care support, we test:

H_0: $\beta_1 = \beta_2 = 0$

12.51 a. The model is $E(y) \doteq \beta_0 + \beta_1 x_1 + \beta_2 x_2 + \beta_3 x_3 + \beta_4 x_4$

where $x_1 = \begin{cases} 1 & \text{if variety A} \\ 0 & \text{if not} \end{cases}$ $x_3 = \begin{cases} 1 & \text{if variety C} \\ 0 & \text{if not} \end{cases}$

$x_2 = \begin{cases} 1 & \text{if variety B} \\ 0 & \text{if not} \end{cases}$ $x_4 = \begin{cases} 1 & \text{if variety D} \\ 0 & \text{if not} \end{cases}$

β_0 = mean yield for variety E
β_1 = difference in mean yield between varieties A and E
β_2 = difference in mean yield between varieties B and E
β_3 = difference in mean yield between varieties C and E
β_4 = difference in mean yield between varieties D and E

b. The least squares model is:

$$\hat{y} = 20.35 + 4.75x_1 + 8.6x_2 + 11.3x_3 + 2.1x_4$$

c. The hypotheses are:

H_0: $\beta_1 = \beta_2 = \beta_3 = \beta_4 = 0$
H_a: At least one $\beta_i \neq 0$, $i = 1, 2, 3, 4$

The null hypothesis says all β_i's are 0 or that the mean yields of varieties A, B, C, and D are not different from the mean yield of variety E.

The alternative hypothesis says at least one $\beta_i \neq 0$ or that the mean yield of at least one of the varieties A, B, C, or D differs from the mean yield of variety E.

d. The test statistic is $F = \dfrac{MSR}{MSE} = \dfrac{85.51}{3.568} = 23.966$

The rejection region requires $\alpha = .05$ in the upper tail of the F-distribution with $v_1 = k = 4$ and $v_2 = n - (k + 1) = 20 - (4 + 1) = 15$. From Table VIII, Appendix B, $F_{.05} = 3.06$. The rejection region is $F > 3.06$.

Since the observed value of the test statistic falls in the rejection region ($F = 23.966 > 3.06$), H_0 is rejected. There is sufficient evidence to indicate a difference in mean yields among the five varieties at $\alpha = .05$.

e. The difference between the means for varieties D and E is β_4. The point estimate of β_4 is $\hat{\beta}_4 = 2.1$. The 95% confidence interval for the difference in the mean yields between variety D and variety E is:

$$\hat{\beta}_4 \pm t_{\alpha/2} s_{\hat{\beta}_4}$$

For confidence coefficient .95, $\alpha = .05$ and $\alpha/2 = .025$. From Table VI, Appendix B, with df = $n - (k + 1) = 20 - (4 + 1) = 15$, $t_{.025} = 2.131$. The confidence interval is:

$$2.1 \pm 2.131(1.3357) \Rightarrow 2.1 \pm 2.846 \Rightarrow (-.746, 4.946)$$

12.53 a. Brand of beer is qualitative.

b. $E(y) = \beta_0 + \beta_1 x_1 + \beta_2 x_2$

where $x_1 = \begin{cases} 1 \text{ if Brand } B_2 \\ 0 \text{ if not} \end{cases}$ $x_2 = \begin{cases} 1 \text{ if Brand } B_3 \\ 0 \text{ if not} \end{cases}$

c. β_0 = mean sales for brand B_1

β_1 = difference in mean sales between brand B_2 and brand B_1

β_2 = difference in mean sales between brand B_3 and brand B_1

Introduction to Model Building

d. From part c, $\beta_0 = \mu_{B_1}$, $\beta_1 = \mu_{B_2} - \mu_{B_1}$, and $\beta_2 = \mu_{B_3} - \mu_{B_1}$

Thus, $\mu_{B_3} = \beta_2 + \beta_0$

12.55 a. To determine if there is a difference in mean monthly sales among the three incentive plans, we test:

H_0: $\beta_1 = \beta_2 = 0$
H_a: At least one $\beta_i \neq 0$, $i = 1, 2$

The test statistic is $F = \dfrac{\text{MSR}}{\text{MSE}} = \dfrac{201.8}{42} = 4.80$

The rejection region requires $\alpha = .05$ in the upper tail of the F-distribution with $\nu_1 = k = 2$ and $\nu_2 = n - (k + 1) = 15 - (2 + 1) = 12$. From Table VIII, Appendix B, $F_{.05} = 3.89$. The rejection region is $F > 3.89$.

Since the observed value of the test statistic falls in the rejection region ($F = 4.80 > 3.89$), H_0 is rejected. There is sufficient evidence to conclude that there is a difference in mean monthly sales among the three incentive plants at $\alpha = .05$.

b. The least squares prediction equation is:

$\hat{y} = 20.0 - 8.60x_1 + 3.80x_2$

$x_1 = 1$ if salesperson is paid a straight salary and $x_2 = 0$.

Thus, an estimate of the mean sales for those on a straight salary is:

$\hat{y} = 20.0 - 8.60(1) + 3.80(0) = 11.4$

Thus, the mean sales is estimated to be $11,400.

c. For those on commission only, $x_1 = 0$ and $x_2 = 0$. The estimate of the mean sales for those on commission only is:

$\hat{y} = 20.0 - 8.60(0) + 3.80(0) = 20.0$

Thus, the mean sales is estimated to be $20,000.

12.57 a. When $x_2 = x_3 = 0$, $E(y) = \beta_0 + \beta_1 x_1$
When $x_2 = 1$ and $x_3 = 0$, $E(y) = \beta_0 + \beta_1 x_1 + \beta_2$
When $x_2 = 0$ and $x_3 = 1$, $E(y) = \beta_0 + \beta_1 x_1 + \beta_3$

b. The least squares prediction equation is:

$\hat{y} = 44.803 + 2.173x_1 + 9.413x_2 + 15.632x_3$

c. For level 1, $\hat{y} = 44.803 + 2.173x_1$
For level 2, $\hat{y} = 44.803 + 2.173x_1 + 9.413$
$= 54.216 + 2.173x_1$
For level 3, $\hat{y} = 44.803 + 2.173x_1 + 15.632$
$= 60.435 + 2.173x_1$

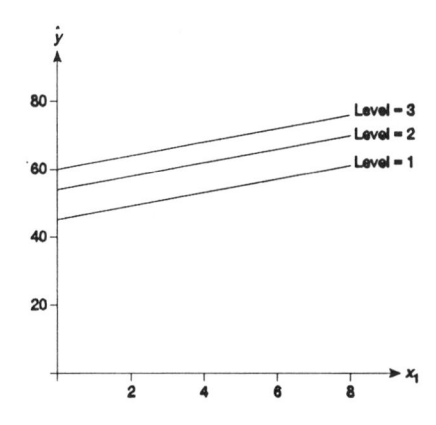

d. To determine if a difference exists between the response lines of the qualitative variable levels, we test:

H_0: $\beta_2 = \beta_3 = 0$
H_a: At least one $\beta_i \neq 0$, $i = 2, 3$

e. The test statistic is $F = \dfrac{(SSE_r - SSE_c)/(k - g)}{SSE_c/[n - (k + 1)]}$

$= \dfrac{(596.0259 - 371.2285)/(3 - 1)}{371.2285/[15 - (3 + 1)]} = \dfrac{112.3987}{33.7480} = 3.33$

The rejection region requires $\alpha = .05$ in the upper tail of the F-distribution with $\nu_1 = k - g = 3 - 1 = 2$ and $\nu_2 = n - (k + 1) = 15 - (3 + 1) = 11$. From Table VIII, Appendix B, $F_{.05} = 3.98$. The rejection region is $F > 3.98$.

Since the observed value of the test statistic does not fall in the rejection region ($F = 3.33 \not> 3.98$), H_0 is not rejected. There is insufficient evidence to indicate a difference exists between the response lines of the qualitative variable levels at $\alpha = .05$.

12.59 a. The type of juice extractor is qualitative.
The size of the orange is quantitative.

b. The model is $E(y) = \beta_0 + \beta_1 x_1 + \beta_2 x_2$

where x_1 = diameter of orange

$x_2 = \begin{cases} 1 \text{ if Brand B} \\ 0 \text{ if not} \end{cases}$

c. To allow the lines to differ, the interaction term is added:

$E(y) = \beta_0 + \beta_1 x_1 + \beta_2 x_2 + \beta_3 x_1 x_2$

Introduction to Model Building

d. For part b:

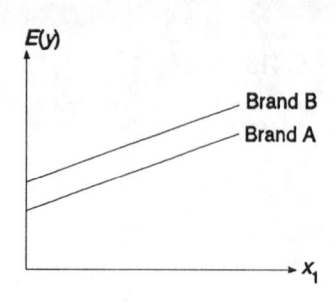

$E(y)$ vs x_1: two parallel increasing lines, Brand B above Brand A.

For part c:

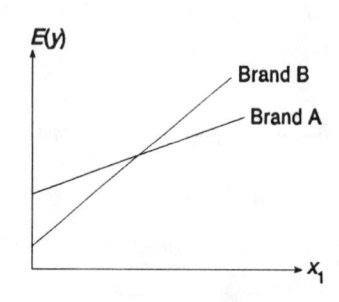

$E(y)$ vs x_1: two increasing lines with different slopes, Brand B steeper than Brand A, crossing.

e. To determine whether the model in part c provides more information for predicting yield than does the model in part b, we test:

H_0: $\beta_3 = 0$
H_a: $\beta_3 \neq 0$

f. The test statistic would be $F = \dfrac{(SSE_r - SSE_c)/(k - g)}{SSE_c/(n - (k + 1))}$

To compute SSE_r: The model in part b is fit and SSE_r is the sum of squares for error.

To compute SSE_c: The model in part c is fit and SSE_c is the sum of squares for error.

$k - g$ = number of parameters in $H_0 = 1$
$n - (k + 1)$ = degrees of freedom for error in the complete model

12.61 a. Let x_1 = initial weight.

The model is $E(y) = \beta_0 + \beta_1 x_1$

A sketch of the response curve might be: $E(y)$ increasing linearly with x_1.

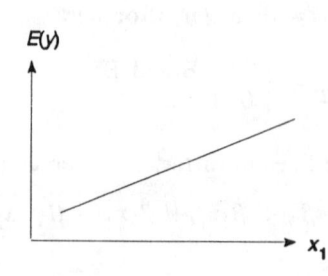

b. The model is $E(y) = \beta_0 + \beta_1 x_1 + \beta_2 x_2 + \beta_3 x_3$

where $x_2 = \begin{cases} 1 & \text{if brand 2} \\ 0 & \text{otherwise} \end{cases}$ $x_3 = \begin{cases} 1 & \text{if brand 3} \\ 0 & \text{otherwise} \end{cases}$

A sketch of the response curve might be:

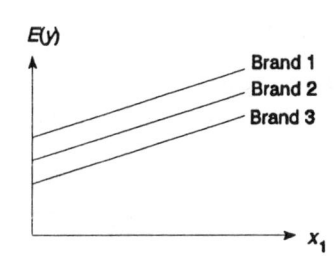

[Graph showing E(y) vs x_1 with three parallel lines labeled Brand 1, Brand 2, Brand 3]

c. The model is $E(y) + \beta_0 + \beta_1 x_1 + \beta_2 x_2 + \beta_3 x_3 + \beta_4 x_1 x_2 + \beta_5 x_1 x_3$

A sketch of the response curve might be:

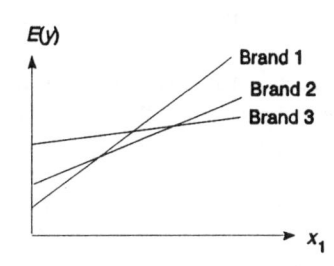

[Graph showing E(y) vs x_1 with three intersecting lines labeled Brand 1, Brand 2, Brand 3]

12.63 a. To determine whether the model is useful in predicting mean time to relief, we test:

H_0: $\beta_1 = \beta_2 = \beta_3 = \beta_4 = \beta_5 = 0$
H_a: At least one $\beta_i \neq 0$, $i = 1, 2, 3, 4, 5$

The test statistic is $F = \dfrac{\text{MSR}}{\text{MSE}} = \dfrac{17.495}{3.574} = 4.90$

The rejection region requires $\alpha = .05$ in the upper tail of the F-distribution with $\nu_1 = k = 5$ and $\nu_2 = n - (k + 1) = 12 - (5 + 1) = 6$. From Table VIII, Appendix B, $F_{.05} = 4.39$. The rejection region is $F > 4.39$.

Since the observed value of the test statistic falls in the rejection region ($F = 4.90 > 4.39$), H_0 is rejected. There is sufficient evidence to indicate the model is useful in predicting mean time to relief at $\alpha = .05$.

b. H_0: $\beta_4 = \beta_5 = 0$
H_a: At least one $\beta_i \neq 0$, $i = 4, 5$

c. The test statistic is $F = \dfrac{(\text{SSE}_r - \text{SSE}_c)/(k - g)}{\text{SSE}_c/[n - (k + 1)]} = \dfrac{(38.289 - 21.443)/(5 - 3)}{21.443/[12 - (5 + 1)]} = 2.36$

The rejection region requires $\alpha = .05$ in the upper tail of the F-distribution with $\nu_1 = k - g = 5 - 3 = 2$ and $\nu_2 = n - (k + 1) = 12 - (5 + 1) = 6$. From Table VIII, Appendix B, $F_{.05} = 5.14$. The rejection region is $F > 5.14$.

Since the observed value of the test statistic does not fall in the rejection region ($F = 2.36 \not> 5.14$), H_0 is not rejected. There is insufficient evidence to indicate the interaction terms should be kept in the model at $\alpha = .05$.

12.65 a. Let $x_2 = \begin{cases} 1 \text{ if program B} \\ 0 \text{ otherwise} \end{cases}$ $x_3 = \begin{cases} 1 \text{ if program C} \\ 0 \text{ otherwise} \end{cases}$

The model is $E(y) = \beta_0 + \beta_1 x_1 + \beta_2 x_2 + \beta_3 x_3$

Introduction to Model Building

b. The hypotheses are:

H_0: $\beta_2 = \beta_3 = 0$
H_a: At least one $\beta_i \neq 0$, $i = 2, 3$

c. The test statistic is $F = \dfrac{(SSE_r - SSE_c)/(k - g)}{SSE_c/[n - (k + 1)]} = \dfrac{(3,113.14 - 1,527.27)/(3 - 1)}{1,527.27/[9 - (3 + 1)]} = 2.60$

The rejection region requires $\alpha = .05$ in the upper tail of the F-distribution with $\nu_1 = k - g = 3 - 1 = 2$ and $\nu_2 = n - (k + 1) = 9 - (3 + 1) = 5$. From Table VIII, Appendix B, $F_{.05} \approx 5.79$. The rejection region is $F > 5.79$.

Since the observed value of the test statistic does not fall in the rejection region ($F = 2.60 \not> 5.79$), H_0 is not rejected. There is insufficient evidence to indicate the mean work-hours lost differ among the three programs at $\alpha = .05$.

12.67 a. From Exercise 12.66, the model is:

$E(y) = \beta_0 + \beta_1 x_1 + \beta_2 x_1^2 + \beta_3 x_2 + \beta_4 x_3 + \beta_5 x_1 x_2 + \beta_6 x_1 x_3 + \beta_7 x_1^2 x_2 + \beta_8 x_1^2 x_3$

where x_1 = quantitative variable

$x_2 = \begin{cases} 1 & \text{if level 2 of qualitative variable} \\ 0 & \text{otherwise} \end{cases}$

$x_3 = \begin{cases} 1 & \text{if level 3 of qualitative variable} \\ 0 & \text{otherwise} \end{cases}$

The response curves will have the same shape if none of the interaction terms are present or if $\beta_5 = \beta_6 = \beta_7 = \beta_8 = 0$.

b. The response curves will be parallel lines if the interaction terms as well as the second-order terms are absent or if $\beta_2 = \beta_5 = \beta_6 = \beta_7 = \beta_8 = 0$.

c. The response curves will be identical if no terms involving the qualitative variable are present or $\beta_3 = \beta_4 = \beta_5 = \beta_6 = \beta_7 = \beta_8 = 0$.

12.69 a. The least squares line is:

$\hat{y} = 48.8 - 3.36x_1 + .075x_1^2 - 2.36x_2 - 7.60x_3 + 3.71x_1 x_2 + 2.66x_1 x_3 - .018x_1^2 x_2 - .037x_1^2 x_3$

b. For $x_2 = 0$ and $x_3 = 0$, $\hat{y} = 48.8 - 3.36x_1 + .075x_1^2$

For $x_2 = 1$ and $x_3 = 0$, $\hat{y} = 48.8 - 3.36x_1 + .075x_1^2 - 2.36(1) + 3.71x_1(1) - .018x_1^2(1)$
$= 46.44 + .35x_1 + .057x_1^2$

For $x_2 = 0$ and $x_3 = 1$, $\hat{y} = 48.8 - 3.36x_1 + .075x_1^2 - 7.60(1) + 2.66x_1(1) - .037x_1^2(1)$
$= 41.2 - .7x_1 + .038x_1^2$

c. The plots of the lines are:

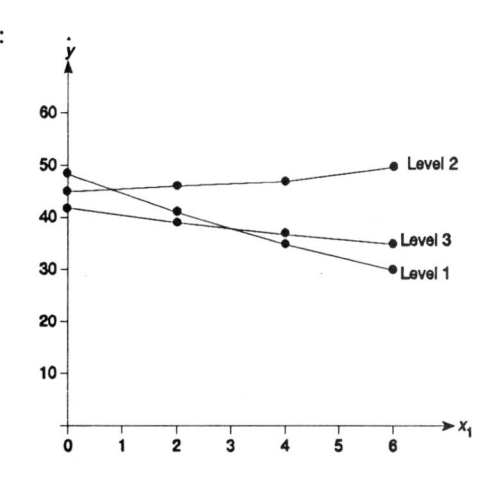

[Graph showing Level 1, Level 2, and Level 3 lines plotted against x_1 from 0 to 6, with y-axis from 0 to 60]

d. H_0: $\beta_3 = \beta_4 = \beta_5 = \beta_6 = \beta_7 = \beta_8 = 0$
H_a: At least one $\beta_i \neq 0$, $i = 3, 4, 5, 6, 7, 8$

e. The test statistic is $F = \dfrac{(SSE_r - SSE_c)/(k - g)}{SSE_c/[n - (k + 1)]} = \dfrac{(14{,}986 - 162.9)/(8 - 2)}{162.9/[25 - (8 + 1)]} = 242.65$

The rejection region requires $\alpha = .05$ in the upper tail of the F-distribution with $\nu_1 = k - g = 8 - 2 = 6$ and $\nu_2 = n - (k + 1) = 25 - (8 + 1) = 16$. From Table VIII, Appendix B, $F_{.05} = 2.74$. The rejection region is $F > 2.74$.

Since the observed value of the test statistic falls in the rejection region ($F = 242.65 > 2.74$), H_0 is rejected. There is sufficient evidence to indicate the second-order response curves differ for the three levels at $\alpha = .05$.

12.71 To determine if the mean salary of faculty members is dependent on gender, we test:

H_0: $\beta_3 = \beta_4 = \beta_5 = 0$
H_a: At least one $\beta_i \neq 0$, $i = 3, 4, 5$

The test statistic is $F = \dfrac{(SSE_r - SSE_c)/(k - g)}{SSE_c/[n - (k + 1)]} = \dfrac{(795.23 - 783.9)/(5 - 2)}{783.9/[200 - (5 + 1)]} = .93$

The rejection region requires $\alpha = .05$ in the upper tail of the F-distribution with $\nu_1 = k - g = 5 - 2 = 3$ and $\nu_2 = n - (k + 1) = 200 - (5 + 1) = 194$. From Table VIII, Appendix B, $F_{.05} \approx 2.60$. The rejection region is $F > 2.60$.

Since the observed value of the test statistic does not fall in the rejection region ($F = .93 \not> 2.60$), H_0 is not rejected. There is insufficient evidence to support the claim that the mean salary of faculty members is dependent on gender at $\alpha = .05$.

12.73 a. The model would be:

$E(y) = \beta_0 + \beta_1 x_1 + \beta_2 x_2 + \beta_3 x_3$

b. The model including the interaction terms is:

$E(y) = \beta_0 + \beta_1 x_1 + \beta_2 x_2 + \beta_3 x_3 + \beta_4 x_1 x_2 + \beta_5 x_1 x_3$

c. For AL, $x_2 = x_3 = 0$. The model would be:

$$E(y) = \beta_0 + \beta_1 x_1 + \beta_2(0) + \beta_3(0) + \beta_4 x_1(0) + \beta_5 x_1(0) = \beta_0 + \beta_1 x_1$$

The slope of the line is β_1.

For TDS-3A, $x_2 = 1$ and $x_3 = 0$. The model would be:

$$E(y) = \beta_0 + \beta_1 x_1 + \beta_2(1) + \beta_3(0) + \beta_4 x_1(1) + \beta_5 x_1(0) = (\beta_0 + \beta_2) + (\beta_1 + \beta_4) x_1$$

The slope of the line is $\beta_1 + \beta_4$.

For FE, $x_2 = 0$ and $x_3 = 1$. The model would be:

$$E(y) = \beta_0 + \beta_1 x_1 + \beta_2(0) + \beta_3(1) + \beta_4 x_1(0) + \beta_5 x_1(1) = (\beta_0 + \beta_3) + (\beta_1 + \beta_5) x_1$$

The slope of the line is $\beta_1 + \beta_5$.

d. To test for the presence of temperature-waste type interaction, we would fit the complete model listed in part b and the reduced model found in part a. The hypotheses would be:

H_0: $\beta_4 = \beta_5 = 0$
H_a: At least one $\beta_i \neq 0$, for $i = 4, 5$

The test statistic would be $F = \dfrac{(SSE_r - SSE_c)/(k - g)}{SSE_c/[n - (k + 1)]}$ where $k = 5$, $g = 3$, SSE_r is the SSE for the reduced model, and SSE_c is the SSE for the complete model.

12.75 a. $\beta_0 = y$ intercept
$\beta_1 =$ location parameter
$\beta_2 =$ change in the rate of change in mean time for each unit change in age
$\beta_3 =$ difference in mean time between the two types of machines

b. To determine if the curvilinear relationship differs for the two types of machines, we test:

H_0: $\beta_3 = 0$
H_a: $\beta_3 \neq 0$

The test statistic is $t = 8.81$.

The rejection region requires $\alpha/2 = .05/2 = .025$ in each tail of the t-distribution with df = $n - (k + 1) = 20 - (3 + 1) = 16$. From Table VI, Appendix B, $t_{.025} = 2.120$. The rejection region is $t < -2.120$ or $t > 2.120$.

Since the observed value of the test statistic falls in the rejection region ($t = 8.81 > 2.120$), H_0 is rejected. There is sufficient evidence to conclude that the curvilinear relationship differs for the two types of machines at $\alpha = .05$.

c. The reduced model would be $E(y) = \beta_0 + \beta_1 x_1 + \beta_2 x_1^2$

12.77 a. The best one-variable predictor of y is the one whose t statistic has the largest absolute value. The t statistics for each of the variables are:

Independent Variable	$t = \dfrac{\hat{\beta}_i}{s_{\hat{\beta}_i}}$
x_1	$t = 1.6/.42 = 3.81$
x_2	$t = -.9/.01 = -90$
x_3	$t = 3.4/1.14 = 2.98$
x_4	$t = 2.5/2.06 = 1.21$
x_5	$t = -4.4/.73 = -6.03$
x_6	$t = .3/.35 = .86$

The variable x_2 is the best one-variable predictor of y. The absolute value of the corresponding t score is 90. This is larger than any of the others.

b. Yes. In the stepwise procedure, the first variable entered is the one which has the largest absolute value of t, provided the absolute value of the t falls in the rejection region.

c. Once x_2 is entered, the next variable that is entered is the one that, in conjunction with x_2, has the largest absolute t value associated with it.

12.79 a. Let x_1 = T-score, x_2 = Mathematics test score, x_3 = SAT score, x_4 = ACT score, x_5 = Verbal test score, x_6 = SCPT score, and x_7 = Trigonometry test score.

The first stage model is $E(y) = \beta_0 + \beta_1 x_1$.

The second stage model is $E(y) = \beta_0 + \beta_1 x_1 + \beta_2 x_2$.

The third stage model is $E(y) = \beta_0 + \beta_1 x_1 + \beta_2 x_2 + \beta_3 x_3$.

The fourth stage model is $E(y) = \beta_0 + \beta_1 x_1 + \beta_2 x_2 + \beta_3 x_3 + \beta_4 x_4$.

b. To determine if the SCPT score comes into the model, we test:

$H_0: \beta_6 = 0$
$H_a: \beta_6 \neq 0$

The test statistic is $F = 1.89$.

The rejection region requires α in the upper tail of the F-distribution with $\nu_1 = 1$ and $\nu_2 = n - (k + 1) = 302 - (6 + 1) = 295$. From Table VIII, Appendix B, $F_{.05} \approx 3.84$. The rejection region is $F > 3.84$.

Since the observed value of the test statistic does not fall in the rejection region ($F = 1.89 \not> 3.84$), H_0 is not rejected. There is insufficient evidence that SCPT contributes information for the prediction of GPA once the first five variables have been entered in the model.

c. The largest correlation coefficient is between GPA and T-score (.37). The rest in order are between GPA and Mathematics test (.34), between GPA and Verbal test (.30), between GPA and SCPT (.29), between GPA and Trigonometry test (.28), between GPA and ACT (.27), and between GPA and SAT (.18). Even though the correlation coefficient between GPA and SCPT

Introduction to Model Building

is greater than the correlation coefficient between GPA and SAT, the SAT variable went into the model before SCPT. This can happen if the SCPT variable is highly correlated to variables already in the model, while the SAT variable is not.

d. The F statistic is $F = \dfrac{R^2/k}{(1 - R^2)/[n - (k + 1)]} = \dfrac{.44/4}{(1 - .44)/[302 - (4 + 1)]} = 58.34$

e. Using Table X, Appendix B, with $\nu_1 = k = 4$ and $\nu_2 = n - (k + 1) = 302 - (4 + 1) = 297$, $P(F \geq 58.34) < .01$. Thus, p-value is less than .01.

12.81 The model-building step is the key to the success or failure of a regression analysis. If the model is a good model, we will have a good predictive model for the dependent variable y. If the model is not a good model, the predictive ability will not be of much use.

12.83 a. $E(y) = 6 + 3x - 2x^2$ — second-order b. $E(y) = 4x$ — first-order

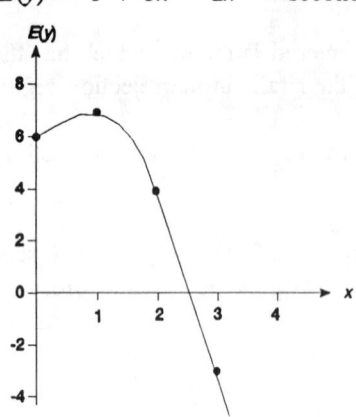

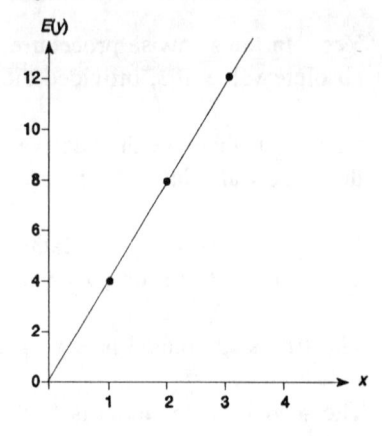

c. $E(y) = x^2$ — second-order 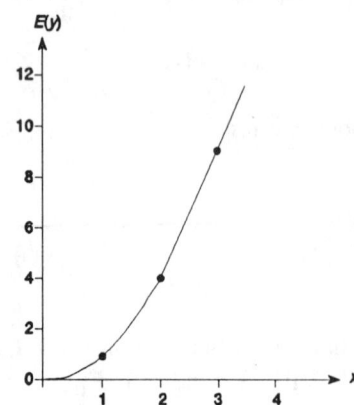 d. $E(y) = 2 - 4x$ — first-order

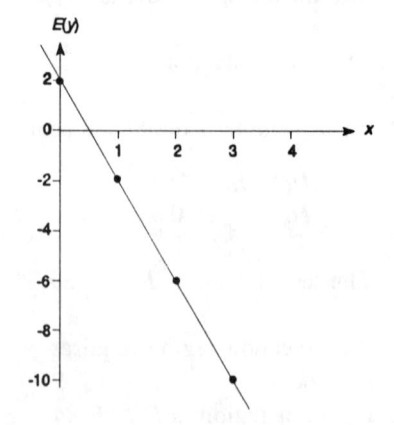

e. $E(y) = 1 + x - x^2 + x^3$ — third-order

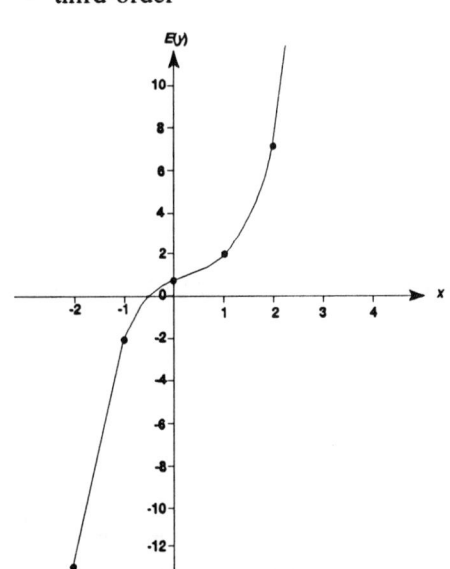

f. $E(y) = 1 - 4x$ — first-order

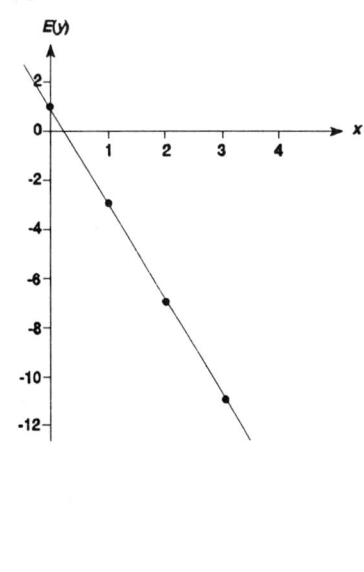

12.85 Quantitative variables are variables that can take on meaningful numerical values. Qualitative variables are variables that can take on only non-numerical or categorical values.

12.87 The stepwise regression method is used to try to find the best model to describe a process. It is a screening procedure that tries to select a small subset of independent variables from a large set of independent variables that will adequately predict the dependent variable. This method is useful in that it can eliminate some unimportant independent variables from consideration.

12.89 Even though SSE = 0, we cannot estimate σ^2 because there are no degrees of freedom corresponding to error. With three data points, there are only two degrees of freedom available. The degrees of freedom corresponding to the model is $k = 2$ and the degrees of freedom corresponding to error is $n - (k + 1) = 3 - (2 + 1) = 0$. Without an estimate for σ^2, no inferences can be made.

12.91 a. Using SAS to fit the model $E(y) = \beta_0 + \beta_1 x_1 + \beta_2 x_2 + \beta_3 x_3$, we get:

DEPENDENT VARIABLE: Y

SOURCE	DF	SUM OF SQUARES	MEAN SQUARE	F VALUE
MODEL	3	13.34333333	4.44777778	63.09
ERROR	20	1.41000000	0.07050000	PR > F
CORRECTED TOTAL	23	14.75333333		0.0001

R-SQUARE	C.V.	ROOT MSE	Y MEAN
0.904428	2.4065	0.26551836	11.03333333

PARAMETER		ESTIMATE	T FOR H0: PARAMETER = 0	PR > |T|	STD ERROR OF ESTIMATE
INTERCEPT		10.23333333	94.41	0.0001	0.10839742
X	VH	0.50000000	3.26	0.0039	0.15329710
	H	2.01666667	13.16	0.0001	0.15329710
	M	0.68333333	4.46	0.0002	0.15329710

Introduction to Model Building

The fitted model is $\hat{y} = 10.2 + .5x_1 + 2.02x_2 + .683x_3$

$$x_1 = \begin{cases} 1 & \text{if VH} \\ 0 & \text{otherwise} \end{cases}$$

$$x_2 = \begin{cases} 1 & \text{if H} \\ 0 & \text{otherwise} \end{cases}$$

$$x_3 = \begin{cases} 1 & \text{if M} \\ 0 & \text{otherwise} \end{cases}$$

b. To determine if the firm's expected market share differs for different levels of advertising exposure, we test:

H_0: $\beta_1 = \beta_2 = \beta_3 = 0$
H_a: At least one $\beta_i \neq 0$, $i = 1, 2, 3$

The test statistic is $F = 63.09$.

The rejection region requires $\alpha = .05$ in the upper tail of the F-distribution with $\nu_1 = k = 3$ and $\nu_2 = n - (k + 1) = 24 - (3 + 1) = 20$. From Table VIII, Appendix B, $F_{.05} = 3.10$. The rejection region is $F > 3.10$.

Since the observed value of the test statistic falls in the rejection region ($F = 63.09 > 3.10$), H_0 is rejected. There is sufficient evidence to indicate the firm's expected market share differs for different levels of advertising exposure at $\alpha = .05$.

12.93 To determine whether the impact of college track on verbal achievement score depends on sector, we would test to see if the interaction term is significant:

H_0: $\beta_3 = 0$
H_a: $\beta_3 \neq 0$

12.95 a. To determine whether the quadratic terms are useful, we test:

H_0: $\beta_2 = \beta_5 = 0$
H_a: At least one β_i parameter $\neq 0$, $i = 2, 5$

b. To determine whether there is a difference in mean delivery time by rail and truck, we test:

H_0: $\beta_3 = \beta_4 = \beta_5 = 0$
H_a: At least one β_i parameter $\neq 0$, $i = 3, 4, 5$

c. To determine if the mean delivery time differs from rail and truck deliveries, we test:

H_0: $\beta_3 = \beta_4 = \beta_5 = 0$
H_a: At least one $\beta_i = 0$, for $i = 3, 4, 5$

The test statistic is $F = \dfrac{(SSE_r - SSE_c)/(k - g)}{SSE_c/[n - (k + 1)]} = \dfrac{(259.34 - 226.12)/(5 - 2)}{226.12/[50 - (5 + 1)]} = 2.15$

The rejection region requires $\alpha = .05$ in the upper tail of the F-distribution with $\nu_1 = k - g = 5 - 2 = 3$ and $\nu_2 = n - (k + 1) = 50 - (5 + 1) = 44$. From Table VIII, Appendix B, $F_{.05} \approx 2.84$. The rejection region is $F > 2.84$.

Since the observed value of the test statistic does not fall in the rejection region ($F = 2.15 \not> 2.84$), H_0 is not rejected. There is insufficient evidence to indicate that the mean delivery time differs from rail and truck deliveries at $\alpha = .05$.

12.97 a. The main effects model is:

$$E(y) = \beta_0 + \beta_1 x_1 + \beta_2 x_2$$

where x_1 = total area of the house

$$x_2 = \begin{cases} 1 & \text{if central air conditioning is to be installed} \\ 0 & \text{otherwise} \end{cases}$$

b. The complete second-order model is:

$$E(y) = \beta_0 + \beta_1 x_1 + \beta_2 x_2 + \beta_3 x_1^2 + \beta_4 x_1 x_2 + \beta_5 x_1^2 x_2$$

c. To determine if the second-order terms are important for predicting mean cost, we test:

$H_0: \beta_3 = \beta_4 = \beta_5 = 0$
$H_a:$ At least one $\beta_i \neq 0$, $i = 3, 4, 5$

The test statistic is $F = \dfrac{(SSE_r - SSE_c)/(k - g)}{SSE_c/[n - (k + 1)]} = \dfrac{(8.548 - 6.133)/(5 - 2)}{6.133/[25 - (5 + 1)]} = 2.49$

The rejection region requires $\alpha = .05$ in the upper tail of the F-distribution with $\nu_1 = k - g = 5 - 2 = 3$ and $\nu_2 = n - (k + 1) = 25 - (5 + 1) = 19$. From Table VIII, Appendix B, $F_{.05} = 3.13$. The rejection region is $F > 3.13$.

Since the observed value of the test statistic does not fall in the rejection region ($F = 2.40 \not> 3.13$), H_0 is not rejected. There is insufficient evidence to indicate that the second-order terms are important for predicting mean cost at $\alpha = .05$.

12.99 a. $H_0: \beta_1 = \beta_2 = \beta_3 = \beta_4 = 0$
$H_a:$ At least one $\beta_i \neq 0$, $i = 1, 2, 3, 4$

The test statistic is $F = \dfrac{MSR}{MSE} = 222.173$

The rejection region requires $\alpha = .05$ in the upper tail of the F-distribution with $\nu_1 = k = 4$ and $\nu_2 = n - (k + 1) = 24 - (4 + 1) = 19$. From Table VIII, Appendix B, $F_{.05} = 2.90$. The rejection region is $F > 2.90$.

Since the observed value of the test statistic falls in the rejection region ($F = 222.173 > 2.90$), H_0 is rejected. There is sufficient evidence to indicate the model is useful at $\alpha = .05$.

b. To determine if the mean weekly sales depends on the city, we test:

$H_0: \beta_2 = \beta_3 = \beta_4 = 0$
$H_a:$ At least one $\beta_i \neq 0$, $i = 2, 3, 4$

The test statistic is $F = \dfrac{(SSE_r - SSE_c)/(k - g)}{SSE_c/[n - (k + 1)]} = \dfrac{(7.8073 - 2.49407)/(4 - 1)}{2.49407/[24 - (4 + 1)]} = \dfrac{1.7711}{.1313}$

$= 13.49$

Introduction to Model Building

The rejection region requires $\alpha = .05$ in the upper tail of the F-distribution with $\nu_1 = k - g = 4 - 1 = 3$ and $\nu_2 = n - (k + 1) = 24 - (4 + 1) = 19$. From Table VIII, Appendix B, $F_{.05} = 3.13$. The rejection region is $F > 3.13$.

Since the observed value of the test statistic falls in the rejection region ($F = 13.49 > 3.13$), H_0 is rejected. There is sufficient evidence to indicate the mean weekly sales depends on the city at $\alpha = .05$.

c. The response lines would be straight and parallel. This model does not imply interaction between city and traffic flow.

d. For $x_2 = 1$, $x_3 = x_4 = 0$,
$$\hat{y} = 1.083 + .104x_1 - 1.216(1) = -.133 + .104x_1$$

For $x_3 = 1$, $x_2 = x_4 = 0$,
$$\hat{y} = 1.083 + .104x_1 - .531(1) = .552 + .104x_1$$

For $x_4 = 1$, $x_2 = x_3 = 0$,
$$\hat{y} = 1.083 + .104x_1 - 1.077(1) = .006 + .104x_1$$

For $x_2 = x_3 = x_4 = 0$, $\hat{y} = 1.083 + .104x_1$

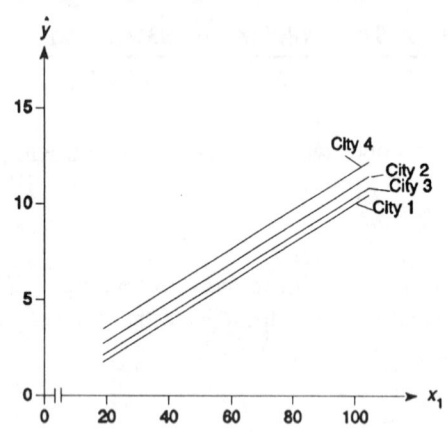

The graphed lines do not suggest an interaction between city and traffic flow because the lines are parallel.

e. The model including the interaction terms is:
$$E(y) = \beta_0 + \beta_1 x_1 + \beta_2 x_2 + \beta_3 x_3 + \beta_4 x_4 + \beta_5 x_1 x_2 + \beta_6 x_1 x_3 + \beta_7 x_1 x_4$$

f. The SAS output from fitting the model is:

```
DEP VARIABLE: Y
ANALYSIS OF VARIANCE

                      SUM OF        MEAN
    SOURCE    DF     SQUARES       SQUARE       F VALUE    PROB>F

    MODEL      7    117.28003   16.75429048    143.387     0.0001
    ERROR     16      1.86954996  0.11684687
    C TOTAL   23    119.14958

           ROOT MSE   0.3418287   R-SQUARE     0.9843
           DEP MEAN   5.995833    ADJ R-SQ     0.9774
           C.V.       5.701104
```

PARAMETER ESTIMATES

VARIABLE	DF	PARAMETER ESTIMATE	STANDARD ERROR	T FOR H0: PARAMETER=0	PROB > |T|
INTERCEP	1	0.70930105	0.47510789	1.493	0.1549
X1	1	0.10920063	0.006646607	16.430	0.0001
X2	1	-0.25198332	0.59854850	-0.421	0.6794
X3	1	-0.61762495	0.78339607	-0.788	0.4420
X4	1	-1.20496297	0.68174490	-1.767	0.0962
X1X2	1	-0.01556934	0.008879560	-1.753	0.0987
X1X3	1	0.005465277	0.01557792	0.351	0.7303
X1X4	1	0.004876956	0.01181063	0.413	0.6851

The fitted model is $\hat{y} = .709 + .109x_1 - .252x_2 - .618x_3 - 1.205x_4 - .016x_1x_2 + .0055x_1x_3 + .0049x_1x_4$

g. To determine if the slopes of the lines differ, we test:

H_0: $\beta_5 = \beta_6 = \beta_7 = 0$
H_a: At least one $\beta_i \neq 0$, $i = 5, 6, 7$

The test statistic is $F = \dfrac{(\text{SSE}_r - \text{SSE}_c)/(k - g)}{\text{SSE}_c/[n - (k + 1)]} = \dfrac{(2.49407 - 1.86955)/(7 - 4)}{1.86955/[24 - (7 + 1)]} = \dfrac{.208173}{.116847} = 1.78$

The rejection region requires $\alpha = .05$ in the upper tail of the F-distribution with $\nu_1 = k - g = 7 - 4 = 3$ and $\nu_2 = n - (k + 1) = 24 - (7 + 1) = 16$. From Table IX, Appendix A, $F_{.05} = 3.24$. The rejection region is $F > 3.24$.

Since the observed value of the test statistic does not fall in the rejection region ($F = 1.78 \not> 3.24$), H_0 is not rejected. There is insufficient evidence to indicate the slopes of the lines differ for at least two of the cities at $\alpha = .05$.

Introduction to Model Building

Methods for Quality Improvement
Chapter 13

13.1   A control chart is a time series plot of individual measurements or means of a quality variable to which a centerline and two other horizontal lines called control limits have been added. The center line represents the mean of the process when the process is in a state of statistical control. The upper control limit and the lower control limit are positioned so that when the process is in control the probability of an individual measurement or mean falling outside the limits is very small. A control chart is used to determine if a process is in control (only common causes of variation present) or not (both common and special causes of variation present). This information helps us to determine when to take action to find and remove special causes of variation and when to leave the process alone.

13.3   When a control chart is first constructed, it is not known whether the process is in control or not. If the process is found not to be in control, then the centerline and control limits should not be used to monitor the process in the future.

13.5   Even if all the points of an $\bar{x}$-chart fall within the control limits, the process may be out of control. Nonrandom patterns may exist among the plotted points that are within the control limits, but are very unlikely if the process is in control. Examples include six points in a row steadily increasing or decreasing and 14 points in a row alternating up and down.

13.7   Rule 1:   One point beyond Zone A: No points are beyond Zone A.
        Rule 2:   Nine points in a row in Zone C or beyond: No sequence of nine points are in Zone C (on one side of the centerline) or beyond.
        Rule 3:   Six points in a row steadily increasing or decreasing: No sequence of six points steadily increase or decrease.
        Rule 4:   Fourteen points in a row alternating up and down: This pattern does not exist.
        Rule 5:   Two out of three points in Zone A or beyond: There are no groups of three consecutive points that have two or more in Zone A or beyond.
        Rule 6:   Four out of five points in a row in Zone B or beyond: Points 18 through 21 are all in Zone B or beyond. This indicates the process is out of control.

Thus, rule 6 indicates this process is out of control.

13.9   Using Table XVII, Appendix B:

    a.   With $n = 3$, $A_2 = 1.023$

    b.   With $n = 10$, $A_2 = 0.308$

    c.   With $n = 22$, $A_2 = 0.167$

13.11   a.   For each sample, we compute $\bar{x} = \dfrac{\sum x}{n}$ and R = range = largest measurement − smallest measurement. The results are listed in the table:

Sample No.	$\bar{x}$	R	Sample No.	$\bar{x}$	R
1	20.225	1.8	11	21.225	3.2
2	19.750	2.8	12	20.475	0.9
3	20.425	3.8	13	19.650	2.6
4	19.725	2.5	14	19.075	4.0
5	20.550	3.7	15	19.400	2.2
6	19.900	5.0	16	20.700	4.3
7	21.325	5.5	17	19.850	3.6
8	19.625	3.5	18	20.200	2.5
9	19.350	2.5	19	20.425	2.2
10	20.550	4.1	20	19.900	5.5

b. $\bar{\bar{x}} = \dfrac{\bar{x}_1 + \bar{x}_2 + \cdots + \bar{x}_{20}}{n} = \dfrac{402.325}{20} = 20.11625$

$\bar{R} = \dfrac{R_1 + R_2 + \cdots + R_{20}}{n} = \dfrac{66.2}{20} = 3.31$

c.   *Centerline* = $\bar{\bar{x}}$ = 20.116

From Table XVII, Appendix B, with $n = 4$, $A_2 = .729$.

Upper control limit = $\bar{\bar{x}} + A_2\bar{R}$ = 20.116 + .729(3.31) = 22.529
Lower control limit = $\bar{\bar{x}} - A_2\bar{R}$ = 20.116 − .729(3.31) = 17.703

d.   *Upper A−B boundary* = $\bar{\bar{x}} + \dfrac{2}{3}(A_2\bar{R})$ = 20.116 + $\dfrac{2}{3}$(.729)(3.31) = 21.725

Lower A−B boundary = $\bar{\bar{x}} - \dfrac{2}{3}(A_2\bar{R})$ = 20.116 − $\dfrac{2}{3}$(.729)(3.31) = 18.507

Upper B−C boundary = $\bar{\bar{x}} + \dfrac{1}{3}(A_2\bar{R})$ = 20.116 + $\dfrac{1}{3}$(.729)(3.31) = 20.920

Lower B−C boundary = $\bar{\bar{x}} - \dfrac{1}{3}(A_2\bar{R})$ = 20.116 − $\dfrac{1}{3}$(.729)(3.31) = 19.312

Methods for Quality Improvement

e. The $\bar{x}$-chart is:

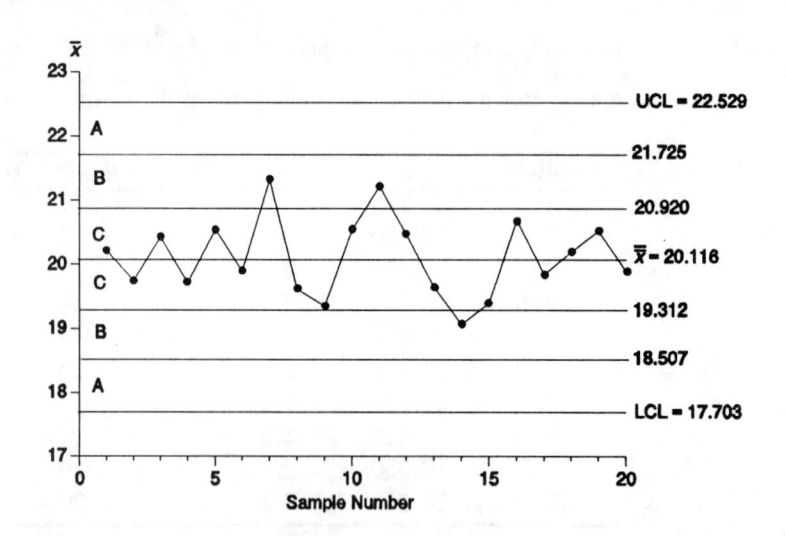

```
                                    UCL = 22.529
                               A
                                    21.725
                               B
                                    20.920
                               C
                                    $\bar{\bar{x}}$ = 20.116
                               C
                                    19.312
                               B
                                    18.507
                               A
                                    LCL = 17.703
```

Rule 1: One point beyond Zone A: No points are beyond Zone A.
Rule 2: Nine points in a row in Zone C or beyond: No sequence of nine points are in Zone C (on one side of the centerline) or beyond.
Rule 3: Six points in a row steadily increasing or decreasing: No sequence of six points steadily increase or decrease.
Rule 4: Fourteen points in a row alternating up and down: This pattern does not exist.
Rule 5: Two out of three points in Zone A or beyond: There are no groups of three consecutive points that have two or more in Zone A or beyond.
Rule 6: Four out of five points in a row in Zone B or beyond: No sequence of five points has four or more in Zone B or beyond.

The process appears to be in control.

13.13 a. $\bar{\bar{x}} = \dfrac{\bar{x}_1 + \bar{x}_2 + \cdots + \bar{x}_{20}}{n} = \dfrac{479.942}{20} = 23.9971$

$\bar{R} = \dfrac{R_1 + R_2 + \cdots + R_{20}}{n} = \dfrac{3.63}{20} = .1815$

Centerline $= \bar{\bar{x}} = 23.9971$

From Table XVII, Appendix B, with $n = 5$, $A_2 = .577$.

Upper control limit $= \bar{\bar{x}} + A_2\bar{R} = 23.9971 + .577(.1815) = 24.102$
Lower control limit $= \bar{\bar{x}} - A_2\bar{R} = 23.9971 - .577(.1815) = 23.892$

Upper A–B *boundary* $= \bar{\bar{x}} + \dfrac{2}{3}(A_2\bar{R}) = 23.9971 + \dfrac{2}{3}(.577)(.1815) = 24.067$

Lower A–B *boundary* $= \bar{\bar{x}} - \dfrac{2}{3}(A_2\bar{R}) = 23.9971 - \dfrac{2}{3}(.577)(.1815) = 23.927$

Upper B–C *boundary* $= \bar{\bar{x}} + \dfrac{1}{3}(A_2\bar{R}) = 23.9971 + \dfrac{1}{3}(.577)(.1815) = 24.032$

Lower B–C *boundary* $= \bar{\bar{x}} - \dfrac{1}{3}(A_2\bar{R}) = 23.9971 - \dfrac{1}{3}(.577)(.1815) = 23.962$

The $\bar{x}$-chart is:

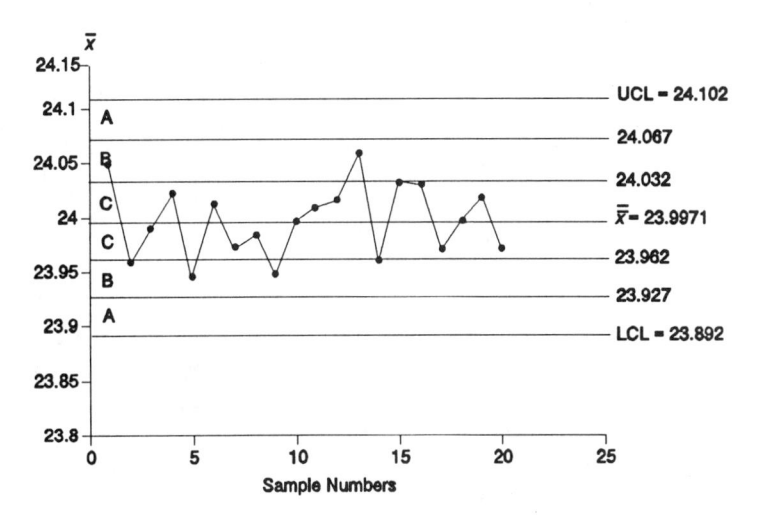

```
x̄
24.15
24.1         A                                                          UCL = 24.102
24.05        B                                                          24.067
             C                                                          24.032
24           C                                                          x̄ = 23.9971
23.95        B                                                          23.962
             A                                                          23.927
23.9                                                                    LCL = 23.892
23.85
23.8
     0    5      10      15      20      25
              Sample Numbers
```

b. To determine if the process is in or out of control, we check the six rules:

Rule 1: One point beyond Zone A: No points are beyond Zone A.

Rule 2: Nine points in a row in Zone C or beyond: No sequence of nine points are in Zone C (on one side of the centerline) or beyond.

Rule 3: Six points in a row steadily increasing or decreasing: No sequence of six points steadily increase or decrease.

Rule 4: Fourteen points in a row alternating up and down: This pattern does not exist.

Rule 5: Two out of three points in Zone A or beyond: There are no groups of three consecutive points that have two or more in Zone A or beyond.

Rule 6: Four out of five points in a row in Zone B or beyond: No sequence of five points has four or more in Zone B or beyond.

The process appears to be in control.

c. Since the process is in control, these limits should be used to monitor future process output.

d. The rational subgrouping strategy used by K-Company will facilitate the identification of process variation caused by differences in the two shifts. All observations within one sample are from the same shift. The shift change is at 3:00 P.M. The samples are selected at 8:00 A.M., 11:00 A.M., 2:00 P.M., 5:00 P.M., and 8:00 P.M. No samples will contain observations from both shifts.

Methods for Quality Improvement

13.15 a. First, we must compute the range for each sample. The range = R = largest measurement − smallest measurement. The results are listed in the table:

Sample No.	R	Sample No.	R	Sample No.	R
1	2.0	25	4.6	49	4.0
2	2.1	26	3.0	50	4.9
3	1.8	27	3.4	51	3.8
4	1.6	28	2.3	52	4.6
5	3.1	29	2.2	53	7.1
6	3.1	30	3.3	54	4.6
7	4.2	31	3.6	55	2.2
8	3.6	32	4.2	56	3.6
9	4.6	33	2.4	57	2.6
10	2.6	34	4.5	58	2.0
11	3.5	35	5.6	59	1.5
12	5.3	36	4.9	60	6.0
13	5.5	37	10.2	61	5.7
14	5.6	38	5.5	62	5.6
15	4.6	39	4.7	63	2.3
16	3.0	40	4.7	64	2.3
17	4.6	41	3.6	65	2.6
18	4.5	42	3.0	66	3.8
19	4.8	43	2.2	67	2.8
20	5.4	44	3.3	68	2.2
21	5.5	45	3.2	69	4.2
22	3.8	46	0.8	70	2.6
23	3.6	47	4.2	71	1.0
24	2.5	48	5.6	72	1.9

$$\bar{\bar{x}} = \frac{\bar{x}_1 + \bar{x}_2 + \cdots + \bar{x}_{72}}{n} = \frac{3537.3}{72} = 49.129$$

$$\bar{R} = \frac{R_1 + R_2 + \cdots + R_{72}}{n} = \frac{268.8}{72} = 3.733$$

Centerline = $\bar{\bar{x}}$ = 49.13

From Table XVII, Appendix B, with $n = 6$, $A_2 = .483$.

Upper control limit = $\bar{\bar{x}} + A_2\bar{R}$ = 49.129 + .483(3.733) = 50.932
Lower control limit = $\bar{\bar{x}} - A_2\bar{R}$ = 49.129 − .483(3.733) = 47.326

Upper A−B *boundary* = $\bar{\bar{x}} + \frac{2}{3}(A_2\bar{R})$ = 49.129 + $\frac{2}{3}$(.483)(3.733) = 50.331

Lower A−B *boundary* = $\bar{\bar{x}} - \frac{2}{3}(A_2\bar{R})$ = 49.129 − $\frac{2}{3}$(.483)(3.733) = 47.927

Upper B−C *boundary* = $\bar{\bar{x}} + \frac{1}{3}(A_2\bar{R})$ = 49.129 + $\frac{1}{3}$(.483)(3.733) = 49.730

Lower B−C *boundary* = $\bar{\bar{x}} - \frac{1}{3}(A_2\bar{R})$ = 49.129 − $\frac{1}{3}$(.483)(3.733) = 48.528

The $\bar{x}$-chart is:

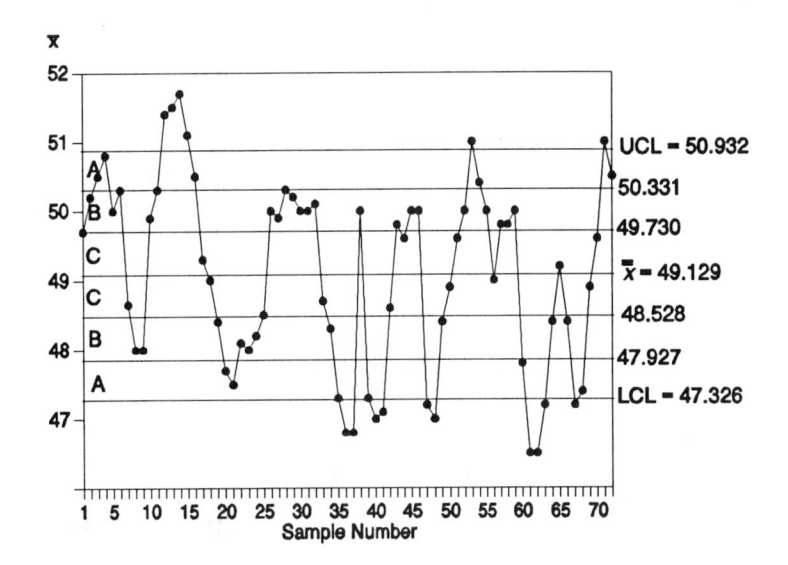

b. To determine if the process is in or out of control, we check the six rules:

Rule 1: One point beyond Zone A: There are a total of 17 points beyond Zone A.

Rule 2: Nine points in a row in Zone C or beyond: No sequence of nine points are in Zone C (on one side of the centerline) or beyond.

Rule 3: Six points in a row steadily increasing or decreasing: There is one sequence of seven points that are steadily increasing—Points 15 through 21.

Rule 4: Fourteen points in a row alternating up and down: This pattern does not exist.

Rule 5: Two out of three points in Zone A or beyond: There are four groups of at least three points in Zone A or beyond—Points 12-16, Points 35-37, Points 39-41, and Points 60-63.

Rule 6: Four out of five points in a row in Zone B or beyond: There are four groups of points that satisfy this rule—Points 10-16, Points 19-24, Points 26-32, and Points 60-64.

The process appears to be out of control. Rules 1, 3, 5, and 6 indicate that the process is out of control.

c. No. The problem does not give the times of the shifts. However, suppose we let the first shift be from 6:00 A.M. to 2:00 P.M., the second shift be from 2:00 P.M. to 10:00 P.M., and the third shift be from 10:00 P.M. to 6:00 A.M. If this is the case, the major problems are during the second shift.

13.17 The R-chart is designed to monitor the variation of the process.

13.19 Using Table XVII, Appendix B:

a. With $n = 4$, $D_3 = 0.000$ $D_4 = 2.282$

b. With $n = 12$, $D_3 = 0.283$ $D_4 = 1.717$

c. With $n = 24$, $D_3 = 0.451$ $D_4 = 1.548$

Methods for Quality Improvement

13.21 a. From Exercise 13.11, the R values are:

Sample No.	R	Sample No.	R
1	1.8	11	3.2
2	2.8	12	0.9
3	3.8	13	2.6
4	2.5	14	4.0
5	3.7	15	2.2
6	5.0	16	4.3
7	5.5	17	3.6
8	3.5	18	2.5
9	2.5	19	2.2
10	4.1	20	5.5

$$\bar{R} = \frac{R_1 + R_2 + \cdots + R_{20}}{n} = \frac{66.2}{20} = 3.31$$

Centerline $= \bar{R} = 3.31$

From Table XVII, Appendix B, with $n = 4$, $D_4 = 2.282$, and $D_3 = 0$.

Upper control limit $= \bar{R}D_4 = 3.31(2.282) = 7.553$

Since $D_3 = 0$, the lower control limit is negative and is not included on the chart.

b. From Table XVII, Appendix B, with $n = 4$, $d_2 = 2.059$, and $d_3 = .880$.

$$\text{Upper A–B boundary} = \bar{R} + 2d_3 \frac{\bar{R}}{d_2} = 3.31 + 2(.880)\frac{3.31}{2.059} = 6.139$$

$$\text{Lower A–B boundary} = \bar{R} - 2d_3 \frac{\bar{R}}{d_2} = 3.31 - 2(.880)\frac{3.31}{2.059} = 0.481$$

$$\text{Upper B–C boundary} = \bar{R} + d_3 \frac{\bar{R}}{d_2} = 3.31 + (.880)\frac{3.31}{2.059} = 4.725$$

$$\text{Lower B–C boundary} = \bar{R} - d_3 \frac{\bar{R}}{d_2} = 3.31 - (.880)\frac{3.31}{2.059} = 1.895$$

c. The *R*-chart is:

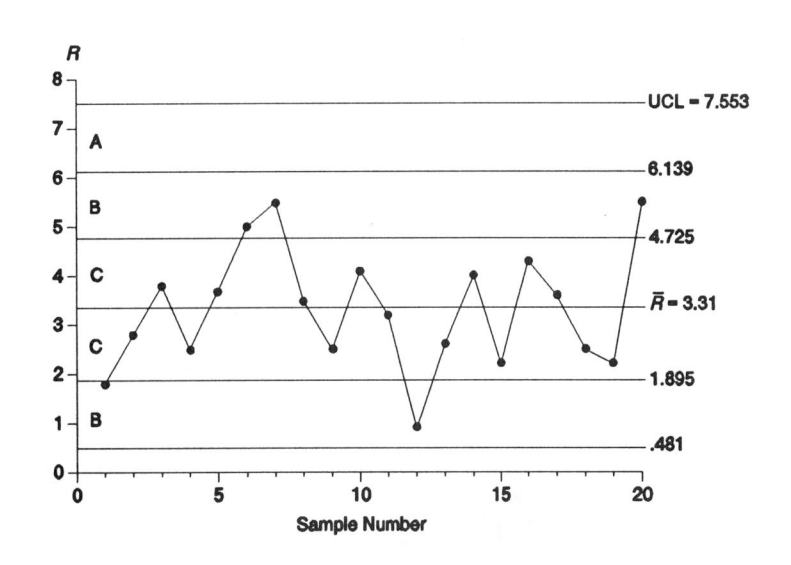

To determine if the process is in or out of control, we check the four rules:

Rule 1: One point beyond Zone A: No points are beyond Zone A.
Rule 2: Nine points in a row in Zone C or beyond: No sequence of nine points are in Zone C (on one side of the centerline) or beyond.
Rule 3: Six points in a row steadily increasing or decreasing: No sequence of six points steadily increase or decrease.
Rule 4: Fourteen points in a row alternating up and down: This pattern does not exist.

The process appears to be in control.

13.23 a. From Table XVII, Appendix B, with $n = 4$, $D_3 = 0$, and $D_4 = 2.282$.

$\bar{R} = .3162$

Upper control limit $= \bar{R}D_4 = .3162(2.282) = .7216$

Since $D_3 = 0$, the lower control limit is negative and is not included on the chart.

b. To determine if special causes of variation are present, we need to complete the *R*-chart.

From Table XVII, Appendix B, with $n = 4$, $d_2 = 2.059$, and $d_3 = .880$.

Upper A–B boundary $= \bar{R} + 2d_3 \dfrac{\bar{R}}{d_2} = .3162 + 2(.880)\dfrac{3.3162}{2.059} = .5865$

Lower A–B boundary $= \bar{R} - 2d_3 \dfrac{\bar{R}}{d_2} = .3162 - 2(.880)\dfrac{3.3162}{2.059} = .0459$

Upper B–C boundary $= \bar{R} + d_3 \dfrac{\bar{R}}{d_2} = .3162 + (.880)\dfrac{3.3162}{2.059} = .4513$

Lower B–C boundary $= \bar{R} - d_3 \dfrac{\bar{R}}{d_2} = .3162 - (.880)\dfrac{3.3162}{2.059} = .1811$

Methods for Quality Improvement

The R-chart is:

R-chart for Pathwidth

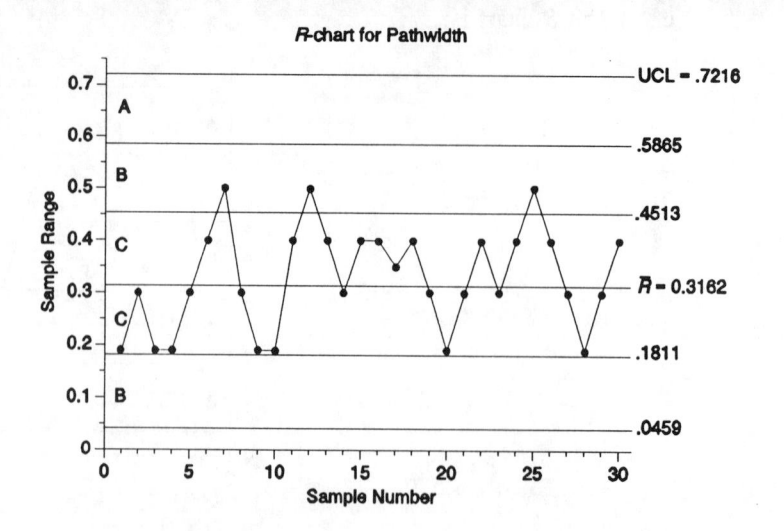

To determine if the process is in control, we check the four rules.

    Rule 1:   One point beyond Zone A: No points are beyond Zone A.
    Rule 2:   Nine points in a row in Zone C or beyond: There are not nine points are in a row in Zone C (on one side of the centerline) or beyond.
    Rule 3:   Six points in a row steadily increasing or decreasing: No sequence of six points steadily increase or decrease.
    Rule 4:   Fourteen points in a row alternating up and down: This pattern does not exist.

It appears that the process is in control.

  c. Yes. This process appears to be in control. Therefore, these control limits could be used to monitor future output.

  d. Of the 30 R values plotted, there are only 6 different values. Most of the R values take on one of three values. This indicates that the data must be discrete (take on a countable number of values), or that the path widths are multiples of each other.

13.25 a. From Table XVII, Appendix B, with $n = 6$, $D_3 = .000$ and $D_4 = 2.004$.

$\bar{R} = 3.733$ (from Exercise 13.15).

Upper control limit $= \bar{R}D_4 = 3.733(2.004) = 7.481$

Since $D_3 = 0$, the lower control limit is negative and is not included on the chart.

From Table XVII, Appendix B, with $n = 6$, $d_2 = 2.534$, and $d_3 = .848$.

Upper A–B *boundary* $= \bar{R} + 2d_3\dfrac{\bar{R}}{d_2} = 3.733 + 2(.848)\dfrac{3.733}{2.534} = 6.231$

Lower A–B *boundary* $= \bar{R} - 2d_3\dfrac{\bar{R}}{d_2} = 3.733 - 2(.848)\dfrac{3.733}{2.534} = 1.235$

Upper B–C *boundary* $= \bar{R} + d_3\dfrac{\bar{R}}{d_2} = 3.733 + (.848)\dfrac{3.733}{2.534} = 4.982$

Lower B–C boundary $= \bar{R} - d_3 \dfrac{\bar{R}}{d_2} = 3.733 - (.848)\dfrac{3.733}{2.534} = 2.484$

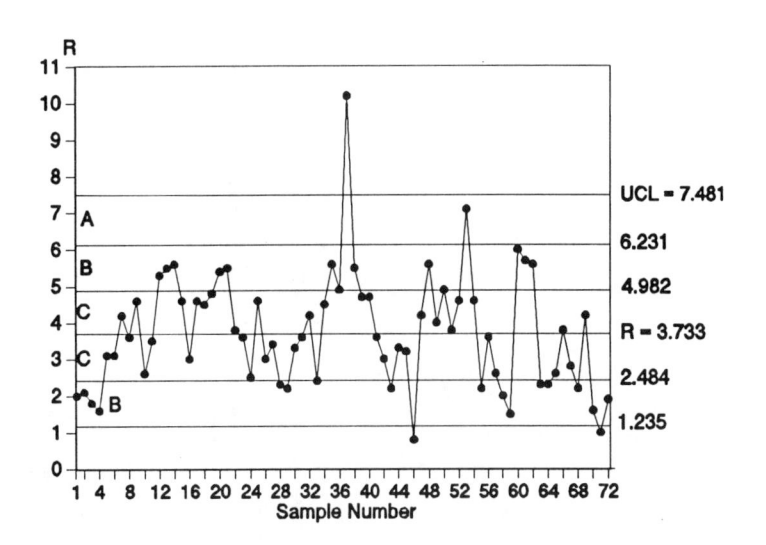

The R-chart is:

b. To determine if the process is in control, we check the four rules.

    Rule 1: One point beyond Zone A: There is 1 point beyond Zone A.
    Rule 2: Nine points in a row in Zone C or beyond: No sequence of nine points are in Zone C (on one side of the centerline) or beyond.
    Rule 3: Six points in a row steadily increasing or decreasing: This pattern is not present.
    Rule 4: Fourteen points in a row alternating up and down: This pattern does not exist.

Rule 1 indicates that the process is out of control. The process is unstable.

c. Yes. The process variation is not under control.

13.27 a. From Table XVII, Appendix B, with $n = 5$, $D_3 = .000$, and $D_4 = 2.114$.

$$\bar{R} = \dfrac{R_1 + R_2 + \cdots + R_5}{n} = \dfrac{62}{5} = 12.4$$

Upper control limit $= \bar{R}D_4 = 12.4(2.114) = 26.214$

Since $D_3 = 0$, the lower control limit is negative and is not included on the chart.

From Table XVII, Appendix B, with $n = 5$, $d_2 = 2.326$, and $d_3 = .864$.

Upper A–B boundary $= \bar{R} + 2d_3 \dfrac{\bar{R}}{d_2} = 12.4 + 2(.864)\dfrac{12.4}{2.326} = 21.612$

Lower A–B boundary $= \bar{R} - 2d_3 \dfrac{\bar{R}}{d_2} = 12.4 - 2(.864)\dfrac{12.4}{2.326} = 3.188$

Upper B–C boundary $= \bar{R} + d_3 \dfrac{\bar{R}}{d_2} = 12.4 + (.864)\dfrac{12.4}{2.326} = 17.006$

Methods for Quality Improvement

Lower B–C boundary $= \bar{R} - d_3 \dfrac{\bar{R}}{d_2} = 12.4 - (.864)\dfrac{12.4}{2.326} = 7.794$

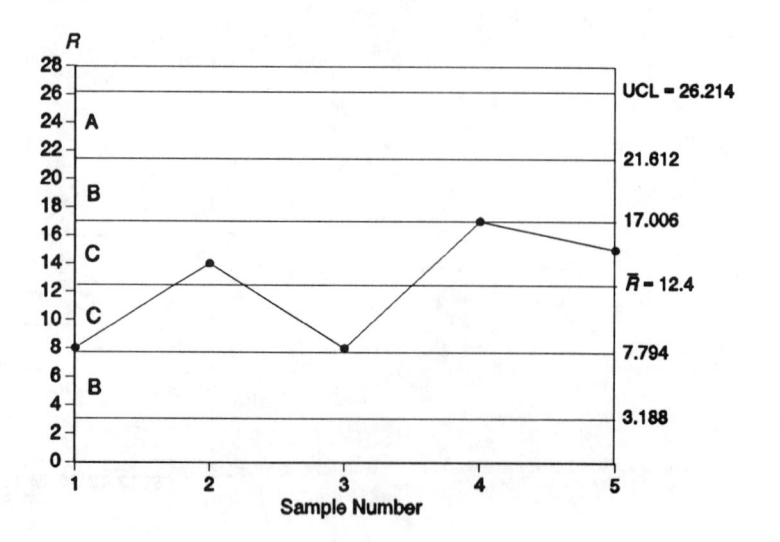

The R-chart is:

$$\bar{\bar{x}} = \dfrac{\bar{x}_1 + \bar{x}_2 + \cdots + \bar{x}_5}{n} = \dfrac{248.2}{5} = 49.64$$

Centerline $= \bar{\bar{x}} = 49.64$

From Table XVII, Appendix B, with $n = 5$, $A_2 = .577$.

Upper control limit $= \bar{\bar{x}} + A_2\bar{R} = 49.64 + .577(12.4) = 56.795$
Lower control limit $= \bar{\bar{x}} - A_2\bar{R} = 49.64 - .577(12.4) = 42.485$

Upper A–B boundary $= \bar{\bar{x}} + \dfrac{2}{3}(A_2\bar{R}) = 49.64 + \dfrac{2}{3}(.577)(12.4) = 54.410$

Lower A–B boundary $= \bar{\bar{x}} - \dfrac{2}{3}(A_2\bar{R}) = 49.64 - \dfrac{2}{3}(.577)(12.4) = 44.870$

Upper B–C boundary $= \bar{\bar{x}} + \dfrac{1}{3}(A_2\bar{R}) = 49.64 + \dfrac{1}{3}(.577)(12.4) = 52.025$

Lower B–C boundary $= \bar{\bar{x}} - \dfrac{1}{3}(A_2\bar{R}) = 49.64 - \dfrac{1}{3}(.577)(12.4) = 47.255$

The $\bar{x}$-chart is:

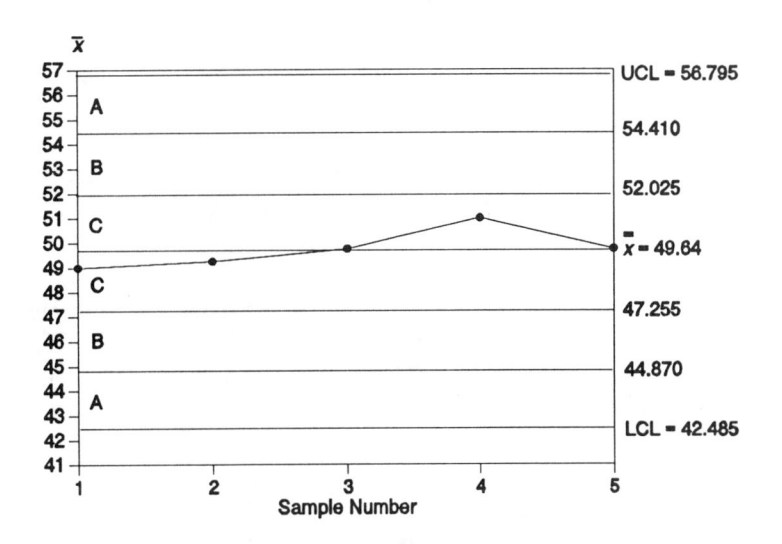

```
  x̄
 57 ┬─────────────────────────────────── UCL = 56.795
 56 ┤    A
 55 ┤
 54 ┤─────────────────────────────────── 54.410
 53 ┤    B
 52 ┤─────────────────────────────────── 52.025
 51 ┤    C              •
 50 ┤         •    •         •          x̄ = 49.64
 49 ┤•
 48 ┤    C
 47 ┤─────────────────────────────────── 47.255
 46 ┤    B
 45 ┤─────────────────────────────────── 44.870
 44 ┤
 43 ┤    A
 42 ┤─────────────────────────────────── LCL = 42.485
 41 ┴──┬─────┬─────┬─────┬─────┬──
       1     2     3     4     5
              Sample Number
```

b. The R-chart should be evaluated first. If the process variation is out of control, the control limits of the $\bar{x}$-chart have little meaning.

c. To determine if the process is in control, we check the four rules for the R-chart.

   Rule 1:   One point beyond Zone A: No points are beyond Zone A.
   Rule 2:   Nine points in a row in Zone C or beyond: No sequence of nine points are in Zone C (on one side of the centerline) or beyond.
   Rule 3:   Six points in a row steadily increasing or decreasing: This pattern is not present.
   Rule 4:   Fourteen points in a row alternating up and down: This pattern does not exist.

The process appears to be in control. Since the process variation appears to be in control, the interpretation of the $\bar{x}$-chart is meaningful.

To determine if the process is in or out of control, we check the six rules:

   Rule 1:   One point beyond Zone A: No points are beyond Zone A.
   Rule 2:   Nine points in a row in Zone C or beyond: No sequence of nine points are in Zone C (on one side of the centerline) or beyond.
   Rule 3:   Six points in a row steadily increasing or decreasing: This pattern does not exist.
   Rule 4:   Fourteen points in a row alternating up and down: This pattern does not exist.
   Rule 5:   Two out of three points in Zone A or beyond: This pattern does not exist.
   Rule 6:   Four out of five points in a row in Zone B or beyond: This pattern does not exist.

The process appears to be in control.

d. No. The five observations each day were from the morning shift only. Thus, no information for the afternoon shift was obtained.

13.29 The sample size is determined as follows:

$$n > \frac{9(1 - p_0)}{p_0} = \frac{9(1 - .08)}{.08} = 103.5 \approx 104$$

13.31 a. We must first calculate $\bar{p}$. To do this, it is necessary to find the total number of defectives in all the samples. To find the number of defectives per sample, we multiple the proportion by the sample size, 150. The number of defectives per sample are shown in the table:

Sample No.	p	No. Defectives	Sample No.	p	No. Defectives
1	.03	4.5	11	.07	10.5
2	.05	7.5	12	.04	6.0
3	.10	15.0	13	.06	9.0
4	.02	3.0	14	.05	7.5
5	.08	12.0	15	.07	10.5
6	.09	13.5	16	.06	9.0
7	.08	12.0	17	.07	10.5
8	.05	7.5	18	.02	3.0
9	.07	10.5	19	.05	7.5
10	.06	9.0	20	.03	4.5

Note: There cannot be a fraction of a defective. The proportions presented in the exercise have been rounded off. I have used the fractions to minimize the roundoff error.

To get the total number of defectives, sum the number of defectives for all 20 samples. The sum is 172.5. To get the total number of units sampled, multiply the sample size by the number of samples: 150(20) = 3000.

$$\bar{p} = \frac{\text{Total defective in all samples}}{\text{Total units sampled}} = \frac{172.5}{3000} = .0575$$

Centerline = $\bar{p}$ = .0575

Upper control limit = $\bar{p} + 3\sqrt{\frac{\bar{p}(1 - \bar{p})}{n}} = .0575 + 3\sqrt{\frac{.0575(.9425)}{150}} = .1145$

Lower control limit = $\bar{p} - 3\sqrt{\frac{\bar{p}(1 - \bar{p})}{n}} = .0575 - 3\sqrt{\frac{.0575(.9425)}{150}} = .0005$

b. Upper A−B boundary = $\bar{p} + 2\sqrt{\frac{\bar{p}(1 - \bar{p})}{n}} = .0575 + 2\sqrt{\frac{.0575(.9425)}{150}} = .0955$

Lower A−B boundary = $\bar{p} - 2\sqrt{\frac{\bar{p}(1 - \bar{p})}{n}} = .0575 - 2\sqrt{\frac{.0575(.9425)}{150}} = .0195$

Upper B−C boundary = $\bar{p} + \sqrt{\frac{\bar{p}(1 - \bar{p})}{n}} = .0575 + \sqrt{\frac{.0575(.9425)}{150}} = .0765$

Lower B−C boundary = $\bar{p} - \sqrt{\frac{\bar{p}(1 - \bar{p})}{n}} = .0575 - \sqrt{\frac{.0575(.9425)}{150}} = .0385$

c. The *p*-chart is:

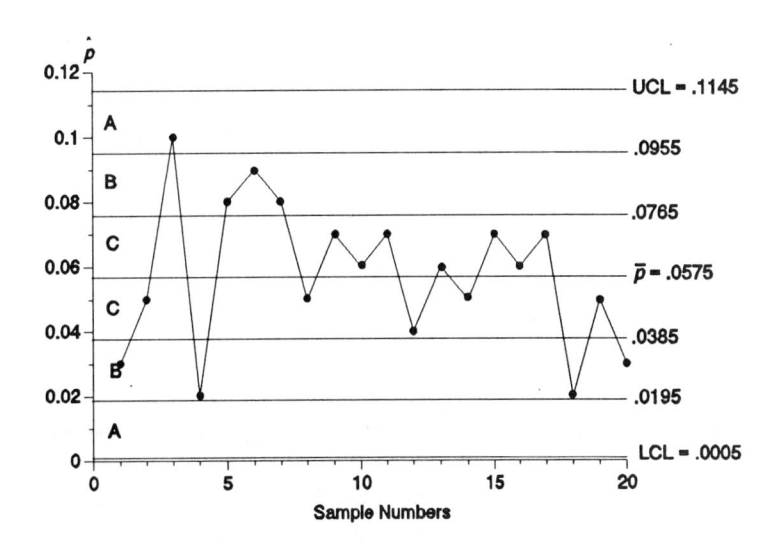

d. To determine if the process is in or out of control, we check the four rules:

Rule 1: One point beyond Zone A: No points are beyond Zone A.
Rule 2: Nine points in a row in Zone C or beyond: No sequence of nine points are in Zone C (on one side of the centerline) or beyond.
Rule 3: Six points in a row steadily increasing or decreasing: No sequence of six points steadily increase or decrease.
Rule 4: Fourteen points in a row alternating up and down: Points 7 through 20 alternate up and down. This indicates the process is out of control.

Rule 4 indicates that the process is out of control.

e. Since the process is out of control, the centerline and control limits should not be used to monitor future process output. The centerline and control limits are intended to represent the behavior of the process when it is under control.

13.33 a. Yes. The minimum sample size necessary so the lower control limit is not negative is:

$$n > \frac{9(1 - p_0)}{p_0}$$

From the data, $p_0 \approx .01$

Thus, $n > \frac{9(1 - .01)}{.01} = 891$. Our sample size was 1000.

b. *Upper control limit* $= \bar{p} + 3\sqrt{\frac{\bar{p}(1 - \bar{p})}{n}} = .01047 + 3\sqrt{\frac{.01047(.98953)}{1000}} = .02013$

Lower control limit $= \bar{p} - 3\sqrt{\frac{\bar{p}(1 - \bar{p})}{n}} = .01047 - 3\sqrt{\frac{.01047(.98953)}{1000}} = .00081$

Methods for Quality Improvement

c. To determine if special causes are present, we must complete the *p*-chart.

$$\text{Upper A-B boundary} = \bar{p} + 2\sqrt{\frac{\bar{p}(1-\bar{p})}{n}} = .01047 + 2\sqrt{\frac{.01047(.98953)}{1000}} = .01691$$

$$\text{Lower A-B boundary} = \bar{p} - 2\sqrt{\frac{\bar{p}(1-\bar{p})}{n}} = .01047 - 2\sqrt{\frac{.01047(.98953)}{1000}} = .00403$$

$$\text{Upper B-C boundary} = \bar{p} + \sqrt{\frac{\bar{p}(1-\bar{p})}{n}} = .01047 + \sqrt{\frac{.01047(.98953)}{1000}} = .01369$$

$$\text{Lower B-C boundary} = \bar{p} - \sqrt{\frac{\bar{p}(1-\bar{p})}{n}} = .01047 - \sqrt{\frac{.01047(.98953)}{1000}} = .00725$$

To determine if the process is in control, we check the four rules.

  Rule 1: One point beyond Zone A: No points are beyond Zone A.
  Rule 2: Nine points in a row in Zone C or beyond: There are not nine points in a row in Zone C (on one side of the centerline) or beyond.
  Rule 3: Six points in a row steadily increasing or decreasing: No sequence of six points steadily increase or decrease.
  Rule 4: Fourteen points in a row alternating up and down: This pattern does not exist.

It appears that the process is in control.

d. The rational subgrouping strategy says that samples should be chosen so that it gives the maximum chance for the measurements in each sample to be similar and so that it gives the maximum chance for the samples to differ. By selecting 1000 consecutive disks each time, this gives the maximum chance for the measurements in the sample to be similar. By selecting the samples every other day, there is a relatively large chance that the samples differ.

13.35 a. To compute the proportion of defectives in each sample, divide the number of defectives by the number in the sample, 100:

$$\hat{p} = \frac{\text{No. of defectives}}{\text{No. in sample}}$$

The sample proportions are listed in the table:

Sample No.	$\hat{p}$	Sample No.	$\hat{p}$
1	.02	16	.02
2	.04	17	.03
3	.10	18	.07
4	.04	19	.03
5	.01	20	.02
6	.01	21	.03
7	.13	22	.07
8	.09	23	.04
9	.11	24	.03
10	.00	25	.02
11	.03	26	.02
12	.04	27	.00
13	.02	28	.01
14	.02	29	.03
15	.08	30	.04

To get the total number of defectives, sum the number of defectives for all 30 samples. The sum is 120. To get the total number of units sampled, multiply the sample size by the number of samples: 100(30) = 3000.

$$\bar{p} = \frac{\text{Total defective in all samples}}{\text{Total units sampled}} = \frac{120}{3000} = .04$$

The centerline is $\bar{p} = .04$

$$\text{Upper control limit} = \bar{p} + 3\sqrt{\frac{\bar{p}(1-\bar{p})}{n}} = .04 + 3\sqrt{\frac{.04(1-.04)}{100}} = .099$$

$$\text{Lower control limit} = \bar{p} - 3\sqrt{\frac{\bar{p}(1-\bar{p})}{n}} = .04 - 3\sqrt{\frac{.04(1-.04)}{100}} = -.019$$

$$\text{Upper A}-\text{B boundary} = \bar{p} + 2\sqrt{\frac{\bar{p}(1-\bar{p})}{n}} = .04 + 2\sqrt{\frac{.04(1-.04)}{100}} = .079$$

$$\text{Lower A}-\text{B boundary} = \bar{p} - 2\sqrt{\frac{\bar{p}(1-\bar{p})}{n}} = .04 - 2\sqrt{\frac{.04(1-.04)}{100}} = .001$$

$$\text{Upper B}-\text{C boundary} = \bar{p} + \sqrt{\frac{\bar{p}(1-\bar{p})}{n}} = .04 + \sqrt{\frac{.04(1-.04)}{100}} = .060$$

$$\text{Lower B}-\text{C boundary} = \bar{p} - \sqrt{\frac{\bar{p}(1-\bar{p})}{n}} = .04 - \sqrt{\frac{.04(1-.04)}{100}} = .020$$

The *p*-chart is:

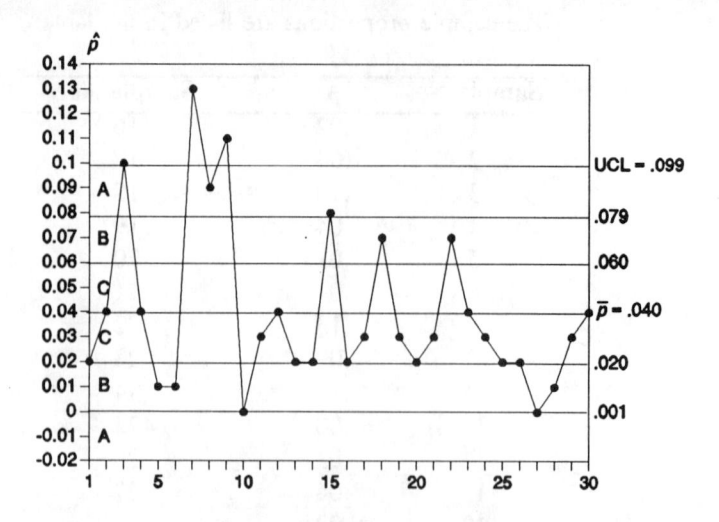

b. To determine if the process is in or out of control, we check the four rules for the *R*-chart.

   Rule 1: One point beyond Zone A: There are 3 points beyond Zone A—points 2, 7, and 9.

   Rule 2: Nine points in a row in Zone C or beyond: No sequence of nine points are in Zone C (on one side of the centerline) or beyond.

   Rule 3: Six points in a row steadily increasing or decreasing: This pattern is not present.

   Rule 4: Fourteen points in a row alternating up and down: This pattern does not exist.

   The process does not appear to be in control. Rule 1 indicates that the process is out of control.

c. No. Since the process is not in control, then these control limits are meaningless.

13.37 A capability analysis is a methodology used to help determine when common cause variation is unacceptably high. If a process is not in statistical control, then both common causes and special causes of variation exist. It would not be possible to determine if the common cause variation is too high because it could not be separated from special cause variation.

13.39 One way to assess the capability of a process is to construct a frequency distribution or stem-and-leaf display for a large sample of individual measurements from the process. Then, the specification limits and the target value for the output variable are added to the graph. This is called a capability analysis diagram. A second way to assess the capability of a process is to quantify capability. The most direct way to quantify capability is to count the number of items that fall outside the specification limits in the capability analysis diagram and report the percentage of such items in the sample. Also, one can construct a capability index. This is the ratio of the difference in the specification spread and the difference in the process spread. This measure is called C_P. If C_P is less than 1, then the process is not capable.

13.41 a. $C_P = 1.00$. For this value, the specification spread is equal to the process spread. This indicates that the process is capable. Approximately 2.7 units per 1,000 will be unacceptable.

b. $C_P = 1.33$. For this value, the specification spread is greater than the process spread. This indicates that the process is capable. Approximately 63 units per 1,000,000 will be unacceptable.

c. $C_P = 0.50$. For this value, the specification spread is less than the process spread. This indicates that the process is not capable.

d. $C_P = 2.00$. For this value, the specification spread is greater than the process spread. This indicates that the process is capable. Approximately 2 units per billion will be unacceptable.

13.43 The process spread is 6σ.

    a. For $\sigma = 21$, the process spread is $6(21) = 126$

    b. For $\sigma = 5.2$, the process spread is $6(5.2) = 31.2$

    c. For $s = 110.06$, the process spread is estimated by $6(110.06) = 660.36$

    d. For $s = .0024$, the process spread is estimated by $6(.0024) = .0144$

13.45 We know that $C_P = \dfrac{USL - LSL}{6\sigma}$

Thus, if $C_P = 2$, then $2 = \dfrac{USL - LSL}{6\sigma} \Rightarrow 12\sigma = USL - LSL$. The process mean is halfway between the USL and the LSL. Since the specification spread covers 12σ, then the USL must be $12\sigma/2 = 6\sigma$ from the process mean.

13.47 a. A capability analysis diagram is:

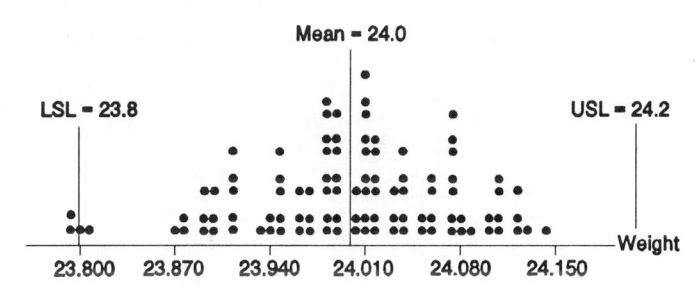

b. From the sample, $\bar{x} = 23.997$ and $s = .077$.

$$C_P = \frac{USL - LSL}{6\sigma} \approx \frac{24.2 - 23.8}{6(.077)} = \frac{.4}{.462} = .866$$

Since the C_P value is less than 1, the process is not capable.

13.49 The quality of a good or service is indicated by the extent to which it satisfies the needs and preferences of its users. Its eight dimensions are: performance, features, reliability, conformance, durability, serviceability, aesthetics, and other perceptions that influence judgments of quality.

13.51 A process is a series of actions or operations that transform inputs to outputs. A process produces output over time. Organizational process: Manufacturing a product. Personnel Process: Balancing a checkbook.

13.53 The six major sources of process variation are: people, machines, materials, methods, measurements, and environment.

Methods for Quality Improvement

13.59 Common causes of variation are the methods, materials, equipment, personnel, and environment that make up a process and the inputs required by the process. That is, common causes are attributable to the design of the process. Special causes of variation are events or actions that are not part of the process design. Typically, they are transient, fleeting events that affect only local areas or operations within the process for a brief period of time. Occasionally, however, such events may have a persistent or recurrent effect on the process.

13.61 Control limits are a function of the natural variability of the process. The position of the limits is a function of the size of the process standard deviation. Specification limits are boundary points that define the acceptable values for an output variable of a particular product or service. They are determined by customers, management, and/or product designers. Specification limits may be either two-sided, with upper and lower limits, or one-sided with either an upper or lower limit. Specification limits are not dependent on the process in any way. The process may not be able to meet the specification limits even when it is under statistical control.

13.63 The C_p statistic is used to assess capability if the process is stable (in control) and if the process is centered on the target value.

13.65 a. The centerline is:

$$\bar{x} = \frac{\sum x}{n} = \frac{96}{15} = 6.4$$

The time series plot is:

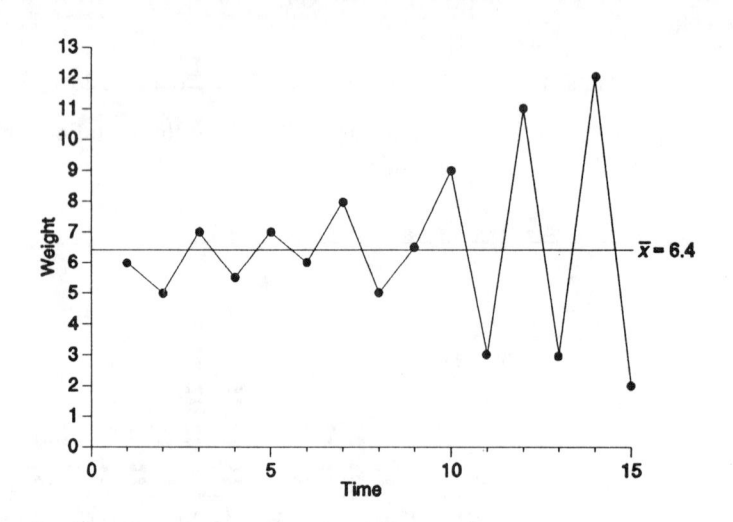

b. The type of variation best described by the pattern in this plot is increasing variance. The spread of the measurements increases with the passing of time.

13.67 To determine if the process is in or out of control, we check the six rules:

Rule 1: One point beyond Zone A: No points are beyond Zone A.
Rule 2: Nine points in a row in Zone C or beyond: Points 8 through 16 are in Zone C (on one side of the centerline) or beyond. This indicates the process is out of control.
Rule 3: Six points in a row steadily increasing or decreasing: No sequence of six points steadily increase or decrease.
Rule 4: Fourteen points in a row alternating up and down: This pattern does not exist.
Rule 5: Two out of three points in Zone A or beyond: No group of three consecutive points have two or more in Zone A or beyond.
Rule 6: Four out of five points in a row in Zone B or beyond: No sequence of five points has four or more in Zone B or beyond.

Rule 2 indicates that the process is out of control. A special cause of variation appears to be present.

13.69 a. To compute the range, subtract the larger score minus the smaller score. The ranges for the samples are listed in the table:

Sample No.	R	$\bar{x}$	Sample No.	R	$\bar{x}$
1	4	343.0	11	5	357.5
2	3	329.5	12	10	330.0
3	12	349.0	13	2	349.0
4	1	351.5	14	1	336.5
5	12	354.0	15	16	337.0
6	6	339.0	16	7	354.5
7	3	329.5	17	1	352.5
8	0	344.0	18	6	337.0
9	25	346.5	19	6	338.0
10	15	353.5	20	13	351.5

The centerline is $\bar{R} = \dfrac{\sum R}{n} = \dfrac{148}{20} = 7.4$

From Table XVII, Appendix B, with $n = 2$, $D_3 = 0$, and $D_4 = 3.267$.

Upper control limit = $\bar{R}D_4 = 7.4(3.267) = 24.1758$

Since $D_3 = 0$, the lower control limit is negative and is not included on the chart.

From Table XVII, Appendix B, with $n = 2$, $d_2 = 1.128$, and $d_3 = .853$.

Upper A-B boundary = $\bar{R} + 2d_3 \dfrac{\bar{R}}{d_2} = 7.4 + 2(.853)\dfrac{(7.4)}{1.128} = 18.5918$

Lower A-B boundary = $\bar{R} - 2d_3 \dfrac{\bar{R}}{d_2} = 7.4 - 2(.853)\dfrac{(7.4)}{1.128} = -3.7918$

Upper B-C boundary = $\bar{R} + d_3 \dfrac{\bar{R}}{d_2} = 7.4 + (.853)\dfrac{(7.4)}{1.128} = 12.9959$

Lower B-C boundary = $\bar{R} - d_3 \dfrac{\bar{R}}{d_2} = 7.4 - (.853)\dfrac{(7.4)}{1.128} = 1.8041$

The R-chart is:

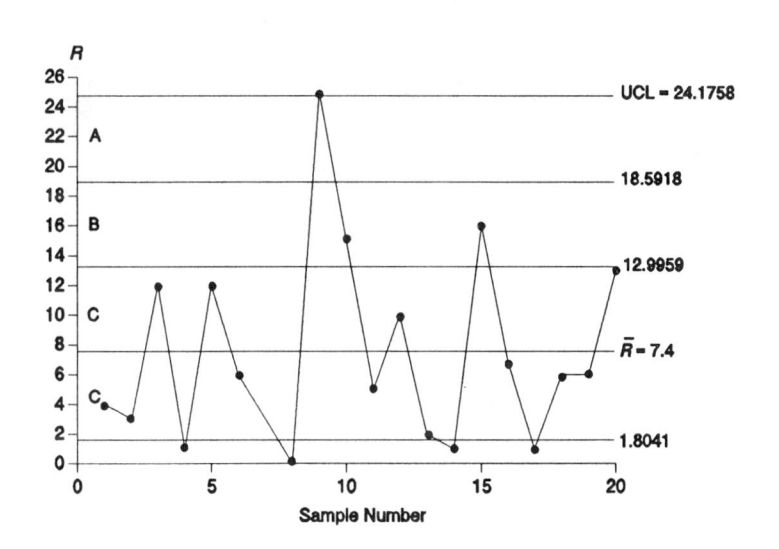

Methods for Quality Improvement

To determine if the process is in control, we check the four rules.

Rule 1: One point beyond Zone A: Point 9 is beyond Zone A. This indicates the process is out of control.
Rule 2: Nine points in a row in Zone C or beyond: There are not nine points in a row in Zone C (on one side of the centerline) or beyond.
Rule 3: Six points in a row steadily increasing or decreasing: No sequence of six points steadily increase or decrease.
Rule 4: Fourteen points in a row alternating up and down: This pattern does not exist.

Rule 1 indicates that the process is out of control. We should not use this to construct the $\bar{x}$-chart.

b. We will construct the $\bar{x}$-chart even though the R-chart indicates the variation is out of control. First, compute the mean for each sample by adding the 2 observations and dividing by 2. These values are in the table in part a.

The centerline is $\bar{\bar{x}} = \dfrac{\sum \bar{x}}{n} = \dfrac{6883}{20} = 344.15$

From Table XVII, Appendix B, with $n = 2$, $A_2 = 1.880$.

$\bar{\bar{x}} = 344.15$ and $\bar{R} = 7.4$

Upper control limit $= \bar{\bar{x}} + A_2\bar{R} = 344.15 + 1.88(7.4) = 358.062$
Lower control limit $= \bar{\bar{x}} - A_2\bar{R} = 344.15 - 1.88(7.4) = 330.238$

Upper A–B boundary $= \bar{\bar{x}} + \dfrac{2}{3}(A_2\bar{R}) = 344.15 + \dfrac{2}{3}(1.88)(7.4) = 353.425$

Lower A–B boundary $= \bar{\bar{x}} - \dfrac{2}{3}(A_2\bar{R}) = 344.15 - \dfrac{2}{3}(1.88)(7.4) = 334.875$

Upper B–C boundary $= \bar{\bar{x}} + \dfrac{1}{3}(A_2\bar{R}) = 344.15 + \dfrac{1}{3}(1.88)(7.4) = 348.787$

Lower B–C boundary $= \bar{\bar{x}} - \dfrac{1}{3}(A_2\bar{R}) = 344.15 - \dfrac{1}{3}(1.88)(7.4) = 339.513$

The $\bar{x}$-chart is:

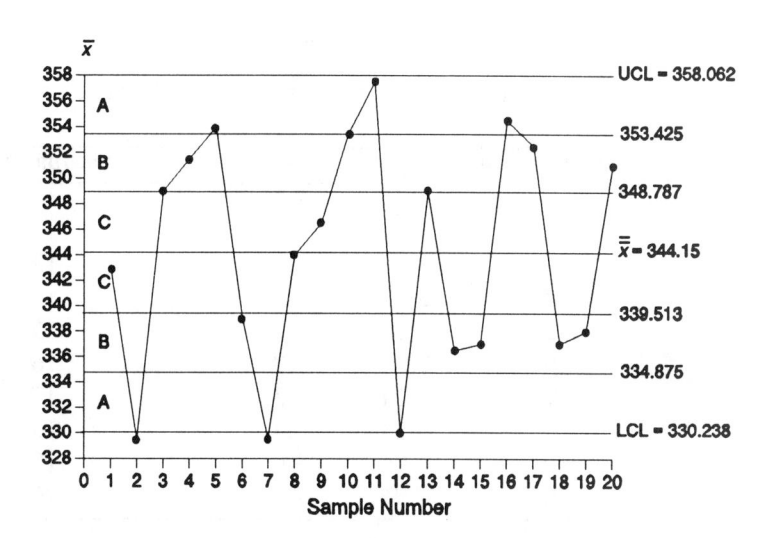

To determine if the process is in control, we check the six rules.

Rule 1: One point beyond Zone A: Points 2 and 7 are beyond Zone A. This indicates the process is out of control.

Rule 2: Nine points in a row in Zone C or beyond: There are nine points (Points 9 through 17) in a row in Zone C (on one side of the centerline) or beyond. This indicates that the process is out of control.

Rule 3: Six points in a row steadily increasing or decreasing: No sequence of six points steadily increase or decrease.

Rule 4: Fourteen points in a row alternating up and down: This pattern does not exist.

Rule 5: Two out of three points in Zone A or beyond: Points 10 and 11 are in Zone 3 or beyond. This indicates that the process is out of control.

Rule 6: Four out of five points in a row in Zone B or beyond: No sequence of five points has four or more in Zone B or beyond.

Rules 1 and 5 indicate the process is out of control. The $\bar{x}$-chart should not be used to monitor the process.

c. These control limits should not be used to monitor future output because both processes are out of control. One or more special causes of variation are affecting the process variation and process mean. These should be identified and eliminated in order to bring the processes into control.

d. Of the 40 patients sampled, 10 received care that did not conform to the hospital's requirement. The proportion is 10/40 = .25.

13.71 a. For each sample, we compute $\bar{x} = \dfrac{\sum x}{n}$ and R = range = largest measurement − smallest measurement. The results are listed in the table:

Sample No.	$\bar{x}$	R	Sample No.	$\bar{x}$	R
1	4.36	7.1	11	3.32	4.8
2	5.10	7.7	12	4.02	4.8
3	4.52	5.0	13	5.24	7.8
4	3.42	5.8	14	3.58	3.9
5	2.62	6.2	15	3.48	5.5
6	3.94	3.9	16	5.00	3.0
7	2.34	5.3	17	3.68	6.2
8	3.26	3.2	18	2.68	3.9
9	4.06	8.0	19	3.66	4.4
10	4.96	7.1	20	4.10	5.5

$$\bar{\bar{x}} = \dfrac{\bar{x}_1 + \bar{x}_2 + \cdots + \bar{x}_{20}}{n} = \dfrac{77.34}{20} = 3.867$$

$$\bar{R} = \dfrac{R_1 + R_2 + \cdots + R_{20}}{n} = \dfrac{109.1}{20} = 5.455$$

First, we construct an R-chart.

Centerline = $\bar{R}$ = 5.455

From Table XVII, Appendix B, with $n = 5$, $D_4 = 2.114$, and $D_3 = 0$.

Upper control limit = $\bar{R} D_4 = 5.455(2.114) = 11.532$

Since $D_3 = 0$, the lower control limit is negative and is not included on the chart.

Upper A–B *boundary* = $\bar{R} + 2d_3 \dfrac{\bar{R}}{d_2} = 5.455 + 2(.864)\dfrac{(5.455)}{2.326} = 9.508$

Lower A–B *boundary* = $\bar{R} - 2d_3 \dfrac{\bar{R}}{d_2} = 5.455 - 2(.864)\dfrac{(5.455)}{2.326} = 1.402$

Upper B–C *boundary* = $\bar{R} + d_3 \dfrac{\bar{R}}{d_2} = 5.455 + (.864)\dfrac{(5.455)}{2.326} = 7.481$

Lower B–C *boundary* = $\bar{R} - d_3 \dfrac{\bar{R}}{d_2} = 5.455 - (.864)\dfrac{(5.455)}{2.326} = 3.429$

The R-chart is:

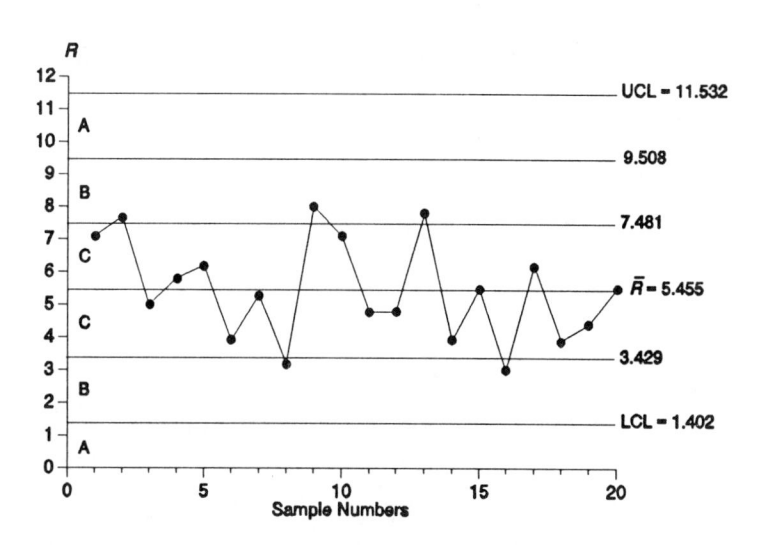

b. To determine if the process is in or out of control, we check the four rules:

Rule 1: One point beyond Zone A: No points are beyond Zone A.
Rule 2: Nine points in a row in Zone C or beyond: No sequence of nine points are in Zone C (on one side of the centerline) or beyond.
Rule 3: Six points in a row steadily increasing or decreasing: No sequence of six points steadily increase or decrease.
Rule 4: Fourteen points in a row alternating up and down: This pattern does not exist.

The process appears to be in control. Since the process variation is in control, it is appropriate to construct the $\bar{x}$-chart.

c. In order for the $\bar{x}$-chart to be valid, the process variation must be in control. The R-chart checks to see if the process variation is in control. For more details, see the answer to Exercise 13.18.

d. To construct an $\bar{x}$-chart, we first calculate the following:

$$\bar{\bar{x}} = \frac{\bar{x}_1 + \bar{x}_2 + \cdots + \bar{x}_{20}}{n} = \frac{77.34}{20} = 3.867$$

$$\bar{R} = \frac{R_1 + R_2 + \cdots + R_{20}}{n} = \frac{109.1}{20} = 5.455$$

Centerline = $\bar{\bar{x}}$ = 3.867

From Table XVII, Appendix B, with $n = 5$, $A_2 = .577$.

Upper control limit = $\bar{\bar{x}} + A_2\bar{R} = 3.867 + .577(5.455) = 7.015$
Lower control limit = $\bar{\bar{x}} - A_2\bar{R} = 3.867 - .577(5.455) = .719$

Upper A–B boundary = $\bar{\bar{x}} + \frac{2}{3}(A_2\bar{R}) = 3.867 + \frac{2}{3}(.577)(5.455) = 5.965$

Lower A–B boundary = $\bar{\bar{x}} - \frac{2}{3}(A_2\bar{R}) = 3.867 - \frac{2}{3}(.577)(5.455) = 1.769$

Methods for Quality Improvement

$$\text{Upper B-C boundary} = \bar{\bar{x}} + \frac{1}{3}\left(A_2\bar{R}\right) = 3.867 + \frac{1}{3}(.577)(5.455) = 4.916$$

$$\text{Lower B-C boundary} = \bar{\bar{x}} - \frac{1}{3}\left(A_2\bar{R}\right) = 3.867 - \frac{1}{3}(.577)(5.455) = 2.818$$

The $\bar{x}$-chart is:

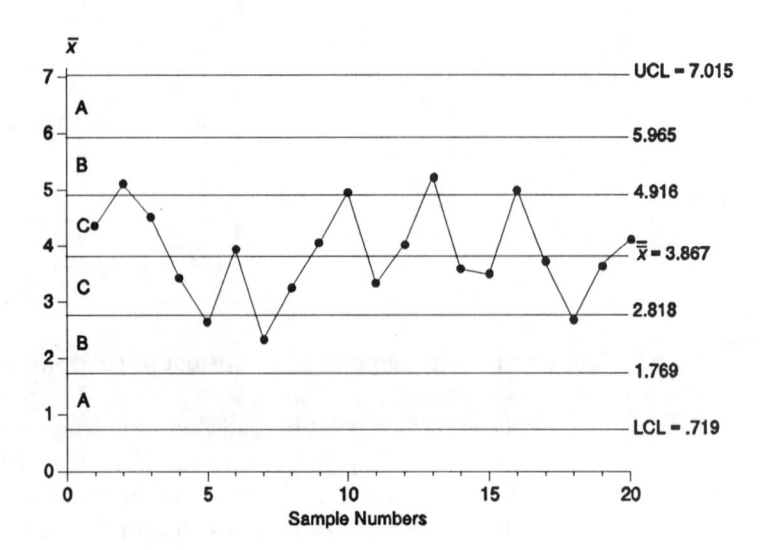

e. To determine if the process is in or out of control, we check the six rules:

    Rule 1:   One point beyond Zone A: No points are beyond Zone A.
    Rule 2:   Nine points in a row in Zone C or beyond: No sequence of nine points are in Zone C (on one side of the centerline) or beyond.
    Rule 3:   Six points in a row steadily increasing or decreasing: No sequence of six points steadily increases or decreases.
    Rule 4:   Fourteen points in a row alternating up and down: This pattern does not exist.
    Rule 5:   Two out of three points in Zone A or beyond: There are no groups of three consecutive points that have two or more in Zone A or beyond.
    Rule 6:   Four out of five points in a row in Zone B or beyond: No sequence of five points has four or more in Zone B or beyond.

The process appears to be in control.

f. Since both the R-chart and the $\bar{x}$-chart are in control, these control limits should be used to monitor future process output.

13.73   a. The sample size is determined by the following:

$$n > \frac{9(1 - p_0)}{p_0} = \frac{9(1 - .06)}{.06} = 141$$

The minimum sample size is 141. Since the sample size of 150 was used, it is large enough.

    b. To compute the proportion of defectives in each sample, divide the number of defectives by the number in the sample, 150:

$$\hat{p} = \frac{\text{No. of defectives}}{\text{No. in sample}}$$

The sample proportions are listed in the table:

Sample No.	$\hat{p}$	Sample No.	$\hat{p}$
1	.060	11	.047
2	.073	12	.040
3	.080	13	.080
4	.053	14	.067
5	.067	15	.073
6	.040	16	.047
7	.087	17	.040
8	.060	18	.080
9	.073	19	.093
10	.033	20	.067

To get the total number of defectives, sum the number of defectives for all 20 samples. The sum is 189. To get the total number of units sampled, multiply the sample size by the number of samples: 150(20) = 3000.

$$\bar{p} = \frac{\text{Total defectives in all samples}}{\text{Total units sampled}} = \frac{189}{3000} = .063$$

Centerline = $\bar{p}$ = .063

$$\text{Upper control limit} = \bar{p} + 3\sqrt{\frac{\bar{p}(1-\bar{p})}{n}} = .063 + 3\sqrt{\frac{.063(.937)}{150}} = .123$$

$$\text{Lower control limit} = \bar{p} - 3\sqrt{\frac{\bar{p}(1-\bar{p})}{n}} = .063 - 3\sqrt{\frac{.063(.937)}{150}} = .003$$

$$\text{Upper A-B boundary} = \bar{p} + 2\sqrt{\frac{\bar{p}(1-\bar{p})}{n}} = .063 + 2\sqrt{\frac{.063(.937)}{150}} = .103$$

$$\text{Lower A-B boundary} = \bar{p} - 2\sqrt{\frac{\bar{p}(1-\bar{p})}{n}} = .063 - 2\sqrt{\frac{.063(.937)}{150}} = .023$$

$$\text{Upper B-C boundary} = \bar{p} + \sqrt{\frac{\bar{p}(1-\bar{p})}{n}} = .063 + \sqrt{\frac{.063(.937)}{150}} = .083$$

$$\text{Lower B-C boundary} = \bar{p} - \sqrt{\frac{\bar{p}(1-\bar{p})}{n}} = .063 - \sqrt{\frac{.063(.937)}{150}} = .043$$

The *p*-chart is:

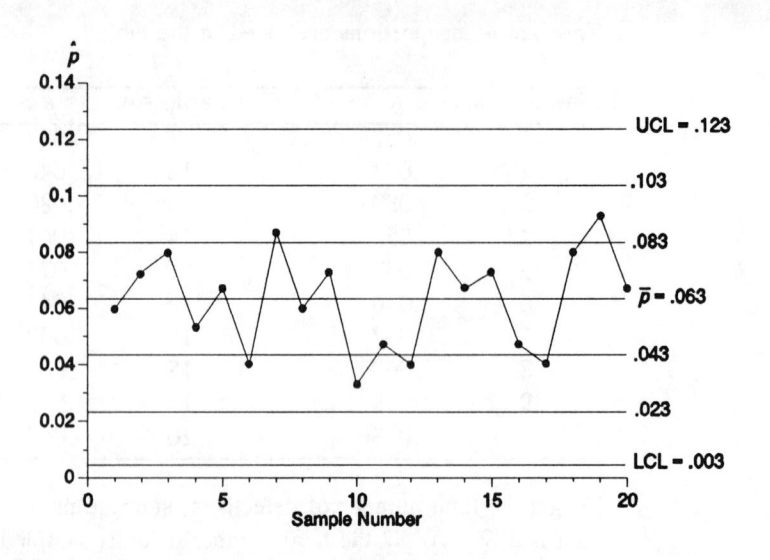

c. To determine if the process is in or out of control, we check the four rules.

    Rule 1: One point beyond Zone A: No points are beyond Zone A.
    Rule 2: Nine points in a row in Zone C or beyond: No sequence of nine points are in Zone C (on one side of the centerline) or beyond.
    Rule 3: Six points in a row steadily increasing or decreasing: No sequence of six points steadily increase or decrease.
    Rule 4: Fourteen points in a row alternating up and down: Points 2 through 16 alternate up and down. This indicates the process is out of control.

Rule 4 indicates the process is out of control. Special causes of variation appear to be present.

e. Since the process is out of control, the control limits should not be used to monitor future process output. It would not be appropriate to evaluate whether the process is in control using control limits determined during a period when the process was out of control.

Time Series: Descriptive Analyses, Models, and Forecasting Chapter 14

14.1　To calculate a simple index number, first obtain the prices or quantities over a time period and select a base year. For each time period, the index number is the number at that time period divided by the value at the base period multiplied by 100.

14.3　A Laspeyres index uses the purchase quantity at the base period as the weights for all other time periods. A Paasche index uses the purchase quantity at each time period as the weight for that time period. The weights at the specified time period are also used with the base period to find the index.

14.5　a.　To compute the simple index, divide each U.S. Beer Production value by the 1977 value, 171, and then multiply by 100.

Year	Simple Index	Year	Simple Index
1970	(133/171) × 100 = 77.78	1983	(195/171) × 100 = 114.04
1971	(137/171) × 100 = 80.12	1984	(192/171) × 100 = 112.28
1972	(141/171) × 100 = 82.46	1985	(194/171) × 100 = 113.45
1973	(149/171) × 100 = 87.13	1986	(194/171) × 100 = 113.45
1974	(156/171) × 100 = 91.23	1987	(196/171) × 100 = 114.62
1975	(161/171) × 100 = 94.15	1988	(197/171) × 100 = 115.20
1976	(164/171) × 100 = 95.91	1989	(198/171) × 100 = 115.79
1977	(171/171) × 100 = 100.00	1990	(202/171) × 100 = 118.13
1978	(179/171) × 100 = 104.68	1991	(204/171) × 100 = 119.30
1979	(184/171) × 100 = 107.60	1992	(202/171) × 100 = 118.13
1980	(194/171) × 100 = 113.45	1993	(202/171) × 100 = 118.13
1981	(194/171) × 100 = 113.45	1994	(203/171) × 100 = 118.71
1982	(196/171) × 100 = 114.62		

　　　b.　This is a quantity index because the numbers collected were the number of barrels produced rather than the price.

　　　c.　To compute the simple index, divide each U.S. Beer Production value by the 1980 value, 194, and then multiply by 100.

Year	Simple Index	Year	Simple Index
1970	(133/194) × 100 = 68.56	1983	(195/194) × 100 = 100.52
1971	(137/194) × 100 = 70.62	1984	(192/194) × 100 = 98.97
1972	(141/194) × 100 = 72.68	1985	(194/194) × 100 = 100.00
1973	(149/194) × 100 = 76.80	1986	(194/194) × 100 = 100.00
1974	(156/194) × 100 = 80.41	1987	(196/194) × 100 = 101.03
1975	(161/194) × 100 = 82.99	1988	(197/194) × 100 = 101.55
1976	(164/194) × 100 = 84.54	1989	(198/194) × 100 = 102.06
1977	(171/194) × 100 = 88.14	1990	(202/194) × 100 = 104.12
1978	(179/194) × 100 = 92.27	1991	(204/194) × 100 = 105.15
1979	(184/194) × 100 = 94.85	1992	(202/194) × 100 = 104.12
1980	(194/194) × 100 = 100.00	1993	(202/194) × 100 = 104.12
1981	(194/194) × 100 = 100.00	1994	(203/194) × 100 = 104.64
1982	(196/194) × 100 = 101.03		

The plots of the two simple indices are:

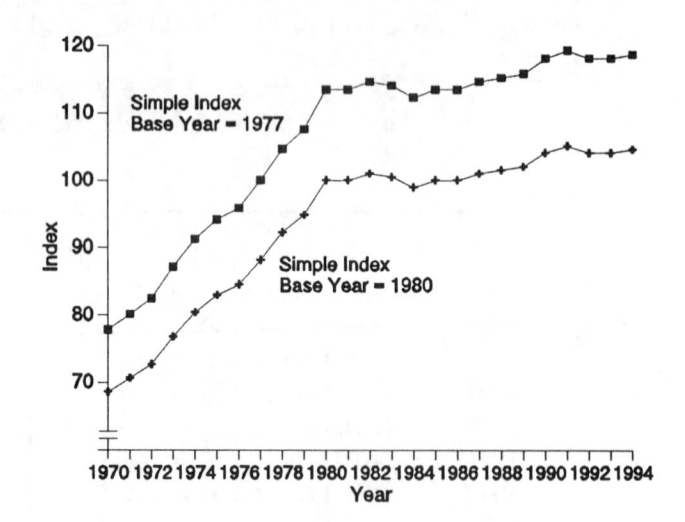

14.7 a. To compute the simple index, divide each closing price by the 1980 value, 56.500, and then multiply by 100.

Year	Simple Index	Year	Simple Index
1980	(56.500/56.5) × 100 = 100.00	1988	(48.010/56.5) × 100 = 84.97
1981	(27.000/56.5) × 100 = 47.79	1989	(64.030/56.5) × 100 = 113.33
1982	(38.750/56.5) × 100 = 68.58	1990	(45.000/56.5) × 100 = 79.65
1983	(45.250/56.5) × 100 = 80.09	1991	(68.070/56.5) × 100 = 120.48
1984	(41.750/56.5) × 100 = 73.89	1992	(30.030/56.5) × 100 = 53.15
1985	(68.375/56.5) × 100 = 121.02	1993	(29.050/56.5) × 100 = 51.42
1986	(45.625/56.5) × 100 = 80.75	1994	(32.050/56.5) × 100 = 56.73
1987	(48.020/56.5) × 100 = 84.99	1995	(41.050/56.5) × 100 = 72.65

b. The value of the index in 1980 is 100 and the value in 1989 is 113.33. Thus, the stock price increased by 113.33 − 100 = 13.33%.

The value of the index in 1991 is 120.48 and the value in 1995 is 72.65. Thus, the stock price decreased by 120.48 − 72.65 = 47.83%.

14.9 a. To compute the simple index for the agricultural data, divide each farm value by the 1980 value, 3,364, and then multiply by 100. To compute the simple index for the nonagricultural data, divide each nonfarm value by the 1980 value, 95,938, and then multiply by 100. The two indices are:

Year	Farm Index	Nonfarm Index
1980	100.00	100.00
1981	100.12	101.14
1982	101.10	100.19
1983	100.56	101.58
1984	98.72	105.99
1985	94.50	108.37
1986	94.02	110.94
1987	95.36	113.86
1988	94.20	116.53
1989	95.10	118.97
1990	94.71	119.59
1991	96.11	118.46
1992	95.33	119.23
1993	91.38	121.15
1994	101.34	124.72

b. The nonfarm segment has shown the greater percentage change in employment over the time period. The nonfarm employment in 1994 was 24.72% greater than in 1980. The farm employment in 1994 was only 1.34% greater than in 1980.

c. To compute the simple composite index, first sum the two values (farm and nonfarm) for every time period. Then, divide each sum by the sum in 1980, 99,302, and then multiply by 100. The simple composite index is:

Year	Sum	Simple Composite Index
1980	99,302	100.00
1981	100,398	101.10
1982	99,526	100.23
1983	100,833	101.54
1984	105,006	105.74
1985	107,150	107.90
1986	109,597	110.37
1987	112,440	113.23
1988	114,969	115.78
1989	117,341	118.17
1990	117,914	118.74
1991	116,877	117.70
1992	117,598	118.42
1993	119,306	120.14
1994	123,060	123.92

d. The simple composite index value in 1990 is 118.74. The composite employment is 18.74% higher in 1990 than in 1980.

14.11 a. The find Laspeyres index, we multiply the durable goods by 10.9, the nondurable goods by 14.02, and the services by 42.6. The three products are then summed. The index is found by dividing the weighted sum at each time period by the weighted sum of 1970, 17,108.86, and then multiplying by 100. The Laspeyres index and the simple composite index for 1970 (computed in Exercise 14.10) are:

Year	Simple Composite Index-1970	Weighted Sum	Laspeyres Index
1960	51.43	8,409.95	49.16
1965	68.77	11,442.51	66.88
1970	100.00	17,108.86	100.00
1975	158.52	27,509.89	160.79
1980	270.39	48,215.53	281.82
1981	297.94	53,543.43	312.96
1982	318.52	58,152.54	339.90
1983	349.19	64,079.28	374.54
1984	380.56	69,781.01	407.86
1985	412.59	76,167.86	445.20
1986	440.93	81,871.36	478.53
1987	472.11	88,329.19	516.28
1988	509.84	95,868.59	560.35
1989	544.95	102,668.37	600.09
1990	581.78	110,254.64	644.43
1991	603.63	115,824.36	676.99
1992	639.89	123,587.96	722.36
1993	677.22	131,182.38	766.75
1994	715.93	138,574.46	809.96

b. The plot of the two indices is:

The two indices are very similar from 1960 to approximately 1983. After 1983, the difference between the two indices becomes larger, with the Laspeyres index increasing faster than the simple composite index.

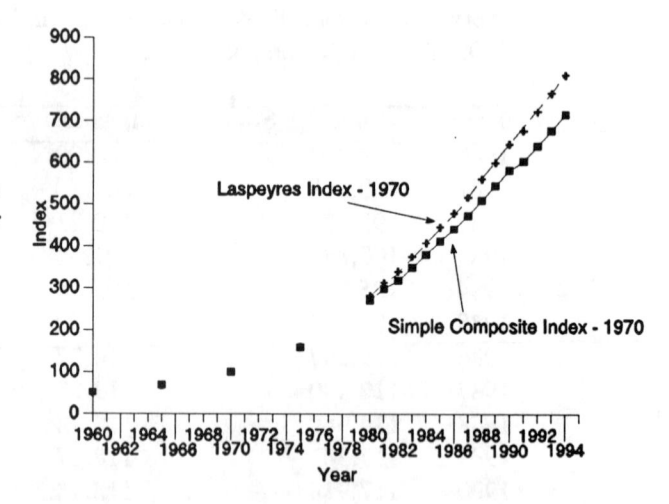

14.13 a. To compute the Laspeyres index, multiply the price for each year by the quantity for each of the utilities for 1988, sum the products for the two utilities, divide by 31,534.05 (the sum for the base period 1988), and multiply by 100. The Laspeyres index is:

Year	Total	Laspeyres Index
1988	31,534.05	100.00
1989	32,374.55	102.67
1990	33,257.40	105.47
1991	33,717.70	106.92
1992	34,037.15	107.94
1993	34,971.55	110.90

b. The following steps are used to compute the Paasche index:

1. First, multiply the price × production for gas and electricity for each month. The numerator of the index is the sum of these quantities at each month.
2. Next, multiply the sales values of gas by 5.29 and the sales of electricity by 7.5. The denominator is the sum of these two quantities at each month.
3. The values of the Paasche index are the ratios of these two values at each month times 100.

The Paasche index is:

Year	Paasche Numerator	Paasche Denominator	Paasche Index
1988	31,534.05	31,534.05	100.00
1989	33,034.70	32,176.42	102.67
1990	32,228.00	30,565.72	105.44
1991	33,393.00	31,232.00	106.92
1992	34,384.06	31,851.26	107.95
1993	38,211.09	34,455.63	110.90

c. The plot of the two indices is:

The two indices are essentially identical.

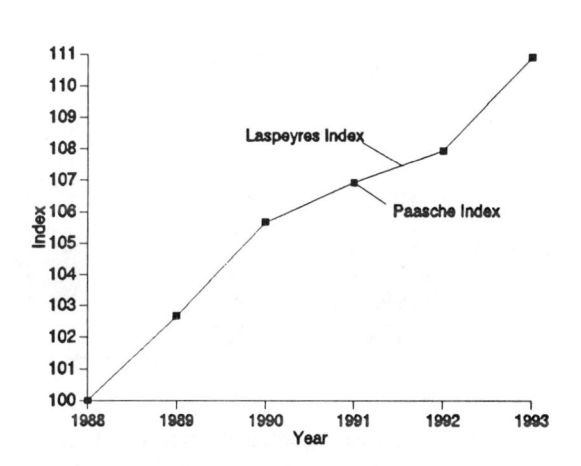

d. The 1993 Laspeyres index value is 110.90. This implies that the price of the utilities has increased 10.9% since 1988, assuming that the 1988 purchase quantities are reasonable weights.

The 1993 Paasche index value is 110.90. This implies that the price of the utilities has increased 10.9%, assuming the purchase quantities are at the 1993 level for both periods.

14.15 The smaller the value of w, the smoother the series. With $w = .2$, the current value receives a weight of .2 while the previous exponentially smoothed value receives a weight of .8. With $w = .8$, the current value receives a weight of .8 while the previous exponentially smoothed value receives a weight of .2. The smaller the value of w, the less chance the series can be affected by large jumps.

14.17 a. The exponentially smoothed beer production for the first period is equal to the beer production for that period. For the rest of the time periods, the exponentially smoothed beer production is found by multiplying .8 times the beer production of that time period by $w = .2$ and adding to that $(1 - .2)$ times the exponentially smoothed value above it. The exponentially smoothed value for the second period is .2(137) + (1 − .2)(133) = 133.8. The rest of the values are shown in the following table.

Year	Beer Production	w = .2 Exponentially Smoothed Production	w = .8 Exponentially Smoothed Production
1970	133	133.00	133.00
1971	137	133.80	136.20
1972	141	135.24	140.04
1973	149	137.99	147.21
1974	156	141.59	154.24
1975	161	145.47	159.65
1976	164	149.18	163.13
1977	171	153.54	169.43
1978	179	158.64	177.09
1979	184	163.71	182.62
1980	194	169.77	191.72
1981	194	174.61	193.54
1982	196	178.89	195.51
1983	195	182.11	195.10
1984	192	184.09	192.62
1985	194	186.07	193.72
1986	194	187.66	193.94
1987	196	189.33	195.59
1988	197	190.86	196.72
1989	198	192.29	197.74
1990	202	194.23	201.15
1991	204	196.18	203.43
1992	202	197.35	202.29
1993	202	198.28	202.06
1994	203	199.22	202.81

b. The exponentially smoothed beer production for the first period is equal to the beer production for that period. For the rest of the time periods, the exponentially smoothed beer production is found by multiplying .8 times the beer production of that time period and adding to that (1 − .8) times the value of the exponentially smoothed beer production figure of the previous time period. The exponentially smoothed beer production for the second time period is .8(137) + (1 − .8)(133) = 136.2. The rest of the values are shown in the table in part a.

c. The plot of the two series is:

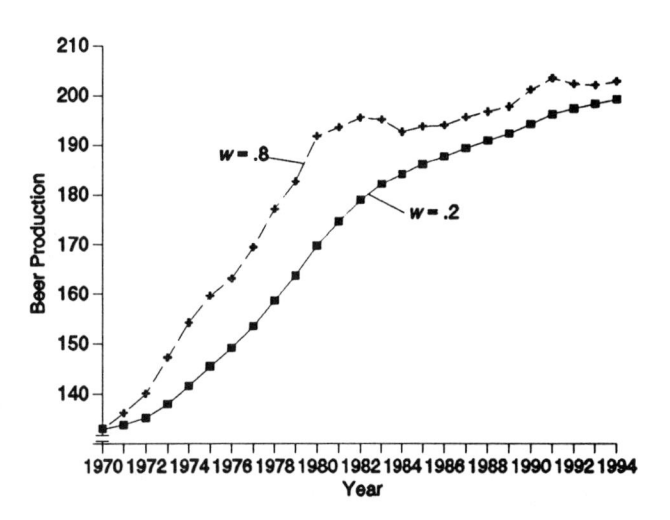

14.19 a. The exponentially smoothed gold price for the first period is equal to the gold price for that period. For the rest of the time periods, the exponentially smoothed gold price is found by multiplying the price for the time period by $w = .8$ and adding to that $(1 - .8)$ times the exponentially smoothed value from the previous time period. The exponentially smoothed value for the second time period is $.8(125) + (1 - .8)(161) = 132.2$. The rest of the values are shown below.

Year	Price	$w = .8$ Exponentially Smoothed Price
1975	161	161.00
1976	125	132.20
1977	148	144.84
1978	194	184.17
1979	308	283.23
1980	613	547.05
1981	460	477.41
1982	376	396.28
1983	424	418.46
1984	361	372.49
1985	318	328.90
1986	368	360.18
1987	448	430.44
1988	438	436.49
1989	383	393.70
1990	385	386.74
1991	363	367.75
1992	345	349.55
1993	361	358.71
1994	387	381.34
1995	385	384.27

Time Series: Descriptive Analyses, Models, and Forecasting

b. The plot of the two series is:

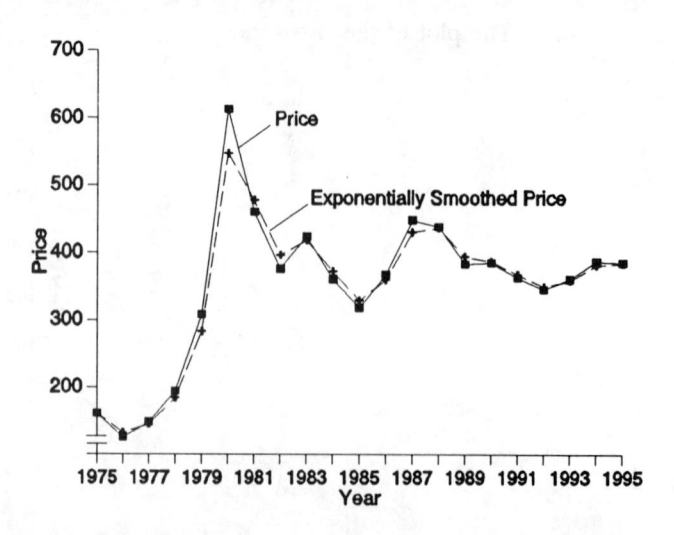

14.21 a. The exponentially smoothed imports/exports for the first period is equal to the imports/exports that period. For the rest of the time periods, the exponentially smoothed imports/exports is found by multiplying $w = .1$ times the imports/exports for that time period and adding to that $(1 - .1)$ times the value of the exponentially smoothed imports/exports figure of the previous time period. The exponentially smoothed imports/exports for the second time period is $.1(1835) + (1 - .1)(2212) = 2174.3$. The rest of the values are shown in the table.

The same procedure is followed for $w = .9$. The exponentially smoothed imports/exports for the second time period is $.9(1835) + (1 - .9)(2212) = 1872.7$. The rest of the values are shown in the table.

Year	Imports/ Exports	$w = .1$ Exponentially Smoothed Series	$w = .9$ Exponentially Smoothed Series
1984	2212	2212.00	2212.00
1985	1835	2174.30	1872.70
1986	2909	2247.77	2805.37
1987	3512	2374.19	3441.34
1988	3348	2471.57	3357.33
1989	2749	2499.32	2809.83
1990	3470	2596.38	3403.98
1991	4195	2756.25	4115.90
1992	4860	2966.62	4785.59
1993	4901	3160.06	4889.46

b. The plot of the three series is:

The smoothed series using $w = .9$ is more like the original series. This is because the original series is getting a weight of .9 for each time period while the previous smoothed value has a weight of only .1.

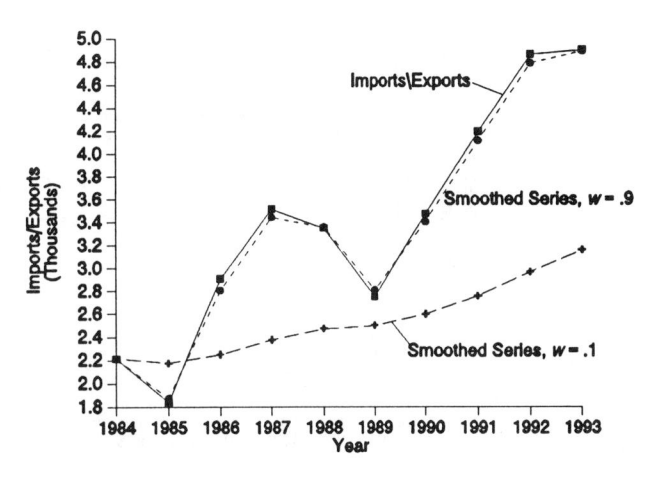

14.23 a. To compute the missing exponentially smoothed value, we follow these steps:

$E_1 = Y_1 = 1160$

$E_i = wY_i + (1 - w)E_{i-1}$ for $i = 2, 3, \ldots, 11$
$E_4 = .6(2020) + (1 - .6)(1746.92) = 1910.77$
$E_6 = .6(1292) + (1 - .6)(1811.31) = 1499.72$
etc.

The values are listed in the table:

Year	Housing Units Started	Exponentially Smoothed $w = .6$
1975	1160	1160.00
1976	1538	1386.80
1977	1987	1746.92
1978	2020	1910.77
1979	1745	1811.31
1980	1292	1499.72
1981	1084	1250.29
1982	1062	1137.32
1983	1703	1476.73
1984	1750	1640.69
1985	1742	1701.48
1986	1805	1763.59
1987	1620	1677.44
1988	1488	1563.77
1989	1376	1451.11
1990	1193	1296.24
1991	1014	1126.90
1992	1200	1170.76
1993	1288	1241.10
1994	1457	1370.64
1995	1354	1360.66

Time Series: Descriptive Analyses, Models, and Forecasting

b.

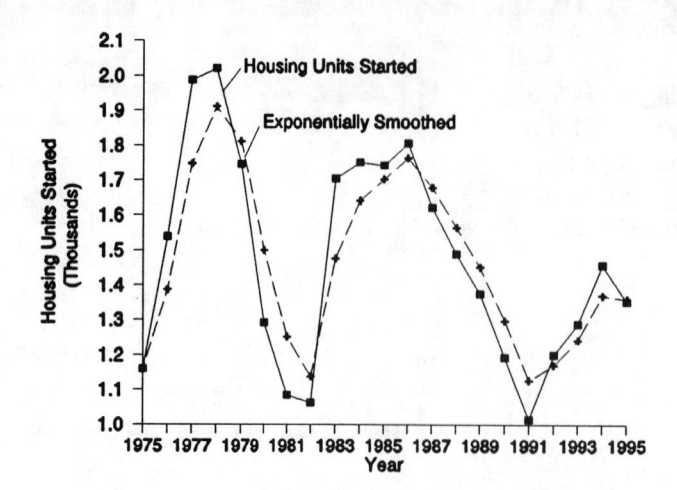

c. The forecast for 1995 is $F_{1995} = E_{1994} = 1370.64$

14.25 To compute the exponentially smoothed values, use the following:

$$E_1 = Y_1$$
$$E_i = wY_i + (1 - w)E_{i-1} \text{ for } i = 2, 3, \ldots$$

With $w = .3$,

$$E_1 = Y_1 = 133$$
$$E_2 = .3(137) + (1 - .3)(131) = 134.20$$
$$E_3 = .3(141) + (1 - .3)(134.2) = 136.24 \text{ etc.}$$

With $w = .7$,

$$E_1 = Y_1 = 133$$
$$E_2 = .7(137) + (1 - .7)(133) = 135.80$$
$$E_3 = .7(141) + (1 - .7)(135.80) = 139.44 \text{ etc.}$$

The rest of the values are found in the table:

Year	Beer Production	Exponentially Smoothed Value $w = .3$	Exponentially Smoothed Value $w = .7$
1970	133	133.00	133.00
1971	137	134.20	135.80
1972	141	136.24	139.44
1973	149	140.07	146.13
1974	156	144.85	153.04
1975	161	149.69	158.61
1976	164	153.99	162.38
1977	171	159.09	168.42
1978	179	165.06	175.82
1979	184	170.74	181.55
1980	194	177.72	190.26
1981	194	182.60	192.88
1982	196	186.62	195.06
1983	195	189.14	195.02
1984	192	190.00	192.91
1985	194	191.20	193.67
1986	194	192.04	193.90
1987	196	193.23	195.37
1988	197	194.36	196.51
1989	198	195.45	197.55
1990	202	197.42	200.67
1991	204	199.39	203.00
1992	202		
1993	202		
1994	203		

$F_{1995} = E_{1991} = 199.39$ for $w = .3$
$\phantom{F_{1995} = E_{1991} = {}} 203.00$ for $w = .7$

14.27 First, we compute the Holt-Winters values for the years 1980–1994.

With $w = .3$ and $v = .5$,

$E_2 = Y_2 = 114.6$
$E_3 = wY_3 + (1 - w)(E_2 + T_2) = .3(126.5) + (1 - .3)(114.6 + 9.9) = 125.10$

$T_2 = Y_2 - Y_1 = 114.6 - 104.7 = 9.9$
$T_3 = v(E_3 - E_2) + (1 - v)T_2 = .5(125.10 - 114.6) + (1 - .5)9.9 = 10.20$

The rest of the E_t's and T_t's appear in the table that follows.

Time Series: Descriptive Analyses, Models, and Forecasting

			Holt-Winters Model 1		Holt-Winters Model 2	
Year	Quarter	S&P500	$E(w = .3)$	$T(v=.5)$	$E(w = .7)$	$T(v=.5)$
1980	I	104.7				
	II	114.6	114.60	9.90	114.60	9.90
	III	126.5	125.10	10.20	125.90	10.60
	IV	133.5	134.76	9.93	134.40	9.55
1981	I	133.2	141.24	8.21	136.42	5.79
	II	132.3	144.30	5.63	135.27	2.32
	III	118.3	140.45	0.89	124.09	−4.43
	IV	123.8	136.07	−1.74	122.56	−2.98
1982	I	110.8	127.27	−5.27	113.43	−6.05
	II	109.7	118.31	−7.12	109.00	−5.24
	III	122.4	114.56	−5.44	116.81	1.28
	IV	139.4	118.20	−0.89	133.01	8.74
1983	I	151.9	127.69	4.29	148.85	12.29
	II	166.4	142.31	9.46	164.82	14.13
	III	167.2	156.39	11.77	170.73	10.02
	IV	164.4	167.04	11.21	169.30	4.30
1984	I	157.4	171.99	8.08	162.26	−1.37
	II	153.1	171.98	4.03	155.44	−4.10
	III	166.1	173.04	2.55	161.67	1.07
	IV	164.5	172.26	0.88	163.97	1.68
1985	I	179.4	175.02	1.82	175.28	6.49
	II	188.9	180.46	3.63	186.76	8.99
	III	184.1	184.09	3.63	187.60	4.91
	IV	207.3	193.60	6.57	202.86	10.09
1986	I	232.3	209.81	11.39	226.50	16.86
	II	245.3	228.43	15.00	244.72	17.54
	III	238.3	241.89	14.23	245.49	9.16
	IV	248.6	253.87	13.11	250.41	7.04
1987	I	292.5	274.63	16.93	281.99	19.31
	II	301.4	294.52	18.41	301.37	19.34
	III	318.7	314.66	19.28	319.30	18.64
	IV	241.0	306.05	5.34	270.08	−15.29
1988	I	265.7	297.68	−1.52	262.43	−11.47
	II	270.7	288.53	−5.34	264.78	−4.56
	III	268.0	278.63	−7.62	265.66	−1.84
	IV	276.5	272.66	−6.79	272.70	2.60
1989	I	292.7	273.92	−2.77	287.48	8.69
	II	323.7	286.91	5.11	315.44	18.33
	III	347.3	308.61	13.40	343.24	23.06
	IV	348.6	329.99	17.39	353.91	16.87
1990	I	338.5	344.72	16.06	348.18	5.57
	II	360.4	360.66	16.00	358.41	7.90
	III	315.4	358.29	6.81	330.67	−9.92
	IV	328.8	354.21	1.37	326.39	−7.10
1991	I	372.3	360.60	3.88	356.39	11.45
	II	378.3	368.62	5.95	375.16	15.11
	III	387.2	378.36	7.84	388.12	14.03
	IV	388.5	386.89	8.19	392.60	9.25

1992	I	407.3	398.75	10.02	405.67	11.16
	II	408.27	408.62	9.95	410.84	8.17
	III	418.48	418.54	9.93	418.64	7.98
	IV	435.64	430.62	11.01	432.93	11.14
1993	I	450.2	444.20	12.29	448.36	13.28
	II	448.1	453.98	11.03	452.16	8.54
	III	459.2	463.27	10.16	459.65	8.02
	IV	466.0	471.20	9.05	466.50	7.43
1994	I	463.8	475.31	6.58	466.84	3.89
	II	454.8	473.77	2.52	459.58	−1.69
	III	467.0	473.50	1.12	464.27	1.50
	IV	455.2	468.80	−1.79	458.37	−2.20
1995	I	493.2				
	II	539.4				
	III	578.8				
	IV	614.6				
1996	I	645.5				
	II	670.63				
	III	687.31				
	IV	740.74				

The forecasts for the four quarters in 1996 are:

$F_{1996,I} = F_{t+5} = E_t + 5T_t = 468.8 + 5(-1.79) = 459.85$
$F_{1996,II} = F_{t+6} = E_t + 6T_t = 468.8 + 6(-1.79) = 458.06$
$F_{1996,III} = F_{t+7} = E_t + 7T_t = 468.8 + 7(-1.79) = 456.27$
$F_{1996,IV} = F_{t+8} = E_t + 8T_t = 468.8 + 8(-1.79) = 454.48$

First, we compute the Holt-Winters values for the years 1980–1994.

With $w = .7$ and $v = .5$,

$E_2 = Y_2 = 114.6$
$E_3 = wY_3 + (1 - w)(E_2 + T_2) = .7(126.5) + (1 - .7)(114.6 + 9.9) = 125.90$

$T_2 = Y_2 - Y_1 = 114.6 - 104.7 = 9.9$
$T_3 = v(E_3 - E_2) + (1 - v)T_2 = .5(125.9 - 114.6) + (1 - .5)9.9 = 10.60$

The rest of the E_t's and T_t's appear in the table above.

The forecasts for the four quarters in 1996 are:

$F_{1996,I} = F_{t+5} = E_t + 5T_t = 458.37 + 5(-2.20) = 447.37$
$F_{1996,II} = F_{t+6} = E_t + 6T_t = 458.37 + 6(-2.20) = 445.17$
$F_{1996,III} = F_{t+7} = E_t + 7T_t = 458.37 + 7(-2.20) = 442.97$
$F_{1996,IV} = F_{t+8} = E_t + 8T_t = 458.37 + 8(-2.20) = 440.77$

Time Series: Descriptive Analyses, Models, and Forecasting

14.29 a. We first compute the exponentially smoothed values $E_1, E_2, \ldots, E_t$ for 1994 through February 1996.

$$E_1 = Y_1 = 16.94$$

For $w = .5$,

$$E_2 = wY_2 + (1 - w)E_1 = .5(16.70) + (1 - .5)16.94 = 16.82$$
$$E_3 = wY_3 + (1 - w)E_2 = .5(18.75) + (1 - .5)16.82 = 17.79$$

The rest of the values appear in the table:

Year	Month	Tires	Exponentially Smoothed $w = .5$
1994	Jan	16.94	16.94
	Feb	16.70	16.82
	Mar	18.75	17.79
	Apr	17.23	17.51
	May	17.81	17.66
	Jun	17.39	17.52
	Jul	14.72	16.12
	Aug	16.53	16.33
	Sep	15.83	16.08
	Oct	17.77	16.92
	Nov	16.45	16.69
	Dec	15.00	15.84
1995	Jan	17.50	16.67
	Feb	17.52	17.10
	Mar	19.34	18.22
	Apr	17.89	18.05
	May	18.16	18.11
	Jun	17.91	18.01
	Jul	15.58	16.79
	Aug	19.25	18.02
	Sep	17.60	17.81
	Oct	18.66	18.24
	Nov	16.88	17.56
	Dec	13.83	15.69
1996	Jan	18.56	17.13
	Feb	17.73	17.43

b. The forecasts for March, April, May, and June are:

$$F_{1996,\text{Mar}} = F_{t+1} = E_t = 17.43$$
$$F_{1996,\text{Apr}} = F_{t+2} = E_t = 17.43$$
$$F_{1996,\text{May}} = F_{t+3} = E_t = 17.43$$
$$F_{1996,\text{Jun}} = F_{t+4} = E_t = 17.43$$

c. The exponentially smoothed forecasts are appropriate only when the trend and seasonal components are relatively insignificant.

14.31 a. From Exercise 14.24a, the forecasts for 1992–1994 using $w = .3$ are:

$$F_{1992} = 199.39$$
$$F_{1993} = 199.39$$
$$F_{1994} = 199.39$$

The errors are the difference between the actual values and the predicted values. Thus, the errors are:

$$Y_{1992} - F_{1992} = 202 - 199.39 = 2.61$$
$$Y_{1993} - F_{1993} = 202 - 199.39 = 2.61$$
$$Y_{1994} - F_{1994} = 203 - 199.39 = 3.61$$

b. From Exercise 14.24 a, the forecasts for 1992–1994 using $w = .7$ are:

$$F_{1992} = 203.00$$
$$F_{1993} = 203.00$$
$$F_{1994} = 203.00$$

The errors are the difference between the actual values and the predicted values. Thus, the errors are:

$$Y_{1992} - F_{1992} = 202 - 203.00 = -1.00$$
$$Y_{1993} - F_{1993} = 202 - 203.00 = -1.00$$
$$Y_{1994} - F_{1994} = 203 - 203.00 = 0.00$$

c. For the smoothed forecasts using $w = .3$,

$$\text{MAD} = \frac{\sum |F_t - Y_t|}{N} = \frac{|199.39 - 202| + |199.39 - 202| + |199.39 - 203|}{3}$$
$$= \frac{8.83}{3} = 2.943$$

d. For the smoothed forecasts using $w = .7$,

$$\text{MAD} = \frac{\sum |F_t - Y_t|}{N} = \frac{|203 - 202| + |203 - 202| + |203 - 203|}{3} = \frac{2}{3} = 0.667$$

e. For the smoothed forecasts using $w = .3$,

$$\text{RMSE} = \sqrt{\frac{\sum (F_t - Y_t)^2}{N}} = \sqrt{\frac{(-2.61)^2 + (-2.61)^2 + (-3.61)^2}{3}} = 2.981$$

f. For the smoothed forecasts using $w = .7$,

$$\text{RMSE} = \sqrt{\frac{\sum (F_t - Y_t)^2}{N}} = \sqrt{\frac{1^2 + 1^2 + 0^2}{3}} = .816$$

14.33 a. We first compute the exponentially smoothed values $E_1, E_2, \ldots, E_t$ for 1993 through 1995.

$$E_1 = Y_1 = 30,100$$

Time Series: Descriptive Analyses, Models, and Forecasting

For $w = .8$,

$$E_2 = wY_2 + (1 - w)E_1 = .8(31,340) + (1 - .8)30,100 = 31,092$$
$$E_3 = wY_3 + (1 - w)E_2 = .8(33,467) + (1 - .8)31,092 = 32,992$$

The rest of the values appear in the table.

Year	Tourists	Exponentially Smoothed $w = .8$	Holt-Winters E_t $w = .8$	T_t $v = .7$
1980	30,100	30,100.00		
1981	31,340	31,092.00	31,340.00	1,240.00
1982	33,467	32,992.00	33,289.60	1,736.72
1983	34,018	33,812.80	34,219.66	1,172.06
1984	35,429	35,105.76	35,421.54	1,192.93
1985	36,748	36,419.55	36,721.30	1,267.71
1986	36,080	36,147.91	36,461.80	198.66
1987	36,974	36,808.78	36,911.29	374.24
1988	38,288	37,992.16	38,087.51	935.62
1989	45,100	43,678.43	43,884.63	4,338.67
1990	52,497	50,733.29	51,642.26	6,731.94
1991	55,041	54,179.46	55,707.64	4,865.35
1992	59,590	58,507.89	59,786.60	4,314.88
1993	61,300			
1994	61,314			
1995	60,000			

The forecasts for 1993–1995 are:

$$F_{1993} = F_{t+1} = E_t = 58,507.89$$
$$F_{1994} = F_{t+2} = E_t = 58,507.89$$
$$F_{1995} = F_{t+3} = E_t = 58,507.89$$

b. First, we compute the Holt-Winters values for the years 1993–1995.

With $w = .8$ and $v = .7$,

$$E_2 = Y_2 = 31,340$$
$$E_3 = wY_3 + (1 - w)(E_2 + T_2) = .8(33,467) + (1 - .8)(31,340 + 1,240)$$
$$= 33,289.60$$

$$T_2 = Y_2 - Y_1 = 31,340 - 30,100 = 1,240$$
$$T_3 = v(E_3 - E_2) + (1 - v)T_2 = .7(33,289.60 - 31,340) + (1 - .7)1,240 = 1,736.72$$

The rest of the E_t's and T_t's appear in the table in part a.

The forecasts for 1993–1995 are:

$$F_{1993} = F_{t+1} = E_t + T_t = 59,786.60 + 4,314.88 = 64,101.48$$
$$F_{1994} = F_{t+2} = E_t + 2T_t = 59,786.60 + 2(4,314.88) = 68,416.36$$
$$F_{1995} = F_{t+3} = E_t + 3T_t = 59,786.60 + 3(4,314.88) = 72,731.24$$

c. For the exponentially smoothed forecasts:

$$\text{MAD} = \frac{\sum |F_t - Y_t|}{N}$$

$$= \frac{|58,507.89 - 61,300| + |58,507.89 - 61,314| + |58,507.89 - 60,000|}{3}$$

$$= \frac{7,090.33}{3} = 2,363.443$$

$$\text{RMSE} = \sqrt{\frac{\sum (F_t - Y_t)^2}{N}} = \sqrt{\frac{(-2,792.11)^2 + (-2,806.11)^2 + (-1,492.11)^2}{3}}$$

$$= 2,442.439$$

For the Holt-Winters forecasts:

$$\text{MAD} = \frac{\sum |F_t - Y_t|}{N}$$

$$= \frac{|64,101.48 - 61,300| + |68,416.36 - 61,314| + |72,731.24 - 60,000|}{3}$$

$$= \frac{22,635.08}{3} = 7,545.027$$

$$\text{RMSE} = \sqrt{\frac{\sum (F_t - Y_t)^2}{N}} = \sqrt{\frac{(2,801.48)^2 + (7,102.36)^2 + (12,731.24)^2}{3}}$$

$$= 8,570.809$$

Based on the MAD and RMSE values, the exponentially smoothed forecasts are better than the Holt-Winters. Both the MAD and RMSE values for the exponentially smoothed forecasts are less than the MAD and RMSE values for the Holt-Winters forecasts.

14.35 a. For the forecasts using $w = .3$ and $v = .5$,

$$\text{MAD} = \frac{\sum |F_t - Y_t|}{N}$$

$$= \frac{|459.85 - 645.5| + |458.06 - 670.63| + |456.27 - 687.31| + |454.48 - 740.74|}{4}$$

$$= \frac{915.52}{4} = 228.88$$

$$\text{RMSE} = \sqrt{\frac{\sum (F_t - Y_t)^2}{N}} = \sqrt{\frac{(-185.65)^2 + (-212.57)^2 + (-231.04)^2 + (-286.26)^2}{4}}$$

$$= 231.828$$

b. For the forecasts using $w = .7$ and $v = .5$,

$$\text{MAD} = \frac{\sum |F_t - Y_t|}{N}$$

$$= \frac{|447.37 - 645.5| + |445.17 - 670.63| + |442.97 - 687.31| + |440.77 - 740.74|}{4}$$

$$= \frac{967.90}{4} = 241.975$$

Time Series: Descriptive Analyses, Models, and Forecasting

$$\text{RMSE} = \sqrt{\frac{\sum(F_t - Y_t)^2}{N}} = \sqrt{\frac{(-198.13)^2 + (-225.46)^2 + (-244.34)^2 + (-299.97)^2}{4}}$$
$$= 244.832$$

    c.   Based on the MAD and RMSE values, the Holt-Winters forecasts using $w = .3$ and $v = .5$ are better than the forecasts using $w = .7$ and $v = .5$. Both the MAD and RMSE values for the Holt-Winters forecasts using $w = .3$ and $v = .5$ are less than the MAD and RMSE values for the forecasts using $w = .7$ and $v = .5$.

14.39 a.   The estimates of the parameters in the model, $E(Y_t) = \beta_0 + \beta_1 t$, are

        $\hat{\beta}_0 = 24.6975$ The price is estimated to be 24.6975 for $t = 0$ or for 1979.
        $\hat{\beta}_1 = .091029$ The price is estimated to increase by .091 for each additional year.

    b.   The forecast for 1996 is:

        Using $t = 17$, $\hat{Y}_{1996} = 24.6975 + .091029(17) = 26.2450$

    The forecast for 1997 is:

        Using $t = 18$, $\hat{Y}_{1997} = 24.6975 + .091029(18) = 26.3360$

Yes, these agree with the predicted values on the printout.

    c.   From the printout, the 95% forecast intervals are:

        1996   (22.6193, 29.8707)
        1997   (22.6358, 30.0363)

We are 95% confident that the actual price in 1996 will be between 22.6193 and 29.870. We are 95% confident that the actual price in 1997 will be between 22.6358 and 30.0363.

14.41 a.   From the printout:

        $\hat{\beta}_0 = 236.989$. The personal income in 1979 is estimated to be 236.989.
        $\hat{\beta}_1 = 23.1824$. For each additional year, the personal income is estimated to increase by 23.1824.

    b.   To determine the model fit, we test:

        $H_0: \beta = 0$
        $H_a: \beta \neq 0$

The test statistic is $t = 46.06$ (from printout).

The p-value is 0.000. Since the p-value is so small, H_0 will be rejected for any reasonable value of α. There is sufficient evidence that the model has an adequate fit.

    c.   The 95% prediction interval for 1994 is (721.71, 777.74). The actual value is 716. The prediction interval does not contain the actual value.

The 95% prediction interval for 1995 is (755.16, 812.66). The actual value is 760. The prediction interval does contain the actual value.

d. There are basically two problems with using simple linear regression for predicting time series data. First, we must predict values of the time series for values of time outside the observed range. We observe data for time periods $1, 2, \ldots, t$ and use the regression model to predict values of the time series for $t + 1, t + 2, \ldots$. The second problem is that simple linear regression does not allow for any cyclical effects such as seasonal trends.

14.43 a. The model that describes the variation in the cement shipments that includes both trend and seasonal components is:

$$E(Y_t) = \beta_0 + \beta_1 t + \beta_2 x_1 + \beta_3 x_2 + \beta_4 x_3 + \beta_5 x_4 + \beta_6 x_5 + \beta_7 x_6 + \beta_8 x_7 + \beta_9 x_8 + \beta_{10} x_9 + \beta_{11} x_{10} + \beta_{12} x_{11}$$

where $t =$ time and

$$x_1 = \begin{cases} 1 & \text{if January} \\ 0 & \text{otherwise} \end{cases} \quad x_2 = \begin{cases} 1 & \text{if February} \\ 0 & \text{otherwise} \end{cases} \quad x_3 = \begin{cases} 1 & \text{if March} \\ 0 & \text{otherwise} \end{cases}$$

$$x_4 = \begin{cases} 1 & \text{if April} \\ 0 & \text{otherwise} \end{cases} \quad x_5 = \begin{cases} 1 & \text{if May} \\ 0 & \text{otherwise} \end{cases} \quad x_6 = \begin{cases} 1 & \text{if June} \\ 0 & \text{otherwise} \end{cases}$$

$$x_7 = \begin{cases} 1 & \text{if July} \\ 0 & \text{otherwise} \end{cases} \quad x_8 = \begin{cases} 1 & \text{if August} \\ 0 & \text{otherwise} \end{cases} \quad x_9 = \begin{cases} 1 & \text{if September} \\ 0 & \text{otherwise} \end{cases}$$

$$x_{10} = \begin{cases} 1 & \text{if October} \\ 0 & \text{otherwise} \end{cases} \quad x_{11} = \begin{cases} 1 & \text{if November} \\ 0 & \text{otherwise} \end{cases}$$

b. Using SAS, the output is:

```
Model: MODEL1
Dependent Variable: Y

                    Analysis of Variance

                       Sum of         Mean
Source         DF     Squares        Square      F Value    Prob>F

Model          12  63199177.667   5266598.1389    9.771     0.0003
Error          11   5929116.8333   539010.62121
C Total        23  69128294.5

   Root MSE       734.17343     R-square       0.9142
   Dep Mean      6912.25000     Adj R-sq       0.8207
   C.V.            10.62134

                    Parameter Estimates

                Parameter      Standard      T for H0:
Variable   DF    Estimate        Error      Parameter=0    Prob > |T|

INTERCEP    1   6060.250000   686.75635677      8.824       0.0001
T           1    -67.902778    24.97708721     -2.719       0.0200
X1          1   -799.930556   783.89863017     -1.020       0.3294
X2          1   -769.527778   775.49733061     -0.992       0.3424
X3          1    465.875000   767.81694886      0.607       0.5563
X4          1   1629.277778   760.87931625      2.141       0.0555
X5          1   2660.180556   754.70491625      3.525       0.0048
X6          1   2878.083333   749.31261640      3.841       0.0027
X7          1   2939.486111   744.71940579      3.947       0.0023
X8          1   3568.388889   740.94014561      4.816       0.0005
X9          1   2697.791667   737.98734080      3.656       0.0038
X10         1   4342.694444   735.87094028      5.901       0.0001
X11         1    797.097222   734.59817322      1.085       0.3011
```

Obs	MONTH	Dep Var Y	Predict Value	Std Err Predict	Lower95% Predict	Upper95% Predict	Residual
1	Jan	5571.0	5192.4	540.337	3186.0	7198.8	378.6
2	Feb	5105.0	5154.9	540.337	3148.5	7161.3	-49.9167
3	Mar	6667.0	6322.4	540.337	4316.0	8328.8	344.6
4	Apr	7343.0	7417.9	540.337	5411.5	9424.3	-74.9167
5	May	8447.0	8380.9	540.337	6374.5	10387.3	66.0833
6	Jun	8748.0	8530.9	540.337	6524.5	10537.3	217.1
7	Jul	8205.0	8524.4	540.337	6518.0	10530.8	-319.4
8	Aug	9206.0	9085.4	540.337	7079.0	11091.8	120.6
9	Sep	7904.0	8146.9	540.337	6140.5	10153.3	-242.9
10	Oct	8676.0	9723.9	540.337	7717.5	11730.3	-1047.9
11	Nov	7184.0	6110.4	540.337	4104.0	8116.8	1073.6
12	Dec	4780.0	5245.4	540.337	3239.0	7251.8	-465.4
13	Jan	3999.0	4377.6	540.337	2371.2	6384.0	-378.6
14	Feb	4390.0	4340.1	540.337	2333.7	6346.5	49.9167
15	Mar	5163.0	5507.6	540.337	3501.2	7514.0	-344.6
16	Apr	6678.0	6603.1	540.337	4596.7	8609.5	74.9167
17	May	7500.0	7566.1	540.337	5559.7	9572.5	-66.0833
18	Jun	7499.0	7716.1	540.337	5709.7	9722.5	-217.1
19	Jul	8029.0	7709.6	540.337	5703.2	9716.0	319.4
20	Aug	8150.0	8270.6	540.337	6264.2	10277.0	-120.6
21	Sep	7575.0	7332.1	540.337	5325.7	9338.5	242.9
22	Oct	9957.0	8909.1	540.337	6902.7	10915.5	1047.9
23	Nov	4222.0	5295.6	540.337	3289.2	7302.0	-1073.6
24	Dec	4896.0	4430.6	540.337	2424.2	6437.0	465.4
25	Jan	.	3562.8	686.756	1350.1	5775.4	.
26	Feb	.	3525.3	686.756	1312.6	5737.9	.
27	Mar	.	4692.8	686.756	2480.1	6905.4	.

Sum of Residuals 0
Sum of Squared Residuals 5929116.8333
Predicted Resid SS (Press) 28224556.165

The fitted model is:

$$\hat{Y}_t = 6060.25 - 67.90t - 799.93x_1 - 769.53x_2 + 465.88x_3 + 1629.28x_4 + 2660.18x_5 \\ + 2878.08x_6 + 2939.49x_7 + 3568.39x_8 + 2697.79x_9 + 4342.69x_{10} + 797.10x_{11}$$

c. The forecasts for January, February, and March 1992 are found at the bottom of the printout above. They are:

January: 3,562.8
February: 3,525.3
March: 4,692.8

d. For the fitted regression model:

$$\text{MAD} = \frac{\sum |F_t - Y_t|}{N}$$

$$= \frac{|3{,}562.8 - 4{,}566| + |3{,}525.3 - 4{,}614| + |4{,}692.8 - 5{,}774|}{3}$$

$$= \frac{3{,}173.1}{3} = 1{,}057.7$$

14.45 a. Using MINITAB, the output is:

```
The regression equation is
Policies = 377 + 0.495 Time

Predictor      Coef      Stdev    t-ratio      p
Constant    377.149      6.075      62.08  0.000
Time         0.4948     0.4252       1.16  0.257

s = 14.42     R-sq = 5.8%     R-sq(adj) = 1.5%
```

```
Analysis of Variance
SOURCE       DF        SS         MS          F       p
Regression    1       281.5      281.5       1.35   0.257
Error        22      4573.8      207.9
Total        23      4855.3

    Fit   Stdev.Fit       95% C.I.           95% P.I.
  389.52     6.08    ( 376.92, 402.12)  ( 357.06, 421.97)

  390.01     6.45    ( 376.63, 403.39)  ( 357.25, 422.78)
```

The fitted model is $\hat{Y} = 377.149 + .4948t$.

b. The forecasted values for 1994 and 1995 are at the bottom of the printout above:

1994:   389.52
1995:   390.01

c. From the printout, the 95% prediction intervals are:

1994:   (357.06, 421.97)
1995:   (357.25, 422.78)

14.47 a. $d = 3.9$ indicates the residuals are very strongly negatively autocorrelated.

b. $d = .2$ indicates the residuals are very strongly positively autocorrelated.

c. $d = 1.99$ indicates the residuals are probably uncorrelated.

14.49 a. The plot of the residuals is:

There is a tendency for the residuals to have long positive runs and negative runs. Residuals 4 through 14 are positive, while residuals 15 through 26 are negative. This indicates the error terms are correlated.

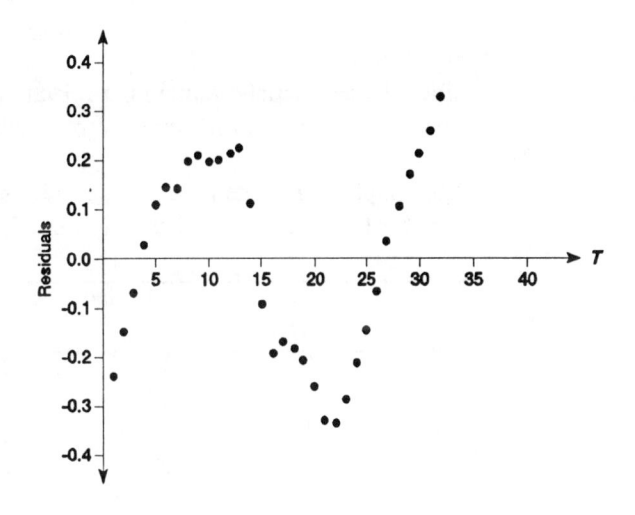

b. From the printout, the Durbin-Watson d is $d = .122$.

To determine if the time series residuals are autocorrelated, we test:

H_0: No first-order autocorrelation of residuals
H_a: Positive or negative first-order autocorrelation of residuals

The test statistic is $d = .122$.

Time Series: Descriptive Analyses, Models, and Forecasting

For $\alpha = .10$, the rejection region is $d < d_{L,\alpha/2} = d_{L,.05} = 1.37$ or $(4 - d) < d_{L,.05} = 1.37$. The value $d_{L,.05}$ is found in Table XIV, Appendix B, with $k = 1$, $n = 32$, and $\alpha = .10$.

Since the observed value of the test statistic falls in the rejection region ($d = .122 < 1.37$), H_0 is rejected. There is sufficient evidence to indicate the time series residuals are autocorrelated at $\alpha = .10$.

c. We must assume the residuals are normally distributed.

14.51 a. The least squares line is $\hat{Y}_t = 42.8678 + .1639t$

$\hat{\beta}_0 = 42.8678$ The estimated mean sales in December 1993 is 42.8678 million dollars.
$\hat{\beta}_1 = .1639$ The estimated increase in mean sales for each month is .1639 million dollars.

b. Root MSE = 4.65119. We would expect to predict annual sales to within $\pm 2s$ or $\pm 2(4.65119)$ or ± 9.30238 of its actual value.

c. To determine if the residuals are autocorrelated, we test:

H_0: No first-order autocorrelation
H_a: Positive or negative first-order autocorrelated

The test statistic is $d = .757$.

For $\alpha = .10$, the rejection region is $d < d_{L,\alpha/2} = d_{L,.05} = 1.27$ or $4 - d < d_{L,.05} = 1.27$. From Table XIV, Appendix B, for $k = 1$, $n = 24$ and $\alpha/2 = .05$.

Since the test statistic falls in the rejection region ($d = .757 < 1.27$), H_0 is rejected. There is sufficient evidence to indicate the residuals are autocorrelated at $\alpha = .10$.

14.53 a. The simple composite index is found by summing the three steel prices, dividing by 64.25, the sum for the base period, 1980, and multiplying by 100. The values appear in the table.

Year	Cold Rolled Price	Hot Rolled Price	Galvanized Price	Price Total	Index
1980	21.91	18.46	23.88	64.25	100.00
1981	23.90	20.15	26.88	70.93	110.40
1982	24.65	20.80	26.75	72.20	112.37
1983	26.36	22.23	28.43	77.02	119.88
1984	28.15	23.75	30.30	82.20	127.94
1985	28.15	23.75	30.30	82.20	127.94
1986	25.65	21.15	30.30	77.10	120.00
1987	27.38	21.64	30.49	79.51	123.75
1988	28.15	21.50	31.05	80.70	125.60
1989	28.15	21.50	32.48	82.13	127.83
1990	25.37	22.25	33.55	81.17	126.33
1991	25.75	22.88	35.35	83.98	130.71
1992	24.03	19.13	30.88	74.04	115.24
1993	23.83	17.25	30.90	71.98	112.03
1994	25.70	17.25	32.24	75.19	117.03

b. This is a price index because it is based on the price of steel rather than quantity.

c. In order to compute the Laspeyres index, we need quantities of steel for the base year 1980. To compute the Paasche index, we need quantities of steel for each of the years.

14.55 a. To compute the Laspeyres index, multiply the price for each year by the quantity for each of the items for 1990, sum the products for the four items, divide by 27.4 (the sum for the base period 1990), and multiply by 100. The Laspeyres index is:

Year	Total	Laspeyres Index
1990	27.40	100.00
1991	26.09	95.22
1992	27.07	98.80
1993	29.07	106.09
1994	29.21	106.61

b. From 1990 to 1994, the "basket" of foods increased by $106.61 - 100 = 6.61\%$.

14.57 a. We first calculate the exponentially smoothed values for 1980–1995.

$$E_1 = Y_1 = 56.50$$
$$E_2 = .8Y_1 + (1 - .8)E_1 = .8(27.0) + .2(56.50) = 32.90$$
$$E_3 = .8Y_2 + (1 - .8)E_2 = .8(38.75) + .2(32.90) = 37.58$$

The rest of the values appear in the table.

Year	Closing Price	Exponentially Smoothed Value ($w = .8$)
1980	56.50	56.50
1981	27.00	32.90
1982	38.75	37.58
1983	45.25	43.72
1984	41.75	42.14
1985	68.37	63.12
1986	45.62	49.12
1987	48.02	48.24
1988	48.01	48.06
1989	64.03	60.84
1990	45.00	48.17
1991	68.07	64.09
1992	30.03	36.84
1993	29.05	30.61
1994	32.05	31.76
1995	41.05	39.19

The forecasts for 1996 and 1997 are:

$$F_{1996} = F_{t+1} = E_t = 39.19$$
$$F_{1997} = F_{t+2} = F_{t+1} = 39.19$$

The expected gain is $F_{1997} - Y_{1995} = 39.19 - 41.05 = -1.86$.

b. We first calculate the Holt-Winters values for 1980–1995.

Time Series: Descriptive Analyses, Models, and Forecasting

For $w = .8$ and $v = .5$,

$$E_2 = Y_2 = 27.00$$
$$E_3 = .8Y_3 + (1 - .8)(E_2 + T_2)$$
$$= .8(38.75) + .2(27 - 29.50) = 30.50$$

$$T_2 = Y_2 - Y_1 = 27.00 - 56.50 = -29.50$$
$$T_3 = .5(E_3 - E_2) + (1 - .5)(T_2)$$
$$= .5(30.50 - 27.00) + .5(-29.50) = -13.00$$

The rest of the values appear in the table.

Year	Closing Price	Holt-Winters $w = .8$ E_t	$v = .5$ T_t
1980	56.50		
1981	27.00	27.00	−29.5
1982	38.75	30.50	−13.00
1983	45.25	39.70	−1.90
1984	41.75	40.96	−0.32
1985	68.37	62.82	10.77
1986	45.62	51.22	−0.42
1987	48.02	48.58	−1.53
1988	48.01	47.82	−1.14
1989	64.03	60.56	5.80
1990	45.00	49.27	−2.74
1991	68.07	63.76	5.87
1992	30.03	37.95	−9.97
1993	29.05	28.84	−9.54
1994	32.05	29.50	−4.44
1995	41.05	37.85	1.96

The forecasts for 1996 and 1997 are:

$$F_{1996} = F_{t+1} = E_t + T_t = 37.85 + 1.96 = 39.81$$
$$F_{1997} = F_{t+2} = E_t + 2T_t = 37.85 + 2(1.96) = 41.77$$

The expected gain is $F_{1997} - Y_{1995} = 41.77 - 41.05 = .72$

14.59 a. To compute the simple index for Canada, divide each Canadian production value by the 1986 value, 56,965, and then multiply by 100. To compute the simple index for Mexico, divide each Mexican production value by the 1986 value, 23,553, and then multiply by 100. The values for the indices are in the table:

Year	Canada	Canada Simple Index	Mexico	Mexico Simple Index
1984	42,800	75.13	23,707	100.65
1985	48,239	84.68	27,403	116.35
1986	56,965	100.00	23,553	100.00
1987	51,682	90.73	23,636	100.35
1988	35,788	62.82	21,067	89.45
1989	48,402	84.97	21,429	90.98
1990	56,797	99.71	25,570	108.56
1991	53,850	94.53	23,616	100.27
1992	49,500	86.90	26,976	114.53
1993	52,241	91.71	25,825	109.65

b. The time series plot is:

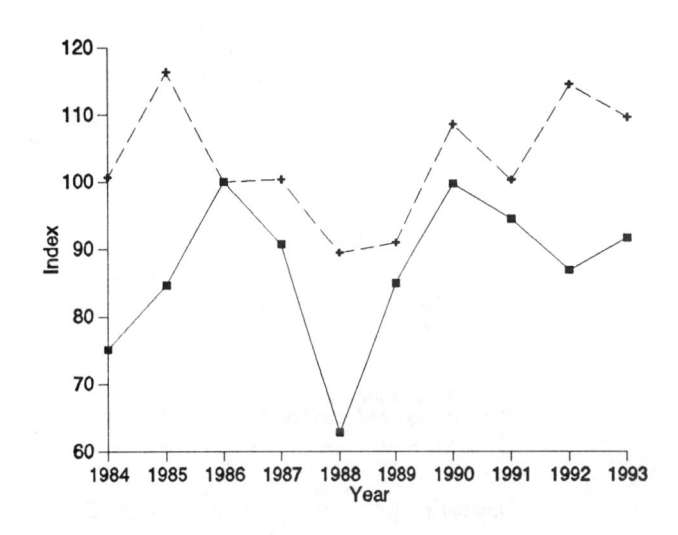

c. The Canadian production values of cereals in 1984 and 1985 were below the production value in 1986, while the Mexican production values in 1984 and 1985 were at or above the 1986 value. The Canadian production values in 1987 and 1988 were well below the 1986 values. The Mexican production values in 1987 and 1988 were at or slightly below the 1986 value. The Mexican production levels did not vary as much as the Canadian.

14.61 a. The following model is fit: $E(Y_t) = \beta_0 + \beta_1 t$. The SAS output is:

```
Model: MODEL1
Dependent Variable: Y

                    Analysis of Variance

                       Sum of         Mean
Source        DF      Squares       Square      F Value      Prob>F

Model          1  119685122.86  119685122.86    8368.142     0.0001
Error         62     886753.28280    14302.47230
C Total       63  120571876.14

       Root MSE      119.59294      R-square     0.9926
       Dep Mean     4799.44844      Adj R-sq     0.9925
       C.V.            2.49181
```

Time Series: Descriptive Analyses, Models, and Forecasting

Parameter Estimates

Variable	DF	Parameter Estimate	Standard Error	T for H0: Parameter=0	Prob > |T|
INTERCEP	1	2393.550893	30.25207365	79.120	0.0001
T	1	74.027617	0.80924354	91.478	0.0001

Obs	Dep Var Y	Predict Value	Std Err Predict	Lower95% Predict	Upper95% Predict	Residual
1	2650.1	2467.6	29.551	2221.3	2713.8	182.5
2	2643.9	2541.6	28.856	2295.7	2787.5	102.3
3	2705.3	2615.6	28.167	2370.0	2861.2	89.6663
4	2832.9	2689.7	27.485	2444.4	2935.0	143.2
5	2953.5	2763.7	26.809	2518.7	3008.7	189.8
6	2993.0	2837.7	26.141	2593.0	3082.4	155.3
.	.	.	.	.	.	.
53	6235.9	6317.0	22.331	6073.8	6560.2	-81.1146
54	6299.9	6391.0	22.939	6147.6	6634.5	-91.1422
55	6359.2	6465.1	23.559	6221.4	6708.7	-105.9
56	6478.1	6539.1	24.189	6295.2	6783.0	-60.9974
57	6772.8	6613.1	24.831	6369.0	6857.3	159.7
58	6885.0	6687.2	25.482	6442.7	6931.6	197.8
59	6987.6	6761.2	26.141	6516.5	7005.9	226.4
60	7080.0	6835.2	26.809	6590.2	7080.2	244.8
61	7147.8	6909.2	27.485	6663.9	7154.5	238.6
62	7196.5	6983.3	28.167	6737.7	7228.9	213.2
63	7298.5	7057.3	28.856	6811.4	7303.2	241.2
64	7348.1	7131.3	29.551	6885.1	7377.6	216.8
65	.	7205.3	30.252	6958.8	7451.9	.
66	.	7279.4	30.958	7032.4	7526.3	.
67	.	7353.4	31.669	7106.1	7600.7	.
68	.	7427.4	32.385	7179.8	7675.1	.

Sum of Residuals   0
Sum of Squared Residuals 886753.2828
Predicted Resid SS (Press) 967038.6601

The estimated regression line is $\hat{Y}_t = 2393.5509 + 74.0276t$.

From the printout, the 1996 quarterly GDP forecasts are:

		Forecast	95% Lower Limit	95% Upper Limit
1991	Q1	7205.3	6958.8	7451.9
	Q2	7279.4	7032.4	7526.3
	Q3	7353.4	7106.1	7600.7
	Q4	7427.4	7179.8	7675.1

b. The following model is fit: $E(Y_t) = \beta_0 + \beta_1 t + \beta_2 Q_1 + \beta_3 Q_2 + \beta_4 Q_3$

where $Q_1 = \begin{cases} 1 \text{ if quarter 1} \\ 0 \text{ otherwise} \end{cases}$ $Q_2 = \begin{cases} 1 \text{ if quarter 2} \\ 0 \text{ otherwise} \end{cases}$ $Q_3 = \begin{cases} 1 \text{ if quarter 3} \\ 0 \text{ otherwise} \end{cases}$

The SAS printout is:

```
Model: MODEL1
Dependent Variable: Y
                           Analysis of Variance

                        Sum of        Mean
   Source        DF    Squares       Square       F Value      Prob>F

   Model          4  119686927.24  29921731.809   1994.897     0.0001
   Error         59     884948.90459   14999.13398
   C Total       63  120571876.14

        Root MSE        122.47095     R-square     0.9927
        Dep Mean       4799.44844     Adj R-sq     0.9922
        C.V.              2.55177

                          Parameter Estimates

                    Parameter     Standard     T for H0:
   Variable   DF    Estimate        Error      Parameter=0    Prob > |T|

   INTERCEP    1   2386.131562    41.64462590     57.297        0.0001
   T           1     74.044844     0.83023999     89.185        0.0001
   Q1          1     14.684531    43.37159708      0.339        0.7361
   Q2          1      7.864688    43.33184673      0.181        0.8566
   Q3          1      4.888594    43.30797900      0.113        0.9105

Durbin-Watson D            0.128
(For Number of Obs.)          64
1st Order Autocorrelation  0.891

        Dep Var    Predict    Std Err    Lower95%   Upper95%
   Obs     Y        Value     Predict    Predict    Predict     Residual

    1    2650.1    2474.9     39.469     2217.4     2732.3       175.2
    2    2643.9    2542.1     39.469     2284.6     2799.6       101.8
    3    2705.3    2613.2     39.469     2355.7     2870.6        92.1453
    4    2832.9    2682.3     39.469     2424.8     2939.8       150.6
    5    2953.5    2771.0     37.462     2514.8     3027.3       182.5
    6    2993.0    2838.3     37.462     2582.0     3094.5       154.7
    .      .         .          .          .          .            .
    .      .         .          .          .          .            .
    .      .         .          .          .          .            .
   53    6235.9    6325.2     35.652     6070.0     6580.4       -89.2928
   54    6299.9    6392.4     35.652     6137.2     6647.7       -92.5178
   55    6359.2    6463.5     35.652     6208.3     6718.7      -104.3
   56    6478.1    6532.6     35.652     6277.4     6787.9       -54.5428
   57    6772.8    6621.4     37.462     6365.1     6877.6       151.4
   58    6885.0    6688.6     37.462     6432.3     6944.9       196.4
   59    6987.6    6759.7     37.462     6503.4     7015.9       227.9
   60    7080.0    6828.8     37.462     6572.5     7085.1       251.2
   61    7147.8    6917.6     39.469     6660.1     7175.0       230.2
   62    7196.5    6984.8     39.469     6727.3     7242.3       211.7
   63    7298.5    7055.8     39.469     6798.4     7313.3       242.7
   64    7348.1    7125.0     39.469     6867.5     7382.5       223.1
   65       .      7213.7     41.645     6954.9     7472.6         .
   66       .      7281.0     41.645     7022.1     7539.8         .
   67       .      7352.0     41.645     7093.2     7610.9         .
   68       .      7421.2     41.645     7162.3     7680.0         .

Sum of Residuals                       0
Sum of Squared Residuals         884948.9046
Predicted Resid SS (Press)      1066341.7262
```

The fitted model is:

$$\hat{Y} = 2386.1316 + 74.0448t + 14.6845Q_1 + 7.8647Q_2 + 4.8886Q_3$$

To determine whether the data indicate a significant seasonal component, we test:

H_0: $\beta_2 = \beta_3 = \beta_4 = 0$
H_a: At least one $\beta_i \neq 0$, $i = 2, 3, 4$

Time Series: Descriptive Analyses, Models, and Forecasting

The test statistic is $F = \dfrac{(SSE_r - SSE_c)/(k - g)}{SSE_c/[n - (k + 1)]}$

$= \dfrac{(886,753.2828 - 884,948.90459)/(4 - 1)}{884,948.90459/[64 - (4 + 1)]} = \dfrac{601.4594333}{14,999.13397} = .040$

The rejection region requires $\alpha = .05$ in the upper tail of the F-distribution with numerator df $= k - g = 4 - 1 = 3$ and denominator df $= n - (k + 1) = 64 - (4 + 1) = 59$. From Table VIII, Appendix B, $F_{.05} \approx 2.76$. The rejection region is $F > 2.76$.

Since the observed value of the test statistic does not fall in the rejection ($F = .040 \ngtr 2.76$), H_0 is not rejected. There is insufficient evidence to indicate a seasonal component at $\alpha = .05$. This supports the assertion that the data have been seasonally adjusted.

c. Using the printout, the 1996 quarterly GDP forecasts are:

		Forecast
1991	Q_1	7213.7
	Q_2	7281.0
	Q_3	7352.0
	Q_4	7421.2

d. From the printout provided in part b, part of the residuals are reported. The Durbin-Watson d is .128 (from the printout).

To determine if the time series residuals are autocorrelated, we test:

H_0: No first-order autocorrelation of residuals
H_a: Positive or negative first-order autocorrelation of residuals

The test statistic is $d = .128$.

For $\alpha = .02$, the rejection region is $d < d_{L,\alpha/2} = d_{L,.01} = 1.31$ or $(4 - d) < d_{L,.01} = 1.31$. The value $d_{L,.01}$ is found in Table XIV, Appendix B, with $k = 4$, $n = 65$, and $\alpha = .02$.

Since the observed value of the test statistic falls in the rejection region ($d = .128 < 1.31$), H_0 is rejected. There is sufficient evidence to indicate the time series residuals are autocorrelated at $\alpha = .02$. (If we reject H_0 for $\alpha = .02$, we will reject H_0 for $\alpha = .05$).

14.63 a. The simple composite index is found by first summing the indexes at each time period. The sums are then divided by the sum for the base period, 1980, and multiplied by 100. The simple composite index value for 1980 is:

$\dfrac{130 + 84 + 98}{130 + 84 + 98} \times 100 = 100.00$

The rest of the values are computed in a similar way and are listed below:

Year	Index of Net Business Formation	Index of Industrial Production	Index of New Private Housing Units	Sum of Three Indices	Composite Index
1980	130	84	98	312	100.00
1981	125	85	102	312	100.00
1982	116	82	105	303	97.12
1983	118	85	108	311	99.68
1984	121	93	111	325	104.17
1985	121	94	115	330	105.77
1986	120	95	119	334	107.05
1987	121	102	123	346	110.90
1988	124	105	125	354	113.46
1989	125	108	128	361	115.71
1990	121	106	131	358	114.74
1991	115	106	133	354	113.46
1992	116	104	136	356	114.10
1993	121	108	140	369	118.27
1994	126	112	144	382	122.44

b. The simple index for each series is computed by dividing each value in the series by the value in the base period and then multiplying by 100. The simple index for the net business formation is found by dividing each value by 130 and multiplying by 100. The simple index for the industrial production is found by dividing each value by 84 and then multiplying by 100. The simple index for the new private housing units is found by dividing each value by 98 and then multiplying by 100. The values are found in the following table:

Year	Index of Net Business Formation	Simple Index	Index of Industrial Production	Simple Index	Index of New Private Housing Units	Simple Index
1980	130	100.00	84	100.00	98	100.00
1981	125	96.15	85	101.19	102	104.08
1982	116	89.23	82	97.62	105	107.14
1983	118	90.77	85	101.19	108	110.20
1984	121	93.08	93	110.71	111	113.27
1985	121	93.08	94	111.90	115	117.35
1986	120	92.31	95	113.10	119	121.43
1987	121	93.08	102	121.43	123	125.51
1988	124	95.38	105	125.00	125	127.55
1989	125	96.15	108	128.57	128	130.61
1990	121	93.08	106	126.19	131	133.67
1991	115	88.46	106	126.19	133	135.71
1992	116	89.23	104	123.81	136	138.78
1993	121	93.08	108	128.57	140	142.86
1994	126	96.92	112	133.33	144	146.94

Time Series: Descriptive Analyses, Models, and Forecasting

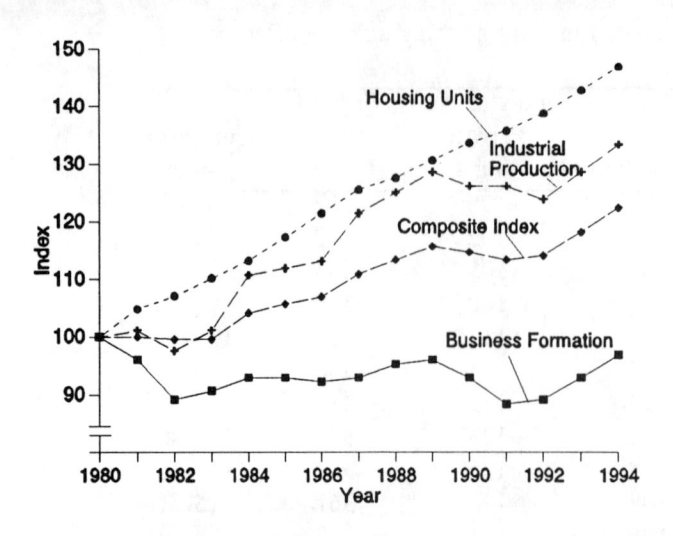

14.65 a. The SAS output for fitting the simple linear regression model for automobile is:

```
Model: MODEL1
Dependent Variable: AUTO

                         Analysis of Variance

                          Sum of          Mean
    Source        DF      Squares         Square        F Value      Prob>F

    Model          1    60602.25889    60602.25889      65.986       0.0001
    Error         13    11939.25844      918.40450
    C Total       14    72541.51733

         Root MSE      30.30519     R-square    0.8354
         Dep Mean     225.55333     Adj R-sq    0.8228
         C.V.          13.43593

                          Parameter Estimates

                   Parameter      Standard      T for H0:
    Variable  DF    Estimate        Error      Parameter=0     Prob > |T|

    INTERCEP   1   107.859048    16.46657201      6.550          0.0001
    T          1    14.711786     1.81108146      8.123          0.0001


           Dep Var    Predict    Std Err    Lower95%    Upper95%
    Obs     AUTO       Value     Predict    Predict     Predict     Residual

      1     112.0      122.6      14.898     49.6171     195.5      -10.5708
      2     119.0      137.3      13.391     65.7059     208.9      -18.2826
      3     125.9      152.0      11.968     81.6038     222.4      -26.0944
      4     143.6      166.7      10.663     97.3011     236.1      -23.1062
      5     173.6      181.4       9.526    112.8        250.0       -7.8180
      6     210.2      196.1       8.622    128.1        264.2       14.0702
      7     247.8      210.8       8.032    143.1        278.6       36.9585
      8     266.3      225.6       7.825    157.9        293.2       40.7467
      9     285.5      240.3       8.032    172.5        308.0       45.2349
     10     292.5      255.0       8.622    186.9        323.0       37.5231
     11     283.1      269.7       9.526    201.1        338.3       13.4113
     12     259.6      284.4      10.663    215.0        353.8      -24.8005
     13     257.7      299.1      11.968    228.7        369.5      -41.4123
     14     282.0      313.8      13.391    242.2        385.4      -31.8240
     15     324.5      328.5      14.898    255.6        401.5       -4.0358
     16       .        343.2      16.467    268.7        417.8         .
     17       .        358.0      18.081    281.7        434.2         .

    Sum of Residuals                        0
    Sum of Squared Residuals          11939.2584
    Predicted Resid SS (Press)        15213.3110
```

The fitted regression line is $\hat{Y}_t = 107.86 + 14.71t$.

The predicted values and 95% prediction intervals for 1995 and 1996 are:

Year	$\hat{Y}_t$	95% Prediction Intervals
1995:	343.2	(268.7, 417.8)
1996:	358.0	(281.7, 434.2)

The SAS output for fitting the simple linear regression model for Other is:

```
Model: MODEL1
Dependent Variable: OTHER

                         Analysis of Variance

                      Sum of          Mean
 Source         DF    Squares        Square       F Value       Prob>F

 Model           1   20508.04889   20508.04889    133.219       0.0001
 Error          13    2001.24711     153.94209
 C Total        14   22509.29600

     Root MSE        12.40734    R-square       0.9111
     Dep Mean       190.14000    Adj R-sq       0.9043
     C.V.             6.52537

                         Parameter Estimates

                 Parameter      Standard    T for H0:
 Variable  DF    Estimate         Error    Parameter=0     Prob > |T|

 INTERCEP   1   121.674286     6.74162948      18.048         0.0001
 T          1     8.558214     0.74148038      11.542         0.0001

        Dep Var   Predict   Std Err   Lower95%  Upper95%
 Obs    OTHER      Value    Predict   Predict   Predict    Residual

   1    131.0     130.2      6.099     100.4     160.1      0.7675
   2    131.2     138.8      5.482     109.5     168.1     -7.5907
   3    133.4     147.3      4.900     118.5     176.2    -13.9489
   4    146.4     155.9      4.366     127.5     184.3     -9.5071
   5    168.8     164.5      3.900     136.4     192.6      4.3346
   6    185.7     173.0      3.530     145.2     200.9     12.6764
   7    188.4     181.6      3.288     153.9     209.3      6.8182
   8    189.3     190.1      3.204     162.5     217.8     -0.8400
   9    203.2     198.7      3.288     171.0     226.4      4.5018
  10    233.3     207.3      3.530     179.4     235.1     26.0436
  11    228.3     215.8      3.900     187.7     243.9     12.4854
  12    223.5     224.4      4.366     196.0     252.8     -0.8729
  13    216.1     232.9      4.900     204.1     261.7    -16.8311
  14    224.4     241.5      5.482     212.2     270.8    -17.0893
  15    249.1     250.0      6.099     220.2     279.9     -0.9475
  16      .       258.6      6.742     228.1     289.1        .
  17      .       267.2      7.402     236.0     298.4        .

 Sum of Residuals                          0
 Sum of Squared Residuals             2001.2471
 Predicted Resid SS (Press)           2618.3416
```

The fitted regression line is $\hat{Y}_t = 121.67 + 8.56t$.

The predicted values and 95% prediction intervals for 1995 and 1996 are:

Year	$\hat{Y}_t$	95% Prediction Intervals
1995:	258.6	(228.1, 289.1)
1996:	267.2	(236.0, 298.4)

The SAS output for fitting the simple linear regression model for Revolve is:

```
Model: MODEL1
Dependent Variable: REVOLVE

                          Analysis of Variance

                       Sum of          Mean
Source         DF     Squares        Square      F Value      Prob>F

Model           1   108795.25889  108795.25889   523.728      0.0001
Error          13     2700.51844     207.73219
C Total        14   111495.77733

     Root MSE       14.41292     R-square     0.9758
     Dep Mean      166.48667     Adj R-sq     0.9739
     C.V.            8.65710

                          Parameter Estimates

                Parameter      Standard     T for H0:
Variable   DF    Estimate         Error    Parameter=0    Prob > |T|

INTERCEP    1    8.792381    7.83137634       1.123         0.2819
T           1   19.711786    0.86133656      22.885         0.0001

         Dep Var    Predict    Std Err   Lower95%   Upper95%
Obs      REVOLVE      Value    Predict    Predict    Predict    Residual

  1       55.1000    28.5042     7.085    -6.1921    63.2004     26.5958
  2       61.1000    48.2160     6.368    14.1746    82.2573     12.8840
  3       66.5000    67.9277     5.692    34.4505   101.4         -1.4277
  4       79.1000    87.6395     5.071    54.6310   120.6         -8.5395
  5      100.3      107.4        4.531    74.7120   140.0         -7.0513
  6      121.8      127.1        4.101    94.6901   159.4         -5.2631
  7      135.8      146.8        3.820   114.6      179.0        -10.9749
  8      153.1      166.5        3.721   134.3      198.6        -13.3867
  9      174.3      186.2        3.820   154.0      218.4        -11.8985
 10      198.5      205.9        4.101   173.5      238.3         -7.4102
 11      223.5      225.6        4.531   193.0      258.3         -2.1220
 12      245.3      245.3        5.071   212.3      278.3         -0.0338
 13      257.3      265.0        5.692   231.6      298.5         -7.7456
 14      287.9      284.8        6.368   250.7      318.8          3.1426
 15      337.7      304.5        7.085   269.8      339.2         33.2308
 16         .       324.2        7.831   288.7      359.6           .
 17         .       343.9        8.599   307.6      380.2           .

Sum of Residuals                            0
Sum of Squared Residuals                 2700.5184
Predicted Resid SS (Press)               4277.2947
```

The fitted regression line is $\hat{Y}_t = 8.79 + 19.71t$.

The predicted values and 95% prediction intervals for 1995 and 1996 are:

Year	$\hat{Y}_t$	95% Prediction Intervals
1995:	324.2	(288.7, 359.6)
1996:	343.9	(307.6, 380.2)

b. The Holt-Winters series is found using the following:

Automobile:

With $w = .7$ and $v = .7$,

$$E_2 = Y_2 = 119.0$$
$$E_3 = wY_3 + (1 - w)(E_2 + T_2) = .7(125.9) + (1 - .7)(119.0 + 7.0) = 125.93$$

$$T_2 = Y_2 - Y_1 = 119.0 - 112.0 = 7$$
$$T_3 = v(E_3 - E_2) + (1 - v)T_2 = .7(125.93 - 119.0) + (1 - .7)7 = 6.95$$

The rest of the E_t's and T_t's appear in the table in part a.

Year	Automobile	Holt-Winters $w = .7$ E_t	$v = .7$ T_t
1980	112.0		
1981	119.0	119.00	7.00
1982	125.9	125.93	6.95
1983	143.6	140.38	12.20
1984	173.6	167.30	22.50
1985	210.2	204.08	32.50
1986	247.8	244.43	38.00
1987	266.3	271.14	30.09
1988	285.5	290.22	22.38
1989	292.5	298.53	12.53
1990	283.1	291.49	−1.17
1991	259.6	268.82	−16.22
1992	257.7	256.17	−13.72
1993	282.0	270.13	5.66
1994	324.5	309.89	29.53

$$F_{1995} = E_{1994} + T_{1994} = 309.89 + 29.53 = 339.42$$
$$F_{1996} = E_{1994} + 2T_{1994} = 309.89 + 2(29.53) = 368.95$$

These predictions are very similar to those using simple linear regression found in **part a**.

Other:

With $w = .7$ and $v = .7$,

$$E_2 = Y_2 = 131.2$$
$$E_3 = wY_3 + (1 - w)(E_2 + T_2) = .7(133.4) + (1 - .7)(131.2 + 0.2) = 132.80$$

$$T_2 = Y_2 - Y_1 = 131.2 - 131.0 = .2$$
$$T_3 = v(E_3 - E_2) + (1 - v)T_2 = .7(132.08 - 131.2) + (1 - .7)(.2) = 1.18$$

The rest of the E_t's and T_t's appear in the table in part a.

	Other	Holt-Winters $w = .7$ E_t	$v = .7$ T_t
Year			
1980	131.0		
1981	131.2	131.20	0.20
1982	133.4	132.80	1.18
1983	146.4	142.67	7.27
1984	168.8	163.14	16.51
1985	185.7	183.88	19.47
1986	188.4	192.89	12.14
1987	189.3	194.02	4.44
1988	203.2	201.78	6.76
1989	233.3	225.87	18.89
1990	228.3	233.24	10.83
1991	223.5	229.67	0.75
1992	216.1	220.40	−6.27
1993	224.4	221.32	−1.23
1994	249.1	240.40	12.98

$F_{1995} = E_{1994} + T_{1994} = 240.40 + 12.98 = 253.38$
$F_{1996} = E_{1994} + 2T_{1994} = 240.40 + 2(12.98) = 266.36$

These predictions are very similar to those using simple linear regression found in part **a**.

Revolve:

With $w = .7$ and $v = .7$,

$E_2 = Y_2 = 61.1$
$E_3 = wY_3 + (1 - w)(E_2 + T_2) = .7(66.5) + (1 - .7)(61.1 + 6.0) = 66.68$

$T_2 = Y_2 - Y_1 = 61.1 - 55.1 = 6$
$T_3 = v(E_3 - E_2) + (1 - v)T_2 = .7(66.8 - 61.1) + (1 - .7)(6) = 5.71$

The rest of the E_t's and T_t's appear in the table in part **a**.

	Revolve	Holt-Winters $w = .7$ E_t	$v = .7$ T_t
Year			
1980	55.1		
1981	61.1	61.10	6.00
1982	66.5	66.68	5.71
1983	79.1	77.09	9.00
1984	100.3	96.03	15.96
1985	121.8	118.86	20.77
1986	135.8	136.95	18.89
1987	153.1	153.92	17.55
1988	174.3	173.45	18.94
1989	198.5	196.67	21.93
1990	223.5	222.03	24.33
1991	245.3	245.62	23.81
1992	257.3	260.94	17.87
1993	287.9	285.17	22.32
1994	337.7	328.64	37.12

$$F_{1995} = E_{1994} + T_{1994} = 328.64 + 37.12 = 365.76$$
$$F_{1996} = E_{1994} + 2T_{1994} = 328.64 + 2(37.12) = 402.88$$

These predictions are somewhat similar to those using simple linear regression found in part a.

14.67   a.   The forecasts for October through December 1996 are:

$$\hat{Y}_{1996,O} = F_{t+1} = E_t = 117.232$$
$$\hat{Y}_{1996,N} = F_{t+2} = E_t = 117.232$$
$$\hat{Y}_{1996,D} = F_{t+3} = E_t = 117.232$$

The forecast errors are the differences between the forecasted value and the actual value. The forecast errors here are:

Year	$\hat{Y}_{t+1}$	F_{t+1}	Difference
1996,O:	129.000	117.232	11.768
1996,N:	159.375	117.232	42.143
1996,D:	151.500	117.232	34.268

b. $\hat{\beta}_0 = 51.3428$ The estimated stock price for December 1993 is 51.3428.
       $\hat{\beta}_1 = 2.094586$ The estimated change in the stock price for each additional month is 2.094586.

c.   The approximate precision is $\pm 2s$ or $\pm 2(7.13079)$ or ± 14.26158

d.   The forecasts and prediction intervals are found at the bottom of the printout.

Year	Month	Prediction	95% Prediction Interval
1996	Oct	122.6	(107.1, 138.0)
	Nov	124.7	(109.1, 140.2)
	Dec	126.7	(111.1, 142.4)

The precision for October is approximately $\dfrac{138.0 - 107.1}{2} = 15.45$

For November $\dfrac{140.2 - 109.1}{2} = 15.55$

For December $\dfrac{142.4 - 111.1}{2} = 15.65$

All of these are close to 14.26158.

e.   The MAD and RMSE for the smoothed series are:

$$\text{MAD} = \frac{\sum |F_t - Y_t|}{N}$$
$$= \frac{|117.232 - 129.000| + |117.232 - 159.375| + |117.232 - 151.500|}{3}$$
$$= \frac{88.179}{3} = 29.393$$

Time Series: Descriptive Analyses, Models, and Forecasting

$$\text{RMSE} = \sqrt{\frac{\sum (F_t - Y_t)^2}{N}} = \sqrt{\frac{(-11.768)^2 + (-42.143)^2 + (-34.268)^2}{3}} = 32.087$$

The MAD and RMSE for the regression model are

$$\text{MAD} = \frac{\sum |F_t - Y_t|}{N}$$

$$= \frac{|122.6 - 129.000| + |124.7 - 159.375| + |126.7 - 151.500|}{3}$$

$$= \frac{65.875}{3} = 21.958$$

$$\text{RMSE} = \sqrt{\frac{\sum (F_t - Y_t)^2}{N}} = \sqrt{\frac{(-6.4)^2 + (-34.675)^2 + (-24.8)^2}{3}} = 24.889$$

The values of both MAD and RMSE for the regression model were smaller than the MAD and RMSE values for the smoothed series. The regression forecasts are made with less error.

f. We have to assume the error terms are independent.

g. To determine if autocorrelation is present, we test:

H_0: Autocorrelation is not present
H_a: Autocorrelation is present

The test statistic is $d = .941$.

Since there is no table for $\alpha = .05$, we will use $\alpha = .02$. The rejection region is $d < d_{L,\alpha/2} = d_{L,.01} = 1.17$ or $4 - d < d_{L,.01} = 1.17$. From Table XV, Appendix B, for $k = 1$, $n = 33$, and $\alpha = .02$.

Since the observed value of the test statistic falls in the rejection region ($d = .941 < 1.17$), H_0 is rejected. There is sufficient evidence to indicate that autocorrelation is present.

Since there is evidence of autocorrelation, the validity of the regression model is questioned.

Design of Experiments and Analysis of Variance — Chapter 15

15.1 Since only one factor is utilized, the treatments are the four levels (A, B, C, D) of the qualitative factor.

15.3 a. College GPA's are measured on college students. The experimental units are college students.

b. Household income is measured on households. The experimental units are households.

c. Gasoline mileage is measured on automobiles. The experimental units are the automobiles of a particular model.

d. The experimental units are the sectors on a computer diskette.

e. The experimental units are the states.

15.5 a. The response is the opinion of the undergraduate student of the value of the discount offer.

b. There are two factors—situation at two levels (advertisements read at home vs. in-store ad) and type of comparison at two levels (comparison to previous price at same store vs. to competitor's price). Both factors are qualitative.

c. The treatments are the $2 \times 2 = 4$ combinations of situation and type of comparison.

d. The experimental units are the college students.

15.7 a. This is an observational experiment. The economist has no control over the factor levels or unemployment rates.

b. This is a designed experiment. The manager chooses only three different incentive programs to compare, and randomly assigns an incentive program to each of nine plants.

c. This is an observational experiment. Even though the marketer chooses the publication, he has no control over who responds to the ads.

d. This is an observational experiment. The load on the facility's generators is only observed, not controlled.

e. This is an observational experiment. One has no control over the distance of the haul, the goods hauled, or the price of diesel fuel.

15.9 a. From Table VIII with $\nu_1 = 4$ and $\nu_2 = 4$, $F_{.05} = 6.39$.

b. From Table X with $\nu_1 = 4$ and $\nu_2 = 4$, $F_{.01} = 15.98$.

c. From Table VII with $\nu_1 = 30$ and $\nu_2 = 40$, $F_{.10} = 1.54$.

d. From Table IX with $\nu_1 = 15$, and $\nu_2 = 12$, $F_{.025} = 3.18$.

15.11 In the second dot diagram b, the difference between the sample means is small relative to the variability within the sample observations. In the first dot diagram a, the values in each of the samples are grouped together with a range of 4, while in the second diagram b, the range of values is 8.

15.13 For each dot diagram, we want to test:

H_0: $\mu_1 = \mu_2$
H_a: $\mu_1 \neq \mu_2$

From Exercise 15.12,

Diagram a	Diagram b
$\bar{x}_1 = 9$	$\bar{x}_1 = 9$
$\bar{x}_2 = 14$	$\bar{x}_2 = 14$
$s_1^2 = 2$	$s_1^2 = 14.4$
$s_2^2 = 2$	$s_2^2 = 14.4$

a.

Diagram a	Diagram b
$s_p^2 = \dfrac{s_1^2 + s_2^2}{2}$	$s_p^2 = \dfrac{s_1^2 + s_2^2}{2}$
$= \dfrac{2 + 2}{2} = 2 \quad (n_1 = n_2)$	$= \dfrac{14.4 + 14.4}{2} = 14.4 \quad (n_1 = n_2)$
In Exercise 15.12, MSE = 2	In Exercise 15.12, MSE = 14.4

The pooled variance for the two-sample t-test is the same as the MSE for the F-test.

b.

Diagram a	Diagram b
$t = \dfrac{\bar{x}_1 - \bar{x}_2}{\sqrt{s_p^2\left(\dfrac{1}{n_1} + \dfrac{1}{n_2}\right)}} = \dfrac{9 - 14}{\sqrt{2\left(\dfrac{1}{6} + \dfrac{1}{6}\right)}}$	$t = \dfrac{\bar{x}_1 - \bar{x}_2}{\sqrt{s_p^2\left(\dfrac{1}{n_1} + \dfrac{1}{n_2}\right)}} = \dfrac{9 - 14}{\sqrt{14.4\left(\dfrac{1}{6} + \dfrac{1}{6}\right)}}$
$= -6.12$	$= -2.28$
In Exercise 15.12, $F = 37.5$	In Exercise 15.12, $F = 5.21$

The test statistic for the F-test is the square of the test statistic for the t-test.

c.

Diagram a	Diagram b
For the t-test, the rejection region requires $\alpha/2 = .05/2 = .025$ in each tail of the t-distribution with df = $n_1 + n_2 - 2 = 6 + 6 - 2 = 10$. From Table VI, Appendix B, $t_{.025} = 2.228$.	For the t-test, the rejection region is the same as Diagram a since we are using the same α, n_1, and n_2 for both tests.

The rejection region is $t < -2.228$ or $t > 2.228$.

In Exercise 15.12, the rejection region for both diagrams using the F-test is $F > 4.96$.

The tabled F value equals the square of the tabled t value.

d.

Diagram a	Diagram b
For the t-test, since the test statistic falls in the rejection region ($t = -6.12 < -2.228$), we would reject H_0. In Exercise 15.12, using the F-test, we rejected H_0.	For the t-test, since the test statistic falls in the rejection region ($t = -2.28 < -2.228$), we would reject H_0. In Exercise 15.12, using the F-test, we rejected H_0.

e. Assumptions for the t-test:

1. Both populations have relative frequency distributions that are approximately normal.
2. The two population variances are equal.
3. Samples are selected randomly and independently from the populations.

Assumptions for the F-test:

1. Both population probability distributions are normal.
2. The two population variances are equal.
3. Samples are selected randomly and independently from the respective populations.

The assumptions are the same for both tests.

15.15 For all parts, the hypotheses are:

H_0: $\mu_1 = \mu_2 = \mu_3 = \mu_4 = \mu_5 = \mu_6$
H_a: At least two treatment means differ

The rejection region for all parts is the same.

The rejection region requires $\alpha = .10$ in the upper tail of the F-distribution with $\nu_1 = p - 1 = 6 - 1 = 5$ and $\nu_2 = n - p = 36 - 6 = 30$. From Table VII, Appendix B, $F_{.10} = 2.05$. The rejection region is $F > 2.05$.

a. $SST = .2(500) = 100$ $SSE = SS(Total) - SST = 500 - 100 = 400$

$MST = \dfrac{SST}{p - 1} = \dfrac{100}{6 - 1} = 20$ $MSE = \dfrac{SSE}{n - p} = \dfrac{400}{36 - 6} = 13.333$

$F = \dfrac{MST}{MSE} = \dfrac{20}{13.333} = 1.5$

Since the observed value of the test statistic does not fall in the rejection region ($F = 1.5 \not> 2.05$), H_0 is not rejected. There is insufficient evidence to indicate differences among the treatment means at $\alpha = .10$.

b. $SST = .5(500) = 250$ $SSE = SS(Total) - SST = 500 - 250 = 250$

$MST = \dfrac{SST}{p - 1} = \dfrac{250}{6 - 1} = 50$ $MSE = \dfrac{SSE}{n - p} = \dfrac{250}{36 - 6} = 8.333$

$F = \dfrac{MST}{MSE} = \dfrac{50}{8.333} = 6$

Since the observed value of the test statistic falls in the rejection region ($F = 6 > 2.05$), H_0 is rejected. There is sufficient evidence to indicate differences among the treatment means at $\alpha = .10$.

Design of Experiments and Analysis of Variance

c. $SST = .8(500) = 400$ $\qquad SSE = SS(Total) - SST = 500 - 400 = 100$

$MST = \dfrac{SST}{p-1} = \dfrac{400}{6-1} = 80 \qquad MSE = \dfrac{SSE}{n-p} = \dfrac{100}{36-6} = 3.333$

$F = \dfrac{MST}{MSE} = \dfrac{80}{3.333} = 24$

Since the observed value of the test statistic falls in the rejection region ($F = 24 > 2.05$), H_0 is rejected. There is sufficient evidence to indicate differences among the treatment means at $\alpha = .10$.

d. The F-ratio increases as the treatment sum of squares increases.

15.17 a. The number of treatments is $3 + 1 = 4$. The total sample size is $37 + 1 = 38$.

b. To determine if the treatment means differ, we test:

H_0: $\mu_1 = \mu_2 = \mu_3 = \mu_4$
H_a: At least two treatment means differ

The test statistic is $F = 14.80$.

The rejection region requires $\alpha = .01$ in the upper tail of the F-distribution with $\nu_1 = p - 1 = 4 - 1 = 3$ and $\nu_2 = n - p = 38 - 4 = 34$. From Table VIII, Appendix B, $F_{.01} \approx 4.51$. The rejection region is $F > 4.51$.

Since the observed value of the test statistic falls in the rejection region ($F = 14.80 > 4.51$), H_0 is rejected. There is sufficient evidence to indicate differences among the treatment means at $\alpha = .01$.

c. We need the sample means to compare specific pairs of treatment means.

15.19 a. This is a completely randomized design.

b. The means presented are the sample means, not the population means. The hypotheses being tested involve the population means. The sample means will almost always be different. What we must do is determine if the sample means are enough different to warrant rejection of the null hypothesis. In this case, although the sample means are different, they are not different enough to reject the null hypothesis.

15.21 a. To determine whether the mean scores of the four groups differ, we test:

H_0: $\mu_1 = \mu_2 = \mu_3 = \mu_4$
H_a: At least two treatment means differ

where μ_i represents the mean of the ith group.

For the variable "Infrequency":

The test statistic is $F = 155.8$.

The rejection region requires $\alpha = .05$ in the upper tail of the F-distribution with $\nu_1 = p - 1 = 4 - 1 = 3$ and $\nu_2 = n - p = 278 - 4 = 274$. Using Table VIII, Appendix B, $F_{.05} \approx 2.60$. The rejection region is $F > 2.60$.

Since the observed value of the test statistic falls in the rejection region ($F = 155.5 > 2.60$), H_0 is rejected. There is sufficient evidence to indicate the mean scores on the "Infrequency" variable differ among the four groups at $\alpha = .05$.

For the variable "Obvious":

The test statistic is $F = 49.7$.

The rejection region is $F > 2.60$. (See above.)

Since the observed value of the test statistic falls in the rejection region ($F = 49.7 > 2.60$), H_0 is rejected. There is sufficient evidence to indicate the mean scores on the "Obvious" variable differ among the four groups at $\alpha = .05$.

For the variable "Subtle":

The test statistic is $F = 10.3$.

The rejection region is $F > 2.60$. (See above.)

Since the observed value of the test statistic falls in the rejection region ($F = 10.3 > 2.60$), H_0 is rejected. There is sufficient evidence to indicate the mean scores on the "Subtle" variable differ among the four groups at $\alpha = .05$.

For the variable "Obvious-Subtle":

The test statistic is $F = 45.4$.

The rejection region is $F > 2.60$. (See above.)

Since the observed value of the test statistic falls in the rejection region ($F = 45.4 > 2.60$), H_0 is rejected. There is sufficient evidence to indicate the mean scores on the "Obvious-Subtle" variable differ among the four groups at $\alpha = .05$.

For the variable "Dissimulation":

The test statistic is $F = 39.1$.

The rejection region is $F > 2.60$. (See above.)

Since the observed value of the test statistic falls in the rejection region ($F = 39.1 > 2.60$), H_0 is rejected. There is sufficient evidence to indicate the mean scores on the "Dissimulation" variable differ among the four groups at $\alpha = .05$.

b. No. No information is provided on the sample means. The test of hypotheses performed in part **a** just indicate differences exist, but do not indicate where. Further analysis would be required.

15.23 a. To determine if the mean level of trust differs among the six treatments, we test:

H_0: $\mu_1 = \mu_2 = \mu_3 = \mu_4 = \mu_5 = \mu_6$
H_a: At least one μ_i differs

b. The test statistic is $F = 2.21$.

The rejection region requires α in the upper tail of the F-distribution with $\nu_1 = p - 1 = 6 - 1 = 5$ and $\nu_2 = n - p = 237 - 6 = 231$. From Table VIII, Appendix B, $F_{.05} \approx 2.21$. The rejection region is $F > 2.21$.

Since the observed value of the test statistic does not fall in the rejection region ($F = 2.21 \not> 2.21$), H_0 is not rejected. There is insufficient evidence to indicate that at least two mean trusts differ at $\alpha = .05$.

c. We must assume that all six samples are drawn from normal populations, the six population variances are the same, and that the samples are independent.

d. I would classify this experiment as designed. Each subject was randomly assigned to receive one of the six scenarios.

15.25 a. Some preliminary calculations are:

$$MST = \frac{SST}{p-1} = \frac{273}{3} = 91 \qquad MSE = \frac{SSE}{n-p} = \frac{494}{94} = 5.2553$$

$$F = \frac{MST}{MSE} = \frac{91}{5.2553} = 17.32$$

To determine whether the mean level of confidence differs among the four forms of auditor association, we test:

H_0: $\mu_1 = \mu_2 = \mu_3 = \mu_4$
H_a: At least two treatment means differ

The test statistic is $F = 17.32$.

The rejection region requires $\alpha = .05$ in the upper tail of the F-distribution with $\nu_1 = p - 1 = 4 - 1 = 3$ and $\nu_2 = n - p = 98 - 4 = 94$. From Table VIII, Appendix B, $F_{.05} \approx 2.76$. The rejection region is $F > 2.76$.

Since the observed value of the test statistic falls in the rejection region ($F = 17.32 > 2.76$), H_0 is rejected. There is sufficient evidence to indicate the mean level of confidence differs among the four forms of auditor association at $\alpha = .05$.

b. The p-value $= P(F \geq 17.32)$. Using Table X, Appendix B, with $\nu_1 = 3$ and $\nu_2 = 94$, $P(F \geq 13.32) < .01$.

c. To determine if the mean level of confidence associated with the audit is significantly higher than the mean for review, we test:

H_0: $\mu_4 - \mu_3 = 0$
H_a: $\mu_4 - \mu_3 > 0$

The test statistic is $t = \dfrac{\bar{y}_4 - \bar{y}_3 - 0}{\sqrt{MSE\left(\dfrac{1}{n_4} + \dfrac{1}{n_3}\right)}} = \dfrac{8.8 - 6.1 - 0}{\sqrt{5.2553\left(\dfrac{1}{27} + \dfrac{1}{25}\right)}} = \dfrac{2.7}{.6363} = 4.24$

The rejection region requires $\alpha = .05$ in the upper tail of the t-distribution with df $= n - p = 94$. From Table VI, Appendix B, $t_{.05} \approx 1.671$. The rejection region is $t > 1.671$.

Since the observed value of the test statistic falls in the rejection region ($t = 4.24 > 1.671$), H_0 is rejected. There is sufficient evidence to indicate the mean level of confidence associated with the audit is significantly higher than the mean for review at $\alpha = .05$.

d. Since there are differences among the treatment means, there is evidence that the auditors were not accepting the same degree of responsibility for each form of financial report.

15.27 The number of pairwise comparisons is equal to $p(p - 1)/2$.

a. For $p = 3$, the number of comparisons is $3(3 - 1)/2 = 3$.

b. For $p = 5$, the number of comparisons is $5(5 - 1)/2 = 10$.

c. For $p = 4$, the number of comparisons is $4(4 - 1)/2 = 6$.

d. For $p = 10$, the number of comparisons is $10(10 - 1)/2 = 45$.

15.29 A comparisonwise error rate is the error rate (or the probability of declaring the means different when, in fact, they are not different) for each individual comparison. That is, if each comparison is run using $\alpha = .05$, then the comparisonwise error rate is .05.

15.31 a. There will be $c = \dfrac{3(3 - 1)}{2} = 3$ pairwise comparisons.

b. The experimentwise error rate is $\alpha = .05$. This means that the probability that at least one pair is declared significantly different when it is not is .05.

c. Yes. All sample sizes are the same. Thus, Tukey's multiple comparison is appropriate.

d. All treatments connected with a line are not significantly different. Thus, the mean cost for client A is significantly higher than the mean cost for clients B and C. No other differences are present.

15.33 a. The experimentwise error rate is given as $\alpha = .05$. This means that the probability of declaring at least two means different that are not different is .05.

b. The confidence interval for the difference between the mean sorption rates of aromatics and esters is 0.3340 and 0.8904. We are 95% confident that the difference in the mean sorption rates of aromatics and esters is between 0.3340 and 0.8904. Since 0 is not in this interval, there is evidence that the mean sorption rate for aromatics is greater than the mean sorption rate of esters.

c. The confidence intervals that do not contain 0 indicate that the pair of means are significantly different. Thus, the mean sorption rates of chloralkanes and esters are significantly different and the mean sorption rates of aromatics and esters are significantly different.

15.35 The mean number of activities for the "successful" firms is significantly greater than that for the "gave up" group and the "still trying" group. No other significant differences exist.

15.37 The mean concern rating for those with post-graduate education is significantly greater than the mean concern rating for the four other education level groups. There are no other significant differences.

Design of Experiments and Analysis of Variance

15.39   a.   The ANOVA table is:

Source	df	SS	MS	F
A	2	.8	.4000	3.69
B	3	5.3	1.7667	16.31
AB	6	9.6	1.6000	14.77
Error	12	1.3	.1083	
Total	23	17.0		

df for A is $a - 1 = 3 - 1 = 2$
df for $B = b - 1 = 4 - 1 = 3$
df for AB is $(a - 1)(b - 1) = 2(3) = 6$
df for Error is $n - ab = 24 - 3(4) = 12$
df for Total is $n - 1 = 24 - 1 = 23$

$SSE = SS(\text{Total}) - SSA - SSB - SSAB = 17.0 - .8 - 5.3 - 9.6 = 1.3$

$MSA = \dfrac{SSA}{a - 1} = \dfrac{.8}{3 - 1} = .40 \qquad MSB = \dfrac{SSB}{b - 1} = \dfrac{5.3}{4 - 1} = 1.7667$

$MSAB = \dfrac{SSAB}{(a - 1)(b - 1)} = \dfrac{9.6}{(3 - 1)(4 - 1)} = 1.60$

$MSE = \dfrac{SSE}{n - ab} = \dfrac{1.3}{24 - 3(4)} = .1083$

$F_A = \dfrac{MSA}{MSE} = \dfrac{.4000}{.1083} = 3.69 \qquad F_B = \dfrac{MSB}{MSE} = \dfrac{1.7667}{.1083} = 16.31$

$F_{AB} = \dfrac{MSAB}{MSE} = \dfrac{1.6000}{.1083} = 14.77$

b.   Sum of Squares for Treatment = $SSA + SSB + SSAB = .8 = 5.3 + 2.6 = 15.7$

$MST = \dfrac{SST}{ab - 1} = \dfrac{15.7}{3(4) - 1} = 1.4273 \qquad F_T = \dfrac{MST}{MSE} = \dfrac{1.4273}{.1083} = 13.18$

To determine if the treatment means differ, we test:

H_0: $\mu_1 = \mu_2 = \cdots = \mu_{12}$
H_a: At least two treatments means differ

The test statistic is $F = 13.18$.

The rejection region requires $\alpha = .05$ in the upper tail of the F-distribution with $\nu_1 = ab - 1 = 3(4) - 1 = 11$ and $\nu_2 = n - ab = 24 - 3(4) = 12$. From Table VIII, Appendix B, $F_{.05} \approx 2.75$. The rejection region is $F > 2.75$.

Since the observed value of the test statistic falls in the rejection region ($F = 13.18 > 2.75$), H_0 is rejected. There is sufficient evidence to indicate the treatment means differ at $\alpha = .05$.

c.   Yes. We need to partition the Treatment Sum of Squares into the Main Effects and Interaction Sum of Squares. Then we test whether factors A and B interact. Depending on the conclusion of the test for interaction, we either test for main effects or compare the treatment means.

d. Two factors are said to interact if the effect of one factor on the dependent variable is not the same at different levels of the second factor. If the factors interact, then tests for main effects are not necessary. We need to compare the treatment means for one factor at each level of the second.

e. To determine if the factors interact, we test:

H_0: Factors A and B do not interact to affect the response mean
H_a: Factors A and B do interact to affect the response mean

The test statistic is $F = \dfrac{\text{MS}AB}{\text{MSE}} = 14.77$

The rejection region requires $\alpha = .05$ in the upper tail of the F-distribution with $\nu_1 = (a-1)(b-1) = (3-1)(4-1) = 6$ and $\nu_2 = n - ab = 24 - 3(4) = 12$. From Table VIII, Appendix B, $F_{.05} = 3.00$. The rejection region is $F > 3.00$.

Since the observed value of the test statistic falls in the rejection region ($F = 14.77 > 3.00$), H_0 is rejected. There is sufficient evidence to indicate the two factors interact to affect the response mean at $\alpha = .05$.

f. No. Testing for main effects is not warranted because interaction is present. Instead, we compare the treatment means of one factor at each level of the second factor.

15.41 a. The treatments for this experiment consist of a level for factor A and a level for factor B. There are six treatments—(1, 1), (1, 2), (1, 3), (2, 1), (2, 2), and (2, 3) where the first number represents the level of factor A and the second number represents the level of factor B.

The treatment means appear to be different because the sample means are quite different. The factors appear to interact because the lines are not parallel.

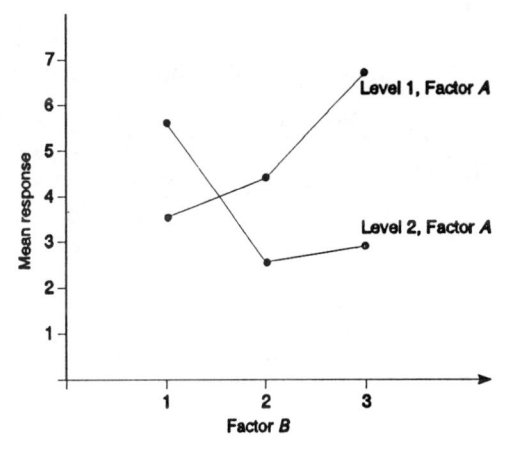

b. $\text{SST} = \text{SS}A + \text{SS}B + \text{SS}AB = 4.441 + 4.127 + 18.007 = 26.575$

$\text{MST} = \dfrac{\text{SST}}{ab - 1} = \dfrac{26.575}{2(3) - 1} = 5.315 \qquad F_T = \dfrac{\text{MST}}{\text{MSE}} = \dfrac{5.315}{.246} = 21.62$

To determine whether the treatment means differ, we test:

H_0: $\mu_1 = \mu_2 = \mu_3 = \mu_4 = \mu_5 = \mu_6$
H_a: At least two treatment means differ

The test statistic is $F = \dfrac{\text{MST}}{\text{MSE}} = 21.62$

The rejection region requires $\alpha = .05$ in the upper tail of the F-distribution with $\nu_1 = ab - 1 = 2(3) - 1 = 5$ and $\nu_2 = n - ab = 12 - 2(3) = 6$. From Table VIII, Appendix B, $F_{.05} = 4.39$. The rejection region is $F > 4.39$.

Design of Experiments and Analysis of Variance

Since the observed value of the test statistic falls in the rejection region ($F = 21.62 > 4.39$), H_0 is rejected. There is sufficient evidence to indicate that the treatment means differ at $\alpha = .05$. This supports the plot in **a**.

c. Yes. Since there are differences among the treatment means, we test for interaction. To determine whether the factors A and B interact, we test:

H_0: Factors A and B do not interact to affect the mean response
H_a: Factors A and B do interact to affect the mean response

The test statistic is $F = \dfrac{\text{MS}AB}{\text{MSE}} = \dfrac{9.003}{.246} = 36.60$

The rejection region requires $\alpha = .05$ in the upper tail of the F-distribution with $\nu_1 = (a-1)(b-1) = (2-1)(3-1) = 2$ and $\nu_2 = n - ab = 12 - 2(3) = 6$. From Table VIII, Appendix B, $F_{.05} = 5.14$. The rejection region is $F > 5.14$.

Since the observed value of the test statistic falls in the rejection region ($F = 36.60 > 5.14$), H_0 is rejected. There is sufficient evidence to indicate that factors A and B interact to affect the response mean at $\alpha = .05$.

d. No. Because interaction is present, the tests for main effects are not warranted.

e. The results of the tests in parts **b** and **c** support the visual interpretation in part **a**.

15.43 a. $\text{SS}A = .2(1000) = 200$, $\text{SS}B = .1(1000) = 100$, $\text{SS}AB = .1(1000) = 100$
$\text{SSE} = \text{SS(Total)} - \text{SS}A - \text{SS}B - \text{SS}AB = 1000 - 200 - 100 - 100 = 600$
$\text{SST} = \text{SS}A + \text{SS}B + \text{SS}AB = 200 + 100 + 100 = 400$

$\text{MS}A = \dfrac{\text{SS}A}{a-1} = \dfrac{200}{3-1} = 100$ $\qquad$ $\text{MS}B = \dfrac{\text{SS}B}{b-1} = \dfrac{100}{3-1} = 50$

$\text{MS}AB = \dfrac{\text{SS}AB}{(a-1)(b-1)} = \dfrac{100}{(3-1)(3-1)} = 25$

$\text{MSE} = \dfrac{\text{SSE}}{n-ab} = \dfrac{600}{27-3(3)} = 33.333$ $\qquad$ $\text{MST} = \dfrac{\text{SST}}{ab-1} = \dfrac{400}{3(3)-1} = 50$

$F_A = \dfrac{\text{MS}A}{\text{MSE}} = \dfrac{100}{33.333} = 3.00$ $\qquad$ $F_B = \dfrac{\text{MS}B}{\text{MSE}} = \dfrac{50}{33.333} = 1.50$

$F_{AB} = \dfrac{\text{MS}AB}{\text{MSE}} = \dfrac{25}{33.333} = .75$ $\qquad$ $F_T = \dfrac{\text{MST}}{\text{MSE}} = \dfrac{50}{33.333} = 1.50$

Source	df	SS	MS	F
A	2	200	100	3.00
B	2	100	50	1.50
AB	4	100	25	.75
Error	18	600	33.333	
Total	26	1000		

To determine whether the treatment means differ, we test:

H_0: $\mu_1 = \mu_2 = \cdots = \mu_9$
H_a: At least two treatment means differ

The test statistic is $F = \dfrac{\text{MST}}{\text{MSE}} = 1.50$

Suppose $\alpha = .05$. The rejection region requires $\alpha = .05$ in the upper tail of the F-distribution with $\nu_1 = ab - 1 = 3(3) - 1 = 8$ and $\nu_2 = n - ab = 27 - 3(3) = 18$. From Table VIII, Appendix B, $F_{.05} = 2.51$. The rejection region is $F > 2.51$.

Since the observed value of the test statistic does not fall in the rejection region ($F = 1.50 \not> 2.51$), H_0 is not rejected. There is insufficient evidence to indicate the treatment means differ at $\alpha = .05$. Since there are no treatment mean differences, we have nothing more to do.

b. $SSA = .1(1000) = 100$, $SSB = .1(1000) = 100$, $SSAB = .5(1000) = 500$
$SSE = SS(\text{Total}) - SSA - SSB - SSAB = 1000 - 100 - 100 - 500 = 300$
$SST = SSA + SSB + SSAB = 100 + 100 + 500 = 700$

$MSA = \dfrac{SSA}{a-1} = \dfrac{100}{3-1} = 50 \qquad MSB = \dfrac{SSB}{b-1} = \dfrac{100}{3-1} = 50$

$MSAB = \dfrac{SSAB}{(a-1)(b-1)} = \dfrac{500}{(3-1)(3-1)} = 125$

$MSE = \dfrac{SSE}{n-ab} = \dfrac{300}{27-3(3)} = 16.667 \qquad MST = \dfrac{SST}{ab-1} = \dfrac{700}{9-1} = 87.5$

$F_A = \dfrac{MSA}{MSE} = \dfrac{50}{16.667} = 3.00 \qquad F_B = \dfrac{MSB}{MSE} = \dfrac{50}{16.667} = 3.00$

$F_{AB} = \dfrac{MSAB}{MSE} = \dfrac{125}{16.667} = 7.50 \qquad F_T = \dfrac{MST}{MSE} = \dfrac{87.5}{16.667} = 5.25$

Source	df	SS	MS	F
A	2	100	50	3.00
B	2	100	50	3.00
AB	4	500	125	7.50
Error	18	300	16.667	
Total	26	1000		

To determine if the treatment means differ, we test:

$H_0: \mu_1 = \mu_2 = \cdots = \mu_9$
$H_a:$ At least two treatment means differ

The test statistic is $F = \dfrac{MST}{MSE} = 5.25$

The rejection region requires $\alpha = .05$ in the upper tail of the F-distribution with $\nu_1 = ab - 1 = 3(3) - 1 = 8$ and $\nu_2 = n - ab = 27 - 3(3) = 18$. From Table VIII, Appendix B, $F_{.05} = 2.51$. The rejection region is $F > 2.51$.

Since the observed value of the test statistic falls in the rejection region ($F = 5.25 > 2.51$), H_0 is rejected. There is sufficient evidence to indicate the treatment means differ at $\alpha = .05$.

Since the treatment means differ, we next test for interaction between factors A and B. To determine if factors A and B interact, we test:

$H_0:$ Factors A and B do not interact to affect the mean response
$H_a:$ Factors A and B do interact to affect the mean response

The test statistic is $F = \dfrac{\text{MS}AB}{\text{MSE}} = 7.50$

The rejection region requires $\alpha = .05$ in the upper tail of the F-distribution with $\nu_1 = (a-1)(b-1) = (3-1)(3-1) = 4$ and $\nu_2 = n - ab = 27 - 3(3) = 18$. From Table VIII, Appendix B, $F_{.05} = 2.93$. The rejection region is $F > 2.93$.

Since the observed value of the test statistic falls in the rejection region ($F = 7.50 > 2.93$), H_0 is rejected. There is sufficient evidence to indicate the factors A and B interact at $\alpha = .05$. Since interaction is present, no tests for main effects are necessary.

c. $\text{SS}A = .4(1000) = 400$, $\text{SS}B = .1(1000) = 100$, $\text{SS}AB = .2(1000) = 200$
$\text{SSE} = \text{SS(Total)} - \text{SS}A - \text{SS}B - \text{SS}AB = 1000 - 400 - 100 - 200 = 300$
$\text{SST} = \text{SS}A + \text{SS}B + \text{SS}AB = 400 + 100 + 200 = 700$

$\text{MS}A = \dfrac{\text{SS}A}{a-1} = \dfrac{400}{3-1} = 50$ \qquad $\text{MS}B = \dfrac{\text{SS}B}{b-1} = \dfrac{100}{3-1} = 50$

$\text{MS}AB = \dfrac{\text{SS}AB}{(a-1)(b-1)} = \dfrac{200}{(3-1)(3-1)} = 50$

$\text{MSE} = \dfrac{\text{SSE}}{n-ab} = \dfrac{300}{27 - 3(3)} = 16.667$ \qquad $\text{MST} = \dfrac{\text{SST}}{ab-1} = \dfrac{700}{3(3)-1} = 87.5$

$F_A = \dfrac{\text{MS}A}{\text{MSE}} = \dfrac{200}{16.667} = 12.00$ \qquad $F_B = \dfrac{\text{MS}B}{\text{MSE}} = \dfrac{50}{16.667} = 3.00$

$F_{AB} = \dfrac{\text{MS}AB}{\text{MSE}} = \dfrac{50}{16.667} = 3.00$ \qquad $F_T = \dfrac{\text{MST}}{\text{MSE}} = \dfrac{87.5}{16.667} = 5.25$

Source	df	SS	MS	F
A	2	400	200	12.00
B	2	100	50	3.00
AB	4	200	50	3.00
Error	18	300	16.667	
Total	26	1000		

To determine if the treatment means differ, we test:

H_0: $\mu_1 = \mu_2 = \cdots = \mu_9$
H_a: At least two treatment means differ

The test statistic is $F = \dfrac{\text{MST}}{\text{MSE}} = 5.25$

The rejection region requires $\alpha = .05$ in the upper tail of the F-distribution with $\nu_1 = ab - 1 = 3(3) - 1 = 8$ and $\nu_2 = n - ab = 27 - 3(3) = 18$. From Table VIII, Appendix B, $F_{.05} = 2.51$. The rejection region is $F > 2.51$.

Since the observed value of the test statistic falls in the rejection region ($F = 5.25 > 2.51$), H_0 is rejected. There is sufficient evidence to indicate the treatment means differ at $\alpha = .05$.

Since the treatment means differ, we next test for interaction between factors A and B. To determine if factors A and B interact, we test:

H_0: Factors A and B do not interact to affect the mean response
H_a: Factors A and B do interact to affect the mean response

The test statistic is $F = \dfrac{MSAB}{MSE} = 3.00$

The rejection region requires $\alpha = .05$ in the upper tail of the F-distribution with $\nu_1 = (a-1)(b-1) = (3-1)(3-1) = 4$ and $\nu_2 = n - ab = 27 - 3(3) = 18$. From Table VIII, Appendix B, $F_{.05} = 2.93$. The rejection region is $F > 2.93$.

Since the observed value of the test statistic falls in the rejection region ($F = 3.00 > 2.93$), H_0 is rejected. There is sufficient evidence to indicate the factors A and B interact at $\alpha = .05$. Since interaction is present, no tests for main effects are necessary.

d. $SSA = .4(1000) = 400$, $SSB = .4(1000) = 400$, $SSAB = .1(1000) = 100$
$SSE = SS(Total) - SSA - SSB - SSAB = 1000 - 400 - 400 - 100 = 100$
$SST = SSA + SSB + SSAB = 400 + 400 + 100 = 900$

$MSA = \dfrac{SSA}{a-1} = \dfrac{400}{3-1} = 200$ $\qquad\qquad MSB = \dfrac{SSB}{b-1} = \dfrac{400}{3-1} = 200$

$MSAB = \dfrac{SSAB}{(a-1)(b-1)} = \dfrac{100}{(3-1)(3-1)} = 25$

$MSE = \dfrac{SSE}{n-ab} = \dfrac{100}{27-3(3)} = 5.556$ $\qquad MST = \dfrac{SST}{ab-1} = \dfrac{900}{3(3)-1} = 112.5$

$F_A = \dfrac{MSA}{MSE} = \dfrac{200}{5.556} = 36.00$ $\qquad\qquad F_B = \dfrac{MSB}{MSE} = \dfrac{200}{5.556} = 36.00$

$F_{AB} = \dfrac{MSAB}{MSE} = \dfrac{25}{5.556} = 4.50$ $\qquad\qquad F_T = \dfrac{MST}{MSE} = \dfrac{112.5}{5.556} = 20.25$

Source	df	SS	MS	F
A	2	400	200	36.00
B	2	400	200	36.00
AB	4	100	25	4.50
Error	18	100	5.556	
Total	26	1000		

To determine if the treatment means differ, we test:

H_0: $\mu_1 = \mu_2 = \cdots = \mu_9$
H_a: At least two treatment means differ

The test statistic is $F = \dfrac{MST}{MSE} = 20.25$

The rejection region requires $\alpha = .05$ in the upper tail of the F-distribution with $\nu_1 = ab - 1 = 3(3) - 1 = 8$ and $\nu_2 = n - ab = 27 - 3(3) = 18$. From Table VIII, Appendix B, $F_{.05} = 2.51$. The rejection region is $F > 2.51$.

Design of Experiments and Analysis of Variance

Since the observed value of the test statistic falls in the rejection region ($F = 20.25 > 2.51$), H_0 is rejected. There is sufficient evidence to indicate the treatment means differ at $\alpha = .05$.

Since the treatment means differ, we next test for interaction between factors A and B. To determine if factors A and B interact, we test:

H_0: Factors A and B do not interact to affect the mean response
H_a: Factors A and B do interact to affect the mean response

The test statistic is $F = \dfrac{\text{MS}AB}{\text{MSE}} = 4.50$

The rejection region requires $\alpha = .05$ in the upper tail of the F-distribution with $\nu_1 = (a - 1)(b - 1) = (3 - 1)(3 - 1) = 4$ and $\nu_2 = n - ab = 27 - 3(3) = 18$. From Table VIII, Appendix B, $F_{.05} = 2.93$. The rejection region is $F > 2.93$.

Since the observed value of the test statistic falls in the rejection region ($F = 4.50 > 2.93$), H_0 is rejected. There is sufficient evidence to indicate the factors A and B interact at $\alpha = .05$. Since interaction is present, no tests for main effects are necessary.

15.45 a. To determine if Herd and Season interact, we test:

H_0: Herd and Season do not interact
H_a: Herd and Season interact

The test statistic is $F = 1.2$.

The p-value is $p > .05$. Since the p-value is greater than $\alpha = .05$, H_0 is not rejected. There is insufficient evidence to indicate that herd and season interact at $\alpha = .05$.

Since the two factors do not interact, the main effect tests are run.

To determine if the mean home range differs among the four herds, we test:

H_0: $\mu_1 = \mu_2 = \mu_3 = \mu_4$
H_a: At least two treatments means differ

where μ_i is the mean home range for herd i.

The test statistic is $F = 17.2$.

The p-value is $p < .001$. Since the p-value is less than $\alpha = .05$, H_0 is rejected. There is sufficient evidence to indicate that the mean home range differs among the four herds at $\alpha = .05$.

To determine if the mean home range differs among the four seasons, we test:

H_0: $\mu_1 = \mu_2 = \mu_3 = \mu_4$
H_a: At least two treatments means differ

where μ_i is the mean home range for season i.

The test statistic is $F = 3.0$.

The p-value is $p > .05$. Since the p-value is greater than $\alpha = .05$, H_0 is not rejected. There is insufficient evidence to indicate that the mean home range differs among the four seasons at $\alpha = .05$.

b. Yes. Since herd and season do not interact, each main effect factor can be treated separately as if the second factor did not exist.

c. The mean home range for herd MTZ is significantly greater than the mean home range for the herds PLC and LGN. The mean home range for herd QMD is significantly greater than the mean home range for the herds PLC and LGN. No other differences exist.

15.47 a. This is a 2×2 factorial experiment.

b. The two factors are the tent type (treated or untreated) and location (inside or outside). There are $2 \times 2 = 4$ treatments. The four treatments are (treated, inside), (treated, outside), (untreated, inside), and (untreated, outside).

c. The response variable is the number of mosquito bites received in a 20 minute interval.

d. There is sufficient evidence to indicate interaction is present. This indicates that the effect of the tent type on the number of mosquito bites depends on whether the person is inside or outside.

15.49 a. We first calculate the total of $n = 8$ pulling force measurements for each of the four categories by multiplying the means in each category by 8.

	Light	Heavy	Totals
Females	146.4	116.0	262.4
Males	104.0	98.0	202.0
Totals	250.4	214.0	

b. $\sum x_i = 146.4 + 116.0 + 104.0 + 98.0 = 464.4$

$$CM = \frac{\left(\sum x_i\right)^2}{n} = \frac{464.4^2}{32} = 6{,}739.605$$

c. $SS(Sex) = \dfrac{\sum A_i^2}{br} - CM = \dfrac{262.4^2}{2(8)} + \dfrac{202.0^2}{2(8)} - 6{,}739.605 = 6{,}853.61 - 6{,}739.605$
$= 114.005$

$SS(Weight) = \dfrac{\sum B_i^2}{ar} - CM = \dfrac{250.4^2}{2(8)} + \dfrac{214.0^2}{2(8)} - 6{,}739.605 = 6{,}781.01 - 6{,}739.605$
$= 41.405$

$SS(Sex \times Weight) = \dfrac{\sum\sum AB_{ij}^2}{r} - SS(Sex) - SS(Weight) - CM$

$= \dfrac{146.4^2}{8} + \dfrac{116.0^2}{8} + \dfrac{104.0^2}{8} + \dfrac{98.0^2}{8} - 114.005 - 41.405$
$- 6{,}739.605 = 18.605$

Design of Experiments and Analysis of Variance

d. The sum of squares of deviations within each sample are found by multiplying the variance by $n - 1 = 8 - 1 = 7$.

	Standard Deviation	Variance	SS
Female, Light	6.81	46.3761	324.6327
Female, Heavy	2.93	8.5849	60.0943
Male, Light	5.04	25.4016	177.8112
Male, Heavy	5.70	32.4900	227.4300
			789.9682

e. SSE = 789.9682

f. SS(Total) = SS(Sex) + SS(Weight) + SS(Sex × Weight) + SSE
    = 114.005 + 41.405 + 18.605 + 789.9682 = 963.9832

g.
Source	df	SS	MS	F
Sex	1	114.005	114.005	4.04
Weight	1	41.405	41.405	1.47
Sex × Weight	1	18.605	18.605	.66
Error	28	789.9682	18.21315	
Total	31	963.9832		

h. SST = SS(Sex) + SS(Weight) + SS(Sex × Weight) = 114.005 + 41.405 + 18.605
    = 174.015

$$MST = \frac{SST}{ab - 1} = \frac{174.015}{2(2) - 1} = 58.005$$

$$F_T = \frac{MST}{MSE} = \frac{58.005}{28.21315} = 2.06$$

To determine if differences exist among the treatment means, we test:

H_0: $\mu_1 = \mu_2 = \mu_3 = \mu_4$
H_a: At least one treatment mean is different

The test statistic is $F = \dfrac{MST}{MSE} = 2.06$

The rejection region requires $\alpha = .05$ in the upper tail of the F-distribution with $\nu_1 = ab - 1 = 2(2) - 1 = 3$ and $\nu_2 = n - ab = 32 - 2(2) = 28$. From Table VIII, Appendix B, $F_{.05} \approx 2.95$. The rejection region is $F > 2.95$.

Since the observed value of the test statistic does not fall in the rejection region ($F = 2.06 \not> 2.95$), H_0 is not rejected. There is insufficient evidence to indicate the treatment means differ at $\alpha = .05$.

Since there is no difference among the treatment means, no further analysis is warranted.

A graph of the means is:

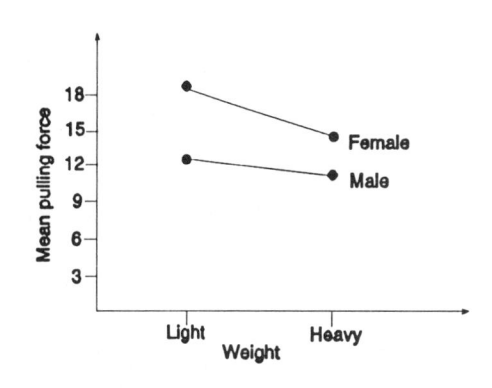

i. We must assume that:
1) The response times for each gender-weight categories are normally distributed.
2) The response time variances are the same for each gender-weight category.
3) Random and independent samples are drawn from each gender-weight category.

15.51 a. Let $x_1 = \begin{cases} 1 & \text{if level 1} \\ 0 & \text{otherwise} \end{cases}$ $x_2 = \begin{cases} 1 & \text{if level 2} \\ 0 & \text{otherwise} \end{cases}$

$x_3 = \begin{cases} 1 & \text{if level 3} \\ 0 & \text{otherwise} \end{cases}$ $x_4 = \begin{cases} 1 & \text{if level 4} \\ 0 & \text{otherwise} \end{cases}$

The model is $E(y) = \beta_0 + \beta_1 x_1 + \beta_2 x_2 + \beta_3 x_3 + \beta_4 x_4$ where

β_0 = mean response for level 5 of factor
β_1 = difference in mean response between levels 1 and 5
β_2 = difference in mean response between levels 2 and 5
β_3 = difference in mean response between levels 3 and 5
β_4 = difference in mean response between levels 4 and 5

b. Error df = $n - (k + 1) = 15 - (4 + 1) = 10$

c. $H_0: \beta_1 = \beta_2 = \beta_3 = \beta_4 = 0$

d. The rejection region requires $\alpha = .10$ in the upper tail of the F-distribution with $\nu_1 = k = 4$ and $\nu_2 = n - (k + 1) = 15 - (4 + 1) = 10$. From Table VII, Appendix B, $F_{.10} = 2.61$. The rejection region is $F > 2.61$.

15.53 a. To determine if the mean costs differ among the three groups, we test:

$H_0: \beta_1 = \beta_2 = 0$
H_a: At least one $\beta_i \neq 0$, $i = 1, 2$

The test statistic is $F = 8.438$.

The rejection region requires $\alpha = .05$ in the upper tail of the F-distribution with $\nu_1 = 2$ and $\nu_2 = 27$. From Table VIII, Appendix B, $F_{.05} = 3.35$. The rejection region is $F > 3.35$.

Since the observed value of the test statistic falls in the rejection region ($F = 8.438 > 3.35$), H_0 is rejected. There is sufficient evidence to indicate a difference in the treatment means among the 3 groups at $\alpha = .05$. This is the same result as found in Exercise 15.20.

b. The observed significance level for this problem is .0014, while the observed significance level for Exercise 15.20 is .0014.

Design of Experiments and Analysis of Variance

c. SST = 318,861.66667 for this problem and SST = 318,861.667 for Exercise 15.20.
SSE = 510,163 for this problem and SSE = 510,163 for Exercise 15.20.

d. $R^2 = .3846$. 38.46% of the sample variation in costs incurred in audits is explained by the three groups.

β_0 = mean costs incurred in audits for group C
β_1 = difference in mean costs incurred in audits between groups A and C
β_2 = difference in mean costs incurred in audits between groups B and C

15.55 a.

Treatment Price, Display	Estimate of Mean Response
Regular, Normal	$\hat{\beta}_0 + \hat{\beta}_1 + \hat{\beta}_3 + \hat{\beta}_5 = 1828.67 - 626 - 250.67 + 62.67 = 1014.67$
Regular, Normal Plus	$\hat{\beta}_0 + \hat{\beta}_1 + \hat{\beta}_4 + \hat{\beta}_6 = 1828.67 - 626 + 681.33 - 669 = 1215$
Regular, Twice Normal	$\hat{\beta}_0 + \hat{\beta}_1 = 1828.67 - 626 = 1202.67$
Reduced, Normal	$\hat{\beta}_0 + \hat{\beta}_2 + \hat{\beta}_3 + \hat{\beta}_7 = 1828.67 - 323.67 - 250.67 + 51.67 = 1202.66$
Reduced, Normal Plus	$\hat{\beta}_0 + \hat{\beta}_2 + \hat{\beta}_4 + \hat{\beta}_8 = 1828.67 - 323.67 + 681.33 - 287.67 = 1898.66$
Reduced, Twice Normal	$\hat{\beta}_0 + \hat{\beta}_2 = 1828.67 - 323.67 = 1505$
Cost, Normal	$\hat{\beta}_0 + \hat{\beta}_3 = 1828.67 - 250.67 = 1578$
Cost, Normal Plus	$\hat{\beta}_0 + \hat{\beta}_4 = 1828.67 + 681.33 = 2510$
Cost, Twice Normal	$\hat{\beta}_0 = 1828.67$

b. The estimate of the standard deviation is $\sqrt{MSE} = \sqrt{495} = 22.2486$.

We expect most of the observed values to fall within $\pm 2s$ or $\pm 2(22.2486)$ or ± 44.4972 of their predicted values.

$R^2 = .999$. 99.9% of the sample variation in unit sales is explained by the nine different display and price combinations.

c. To determine if the mean unit sales differ for the nine treatments, we test:

H_0: $\beta_1 = \beta_2 = \beta_3 = \cdots = \beta_8 = 0$
H_a: At least one $\beta_i \neq 0$, $i = 1, 2, \ldots, 8$

The test statistic is $F = \dfrac{MSR}{MSE} = 1336.85$

The rejection region requires $\alpha = .10$ in the upper tail of the F-distribution with $\nu_1 = 8$ and $\nu_2 = 18$. From Table VII, Appendix B, $F_{.10} = 2.04$. The rejection region is $F > 2.04$.

Since the observed value of the test statistic falls in the rejection region ($F = 1336.85 > 2.04$), H_0 is rejected. There is sufficient evidence to indicate there are differences in mean unit sales among the 9 treatments at $\alpha = .10$. This is the same result as in Exercise 15.36.

d. The null hypothesis used to test for interaction is:

H_0: $\beta_5 = \beta_6 = \beta_7 = \beta_8 = 0$

The test statistic is $F = \dfrac{(SSE_r - SSE_c)/(k - g)}{SSE_c/[n - (k + 1)]}$

The rejection region requires $\alpha = .10$ in the upper tail of the F-distribution with $\nu_1 = 4$ and $\nu_2 = 18$. From Table VII, Appendix B, $F_{.10} = 2.29$. The rejection region is $F > 2.29$.

e. $F = \dfrac{(519610.1481 - 8905.3333)/(8 - 4)}{8905.3333/[27 - (8 + 1)]} = \dfrac{127{,}676.2037}{494.7407} = 258.07$

Since the observed value of the test statistic falls in the rejection region ($F = 258.07 > 2.29$), H_0 is rejected. There is sufficient evidence to indicate interaction is present at $\alpha = .10$. This is the same result as in Exercise 15.46.

f. No further testing is necessary. Our next step would be to compare the treatment means using Bonferroni's multiple comparisons procedure.

15.57 There are $3 \times 2 = 6$ treatments. They are A_1B_1, A_1B_2, A_2B_1, A_2B_2, A_3B_1, and A_3B_2.

15.59 a. SSE = SSTot − SST = 62.55 − 36.95 = 25.60

df Treatment = $p - 1 = 4 - 1 = 3$
df Error = $n - p = 20 - 4 = 16$
df Total = $n - 1 = 20 - 1 = 19$

MST = SST/df = $\dfrac{36.95}{3} = 12.32$

MSE = SSE/df = $\dfrac{25.60}{16} = 1.60$

$F = \dfrac{MST}{MSE} = \dfrac{12.32}{1.60} = 7.70$

The ANOVA table:

Source	df	SS	MS	F
Treatment	3	36.95	12.32	7.70
Error	16	25.60	1.60	
Total	19	62.55		

b. To determine if there is a difference in the treatment means, we test:

H_0: $\mu_1 = \mu_2 = \mu_3 = \mu_4$
H_a: At least two of the means differ

where the μ_i represents the mean for the ith treatment.

The test statistic is $F = \dfrac{MST}{MSE} = 7.70$

The rejection region requires $\alpha = .10$ in the upper tail of the F-distribution with $\nu_1 = (p - 1) = (4 - 1) = 3$ and $\nu_2 = (n - p) = (20 - 4) = 16$. From Table VII, Appendix B, $F_{.10} = 2.46$. The rejection region is $F > 2.46$.

Since the observed value of the test statistic falls in the rejection region ($F = 7.70 > 2.46$), H_0 is rejected. There is sufficient evidence to conclude that at least two of the means differ at $\alpha = .10$.

c. $\bar{x}_4 = \dfrac{\sum x_4}{n_4} = \dfrac{57}{5} = 11.4$

For confidence level .90, $\alpha = .10$ and $\alpha/2 = .10/2 = .05$. From Table VI, Appendix B, with df = 16, $t_{.05} = 1.746$. The confidence interval is:

$\bar{x}_4 \pm t_{.05} \cdot \sqrt{MSE/n_4} \Rightarrow 11.4 \pm 1.746 \cdot \sqrt{1.6/5} \Rightarrow 11.4 \pm .99 \Rightarrow (10.41, 12.39)$

15.61 a. The data are collected as a completely randomized design because five boxes of each size were randomly selected and tested.

b. Yes. The confidence intervals surrounding each of the means do not overlap. This would indicate that there is a difference in the means for the two sizes.

c. No. Several of the confidence intervals overlap. This would indicate that the mean compression strengths of the sizes that have intervals that overlap are not significantly different.

15.63 a. To determine if leadership style affects behavior of subordinates, we test:

H_0: All four treatment means are the same
H_a: At least two treatment means differ

The test statistic is $F = 30.4$.

The rejection region requires $\alpha = .05$ in the upper tail of the F-distribution with $\nu_1 = ab - 1 = 2(2) - 1 = 3$ and $\nu_2 = n - ab = 257 - 2(2) = 253$. From Table VIII, Appendix B, $F_{.05} \approx 2.60$. The rejection region is $F > 2.60$.

Since the observed value of the test statistic falls in the rejection region ($F = 30.4 > 2.60$), H_0 is rejected. There is sufficient evidence to indicate that leadership style affects behavior of subordinates at $\alpha = .05$.

b. From the table, the mean response for High control, low consideration is significantly higher than for any other treatment. The mean response for Low control, low consideration is significantly higher than that for High control, high consideration and for Low control, high consideration. No other significant differences exist.

c. The assumptions for Bonferroni's method are the same as those for the ANOVA. Thus, we must assume that:

i. The populations sampled from are normal.
ii. The population variances are the same.
iii. The samples are independent.

15.65 a. The type of experimental design is completely randomized and a two-factor complete factorial.

b. The degrees of freedom associated with SSE = $n - ab = 120 - 2(2) = 116$.

c. To determine whether the salesperson's territory and level of effort interact, we test:

H_0: Territory and level of effort do not interact to affect the perception of performance
H_a: Territory and level of effort do interact to affect the perception of performance

The test statistic is $F = 1.95$.

The rejection region requires $\alpha = .05$ in the upper tail of the F-distribution with $\nu_1 = (a-1)(b-1) = (2-1)(2-1) = 1$ and $\nu_2 = n - ab = 120 - 2(2) = 116$. From Table VIII, Appendix B, $F_{.05} \approx 3.92$. The rejection region is $F > 3.92$.

Since the observed value of the test statistic does not fall in the rejection region ($F = 1.95 \not> 3.92$), H_0 is not rejected. There is insufficient evidence to indicate territory and level of effort interact at $\alpha = .05$.

d. To determine whether the salesperson's territory influences performance ratings, we test:

H_0: $\mu_1 = \mu_2$
H_a: $\mu_1 \neq \mu_2$

The test statistic is $F = .39$.

The rejection region requires $\alpha = .05$ in the upper tail of the F-distribution with $\nu_1 = (a-1) = 2 - 1 = 1$ and $\nu_2 = n - ab = 120 - 2(2) = 116$. From Table VIII, Appendix B, $F_{.05} \approx 3.92$. The rejection region is $F > 3.92$.

Since the observed value of the test statistic does not fall in the rejection region ($F = .39 \not> 3.92$), H_0 is not rejected. There is insufficient evidence to indicate a salesperson's territory influences performance ratings at $\alpha = .05$.

e. To determine whether the salesperson's level of effort influences performance ratings, we test:

H_0: $\mu_1 = \mu_2$
H_a: $\mu_1 \neq \mu_2$

The test statistic is $F = 53.27$.

The rejection region requires $\alpha = .05$ in the upper tail of the F-distribution with $\nu_1 = (b-1) = 2 - 1 = 1$ and $\nu_2 = n - ab = 120 - 2(2) = 116$. From Table VIII, Appendix B, $F_{.05} \approx 3.92$. The rejection region is $F > 3.92$.

Since the observed value of the test statistic falls in the rejection region ($F = 53.27 > 3.92$), H_0 is rejected. There is sufficient evidence to indicate a salesperson's level of effort influences performance ratings at $\alpha = .05$.

f. The results confirm the hypothesis of Mowen, et al. They suggested that managers underutilize data on the salesperson's territory and rely on data associated with how much effort the salesperson expended. The tests showed that territory did not affect the perceived performance, implying the managers do not take territory into account.

g. We must assume:
    1. The response distribution for each factor level combination is normal.
    2. The response variance is constant for all treatments.

3. Random and independent samples of experimental units are associated with each treatment.

15.67 a. This is a completely randomized design with a complete four-factor factorial design.

b. There are a total of $2 \times 2 \times 2 \times 2 = 16$ treatments.

c. Using SAS, the output is:

Analysis of Variance Procedure

Dependent Variable: Y

Source	DF	Sum of Squares	Mean Square	F Value	Pr > F
Model	15	546745.50	36449.70	5.11	0.0012
Error	16	114062.00	7128.88		
Corrected Total	31	660807.50			

R-Square	C.V.	Root MSE	Y Mean
0.827390	41.46478	84.433	203.63

Source	DF	Anova SS	Mean Square	F Value	Pr > F
SPEED	1	56784.50	56784.50	7.97	0.0123
FEED	1	21218.00	21218.00	2.98	0.1037
SPEED*FEED	1	55444.50	55444.50	7.78	0.0131
COLLET	1	165025.13	165025.13	23.15	0.0002
SPEED*COLLET	1	44253.13	44253.13	6.21	0.0241
FEED*COLLET	1	142311.13	142311.13	19.96	0.0004
SPEED*FEED*COLLET	1	54946.13	54946.13	7.71	0.0135
WEAR	1	378.13	378.13	0.05	0.8208
SPEED*WEAR	1	1540.13	1540.13	0.22	0.6483
FEED*WEAR	1	946.13	946.13	0.13	0.7204
SPEED*FEED*WEAR	1	528.13	528.13	0.07	0.7890
COLLET*WEAR	1	1682.00	1682.00	0.24	0.6337
SPEED*COLLET*WEAR	1	512.00	512.00	0.07	0.7921
FEED*COLLET*WEAR	1	72.00	72.00	0.01	0.9212
SPEE*FEED*COLLE*WEAR	1	1104.50	1104.50	0.15	0.6991

d. To determine if the interaction terms are significant, we must add together the sum of squares for all interaction terms as well as the degrees of freedom.

SS(Interaction) = 55,444.50 + 44,253.13 + 142,311.13 + 54,946.13 + 1,540.13 + 946.13
   + 528.13 + 1,682.00 + 512.00 + 72.00 + 1,104.50
   = 303,339.78

df(Interacton) = 11

$$\text{MS(Interaction)} = \frac{\text{SS(Interacton)}}{\text{df(Interaction)}} = \frac{303{,}339.78}{11} = 27{,}576.34364$$

$$\text{F(Interacton)} = \frac{\text{MS(Interaction)}}{\text{MSE}} = \frac{27{,}576.34364}{7128.88} = 3.87$$

To determine if interaction effects are present, we test:

H_0: No interaction effects exist
H_a: Interaction effects exist

The test statistic is $F = 3.87$.

The rejection region requires $\alpha = .05$ in the upper tail of the F-distribution with $\nu_1 = 11$ and $\nu_2 = 16$. From Table VIII, Appendix B, $F_{.05} \approx 2.49$. The rejection region is $F > 2.49$.

Since the observed value of the test statistic falls in the rejection region ($F = 3.87 > 2.49$), H_0 is rejected. There is sufficient evidence to indicate that interaction effects exist at $\alpha = .05$.

Since the sums of squares for a balanced factorial design are independent of each other, we can look at the SAS output to determine which of the interaction effects are significant. The three-way interaction between speed, feed, and collet is significant ($p = .0135$). There are three two-way interactions with p-values less than .05. However, all of these two-way interaction terms are imbedded in the significant three-way interaction term.

e. Yes. Since the significant interaction terms do not include wear, it would be necessary to perform the main effect test for wear. All other main effects are contained in a significant interaction term.

To determine if the mean finish measurements differ for the different levels of wear, we test:

H_0: The mean finish measurements for the two levels of wear are the same
H_a: The mean finish measurements for the two levels of wear are different

The test statistic is $t = 0.05$.

The rejection region requires $\alpha = .05$ in the upper tail of the F-distribution with $\nu_1 = 1$ and $\nu_2 = 16$. From Table VIII, Appendix B, $F_{.05} = 4.49$. The rejection region is $F > 4.49$.

Since the observed value of the test statistic does not fall in the rejection region ($F = .05 \not> 4.49$), H_0 is not rejected. There is insufficient evidence to indicate that the mean finish measurements differ for the different levels of wear at $\alpha = .05$.

f. We must assume that:
   i. The populations sampled from are normal.
   ii. The population variances are the same.
   iii. The samples are random and independent.

15.69 a. df(Companies) $= p - 1 = 2 - 1 = 1$
df(Error) $= n - p = 100 - 2 = 98$

$$\text{MST} = \frac{\text{SST}}{p-1} = \frac{3237.2}{2-1} = 3237.2 \qquad \text{MSE} = \frac{\text{SSE}}{n-p} = \frac{16167.7}{100-2} = 164.9765$$

$$F = \frac{\text{MST}}{\text{MSE}} = \frac{3237.2}{164.9765} = 19.62$$

Source	df	SS	MS	F
Companies	1	3237.2	3237.2	19.62
Error	98	16167.7	164.9765	
Total	99	19404.9		

b. To determine if the mean number of hours missed differs for employees of the two companies, we test:

H_0: $\mu_1 = \mu_2$
H_a: $\mu_1 \neq \mu_2$

The test statistic is $F = \dfrac{\text{MST}}{\text{MSE}} = 19.62$

The rejection region requires $\alpha = .05$ in the upper tail of the F-distribution with $\nu_1 = p - 1 = 2 - 1 = 1$ and $\nu_2 = n - p = 100 - 2 = 98$. From Table VIII, Appendix B, $F_{.05} \approx 4.00$. The rejection region is $F > 4.00$.

Since the observed value of the test statistic falls in the rejection region ($F = 19.62 > 4.00$), H_0 is rejected. There is sufficient evidence to indicate the mean number of hours missed differs for employees of the two companies at $\alpha = .05$.

c. No. We need the sample means for the two companies.

15.71 a. The experiment is completely randomized. The response is the attitude test score after 1 month. The two factors are scheduling (2 levels) and payment (2 levels). Both factors are qualitative. There are $2 \times 2 = 4$ different treatments, where each treatment consists of a level of each factor, A_1B_1, A_1B_2, A_2B_1, and A_2B_2. The experimental units are the workers.

b. To determine if the treatment means differ, we test:

H_0: $\mu_1 = \mu_2 = \mu_3 = \mu_4$
H_a: At least one treatment mean differs

The test statistic is $F = \dfrac{\text{MST}}{\text{MSE}} = 12.29$

The rejection region requires $\alpha = .05$ in the upper tail of the F-distribution with $\nu_1 = ab - 1 = 2(2) - 1 = 3$ and $\nu_2 = n - ab = 16 - 2(2) = 12$. From Table VIII, Appendix B, $F_{.05} = 3.49$. The rejection region is $F > 3.49$.

Since the observed value of the test statistic falls in the rejection region ($F = 12.29 > 3.49$), H_0 is rejected. There is sufficient evidence to indicate the treatment means differ at $\alpha = .05$.

c. To determine if the factors interact, we test:

H_0: Factor A and factor B do not interact to affect the response mean
H_a: Factors A and B do interact to affect the response mean

The test statistic is $F = \dfrac{\text{MS}AB}{\text{MSE}} = .02$

The rejection region requires $\alpha = .05$ in the upper tail of the F-distribution with $\nu_1 = (a - 1)(b - 1) = (2 - 1)(2 - 1) = 1$ and $\nu_2 = n - ab = 16 - 2(2) = 12$. From Table VIII, Appendix B, $F_{.05} = 4.75$. The rejection region is $F > 4.75$.

Since the observed value of the test statistic does not fall in the rejection region ($F = .02 \not> 4.75$), H_0 is not rejected. There is insufficient evidence to indicate the factors interact at $\alpha = .05$.

To determine if the mean attitude test scores differ for the two types of scheduling, we test:

H_0: $\mu_1 = \mu_2$
H_a: $\mu_1 \ne \mu_2$

The test statistic is $F = \dfrac{\text{MS(Schedule)}}{\text{MSE}} = 7.37$

The rejection region requires $\alpha = .05$ in the upper tail of the F-distribution with $\nu_1 = (a - 1) = 2 - 1 = 1$ and $\nu_2 = n - ab = 16 - 2(2) = 12$. From Table VIII, Appendix B, $F_{.05} = 4.75$. The rejection region is $F > 4.75$.

Since the observed value of the test statistic falls in the rejection region ($F = 7.37 > 4.75$), H_0 is rejected. There is sufficient evidence to indicate the mean attitude test scores differ for the two types of scheduling at $\alpha = .05$.

To determine if the mean attitude test scores differ for the two types of payments, we test:

H_0: $\mu_1 = \mu_2$
H_a: $\mu_1 \neq \mu_2$

The test statistic is $F = \dfrac{\text{MS(Payment)}}{\text{MSE}} = 29.47$

The rejection region requires $\alpha = .05$ in the upper tail of the F-distribution with $\nu_1 = b - 1 = 2 - 1 = 1$ and $\nu_2 = n - ab = 16 - 2(2) = 12$. From Table VIII, Appendix B, $F_{.05} = 4.75$. The rejection region is $F > 4.75$.

Since the observed value of the test statistic falls in the rejection region ($F = 29.47 > 4.75$), H_0 is rejected. There is sufficient evidence to indicate the mean attitude test scores differ for the two types of payment at $\alpha = .05$.

Since the mean attitude test scores for 8-5 is $558/8 = 69.75$ and the mean for worker-modified schedules is $634/8 = 79.25$, the mean attitude test scores for those on worker-modified schedules is significantly higher than for those on 8-5 schedules.

Since the mean attitude test scores for those on hourly rate is $520/8 = 65$ and the mean for those on hourly and piece rate is $672/8 = 84$, the mean attitude test scores for those on hourly and piece rate is significantly higher than for those on hourly rate.

d. The necessary assumptions are:

1. The probability distributions for each schedule-payment combination is normal.
2. The variances for each distribution are equal.
3. The samples are random and independent.

15.73 a. This is an observational experiment and is completely randomized.

b. To determine if the mean closing price differed among the three markets, we test:

H_0: $\mu_1 = \mu_2 = \mu_3$
H_a: At least two treatment means differ

The test statistic is $F = \dfrac{\text{MST}}{\text{MSE}} = 3.34$

The rejection region requires $\alpha = .10$ in the upper tail of the F-distribution with $\nu_1 = p - 1 = 3 - 1 = 2$ and $\nu_2 = n - p = 108 - 3 = 105$. From Table VII, Appendix B, $F_{.10} \approx 2.39$. The rejection region is $F > 2.39$.

Since the observed value of the test statistic falls in the rejection region ($F = 3.34 > 2.39$), H_0 is rejected. There is sufficient evidence to indicate the mean closing price differed among the three markets at $\alpha = .10$.

c. From the printout, the mean closing price for the NYSE is significantly higher than the mean closing price for the ASE. No other significant differences exist.

The experimentwise error rate is $\alpha = .05$.

15.75 a. This is a completely randomized design.

b. Using the formulas in Appendix B:

$$CM = \frac{(\sum y_i)^2}{n} = \frac{497^2}{17} = 14{,}529.9412$$

$$SS(\text{Total}) = \sum y_i^2 - CM = 14{,}713 - 14{,}529.9412 = 183.059$$

$$SST = SS(\text{Plan}) = \frac{T_1^2}{n_1} + \frac{T_2^2}{n_2} + \frac{T_3^2}{n_3} + \frac{T_4^2}{n_4} - CM$$

$$= \frac{107^2}{4} + \frac{134^2}{5} + \frac{162^2}{5} + \frac{94^2}{3} - 14{,}529.9412 = 117.642$$

$$SSE = SS(\text{Total}) - SS(\text{Plan}) = 183.059 - 117.642 = 65.417$$

$$MST = MS(\text{Plan}) = \frac{SS(\text{Plan})}{p-1} = \frac{117.642}{4-1} = 39.214, \quad df = p - 1 = 3$$

$$MSE = \frac{SSE}{n-p} = \frac{65.417}{17-4} = 5.032, \quad df = n - p = 13$$

$$F = \frac{MS(\text{Plan})}{MSE} = \frac{39.214}{5.032} = 7.79$$

Source	df	SS	MS	F
Treatment	3	117.642	39.214	7.79
Error	13	65.417	5.032	
Total	16	183.059		

c. To determine if the mean travel times for the four plans differ, we test:

H_0: $\mu_1 = \mu_2 = \mu_3 = \mu_4$
H_a: At least two of the mean travel times differ

The test statistic is $F = \dfrac{MS(\text{Plan})}{MSE} = 7.79$

The rejection region requires $\alpha = .01$ in the upper tail of the F-distribution with $\nu_1 = p - 1 = 4 - 1 = 3$ and $\nu_2 = n - p = 17 - 4 = 13$. From Table X, Appendix B, $F_{.01} = 5.74$. The rejection region is $F > 5.74$.

Since the observed value of the test statistic falls in the rejection region ($F = 7.79 > 5.74$), H_0 is rejected. There is sufficient evidence of a difference in mean travel times for the plans at $\alpha = .01$.

d. Using SAS and $\alpha = .05$, the Tukey's multiple comparison is:

```
                Analysis of Variance Procedure

        Tukey's Studentized Range (HSD) Test for variable:  Y

    NOTE:  This test controls the type I experimentwise error rate.

            Alpha= 0.05  Confidence= 0.95  df= 13  MSE= 5.032051
                 Critical Value of Studentized Range= 4.151

    Comparisons significant at the 0.05 level are indicated by '***'.

                       Simultaneous                    Simultaneous
                          Lower       Difference          Upper
            PLAN        Confidence     Between         Confidence
         Comparison       Limit         Means             Limit

           3  -  4       -3.742         1.067            5.875
           3  -  2        1.436         5.600            9.764      ***
           3  -  1        1.233         5.650           10.067      ***

           4  -  3       -5.875        -1.067            3.742
           4  -  2       -0.275         4.533            9.342
           4  -  1       -0.445         4.583            9.612

           2  -  3       -9.764        -5.600           -1.436      ***
           2  -  4       -9.342        -4.533            0.275
           2  -  1       -4.367         0.050            4.467

           1  -  3      -10.067        -5.650           -1.233      ***
           1  -  4       -9.612        -4.583            0.445
           1  -  2       -4.467        -0.050            4.367
```

From the output, the confidence intervals that do not contain 0 indicate that the means are significantly different. The mean travel time for Plan 3 is significantly longer than the mean travel times for Plans 1 and 2. No other significant differences exist.

Design of Experiments and Analysis of Variance

Nonparametric Statistics — Chapter 16

16.1 The sign test is preferred to the *t*-test when the population from which the sample is selected is not normal.

16.3 a. $P(x \geq 7) = 1 - P(x \leq 6) = 1 - .965 = .035$

  b. $P(x \geq 5) = 1 - P(x \leq 4) = 1 - .637 = .363$

  c. $P(x \geq 8) = 1 - P(x \leq 7) = 1 - .996 = .004$

  d. $P(x \geq 10) = 1 - P(x \leq 9) = 1 - .849 = .151$

  $\mu = np = 15(.5) = 7.5$ and $\sigma = \sqrt{npq} = \sqrt{15(.5)(.5)} = 1.9365$

  $P(x \geq 10) \approx P\left(z \geq \dfrac{(10 - .5) - 7.5}{1.9365}\right) = P(z \geq 1.03) = .5 - .3485 = .1515$

  e. $P(x \geq 15) = 1 - P(x \leq 14) = 1 - .788 = .212$

  $\mu = np = 25(.5) = 12.5$ and $\sigma = \sqrt{npq} = \sqrt{25(.5)(.5)} = 2.5$

  $P(x \geq 15) \approx P\left(z \geq \dfrac{(15 - .5) - 12.5}{2.5}\right) = P(z \geq .80) = .5 - .2881 = .2119$

16.5 To determine if the median is greater than 75, we test:

$H_0: \eta = 75$
$H_a: \eta > 75$

The test statistic is S = number of measurements greater than $75 = 17$.

The *p*-value = $P(x \geq 17)$ where x is a binomial random variable with $n = 25$ and $p = .5$. From Table II,

$p\text{-value} = P(x \geq 17) = 1 - P(x \leq 16) = 1 - .946 = .054$

Since the *p*-value = $.054 < \alpha = .10$, H_0 is rejected. There is sufficient evidence to indicate the median is greater than 75 at $\alpha = .10$.

We must assume the sample was randomly selected from a continuous probability distribution.

Note: Since $n \geq 10$, we could use the large-sample approximation.

16.7 a. To determine whether the median biting rate is higher in bright, sunny weather, we test:

$H_0: \eta = 5$
$H_a: \eta > 5$

b. The test statistic is $z = \dfrac{(S - .5) - .5n}{.5\sqrt{n}} = \dfrac{(95 - .5) - .5(122)}{.5\sqrt{122}} = 6.07$

(where $S =$ number of observations greater than 5)

The p-value is $p = P(z \geq 6.07)$. From Table IV, Appendix B, $p = P(z \geq 6.07) \approx 0.0000$.

c. Since the observed p-value is less than α ($p = 0.0000 < .01$), H_0 is rejected. There is sufficient evidence to indicate that the median biting rate in bright, sunny weather is greater than 5 at $\alpha = .01$.

16.9 a. I would recommend the sign test because five of the sample measurements are of similar magnitude, but the 6th is about three times as large as the others. It would be very unlikely to observe this sample if the population were normal.

b. To determine if the airline is meeting the requirement, we test:

$H_0: \eta = 30$
$H_a: \eta < 30$

c. The test statistic is $S =$ number of measurements less than $30 = 5$.

H_0 will be rejected if the p-value $< \alpha = .01$.

d. The test statistic is $S = 5$.

The p-value $= P(x \geq 5)$ where x is a binomial random variable with $n = 6$ and $p = .5$. From Table II,

p-value $= P(x \geq 5) = 1 - P(x \leq 4) = 1 - .891 = .109$

Since the p-value $= .109$ is not less than $\alpha = .01$, H_0 is not rejected. There is insufficient evidence to indicate the airline is meeting the maintenance requirement at $\alpha = .01$.

16.11 a. The test statistic is T_B, the rank sum of population B (because $n_B < n_A$).

The rejection region is $T_B \leq 35$ or $T_B \geq 67$, from Table XI, Appendix B, with $n_A = 10$, $n_B = 6$, and $\alpha = .10$.

b. The test statistic is T_A, the rank sum of population A (because $n_A < n_B$).

The rejection region is $T_A \geq 43$, from Table XI, Appendix B, with $n_A = 5$, $n_B = 7$, and $\alpha = .05$.

c. The test statistic is T_B, the rank sum of population B (because $n_B < n_A$).

The rejection region is $T_B \geq 93$, from Table XI, Appendix B, with $n_A = 9$, $n_B = 8$, and $\alpha = .025$.

d. Since $n_A = n_B = 15$, the test statistic is:

$$z = \frac{T_A - \frac{n_1(n_1 + n_2 + 1)}{2}}{\sqrt{\frac{n_1 n_2(n_1 + n_2 + 1)}{12}}}$$

The rejection region is $z < -z_{\alpha/2}$ or $z > z_{\alpha/2}$. For $\alpha = .05$ and $\alpha/2 = .05/2 = .025$, $z_{.025} = 1.96$ from Table IV, Appendix B. The rejection region is $z < -1.96$ or $z > 1.96$.

16.13 The Wilcoxon rank sum test is a test of the location (center) of a distribution. The one-tailed test deals specifically with the center of one distribution being shifted in one direction (right or left) from the other distribution. The two-tailed test does not specify a particular direction of shift; we consider the possibility of a shift in either direction.

16.15 a. Some preliminary calculations:

Private Sector	Rank	Public Sector	Rank
2.58	10	5.40	15
5.05	13	2.55	9
0.05	1	9.00	16
2.10	5	10.55	17
4.30	12	1.02	2
2.25	6	5.11	14
2.50	8	12.42	18
1.94	4	1.67	3
2.33	7	3.33	11
	$T_1 = 66$		$T_2 = 105$

To determine if the distribution for public sector organizations is located to the right of the distribution for private sector firms, we test:

H_0: The two sampled populations have identical probability distributions
H_a: The probability distribution of the public sector is located to the right of that for the private sector

The test statistic is $T_2 = 105$.

The null hypothesis will be rejected if $T_2 \geq T_U$ where T_U corresponds to $\alpha = .025$ (one-tailed), and $n_1 = n_2 = 9$. From Table XI, Appendix B, $T_U = 108$. (There is no table for $\alpha = .01$. However, if we do not reject H_0 for $\alpha = .025$, we will not reject H_0 for $\alpha = .01$.)

Reject H_0 if $T_2 \geq 108$.

Since $T_2 = 105 \not\geq 108$, H_0 is not rejected. There is insufficient evidence to indicate that the distribution for public sector organizations is located to the right of the distribution for private sector firms at $\alpha = .01$.

b. The null hypothesis will be rejected if $T_2 \geq T_U$ where T_U corresponds to $\alpha = .05$ (one-tailed), and $n_1 = n_2 = 9$. From Table XI, Appendix B, $T_U = 105$. Since $T_1 = 105$, we would reject H_0. Thus, the p-value is less than or equal to $\alpha = .05$.

c. The assumptions necessary for the test are:
1. The two samples are random and independent.
2. The two probability distributions from which the samples were drawn are continuous.

16.17

Neighborhood A	Rank	Neighborhood B	Rank
.850	11	.911	16
1.060	18	.770	3
.910	15	.815	8
.813	7	.748	2
.737	1	.835	9
.880	13	.800	6
.895	14	.793	4
.844	10	.796	5
.965	17		
.875	12		
	$T_A = 118$		$T_B = 53$

a. H_0: The two sampled neighborhoods have identical probability distributions
H_a: The probability distribution for neighborhood A is shifted to the right or left of neighborhood B

The test statistic is $T_B = 53$.

The null hypothesis will be rejected if $T_B \leq T_L$ or $T_B \geq T_U$ where $\alpha = .05$ (two-tailed), $n_1 = 8$ and $n_2 = 10$. From Table XI, Appendix B, $T_L = 54$ and $T_U = 98$.

Reject H_0 if $T_B \leq 54$ or $T_B \geq 98$.

Since $T_B = 53 \leq 54$, we reject H_0 and conclude there is sufficient evidence to indicate neighborhood A is shifted to the right or left of neighborhood B at $\alpha = .05$.

b. The two independent sample t-test is based on the assumptions of:
1. random, independent samples from
2. normally distributed populations with
3. equal variances.

The assumption of normal populations with equal variances would be necessary to use the t-test.

c. 1. The two samples are random and independent.
2. The two probability distributions from which the samples are drawn are continuous.

16.19

U.S. Plants		Japanese Plants	
Observation	Rank	Observation	Rank
7.11	9	3.52	4
6.06	7	2.02	2
8.00	10	4.91	6
6.87	8	3.22	3
4.77	5	1.92	1
	$T_A = 39$		$T_B = 16$

Nonparametric Statistics

To determine if the distribution of American plants is shifted to the right of that for Japanese plants, we test:

H_0: The two sampled population have identical probability distributions
H_a: The probability distribution for American plants is shifted to the right of that for Japanese plants

The test statistic is $T_A = 39$.

The rejection region is $T_A \geq 36$ from Table XI, Appendix B, with $n_A = n_B = 5$, and $\alpha = .05$.

Since the observed value of the test statistic falls in the rejection region ($T_A = 39 \geq 36$), H_0 is rejected. There is sufficient evidence to indicate the probability distribution for U.S. plants is shifted to the right of that for Japanese plants at $\alpha = .05$.

This result agrees with that from Exercise 9.21.

16.21 a. We first rank all the data:

\multicolumn{4}{c	}{Firms with Successful MIS (A)}	\multicolumn{4}{c}{Firms with Unsuccessful MIS (B)}
Score	Rank	Score	Rank	Score	Rank	Score	Rank
52	5	90	25.5	60	10.5	65	12.5
70	15	75	17	50	4	55	7
40	1.5	80	19	55	7	70	15
80	19	95	29.5	70	15	90	25.5
82	21	90	25.5	41	3	85	22
65	12.5	86	23	40	1.5	80	19
59	9	95	29.5	55	7	90	25.5
60	10.5	93	28				
\multicolumn{4}{c	}{$T_A = 290.5$}	\multicolumn{4}{c}{$T_B = 174.5$}

To determine whether the distribution of quality scores for successfully implemented systems lies above that for unsuccessfully implemented systems, we test:

H_0: The two sampled populations have identical probability distributions
H_a: The probability distribution for successful MIS is shifted to the right of that for the unsuccessful MIS

The test statistic is $z = -1.75103$ (from printout).

The rejection region requires $\alpha = .05$ in the upper tail of the z-distribution. From Table IV, Appendix B, $z_{.05} = 1.645$. The rejection region is $z > -1.645$.

Since the observed value of the test statistic falls in the rejection region ($z = -1.75103 < -1.645$), H_0 is rejected. There is sufficient evidence to indicate the distribution of quality scores for successfully or good implemented systems lies above that for the unsuccessfully or poor implemented systems at $\alpha = .05$.

b. We could use the two-sample t-test if:

1. Both populations are normal.
2. The variances of the two populations are the same.

16.23 a. The hypotheses are:

H_0: The two sampled populations have identical probability distributions
H_a: The probability distributions for population A is shifted to the right of that for population B

b. Some preliminary calculations are:

Treatment		Difference	Rank of Absolute
A	B	A − B	Difference
54	45	9	5
60	45	15	10
98	87	11	7
43	31	12	9
82	71	11	7
77	75	2	2.5
74	63	11	7
29	30	−1	1
63	59	4	4
80	82	−2	2.5
			$T_- = 3.5$

The test statistic is $T_- = 3.5$

The rejection region is $T_- \leq 8$, from Table XII, Appendix B, with $n = 10$ and $\alpha = .025$.

Since the observed value of the test statistic falls in the rejection region ($T_- = 3.5 \leq 8$), H_0 is rejected. There is sufficient evidence to indicate the responses for A tend to be larger than those for B at $\alpha = .025$.

16.25 We assume that the probability distribution of differences is continuous so that the absolute differences will have unique ranks. Although tied (absolute) differences can be assigned average ranks, the number of ties should be small relative to the number of observations to assure validity.

16.27 a. H_0: The two sampled populations have identical probability distributions
H_a: The probability distribution for population A is located to the right of that for population B

b. The test statistic is:

$$z = \frac{T_+ - \frac{n(n+1)}{4}}{\sqrt{\frac{n(n+1)(2n+1)}{24}}} = \frac{354 - \frac{30(30+1)}{4}}{\sqrt{\frac{30(30+1)(60+1)}{24}}} = \frac{121.5}{48.6184} = 2.499$$

The rejection region requires $\alpha = .05$ in the upper tail of the z-distribution. From Table IV, Appendix B, $z = 1.645$. The rejection region is $z > 1.645$.

Since the observed value of the test statistic falls in the rejection region ($z = 2.499 > 1.645$), H_0 is rejected. There is sufficient evidence to indicate population A is located to the right of that for population B at $\alpha = .05$.

c. The p-value $= P(z \geq 2.499) = .5 - .4938 = .0062$ (using Table IV, Appendix B).

d. The necessary assumptions are:
   1. The sample of differences is randomly selected from the population of differences.
   2. The probability distribution from which the sample of paired differences is drawn is continuous.

16.29 a. This is a paired difference problem.

b. To determine if the problem-solving performance of video teleconferencing groups is superior to face-to-face groups, we test:

H_0: The two sampled populations have identical probability distributions
H_a: The probability distribution for population A (face-to-face) is shifted to the left of that for population B (video teleconferencing)

c. Some preliminary calculations:

Group	Face-To-Face	Video Teleconferencing	Difference	Rank of Absolute Difference
1	65	75	−10	7.5
2	82	80	2	1
3	54	60	−6	6
4	69	65	4	2.5
5	40	55	−15	9
6	85	90	−5	4.5
7	98	98	0	(eliminated)
8	35	40	−5	4.5
9	85	89	−4	2.5
10	70	80	−10	7.5

Negative rank sum $T_- = 41.5$
Positive rank sum $T_+ = 3.5$

The test statistic is $T_+ = 3.5$.

The null hypothesis will be rejected if $T_+ \leq T_0$ where T_0 corresponds to $\alpha = .05$ (one-tailed) and $n = 9$. From Table XII, Appendix B, $T_0 = 8$.

Reject H_0 if $T_+ \leq 8$.

Since the observed value of the test statistic falls in the rejection region ($T_+ = 3.5 \leq 8$), H_0 is rejected. There is sufficient evidence to indicate that problem-solving performance of video teleconferencing groups is superior to that of groups that interact face-to-face at $\alpha = .05$.

d. p-value $= P(T_+ \leq 3.5)$ where $n = 9$ and the test is one-tailed. Using Table XII, locate the appropriate column for n, then find the values in that column that include the test statistic (in this case, 6 and 3). Then read the α level corresponding to these values. Thus,

$.01 < p$-value $< .025$

16.31 Some preliminary calculations are:

Employee	Before Flextime	After Flextime	Difference (B − A)	Difference
1	54	68	−14	7
2	25	42	−17	9
3	80	80	0	(Eliminated)
4	76	91	−15	8
5	63	70	−7	5
6	82	88	−6	3.5
7	94	90	4	2
8	72	81	−9	6
9	33	39	−6	3.5
10	90	93	−3	1
				$T_+ = 2$

To determine if the pilot flextime program is a success, we test:

H_0: The two probability distributions are identical
H_a: The probability distribution before is shifted to the left of that after

The test statistic is $T_+ = 2$.

The rejection region is $T_+ \leq 8$, from Table XII, Appendix B, with $n = 9$ and $\alpha = .05$.

Since the observed value of the test statistic falls in the rejection region ($T_+ = 2 \leq 8$), H_0 is rejected. There is sufficient evidence to indicate the pilot flextime program has been a success at $\alpha = .05$.

16.33 To determine if one of the measuring facilities tends to read higher or lower than the other, we test:

H_0: The exhalation rate measurements for the two facilities are the same
H_a: The exhalation rate measurements by PCHD are shifted to the right or left of those by EERF

The test statistic is $z = -1.3631$ (from printout).

The p-value is $p = .1728$. Since the p-value is not less than α, ($p = .1728 \not< \alpha = .05$), H_0 is not rejected.

There is insufficient evidence to indicate a difference in the exhalation rate measurements for the two facilities at $\alpha = .05$.

16.35 Using Table XIII, Appendix B,

a. $P(\chi^2 \geq 3.07382) = .995$

b. $P(\chi^2 \leq 24.4331) = 1 - .975 = .025$

c. $P(\chi^2 \geq 14.6837) = .10$

d. $P(\chi^2 < 34.1696) = 1 - .025 = .975$

e. $P(\chi^2 < 6.26214) = 1 - .975 = .025$

f. $P(\chi^2 \le .584375) = 1 - .90 = .10$

16.37   a. A completely randomized design was used.

b. The hypotheses are:

H_0: The three probability distributions are identical
H_a: At least two of the three probability distributions differ in location

c. The rejection region requires $\alpha = .01$ in the upper tail of the χ^2 distribution with df $= p - 1 = 3 - 1 = 2$. From Table XIII, Appendix B, $\chi^2_{.01} = 9.21034$. The rejection region is $H > 9.21034$.

d. Some preliminary calculations are:

I		II		III	
Observation	Rank	Observation	Rank	Observation	Rank
66	13	19	2	75	14.5
23	3	31	6	96	19
55	10	16	1	102	21
88	18	29	4	75	14.5
58	11	30	5	98	20
62	12	33	7	78	16
79	17	40	8		
49	9				
	$R_A = 93$		$R_B = 33$		$R_C = 105$

The test statistic is:

$$H = \frac{12}{n(n+1)} \sum \frac{R_j^2}{n_j} - 3(n+1)$$

$$= \frac{12}{21(21+1)} \left[\frac{93^2}{8} + \frac{33^2}{7} + \frac{105^2}{6} \right] - 3(21+1) = 79.85 - 66 = 13.85$$

Since the observed value of the test statistic falls in the rejection region ($H = 13.85 > 9.21034$), H_0 is rejected. There is sufficient evidence to indicate at least two of the three probability distributions differ in location at $\alpha = .01$.

16.39   a. $H = \frac{12}{n(n+1)} \sum \frac{R_j^2}{n_j} - 3(n+1)$

$= \frac{12}{217(217+1)} \left[\frac{1804^2}{11} + \frac{6398^2}{49} + \frac{7328^2}{62} + \frac{4075^2}{39} + \frac{2660^2}{35} + \frac{1388^2}{21} \right] - 3(217+1)$
$= 35.23$

b. The rejection region requires $\alpha = .01$ in the upper tail of the χ^2 distribution with df $= p - 1 = 6 - 1 = 5$. From Table XIII, Appendix B, $\chi^2_{.01} = 15.0863$. The rejection region is $H > 15.0863$.

c. To determine if the biting rates for the six wind speed conditions differ, we test:

H_0: The probability distributions of the number of bites are the same for the six wind speed conditions
H_a: At least two of the six probability distributions differ in location

Since the observed value of the test statistic falls in the rejection region ($H = 35.23 > 15.0863$), H_0 is rejected. There is sufficient evidence to indicate that the biting rates for the six wind speed conditions differ at $\alpha = .01$.

d. The p-value is $p < .01$. Since the p-value is less than $\alpha = .01$, H_0 is rejected. This supports the inference in part c.

16.41 a. Some preliminary calculations are:

Growth		Income		Value	
Rate	Rank	Rate	Rank	Rate	Rank
22.7%	19	14.9%	5	13.2%	3
15.1	6	16.0	8	19.7	16
16.5	10	16.8	12	17.2	13
16.1	9	10.2	1	18.3	14
14.0	4	15.8	7	21.8	18
18.6	15	24.1	20	12.8	2
43.1	21	16.6	11	20.4	17
$R_A = 84$		$R_B = 64$		$R_C = 83$	

To determine if the rate-of-return distributions differ among the three types of mutual funds, we test:

H_0: The three probability distributions are identical
H_a: At least two of the rate-of-return distributions differ

The test statistic is:

$$H = \frac{12}{n(n+1)} \sum \frac{R_j^2}{n_j} - 3(n+1)$$

$$= \frac{12}{21(21+1)} \left[\frac{84^2}{7} + \frac{64^2}{7} + \frac{83^2}{7} \right] - 3(21+1) = 66.9425 - 66 = .9425$$

The rejection region requires $\alpha = .05$ in the upper tail of the χ^2 distribution with df = $p - 1$ = 3 − 1 = 2. From Table XIII, Appendix B, $\chi^2_{.05} = 5.99147$. The rejection region is $H > 5.99147$.

Since the observed value of the test statistic does not fall in the rejection region ($H = .9425 \not> 5.99147$), H_0 is not rejected. There is insufficient evidence to indicate the rate-of-return distributions differ among the three types of mutual funds at $\alpha = .05$.

b. The necessary assumptions are:

1. The three samples are random and independent.
2. There are five or more measurements in each sample.
3. The three probability distributions from which the samples are drawn are continuous.

c. A Type I error would be concluding at least two of the rate-of-return distributions differ when they do not.

A Type II error would be concluding the three rate-of-return distributions are identical when they are not.

d. The F-test could be used if the three distributions were normal with equal variances.

16.43 a. The assumptions for the F-test are:

1. All p population probability distributions are normal.
2. The p population variances are equal.
3. Samples are selected randomly and independently from the respective populations.

The assumptions for the Kruskal-Wallis H-test are:

1. The k samples are random and independent.
2. There are five or more measurements in each sample.
3. The observations can be ranked.

The assumptions for the Kruskal-Wallis H-test are less restrictive than those for the F-test.

b. Some preliminary calculations are:

Aerospace & Defense	Rank	Electric Utilities	Rank	Retailing	Rank	Chemical	Rank
26.1	3	37.3	10	46.3	18	32.7	8
19.7	2	37.4	11	38.6	14	44.9	17
76.8	23	34.5	9	59.8	20	32.5	7
0.6	1	31.2	4	65.5	21	59.7	19
31.5	5	32.1	6	43.7	16	41.5	15
75.4	22	37.7	12				
		38.5	13				
$R_A = 56$		$R_B = 65$		$R_C = 89$		$R_D = 66$	

To determine whether debt/capital ratios differ among the four industries, we test:

H_0: The four probability distributions are identical
H_a: At least two of the four probability distributions differ in location

The test statistic is $H = \dfrac{12}{n(n+1)} \sum \dfrac{R_j^2}{n_j} - 3(n+1)$

$= \dfrac{12}{23(24)} \left[\dfrac{56^2}{6} + \dfrac{65^2}{7} + \dfrac{89^2}{5} + \dfrac{66^2}{5} \right] - 3(24)$

$= 77.8617 - 72 = 5.8617$

The rejection region requires $\alpha = .05$ in the upper tail of the χ^2 distribution with df $= p - 1 = 4 - 1 = 3$. From Table XIII, Appendix B, $\chi^2_{.05} = 7.81473$. The rejection region is $H > 7.81473$.

Since the observed value of the test statistic does not fall in the rejection region ($H = 5.8617 \not> 7.81473$), H_0 is not rejected. There is insufficient evidence to indicate the debt/capital ratios differ among the four industries at $\alpha = .05$.

c. The distributions of debt/capital ratios for the retailing and chemical industries could be compared using the Wilcoxon rank sum test.

16.45 a. From Table XVI with $n = 10$, $r_{s,\alpha/2} = r_{s,.025} = .648$. The rejection region is $r_s > .648$ or $r_s < -.648$.

b. From Table XVI with $n = 20$, $r_{s,\alpha} = r_{s,.025} = .450$. The rejection region is $r_s > .450$.

c. From Table XVI with $n = 30$, $r_{s,\alpha} = r_{s,.01} = .432$. The rejection region is $r_s < -.432$.

16.47 a. $H_0: \rho_s = 0$
$H_a: \rho_s \neq 0$

b. The test statistic is $r_s = \dfrac{SS_{uv}}{\sqrt{SS_{uu}SS_{vv}}}$

x	Rank, u	y	Rank, v	u^2	v^2	uv
0	3	0	1.5	9	2.25	45
3	5.5	2	5	30.25	25	27.5
0	3	2	5	9	25	15
-4	1	0	1.5	1	2.25	1.5
3	5.5	3	7	30.25	49	38.5
0	3	1	3	9	9	9
4	7	2	5	49	25	35
	$\sum u = 28$		$\sum v = 28$	$\sum u^2 = 137.5$	$\sum v^2 = 137.5$	$\sum uv = 131$

$$SS_{uv} = \sum uv - \dfrac{(\sum u)(\sum v)}{n} = 131 - \dfrac{28(28)}{7} = 19$$

$$SS_{uu} = \sum u^2 - \dfrac{(\sum u)^2}{n} = 137.5 - \dfrac{(28)^2}{7} = 25.5$$

$$SS_{vv} = \sum v^2 - \dfrac{(\sum v)^2}{n} = 137.5 - \dfrac{(28)^2}{7} = 25.5$$

$$r_s = \dfrac{19}{\sqrt{25.5(25.5)}} = .745$$

Reject H_0 if $r_s < -r_{s,\alpha/2}$ or $r_s > r_{s,\alpha/2}$ where $\alpha/2 = .025$ and $n = 7$:

Reject H_0 if $r_s < -.786$ or $r_s > .786$ (from Table XVI, Appendix B).

Since the observed value of the test statistic does not fall in the rejection region, ($r_s = .745 \not> .786$), do not reject H_0. There is insufficient evidence to indicate x and y are correlated at $\alpha = .05$.

c. The p-value is $P(r_s \geq .745) + P(r_s \leq -.745)$. For $n = 7$, $r_s = .745$ is above $r_{s,.025}$ where $\alpha/2 = .025$ and below $r_{s,.05}$ where $\alpha/2 = .05$. Therefore, $2(.025) = .05 < p\text{-value} < 2(.05) = .10$.

Nonparametric Statistics

d. The assumptions of the test are that the samples are randomly selected and the probability distributions of the two variables are continuous.

16.49 a. Some preliminary calculations:

University	u_i	v_i	Differences $d_i = u_i - v_i$	d_i^2
1	10	7	3	9
2	9	9	0	0
3	8	10	-2	4
4	7	1	6	36
5	6	6	0	0
6	5	3	2	4
7	4	5	-1	1
8	3	8	-5	25
9	2	4	-2	4
10	1	2	-1	1
				$\sum d_i^2 = 84$

$$r_s = 1 - \frac{6 \sum d_i^2}{n(n^2 - 1)} = 1 - \frac{6(84)}{10(10^2 - 1)} = .491$$

To determine if total fundraising and alumni contributions are correlated, we test:

$H_0: \rho_s = 0$
$H_a: \rho_s \neq 0$

The test statistic is $r_s = .491$.

From Table XVI, Appendix B, $r_{s,.025} = .648$, with $n = 10$. The rejection region is $r_s > .648$ or $r_s < -.648$.

Since the observed value of the test statistic does not fall in the rejection region ($r_s = .491 \not> .648$), H_0 is not rejected. There is insufficient evidence to indicate that total fundraising and alumni contributions are correlated at $\alpha = .05$.

b. We must assume:

1. The sample is randomly selected.
2. The probability distributions of both of the variables are continuous.

16.51 b. Some preliminary calculations:

Involvement	u_i	v_i	Differences $d_i = u_i - v_i$	d_i^2
1	8	9	−1	1
2	6	7	−1	1
3	10	10	0	0
4	2	1	1	1
5	5	5	0	0
6	9	8	1	1
7	1	2	−1	1
8	4	4	0	0
9	7	6	1	1
10	11	11	0	0
11	3	3	0	1

$$\sum d_i^2 = 6$$

$$r_s = 1 - \frac{6\sum d_i^2}{n(n^2 - 1)} = 1 - \frac{6(6)}{11(11^2 - 1)} = .972$$

To determine if a positive relationship exists between participation rates and cost savings rates, we test:

H_0: $\rho_s = 0$
H_a: $\rho_s > 0$

The test statistic is $r_s = .972$.

From Table XVI, Appendix B, $r_{s,.01} = .736$, with $n = 11$. The rejection region is $r_s > .736$.

Since the observed value of the test statistic does falls in the rejection region ($r_s = .972 > .736$), H_0 is rejected. There is sufficient evidence to indicate that a positive relationship exists between participation rates and cost savings rates at $\alpha = .01$.

c. In order for the above test to be valid, we must assume:

1. The sample is randomly selected.
2. The probability distributions of both of the variables are continuous.

In order to use the Pearson correlation coefficient, we must assume that both populations are normally distributed. It is very unlikely that the data are normally distributed.

16.53 Since there are no ties, we can use the formula:

$$r_s = 1 - \frac{6\sum d_i^2}{n(n^2 - 1)}$$

Nonparametric Statistics

Differences $d_i = u_i - v_i$	d_i^2
0	0
0	0
−1	1
−1	1
2	4
−1	1
−1	1
−2	4
3	9
1	1
−1	1
1	1
0	0
$\sum d_i^2 = 24$	

$$r_s = 1 - \frac{6 \sum d_i^2}{n(n^2 - 1)}$$
$$= 1 - \frac{6(24)}{13(13^2 - 1)}$$
$$= 1 - .0659 = .9341$$

The rankings of the manufacturers locating in Arkansas and the ranking of the manufacturers locating elsewhere are positively related. Because $r_s = .9341$, this relationship is very strong.

16.55 It is appropriate to use the t and F tests for comparing two or more population means when the populations sampled are normal and the population variances are equal.

16.57 a. Some preliminary calculations are:

Pair	X	Rank u_i	Y	Rank v_i	u_i^2	v_i^2	$u_i v_i$
1	19	5	12	5	25	25	25
2	27	7	19	8	49	64	56
3	15	2	7	1	4	1	2
4	35	9	25	9	81	81	81
5	13	1	11	4	1	16	4
6	29	8	10	2.5	64	6.25	20
7	16	3.5	16	6	12.25	36	21
8	22	6	10	2.5	36	6.25	15
9	16	3.5	18	7	12.25	49	24.5
	$\sum u_i = 45$		$\sum v_i = 45$		$\sum u_i^2 = 284.5$	$\sum v_i^2 = 284.5$	$\sum u_i v_i = 248.5$

$$SS_{uv} = \sum u_i v_i - \frac{\sum u_i v_i}{n} = 248.5 - \frac{45(45)}{9} = 23.5$$

$$SS_{uu} = \sum u_i^2 - \frac{\left(\sum u_i\right)^2}{n} = 284.5 - \frac{45^2}{9} = 59.5$$

$$SS_{vv} = \sum v_i^2 - \frac{\left(\sum v_i\right)^2}{n} = 284.5 - \frac{45^2}{9} = 59.5$$

To determine if the Spearman rank correlation differs from 0, we test:

$H_0: \rho_s = 0$
$H_a: \rho_s \neq 0$

The test statistic is $r_s = \dfrac{SS_{uv}}{\sqrt{SS_{uu}SS_{vv}}} = \dfrac{23.5}{\sqrt{59.5(59.5)}} = .40$

Reject H_0 if $r_s < -r_{s,\alpha/2}$ or if $r_s > r_{s,\alpha/2}$ where $\alpha/2 = .025$ and $n = 9$:

Reject H_0 if $r_s < -.683$ or if $r_s > .683$ (from Table XVI, Appendix B)

Since the observed value of the test statistic does not fall in the rejection region ($r_s = .40 \not> .683$), H_0 is not rejected. There is insufficient evidence to indicate that Spearman's rank correlation between x and y is significantly different from 0 at $\alpha = .05$.

b. Use the Wilcoxon signed rank test. Some preliminary calculations are:

Pair	X	Y	Difference	Rank of Absolute Difference
1	19	12	7	3
2	27	19	8	4.5
3	15	7	8	4.5
4	35	25	10	6
5	13	11	2	1.5
6	29	10	19	8
7	16	16	0	(eliminated)
8	22	10	12	7
9	16	18	−2	1.5
				$T_- = 1.5$

To determine if the probability distribution of x is shifted to the right of that for y, we test:

H_0: The probability distributions are identical for the two variables
H_a: The probability distribution of x is shifted to the right of the probability distribution of y

The test statistic is $T = T_- = 1.5$.

Reject H_0 if $T \leq T_0$ where T_0 is based on $\alpha = .05$ and $n = 8$ (one-tailed):

Reject H_0 if $T \leq 6$ (from Table XII, Appendix B).

Since the observed value of the test statistic falls in the rejection region ($T = 1.5 \leq 6$), reject H_0 at $\alpha = .05$. There is sufficient evidence to conclude that the probability distribution of x is shifted to the right of that for y.

16.59 Some preliminary calculations:

A		B		C	
Urban	Rank	Suburban	Rank	Rural	Rank
4.3	4.5	5.9	14	5.1	9
5.2	10.5	6.7	17	4.8	7
6.2	15.5	7.6	19	3.9	2
5.6	12	4.9	8	6.2	15.5
3.8	1	5.2	10.5	4.2	3
5.8	13	6.8	18	4.3	4.5
4.7	6				
	$R_A = 62.5$		$R_B = 86.5$		$R_C = 41$

To determine if there is a difference in the level of property taxes among the three types of school districts, we test:

H_0: The three probability distributions are identical
H_a: At least two of the three probability distributions differ in location

The test statistic is $H = \dfrac{12}{n(n+1)} \sum \dfrac{R_j^2}{n_j} - 3(n+1)$

$= \dfrac{12}{19(19+1)} \left[\dfrac{62.5^2}{7} + \dfrac{86.5^2}{6} + \dfrac{41^2}{6} \right] - 3(20) = 65.8498 - 60$

$= 5.8498$

The rejection region requires $\alpha = .05$ in the upper tail of the χ^2 distribution with df $= p - 1 = 3 - 1 = 2$. From Table XIII, Appendix B, $\chi^2_{.05} = 5.99147$. The rejection region is $H > 5.99147$.

Since the observed value of the test statistic does not fall in the rejection region ($H = 5.8498 \not> 5.99147$), H_0 is not rejected. There is insufficient evidence to indicate that there is a difference in the level of property taxes among the three types of school districts at $\alpha = .05$.

16.61 The appropriate test for paired samples is the Wilcoxon signed rank test. Some preliminary calculations are:

Subject	Aspirin	Drug	Difference	Rank of Absolute Difference
1	15	7	8	6
2	20	14	6	3.5
3	12	13	−1	1
4	20	11	9	7
5	17	10	7	5
6	14	16	−2	2
7	17	11	6	3.5
				$T_- = 3.0$
				$T_+ = 25.0$

To determine if the probability distribution of the times required to obtain relief with aspirin is shifted to the right of the probability distribution of the times required to obtain relief with the drug, we test:

H_0: The probability distributions of length of time required for pain relief are identical for aspirin and the new drug

H_a: The probability distribution of the length of time required for pain relief with aspirin is shifted to the right of that for the new drug

The test statistic is $T_- = 3$.

Reject H_0 if $T_- \leq T_0$ where $\alpha = .05$ (one-tailed) and $n = 7$:

Reject H_0 if $T_- \leq 4$ (from Table XII, Appendix B).

Since $T_- = 3 \leq 4$, reject H_0. There is sufficient evidence to indicate the probability distribution of time required to obtain relief with aspirin is shifted to the right of that for the new drug at $\alpha = .05$.

16.63 a. Some preliminary calculations:

Difference B − A	Rank of Absolute Difference
14.92	14
6.65	13
3.90	12
3.60	11
3.37	10
1.95	9
1.30	8
−.95	7
.91	6
−.90	4.5
−.90	4.5
−.45	3
−.40	2
−.05	1
	$T_- = 22$

To determine if the populations of differences before and after differ in location, we test:

H_0: The populations of differences before and after have identical probability distributions

H_a: The population of differences after is shifted to the left of that for before

The test statistic is $T_- = 22$

The rejection region is $T_- \leq 26$ from Table XII, Appendix B, with $n = 14$ and $\alpha = .05$.

Since the observed value of the test statistic falls in the rejection region ($T_- = 22 \leq 26$), H_0 is rejected. There is sufficient evidence to indicate the population of differences after is shifted to the left of that for before at $\alpha = .05$. This supports Teece's findings.

b. The p-value is $P(T_- \leq 22)$. From Table XII, Appendix B, with $n = 14$,
$.025 < P(T_- \leq 22) < .05$.

c. The assumptions necessary are:

1. The sample of differences is randomly selected from the population of differences.
2. The probability distribution from which the sample of paired differences is drawn is continuous.

16.65 Some preliminary calculations are:

Type A	Rank	Type B	Rank
95	1	110	6
122	10	102	4
102	3	115	8
99	2	112	7
108	5	120	9
$T_A = 21$		$T_B = 34$	

To determine if print type A is easier to read, we test:

H_0: The two sampled populations have identical probability distributions
H_a: The probability distribution for print type A is shifted to the left of that for print type B

The test statistic is $T_A = 21$.

The rejection region is $T_A \leq 19$ form Table XI, Appendix B, with $n_A = 5$ and $n_B = 5$, and $\alpha = .05$.

Since the observed value of the test statistic does not fall in the rejection region ($T_A = 21 \nleq 19$), H_0 is not rejected. There is insufficient evidence to indicate print type A is easier to read at $\alpha = .05$.

16.67 Some preliminary calculations are:

				Supervisor				
1	Rank	2	Rank	3	Rank	4	Rank
20	21.5	17	16.5	16	14.5	8	1
19	20	11	5.5	15	12.5	12	7
20	21.5	13	8.5	13	8.5	10	3.5
18	18.5	15	12.5	18	18.5	14	10.5
17	16.5	14	10.5	11	5.5	9	2
		16	14.5			10	3.5
$R_A = 98$		$R_B = 68$		$R_C = 59.5$		$R_D = 27.5$	

a. The type of experimental design is completely randomized. The response is the rating of the leader. The factor is personality type, which has four levels and is qualitative. The treatments correspond to the four factor levels. The experimental units are the employees selected to do the ratings.

b. To determine whether the probability distributions of ratings differ for at least two of the four supervisors, we test:

H_0: The four probability distributions are identical
H_a: At least two of the four probability distributions differ in location

The test statistic is $H = \dfrac{12}{n(n+1)} \sum \dfrac{R_j^2}{n_j} - 3(n+1)$

$$= \dfrac{12}{22(23)} \left[\dfrac{98^2}{5} + \dfrac{68^2}{6} + \dfrac{59.5^2}{5} + \dfrac{27.5^2}{6} \right] - 3(22+1)$$

$$= 83.6101 - 69 = 14.6101$$

The rejection region requires $\alpha = .05$ in the upper tail of the χ^2 distribution with df = $p - 1 = 4 - 1 = 3$. From Table XIII, Appendix B, $\chi^2_{.05} = 7.81473$. The rejection region is $H > 7.81473$.

Since the observed value of the test statistic falls in the rejection region ($H = 14.6101 > 7.81473$), H_0 is rejected. There is sufficient evidence to indicate the probability distributions of ratings differ for at least two of the four supervisors at $\alpha = .05$.

c. The necessary assumptions are:

1. The four samples are random and independent.
2. There are five or more measurements in each sample.
3. The four probability distributions from which the samples are drawn are continuous.

d. Since we rejected H_0 in part b, we need to compare all pairs.

Some preliminary calculations are:

Supervisor 1	Rank	2	Rank	Supervisor 1	Rank	3	Rank	Supervisor 1	Rank	4	Rank
20	10.5	17	6.5	20	9.5	16	4	20	10.5	8	1
19	9	11	1	19	8	15	3	19	9	12	5
20	10.5	13	2	20	9.5	13	2	20	10.5	10	3.5
18	8	15	4	18	6.5	18	6.5	18	8	14	6
17	6.5	14	3	17	5	11	1	17	7	9	2
		16	5							10	3.5
$T_A = 44.5$		$T_B = 21.5$		$T_A = 38.5$		$T_C = 16.5$		$T_A = 45$		$T_D = 21$	

Supervisor 2	Rank	3	Rank	Supervisor 2	Rank	4	Rank	Supervisor 3	Rank	4	Rank
17	10	16	8.5	17	12	8	1	16	10	8	1
11	1.5	15	6.5	11	5	12	6	15	9	12	6
13	3.5	13	3.5	13	7	10	3.5	13	7	10	3.5
15	6.5	18	11	15	10	14	8.5	18	11	14	8
14	5	11	1.5	14	8.5	9	2	11	5	9	2
16	8.5			16	11	10	3.5			10	3.5
$T_B = 35$		$T_C = 31$		$T_B = 53.5$		$T_D = 24.5$		$T_C = 42$		$T_D = 24$	

For each pair, we test:

H_0: The two sampled populations have identical probability distributions
H_a: The probability distribution for one sampled population is shifted to the right or the left of that of the other

For supervisors 1 and 2:

The test statistic is $T_A = 44.5$.

The rejection region is $T_A \leq 19$ or $T_A \geq 41$ from Table XI, Appendix B, with $n_A = 5$, $n_B = 6$, and $\alpha = .05$.

Since the observed value of the test statistic falls in the rejection region ($T_A = 44.5 \geq 41$), H_0 is rejected. There is sufficient evidence to indicate the probability distribution of supervisor 1 is shifted to the right of that for supervisor 2 at $\alpha = .05$.

For supervisors 1 and 3:

The test statistic is $T_A = 38.5$.

The rejection region is $T_A \leq 18$ or $T_A \geq 37$ from Table XI, Appendix B, with $n_A = n_C = 5$ and $\alpha = .05$.

Since the observed value of the test statistic falls in the rejection region ($T_A = 38.5 \geq 37$), H_0 is rejected. There is sufficient evidence to indicate the probability distribution of supervisor 1 is shifted to the right of that for supervisor 3.

For supervisors 1 and 4:

The test statistic is $T_A = 45$.

The rejection region is $T_A \leq 19$ or $T_A \geq 41$ from Table XI, Appendix B, with $n_A = 5$, $n_D = 6$, and $\alpha = .05$.

Since the observed value of the test statistic falls in the rejection region ($T_A = 45 \geq 41$), H_0 is rejected. There is sufficient evidence to indicate the probability distribution of supervisor 1 is shifted to the right of that for supervisor 4 at $\alpha = .05$.

For supervisors 2 and 3:

The test statistic is $T_C = 31$.

The rejection region is $T_C \leq 19$ or $T_C \geq 41$ from Table XI, Appendix B, with $n = 6$, $n = 5$, and $\alpha = .05$.

Since the observed value of the test statistic does not fall in the rejection region ($T_C = 31 \not\leq 19$ and $\not\geq 41$), H_0 is not rejected. There is insufficient evidence to indicate the probability distribution of supervisor 2 is shifted to the right or left of that for supervisor 3 at $\alpha = .05$.

For supervisors 2 and 4:

The test statistic is $T_D = 24.5$.

The rejection region is $T_D \leq 26$ or $T_D \geq 52$ from Table XI, Appendix B, with $n_B = n_D = 6$ and $\alpha = .05$.

Since the observed value of the test statistic falls in the rejection region ($T_D = 24.5 \leq 26$), H_0 is rejected. There is sufficient evidence to indicate the probability distribution for supervisor 2 is shifted to the right of that for supervisor 4.

For supervisors 3 and 4:

The test statistic is $T_C = 42$.

The rejection region is $T_C \leq 19$ or $T_C \geq 41$ from Table XI, Appendix B, with $n_C = 5$, $n_D = 6$, and $\alpha = .05$.

Since the observed value of the test statistic falls in the rejection region ($T_C = 42 \geq 41$), H_0 is rejected. There is sufficient evidence to indicate the probability distribution for supervisor 3 is shifted to the right of that for supervisor 4.

Supervisor 1 is rated significantly higher than any of the others.

16.69 The appropriate test for this completely random design is the Kruskal-Wallis H-test. Some preliminary calculations are:

A	Rank	B	Rank	C	Rank
10.8	3.5	22.3	27	9.8	1.5
15.6	11	19.5	21	12.3	7
19.2	19	18.6	17	16.2	12
17.9	15	24.3	30	14.1	8
18.3	16	19.9	23	15.3	10
9.8	1.5	20.4	25	10.8	3.5
16.7	13	23.6	29	12.2	6
19.0	18	21.2	26	17.3	14
20.3	24	19.8	22	15.1	9
19.4	20	22.6	28	11.3	5
$R_1 = 141.0$		$R_2 = 248.0$		$R_3 = 76.0$	

To determine if there is a difference in location among the distribution of damage rates among the three treatments, we test:

H_0: The probability distributions of damage rates are identical for the three treatments
H_a: At least two of the probability distributions differ in location

The test statistic is $H = \dfrac{12}{n(n+1)} \sum \dfrac{R_j^2}{n_j} - 3(n+1)$

$= \dfrac{12}{30(30+1)} \left[\dfrac{(141.0)^2}{10} + \dfrac{(248.0)^2}{10} + \dfrac{(76.0)^2}{10} \right] - 3(30+1) = 112.466 - 93 = 19.466$

The rejection region requires $\alpha = .05$ in the upper tail of the χ^2 distribution with df $= p - 1 = 3 - 1 = 2$. From Table XIII, Appendix B, $\chi^2_{.05} = 5.99147$. The rejection region is $H > 5.99147$.

Nonparametric Statistics

Since the observed value of the test statistic falls in the rejection region ($H = 19.466 > 5.99147$), reject H_0. There is sufficient evidence to indicate a difference in the damage rates for the three treatments at $\alpha = .05$.

16.71 Some preliminary calculations are:

Before		After	
Observation	Rank	Observation	Rank
10	19	4	5.5
5	8.5	3	3.5
3	3.5	8	16.5
6	12	5	8.5
7	14.5	6	12
11	20	4	5.5
8	16.5	2	2
9	18	5	8.5
6	12	7	14.5
5	8.5	1	1
$T_{Before} = 132.5$		$T_{After} = 77.5$	

To determine if the situation has improved under the new policy, we test:

H_0: The two sampled population probability distributions are identical
H_a: The probability distribution associated with after the policy was instituted is shifted to the left of that before

The test statistic is $T_{Before} = 132.5$.

The rejection region is $T_{Before} \geq 127$ from Table XI, Appendix B, with $n_A = n_B = 10$ and $\alpha = .05$.

Since the observed value of the test statistic falls in the rejection region ($T_{Before} = 132.5 \geq 127$), H_0 is rejected. There is sufficient evidence to indicate the situation has improved under the new policy at $\alpha = .05$.

16.73 a. To determine if the median hourly fraction defective exceeds .05, we test:

H_0: $\eta = .05$
H_a: $\eta > .05$

The test statistic is S = number of measurements greater than $.05 = 5$.

The p-value $= P(x \geq 5)$ where x is a binomial random variable with $n = 8$ and $p = .5$. From Table II,

p-value $= P(x \geq 5) = 1 - P(x \leq 4) = 1 - .637 = .363$

Since the p-value $= .363 > \alpha = .10$, H_0 is not rejected. There is insufficient evidence to indicate the median hourly fraction defective exceeds .05 at $\alpha = .10$.

b. The manufacturer might want to use a relatively high level of significance so that it is easier to reject H_0. The manufacturer would rather reject H_0 when it is true (conclude the median fraction of defective exceeds .05 when it does not) than not reject H_0 when it is false (conclude the median fraction defective is .05 when it exceeds .05). The manufacturer would rather be conservative and declare too many defectives, shut down the process and correct it, than say the process is working correctly and let too many defectives be produced.

c. We must assume the sample was randomly selected from a continuous distribution of defective rates. In order to conduct a t-test, we must also assume the population of defective rates is normally distributed.

16.75 Some preliminary calculations are:

Candidate	u_i	v_i	Difference $d_i = u_i - v_i$	d_i^2
1	6	4	2	4
2	4	5	-1	1
3	5	6	-1	1
4	1	2	-1	1
5	2	1	1	1
6	3	3	0	0
				$\sum d_i^2 = 8$

$$r_s = 1 - \frac{6 \sum d_i^2}{n(n^2 - 1)} = 1 - \frac{6(8)}{6(36 - 1)} = .7714$$

To determine if the candidates' qualification scores are related to their interview performance, we test:

H_0: $\rho_s = 0$
H_a: $\rho_s \neq 0$

The test statistic is $r_s = .7714$

From Table XVI, Appendix B, for $\alpha/2 = .10/2 = .05$, $r_{s,.05} = .829$ for $n = 6$. The rejection region is $r_s < -.829$ or $r_s > .829$. Since the observed value of the test statistic does not fall in the rejection region ($r_s = .7714 \not> .829$), H_0 is not rejected. There is insufficient evidence to indicate the qualification scores are related to the interview performance at $\alpha = .10$.

16.77 a. Since there are no ties, we can use the formula

$$r_s = 1 - \frac{6 \sum d_i^2}{n(n^2 - 1)}$$

Nonparametric Statistics

		Differences	
u_i	v_i	$d_i = u_i - v_i$	d_i^2
15	14	1	1
6	9	-3	9
14	15	-1	1
8	4	4	16
12	13	-1	1
2	1	1	1
3	3	0	0
11	11	0	0
5	6	-1	1
9	12	-3	9
7	8	-1	1
4	2	2	4
13	10	3	9
1	5	-4	16
10	7	3	9
		$\sum d_i^2 = 78$	

$$r_s = 1 - \frac{6\sum d_i^2}{(n^2 - 1)}$$
$$= 1 - \frac{6(78)}{15(15^2 - 1)}$$
$$= 1 - .139 = .861$$

b. To determine if job satisfaction and income are positively correlated, we test:

H_0: $\rho_s = 0$
H_a: $\rho_s > 0$

The test statistic is $r_s = .861$.

From Table XVI, Appendix B, $r_{s,.05} = .441$, with $n = 15$. The rejection region is $r_s > .441$.

Since the observed value of the test statistic falls in the rejection region ($r_s = .861 > .441$), H_0 is rejected. There is sufficient evidence to indicate job satisfaction and income are positively correlated at $\alpha = .05$.

c. To determine if the median job score exceeds 75, we test:

H_0: $\eta = 75$
H_a: $\eta > 75$

The test statistic is S = number of measurements greater than 75 = 4.

The p-value = $P(x \geq 4)$ where x is a binomial random variable with $n = 15$ and $p = .5$. From Table II, Appendix B,

p-value = $P(x \geq 4) = 1 - P(x \leq 3) = 1 - .018 = .982$.

Since the p-value = $.982 > \alpha = .05$, H_0 is not rejected. There is insufficient evidence to indicate that the median job score exceed 75 at $\alpha = .05$.

The Chi-Square Test and the Analysis of Contingency Tables   Chapter 17

17.1   a.   For df = 17, $\chi^2_{.05} = 27.5871$

       b.   For df = 100, $\chi^2_{.990} = 70.0648$

       c.   For df = 15, $\chi^2_{.10} = 22.3072$

       d.   For df = 3, $\chi^2_{.005} = 12.8381$

17.3   a.   The rejection region requires $\alpha = .05$ in the upper tail of the χ^2 distribution with df = $k - 1$ = 3 - 1 = 2. From Table XIII, Appendix B, $\chi^2_{.05} = 5.99147$. The rejection region is $\chi^2 > 5.99147$.

       b.   The rejection region requires $\alpha = .10$ in the upper tail of the χ^2 distribution with df = $k - 1$ = 5 - 1 = 4. From Table XIII, Appendix B, $\chi^2_{.10} = 7.77944$. The rejection region is $\chi^2 > 7.77944$.

       c.   The rejection region requires $\alpha = .01$ in the upper tail of the χ^2 distribution with df = $k - 1$ = 4 - 1 = 3. From Table XIII, Appendix B, $\chi^2_{.01} = 11.3449$. The rejection region is $\chi^2 > 11.3449$.

17.5   The sample size n will be large enough so that, for every cell, the expected cell count, $E(n_i)$, will be equal to 5 or more.

17.7   Some preliminary calculations are:

       If the probabilities are the same, $p_{1,0} = p_{2,0} = p_{3,0} = p_{4,0} = .25$

$$E(n_1) = np_{1,0} = 205(.25) = 51.25$$
$$E(n_2) = E(n_3) = E(n_4) = 205(.25) = 51.25$$

       a.   To determine if the multinomial probabilities differ, we test:

H_0: $p_1 = p_2 = p_3 = p_4 = .25$
H_a: At least one of the probabilities differs from .25

The test statistic is $\chi^2 = \sum \dfrac{[n_i - E(n_i)]^2}{E(n_i)}$

$$= \frac{(43 - 51.25)^2}{51.25} + \frac{(56 - 51.25)^2}{51.25} + \frac{(59 - 51.25)^2}{51.25} + \frac{(47 - 51.25)^2}{51.25} = 3.293$$

The rejection region requires $\alpha = .05$ in the upper tail of the χ^2 distribution with df $= k - 1 = 4 - 1 = 3$. From Table XIII, Appendix B, $\chi^2_{.05} = 7.81473$. The rejection region is $\chi^2 > 7.81473$.

Since the observed value of the test statistic does not fall in the rejection region ($\chi^2 = 3.293 \not> 7.81473$), H_0 is not rejected. There is insufficient evidence to indicate the multinomial probabilities differ at $\alpha = .05$.

b. The Type I error is concluding the multinomial probabilities differ when, in fact, they do not.

The Type II error is concluding the multinomial probabilities are equal, when, in fact, they are not.

17.9 a. To determine if the opinions of Internet users are evenly divided among the four categories, we test:

H_0: $p_1 = p_2 = p_3 = p_4 = .25$
H_a: At least one $p_i \neq .25$, for $i = 1, 2, 3, 4$

b. Some preliminary calculations are:

$E(n_1) = np_{1,0} = 328(.25) = 82$
$E(n_2) = E(n_3) = E(n_4) = 328(.25) = 82$

The test statistic is $\chi^2 = \sum \dfrac{[n_i - E(n_i)]^2}{E(n_i)}$

$= \dfrac{(59 - 82)^2}{82} + \dfrac{(108 - 82)^2}{82} + \dfrac{(82 - 82)^2}{82} + \dfrac{(79 - 82)^2}{82} = 14.805$

The rejection region requires $\alpha = .05$ in the upper tail of the χ^2 distribution with df $= k - 1 = 4 - 1 = 3$. From Table XIII, Appendix B, $\chi^2_{.05} = 7.81473$. The rejection region is $\chi^2 > 7.81473$.

Since the observed value of the test statistic falls in the rejection region ($\chi^2 = 14.805 > 7.81473$), H_0 is rejected. There is sufficient evidence to indicate that the opinions of Internet users are not evenly divided among the four categories at $\alpha = .05$.

c. A Type I error would be to conclude that the opinions of Internet users are not evenly divided among the four categories when, in fact, they are evenly divided.

A Type II error would be to conclude that the opinions of Internet users are evenly divided among the four categories when, in fact, they are not evenly divided.

d. We must assume that:

1. A multinomial experiment was conducted. This is generally satisfied by taking a random sample from the population of interest.
2. The sample size n will be large enough so that, for every cell, the expected cell count, $E(n_i)$, will be equal to 5 or more.

17.11 To determine if the true percentages of ADEs in the five "cause" categories are different, we test:

H_0: $p_1 = p_2 = p_3 = p_4 = p_5 = .2$
H_a: At least one p_i differs from .2, $i = 1, 2, 3, 4, 5$

The test statistic is $\chi^2 = 16$ (from printout).

The p-value of the test is $p = .003019$.

Since the p-value is less than α ($p = .003019 < .10$), H_0 is rejected. There is sufficient evidence to indicate that at least one percentage of ADEs in the five "cause" categories is different at $\alpha = .10$.

17.13 a. To determine if a difference in the preference of entrepreneurs for the cars, we test:

H_0: $p_1 = p_2 = p_3 = 1/3$
H_a: At least one of the multinomial probabilities does not equal 1/3

Where p_1 = proportion who prefer U.S. cars
p_2 = proportion who prefer European cars
p_3 = proportion who prefer Japanese cars

$$E(n_1) = np_{1,0} = 100\left[\frac{1}{3}\right] = 33\frac{1}{3}$$

$$E(n_2) = np_{2,0} = 100\left[\frac{1}{3}\right] = 33\frac{1}{3}$$

$$E(n_3) = np_{3,0} = 100\left[\frac{1}{3}\right] = 33\frac{1}{3}$$

The test statistic is $\chi^2 = \sum \frac{[n_i - E(n_i)]^2}{E(n_i)}$

$$= \frac{\left[45 - 33\frac{1}{3}\right]^2}{33\frac{1}{3}} + \frac{\left[46 - 33\frac{1}{3}\right]^2}{33\frac{1}{3}} + \frac{\left[9 - 33\frac{1}{3}\right]^2}{33\frac{1}{3}} = 26.66$$

The rejection region requires $\alpha = .05$ in the upper tail of the χ^2 distribution with df $= k - 1 = 3 - 1 = 2$. From Table XIII, Appendix B, $\chi^2_{.05} = 5.99147$. The rejection region is $\chi^2 > 5.99147$.

Since the observed value of the test statistic falls in the rejection region ($\chi^2 = 26.66 > 5.99147$), H_0 is rejected. There is sufficient evidence to indicate a difference in the preference of entrepreneurs for the cars at $\alpha = .05$.

b. To determine if there is a difference in the preference of entrepreneurs for domestic versus foreign cars, we test:

H_0: $p_1 = p_2 = .5$
H_a: At least one probability differs from .5

Where p_1 = proportion who prefer U.S. cars
p_2 = proportion who prefer foreign cars

The Chi-Square Test and the Analysis of Contingency Tables

$$E(n_1) = np_{1,0} = 100(.5) = 50$$
$$E(n_2) = np_{2,0} = 100(.5) = 50$$

The test statistic is $\chi^2 = \sum \dfrac{[n_i - E(n_i)]^2}{E(n_i)} = \dfrac{(45 - 50)^2}{50} + \dfrac{(55 - 50)^2}{50} = 1$

The rejection region requires $\alpha = .05$ in the upper tail of the χ^2 distribution with df = $k - 1$ = 2 - 1 = 1. From Table XIII, Appendix .B, $\chi^2_{.05} = 3.84146$. The rejection region is $\chi^2 > 3.84146$.

Since the observed value of the test statistic does not fall in the rejection region ($\chi^2 = 1 \not> 3.84146$), H_0 is not rejected. There is insufficient evidence to indicate a difference in the preference of entrepreneurs for domestic and foreign cars at $\alpha = .05$.

c. We must assume that:

1. The sample size n is large enough so that the expected cell count, $E(n_i)$, will be equal to 5 or more for every cell.
2. A multinomial experiment was conducted.

17.15 a. To determine if the number of overweight trucks per week is distributed over the 7 days of the week in direct proportion to the volume of truck traffic, we test:

H_0: $p_1 = .191, p_2 = .198, p_3 = .187, p_4 = .180, p_5 = .155, p_6 = .043, p_7 = .046$
H_a: At least one of the probabilities differs from the hypothesized value

$E(n_1) = np_{1,0} = 414(.191) = 79.074$
$E(n_2) = np_{2,0} = 414(.198) = 81.972$
$E(n_3) = np_{3,0} = 414(.187) = 77.418$
$E(n_4) = np_{4,0} = 414(.180) = 74.520$
$E(n_5) = np_{5,0} = 414(.155) = 64.170$
$E(n_6) = np_{6,0} = 414(.043) = 17.802$
$E(n_7) = np_{7,0} = 414(.046) = 19.044$

The test statistic is $\chi^2 = \sum \dfrac{[n_i - E(n_i)]^2}{E(n_i)} = \dfrac{(90 - 79.074)^2}{79.074} + \dfrac{(82 - 81.972)^2}{81.972}$

$+ \dfrac{(72 - 77.418)^2}{77.418} + \dfrac{(70 - 74.520)^2}{74.520} + \dfrac{(51 - 64.170)^2}{64.170} + \dfrac{(18 - 17.802)^2}{17.802}$

$+ \dfrac{(31 - 19.044)^2}{19.044} = 12.374$

The rejection region requires $\alpha = .05$ in the upper tail of the χ^2 distribution with df = $k - 1$ = 7 - 1 = 6. From Table XIII, Appendix B, $\chi^2_{.05} = 12.5916$. The rejection region is $\chi^2 > 12.5916$.

Since the observed value of the test statistic does not fall in the rejection region ($\chi^2 = 12.374 \not> 12.5916$), H_0 is not rejected. There is insufficient evidence to indicate the number of overweight trucks per week is distributed over the 7 days of the week is not in direct proportion to the volume of truck traffic at $\alpha = .05$.

b. The *p*-value is $P(\chi^2 \geq 12.374)$. From Table XIII, Appendix B, with df $= k - 1 = 7 - 1 = 6$, $.05 < P(\chi^2 \geq 12.374) < .10$.

17.17 If the die is balanced, $p_1 = p_2 = p_3 = p_4 = p_5 = p_6 = 1/6$

Some preliminary calculations are:

$$E(n_1) = E(n_2) = E(n_3) = E(n_4) = E(n_5) = E(n_6) = np_{i,0} = 120(1/6) = 20$$

To determine if the die is fair, we test:

H_0: $p_1 = p_2 = p_3 = p_4 = p_5 = p_6 = 1/6$
H_a: At least one of the multinomial probabilities does not equal 1/6

The test statistic is $\chi^2 = \sum \dfrac{[n_i - E(n_i)]^2}{E(n_i)} = \dfrac{(28-20)^2}{20} + \dfrac{(27-20)^2}{20} + \dfrac{(20-20)^2}{20}$

$+ \dfrac{(18-20)^2}{20} + \dfrac{(15-20)^2}{20} + \dfrac{(12-20)^2}{20} = 10.3$

The rejection region requires $\alpha = .10$ in the upper tail of the χ^2 distribution with df $= k - 1 = 6 - 1 = 5$. From Table XIII, Appendix B, $\chi^2_{.10} = 9.23635$. The rejection region is $\chi^2 > 9.23635$.

Since the observed value of the test statistic falls in the rejection region ($\chi^2 = 10.3 > 9.23635$), H_0 is rejected. There is sufficient evidence to indicate the die is not fair at $\alpha = .10$.

17.19 a. H_0: The row and column classifications are independent
H_a: The row and column classifications are dependent

b. The test statistic is $\chi^2 = \sum\sum \dfrac{[n_{ij} - \hat{E}(n_{ij})]^2}{\hat{E}(n_{ij})}$

The rejection region requires $\alpha = .01$ in the upper tail of the χ^2 distribution with df $= (r-1)(c-1) = (2-1)(3-1) = 2$. From Table XIII, Appendix B, $\chi^2_{.01} = 9.21034$. The rejection region is $\chi^2 > 9.21034$.

c. The expected cell counts are:

$\hat{E}(n_{11}) = \dfrac{r_1 c_1}{n} = \dfrac{96(25)}{167} = 14.37 \qquad \hat{E}(n_{21}) = \dfrac{r_2 c_1}{n} = \dfrac{71(25)}{167} = 10.63$

$\hat{E}(n_{12}) = \dfrac{r_1 c_2}{n} = \dfrac{96(64)}{167} = 36.79 \qquad \hat{E}(n_{22}) = \dfrac{r_2 c_2}{n} = \dfrac{71(64)}{167} = 27.21$

$\hat{E}(n_{13}) = \dfrac{r_1 c_3}{n} = \dfrac{96(78)}{167} = 44.84 \qquad \hat{E}(n_{23}) = \dfrac{r_2 c_3}{n} = \dfrac{71(78)}{167} = 33.16$

The Chi-Square Test and the Analysis of Contingency Tables

d. The test statistic is $\chi^2 = \sum\sum \dfrac{[n_{ij} - \hat{E}(n_{ij})]^2}{\hat{E}(n_{ij})}$

$$= \dfrac{(9 - 14.37)^2}{14.37} + \dfrac{(34 - 36.79)^2}{36.79} + \dfrac{(53 - 44.84)^2}{44.84} + \dfrac{(16 - 10.63)^2}{10.63}$$

$$+ \dfrac{(30 - 27.21)^2}{27.21} + \dfrac{(25 - 33.16)^2}{33.16} = 8.71$$

Since the observed value of the test statistic does not fall in the rejection region ($\chi^2 = 8.71 \not> 9.21034$), H_0 is not rejected. There is insufficient evidence to indicate the row and column classifications are dependent at $\alpha = .01$.

17.21 Some preliminary calculations are:

$\hat{E}(n_{11}) = \dfrac{r_1 c_1}{n} = \dfrac{154(134)}{439} = 47.007 \qquad \hat{E}(n_{21}) = \dfrac{186(134)}{439} = 56.774$

$\hat{E}(n_{12}) = \dfrac{154(163)}{439} = 57.180 \qquad \hat{E}(n_{22}) = \dfrac{186(163)}{439} = 69.062$

$\hat{E}(n_{13}) = \dfrac{154(142)}{439} = 49.813 \qquad \hat{E}(n_{23}) = \dfrac{186(142)}{439} = 60.164$

$\hat{E}(n_{31}) = \dfrac{99(134)}{439} = 30.219 \qquad \hat{E}(n_{33}) = \dfrac{99(142)}{439} = 32.023$

$\hat{E}(n_{32}) = \dfrac{99(163)}{439} = 36.759$

To determine if the row and column classifications are dependent, we test:

H_0: The row and column classifications are independent
H_a: The row and column classifications are dependent

The test statistic is $\chi^2 = \sum\sum \dfrac{[n_{ij} - \hat{E}(n_{ij})]^2}{\hat{E}(n_{ij})}$

$$= \dfrac{(40 - 47.007)^2}{47.007} + \dfrac{(72 - 57.180)^2}{57.180} + \dfrac{(42 - 49.813)^2}{49.813} + \dfrac{(63 - 56.774)^2}{56.774}$$

$$+ \dfrac{(53 - 69.062)^2}{69.062} + \dfrac{(70 - 60.164)^2}{60.164} + \dfrac{(31 - 30.219)^2}{30.219}$$

$$+ \dfrac{(38 - 36.759)^2}{36.759} + \dfrac{(30 - 32.023)^2}{32.023} = 12.36$$

The rejection region requires $\alpha = .05$ in the upper tail of the χ^2 distribution with df = $(r - 1)(c - 1) = (3 - 1)(3 - 1) = 4$. From Table XIII, Appendix B, $\chi^2_{.05} = 9.48773$. The rejection region is $\chi^2 > 9.48773$.

Since the observed value of the test statistic falls in the rejection region ($\chi^2 = 12.36 > 9.48773$), H_0 is rejected. There is sufficient evidence to indicate the row and column classification are dependent at $\alpha = .05$.

17.23 a. The sample proportion of injured Hispanic children who were not wearing seatbelts during the accident is:

$\hat{p} = 283/314 = .901$

b. The sample proportion of injured non-Hispanic white children who were not wearing seatbelts during the accident is:

$$\hat{p} = 330/478 = .690$$

c. Since the proportion of injured Hispanic children who were not wearing seatbelts during the accident (.901) is .211 higher than the proportion of injured non-Hispanic white children who were not wearing seatbelts during the accident (.690), the proportions probably differ.

d. Some preliminary calculations are:

$$\hat{E}(n_{11}) = \frac{r_1 c_1}{n} = \frac{179(314)}{792} = 70.97 \qquad \hat{E}(n_{12}) = \frac{r_1 c_2}{n} = \frac{179(478)}{792} = 108.03$$

$$\hat{E}(n_{21}) = \frac{r_2 c_1}{n} = \frac{613(314)}{792} = 243.03 \qquad \hat{E}(n_{22}) = \frac{r_2 c_2}{n} = \frac{613(478)}{792} = 369.97$$

To determine whether seatbelt usage in motor vehicle accidents depends on ethnic status in the San Diego County Regionalized Trauma System, we test:

H_0: Seatbelt usage in motor vehicle accidents and ethnic status in the San Diego County Regionalized Trauma System are independent
H_a: Seatbelt usage in motor vehicle accidents and ethnic status in the San Diego County Regionalized Trauma System are dependent

The test statistic is $\chi^2 = \sum\sum \dfrac{\left[n_{ij} - \hat{E}(n_{ij})\right]^2}{\hat{E}(n_{ij})^2}$

$$= \frac{(31 - 70.97)^2}{70.97} + \frac{(148 - 108.03)^2}{108.03} + \frac{(283 - 243.03)^2}{243.03} + \frac{(330 - 369.97)^2}{369.97} = 48.191$$

The rejection region requires $\alpha = .01$ in the upper tail of the χ^2 distribution with df = $(r - 1)(c - 1) = (2 - 1)(2 - 1) = 1$. From Table XIII, Appendix B, $\chi^2_{.01} = 6.63490$. The rejection region is $\chi^2 > 6.63490$.

Since the observed value of the test statistic falls in the rejection region ($\chi^2 = 48.191 > 6.63490$), H_0 is rejected. There is sufficient evidence to indicate seatbelt usage in motor vehicle accidents depends on ethnic status in the San Diego County Regionalized Trauma System at $\alpha = .01$.

e. For confidence coefficient .99, $\alpha = .01$ and $\alpha/2 = .01/2 = .005$. From Table IV, Appendix B, $z_{.005} = 2.58$. The confidence interval is:

$$(\hat{p}_1 - \hat{p}_2) \pm z_{.005}\sqrt{\frac{\hat{p}_1 \hat{q}_1}{n_1} + \frac{\hat{p}_2 \hat{q}_2}{n_2}} \Rightarrow (.901 - .690) \pm 2.58\sqrt{\frac{.901(.099)}{314} + \frac{.690(.310)}{478}}$$

$$\Rightarrow .211 \pm .070 \Rightarrow (.141, .281)$$

We are 99% confident that the difference in the proportion of injured Hispanic children who were not wearing seatbelts and the proportion of injured non-Hispanic white children who were not wearing seatbelts is between .141 and .281.

17.25 a. Some preliminary calculations are:

$$\hat{E}(n_{11}) = \frac{r_1 c_1}{n} = \frac{31(70)}{117} = 18.55 \quad \hat{E}(n_{21}) = \frac{86(70)}{117} = 51.45$$

$$\hat{E}(n_{12}) = \frac{31(30)}{117} = 7.95 \quad \hat{E}(n_{22}) = \frac{86(30)}{117} = 22.05$$

$$\hat{E}(n_{13}) = \frac{31(17)}{117} = 4.50 \quad \hat{E}(n_{23}) = \frac{86(17)}{117} = 12.50$$

To determine if there is a relationship between an employee's age and the kind of accident, we test:

H_0: Age and kind of accident are independent
H_a: Age and kind of accident are dependent

The test statistic is $\chi^2 = \sum\sum \frac{[n_{ij} - \hat{E}(n_{ij})]^2}{\hat{E}(n_{ij})} = \frac{(9 - 18.55)^2}{18.55} + \frac{(61 - 51.45)^2}{51.45}$

$+ \frac{(17 - 7.95)^2}{7.95} + \frac{(13 - 22.05)^2}{22.05} + \frac{(5 - 4.50)^2}{4.50} + \frac{(12 - 12.5)^2}{12.5} = 20.78$

The rejection region requires $\alpha = .05$ in the upper tail of the χ^2 distribution with df = $(r - 1)(c - 1) = (2 - 1)(3 - 1) = 2$. From Table XIII, Appendix B, $\chi^2_{.05} = 5.99147$. The rejection region is $\chi^2 > 5.99147$.

Since the observed value of the test statistic falls in the rejection region ($\chi^2 = 20.78 > 5.99147$), H_0 is rejected. There is sufficient evidence to indicate a relationship exists between an employee's age and the kind of accident that the employee had at $\alpha = .05$.

b. The most frequent type of accident is sprain (total sprains is 70). Of the 70 people who suffered sprains, 61 are 25 or over while only 9 are under 25. Thus, older employees are more likely to have sprains.

Of the 30 people who suffered burns, 17 are under 25 while 13 are 25 and over. Thus, younger employees are more likely to suffer burns.

c. The necessary assumptions are:

1. The n observed counts are a random sample from the population of interest. We may then consider this to be a multinomial experiment with $r \times c = 2(3) = 6$ possible outcomes.
2. The sample size, n, will be large enough so that, for every cell, the expected cell count, $E(n_{ij})$, will be equal to 5 or more.

d. To find the percentages of those under 25 who are injured, divide the number under 25 in each column by the column total and multiply by 100.

The percentages are:

	Kind of Accident			Total
	Sprain	Burn	Cut	
Under 25	$\frac{9}{70} \cdot 100 = 12.9\%$	$\frac{17}{30} \cdot 100 = 56.7\%$	$\frac{5}{17} \cdot 100 = 29.4\%$	$\frac{31}{117} \cdot 100 = 26.50\%$

Since the row percentages in each column are not similar to the row total percentage, the graph indicates the variables are dependent.

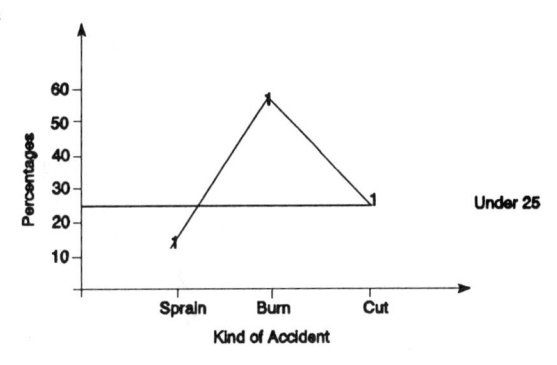

17.27 a. Some preliminary calculations are:

$$\hat{E}(n_{11}) = \frac{r_1 c_1}{n} = \frac{136(150)}{300} = 68 \qquad \hat{E}(n_{21}) = \frac{r_2 c_1}{n} = \frac{164(150)}{300} = 82$$

$$\hat{E}(n_{12}) = \frac{r_1 c_2}{n} = \frac{136(150)}{300} = 68 \qquad \hat{E}(n_{22}) = \frac{r_2 c_2}{n} = \frac{164(150)}{300} = 82$$

To determine whether audience gender and product identification are dependent factors for male spokespersons, we test:

H_0: Audience gender and product identification are independent factors
H_a: Audience gender and product identification are dependent factors

The test statistic is $\chi^2 = \sum\sum \dfrac{[n_{ij} - \hat{E}(n_{ij})]^2}{\hat{E}(n_{ij})^2}$

$$= \frac{(95-68)^3}{68} + \frac{(41-68)^2}{68} + \frac{(55-82)^2}{82} + \frac{(109-82)^2}{82} = 39.22$$

The rejection region requires $\alpha = .05$ in the upper tail of the χ^2 distribution with df = $(r-1)(c-1) = (2-1)(2-1) = 1$. From Table XIII, Appendix B, $\chi^2_{.05} = 3.84146$. The rejection region is $\chi^2 > 3.84146$.

Since the observed value of the test statistic falls in the rejection region ($\chi^2 = 39.22 > 3.84146$), H_0 is rejected. There is sufficient evidence to indicate audience gender and product identification are dependent factors for $\alpha = .05$.

b. Some preliminary calculations are:

$$\hat{E}(n_{11}) = \frac{r_1 c_1}{n} = \frac{108(150)}{300} = 54 \qquad \hat{E}(n_{21}) = \frac{r_2 c_1}{n} = \frac{192(150)}{300} = 96$$

$$\hat{E}(n_{12}) = \frac{r_1 c_2}{n} = \frac{108(150)}{300} = 54 \qquad \hat{E}(n_{22}) = \frac{r_2 c_2}{n} = \frac{192(150)}{300} = 96$$

To determine whether audience gender and product identification are dependent factors for female spokespersons, we test:

H_0: Audience gender and product identification are independent factors
H_a: Audience gender and product identification are dependent factors

The test statistic is $\chi^2 = \sum\sum \dfrac{[n_{ij} - \hat{E}(n_{ij})]^2}{\hat{E}(n_{ij})}$

$= \dfrac{(47-54)^2}{54} + \dfrac{(61-54)^2}{54} + \dfrac{(103-96)^2}{96} + \dfrac{(89-96)^2}{96} = 2.84$

The rejection region requires $\alpha = .05$ in the upper tail of the χ^2 distribution with df = $(r-1)(c-1) = (2-1)(2-1) = 1$. From Table XIII, Appendix B, $\chi^2_{.05} = 3.84146$. The rejection region is $\chi^2 > 3.84146$.

Since the observed value of the test statistic does not fall in the rejection region ($\chi^2 = 2.84 \not> 3.84146$), H_0 is not rejected. There is insufficient evidence to indicate audience gender and product identification are dependent factors for $\alpha = .05$.

c. When a male spokesperson is used in an advertisement, audience gender and product identification are dependent. Males tended to identify the product more frequently than females.

When a female spokesperson is used in an advertisement, there is no evidence that audience gender and product identification are dependent. Males and females tend to identify the product at the same rate.

17.29 First, we must set up the contingency table. The proportions given are the proportions of the whole group who show signs of stress and fall into a particular fitness level. Thus, the number of people showing signs of stress and falling in the poor fitness level is $np_1 = 549(.155) = 85$. The number of people showing signs of stress and falling in the average fitness level is $np_2 = 549(.133) = 73$. The number of people showing signs of stress and falling in the good fitness level is $np_3 = 549(.108) = 59$.

The contingency table is:

Fitness level	Stress — No stress	Stress — Signs of stress	Total
Poor	157	85	242
Average	139	73	212
Good	36	59	95
Total	332	217	549

Some preliminary calculations are:

$\hat{E}(n_{11}) = \dfrac{r_1 c_1}{n} = \dfrac{242(332)}{549} = 146.346 \qquad \hat{E}(n_{12}) = \dfrac{r_1 c_2}{n} = \dfrac{242(217)}{549} = 95.654$

$\hat{E}(n_{21}) = \dfrac{r_2 c_1}{n} = \dfrac{212(332)}{549} = 128.204 \qquad \hat{E}(n_{22}) = \dfrac{r_2 c_2}{n} = \dfrac{212(217)}{549} = 83.796$

$\hat{E}(n_{31}) = \dfrac{r_3 c_1}{n} = \dfrac{95(332)}{549} = 57.45 \qquad \hat{E}(n_{32}) = \dfrac{r_3 c_2}{n} = \dfrac{95(217)}{549} = 37.55$

To determine whether the likelihood for stress is dependent on an employee's fitness level, we test:

H_0: Likelihood for stress is independent of an employee's fitness level
H_a: Likelihood for stress is dependent on an employee's fitness level

The test statistic is $\chi^2 = \sum\sum \dfrac{[n_{ij} - \hat{E}(n_{ij})]^2}{\hat{E}(n_{ij})}$

$= \dfrac{(157 - 146.346)^2}{146.346} + \dfrac{(85 - 95.654)^2}{95.654} + \dfrac{(139 - 128.204)^2}{128.204}$

$+ \dfrac{(73 - 83.796)^2}{83.796} + \dfrac{(36 - 57.45)^2}{57.45} + \dfrac{(59 - 37.55)^2}{37.55} = 24.524$

The rejection region requires $\alpha = .05$ in the upper tail of the χ^2 distribution with df = $(r-1)(c-1) = (3-1)(2-1) = 2$. From Table XIII, Appendix B, $\chi^2_{.05} = 5.99147$. The rejection region is $\chi^2 > 5.99147$.

Since the observed value of the test statistic falls in the rejection region ($\chi^2 = 24.524 > 5.99147$), H_0 is rejected. There is sufficient evidence to indicate the likelihood for stress is dependent on an employee's fitness level for $\alpha = .05$.

17.31 a. No. In a multinomial experiment, each trial results in one of $k = 8$ possible outcomes. In this experiment, each trial cannot result in one of all of the eight possible outcomes. The people are assigned to a particular diet before the experiment. Once the people are assigned to a particular diet, there are only two possible outcomes, cancer tumors or no cancer tumors.

b. The expected cell counts are:

$\hat{E}(n_{11}) = \dfrac{r_1 c_1}{n} = \dfrac{80(30)}{120} = 20 \qquad \hat{E}(n_{21}) = \dfrac{r_2 c_1}{n} = \dfrac{40(30)}{120} = 10$

$\hat{E}(n_{12}) = \dfrac{r_1 c_2}{n} = \dfrac{80(30)}{120} = 20 \qquad \hat{E}(n_{22}) = \dfrac{r_2 c_2}{n} = \dfrac{40(30)}{120} = 10$

$\hat{E}(n_{13}) = \dfrac{r_1 c_3}{n} = \dfrac{80(30)}{120} = 20 \qquad \hat{E}(n_{23}) = \dfrac{r_2 c_3}{n} = \dfrac{40(30)}{120} = 10$

$\hat{E}(n_{14}) = \dfrac{r_1 c_4}{n} = \dfrac{80(30)}{120} = 20 \qquad \hat{E}(n_{24}) = \dfrac{r_2 c_4}{n} = \dfrac{40(30)}{120} = 10$

c. The test statistic is $\chi^2 = \sum\sum \dfrac{[n_{ij} - \hat{E}(n_{ij})]^2}{\hat{E}(n_{ij})}$

$= \dfrac{(27-20)^2}{20} + \dfrac{(20-20)^2}{20} + \dfrac{(19-20)^2}{20} + \dfrac{(14-20)^2}{20} + \dfrac{(3-10)^2}{10} + \dfrac{(10-10)^2}{10}$

$+ \dfrac{(11-10)^2}{10} + \dfrac{(16-10)^2}{10} = 12.9$

d. To determine if diet and presence/absence of cancer are independent, we test:

H_0: Diet and presence/absence of cancer are independent
H_a: Diet and presence/absence of cancer are dependent

The test statistic is $\chi^2 = 12.9$ (from part c).

The Chi-Square Test and the Analysis of Contingency Tables

The rejection region requires $\alpha = .05$ in the upper tail of the χ^2 distribution with df = $(r-1)(c-1) = (2-1)(4-1) = 3$. From Table XIII, Appendix B, $\chi^2_{.05} = 7.81473$. The rejection region is $\chi^2 > 7.81473$.

Since the observed value of the test statistic falls in the rejection region ($\chi^2 = 12.9 > 7.81473$), H_0 is rejected. There is sufficient evidence to indicate that diet and presence/absence of cancer are dependent for $\alpha = .05$.

e. $\hat{p}_1 = 27/30 = .9; \hat{p}_2 = 20/30 = .667$

For confidence coefficient .95, $\alpha = .05$ and $\alpha/2 = .05/2 = .025$. From Table IV, Appendix B, $z_{.025} = 1.96$. The confidence interval is:

$$(\hat{p}_1 - \hat{p}_2) \pm z_{.005} \sqrt{\frac{\hat{p}_1 \hat{q}_1}{n_1} + \frac{\hat{p}_2 \hat{q}_2}{n_2}} \Rightarrow (.900 - .667) \pm 1.96 \sqrt{\frac{.900(.100)}{30} + \frac{.667(.333)}{30}}$$
$$\Rightarrow .233 \pm .200 \Rightarrow (.033, .433)$$

We are 95% confident that the difference in the percentage of rats on a high fat/no fiber diet with cancer and the percentage of rats on a high fat/fiber diet with cancer is between 3.3% and 43.3%.

17.33 a. Some preliminary calculations are:

If all the categories are equally likely,

$$p_{1,0} = p_{2,0} = p_{3,0} = p_{4,0} = p_{5,0} = .2$$

$$E(n_1) = E(n_2) = E(n_3) = E(n_4) = E(n_5) = np_{1,0} = 150(.2) = 30$$

To determine if the categories are not equally likely, we test:

H_0: $p_1 = p_2 = p_3 = p_4 = p_5 = .2$
H_a: At least one probability is different from .2

The test statistic is $\chi^2 = \sum \dfrac{[n_i - E(n_i)]^2}{E(n_i)}$

$$= \frac{(28-30)^2}{30} + \frac{(35-30)^2}{30} + \frac{(33-30)^2}{30} + \frac{(25-30)^2}{30} + \frac{(29-30)^2}{30} = 2.133$$

The rejection region requires $\alpha = .10$ in the upper tail of the χ^2 distribution with df = $k - 1 = 5 - 1 = 4$. From Table XIII, Appendix B, $\chi^2_{.10} = 7.77944$. The rejection region is $\chi^2 > 7.77944$.

Since the observed value of the test statistic does not fall in the rejection region ($\chi^2 = 2.133 \not> 7.77944$), H_0 is not rejected. There is insufficient evidence to indicate the categories are not equally likely at $\alpha = .10$.

b. $\hat{p}_2 = \dfrac{35}{150} = .233$

For confidence coefficient .90, $\alpha = .10$ and $\alpha/2 = .05$. From Table IV, Appendix B, $z_{.05} = 1.645$. The confidence interval is:

$$\hat{p}_2 \pm z_{.05}\sqrt{\frac{\hat{p}_2\hat{q}_2}{n_2}} \Rightarrow .233 \pm 1.645\sqrt{\frac{.233(.767)}{150}} \Rightarrow .233 \pm .057 \Rightarrow (.176, .290)$$

17.35 For union members:

H_0: Level of confidence and job satisfaction are independent
H_a: Level of confidence and job satisfaction are dependent

The test statistic is $\chi^2 = 13.36744$ (from printout).

The rejection region requires $\alpha = .05$ in the upper tail of the χ^2 distribution with df = $(r - 1)(c - 1) = (3 - 1)(4 - 1) = 6$. From Table XIII, Appendix B, $\chi^2_{.05} = 12.5916$. The rejection region is $\chi^2 > 12.5916$.

Since the observed value of the test statistic falls in the rejection region ($\chi^2 = 13.36 > 12.5916$), H_0 is rejected. There is sufficient evidence to indicate the level of confidence and job satisfaction are related at $\alpha = .05$ for union members.

Note: This test should be viewed cautiously since three cells have expected values less than 5.

For nonunion members:

H_0: Level of confidence and job satisfaction are independent
H_a: Level of confidence and job satisfaction are dependent

The test statistic is $\chi^2 = 9.63514$ (from printout).

The rejection region is $\chi^2 > 12.5916$. Since the observed value of the test statistic does not fall in the rejection region ($\chi^2 = 9.64 \not> 12.5916$), H_0 is not rejected. There is insufficient evidence to indicate the level of confidence and job satisfaction are related for nonunion workers at $\alpha = .05$.

17.37 a. No. If January change is down, half the next 11-month changes are up and half are down.

b. The percentages of years for which the 11-month movement is up based on January change are found by dividing the numbers in the first column by the corresponding row total and multiplying by 100. We also divide the first column total by the overall total and multiply by 100.

January Change:

Up $\quad \frac{25}{35} \cdot 100 = 71.4\%$

Down $\quad \frac{9}{18} \cdot 100 = 50\%$

Total $\quad \frac{34}{53} \cdot 100 = 64.2\%$

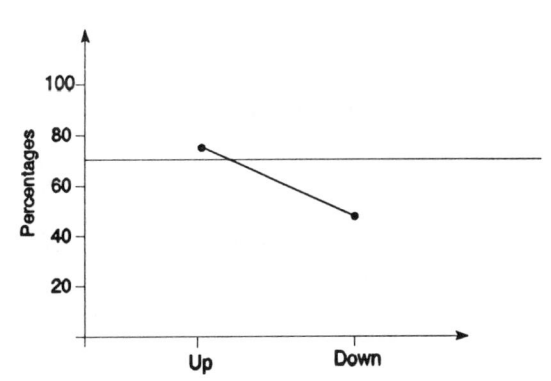

The Chi-Square Test and the Analysis of Contingency Tables

c. H_0: The January change and the next 11-month change are independent
H_a: The January change and the next 11-month change are dependent

d. Some preliminary calculations are:

$$\hat{E}(n_{11}) = \frac{r_1 c_1}{n} = \frac{35(34)}{53} = 22.453 \qquad \hat{E}(n_{12}) = \frac{35(19)}{53} = 12.547$$

$$\hat{E}(n_{21}) = \frac{18(34)}{53} = 11.547 \qquad \hat{E}(n_{22}) = \frac{18(19)}{53} = 6.453$$

The test statistic is $\chi^2 = \sum\sum \frac{[n_{ij} - \hat{E}(n_{ij})]^2}{\hat{E}(n_{ij})} = \frac{(25 - 22.453)^2}{22.453} + \frac{(9 - 11.547)^2}{11.547}$

$+ \frac{(10 - 12.547)^2}{12.547} + \frac{(9 - 6.453)^2}{6.453} = 2.373$

The rejection region requires $\alpha = .05$ in the upper tail of the χ^2 distribution with df = $(r - 1)(c - 1) = (2 - 1)(2 - 1) = 1$. From Table XIII, Appendix B, $\chi^2_{.05} = 3.84146$. The rejection region is $\chi^2 > 3.84146$.

Since the observed value of the test statistic does not fall in the rejection region ($\chi^2 = 2.373 \not> 3.84146$), H_0 is not rejected. There is insufficient evidence to indicate the January change and the next 11-month change are dependent at $\alpha = .05$.

e. Yes. For $\alpha = .10$, the rejection region is $\chi^2 > \chi^2_{.10} = 2.70554$, from Table XIII, Appendix B, with df = 1. Since the observed value of the test statistic does not fall in the rejection region ($\chi^2 = 2.373 \not> 2.70554$), H_0 is not rejected. The conclusion is the same.

17.39 a. The contingency table is:

		Committee		
		Acceptable	Rejected	Totals
Inspector	Acceptable	101	23	124
	Rejected	10	19	29
	Totals	111	42	153

b. Yes. To plot the percentages, first convert frequencies to percentages by dividing the numbers in each column by the column total and multiplying by 100. Also, divide the row totals by the overall total and multiply by 100.

		Acceptable	Rejected	Totals
Inspector	Acceptable	$\frac{101}{111} \cdot 100 = 90.99\%$	$\frac{23}{42} \cdot 100 = 54.76\%$	$\frac{124}{153} \cdot 100 = 81.05\%$
	Rejected	$\frac{10}{111} \cdot 100 = 9.01\%$	$\frac{19}{42} \cdot 100 = 45.23\%$	$\frac{29}{153} \cdot 100 = 18.95\%$

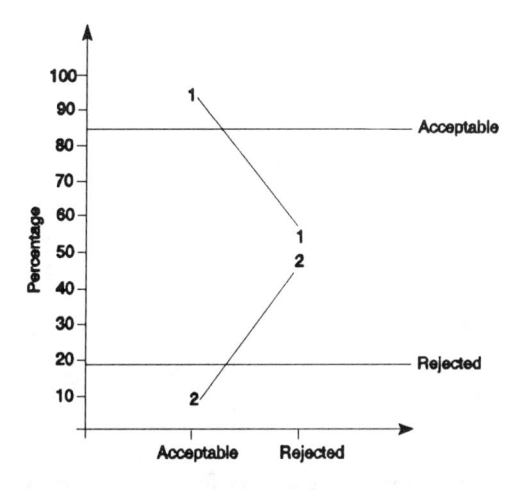

From the plot, it appears there is a relationship.

c. Some preliminary calculations are:

$$\hat{E}(n_{11}) = \frac{r_1 c_1}{n} = \frac{124(111)}{153} = 89.691 \qquad \hat{E}(n_{12}) = \frac{r_1 c_2}{n} = \frac{124(42)}{153} = 34.039$$

$$\hat{E}(n_{21}) = \frac{r_2 c_1}{n} = \frac{29(111)}{153} = 21.039 \qquad \hat{E}(n_{22}) = \frac{r_2 c_2}{n} = \frac{29(42)}{153} = 7.961$$

To determine if the inspector's classifications and the committee's classifications are related, we test:

H_0: The inspector's and committee's classification are independent
H_a: The inspector's and committee's classifications are dependent

The test statistic is $\chi^2 = \sum\sum \frac{[n_{ij} - \hat{E}(n_{ij})]^2}{\hat{E}(n_{ij})}$

$$= \frac{(101 - 89.961)^2}{89.961} + \frac{(23 - 34.039)^2}{34.039} + \frac{(10 - 21.039)^2}{21.039} + \frac{(19 - 7.961)^2}{7.961}$$
$$= 26.034$$

The rejection region requires $\alpha = .05$ in the upper tail of the χ^2 distribution with df = $(r - 1)(c - 1) = (2 - 1)(2 - 1) = 1$. From Table XIII, Appendix B, $\chi^2_{.05} = 3.84146$. The rejection region is $\chi^2 > 3.84146$.

Since the observed value of the test statistic falls in the rejection region ($\chi^2 = 26.034 > 3.84146$), H_0 is rejected. There is sufficient evidence to indicate the inspector's and committee's classifications are related at $\alpha = .05$. This indicates that the inspector and committee tend to make the same decisions.

The Chi-Square Test and the Analysis of Contingency Tables

17.41   a.   Some preliminary calculations are:

$$\hat{E}(n_{11}) = \frac{r_1 c_1}{n} = \frac{99(258)}{314} = 81.34 \qquad \hat{E}(n_{12}) = \frac{r_1 c_2}{n} = \frac{99(56)}{314} = 17.66$$

$$\hat{E}(n_{21}) = \frac{r_2 c_1}{n} = \frac{67(258)}{314} = 55.05 \qquad \hat{E}(n_{22}) = \frac{r_2 c_2}{n} = \frac{67(56)}{314} = 11.95$$

$$\hat{E}(n_{31}) = \frac{r_3 c_1}{n} = \frac{55(258)}{314} = 45.19 \qquad \hat{E}(n_{32}) = \frac{r_3 c_2}{n} = \frac{55(56)}{314} = 9.81$$

$$\hat{E}(n_{41}) = \frac{r_4 c_1}{n} = \frac{45(258)}{314} = 36.97 \qquad \hat{E}(n_{42}) = \frac{r_4 c_2}{n} = \frac{45(56)}{314} = 8.03$$

$$\hat{E}(n_{51}) = \frac{r_5 c_1}{n} = \frac{48(258)}{314} = 39.44 \qquad \hat{E}(n_{52}) = \frac{r_5 c_2}{n} = \frac{48(56)}{314} = 8.56$$

To determine if the proportion of correctly priced items differs for at least two types of stores, we test:

H_0:   Correctness of pricing and type of store are independent
H_a: Correctness of pricing and type of store are dependent

The test statistic is $\chi^2 = \sum\sum \frac{[n_{ij} - \hat{E}(n_{ij})]^2}{\hat{E}(n_{ij})} = \frac{(89 - 81.34)^2}{81.34} + \cdots + \frac{(7 - 8.56)^2}{8.56} = 9.16$

The rejection region requires $\alpha = .10$ in the upper tail of the χ^2 distribution with df = $(r-1)(c-1) = (5-1)(2-1) = 4$. From Table XIII, Appendix B, $\chi^2_{.10} = 7.77944$. The rejection region is $\chi^2 > 7.77944$.

Since the observed value of the test statistic falls in the rejection region ($\chi^2 = 9.16 > 7.77944$), H_0 is rejected. There is sufficient evidence to indicate a dependence between correctness of pricing and type of store at $\alpha = .10$.

   b.   Let p = the proportion of correctly priced items in the stores in the national chain category.

$$\hat{p} = \frac{x}{n} = \frac{89}{99} = .90$$

For confidence coefficient .95, $\alpha = .05$ and $\alpha/2 = .025$. From Table IV, Appendix B, $z_{.025} = 1.96$. The confidence interval is:

$$\hat{p} \pm z_{\alpha/2}\sqrt{\frac{\hat{p}\hat{q}}{n}} \Rightarrow .90 \pm 1.96\sqrt{\frac{(.90)(.10)}{99}} \Rightarrow .90 \pm .06 \Rightarrow (.84, .96)$$

17.43   Some preliminary calculations are:

If the transactions are randomly assigned to each of the locations, then $p_{i,0} = .20$ for $i = 1, 2, 3, 4,$ and 5.

$$E(n_i) = np_{i,0} = 425(.2) = 85$$

To determine if there is a difference in the proportions of transactions assigned to the five memory locations, we test:

H_0: $p_1 = p_2 = p_3 = p_4 = p_5 = .2$
H_a: At least one of the proportions differ from .2

The test statistic is $\chi^2 = \sum \dfrac{[n_i - E(n_i)]^2}{E(n_i)}$

$= \dfrac{(90-85)^2}{85} + \dfrac{(78-85)^2}{85} + \dfrac{(100-85)^2}{85} + \dfrac{(72-85)^2}{85} + \dfrac{(85-85)^2}{85}$

$= 5.506$

The rejection region requires $\alpha = .025$ in the upper tail of the χ^2 distribution with df $= k - 1 = 5 - 1 = 4$. From Table XIII, Appendix B, $\chi^2_{.025} = 11.1433$. The rejection region is $\chi^2 > 11.1433$.

Since the observed value of the test statistic does not fall in the rejection region ($\chi^2 = 5.506 \not> 11.1433$), H_0 is not rejected. There is insufficient evidence to indicate the proportions of transactions assigned to the five memory locations differ at $\alpha = .025$.

17.45 a. Some preliminary calculations are:

$E(n_1) = np_{1,0} = 200(.65) = 130$ $\quad n_1 = np_1 = 200(.78) = 156$
$E(n_2) = np_{2,0} = 200(.15) = 30$ $\quad n_2 = np_2 = 200(.12) = 24$
$E(n_3) = np_{3,0} = 200(.10) = 20$ $\quad n_3 = np_3 = 200(.05) = 10$
$E(n_4) = np_{4,0} = 200(.07) = 14$ $\quad n_4 = np_4 = 200(.02) = 4$
$E(n_5) = np_{5,0} = 200(.03) = 6$ $\quad n_5 = np_5 = 200(.03) = 6$

To determine if the increase in interest rates affected the timing of buyers' payments, we test:

H_0: $p_1 = .65, p_2 = .15, p_3 = .10, p_4 = .07,$ and $p_5 = .03$
H_a: At least one proportion differs from its hypothesized value

The test statistic is $\chi^2 = \sum \dfrac{(n_i - E(n_i))^2}{E(n_i)}$

$= \dfrac{(156-130)^2}{130} + \dfrac{(24-30)^2}{30} + \dfrac{(10-20)^2}{20} + \dfrac{(4-14)^2}{14} + \dfrac{(6-6)^2}{6} = 18.54$

The rejection region requires $\alpha = .10$ in the upper tail of the χ^2 distribution with df $= k - 1 = 5 - 1 = 4$. From Table XIII, Appendix B, $\chi^2_{.10} = 7.77944$. The rejection region is $\chi^2 > 7.77944$.

Since the observed value of the test statistic falls in the rejection region ($\chi^2 = 18.54 > 7.77944$), H_0 is rejected. There is sufficient evidence to indicate the increase in interest rates affected the timing of buyers' payments at $\alpha = .10$.

b. The observed significance level is $P(\chi^2 \geq 18.54)$. From Table XIII, Appendix B, with df $= 4$, $P(\chi^2 \geq 18.54) = p$-value $< .005$.

17.47 a. Some preliminary calculations are:

The contingency table is:

	Defectives	Non-Defectives	
Shift 1	25	175	200
Shift 2	35	165	200
Shift 3	80	120	200
	140	460	600

$$\hat{E}(n_{11}) = \frac{r_1 c_1}{n} = \frac{200(140)}{600} = 46.667$$

$$\hat{E}(n_{21}) = \hat{E}(n_{31}) = \frac{200(140)}{600} = 46.667$$

$$\hat{E}(n_{12}) = \hat{E}(n_{22}) = \hat{E}(n_{32}) = \frac{200(460)}{600} = 153.333$$

To determine if quality of the filters are related to shift, we test:

H_0: Quality of filters and shift are independent
H_a: Quality of filters and shift are dependent

The test statistic is $\chi^2 = \sum\sum \frac{[n_{ij} - \hat{E}(n_{ij})]^2}{\hat{E}(n_{ij})} = \frac{(25 - 46.667)^2}{46.667} + \frac{(35 - 46.667)^2}{46.667}$

$+ \frac{(80 - 46.667)^2}{46.667} + \frac{(175 - 153.333)^2}{153.333} + \frac{(165 - 153.333)^2}{153.333} + \frac{(120 - 153.333)^2}{153.333}$

$= 47.98$

The rejection region requires $\alpha = .05$ in the upper tail of the χ^2 distribution with df = $(r - 1)(c - 1) = (3 - 1)(2 - 1) = 2$. From Table XIII, Appendix B, $\chi^2_{.05} = 5.99147$. The rejection region is $\chi^2 > 5.99147$.

Since the observed value of the test statistic falls in the rejection region ($\chi^2 = 47.98 > 5.99147$), H_0 is rejected. There is sufficient evidence to indicate quality of filters and shift are related at $\alpha = .05$.

b. The form of the confidence interval for p is:

$$\hat{p}_1 \pm z_{\alpha/2}\sqrt{\frac{\hat{p}_1 \hat{q}_1}{n}} \text{ where } \hat{p}_1 = \frac{25}{200} = .125$$

For confidence coefficient .95, $\alpha = 1 - .95 = .05$ and $\alpha/2 = .05/2 = .025$. From Table IV, Appendix B, $z_{.025} = 1.96$. The 95% confidence interval is:

$$.125 \pm 1.96\sqrt{\frac{.125(.875)}{200}} \Rightarrow .125 \pm .046 \Rightarrow (.079, .171)$$

17.49 a. Some preliminary calculations are:

$$\hat{E}(n_{11}) = \frac{r_1 c_1}{n} = \frac{117(155)}{300} = 60.45 \qquad \hat{E}(n_{13}) = \frac{117(31)}{300} = 12.09$$

$$\hat{E}(n_{21}) = \frac{120(155)}{300} = 62 \qquad \hat{E}(n_{23}) = \frac{120(31)}{300} = 12.4$$

$$\hat{E}(n_{31}) = \frac{63(155)}{300} = 32.55 \qquad \hat{E}(n_{33}) = \frac{63(31)}{300} = 6.51$$

$$\hat{E}(n_{12}) = \frac{117(114)}{300} = 44.46$$

$$\hat{E}(n_{22}) = \frac{120(114)}{300} = 45.6$$

$$\hat{E}(n_{32}) = \frac{63(114)}{300} = 23.94$$

To determine if time and size of purchase are related, we test:

H_0: Time and size of purchase are independent
H_a: Time and size of purchase are dependent

The test statistic is $\chi^2 = \sum\sum \frac{[n_{ij} - \hat{E}(n_{ij})]^2}{\hat{E}(n_{ij})} = \frac{(65 - 60.45)^2}{60.45} + \frac{(61 - 62)^2}{62}$

$$+ \frac{(29 - 32.55)^2}{32.55} + \ldots + \frac{(7 - 6.51)^2}{6.51} = 3.13$$

The rejection region requires $\alpha = .05$ in the upper tail of the χ^2 distribution with df = $(r - 1)(c - 1) = (3 - 1)(3 - 1) = 4$. From Table XIII, Appendix B, $\chi^2_{.05} = 9.48773$. The rejection region is $\chi^2 > 9.48773$.

Since the observed value of the test statistic does not fall in the rejection region ($\chi^2 = 3.13 \not> 9.48773$), H_0 is not rejected. There is insufficient evidence to indicate time and size of purchase are related at $\alpha = .05$.

b. Let p_1 = proportion of customers spending \$2 or less for the time period 8 A.M. to 3:59 P.M. and p_2 = proportion of customers spending \$2 or less for the time period 12 midnight to 7:59 A.M.

$$\hat{p}_1 = \frac{65}{117} = .556 \qquad \hat{p}_2 = \frac{29}{63} = .460$$

For confidence level .90, $\alpha = 1 - .90 = .10$ and $\alpha/2 = .10/2 = .05$. From Table IV, Appendix B, $z_{.05} = 1.645$. The 90% confidence interval is:

$$(\hat{p}_1 - \hat{p}_2) \pm z_{.05} \sqrt{\frac{p_1(1 - p_1)}{n_1} + \frac{p_2(1 - p_2)}{n_2}}$$

$$\Rightarrow (.556 - .460) \pm 1.645 \sqrt{\frac{.556(.444)}{117} + \frac{.460(.540)}{63}} \Rightarrow .096 \pm .128$$

$$\Rightarrow (-.032, .224)$$

We are 90% confident that the difference between the proportions of customers who spend \$2 or less for the time periods 8 A.M. to 3:59 P.M. and 12 midnight to 7:59 A.M. is between $-.032$ and $.224$.

The Chi-Square Test and the Analysis of Contingency Tables

Decision Analysis — Chapter 18

18.3   a. This problem is decision-making under uncertainty. The management does not know whether the applicant will default on the loan or not.

b. This problem is decision-making under conflict. The manufacturer is "playing against" his competitors.

c. This problem is decision-making under certainty. The company knows the outcomes of the possible decisions.

18.5 This would be decision-making under uncertainty. The firms do not know whether investment in the emerging competitive markets will be successful or not.

18.7 Mutually exclusive and collectively exhaustive means that the states of nature cover all possibilities and that no two states of nature overlap each other.

18.9 a. Actions: Introduce low-cost dinner wine or Do not introduce low-cost dinner wine
States of Nature: Sales ranging from 5 to 25 million bottles per year
Outcomes: Profits made (or lost) from the sale of the wine
Objective Variable: Profits

b. Actions: Level of fines set
States of Nature: Ability or non-ability to pay fine
Outcomes: Firms driven out of business or waterways polluted
Objective Variable: Cost to firm

18.11 Actions: Invest heavily in emerging competitive markets or Do not invest
States of Nature: This is not given in the problem. The states of nature could be the different climates of the economy.
Outcomes: Increase in value of 55% or 120% or a decrease in value of 40% or 10%
Objective variable: Base value of the firm

18.13 The payoffs are the outcomes that reflect the actual reward to the decision-maker in terms of the objective variable. The opportunity loss is the difference between the payoff a decision-maker receives for a chosen action and the maximum that the decision-maker could have received for choosing the action yielding the highest payoff for the state of nature that occurred.

18.15 Action a_3 is inadmissible because it is dominated by action a_2. That is, for each state of nature, the payoff for a_2 is greater than or equal to the payoff for a_3.

The opportunity losses are calculated as shown in the table below.

		State of Nature			
		S_1	S_2	S_3	S_4
Action	a_1	0	0	$40 - 0 = 40$	$80 - 50 = 30$
	a_2	$-58 - (-69) = 11$	$-2 - (-10) = 8$	0	$80 - 71 = 9$
	a_4	$-58 - (-100) = 42$	$-2 - (-40) = 38$	$40 - (-10) = 50$	0

18.17 a. Action a_4 is dominated by action a_2 and thus is inadmissible.

b. For each action-state combination (a_i, S_j), the opportunity loss table displays the difference between the payoff received for action a and the maximum payoff attainable for state S_j. From this information, it is not possible to determine the original payoffs.

18.19 a.
Actions: Replace PCB transformer and Do not replace PCB transformer.
States of Nature: Major fire occurs or not
Outcomes: Costs of 0, $75,000, $20,075,000, and $30,000,000
Objective variable: Cost of cleanup

The payoff table is:

		State of Nature	
		Fire	No Fire
Action	Replace PCB Transformer	$-\$20,075,000$	$-\$75,000$
	Do Not Replace PCB Transformer	$-\$30,000,000$	0

b. To convert the payoff table to an opportunity loss table, we subtract the actual payoff from the maximum payoff in each state of nature. The opportunity loss table is:

		State of Nature	
		Fire	No Fire
Action	Replace PCB Transformer	$-\$20,075,000 - (-\$20,075,000) = \$0$	$0 - (-\$75,000) = \$75,000$
	Do Not Replace PCB Transformer	$-\$20,075,000 - (-\$30,000,000) = \$9,925,000$	$\$0 - \$0 = \$0$

Decision Analysis

c. The decision tree would be:

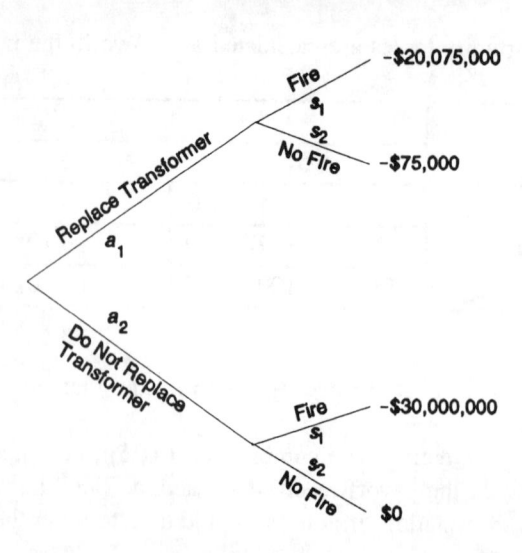

```
                                          Fire
                          Replace        s₁
                          Transformer  ───────── -$20,075,000
                             a₁          s₂
                                       No Fire
                                       ───────── -$75,000
                              
                             a₂
                          Do Not Replace
                          Transformer      Fire
                                          s₁
                                       ───────── -$30,000,000
                                          s₂
                                       No Fire
                                       ───────── $0
```

18.21 The payoff is $15 million if the laptop computer is not marketed in Europe. If it is marketed in Europe, and a 3% market share is attained, the company profits $3 million (or $18 million for the company), 2% market share gives $1 million profit ($16 million), 1% market share gives $1 million loss ($14 million). The payoff table is:

		State of Nature		
		1%	2%	3%
Action	Market	14	16	18
	Do Not Market	15	15	15

The opportunity losses are calculated as shown in the following table.

		State of Nature		
		1%	2%	3%
Action	Market	15 − 14 = 1	0	0
	Do Not Market	0	16 − 15 = 1	18 − 15 = 3

18.23 a. The payoffs when the guarantee is not bought are equal to the number of defective items times −$10. When the guarantee is bought, the payoff is −$1000 minus $10 times the number of defective items (up to a maximum of 50). The payoff table is:

		State of Nature		
		5%(25)	10%(50)	50%(250)
Action	Guarantee	−1,250	−1,500	−1,500
	No guarantee	−250	−500	−2,500

b. The decision tree is:

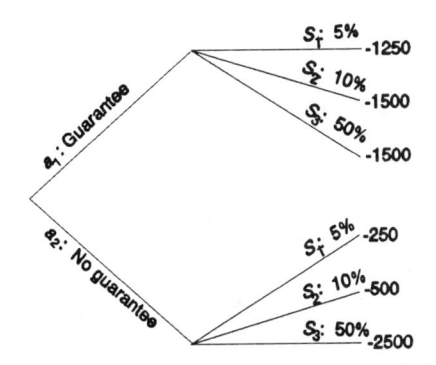

```
                               S₁: 5%
                              ╱──── -1250
                    a₁: Guarantee  S₂: 10%
                          ╱────────── -1500
                         ╱    S₃: 50%
                        ╱────────────── -1500
                       ╱
                      ╱         S₁: 5%
                       ╲       ╱──── -250
                        ╲     ╱ S₂: 10%
                  a₂: No guarantee ──── -500
                          ╲    S₃: 50%
                           ╲────────── -2500
```

18.25 $E(x) = \sum_{\text{All } x} xp(x)$

$EP(a_1) = (-150)(.1) + (-500)(.3) + (10)(.4) + (300)(.2) = -101$
$EP(a_2) = (-200)(.1) + (-100)(.3) + (300)(.4) + (100)(.2) = 90$
$EP(a_3) = (-150)(.1) + (-40)(.3) + (-10)(.4) + (85)(.2) = -14$

We would choose a_2, the action that produced the largest expected payoff.

18.27 Using the expected payoffs from Exercise 18.27, the decision tree is:

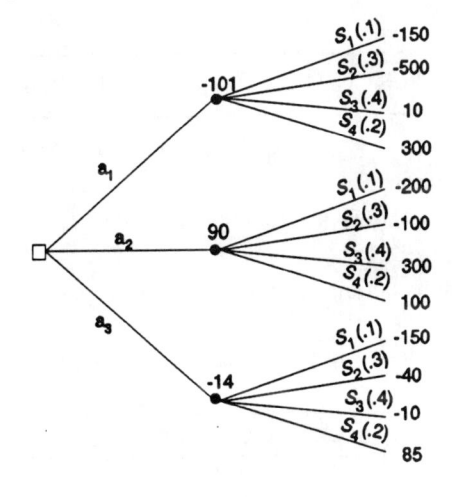

```
                       S₁(.1) -150
              -101  ╱── S₂(.3) -500
                ●──── S₃(.4)  10
                    ╲── S₄(.2) 300
           ╱a₁
          ╱              S₁(.1) -200
         ╱        90  ╱── S₂(.3) -100
        ╱─── a₂ ●──── S₃(.4)  300
       □              ╲── S₄(.2)  100
        ╲
         ╲a₃            S₁(.1) -150
          ╲    -14  ╱── S₂(.3) -40
               ●──── S₃(.4) -10
                   ╲── S₄(.2)  85
```

18.29 $EOL(a_1) = (56)(.6) + (0)(.4) = 33.6$
$EOL(a_2) = (0)(.6) + (70)(.4) = 28.0$

We would choose a_2, since it produces the smallest expected opportunity loss.

18.31 a. In this exercise, the probabilities of the states of nature differ for different actions. The expected payoffs for the two actions are:

$EP(a_1$: Replace transformer$) = .0005(-20,075,000) + .9995(-75,000) = -\$85,000$
$EP(a_2$: Do not replace transformer$) = .0025(-30,000,000) + .9975(0) = -\$75,000$

The action selected by the expected payoff criterion is action a_2, do not replace the transformer.

b. For action a_2, do not replace transformer, the expected payoff is $-\$75,000$. If we were to make this decision a large number of times, the average payoff per decision is $\$-75,000$.

c. To find the expected opportunity loss, we use the same probabilities as in part a:

$$EOL(a_1) = .0005(0) + .9995(75,000) = \$74,962.50$$
$$EOL(a_2) = .0025(9,925,000) + .9975(0) = \$24,812.50$$

The action with the smallest opportunity loss is action a_2, do not replace the transformer.

d. The company should not replace the transformer.

18.33 a. No, both actions are admissible. Neither action dominates the other.

b. $EP(a_1) = .09(26,500,000) + .91(-725,000) = 1,725,250$
$EP(a_2) = .09(13,980) + .91(-175,000) = -157,991.80$

The action with the highest expected payoff is action a_1, drill with 100% participation.

c. To convert the payoff table to an opportunity loss table, we subtract the actual payoff from the maximum payoff in each state of nature. The opportunity loss table is:

		State of Nature	
		35 BCF (.09)	Dry Hole (.91)
Action	Drill – 100% Participation	$26,500,000 – ($26,500,000) = $0	–$175,000 – (–$725,000) = $550,000
	Drill – 50% Participation	$26,500,000 – (–$13,980) = $26,486,020	–$175,000 – (–$175,000) = $0

d. $EOL(a_1) = .09(0) + .91(550,000) = \$500,500$
$EOL(a_2) = .09(26,486,020) + .91(0) = \$2,383,741.80$

The action with the smallest opportunity loss is action a_1, drill with 100% participation.

18.35 The payoff table, with state of nature probabilities shown in parentheses is given below.

		State (Percent Defective)		
		5% (.55)	10% (.24)	50% (.21)
Action	a_1: Purchase the Guarantee	–1250	–1500	–1500
	a_2: Do Not Purchase the Guarantee	–250	–500	–2500

$EP(a_1) = -1250(.55) - 1500(.24) - 1500(.21) = -1362.5$
$EP(a_2) = -250(.55) - 500(.24) - 2500(.21) = -782.5$

The greater expected payoff is associated with action a_2: Do not purchase the guarantee.

18.37 a. Utilities were computed using the function $U(x) = x^2$, and are shown in the following table.

		State of Nature		
		S_1 (.25)	S_2 (.30)	S_3 (.45)
Action	a_1	10,000	5,625	625
	a_2	4,900	9,025	0

b. $EU(a_1) = 10000(.25) + 5625(.30) + 625(.45) = 4469.05$
$EU(a_2) = 4900(.25) + 9025(.30) + 0(.45) = 3932.5$

Therefore, the expected utility criterion selects action a_1.

18.39 a. Utilities were computed using the function $U(x) = -1 + .01x$, and are shown in the following table.

		State of Nature			
		S_1 (.30)	S_2 (.05)	S_3 (.45)	S_4 (.20)
	a_1	.50	.80	0	−.20
Action	a_2	.30	.65	.90	.40
	a_3	.15	.20	.60	1.10

Note: The utility function is defined for $100 \leq x \leq 200$. Thus, even though the actual payoff in a_3, s_4 is greater than 200, only 200 can be used to find the utility.

b. $EU(a_1) = (.50)(.30) + (.80)(.05) + (0)(.45) + (-.20)(.20) = .1500$
$EU(a_2) = (.30)(.30) + (.65)(.05) + (.90)(.45) + (.40)(.20) = .6075$
$EU(a_3) = (.15)(.30) + (.20)(.05) + (.60)(.45) + (1.10)(.20) = .5450$

The expected utility criterion selects action a_2.

18.41 a. $U(\$600,000) = p = .9$
$U(\$0) = p = .8$

b. We know $U(-500,000) = 0$ and $U(1,500,000) = 1$

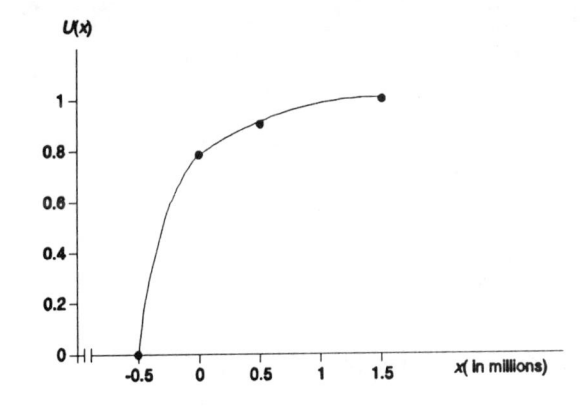

Decision Analysis

18.43 Using the payoffs found in Exercise 18.34 and $U(x) = \dfrac{\sqrt{x + 2000}}{110}$, the utiles are:

		State of Nature					
		3 doz	4 doz	5 doz	6 doz	7 doz	8 doz
Action	3 doz	.474	.474	.474	.474	.474	.474
	4 doz	.469	.495	.495	.495	.495	.495
	5 doz	.464	.490	.514	.514	.514	.514
	6 doz	.458	.484	.509	.533	.533	.533
	7 doz	.453	.479	.505	.529	.551	.551
	8 doz	.447	.474	.500	.524	.547	.569

The probabilities of the states of nature are found in Exercise 18.34.

$EU(3) = .15(.474) + .25(.474) + .30(.474) + .15(.474) + .10(.474) + .05(.474) = .4740$
$EU(4) = .15(.469) + .25(.495) + .30(.495) + .15(.495) + .10(.495) + .05(.495) = .4911$
$EU(5) = .15(.464) + .25(.490) + .30(.514) + .15(.514) + .10(.514) + .05(.514) = .5005$
$EU(6) = .15(.458) + .25(.484) + .30(.509) + .15(.533) + .10(.533) + .05(.533) = .5023$
$EU(7) = .15(.453) + .25(.479) + .30(.505) + .15(.529) + .10(.551) + .05(.551) = .5012$
$EU(8) = .15(.447) + .25(.474) + .30(.500) + .15(.524) + .10(.547) + .05(.569) = .4973$

The expected utility criterion selects buy 6 dozen dresses.

18.45 a.

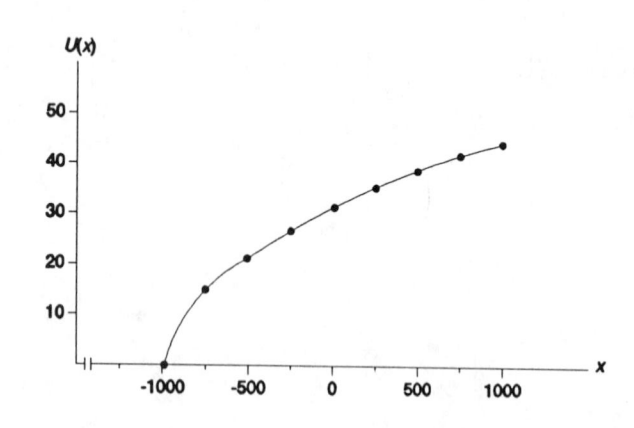

b. The graph is concave indicating the decision-maker is a risk-avoider.

c. Using the utility function, $U(x) = (x + 1000)^{1/2}$ the utiles are:

		State of Nature		
		S_1 (.1)	S_2 (.5)	S_3 (.4)
Action	a_1	20.000	44.721	36.056
	a_2	14.142	31.623	41.833
	a_3	32.558	28.723	40.125

$$EU(a_1) = .1(20.000) + .5(44.721) + .4(36.056) = 38.7829$$
$$EU(a_2) = .1(14.142) + .5(31.623) + .4(41.833) = 33.9589$$
$$EU(a_3) = .1(32.558) + .5(28.723) + .4(40.125) = 33.6673$$

The expected utility criterion selects action a_1.

18.47   a.   Since the payoffs range from $-\$30,000,000$ to $\$0$, we will use this as the range for x.

$$U(-20,075,000) = 1 + (1/30,000,000)(-20,075,000) = .3308$$
$$U(-75,000) = 1 + (1/30,000,000)(-75,000) = .9975$$
$$U(-30,000,000) = 1 + (1/30,000,000)(-30,000,000) = 0$$
$$U(0) = 1 + (1/30,000,000)(0) = 1$$

The graph is:

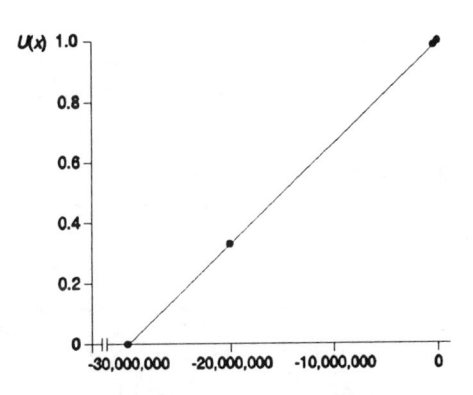

b.   Since the function is a straight line, the manager is risk-neutral.

c. $EU(a_1) = .0005(.3308) + .9995(.9975) = .9972$
       $EU(a_2) = .0025(0) + .9975(1) = .9975$

The expected utility criterion selects action a_2, do not replace the transformer.

18.49   a.

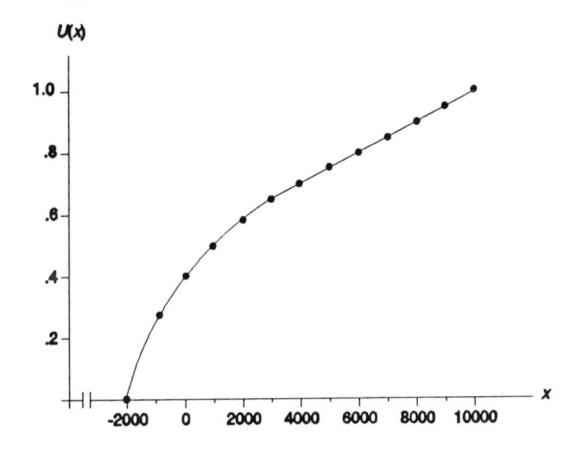

b.   The graph is concave implying the decision maker is a risk-avoider

Decision Analysis

18.51 Bayes' Rule for three states of nature and information I is:

$$P(S_i \mid I) = \frac{P(I \cap S_i)}{P(I)} = \frac{P(I \mid S_i)P(S_i)}{\sum P(I \mid S_i)P(S_i)}$$

18.53

(1) State of Nature	(2) Prior Probability	(3) Conditional Probability of Sample Information	(4) (2) × (3)	(5) Posterior Probability (4) ÷ Total of (4)
S_1	.10	.90	.0900	.1925
S_2	.25	.10	.0250	.0535
S_3	.45	.65	.2925	.6257
S_4	.20	.30	.0600	.1283
	1.00		.4675	1.0000

18.55 Prior information is information available before any sample information is obtained. Posterior information is additional information obtained from sampling.

18.57

(1) State of Nature	(2) Prior Probability	(3) Conditional Probability	(4) Probability of Intersection (2) × (3)	(5) Posterior Probability (4) ÷ Total of (4)
S_1: Correctly Adjusted	.9	.05	.045	.474
S_2: Incorrectly Adjusted	.1	.50	.050	.526
	1.00		.095	1.000

The probability that the machine is incorrectly adjusted is .526.

18.59 a.

p	Prior Probability
.01	$p = .25$
.05	$2p = .50$
.10	$p = .25$
	$4p = 1$
	$\Rightarrow p = .25$

b. $P(I \mid S_1) = P(x = 3 \mid p = .01) = \binom{5}{3}(.01)^3(.99)^2 = .0000098$

$P(I \mid S_2) = P(x = 3 \mid p = .05) = \binom{5}{3}(.05)^3(.95)^2 = .0011281$

$P(I \mid S_3) = P(x = 3 \mid p = .10) = \binom{5}{3}(.10)^3(.90)^2 = .0081000$

	(1)	(2)	(3)	(4)	(5)
	State of Nature	Prior Probability	Conditional Probability	Probability of Intersection (2) × (3)	Posterior Probability (4) ÷ Total of (4)
	S_1: $p = .01$	.25	.0000098	.0000025	.00096
	S_2: $p = .05$	.50	.0011281	.0005641	.21766
	S_3: $p = .10$	.25	.0081000	.0020250	.78137
		1.00		.0025916	1.00000

18.61 $EP(a_1) = \sum_{\text{All states}}$ (Payoff)(Posterior probability of state)
$= (30)(.1925) + (20)(.0535) + (0)(.6257) + (15)(.1283) = 8.7695$
$EP(a_2) = (40)(.1925) + (20)(.0535) + (5)(.6257) + (0)(.1283) = 11.8985$
$EP(a_3) = (9)(.1925) + (15)(.0535) + (-21)(.6257) + (25)(.1283) = -7.3972$

The action with the highest expected payoff is a_2.

18.63 a. $EP(a_1) = (-150)(.5) + (225)(.3) + (120)(.2) = 16.5$
$EP(a_2) = (200)(.5) + (-172)(.3) + (100)(.2) = 68.4$
$EP(a_3) = (300)(.5) + (80)(.3) + (-100)(.2) = 154$

The action with the highest expected payoff is a_3.

b.
(1)	(2)	(3)	(4)	(5)
State	Prior Probability	Conditional Probability	Probability of Intersection (2) × (3)	Posterior Probability (4) ÷ Total of (4)
S_1	.5	.2	.10	.3125
S_2	.3	.6	.18	.5625
S_3	.2	.2	.04	.1250
			.32	1.0000

c. $EP(a_1) = (-150)(.3125) + 225(.5625) + 120(.1250) = 94.6875$
$EP(a_2) = (200)(.3125) + (-172)(.5625) + 100(.1250) = -21.75$
$EP(a_3) = (300)(.3125) + (80)(.5625) + (-100)(.1250) = 126.25$

The action with the highest expected payoff is a_3.

18.65 Payoffs are in millions of dollars.

a.
Action	State of Nature (Prior Probabilities in Parentheses)	
	Pass Bill (.6)	Do Not Pass Bill (.4)
a_1: Stay in Business	2.5	-1.5
a_2: Lease Facility	.5	.5

Decision Analysis

b.

(1)	(2)	(3)	(4)	(5)
State of Nature	Prior Probability	Conditional Probability	Probability of Intersection (2) × (3)	Posterior Probability (4) ÷ Total of (4)
S_1	.6	.8	.48	.923
S_2	.4	.1	.04	.077
			.52	1.000

d. $EP(a_1) = 2.5(.923) + (-1.5)(.077) = 2.192$ million dollars
$EP(a_2) = .5(.923) + .5(.077) = .5$ million dollars

The action having the highest expected payoff is a_1: Stay in business

18.67 a. First we construct the probability revision tables to derive posterior probabilities for each of the two sample outcomes:

(1)	(2)	(3)	(4)	(5)
State of Nature	Prior Probability	Conditional Probability	Probability of Intersection (2) × (3)	Posterior Probability (4) ÷ Total of (4)
Sample Outcome: S_1 True				
S_1	.4	.4	.16	.4706
S_2	.6	.3	.18	.5294
			.34	1.0000
Sample Outcome: S_2 True				
S_1	.4	.6	.24	.3636
S_2	.6	.7	.42	.6364
			.66	1.0000

From the upper portion of the previous table,

$EP(a_1 \mid$ Sample information indicates S_1 True$) = 600(.4706) - 100(.5294) = \$229.42$
$EP(a_2 \mid$ Sample information indicates S_1 True$) = -200(.4706) + 300(.5294) = \$64.70$

The expected payoff criterion selects action a_1, when the sample information indicates S_1 is the true state of nature.

From the lower portion of the table,

$EP(a_1 \mid$ Sample information indicates S_2 True$) = 600(.3636) - 100(.6364) = \$154.52$
$EP(a_2 \mid$ Sample information indicates S_2 True$) = -200(.3636) + 300(.6364) = \$118.20$

The expected payoff criterion selects action a_1, when the sample information indicates S_2 is the true state of nature.

The expected payoff of sampling (EPS) is computed as follows:

EPS = 229.42(.34) + 154.52(.66) = $179.986
EVSI = EPS − EPNS = 179.986 − 180 = −.014
(EPNS = 180 is from Exercise 18.66)
ENGS = EVSI − CS = −.014 − 10 = −10.014

b. Since the ENGS for the second source is smaller than for the first source, the decision maker should choose the first source.

18.69 a. We now construct probability revision tables to derive posterior probabilities for each of the four possible sample outcomes.

(1)	(2)	(3)	(4)	(5)
State of Nature	Prior Probability	Conditional Probability	Probability of Intersection (2) × (3)	Posterior Probability (4) ÷ Total of (4)
Sample Outcome: Product is "Very Successful"				
Failure	.6	.1	.06	1/3
Successful	.3	.2	.06	1/3
Very Successful	.1	.6	.06	1/3
			.18	1
Sample Outcome: Product is "Successful"				
Failure	.6	.1	.06	.300
Successful	.3	.4	.12	.600
Very Successful	.1	.2	.02	.100
			.20	1.000
Sample Outcome: Product is "Failure"				
Failure	.6	.5	.30	.811
Successful	.3	.2	.06	.612
Very Successful	.1	.1	.01	.027
			.37	1.000
Sample Outcome: Product is "Uncertain"				
Failure	.6	.3	.18	.72
Successful	.3	.2	.06	.24
Very Successful	.1	.1	.01	.04
			.25	1.00

From the first portion of the table, Product is "Very Successful,"

$EP(a_1) = -200{,}000(1/3) + 300{,}000(1/3) + 600{,}000(1/3) = \$233{,}333.33$
$EP(a_2) = 0(1/3) + 0(1/3) + 0(1/3) = 0$

The expected payoff criterion selects action a_1.

From the second portion of the table, Product is "Successful,"

$EP(a_1) = -200{,}000(.3) + 300{,}000(.6) + 600{,}000(.1) = \$180{,}000$
$EP(a_2) = 0(.3) + 0(.6) + 0(.1) = 0$

The expected payoff criterion selects action a_1.

From the third portion of the table, Product is "Failure,"

$EP(a_1) = -200{,}000(.811) + 300{,}000(.162) + 600{,}000(.027) = \$-97{,}400$
$EP(a_2) = 0(.811) + 0(.162) + 0(.027) = 0$

The expected payoff criterion selects action a_2.

Decision Analysis

From the fourth portion of the table, Product is "Uncertain,"

$$EP(a_1) = -200,000(.72) + 300,000(.24) + 600,000(.04) = \$-48,000$$
$$EP(a_2) = 0(.72) + 0(.24) + 0(.04) = 0$$

The expected payoff criterion selects action a_2.

The expected payoff of sampling is:

$$EPS = 233,333.33(.18) + 180,000(.20) + 0(.37) + 0(.25) = \$78,000.00$$

The expected payoff with no sampling is:

$$EP(a_1) = -200,000(.6) + 300,000(.3) + 600,000(.1) = \$30,000$$
$$EP(a_2) = 0(.6) + 0(.3) + 0(.1) = 0$$

The EPNS = \$30,000

Thus, EVSI = EPS − EPNS = 78,000 − 30,000 = \$48,000

The most the company should pay for sampling information is \$48,000.

b. ENGS = EVSI − CS(Cost of Sampling) = \$48,000 − \$30,000 = \$18,000.

Since this is a positive, the company should undertake the proposed market survey.

18.71 From Exercise 18.64, EPS = .06(−45,332) + .94(−42,210) = −42,397.32

EVSI = EPS − EPNS = −42,397.32 − (−42,400) = 2.68

Thus, it is worth \$2.68 for the hospital to be able to test one of the 100 television sets.

(If we round off EPS to the nearest \$1000, EVSI = 0).

18.73 a.

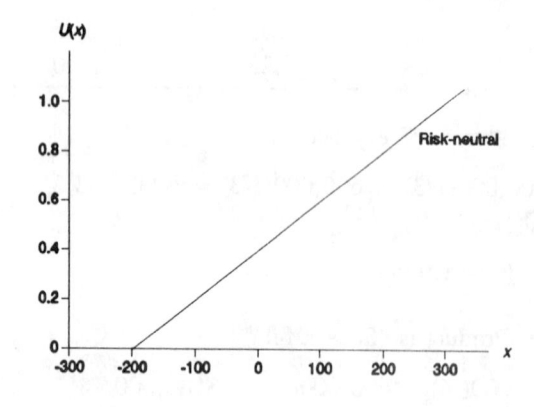

b.

Graph of U(x) vs x for Risk-avoider: concave curve passing through points approximately (-100, 0), (0, 0.5), (100, 0.75), (200, 0.9), (300, 1.0).

c.

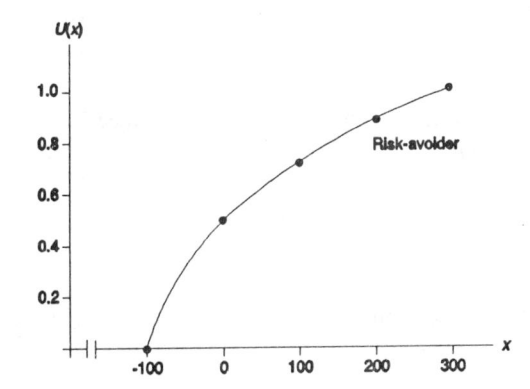

Graph of U(x) vs x for Risk-taker: convex curve from (0, 0) rising slowly then steeply to (10, 1.0).

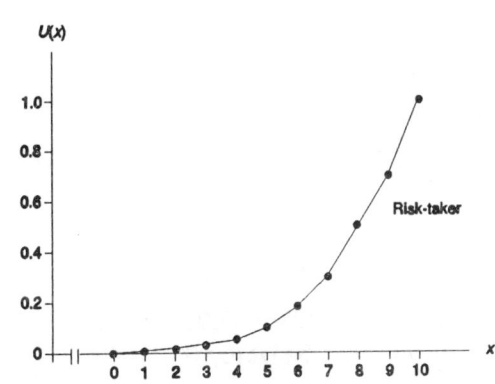

d.

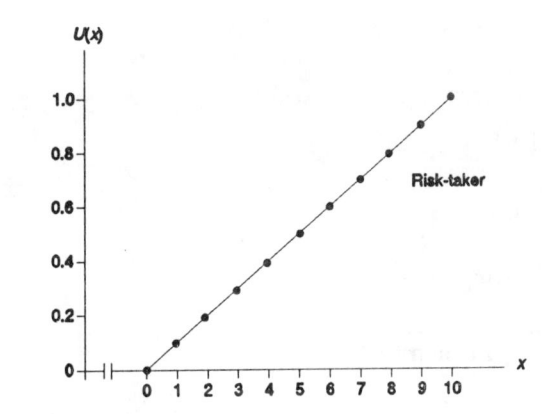

Graph of U(x) vs x labeled Risk-taker: linear line from (0, 0) to (10, 1.0).

18.75   a.   The expected cost is found the same way as the expected payoff. The expected costs are:

Let a_1 = {No preventative maintenance}, a_2 = {Oil Analysis}, and a_3 = {Change Oil}.

$E(a_1) = .1(4,000) + .9(0) = \$400$
$E(a_2) = .02(.7)(1,100) + .02(.3)(2,100) + .98(.2)(1,100) + .98(.8)(100) = 322$
$E(a_3) = .04(3,200) + .96(200) = \$320$

     b.   Using the expected cost criterion, we would select action a_2, change oil.

     c.   To recompute the expected cost for oil analysis, we must change the probabilities on the third branches—change .7 to .9, change .3 to .1, change .2 to .05, and change .8 to .95. The new expected cost is:

$E(a_2) = .02(.9)(1,100) + .02(.1)(2,100) + .98(.05)(1,100) + .98(.95)(100) = \$171$

Using the new probabilities, the answer to part b would now be action a_2, do oil analysis.

Decision Analysis

18.77 a. We would use relative frequency. We could obtain the information from previous insurance claims.

b. Since we have no access to prior information, we would have to use subjective values. These could be obtained by your knowledge of market shares from similar new products.

c. Since no prior information is available, we would have to use subjective values. These values could be obtained by your suspicions of how successful the research will be.

d. Since previous bank records are available, we would use relative frequency to obtain probabilities.

18.79 a. $P(\text{repaid}) = \dfrac{1104}{1280} = .8625$

$P(\text{repaid with difficulty}) = \dfrac{120}{1280} = .09375$

$P(\text{defaulted}) = \dfrac{56}{1280} = .04375$

b. Using the payoff table in Exercise 18.78, the expected payoffs are:

$EP(\text{loan}) = .8625(7500) + .09375(6500) + .04375(-30{,}000) = 5765.625$
$EP(\text{no loan}) = .8625(6000) + .09375(6000) + .04375(6{,}000) = 6000$

The expected payoff criterion selects action a_2, do not make loan.

18.81 a. We will first determine the quantity q of stockings demanded using the equations

$q = 10 - 2p$ for Economist 1

and

$q = 16 - 4p$ for Economist 2

These **quantities** are shown in the following table.

		Economist 1	Economist 2
	.99	8.02	12.04
Price	1.98	6.04	8.08
($)	2.75	4.50	5.00
	3.50	3.00	2.00

These quantities can now be used to determine **payoffs**, as illustrated in the following table.

		State of Nature	
		Economist 1 (.5)	Economist 2 (.5)
	a_1: .99	.99(8.02) = 7.94	.99(12.04) = 11.92
Action	a_2: 1.98	1.98(6.04) = 11.96	1.98(8.08) = 16.00
(Price, $)	a_3: 2.75	2.75(4.50) = 12.38	2.75(5.00) = 13.75
	a_4: 3.50	3.50(3.00) = 10.50	3.50(2.00) = 7.00

b. The opportunity loss is found by subtracting the payoffs in each state from the maximum payoff in each state. The opportunity loss table is:

		State of Nature	
		Economist 1 (.5)	Economist 2 (.5)
Action (Price, $)	a_1: .99	4.44	4.08
	a_2: 1.98	.42	0
	a_3: 2.75	0	2.25
	a_4: 3.50	1.88	9.00

c. $EP(a_1) = 7.94(.5) + 11.92(.5) = 9.93$
    $EP(a_2) = 11.96(.5) + 16.00(.5) = 13.98$
    $EP(a_3) = 12.38(.5) + 13.75(.5) = 13.07$
    $EP(a_4) = 10.50(.5) + 7.00(.5) = 8.75$

According to the expected payoff criterion, the company should choose action a_2: Set the price at $1.98.

18.83 a. Expected profit = $25,000 \times 5$ years $\times E(x)$
    $= 25,000(5)[0(.01) + 10(.04) + \cdots + 90(.05)]$
    $= 125,000(47.9) = \$5,987,500$

b. The payoff table for this problem would be:

		State of Nature	
		Use (.2)	Not Use (.8)
Action	a_1: Purchase	4,487,500	−1,500,000
	a_2: Do not purchase	0	0

$EP(a_1) = .2(4,487,500) - .8(1,500,000) = -302,500$
$EP(a_2) = .2(0) + .8(0) = 0$

The expected payoff criterion selects action a_2, do not purchase.

c. We will construct probability tables to derive posterior probabilities for each of the 2 possible outcomes.

Decision Analysis

	(1)	(2)	(3)	(4)	(5)
	State of Nature	Prior Probability	Conditional Probability	Probability of Intersection (2) × (3)	Posterior Probability (4) ÷ Total of (4)
		Sample Outcome:	Will use system		
Use		.2	.7	.14	.636
Do not use		.8	.1	.08	.364
				.22	1.000
		Sample Outcome:	Will not use system		
Use		.2	.3	.06	.077
Do not use		.8	.9	.72	.923
				.78	1.000

$EP(a_1 \mid \text{will use system}) = 4{,}487{,}500(.636) - 1{,}500{,}000(.364) = 2{,}308{,}050$
$EP(a_2 \mid \text{will use system}) = 0(.636) + 0(.364) = 0$

The expected payoff criterion selects action a_1, purchase.

$EP(a_1 \mid \text{will not use system}) = 4{,}487{,}500(.077) - 1{,}500{,}000(.923) = -1{,}038{,}962.5$
$EP(a_2 \mid \text{will not use system}) = 0(.077) + 0(.923) = 0$

The expected payoff criterion selects action a_2, do not purchase system.

The expected payoff for sampling is:

$\text{EPS} = .22(2{,}308{,}050) + .78(0) = 507{,}771$

The $\text{EVSI} = \text{EPS} - \text{EPNS} = 507{,}771 - 0 = 507{,}771$

$\text{ENGS} = \text{EVSI} - \text{CS} = 507{,}771 - 50{,}000 = 457{,}771$

Since this is a positive number, the bank should purchase the survey.

18.85 a. First we will construct probability tables to derive posterior probabilities for each of the four possible outcomes.

$P(x = 0 \mid p = .05) = \binom{3}{0} .05^0 .95^3 = .8574$

$P(x = 0 \mid p = .10) = \binom{3}{0} .10^0 .90^3 = .729$

$P(x = 1 \mid p = .05) = \binom{3}{1} .05^1 .95^2 = .1354$

$P(x = 1 \mid p = .10) = \binom{3}{1} .10^1 .90^2 = .243$

$P(x = 2 \mid p = .05) = \binom{3}{2} .05^2 .95 = .0071$

$P(x = 2 \mid p = .10) = \binom{3}{2} .10^2 .90 = .027$

$$P(x = 3 \mid p = .05) = \begin{pmatrix} 3 \\ 3 \end{pmatrix} .05^3 .95^0 = .0001$$

$$P(x = 3 \mid p = .10) = \begin{pmatrix} 3 \\ 3 \end{pmatrix} .10^3 .90^0 = .001$$

(1)	(2)	(3)	(4)	(5)
State of Nature	Prior Probability	Conditional Probability	Probability of Intersection (2) × (3)	Posterior Probability (4) ÷ Total of (4)
Sample Outcome: $x = 0$ defectives					
S_1	.8	.8574	.6859	.8247
S_2	.2	.7290	.1458	.1753
			.8317	1.0000
Sample Outcome: $x = 1$ defective					
S_1	.8	.1354	.1083	.6902
S_2	.2	.2430	.0486	.3098
			.1569	1.0000
Sample Outcome: $x = 2$ defectives					
S_1	.8	.0071	.0057	.5135
S_2	.2	.0270	.0054	.4865
			.0111	1.0000
Sample Outcome: $x = 3$ defectives					
S_1	.8	.0001	.00008	.2857
S_2	.2	.0010	.00020	.7143
			.00028	1.0000

$EP(a_1 \mid x = 0) = .8247(-1000) + .1753(0) = -824.7$
$EP(a_2 \mid x = 0) = .8247(0) + .1753(-4100) = -718.73$

The expected payoff criterion selects action a_2.

$EP(a_1 \mid x = 1) = .6902(-1000) + .3098(0) = -690.2$
$EP(a_2 \mid x = 1) = .6902(0) + .3098(-4100) = -1270.18$

The expected payoff criterion selects action a_1.

$EP(a_1 \mid x = 2) = .5135(-1000) + .4865(0) = -513.5$
$EP(a_2 \mid x = 2) = .5135(0) + .4865(-4100) = -1994.65$

The expected payoff criterion selects action a_1.

$EP(a_1 \mid x = 3) = .2857(-1000) + .7143(0) = -285.7$
$EP(a_2 \mid x = 3) = .2857(0) + .7143(-4100) = -2928.63$

The expected payoff criterion selects action a_1.

EPS = $.8317(-718.73) + .1569(-690.2) + .0111(-513.5) + .00028(-285.7) = -711.84$

EVSI = EPS − EPNS = $-711.84 - (-800) = 88.16$

[Decision tree diagram with branches:

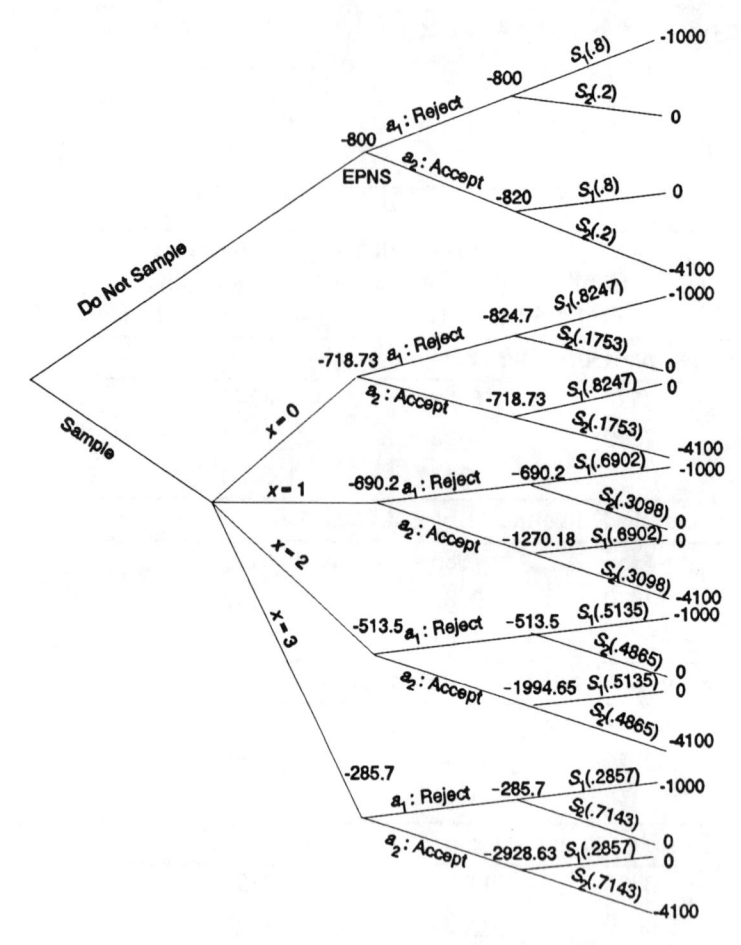

Do Not Sample branch (EPNS = -800):
- a_1: Reject (-800): $S_1(.8)$ → -1000, $S_2(.2)$ → 0
- a_2: Accept (-820): $S_1(.8)$ → 0, $S_2(.2)$ → -4100

Sample branch:
- $x = 0$ (-718.73):
  - a_1: Reject (-824.7): $S_1(.8247)$ → -1000, $S_2(.1753)$ → 0
  - a_2: Accept (-718.73): $S_1(.8247)$ → 0, $S_2(.1753)$ → -4100
- $x = 1$ (-690.2):
  - a_1: Reject (-690.2): $S_1(.6902)$ → -1000, $S_2(.3098)$ → 0
  - a_2: Accept (-1270.18): $S_1(.6902)$ → 0, $S_2(.3098)$ → -4100
- $x = 2$ (-513.5):
  - a_1: Reject (-513.5): $S_1(.5135)$ → -1000, $S_2(.4865)$ → 0
  - a_2: Accept (-1994.65): $S_1(.5135)$ → 0, $S_2(.4865)$ → -4100
- $x = 3$ (-285.7):
  - a_1: Reject (-285.7): $S_1(.2857)$ → -1000, $S_2(.7143)$ → 0
  - a_2: Accept (-2928.63): $S_1(.2857)$ → 0, $S_2(.7143)$ → -4100]

b. ENGS = EVSI − CS = 88.16 − (10 + 3(10)) = $48.16

18.87 a. Using the midpoints as states of nature, 55,000 trees might need to be cut. Since the forester's staff can cut 15,000 trees, 40,000 might need to be cut down by private contractors. Since each contractor can cut 6,000 trees, between one and seven contractors might be needed. Thus, there are eight actions possible—$a_0 - a_7$— corresponding to the number of contractors to hire, that is, between 0 and seven. If no contractors are hired, there is no loss for the first three states of nature: 2500, 7500, or 15,000. After that, the loss is $300 per tree. If contractors are hired, the loss for the first three states of nature is $2000 per contractor. If one contractor is hired, then $2000 is the loss for the first three states of nature, since the foresters can handle these. The next state of nature is 25,000 trees. This leaves 10,000 trees that the forester's staff cannot cut. One contractor can cut 6,000 of these ($2,000 for the contract and $250 per tree). This leaves 4,000 trees for which the city will be fined $300 each. Thus, for $S_4 a_2$, the payoff is:

$$-2000 + (-250)(6000) + (-300)(4000) = -2,702,000$$

The other payoffs are calculated similarly. The payoff table then is (in thousands of dollars):

	State of Nature						
	(.05) S_1 (2500)	(.20) S_2 (7500)	(.30) S_3 (15,000)	(.20) S_4 (25,000)	(.10) S_5 (35,000)	(.08) S_6 (45,000)	(.07) S_7 (55,000)
$0 = a_1$	0	0	0	−3000	−6000	−9000	−12,000
$1 = a_2$	−2	−2	−2	−2702	−5702	−8702	−11,702
$2 = a_3$	−4	−4	−4	−2504	−5404	−8404	−11,404
$3 = a_4$	−6	−6	−6	−2506	−5106	−8106	−11,106
Action $4 = a_5$	−8	−8	−8	−2508	−5008	−7808	−10,808
$5 = a_6$	−10	−10	−10	−2510	−5010	−7510	−10,510
$6 = a_7$	−12	−12	−12	−2512	−5012	−7512	−10,212
$7 = a_8$	−14	−14	−14	−2514	−5014	−7514	−10,014

c. $EP(a_0) = (0)(.05) + (0)(.20) + (0)(.30) + (-3000)(.20) + (-6000)(.10) + (-9000)(.08)$
    $+ (-12,000)(.07) = -2760$
    $EP(a_1) = (-2)(.05) + (-2)(.20) + (-2)(.30) + (-2702)(.20) + (-5702)(.10)$
    $+ (-8702)(.08) + (11,702)(.07) = -2627$

Similarly,

$EP(a_2) = -2514$ $EP(a_5) = -2345$
$EP(a_3) = -2441$ $EP(a_6) = -2326$
$EP(a_3) = -2388$ $EP(a_7) = -2314$

The expected payoff criterion selects a_7, that is, hire seven contractors.

18.89 a. The payoff table is:

		State of Nature	
		Errors (S_1)	No Errors (S_2)
Action	a_1: Certify	−10	0
	a_2: Do not certify	0	−2

(Amounts in millions of dollars)

b. One could sample previous audits to see what proportion contained errors and what proportion did not.

c. $P(S_1) = .1$ $P(S_2) = .9$
    $EP(a_1) = -10(.1) + 0(.9) = -1$ million
    $EP(a_2) = 0(.1) + -2(.9) = -1.8$ million

The expected payoff criterion would select action a_1, certify the account.

d. We will construct probability tables to derive posterior probabilities for each of the two possible outcomes. If we have perfect information, then the conditional probabilities are 0 and 1.

Decision Analysis

(1) State of Nature	(2) Prior Probability	(3) Conditional Probability	(4) Probability of Intersection (2) × (3)	(5) Posterior Probability (4) ÷ Total of (4)
Sample Outcome: Errors Present					
Errors	.1	1	.1	1
No Errors	.9	0	0	0
			.1	1
Sample Outcome: No Errors					
Errors	.1	0	0	0
No Errors	.9	1	.9	1
			.9	1

$EP(a_1 \mid \text{Errors}) = 1(-10) + 0(0) = -10$
$EP(a_2 \mid \text{Errors}) = 1(0) + 0(-2) = 0$

The expected payoff criterion selects action a_2, do not certify.

$EP(a_1 \mid \text{No errors}) = 0(-10) + 1(0) = 0$
$EP(a_2 \mid \text{No errors}) = 0(0) + 1(-2) = -2$

The expected payoff criterion selects action a_1, certify.

The expected payoff for perfect information is:

$\quad$ EPS $= .1(0) + .9(0) = 0$

The EVSI = EPS − EPNS = EPS − $EP(a_1)$ = 0 − (−\$1 million) = \$1 million.

One should be willing too pay 1 million dollars for perfect information.